The students have found your book to be easy to read and understand—a great accomplishment.

—Al Cawns, Webster University, MO

Dear Professor Gaddis: I'm a Tufts University student. I have to say that your book is a great resource. I (and many others) like the short examples that quickly get to the point they're trying to make.

—Jonathan King, student

I listen to what students say about the books I select. Their response to Gaddis is unusually positive. They really like the book.

—Jeffrey A. Kent, Los Angeles Valley College, CA

...just wanted to tell you that your book has made a lot of difference in my life. Your book is absolutely "Awesome". You have a lot of examples in the book which help a lot. Thanks again!

—Saud Faisal, student

Gaddis is an *extraordinary writer*. Gaddis' text is working much better than I expected. The ancillary materials especially the test bank and Power Point presentations add greatly to our ability to do some solid, diverse, and effective teaching.

—George Harrison, Norfolk State University, VA

Dear Mr.Gaddis:

I use your book at the University of Texas at Dallas. Your book is GREAT!! . Good presentation, takes care that we know the details. Thanks!

—Jim Burke, student

I have adopted this book for courses at both Inver Hills Community College and Century College in Minnesota this semester. I have not been disappointed. It works for-me."

—Ray Larson, Century College, MN

I have been teaching using the GUI/event driven model introduced right from the beginning for 2 years now. I am looking to change ... I think this book is easier to read and understand. Students can learn basic concepts at the beginning without being overwhelmed by the amount of code required for GUI programming.

I have used examples from Tony Gaddis's book when we taught our introductory courses in C++. When we switched to Java, the department decided to try teaching using an event driven/GUI approach from the very beginning. It has been two years with this approach now, and I am finding less than desirable results with our students. We will be evaluating our results and rethinking our strategy this year, with an expected change in textbook in fall 2004.

...the more of it I read, the more I like it.

—Diane Christie, University of Wisconsin Stout

For me, the most important feature of the text is the exercises, and there Gaddis seems to be strong.

—Michael Fry, Lebanon Valley College

I like Gaddis better than either the Horstmann or Lewis & Loftus books.

—Bryson Payne, North Georgia College and State University

As regards completeness, this author displayed a good knack for catching all the loose ends without Deiteling the book.

Nice job with flowcharts. Usual easy to understand prose. Good job introducing indentation exactly where it should be

The lengthy examples are absolutely appropriate. This is again in contrast to the Deitels, who, while being thorough, make their texts very tiring to read. Gaddis doesn't allow this to happen.

Gaddis is an excellent writer. He writes thorough, yet un-Deitelish texts that are fully understandable.

—Daniel S. Spiegel, Kutztown University

"I have found the Gaddis book to be a wonderful textbook for our students. It is highly readable, and I .... students are actually reading the text."

Gaddis' Java book is wel......................
examples for a student i...........................
ter exercises, multiple ch..................

Teaching out of Gaddis' Java text, I have g................ ....
order they are given in the book, and let the students use the boo...
their memory or look at the material stated in a different fashion from the way I did. I took a quick snap poll, and most of the students also feel very positively about the book.

A number of features that have impressed me with Gaddis:

—The general organization of topics. It follows a logical order, easy to work through, one subject leading to the next.

—The general layout is good, with the chapter introduction and list of topics at the beginning of each chapter. The colored thumb guides at the side of the book can be useful, although I haven't used them much myself— probably mostly due to my not being used to having them there.

—The code listings are clear and easy to read. I also appreciate the use of javadoc comments from early on. It makes it easy for me to bring that to the students' attention.

—The tables and figures are clear, and well-placed in the text. It's easy to correlate them with thematerial they refer to.

To summarize--I and my students both enjoyed using Gaddis' Java book. It was well laid out, easy to use, and up-to-date.

—Sander Eller
California Polytechnic University–Pomona

I am using this book for the first time at Cal Poly Pomona (my part-time job). I really like the book and I am considering this book at Mt. San Antonio College as well (my home institution).

—Tuan A Vo
Mt. San Antonio College

I have taught Java for about eight years and have probably used a different textbook each term that I've taught the course. I have to say that the Gaddis book is the best one that I've used.

The first chapter on GUI applications is well done. By this time the students are ready for something besides a console application. Most of my students come directly out of Visual Basic so the GUI app is for many of them their only perspective on a computer program. Getting into a GUI sooner than later seems like a good choice to me. By the time my students have finished the decision structure chapter, they have had at least three assignments in which they must create their own class. By introducing GUI apps next, I can have them code a windows-type program that makes use of a class that they have created in a previous assignment. There is s ome nice synergy in that type of relationship.

—Merrill Parker
Chattaonooga State Technical Community College

I've been thinking about improvements for Starting Out With Java after teaching out it, and, to be honest, have come up with very little.

We're in our third term using the book and the experience has been overwhelmingly positive for me and for the students. I'm looking forward to the new "kitchen sink" edition in the hope we'll be able to use it for both our first and second Java courses. This book has (and will continue to be, I'm sure) a great help to us is getting the students started "right". Our thanks to you guys and to Tony for making it available!

—Peter H.Van Der Goes
Rose State College

"I want to tell you that I believe your C++ text is the most thorough one available. I have used 5 different ones since 1992 and every one assumes the students know things that they do not. You cover every detail. Thank you."
—David McLeod, Belmont Technical College

"Gaddis's book is a good, solid book and teachers should be successful using it. Students in our Bachelors program find the book clear, easy to follow and therefore, they like it very much."
—Miriam Plonczak, Touro College

"My students say Gaddis is the best thing they've seen since sliced bread."
—Tom Gilman, College of the Desert,

The GADDIS book is the BEST C++ book I have ever found. THANKS! I tried at least half a dozen other C++ books before I found GADDIS. NONE of them is as effective or thorough!
—Dr. Cherie M. Stevens, Professor, Computer Science, South Florida Community College

---

...and that's just what people have told us directly. Go to the reviews at Amazon.Com, and you'll read more of the same:

This book is very, very exhaustive in its coverage. I didn't even go through a part of it. But aside from its bulk, it was a very good introduction to programming. Gaddis does an excellent job of showing how to program step-by-step, and makes it easy to teach yourself.

The book also contains a quick reference section where you can look up frequently used commands without having to find them in the text. This book is highly recommended for beginning (and even continuing) programmers.
—Reviewer: from Utah, USA

Easy reading - Best technical book I've read,
I used this text in a lecture driven course taken at a university. This text is by far the best technical book I've read and I've read my fair share of technical resources in route to receiving my MCSE, MCDBA, CCSA, and CCA certifications. The subject matters were clearly stated and the examples were informative and useful. The authors did a fantastic job covering the material.
—Reviewer: Kelsey Stidham from Chicago, IL

As an instructor in the community-college system, I have students with wide-ranging abilities—from remedial to advanced. Though I haven't had time to study the whole book (yet), it has many good features, all of which I can't list.

The most important to me is how the book proceeds. Though this book is exhaustive (i.e., covers each of its topics very thoroughly), it goes step-by-step to teach the basics of the programming process in an organized fashion. Such a progressive approach is MUCH better than a "here's EVERYTHING on one topic" approach (see any book by the Deitels); beginning students don't NEED to know the details. Any programming instructor who thinks about how he/she learned will recognize that he/she learned broad, general basics and only picked up the details through practice
—Reviewer from Wake Technical Community College, Raleigh, NC

After teaching out of Gaddis' Java book, I recommend not changing much. By the first test, we had covered the first 5 chapters. It is the first time I can recall that everyone in my class passed the first test! Do not change the order of topics in the first 6 chapters. These work beautifully.
—Diane Christie University of Wisconsin Stout

Some texts do too much too quickly and that is easy to do when classes are introduced early.

Gaddis does another very good job of spiraling classes and keeping them going through several chapters adding on more depth as he goes. Some other texts introduce classes early, but I fear that students would be intimidated.

Our programming I course has a wide range of student backgrounds and abilities and I think that objects early is good and I prefer it, but that few texts do it well. I can't think of a way to improve the Gaddis approach to early classes. It is really good - one of the best I've seen.

The pedagogy is sound. The writing style is clear and the topics are explained at the right level. The examples are appropriate for the topic.
—Jeanne M. Douglas, University of Vermont

(Gaddis) does a particularly good job of explaining the development of classes.

Arrays are discussed in detail-good job of noting how invalid subscripts occur-also, good illustration of how to create a variable size array.

—Good practical examples applicable to any programming language-good "transferability" of skills...

—Overall, very strong-a refreshing book that teaches Java plus does an excellent job of teaching general programming skills applicable to any language. Very sound theoretically and practically implemented with sound programming exercises.
—Brad Chilton, Tarleton State University

The writing is very clear, Gaddis did an excellent job on making the material easy to be understood. I think the majority of the students would find this book is easy to digest even if they never had programming experience before. Starting Out with Java is definitely one of the textbooks that I have seen so far that made lots of efforts on making it easy for the students to understand the material.

I would definitely recommend this book as the non-major first semester programming textbook, because it is very easy to understand even for someone who have never had any programming experience, I am sure the students will like that.

For an entry level programming course, the material covered in this book is more than sufficient.
—Xiaoying Wang, University of Mississippi

"I love this book - Dietel & Dietel just about killed my students."
—Frank Lucent, Westmorland County Community College

For 2 years previous to this one, I was a full-time instructor at St. Petersburg College in St. Pete and used your books. I love them !
—Amy Patterson, Computer Science Teacher, Shorecrest Prep. School

I especially like the use of flowcharts! I have found that often students have a much more difficult time understanding control structures than I expect. Flow charts seem to work well in explaining how if-else works, but few texts that I have looked at make much use of them........ The exercises and examples are great! I also like the programming problems. Some are quick and easy and some a little more involved which is exactly what we need!

I find the common errors feature and error finding very helpful! We have often provided our students with code to be debugged in labs. Coming up with this code is not easy and takes a great deal of time. I like the idea of having lots of this kind of stuff in the text for students to explore on their own.
—Shirley White, Illinois State U university

"I am a Sophomore at Augusta State University and my school's first programming class uses 'Starting out with C++.' I love your C++ book-it makes everything so easy to understand! "
—Christopher Savage, Student

"I have adopted and am currently teaching from the Gaddis second edition textbook. This is by far the best C++ book that I have taught with."
—Deedee Herrera, Dodge City CC

STARTING OUT WITH

C#

James Chegwidden
Tony Gaddis

This title is now offered by Addison-Wesley. Student companion files can be downloaded from:
http://www.aw-bc.com/cssupport

Instructor supplements are available on the catalog page for this title at:
http://www.aw-bc.com

Instructor supplements require a password. Instructors can obtain a password through the local Addison-Wesley representative. For further information contact computing@aw.com

Starting Out with C#
James Chegwidden
Tarrant County College-Southeast

Tony Gaddis
Haywood Community College

Copyright 2005 Scott/Jones, Inc.

Printed in USA.
ePac, San Leandro, CA

ZYX 456
ISBN: 1-57676-161-4

The publisher wishes to acknowledge the memory and influence of James F. Leisy. Thanks, Jim. We miss you.

Cover Design: Nicole Clayton
Kirstin Furino: Proofreading
Robert A. Saigh: Index
Composition: Stephen Adams
Book Manufacturing:

Scott/Jones Publishing Company
Editorial Group: Richard Jones, Denise Simon, and Patricia Miyaki
Production Management: Mario Rodriguez
Marketing and Sales: Victoria Chamberlin, Richard Jones, and Leata Holloway
Business Operations: Michelle Robelet, Cathy Glenn, and Bill Overfelt

A Word About Trademarks
All product names identified in this book are trademarks or registered trademarks of their respective companies. We have used the names in an editorial fashion only, and to the benefit of the trademark owner, with no intention of infringing the trademark.

Additional Titles of Interest from Scott/Jones
Starting Out with C++ 4th, 2005 update
Starting Out with C++ 4th Brief Edition, 2005 update (with Barret Krupnow)
Starting Out with C++ 4th Alternate Edition, 2005 update
(with Judy Walters and Godfrey Muganda)

Java
Starting out with Java 5: from Controls to Objects
Starting out with Java 5: from Objects to Controls
Starting out with Java 5: the Control and Structure of Data (CS1 & CS2)
Starting out with Java 5: Industrial Strength (with James Chegwidden)
Starting out with Java 5: Brief Ed. (with Irene Bruno)

Visual Basic
Starting Out with Visual Basic 6
Starting Out with Visual Basic .Net (with Kip Irvine and Bruce Denton)
Advanced Visual Basic .Net (with Kip Irvine)
Starting Out with Visual Basic .Net, Brief Edition
Visual Basic .Net for Engineers

Preface

Starting Out with C# is intended for a one-semester CS1 course, or a two-quarter sequence. Although it is written for students with no prior programming background, even experienced students will benefit from its depth of detail.

This text first introduces the student to the fundamentals of data types, input and output, control structures, methods, and objects created from standard library classes. Then the student learns to write his or her own classes. Next, the student learns to use arrays of simple and reference types. After this, the student progresses through more advanced topics, such as inheritance, polymorphism, the creation and management of namespaces. Finally the student is exposed to Windows programming in C#.

As with all the books in the *Starting Out* series, the hallmark of this text is its clear, friendly, and easy-to-understand writing. In addition, it is rich in example programs that are concise and practical.

Organization of the Text

This text teaches C# in a step-by-step fashion. Each chapter covers a major set of topics and builds knowledge as the student progresses through the book. Although the chapters can be easily taught in their existing sequence, some flexibility is provided. The following diagram shows the dependencies that exist among the chapters.

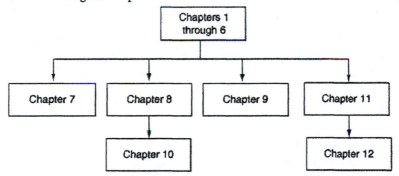

From the diagram you can see that Chapters 7, 8, 9, and 11 depend on Chapters 1 through 6. Chapter 10 depends on Chapter 8. Chapter 12 depends on Chapter 11.

Brief Overview of Each Chapter:

Chapter 1: Introduction to Computers and C#. This chapter provides an introduction to the field of computer science, and covers the fundamentals of hardware, software, and programming languages. The elements of a program, such as key words, variables, operators, and punctuation are discussed through the examination of a simple program. An overview of entering source code, compiling it, and executing it is presented.

Chapter 2: C# Fundamentals. This chapter gets the student started in C# by introducing data types, identifiers, variable declarations, constants, comments, program output, and simple arithmetic operations. The conventions of programming style are also introduced. The student learns to read console input with the appropriate C# classes.

Chapter 3: Methods. The student learns how to write void methods, value-returning methods, no-arg methods, and methods that that accept arguments. The concept of functional decomposition is discussed. Formatting numeric output in C# is also covered.

Chapter 4: A First Look at Classes and Objects. This chapter introduces the student to designing classes for the purpose of instantiating objects. The student learns about class fields and methods, and UML diagrams are introduced as a design tool. Constructors and overloading are then discussed. The use of properties in C# is also demonstrated. A BankAccount class is presented as a case study.

Chapter 5: Decision Structures. Here the student explores relational operators, relational expressions and is shown how to control the flow of a program with the if, if/else, and if/else if statements. The conditional operator and the switch statement are also covered. This chapter also discusses how to compare string objects using various methods.

Chapter 6: Loops and Files. This chapter covers C#'s repetition control structures. The while loop, do-while loop, and for loop are taught, along with common uses for these devices. Counters, accumulators, and other application-related topics are discussed. Simple file operations for reading and writing text files are also covered.

Chapter 7: Arrays. Here the student learns to create and work with single and multi-dimensional arrays. Numerous array-processing techniques are demonstrated, such as summing the elements in an array, and finding the highest and lowest values. The linear search, binary search, and selection sort algorithms are also discussed. Passing values to the command line are also mentioned.

Chapter 8: A Second Look at Classes and Objects. This chapter shows the student how to write classes with added capabilities. Static methods and fields are discussed. Interaction between objects, passing objects as arguments, and returning objects from methods is discussed. Aggregation and the "has a" relationship is then covered. This chapter also explains namespaces, and shows the student how to create them.

Chapter 9: Text Processing, Exceptions, and Files. This chapter discusses techniques for manipulating and searching strings are discussed. More `string` class methods are also covered. Handling an exception is covered, as well as developing and throwing exceptions. This chapter also discusses advanced techniques for working with sequential access, random access, text, and binary files.

Chapter 10: Inheritance. The study of classes continues in this chapter with the subjects of inheritance and polymorphism. The topics covered include base classes, derived classes, how constructors work in inheritance, method overriding, polymorphism and dynamic binding, protected access, class hierarchies, abstract classes and methods, and interfaces.

Chapter 11: A First Look at Windows Applications. Here the student is introduced to creating Windows-based applications. The student is also introduced to event-driven programming and the Visual C# .NET environment. Tutorials are used to demonstrate various windows components.

Chapter 12: Windows Applications—Part II. This chapter continues the study of windows components. The student will learn about inputting text, Message Boxes, Radio Buttons, Check Boxes, Input Boxes, List Boxes, Checked List Boxes, and Combo Boxes.

Appendices on CD-ROM:

- **Appendix A:** The ASCII and Unicode Characters
- **Appendix B:** Operator Precedence Table & Associativity
- **Appendix C:** C# Key Words
- **Appendix D:** Introduction to .NET Framework SDK
- **Appendix E:** Introduction to Microsoft Visual C# .NET

Appendices in the Textbook:

- **Appendix F:** Answers to Checkpoints
- **Appendix G:** Answers to Odd Number Review Questions

Features of the Text

 Concept Statements Each major section of the text starts with a concept statement. This statement concisely summarizes the meaning of the section.

Example Programs The text has an abundant number of complete and partial example programs, each designed to highlight the topic currently being studied. In most cases, the programs are practical, real-world examples.

Program Output

After each example program is a sample of its screen output. This immediately shows the student how the program functions.

 ## CHECKPOINTS

Checkpoints are questions placed at intervals throughout each chapter. They are designed to query the student's knowledge quickly after learning a new topic.

 NOTE: Notes appear throughout the text. They are short explanations of interesting or often misunderstood points relevant to the topic at hand.

 WARNING! Warnings are notes that caution the student about certain C++ features, programming techniques, or practices that can lead to malfunctioning programs or lost data.

Case Studies Case studies that simulate real-world business applications are placed throughout the text. These case studies are designed to highlight the major topics of each chapter they appear in.

Review Questions Each chapter presents a thorough and diverse set of review questions. The format of these includes fill-in-the-blank, true–false, multiple choice, short answer, and find the error.

Programming Challenges Each chapter offers a pool of programming exercises designed to solidify the student's knowledge of topics at hand. In most cases the assignments present real-world problems to be solved. When applicable, these exercises also include input validation rules.

Student CDs

When purchased new this book comes with one or more CDs containing the following items:

- The source code for each example program in the book

- Appendices A-E

Supplements

The following supplementary material is also available for this textbook:

- Instructor's resources, containing answers to all of the Review Questions and solutions for the programming challenges, Powerpoint slides, and a test bank.

Web Resources

The web site for *Starting Out with C#* is located at the following URL:

```
http://www.gaddisbooks.com/csharp
```

This site contains various pages, including a list of corrections for the book and a password-protected instructor page.

Acknowledgments

There have been many helping hands in the development and publication of this text. We would like to thank the following faculty reviewers for their helpful suggestions and expertise during the production of this manuscript:

Randal August
Northeastern University

Scott Bing
Albuquerque Technical Vocational Institute

Lik Mui
San Francisco State University

Alison Pechenick
University of Vermont

Greg Stefanelli
Carroll County CC

A special thanks goes to:

- Peter vander Goes at Rose State College for his detailed attention to this project

The authors would also like to thank everyone at Scott/Jones for making the *Starting Out* books so successful. Specifically, we thank Richard Jones, our publisher, for his expertise, ideas, and mentorship. Leata Holloway, as always, helped to make this the best book it can be. Jean Coston worked tirelessly guiding this project through its development, and did her best to keep me on track. Mario Rodriguez did a superb job leading the production process. Stephen Adams did a great job with the layout composition. We truly appreciate Kristin Furino's hard work as proofreader.

James would like to thank his mother Beverley for all the sacrifices she has made over the years.

In addition he would like to thank his division chair Sheryl Harris at TCC for giving the nervous young man who sat in her office many years ago the opportunity to prove himself in the classroom.

Finally, James wants to thank his colleagues at TCC-SE: Ernie, Garry, Charles, Nick, James D, and Lydia, for their friendship, support, and patience over the years. He dedicates this book to all of them.

Tony would like to thank his students at Haywood Community College for giving him the inspiration to write student-friendly textbooks. Most of all, he thanks his family for all of their patience, love, and support.

About the Authors

James Chegwidden is currently an instructor at Tarrant County College-Southeast in Arlington, Texas. He teaches courses in C, C++ and Java as well as computer applications. He also has reviewed many professional and academic publications, and is a faculty reader for the APCS exam. James is member of the ACM, SIGCSE, and IEEE Computer Affiliate.

Tony Gaddis teaches computer science courses at Haywood Community College in North Carolina. He has also taught computer programming for several corporations and government agencies, including NASA's Kennedy Space Center. Tony is a highly acclaimed instructor who was selected as the North Carolina Community College "Teacher of the Year" in 1994, and received the Teaching Excellence award from the National Institute for Staff and Organizational Development in 1997. He is the author of the *Starting Out with Java* series, the principal author of the *Starting Out with C++* series, and a coauthor of *Starting Out with Visual Basic*, all published by Scott/Jones.

Contents

Preface   **v**

About the Authors   **xi**

CHAPTER 1   **Introduction to Computers and C#**   **1**
   1.1   Introduction   **1**
   1.2   Why Program?   **2**
   1.3   Computer Systems: Hardware and Software   **3**
   1.4   Programming Languages   **7**
   1.5   What Is a Program Made of?   **9**
   1.6   The Programming Process   **15**
   1.7   Object-Oriented Programming   **18**
      Review Questions and Exercises   **21**
      Programming Challenges   **25**

CHAPTER 2   **C# Fundamentals**   **27**
   2.1   The Parts of a C# Program   **28**
   2.2   The `Write` and `WriteLine` Methods, and the .NET Framework Class Library (FCL)   **34**
   2.3   Variables and Literals   **40**
   2.4   C# Data Types   **47**
   2.5   Arithmetic Operators   **59**
   2.6   Combined Assignment Operators   **65**
   2.7   Conversion Between Data Types   **67**
   2.8   Creating Named Constants with `const`   **72**
   2.9   The `string` Type   **73**
   2.10   Scope   **79**
   2.11   Comments   **80**
   2.12   Programming Style   **83**
   2.13   Reading Keyboard Input   **85**
   2.14   Common Errors   **89**
      Review Questions and Exercises   **91**
      Programming Challenges   **96**

CHAPTER 3   **Methods**   **99**
   3.1   Introduction to Methods   **100**
   3.2   Passing Arguments to a Method   **110**
   3.3   More About Local Variables   **122**
   3.4   Returning a Value from a Method   **124**
   3.5   Problem Solving with Methods   **130**

3.6   Recursion **133**
3.7   Formatting Numbers **140**
3.8   Common Errors **143**
         Review Questions and Exercises **144**
         Programming Challenges **148**

CHAPTER 4   **A First Look at Classes and Objects** **153**
4.1   Classes and Objects **154**
4.2   Instance Fields and Methods **175**
4.3   Constructors **179**
4.4   Overloading Methods and Constructors **184**
4.5   Scope of Instance Fields **192**
4.6   Using get and set **194**
4.7   Common Errors **197**
         Review Questions **198**
         Programming Challenges **202**

CHAPTER 5   **Decision Structures** **209**
5.1   The if Statement **210**
5.2   The if-else Statement **219**
5.3   The if-else-if Statement **222**
5.4   Nested if Statements **228**
5.5   Logical Operators **231**
5.6   Comparing string Objects **241**
5.7   More About Variable Declaration and Scope **247**
5.8   The Conditional Operator **248**
5.9   The switch Statement **250**
5.10   Common Errors **258**
         Review Questions **259**
         Programming Challenges **264**

CHAPTER 6   **Loops and Files** **269**
6.1   The Increment and Decrement Operators **270**
6.2   The while Loop **273**
6.3   Using the while Loop for Input Validation **279**
6.4   The do-while Loop **282**
6.5   The for Loop **285**
6.6   Running Totals and Sentinel Values **294**
6.7   Nested Loops **298**
6.8   The break and continue Statements (*Optional*) **300**
6.9   Deciding Which Loop to Use **300**
6.10   Introduction to File Input and Output **301**
6.11   Common Errors **315**
         Review Questions and Exercises **316**
         Programming Challenges **322**

CHAPTER 7	**Arrays 327**	
7.1	Introduction to Arrays **328**	
7.2	Processing Array Contents **337**	
7.3	The foreach Loop **346**	
7.4	Passing Arrays as Arguments to Methods **348**	
7.5	Returning Arrays from Methods **352**	
7.6	Arrays of Objects **353**	
7.7	Searching and Sorting Arrays **357**	
7.8	Multidimensional Arrays **365**	
7.9	Command-Line Arguments **377**	
7.10	Common Errors **379**	
	Review Questions and Exercises **379**	
	Programming Challenges **383**	
CHAPTER 8	**A Second Look at Classes and Objects 389**	
8.1	Static Class Members **390**	
8.2	Passing Objects as Arguments to Methods **396**	
8.3	Returning Objects from Methods **400**	
8.4	The ToString Method, the Equals Method, and Same Class Operations **403**	
8.5	Aggregation **417**	
8.6	The this Reference Variable **429**	
8.7	Namespaces **431**	
8.8	Common Errors **435**	
	Review Questions and Exercises **436**	
	Programming Challenges **439**	
CHAPTER 9	**Text Processing, Exceptions and More Files 445**	
9.1	Character-testing and Conversion with the Char Class **446**	
9.2	More string Methods **454**	
9.3	The StringBuilder Class **466**	
9.4	Using the Split Method to parse strings. **472**	
9.5	Handling and Throwing Exceptions **475**	
9.6	Advanced File Operations: Binary Files and Random Access Files **488**	
9.7	Common Errors **497**	
	Review Questions and Exercises **498**	
	Programming Challenges **503**	
CHAPTER 10	**Inheritance 509**	
10.1	What Is Inheritance? **510**	
10.2	Calling the Base Class Constructor **522**	
10.3	Overriding Base Class Methods **531**	
10.4	Protected Members **540**	
10.5	Chains of Inheritance **546**	

10.6   The `Object` Class   **552**
10.7   Polymorphism   **555**
10.8   Abstract Classes and Abstract Methods   **559**
10.9   Interfaces   **565**
10.10   Common Errors   **576**
             Review Questions and Exercises   **577**
             Programming Challenges   **582**

CHAPTER 11   **A First Look at Windows Applications   587**
11.1   Introduction   **587**
11.2   Event-Driven Programming   **588**
11.3   Visual Studio and the Visual C# .NET Environment   **594**
11.4   More About Controls and Programming   **609**
11.5   Focus on Problem Solving: Building the Hotel Directions Application   **614**
11.6   Focus on Problem Solving: Responding to Events   **634**
11.7   Modifying the `Text` Property with Code   **651**
11.8   Using Visual C# .NET Help   **654**
             Review Questions and Exercises   **658**
             Programming Challenges   **659**

CHAPTER 12   **Windows Applications—Part II   661**
12.1   Gathering Text Input   **661**
12.2   Group Boxes and Form Formatting   **675**
12.3   Focus on GUI Design: The Message Box   **681**
12.4   Focus on GUI Design: Radio Buttons and Check Boxes   **686**
12.5   Input Boxes and List Boxes   **691**
12.6   Checked List Boxes and Combo Boxes   **701**
             Review Questions and Exercises   **708**
             Programming Challenges   **711**

             Appendix A: ASCII/Unicode Characters   717

             Appendix B: Operator Precedence and Associativity   718

             Appendix C: C# Key Words   720

             Appendix D: Introduction to .NET Framework SDK   721

             Appendix E: Introduction to Microsoft Visual C# .NET   726

             Appendix F: Answers to Checkpoints   732

             Appendix G: Answers to Odd-Numbered Review Questions   752

             Index   773

1

Introduction to Computers and C#

Chapter Objectives

- To recognize why it is necessary to program computers
- To realize the difference between hardware and software
- To know the common components and organization of computer systems
- To understand the role of the operating system and application software
- To appreciate why programming languages are necessary
- To become familiar with the common elements of all programming languages
- To be able to compile and execute a C# program using the Microsoft .NET SDK
- To learn about the various steps involved in creating a program
- To understand the fundamental concepts and terms of object-oriented programming

Topics in this Chapter

1.1	Introduction	1.5	What Is a Program Made of?
1.2	Why Program?	1.6	The Programming Process
1.3	Computer Systems: Hardware and Software	1.7	Object-Oriented Programming
		Review Questions and Exercises	
1.4	Programming Languages		

1.1 Introduction

This book teaches programming using C#. C# is a powerful language that runs on the Microsoft Windows .NET platform. It can be used to create console-, window-, and Web-based applications known as ASP .NET as well as numerous other software components. Before plunging right into learning C#, however, this chapter will review the fundamentals of computer hardware and software, and then take a broad look at computer programming in general.

1.2 Why Program?

CONCEPT Computers can do many different jobs because they are programmable.

Every profession has tools that make the job easier to do. Carpenters use hammers, saws, and measuring tapes. Mechanics use wrenches, screwdrivers, and ratchets. Electronics technicians use probes, scopes, and meters. Some tools are unique and can be categorized as belonging to a single profession. For example, surgeons have certain tools that are designed specifically for surgical operations. Those tools probably aren't used by anyone other than surgeons. There are some tools, however, that are used in several professions. Screwdrivers, for instance, are used by mechanics, carpenters, and, electricians, among others.

The computer is a tool used in so many professions that it cannot be easily categorized. It can perform so many different jobs that it is perhaps the most versatile tool ever made. For the accountant, computers balance books, analyze profits and losses, and prepare tax reports. For the factory worker, computers control manufacturing machines and track production. For the mechanic, computers analyze the various systems in an automobile and pinpoint hard-to-find problems. The computer can do such a wide variety of tasks because it can be *programmed*. It is a machine specifically designed to follow instructions. Because of the computer's programmability, it doesn't belong to any single profession. Computers are designed to do whatever job their programs, or *software*, tell them to do.

Computer programmers do a very important job. They create software that transforms computers into the specialized tools of many trades. Without programmers, the users of computers would have no software, and without software, computers would not be able to do anything.

Computer programming is both an art and a science. It is an art because every aspect of a program should be carefully designed. Here are a few of the things that must be designed for any real-world computer program:

- The logical flow of the instructions
- The mathematical procedures
- The layout of the programming statements
- The appearance of the screens
- The way information is presented to the user
- The program's user friendliness
- Manuals, help systems, and/or other forms of written documentation

There is also a science to programming. Because programs rarely work right the first time they are run, a lot of analyzing, experimenting, correcting, and redesigning is required. This demands patience and persistence of the programmer. Writing software demands discipline as well. Programmers must learn special languages such as C# because computers do not understand English or other human languages. Programming languages have strict rules that must be carefully followed.

Both the artistic and scientific nature of programming makes writing computer software like designing a car: Both cars and programs should be functional, efficient, powerful, easy to use, and pleasing to look at.

1.3 Computer Systems: Hardware and Software

CONCEPT All computer systems consist of similar hardware devices and software components.

Hardware

Hardware refers to the physical components that a computer is made of. A computer, as we generally think of it, is not an individual device, but a system of devices. Like the instruments in a symphony orchestra, each device plays its own part. A typical computer system consists of the following major components:

- Central processing unit (CPU)
- Main memory
- Secondary storage devices
- Input devices
- Output devices

The organization of a computer system is depicted in Figure 1-1.

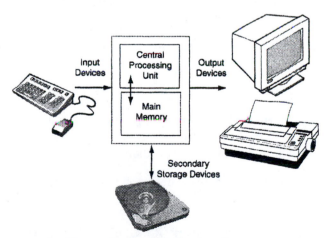

Figure 1-1 The organization of a computer system

Let's take a closer look at each of these devices.

The CPU

At the heart of a computer is its *central processing unit (CPU)*. The CPU's job is to fetch instructions, follow the instructions, and produce some resulting data. Internally, the CPU consists of two parts: the *control unit* and the *arithmetic and logic unit (ALU)*. The control unit coordinates all of the computer's operations. It is responsible for determining where to get the next instruction and for regulating the other major components of the computer with control signals. The arithmetic and logic unit, as its name suggests, is designed to perform mathematical operations. The organization of the CPU is shown in Figure 1-2.

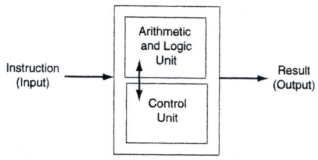

Figure 1-2   The organization of the CPU

A program is a sequence of instructions stored in the computer's memory. When a computer is running a program, the CPU is engaged in a process known formally as the *fetch/decode/execute cycle*. The steps in the fetch/decode/execute cycle are as follows:

Fetch	The CPU's control unit fetches, from main memory, the next instruction in the sequence of program instructions.
Decode	The instruction is encoded in the form of a number. The control unit decodes the instruction and generates an electronic signal.
Execute	The signal is routed to the appropriate component of the computer (such as the ALU, a disk drive, or some other device). The signal causes the component to perform an operation.

These steps are repeated as long as there are instructions to perform.

Main Memory

Commonly known as *random-access memory (RAM)*, the computer's main memory is a device that holds information. Specifically, RAM holds the sequences of instructions in the programs that are running and the data those programs are using.

Memory is divided into sections that hold an equal amount of data. Each section is made of eight "switches" that may be either on or off. A switch that is in the on position usually represents the number 1, while a switch in the off position usually represents the number 0. The computer stores data by setting the switches in a memory location to a pattern that represents a character or a number. Each of these switches is known as a *bit*, which stands for *binary digit*. Each section of memory, which is a collection of eight bits, is known as a *byte*. Each byte is assigned a unique number known as an *address*. The addresses are ordered from lowest to highest. A byte is identified by its address in much the same way a post office box is identified by an address. Figure 1-3 shows a series of bytes with their addresses. In the illustration, sample data is stored in memory. The number 149 is stored in the byte with the address 16, and the number 72 is stored in the byte at address 23.

RAM is usually a volatile type of memory, used only for temporary storage. When the computer is turned off, the contents of RAM are erased.

0	1	2	3	4	5	6	7	8	9
10	11	12	13	14	15	16 149	17	18	19
20	21	22	23 72	24	25	26	27	28	29

Figure 1-3 Memory bytes and their addresses

Secondary Storage

Secondary storage is a type of memory that can hold data for long periods of time—even when there is no power to the computer. Frequently used programs are stored in secondary memory and loaded into main memory as needed. Important data, such as word processing documents, payroll data, and inventory figures, is saved to secondary storage as well.

The most common type of secondary storage device is the *disk drive*. A disk drive stores data by magnetically encoding it onto a circular disk. There are several different types of disks, each with advantages and disadvantages. The most common types are hard disks, floppy disks, and ZIP disks. Hard disks are capable of storing very large amounts of data and data on them can be accessed quickly. Hard disks are not usually portable, however. Floppy disks are small and portable, but hold only a small amount of data. Also, a floppy disk drive's access speed is considerably slower than that of a hard disk. A ZIP disk is a small portable device that holds much more data than a floppy disk.

Optical devices such as the compact disc (CD) are also popular for data storage. Data is not recorded magnetically on a CD, but is encoded as a series of pits on the disc surface. The CD drive uses a laser to detect the pits and thus reads the encoded data. CDs hold large amounts of data, and because recordable CD drives are now commonplace, they make a suitable backup medium.

Input Devices

Input is any data the computer collects from the outside world. The device that collects the data and sends it to the computer is called an *input device*. Common input devices are the keyboard, mouse, scanner, and digital camera. Disk drives and CD drives can also be considered input devices because programs and data are retrieved from them and loaded into the computer's memory.

Output Devices

Output is any data the computer sends to the outside world. It might be a sales report, a list of names, or a graphic image. The data is sent to an *output device*, which formats and presents it. Common output devices are monitors and printers. Disk drives and CD recorders can also be considered output devices because the CPU sends data to them to be saved.

Software

As previously mentioned, *software* refers to the programs that run on a computer. There are two general categories of software: *operating systems* and *application software*. An operating system is a set of programs that manages the computer's hardware devices and controls their processes. Almost all modern operating systems are *multitasking*, which means they are capable of running multiple programs at once. Through a technique called *time sharing*, a multitasking system divides the allocation of hardware resources and the attention of the CPU among all the executing programs. UNIX, Linux, and modern versions of Windows are multitasking operating systems.

Application software refers to programs that make the computer useful to the user. These programs solve specific problems or perform general operations that satisfy the needs of the user. Word processing, spreadsheet, and database packages are all examples of application software.

 ## CHECKPOINT

1.1 Why is the computer used in so many different professions?

1.2 List the five major hardware components of a computer system.

1.3 Internally, the CPU consists of what two units?

1.4 Describe the steps in the fetch/decode/execute cycle.

1.5 What is a memory address? What is its purpose?

1.6 Explain why computers have both main memory and secondary storage.

1.7 What does the term *multitasking* mean?

1.4   Programming Languages

CONCEPT A program is a set of instructions a computer follows in order to perform a task. A programming language is a special language used to write computer programs.

What Is a Program?

Computers are designed to follow instructions. A computer program is a set of instructions that enable the computer to solve a problem or perform a task. For example, suppose we want the computer to calculate someone's gross pay. The following is a list of things the computer should do to perform this task.

1. Display a message on the screen: "How many hours did you work?"
2. Allow the user to enter the number of hours worked.
3. Once the user enters a number, store it in memory.
4. Display a message on the screen: "How much do you get paid per hour?"
5. Allow the user to enter an hourly pay rate.
6. Once the user enters a number, store it in memory.
7. Once both the number of hours worked and the hourly pay rate are entered, multiply the two numbers and store the result in memory.
8. Display a message on the screen that shows the amount of money earned. The message must include the result of the calculation performed in Step 7.

Collectively, these instructions are called an *algorithm*. An algorithm is a set of well-defined steps for performing a task or solving a problem. Notice these steps are sequentially ordered. Step 1 should be performed before Step 2, and so forth. It is important that these instructions be performed in their proper sequence.

Although you and I might easily understand the instructions in the pay-calculating algorithm, it is not ready to be executed on a computer. A computer's CPU can only process instructions that are written in *machine language*. If you were to look at a machine language program, you would see a stream of *binary numbers* (numbers consisting of only 1s and 0s). The binary numbers form machine language instructions, which the CPU interprets as commands. Here is an example of what a machine language instruction might look like:

1011010000000101

As you can imagine, the process of encoding an algorithm in machine language is very tedious and difficult. In addition, each type of CPU has its own machine language. If you wrote a machine language program for computer A and then wanted to run it on computer B, which has a different type of CPU, you would have to rewrite the program in computer B's machine language.

Programming languages, which use words instead of numbers, were invented to ease the task of programming. A program can be written in a programming language, which is much easier to understand than machine language, and then be translated into machine language. Programmers use software to perform this translation. Many programming languages have been created. Table 1-1 lists a few of the well-known ones.

Table 1-1 Programming languages

Language	Description
BASIC	Beginners All-purpose Symbolic Instruction Code is a general-purpose, procedural programming language. It was originally designed to be simple enough for beginners to learn.
FORTRAN	FORmula TRANslator is a procedural language designed for programming complex mathematical algorithms.
COBOL	COmmon Business-Oriented Language is a procedural language designed for business applications.
Pascal	Pascal is a structured, general-purpose, procedural language designed primarily for teaching programming.
C	C is a structured, general-purpose, procedural language developed at Bell Laboratories.
C++	Based on the C language, C++ offers object-oriented features not found in C. C++ was also invented at Bell Laboratories.
C#	Pronounced "C sharp," C# is a language invented by Microsoft for developing applications based on the Microsoft .NET platform.
Java	Java is an object-oriented language invented at Sun Microsystems. It may be used to develop stand-alone applications that operate on a single computer, applications that run over the Internet from a Web server, or applets that run in a Web browser.
JavaScript	JavaScript is a programming language that can be used in a Web site to perform simple operations. Despite its name, JavaScript is not related to Java.
Perl	Perl is general-purpose programming language that is widely used on Internet servers.
Visual Basic	Visual Basic is a Microsoft programming language and software development environment that allows programmers to quickly create Windows-based applications.

1.5 What Is a Program Made of?

CONCEPT There are certain elements that are common to all programming languages.

Language Elements

All programming languages have some things in common. Table 1-2 lists the common elements you will find in almost every language.

Table 1-2 The common elements of a programming language

Language Element	Description
Key Words	These are words that have a special meaning in the programming language. They may be used only for their intended purpose. Key words are also known as reserved words.
Operators	Operators are symbols or words that perform operations on one or more operands. An operand is usually an item of data, such as a number.
Punctuation	Most programming languages require the use of punctuation characters. These characters serve specific purposes, such as marking the beginning or ending of a statement, or separating items in a list.
Programmer-Defined Names	Unlike key words, which are part of the programming language, these are words or names that are defined by the programmer. They are used to identify storage locations in memory and parts of the program that are created by the programmer. Programmer-defined names are often called *identifiers*.
Syntax	Rules that must be followed when writing a program. Syntax dictates how key words and operators may be used, and where punctuation symbols must appear.

Let's look at an example C# program and identify an instance of each of these elements. Code Listing 1-1 shows the program with each line numbered.

 NOTE: The line numbers are *not* part of the program. They are included to help point out specific parts of the program.

Code Listing 1-1 Payroll.cs

```
1 using System;
2
3 public class Payroll
4 {
5    public static void Main()
6    {
7        int hours = 40;
8        double grossPay, payRate = 25.0;
9
10       grossPay = hours * payRate;
11       Console.WriteLine("Your gross pay is ${0}", grossPay);
12   }
13 }
```

Key Words (Reserved Words)

Three of C#'s key words appear in lines 1 and 3: using, public and class. In line 5 the words public, static, and void are all key words. The word int in line 7 and double in line 8 are also key words. These words, which are always written in lowercase, each have a special meaning in C# and can only be used for their intended purpose. As you will see, the programmer is allowed to make up his or her own names for certain things in a program. Key words, however, are reserved and cannot be used for anything other than their designated purpose. Part of learning a programming language is learning the commonly used key words, what they mean, and how they are used.

Programmer-Defined Names

The words hours, payRate, and grossPay that appear in the program in lines 8, 10, and 11 are programmer-defined names. They are not part of the C# language but are names made up by the programmer. In this particular program, these are the names of variables. As you will learn later in this chapter, variables are the names of memory locations that may hold data.

Operators

In line 10 the following line appears:

```
grossPay = hours * payRate;
```

The = and * symbols are *operators*. They perform operations on items of data, known as *operands*. The * operator multiplies its two operands, which in this example are the variables hours and payRate. The = symbol is called the *assignment operator*. It takes the value of the expression that appears at its right and stores it in the variable whose name appears at its the left. In this example, the = operator stores in the grossPay variable the result of the hours variable multiplied by the payRate variable. In other words, the statement says, "the grossPay variable is assigned the value of hours times payRate."

Punctuation

Notice that lines 7, 8, 10, and 11 end with a semicolon. A semicolon in C# is similar to a period in English: It marks the end of a complete sentence (or *statement*, as it is called in programming jargon). Semicolons do not appear at the end of every line in a C# program, however. There are rules that govern where semicolons are required and where they are not. Part of learning C# is learning where to place semicolons and other punctuation symbols.

Lines and Statements

Often, the contents of a program are thought of in terms of lines and statements. A *line* is just that—a single line as it appears in the body of a program. Code Listing 1-1 is shown with each of its lines numbered. Most of the lines contain something meaningful; however, line 9 is empty. Blank lines are only used to make a program more readable to a person.

A *statement* is a complete instruction that causes the computer to perform some action. Here is the statement that appears in line 11 of Code Listing 1-1:

```
Console.WriteLine("Your gross pay is ${0}", grossPay);
```

This statement causes the computer to display a message on the screen. Statements can be a combination of key words, operators, and programmer-defined names. Statements often occupy only one line in a program, but sometimes they are spread out over more than one line.

Variables

The most fundamental way that a C# program stores an item of data in memory is with a variable. A *variable* is a named storage location in the computer's memory. The data stored in a variable may change while the program is running (hence the name "variable"). Notice that in Code Listing 1-1 the programmer-defined names hours, grossPay, and payRate appear in several places. All three of these are the names of variables. The hours variable is used to store the number of hours the user has worked. The payRate variable stores the user's hourly pay rate. The grossPay variable holds the result of hours multiplied by payRate, which is the user's gross pay.

Variables are symbolic names made up by the programmer that represent locations in the computer's RAM. When data is stored in a variable, it is actually stored in RAM. Assume that a program has a variable named length. Figure 1-4 illustrates the way the variable name represents a memory location.

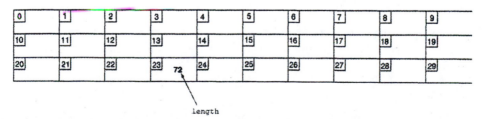

Figure 1-4   A variable name represents a location in memory

In Figure 1-4, the variable length is holding the value 72. The number 72 is actually stored in RAM at address 23, but the name length symbolically represents this storage location. If it helps, you can think of a variable as a box that holds data. In Figure 1-4, the number 72 is stored in the box named length. Only one item may be stored in the box at any given time. If the program stores another value in the box, it will take the place of the number 72.

The Compiler and the C# Virtual Machine

When a C# program is written, it must be typed into the computer and saved to a file. A *text editor*, which is similar to a word processing program, is used for this task. The C# programming statements written by the programmer are called *source code*, and the file they are saved in is called a *source file*. C# source files end with the .cs extension.

After the programmer saves the source code to a file, he or she runs the C# compiler. A *compiler* is a program that translates source code into an executable form. During the translation process, the compiler uncovers any syntax errors that may be in the program. *Syntax errors* are mistakes that the programmer has made that violate the rules of the programming language. These errors must be corrected before the compiler can translate the source code. Once the program is free of syntax errors, the compiler creates another file that holds the translated instructions.

Most programming language compilers translate source code directly into files that contain machine language instructions. These files are called *executable files* because they may be executed directly by the computer's CPU. The C# compiler, however, translates a C# source file into an intermediate language called Microsoft Intermediate Language (MSIL), which is similar to byte-code found in Java. This intermediate code is translated via the just-in-time (JIT) compiler into machine code. The JIT compiler compiles only certain parts from the intermediate code for execution. The machine code is finally executed by the machine. Figure 1-5 shows the C# program development process.

Compiling and Running a C# Program

Compiling a C# program is a simple process. Using the Microsoft .NET SDK, which is included on the Student CD that accompanies this book, you first go to your operating system's command prompt.

 Tip: In Windows XP, click Start, go to All Programs, then go to Accessories. Click Command Prompt on the Accessories menu. A command prompt window should open.

At the operating system command prompt, make sure you are in the directory or folder where the C# program that you want to compile is located. Then use the csc command, in the following form:

```
csc Filename
```

Filename is the name of a file that contains the C# source code. As mentioned earlier, this file has the .cs extension. For example, if you want to compile the Payroll.cs file, you would execute the following command:

```
csc Payroll.cs
```

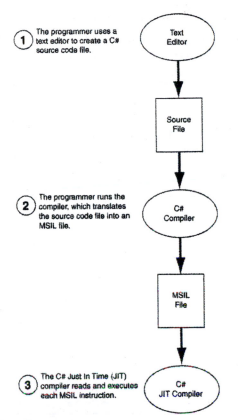

Figure 1-5   Program development process

This command runs the compiler. If the file contains any syntax errors, you will see one or more error messages and the compiler will not translate the file into an executable file. When this happens you must open the source file in a text editor and fix the error. Then you can run the compiler again. If the file has no syntax errors, the compiler will translate it into executable code.

To run the C# program, you type in the class file name:

ClassFilename

ClassFilename is the name of the .exe file that you wish to execute. However, you do not type the .exe extension. For example, to run the program that is stored in the Payroll.exe file, you would enter the following command:

Payroll

This command runs the.exe file and executes the program.

 NOTE: See Appendix D for a complete explanation on executing programs via the command line.

Integrated Development Environments

In addition to the command prompt program, there are also several C# *integrated development environments* (*IDEs*). These environments consist of a text editor, compiler, debugger, and other utilities integrated into a package with a single set of menus. A program is compiled and executed with a single click of a button, or by selecting a single item from a menu. Figure 1-6 shows a screen from the Visual Studio .NET IDE.

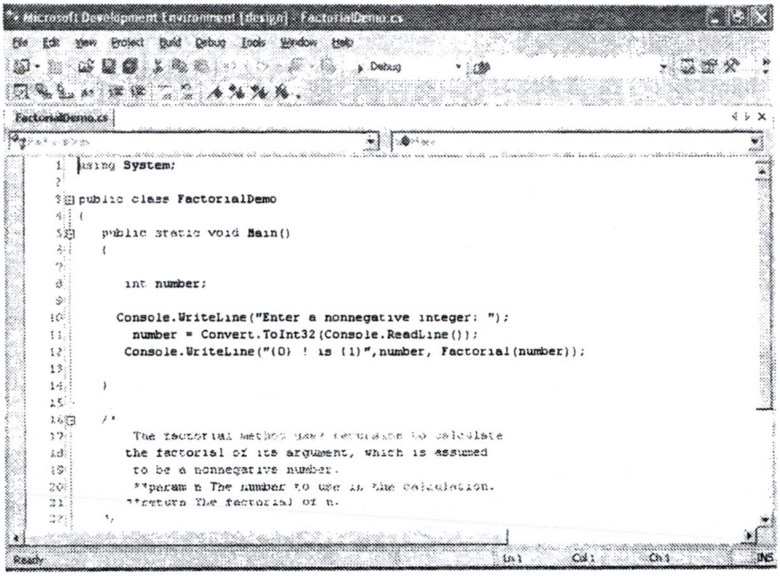

Figure 1-6 An integrated development environment (IDE)

In addition to Visual Studio .NET from Microsoft, Borland has its own C# IDE called C# Builder.

 ## CHECKPOINT

1.8 Describe the difference between a key word and a programmer-defined symbol.

1.9 Describe the difference between operators and punctuation symbols.

1.10 Describe the difference between a program line and a statement.

1.11 Why are variables called "variable"?

1.12 What happens to a variable's current contents when a new value is stored there?

1.13 What is a compiler?

1.14 What is a syntax error?

1.15 What is MSIL?

1.16 What is the JIT?

1.6 The Programming Process

CONCEPT The programming process consists of several steps, which include design, creation, testing, and debugging activities.

Now that you have been introduced to what a program is, it's time to consider the process of creating a program. Quite often when inexperienced students are given programming assignments, they have trouble getting started because they don't know what to do first. If you find yourself in this dilemma, the following steps may help.

1. Clearly define what the program is to do.
2. Visualize the program running on the computer.
3. Use design tools to create a model of the program.
4. Check the model for logical errors.
5. Enter the code and compile it.
6. Correct any errors found during compilation. Repeat Steps 5 and 6 as many times as necessary.
7. Run the program with test data for input.
8. Correct any runtime errors found while running the program. Repeat Steps 5 through 8 as many times as necessary.
9. Validate the results of the program.

These steps emphasize the importance of planning. Just as there are good ways and bad ways to paint a house, there are good ways and bad ways to create a program. A good program always begins with planning. With the pay-calculating algorithm that was presented earlier in this chapter serving as our example, let's look at each of the steps in more detail.

1. Clearly define what the program is to do.

This step commonly requires you to identify the purpose of the program, the data that is to be input, the processing that is to take place, and the desired output. Let's examine each of these requirements for the pay-calculating algorithm.

Purpose	To calculate the user's gross pay
Input	Number of hours worked, hourly pay rate
Process	Number of hours worked multiplied by hourly pay rate to give a result that is the user's gross pay
Output	A displayed message indicating the user's gross pay

2. Visualize the program running on the computer.

Before you create a program on the computer, you should first create it in your mind. Try to imagine what the computer screen will look like while the program is running. If it helps, draw pictures of the screen, with sample input and output, at various points in the program. For instance, Figure 1-7 shows the screen we might want produced by a program that implements the pay-calculating algorithm.

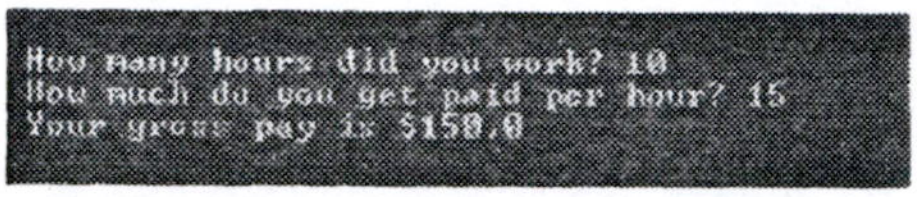

Figure 1-7   Screen produced by the pay-calculating algorithm

In this step, you must put yourself in the shoes of the user. What messages should the program display? What questions should it ask? By addressing these concerns, you will have already determined most of the program's output.

3. Use design tools to create a model of the program.

The programmer uses one or more design tools to create a model of the program. For example, the programmer may use *pseudocode*, a cross between human language and a programming language that especially helpful for designing an algorithm. Although the computer can't understand pseudocode, programmers often find it helpful to write an algorithm in a language that's "almost" a programming language, but still very similar to natural language. For example, here is pseudocode that describes the pay-calculating algorithm:

```
Get payroll data.
Calculate gross pay.
Display gross pay.
```

Although this pseudocode gives a broad view of the program, it doesn't reveal all the program's details. A more detailed version of the pseudocode follows.

```
Display "How many hours did you work?".
Input hours.
Display "How much do you get paid per hour?".
Input rate.
Store the value of hours times rate in the pay variable.
Display the value in the pay variable.
```

Notice that the pseudocode uses statements that look more like commands than the English statements that describe the algorithm in Section 1.4. The pseudocode even names variables and describes mathematical operations.

4. Check the model for logical errors.

Logical errors are mistakes that cause the program to produce erroneous results. Once a model of the program is assembled, it should be checked for these errors. For example, if pseudocode is used, the programmer should trace through it, checking the logic of each step. If an error is found, the model can be corrected before the next step is attempted.

5. Enter the code and compile it.

Once a model of the program has been created, checked, and corrected, the programmer is ready to write source code on the computer. The programmer saves the source code to a file and begins the process of compiling it. During this step the compiler will find any syntax errors that may exist in the program.

6. Correct any errors found during compilation. Repeat Steps 5 and 6 as many times as necessary.

If the compiler reports any errors, they must be corrected. Steps 5 and 6 must be repeated until the program is free of compile-time errors.

7. Run the program with test data for input.

Once an executable file is generated, the program is ready to be tested for runtime errors. A runtime error is an error that occurs while the program is running. These are usually logical errors, such as mathematical mistakes.

Testing for runtime errors requires that the program be executed with sample data or sample input. **The sample data should be such that the correct output can be predicted.** If the program does not produce the correct output, a logical error is present in the program.

8. Correct any runtime errors found while running the program. Repeat Steps 5 through 8 as many times as necessary.

When runtime errors are found in a program, they must be corrected. You must identify the step where the error occurred and determine the cause. If an error is a result of incorrect logic (such as an improperly stated math formula), you must correct the statement or statements involved in the logic. If an error is due to an incomplete understanding of the program requirements, then you must restate the program purpose, modify the program model and source code. The program must then be saved, recompiled and retested. This means Steps 5 though 8 must be repeated until the program reliably produces satisfactory results.

9. Validate the results of the program.

When you believe you have corrected all the runtime errors, enter test data and determine whether the program solves the original problem.

Software Engineering

The field of software engineering encompasses the whole process of crafting computer software. It includes designing, writing, testing, debugging, documenting, modifying, and maintaining complex software development projects. Like traditional engineers, software engineers use a number of tools in their craft. Here are a few examples:

- Program specifications
- Diagrams of screen output
- Diagrams representing the program components and the flow of data
- Pseudocode
- Examples of expected input and desired output
- Special software designed for testing programs

Most commercial software applications are large and complex. Usually a team of programmers, not a single individual, develops them. It is important that the program requirements be thoroughly analyzed and divided into subtasks that are handled by individual teams, or individuals within a team.

 CHECKPOINT

1.17 What four items should you identify when defining what a program is to do?

1.18 What does it mean to "visualize a program running"? What is the value of such an activity?

1.19 What is pseudocode?

1.20 Describe what a compiler does with a program's source code.

1.21 What is a runtime error?

1.22 Is a syntax error (such as misspelling a key word) found by the compiler or when the program is running?

1.23 What is the purpose of testing a program with sample data or input?

1.7 Object-Oriented Programming

 C# is an object-oriented programming (OOP) language. OOP is a method of software development that has its own practices, concepts, and vocabulary.

There are primarily two methods of programming in use today: procedural and object-oriented. The earliest programming languages were procedural, meaning a program was made of one or more procedures. A *procedure* is a set of programming statements that, together, perform a specific task. The statements might gather input from the user, manipulate data stored in the computer's memory, and perform calculations or any other operation necessary to complete its task.

Procedures typically operate on data items that are separate from the procedures. In a procedural program, the data items are commonly passed from one procedure to another, as illustrated in Figure 1-8.

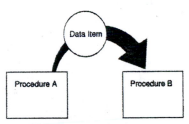

Figure 1-8   Data is passed among procedures

As you might imagine, the focus of procedural programming is on the creation of procedures that operate on the program's data. The separation of data and the code that operates on the data often leads to problems, however. For example, the data is stored in a particular format, which consists of variables and more complex structures that are created from variables. The procedures that operate on the data must be designed with that format in mind. But, what happens if the format of the data is altered? Quite often, a program's specifications change, resulting in a redesigned data format. When the structure of the data changes, the code that operates on the data must also be changed to accept the new format. This results in added work for programmers and a greater opportunity for bugs to appear in the code.

This has helped influence the shift from procedural programming to object-oriented programming (OOP). Whereas procedural programming is centered on creating procedures, object-oriented programming is centered on creating objects. An *object* is a software entity that contains data and procedures. The data contained in an object is known as the object's *attributes*. The procedures, or behaviors, that an object performs are known as the object's *methods*. The object is, conceptually, a self-contained unit consisting of data (attributes) and procedures (methods). This is illustrated in Figure 1-9.

OOP addresses the problem of code/data separation through encapsulation and data hiding. *Encapsulation* refers to the combining of data and code into a single object. *Data hiding* refers to an object's ability to hide its data from code that is outside the object. Only the object's methods may then directly access and make changes to the object's data. An object typically hides its data, but allows outside code to access the methods that operate on the data. As shown in Figure 1-10, the object's methods provide programming statements that are outside the object to have indirect access to the object's data.

When an object's internal data is hidden from outside code and access to that data is restricted to the object's methods, the data is protected from accidental corruption. In addition, the programming code outside the object does not need to know about the format or internal structure of the object's data. The code only needs to interact with the object's methods. When a programmer changes the structure of an object's internal data, he or she also modifies the object's

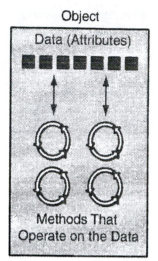

Figure 1-9 An object contains data and procedures

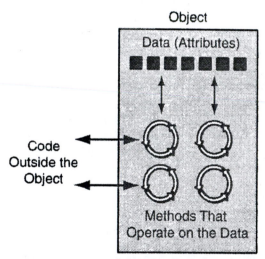

Figure 1-10 Code outside the object interacts with the object's methods

methods so they may properly operate on the data. The way in which outside code interacts with the methods, however, does not change.

These are just a few of the benefits of object-oriented programming. Because C# is fully object-oriented, you will learn much more about OOP practices, concepts, and terms as you progress through this book.

CHECKPOINT

1.24 In procedural programming, what two parts of a program are typically separated?

1.25 What are an object's attributes?

1.26 What are an object's methods?

1.27 What is encapsulation?

1.28 What is data hiding?

Review Questions and Exercises

Multiple Choice

1. This part of the computer fetches instructions, carries out the operations commanded by the instructions, and produces some outcome or resultant information.

    a) Memory   b) CPU
    c) Secondary storage   d) Input device

2. A byte is made up of eight

    a) CPUs   b) Addresses
    c) Variables   d) Bits

3. Each byte is assigned a unique

    a) Address   b) CPU
    c) Bit   d) Variable

4. This type of memory can hold data for long periods of time—even when there is no power to the computer.

    a) RAM   b) Primary storage
    c) Secondary storage   d) CPU storage

5. If you were to look at a machine language program, you would see

    a) C# source code.   b) a stream of binary numbers.
    c) English words.   d) circuits.

6. These are words that have a special meaning in the programming language.

    a) Punctuation   b) Programmer-defined names
    c) Key words   d) Operators

7. These are symbols or words that perform operations on one or more operands.

    a) Punctuation   b) Programmer-defined names
    c) Key words   d) Operators

8. These characters serve specific purposes, such as marking the beginning or ending of a statement, or separating items in a list.

   a) Punctuation   b) Programmer-defined names
   c) Key words   d) Operators

9. These are words or names that are used to identify storage locations in memory and parts of the program that are created by the programmer.

   a) Punctuation   b) Programmer-defined names
   c) Key words   d) Operators

10. These are the rules that must be followed when writing a program.

    a) Syntax   b) Punctuation
    c) Key words   d) Operators

11. This is a named storage location in the computer's memory.

    a) Class   b) Key word
    c) Variable   d) Operator

12. The C# compiler generates

    a) machine code.   b) MSIL.
    c) source code.   d) HTML.

13. JIT stands for

    a) java integrated technology.   b) just Integrated technology.
    c) just in technology.   d) just in-time.

Find the Error

1. The following pseudocode algorithm has an error. The program is supposed to ask the user for the length and width of a rectangular room, and then display the room's area. The program must multiply the width by the length in order to determine the area. Find the error.

```
area = width  length.
Display "What is the room's width?".
Input width.
Display "What is the room's length?".
Input length.
Display area.
```

Algorithm Workbench

Write pseudocode algorithms for the programs described as follows:

1. Available Credit

   A program that calculates a customer's available credit should ask the user for

   ■ The customer's maximum amount of credit

   ■ The amount of credit used by the customer

Once these items have been entered, the program should calculate and display the customer's available credit. You can calculate available credit by subtracting the amount of credit used from the maximum amount of credit.

2. Sales Tax

A program that calculates the total of a retail sale should ask the user for

▪ The retail price of the item being purchased

▪ The sales tax rate

Once these items have been entered, the program should calculate and display

▪ The sales tax for the purchase

▪ The total of the sale

3. Account Balance

A program that calculates the current balance in a savings account must ask the user for:

▪ The starting balance

▪ The total dollar amount of deposits made

▪ The total dollar amount of withdrawals made

▪ The monthly interest rate

Once the program calculates the current balance, it should be displayed on the screen.

Predict the Result

The following are programs expressed as English statements. What would each display on the screen if they were actual programs?

1. The variable x starts with the value 0.
   The variable y starts with the value 5.

   Add 1 to x.

   Add 1 to y.

   Add x and y, and store the result in y.

   Display the value in y on the screen.

2. The variable a starts with the value 10.
   The variable b starts with the value 2.

   The variable c starts with the value 4.

   Store the value of a times b in a.

   Store the value of b times c in c.

   Add a and c, and store the result in b.

   Display the value in b on the screen.

Short Answer

1. Both main memory and secondary storage are types of memory. Describe the difference between the two.

2. What type of memory is usually volatile?

3. What is the difference between operating system software and application software?

4. Why must programs written in a high-level language be translated into machine language before they can be run?

5. Why is it easier to write a program in a high-level language than in machine language?

6. What is a source file?

7. What is the difference between a syntax error and a logical error?

8. What is an algorithm?

9. What is a compiler?

10. What must a computer have in order for it to execute C# programs?

11. What is the difference between machine language code and intermediate code?

12. What does MSIL contain?

13. Is encapsulation a characteristic of procedural or object-oriented programming?

14. Why should an object hide its data?

15. What part of an object forms an interface through which outside code may access the object's data?

16. What type of program do you use to write C# source code?

17. Will the C# compiler translate a source file that contains syntax errors?

18. What does the C# compiler translate C# source code to?

19. Assuming you are using the Microsoft .NET SDK, what command would you type at the operating system command prompt to compile the program LabAssignment.cs?

20. Assuming there are no syntax errors in the LabAssignment.cs program when it is compiled, answer the following questions.

   a) What file will be produced?

   b) What will the file contain?

   c) What command would you type at the operating system command prompt to run the program?

Programming Challenges

1. Your First C# Program

This assignment will help you get acquainted with your C# development software. Here is the C# program you will enter:

```
// This is my first C# program.
using System;
public class MyFirstProgram
{
    public static void Main()
    {
        Console.WriteLine("Hello world!");
    }
}
```

If you are using the Microsoft .NET SDK:

1. Use a text editor to type the source code exactly as it is shown. Be sure to place all the punctuation characters and be careful to match the case of the letters as they are shown. Save it to a file named MyFirstProgram.cs.

2. After saving the program, go to your operating system's command prompt and change your current directory or folder to the one that contains the C# program you just created. Then use the following command to compile the program:

```
csc MyFirstProgram.cs
```

If you typed the contents of the file exactly as shown, you shouldn't have any syntax errors. If you do see error messages, open the file in the editor and compare your code to that shown. Correct any mistakes you have made, save the file, and run the compiler again. If you see no error messages, the file was successfully compiled.

3. Next, enter the following command to run the program:

```
MyFirstProgram
```

Be sure to use the capitalization of MyFirstProgram exactly as it is shown here. You should see the message "Hello World" displayed on the screen.

If you are using Visual Studio .NET:

See the Appendix E for a step-by-step discussion on how to create a C# application in Visual Studio .NET.

2

C# Fundamentals

Chapter Objectives

- To learn the meaning and placement of the parts of a simple C# program
- To write statements that display console output
- To understand the use of variables
- To know the system data types
- To recognize the use of literals and the different types of literals
- To be able to identify the arithmetic operators and the order of operations, and to understand how to use parentheses to group parts of a mathematical expression
- To write statements using combined assignment operators
- To understand data type ranking and know how C# performs widening conversions, and how to write statements using cast operators to perform conversions manually
- To create named constants using the const key word
- To be able to create and use string objects
- To recognize the difference between a primitive data type variable and a reference variable
- To grasp the concept of scope
- To write single-line, multi-line, and documentation comments
- To understand the uses of indentations, spaces, and blank lines in a program to reflect a programming style
- To know how to read console keyboard input

Topics in this Chapter

2.1 The Parts of a C# Program

2.2 The Write and WriteLine Methods, and the .NET Framework Class Library (FCL)

2.3 Variables and Literals

2.4 C# Data Types

2.5 Arithmetic Operators

2.6 Combined Assignment Operators

2.7 Conversion Between Data Types

2.8 Creating Named Constants with const

2.9 The string Type

2.10 Scope

2.11 Comments

2.12 Programming Style

2.13 Reading Keyboard Input

2.14 Common Errors to Avoid

Review Questions and Exercises

2.1 The Parts of a C# Program

CONCEPT A C# program has parts that serve specific purposes.

C# programs are made up of different parts. Your first step in learning C# is to learn what the parts are. We will begin by looking at a simple example, shown in Code Listing 2-1.

Code Listing 2-1   Simple.cs

```
1 // This is a simple C# program.
2
3 using System;
4
5 public class Simple
6 {
7     public static void Main()
8     {
9         Console.Write("Programming is great fun!");
10    }
11 }
```

 TIP: Remember, the line numbers shown in the programs are not part of the program. The numbers are shown so we can refer to specific lines in the programs.

As mentioned in Chapter 1, the names of C# source code files end with .cs. The program shown in Code Listing 2-1 is named Simple.cs. Using the Microsoft .NET SDK compiler, this program may be compiled with the following command:

```
csc Simple.cs
```

The compiler will create another file named `Simple.exe`, which contains the translated C# intermediate code. This file can be executed with the following command:

```
Simple
```

 TIP: Remember, you do not type the `.exe` extension when executing the program.

The output of the program is as follows. This is what appears on the screen when the program runs.

Program Output
```
Programming is great fun!
```

Let's examine the program line by line. Here's the statement in line 1:

```
// This is a simple C# program.
```

Other than the two slash marks that begin this line, it looks pretty much like an ordinary sentence. The // defines the beginning of a *comment*. The compiler ignores everything from the double slash marks to the end of the line. This means you can type anything you want on that line and the compiler never complains. Although comments are not required, they are very important to programmers. Real programs are much more complicated than this example, and comments help explain to future code readers what's going on.

Line 2 is blank. Programmers often insert blank lines in programs to make them easier to read. Because the compiler ignores whitespace, thus blank lines can be added anywhere to separate code areas.

Line 3 reads

```
using System;
```

Here we are using the `System` namespace found in the .NET Framework. A namespace is like a package for code that contains a variety of similar classes. The fundamental classes we will use will be contained in the `System` namespace. The using key word allows us to refer to the `WriteLine()` method without the namespace qualifier. So instead of saying

```
System.Console.WriteLine("Hi");
```

by adding the statement `using System;` we can now say

```
Console.WriteLine("Hi");
```

 NOTE: You can apply the using key word only to namespaces, not to classes.

Line 5 reads

```
public class Simple
```

This line is known as a *class header*, and it marks the beginning of a *class definition*. One of the uses of a class is to serve as a container for an application. As you progress through this book you will learn more and more about classes. For now, just remember that a C# program must have at least one class definition. This line of code consists of three words: `public`, `class`, and `Simple`. Let's take a closer look at each word.

- `public` is a C# key word, and it must be written in all lowercase letters. It is known as an *access specifier*, and it controls where the class may be accessed. The `public` specifier means access to the class is unrestricted. (In other words, the class is "open to the public.")

- `class`, which must also be written in lowercase letters, is a C# key word that indicates the beginning of a class definition.

- `Simple` is the class name. This name was made up by the programmer. The class could have been called `Pizza`, or `Dog`, or anything else the programmer wanted. Programmer-defined names may be written in lowercase letters, uppercase letters, or a mixture of both.

In a nutshell, this line of code tells the compiler that a publicly accessible class named `Simple` is being defined. Here are a couple more points to know about classes:

- You may create more than one class in a file, but you may only have one public class per C# file.

- When a C# file has a public class, the name of the public class must be the same as the name of the file (without the `.cs` extension). For instance, the program in Code Listing 2-1 has a public class named `Simple`, so it is stored in a file named `Simple.cs`.

 NOTE: C# is a case-sensitive language. That means it regards uppercase letters as being entirely different characters than their lowercase counterparts. The word `Public` is not the same as `public`, and `Class` is not the same as `class`. Some words in a C# program must be entirely in lowercase, while other words may use a combination of lower and uppercase characters. Later in this chapter you will see a list of all the C# key words, which must appear in lowercase.

Line 6 contains only a single character:

```
{
```

This is called a *left brace*, or an *opening brace*, and is associated with the beginning of the class definition. Every programming statement that is part of the class is enclosed in a set of braces. If you glance at the last line in the program, line 11, you'll see the closing brace. Everything between the two braces is the *body* of the class named `Simple`. Here is the program code again; this time the body of the class definition is shaded.

```
// This is a simple C# program.
using System;
public class Simple
{
public static void Main()
    {
        Console.Write("Programming is great fun!");
    }
}
```

 CAUTION: Make sure you have a closing brace for every opening brace in your program!

Line 7 reads

```
public static void Main()
```

This line is known as a *method header*. It marks the beginning of a *method*. A method can be thought of as a group of one or more programming statements that have a collective name. When creating a method, you must tell the compiler several things about it. That is why this line contains so many words. At this point, the only thing you should be concerned about is that the name of the method is Main, and the rest of the words are required in order for the method to be properly defined. This is illustrated in Figure 2-1.

Name of the method

```
public static void Main ()
```

The other parts of this line are necessary
for the method to be properly defined.

Figure 2-1   The Main method header

Every C# console application must have a method named Main. The Main method is the starting point of a console application. If you are ever reading the code for someone else's application and want to find where it starts, just look for the method named Main.

 NOTE: For the time being, all the programs you write consist of a class with a Main method whose header looks exactly like the one shown in Code Listing 2-1. As you progress through this book you will learn what public static void means. For now, just assume that you are learning a recipe for assembling a C# program.

Line 8 has another opening brace:

```
{
```

This opening brace belongs to the Main method. Remember that braces enclose statements, and every opening brace must have an accompanying closing brace. If you look at line 10 you will see the closing brace that corresponds with this opening brace. Everything between these braces is the *body* of the Main method.

Line 9 appears as follows:

```
Console.Write("Programming is great fun!");
```

To put it simply, this line displays a message on the screen. The message, "Programming is great fun!" is printed without the quotation marks. In programming terms, the group of characters inside the quotation marks is called a *string literal*.

NOTE: This is the only line in the program that causes anything to be printed on the screen. The other lines, like `public class Simple` and `public static void Main()`, are necessary for the framework of your program, but they do not cause any screen output. Remember, a program is a set of instructions for the computer. If something is to be displayed on the screen, you must use a programming statement for that purpose.

At the end of the line is a *semicolon*. Just as a period marks the end of a sentence, a semicolon marks the end of a statement in C#. Not every line of code ends with a semicolon, however. Here is a summary of where you do *not* place a semicolon:

- Comments do not have to end with a semicolon because they are ignored by the compiler.
- Class headers and method headers do not end with a semicolon because they are terminated with a body of code inside braces.
- The brace characters, { and }, are not statements, so you do not place a semicolon after them.

It might seem that the rules for where to put a semicolon are not clear at all. For now, just concentrate on learning the parts of a program. You'll soon get a feel for where you should and should not use semicolons.

As has already been pointed out, lines 10 and 11 contain the closing braces for the Main method and the class definition:

```
    }
}
```

Before continuing, let's review the points we just covered, including some of the more elusive rules.

- `System` is a namespace that holds a wide range of classes.
- C# is a case-sensitive language. It does not regard uppercase letters as being the same character as their lowercase equivalents.

- All C# programs must be stored in a file with a name that ends with `.cs`.

- Comments are ignored by the compiler.

- A `.cs` file may contain many classes, but it may only have one `public` class. If a `.cs` file has a public class, the class must have the same name as the file. For instance, if the file `Pizza.cs` contains a public class, the class's name would be `Pizza`.

- Every C# application program must have a method named `Main`.

- For every left brace, or opening brace, there must be a corresponding right brace, or closing brace.

- Statements are terminated with semicolons. This does not include comments, class headers, method headers, or braces.

In the sample program you encountered several special characters. Table 2-1 summarizes how they were used.

Table 2-1 Special characters

Characters	Name	Meaning
//	Double slash	Marks the beginning of a comment
( )	Opening and closing parentheses	Used in a method header
{ }	Opening and closing braces	Enclose a group of statements, such as the contents of a class or a method
" "	Quotation marks	Enclose a string of characters, such as a message that is to be printed on the screen
;	Semicolon	Marks the end of a complete programming statement

 CHECKPOINT

2.1   The following program will not compile because the lines have been mixed up.

```
public static void Main()
}
using System;
// A crazy mixed up program
public class Columbus
{
Console.WriteLine("In 1492 Columbus sailed the ocean blue.");
{
```

When the lines are properly arranged the program should display the following on the screen:

```
In 1492 Columbus sailed the ocean blue.
```

Arrange the lines in the correct order. Test the program by entering it on the computer, compiling it, and running it.

2.2 When the program in Question 2.1 is saved to a file, what could you name the file?

2.3 Complete the following program skeleton so it displays the message "Hello World" on the screen.

```
using System;
public class Hello
{
    public static void Main()
    {
        // Insert code here to complete the program
    }
}
```

2.4 On paper, write a program that will display your name on the screen. Place a comment with today's date at the top of the program. Test your program by entering, compiling, and running it.

2.5 All C# source code filenames must end with

a) a semicolon.   b) .class.

c) .cs.   d) none of the above

2.6 Every C# program must have

a) a method named Main.   b) more than one class definition.

c) one or more comments.   d) none of the above.

2.2 The Write and WriteLine Methods, and the .NET Framework Class Library (FCL)

 The Write and WriteLine methods are used to display text output. They are part of the .NET FCL, which is a collection of prewritten classes and methods for performing specific operations.

One of the primary jobs of a computer is to produce output for the user. When a program is ready to send data to the outside world, it must have a way to transmit that data to an output device. The *console* is normally considered the *standard output* and *standard input device*, and it usually refers to your monitor and keyboard.

Performing output in C#, as well as many other tasks, is accomplished by using the .NET FCL. The FCL is a standard library of prewritten classes for performing specific operations. These classes and their methods are available to all C# programs. The `Write` and `WriteLine` methods are part of the FCL and provide ways for output to be displayed on the standard output device.

 NOTE: C# uses the .NET class libraries. All non user-defined classes in C# are derived from the .NET FCL.

The program in Code Listing 2-1 (`Simple.cs`) uses the following statement to print a message on the screen:

```
Console.WriteLine("Programming is great fun!");
```

`Console` is a class that is part of the .NET FCL. The Console class contains objects and methods that perform system-level operations. The Console class has methods, such as `Write` and `WriteLine`, for performing output on the system console, or standard output device. The sequence `Console.WriteLine` specifies `WriteLine` as a method that is a member of the Console class.

 NOTE: The period that separates the names of the objects is pronounced "dot." `Console.Write` is pronounced "console dot write."

The value that is to be displayed on the screen is placed inside the parentheses. This value is known as an *argument*. For example, the following statement executes the `WriteLine` method using the string "King Arthur" as its argument. This will print "King Arthur" on the screen. (The quotation marks are not displayed.)

```
Console.WriteLine("King Arthur");
```

An important thing to know about the `WriteLine` method is that after it displays its message, it advances the cursor to the beginning of the next line. The next item printed on the screen will begin in this position. For example, look at the program in Code Listing 2-2.

Code Listing 2-2   TwoLines.cs

```
1 // This is another simple C# program.
2
3 using System;
4
5 public class TwoLines
6 {
7     public static void Main()
8     {
9         Console.WriteLine("Programming is great fun!");
10        Console.WriteLine("I can't get enough of it!");
11    }
12 }
```

(code listing continues)

Code Listing 2-2   TwoLines.cs *(continued)*

Program Output
```
Programming is great fun!
I can't get enough of it!
```

Because each string was printed with separate WriteLine statements, the strings appear on separate lines.

The Write Method

The Write method, which is also part of the Console class, serves a purpose similar to that of WriteLine: to display output on the screen. The Write method, however, does not advance the cursor to the next line after its message is displayed. Look at Code Listing 2-3.

Code Listing 2-3   GreatFun.cs

```
1 // This is another simple C# program.
2
3 using System;
4
5 public class GreatFun
6 {
7       public static void Main()
8       {
9             Console.Write("Programming is ");
10            Console.WriteLine("great fun!");
11      }
12 }
```

Program Output
```
Programming is great fun!
```

An important concept to understand about Code Listing 2-3 is that, although the output is in two programming statements, this program will still display the message on one line. The data that you send to the Write method is displayed in a continuous stream. Sometimes this can produce less-than-desirable results. The program in Code Listing 2-4 is an example.

Code Listing 2-4   Unruly.cs

```
1 // An unruly printing program
2
3 using System;
4
```

(code listing continues)

Code Listing 2-4   Unruly.cs *(continued)*

```
 5 public class Unruly
 6 {
 7      public static void Main()
 8      {
 9              Console.Write("These are our top sellers:");
10              Console.Write("Computer games");
11              Console.Write("Coffee");
12              Console.WriteLine("Aspirin");
13      }
14 }
```

Program Output

```
These are our top sellers:Computer gamesCoffeeAspirin
```

The layout of the output looks nothing like the arrangement of the strings in the source code. First, even though the output is broken into four lines in the source code (lines 9 through 12), it comes out on the screen as one line. Second, notice that some of the words that are displayed are not separated by spaces. The strings are displayed exactly as they are sent to the Write method. If spaces are to be displayed, they must appear in the strings.

There are two ways to fix this program. The most obvious way is to use WriteLine methods instead of Write methods. Another way is to use escape sequences to separate the output into different lines. An *escape sequence* starts with the backslash character (\) and is followed by one or more *control characters*. An escape sequence allows you to control the way output is displayed by embedding commands within the string itself. The escape sequence that causes the output cursor to go to the next line is \n. Code Listing 2-5 illustrates its use.

Code Listing 2-5   Adjusted.cs

```
 1 // A well-adjusted printing program
 2
 3 using System;
 4
 5 public class Adjusted
 6 {
 7    public static void Main()
 8    {
 9        Console.Write("These are our top sellers:\n");
10        Console.Write("Computer games\nCoffee\n");
11        Console.WriteLine("Aspirin");
12    }
13 }
```

Code Listing 2-5   Adjusted.cs

Program Output

```
These are our top sellers:
Computer games
Coffee
Aspirin
```

The \n characters are called the *newline escape sequence*. When the Write or WriteLine method encounters \n in a string, it doesn't print \n on the screen, but interprets it as a special command to advance the output cursor to the next line. There are several other escape sequences as well. For instance, \t is the tab escape sequence. When Write or WriteLine encounters \t in a string, it causes the output cursor to advance to the next tab position.

Code Listing 2-6 shows \n and \t in use.

Code Listing 2-6   Tabs.cs

```
1 // Another well-adjusted printing program
2
3 using System;
4
5 public class Tabs
6 {
7     public static void Main()
8     {
9         Console.Write("These are our top sellers:\n");
10        Console.Write("\tComputer games\n\tCoffee\n ");
11        Console.WriteLine("\tAspirin");
12    }
13 }
```

Program Output

```
These are our top sellers:
    Computer games
    Coffee
    Aspirin
```

 NOTE: Although you have to type two characters to write an escape sequence, they are stored in memory as a single character.

Table 2-2 lists and describes the common escape sequences.

 WARNING! Do not confuse the backslash (\) with the forward slash (/). An escape sequence will not work if you accidentally start it with a forward slash. Also, do not put a space between the backslash and the control character.

Table 2-2 Common escape sequences

Escape Sequence	Name	Description
\n	Newline	Advances the cursor to the next line for subsequent printing
\t	Horizontal tab	Causes the cursor to skip over to the next tab stop
\b	Backspace	Causes the cursor to back up, or move left, one position
\r	Return	Causes the cursor to go to the beginning of the current line, not the next line
\\	Backslash	Causes a backslash to be printed
\'	Single quote	Causes a single quotation mark to be printed
\"	Double quote	Causes a double quotation mark to be printed

 ## CHECKPOINT

2.7 The following program will not compile because the lines have been mixed up.

```
using System;
Console.Write("Success\n");
}
public class Success
{
Console.Write("Success\n");
public static void Main()
Console.Write("Success");
}
// It's a mad, mad program.
Console.Write("\nSuccess");
{
```

When the lines are arranged properly the program should display the following output on the screen:

Program Output

```
Success
Success Success

Success
```

Arrange the lines in the correct order. Test the program by entering it on the computer, compiling it, and running it.

2.8 Study the following program and show what it will print on the screen.

```
// The Works of Wolfgang
using System;
public class Wolfgang
{
    public static void Main()
    {
        Console.Write("The works of Wolfgang\n include ");
        Console.Write("the following");
        Console.Write("\n The Turkish March");
        Console.Write("and Symphony No. 40 ");
        Console.WriteLine("in G minor.");
    }
}
```

2.9 On paper, write a program that will display your name on the first line; your street address on the second line; your city, state, and ZIP code on the third line; and your telephone number on the forth line. Place a comment with today's date at the top of the program. Test your program by entering, compiling, and running it.

2.3 Variables and Literals

 A variable is a named storage location in the computer's memory. A literal is a value that is written into the code of a program.

As you discovered in Chapter 1, variables allow you to store and work with data in the computer's memory. Part of the job of programming is to determine how many variables a program will need and what types of data they will hold. The program in Code Listing 2-7 is an example of a C# program with a variable.

Code Listing 2-7 Variable.cs

```
1 // This program has a variable.
2
3 using System;
4
5 public class Variable
6 {
7     public static void Main()
8     {
9         int value;
10
11         value = 5;
12         Console.Write("The value is ");
13         Console.WriteLine(value);
14     }
15 }
```

(code listing continues)

Code Listing 2-7 Variable.cs

Program Output
The value is 5

Let's look more closely at this program. Here is line 9:

```
int value;
```

This is called a *variable declaration*. Variables must be declared before they can be used. A variable declaration tells the compiler the variable's name and the type of data it will hold. This line indicates the variable's name is value. The word int stands for integer, so value will only be used to hold integer numbers. Notice that variable declarations end with a semicolon. The next statement in this program appears in line 11:

```
value = 5;
```

This is called an *assignment statement*. The equal sign is an operator that stores the value on its right (in this case 5) in the variable named on its left. After this line executes, the value variable will contain the value 5.

 NOTE: This line does not print anything on the computer screen. It runs silently behind the scenes.

Now look at lines 12 and 13:

```
Console.Write("The value is ");
Console.WriteLine(value);
```

The statement in line 12 sends the string literal "The value is" to the Write method. The statement in line 13 sends the name of the value variable to the WriteLine method. When you send a variable name to Write or WriteLine, the variable's contents are displayed. Notice there are no quotation marks around value. Look at what happens in Code Listing 2-8.

Code Listing 2-8 Variable2.cs

```
1 // This program has a variable.
2
3 using System;
4
```

(code listing continues)

Code Listing 2-8 Variable2.cs *(continued)*

```
5 public class Variable2
6 {
7    public static void Main()
8    {
9       int value;
10
11      value = 5;
12      Console.Write("The value is ");
13      Console.WriteLine("value");
14   }
15 }
```

Program Output

```
The value is value
```

When double quotation marks are placed around the word value it becomes a string literal, not a variable name. When string literals are sent to Write or WriteLine, they are displayed exactly as they appear inside the quotation marks.

Displaying Multiple Items in Output

What if we want to display one or multiple items on the screen? We could use multiple Write or WriteLine statements such as

```
value = 5;
Console.Write("The value is ");
Console.WriteLine(value);
```

This statement will print

```
The value is 5
```

To prevent us from having multiple statements for output, we can combine strings and values of variables into one output statement via a format specifier. The format specifier is a placeholder for the variables in a string. The following code shows an example.

```
number = 5;
Console.WriteLine("The value is {0}", number);
```

The second line uses the format specifier, surrounded by curly braces, to state the position of the number in relation to the variable list following the string. The output that will be displayed is

```
The value is 5
```

 NOTE: The value in the curly braces must be less than the number of values in the list of values after the format string. Thus, if you have two variables in the

variable list the placeholders will be {0} and {1}, respectively. Example:

```
Console.WriteLine("The values are {0} and {1}", x, y);
```

Sometimes the argument you use with `Write` or `WriteLine` is too long to fit on one line in your program code. However, a string literal cannot begin on one line and end on another. For example, the following will cause an error.

```
// This is an error!
Console.WriteLine("Enter a value that is greater than zero
      and less than 10." );
```

You can remedy this problem by breaking the argument into smaller string literals and then using the string concatenation operator, the +, to spread them out over more than one line. Here is an example.

```
Console.WriteLine("Enter a value that is " +
    "greater than zero and less " +
    "than 10." );
```

In this statement, the argument is broken up into three strings and joined together using the + operator. The following example shows the same technique used when the contents of a variable are part of the concatenation.

```
sum = 249;
Console.WriteLine("The sum of the three " +
    "numbers is {0}", sum);
```

 NOTE: In C#, we could also use the + operator to combine a string and variables the way Java does. However, most C# books use the format specifier notation. This book will use such notation.

Quotation Marks

As shown in Code Listing 2-8, placing quotation marks around a variable name changes the program's results. In fact, placing double quotation marks around anything that is not intended to be a string literal will create an error of some type. For example, in Programs 2-7 and 2-8, the number 5 was assigned to the variable `value`. It would have been an error to perform the assignment this way:

```
value = "5";     // Error!
```

In this statement, 5 is no longer an integer, but a string literal. Because `value` was declared as an integer variable, you can only store integers in it. In other words, 5 and "5" are not the same thing.

The fact that numbers can be represented as strings frequently confuses students who are new to programming. Just remember that strings are intended for humans to read. They are to be printed on computer screens or paper. Numbers, however, are intended primarily for mathematical operations. You cannot perform math on strings, and before numbers can be displayed on the screen, they must first be converted to strings. (Fortunately, `Write` and `WriteLine` handle the conversion automatically when you send numbers to them.) Don't fret if this still bothers you. Later in this chapter we will shed more light on the differences among numbers, characters, and strings by discussing their internal storage.

More About Literals

A literal is a value that is written in the code of a program. Literals are commonly assigned to variables or displayed. Code Listing 2-9 contains both literals and a variable.

Code Listing 2-9 Literals.cs

```
 1 // This program has literals and a variable.
 2
 3 using System;
 4
 5 public class Literals
 6 {
 7    public static void Main()
 8    {
 9       int apples;
10
11       apples = 20;
12       Console.WriteLine("Today we sold {0} bushels of
                 apples.", apples);
13    }
14 }
```

Program Output
Today we sold 20 bushels of apples.

Of course, the variable in this program is `apples`. It is declared as an integer. Table 2-3 lists the literals found in the program.

Table 2-3 Literals

Literal	Type of Literal
20	integer literal
"Today we sold"	string literal
"bushels of apples."	string literal

Identifiers

An *identifier* is a programmer-defined name that represents some element of a program. Variable names and class names are examples of identifiers. You may choose your own variable names and class names in C#, as long as you do not use any of the C# *key words*. The key words make up the core of the language and each has a specific purpose. Table 2-4 shows a complete list of the C# key words.

Table 2-4   The C# key words

abstract	as	base	bool	break	byte	case
catch	char	checked	class	const	continue	decimal
default	delegate	do	double	else	enum	event
explicit	extern	false	finally	fixed	float	for
foreach	goto	if	implicit	in	int	interface
internal	is	lock	long	namespace	new	null
object	operator	out	override	params	private	protected
public	readonly	ref	return	sbyte	sealed	short
sizeof	stackalloc	static	string	struct	switch	this
throw	true	try	typeof	uint	ulong	unchecked
unsafe	ushort	using	virtual	void	volatile	while

You should always choose names for your variables that indicate what they are used for. You may be tempted to declare variables with names like this:

```
int x;
```

The rather nondescript name, x, gives no clue as to what the variable's purpose is. Here is a better example.

```
int itemsOrdered;
```

The name itemsOrdered gives anyone reading the program an idea of what the variable is used for. This method of coding helps produce *self-documenting programs*, which means a person can understand what the program is doing just by reading its code. Because real-world programs usually have thousands of lines of code, it is important that they be as self-documenting as possible.

You have probably noticed the mixture of uppercase and lowercase letters in the name itemsOrdered. Although all of C#'s key words must be written in lowercase, you may use uppercase letters in variable names. The reason the O in itemsOrdered is capitalized is to improve readability. Normally "items ordered" is two words. Variable names cannot contain spaces, however, so the two words must be combined into one. When "items" and "ordered" are stuck together, you get a variable declaration like this:

```
int itemsordered;
```

Capitalization of the letter O makes itemsOrdered easier to read. Typically, variable names begin with a lowercase letter, and after that, the first letter of each individual word that makes up the variable name is capitalized.

Here are some specific rules that must be followed with all identifiers.

■ The first character must be one of the letters a–z, A–Z, or an underscore (_).

■ After the first character, you may use the letters a–z or A–Z, the digits 0–9, or underscores (_).

■ Uppercase and lowercase characters are distinct. This means itemsOrdered is not the same as itemsordered.

■ Identifiers cannot include spaces.

Table 2-5 lists variable names and identifies whether each is legal or illegal in C#.

Table 2-5 Some variable names

Variable Name	Legal or Illegal?
dayOfWeek	Legal
3dGraph	Illegal because identifiers cannot begin with a digit
june1997	Legal
mixture#3	Illegal because identifiers may only use alphabetic letters, digits, or underscores
week day	Illegal because identifiers cannot contain spaces

Class Names

As mentioned before, it is standard practice to begin variable names with a lowercase letter, and then capitalize the first letter of each subsequent word that makes up the name. It is also a standard practice to capitalize the first letter of a class name, as well as the first letter of each subsequent word it contains. This helps differentiate the names of variables from the names of classes. For example, payRate would be a variable name, and Employee would be a class name.

 CHECKPOINT

2.10 Examine the following program.

```
// This program uses variables and literals.
using System;
public class BigLittle
{
    public static void Main()
    {
        int little;
        int big;

        little = 2;
        big = 2000;
        Console.WriteLine("The little number is {0}", little);
        Console.WriteLine("The big number is {0}", big);
    }
}
```

List the variables and literals found in the program.

2.11 What will the following program display on the screen?

```
using System;
public class CheckPoint
{
    using System;
    public static void Main()
    {
        int number;

        number = 712;
        Console.WriteLine("The value is {0}" + "number");
    }
}
```

2.4   C# Data Types

CONCEPT   There are many different types of data. Variables are classified according to their data type, which determines the kind of data that may be stored in them.

Computer programs collect pieces of data from the real world and manipulate them in various ways. There are many different types of data. In the realm of numeric data, for example, there are whole and fractional numbers, negative and positive numbers; and numbers so large and others so small that they don't even have a name. Then there is textual information. Names and addresses, for instance, are stored as strings of characters. When you write a program you must determine what types of data it will be likely to encounter.

Each variable has a *data type*, which is the type of data that the variable can hold. Selecting the proper data type is important because a variable's data type determines the amount of memory the variable uses, and the way the variable formats and stores data. It is important to select a data type that is appropriate for the type of data that your program will work with. If you are writing a program to calculate the number of miles to a distant star, you need variables that can hold very large numbers. If you are designing software to record microscopic dimensions, you need variables that store very small and precise numbers. If you are writing a program that must perform thousands of intensive calculations, you want variables that can be processed quickly. The data type of a variable determines all of these factors.

Table 2-6 shows all of the C# value data types.

Table 2-6 C# value data types

Data Type	Alias of	Size	Range
sbyte	System.Sbyte	1 byte	Integers in the range of −128 to +127
byte	System.Byte	I byte	Integers in the range of 0 to 255
short	System.Int16	2 bytes	Integers in the range of −32,768 to +32,767
ushort	System.UInt16	2 bytes	Integers in the range of 0 to 65535
int	System.Int32	4 bytes	Integers in the range of −2,147,483,648 to +2,147,483,647
uint	System.UInt32	4 bytes	Integers in the range of 0 to 4294967295
long	System.Int64	8 bytes	Integers in the range of −9,223,372,036,854,775,808 to +9,223,372,036,854,775,807
ulong	System.UInt64	8 bytes	Integers in the range of 0 to 18446744073709551615
float	System.Single	4 bytes	Floating-point numbers in the range of $\pm1.5\times10^{-45}$ to $\pm3.4\times10^{38}$, with seven digits of accuracy
double	System.Double	8 bytes	Floating-point numbers in the range of $\pm5.0\times10^{-324}$ to $\pm3.4\times10^{30}$, with 15 digits of accuracy
decimal	System.Decimal	16 bytes	Floating-point numbers in the range of $\pm1.0\times10^{-28}$ to $\pm7.9\times10^{28}$
char	System.Char	2 bytes	Unicode
bool	System.Boolean	1 byte	Values true or false only

The words listed in the left column of Table 2-6 are the key words you use in variable declarations. A variable declaration takes the following general format:

```
DataType VariableName;
```

DataType is the name of the data type and VariableName is the name of the variable. Here are some examples of variable declarations:

```
byte inches;

int speed;

short month;

float salesCommission;

double distance;
```

The second column, Alias of, is another name for the type stated in the .NET Framework Common Language Specification (CLS). Thus int is an alias for the System.Int32 type. This basically means all of C# simple data types are technically objects.

The size column in Table 2-6 shows the number of bytes that a variable of each of the data types uses. For example, an int variable uses 4 bytes, and a double variable uses 8 bytes. The range column shows the ranges of numbers that may be stored in variables of each data type. For example, an int variable can hold numbers from -2,147,483,648 up to +2,147,483,647. One of the appealing characteristics of the C# language is that the sizes and ranges of all the data types are the same on all computers.

NOTE: There is no distinction between the simple data types and reference types, as there is in Java. Therefore, C# is a true object-oriented language.

The Integer Data Types

The first eight data types listed in Table 2-6, sbyte, byte, int, uint, short, ushort, and long, ulong, are integer data types. An integer variable can hold whole numbers such as 7, 125, −14, and 6928. The program in Code Listing 2-10 shows several variables of different integer data types being used.

Code Listing 2-10   IntegerVariables.cs

```
1 // This program has variables of several of the integer types.
2
3 using System;
4
```

(code listing continues)

Code Listing 2-10   IntegerVariables.cs *(continued)*

```
 5 public class IntegerVariables
 6 {
 7    public static void Main()
 8    {
 9       int checking;   // Declare an int variable named checking.
10       byte miles;     // Declare a byte variable named miles.
11       short minutes;  // Declare a short variable named minutes.
12       long days;      // Declare a long variable named days.
13
14       checking = -20;
15       miles = 105;
16       minutes = 120;
17       days = 185000;
18       Console.WriteLine("We have made a journey of {0}
              miles.", miles);
19       Console.WriteLine("It took us {0} minutes.", minutes);
20       Console.WriteLine("Our account balance is ${0}",
              checking);
21       Console.WriteLine("About {0} days ago Columbus stood on
              this spot.", days);
22    }
23 }
```

Program Output

```
We have made a journey of 105 miles.
It took us 120 minutes.
Our account balance is $-20
About 185000 days ago Columbus stood on this spot.
```

 NOTE: The u in front of the data types stands for "unsigned." Unsigned numbers hold only positive values. We will not use unsigned numbers in this text.

In most programs you will need more than one variable of any given data type. If a program uses three integers, such as length, width, and area, they could be declared separately, like this:

```
int length;
```

```
int width;
```

```
int area;
```

It is easier, however, to combine the three variable declarations:

```
int length, width, area;
```

You can declare several variables of the same type, simply by separating their names with commas.

Integer Literals

When you write an integer literal in your program code, C# assumes it to be of the int data type. For example, in Code Listing 2-10, the literals –20, 105, 120, and 185000 are all treated as int values. You can force an integer literal to be treated as a long, however, by suffixing it with the letter L. For example, the value 57L would be treated as a long. You can use either an uppercase or lowercase L. The lowercase l looks too much like the number 1, so you should always use the uppercase L.

 WARNING! You cannot embed commas in numeric literals. For example, the following statement will cause an error:

```
number = 1,257,649;        // ERROR!
```

This statement must be written as:

```
number = 1257649;          // Correct.
```

Floating-Point Data Types

Whole numbers are not adequate for many jobs. If you are writing a program that works with dollar amounts or precise measurements, you need a data type that allows fractional values. In programming terms, these are called *floating-point numbers*. Values such as 1.7 and –45.316 are floating-point numbers.

In C# there are three data types that can represent floating-point numbers. They are float, double, and decimal. The float data type is considered a *single precision data type*. It can store a floating-point number with seven digits of accuracy. The double data type is considered a *double precision data type*. It can store a floating-point number with 15 digits of accuracy. The double data type uses twice the memory as the float data type, however. A float variable occupies 4 bytes of memory, whereas a double variable uses 8 bytes. The decimal data type occupies 16 bytes of memory and has a smaller range and greater precision than both the float and double types. This means the decimal type has greater accuracy but cannot hold values as large as a double. The decimal type is typically used for money and finance calculations.

Code Listing 2-11 shows a program that uses three double variables.

Code Listing 2-11 Sale.cs

```
1 Code Listing 2-11 (Sale.cs)
2 // This program demonstrates the double data type.
3
4 using System;
5
```

(code listing continues)

Code Listing 2-11   Sale.cs *(continued)*

```
 6 public class Sale
 7 {
 8    public static void Main()
 9    {
10       double price, tax, total;
11
12       price = 29.75;
13       tax = 1.76;
14       total = 31.51;
15       Console.WriteLine("The price of the item is {0}",
               price);
16       Console.WriteLine("The tax is {0}", tax);
17       Console.WriteLine("The total is {0}", total);
18    }
19 }
```

Program Output

```
The price of the item is 29.75
The tax is 1.76
The total is 31.51
```

Floating-Point Literals

When you write a floating-point literal in your program code, C# assumes it to be of the double data type. For example, in Code Listing 2-11, the literals 29.75, 1.76, and 31.51 are all treated as double values. Because of this, a problem can arise when a floating-point literal is assigned to a float variable. C# is a *strongly typed language*, which means that it only allows you to store values of compatible data types in variables. A double value is not compatible with a float variable because a double can be much larger or much smaller than the allowable range for a float. As a result, code such as the following will cause an error.

```
float number;
number = 23.5;         // Error!
```

You can force a double literal to be treated as a float, however, by suffixing it with the letter F or f. The preceding code can be rewritten in the following manner to prevent an error.

```
float number;
number = 23.5F;        // This will work.
```

You can force a double literal to be treated as a decimal, however, by suffixing it with the letter M or m.

```
float number;
number = 23.5M;        // This will work as well.
```

WARNING! If you are working with literals that represent dollar amounts, remember that you cannot embed currency symbols (such as $) or commas in the literal. For example, the following statement will cause an error:

```
grossPay = $1,257.00;    // ERROR!
```

This statement must be written as

```
grossPay = 1257.00;      // Correct.
```

Scientific and E Notation

Floating-point literals can be represented in *scientific notation*. Take the number 47,281.97. In scientific notation this number is 4.728197×10^4. (10^4 is equal to 10,000, and $4.728197 \times 10,000$ is 47,281.97.)

C# uses *E notation* to represent values in scientific notation. In E notation, the number 4.728197×10^4 would be 4.728197E4. Table 2-7 shows other numbers represented in scientific and E notation.

Table 2-7 Floating-point representations

Decimal Notation	Scientific Notation	E Notation
247.91	2.4791×10^2	2.4791E2
0.00072	7.2×10^{-4}	7.2E-4
2,900,000	2.9×10^6	2.9E6

 NOTE: The E can be upper- or lowercase.

Code Listing 2-12 demonstrates the use of floating-point literals expressed in E notation.

Code Listing 2-12 SunFacts.cs

```
1 // This program uses E notation.
2
3 using System;
4
```

(code listing continues)

Code Listing 2-12   SunFacts.cs

```
 5 public class SunFacts
 6 {
 7    public static void Main()
 8    {
 9        double distance, mass;
10
11        distance = 1.495979E11;
12        mass = 1.989E30;
13        Console.WriteLine("The Sun is {0} meters
              away.",distance);
14        Console.WriteLine("The Sun's mass is {0} kilograms.",
              mass);
15    }
16 }
```

Program Output

```
The Sun is 149597900000 meters away.
The Sun's mass is 1.989E+30 kilograms.
```

The boolean Data Type

The boolean data type allows you to create variables that may hold one of two possible values: true or false. Code Listing 2-13 demonstrates the declaration and assignment of a boolean variable.

Code Listing 2-13   TrueFalse.cs

```
 1 // A program for demonstrating boolean variables
 2
 3 using System;
 4
 5 public class TrueFalse
 6 {
 7    public static void Main()
 8    {
 9        bool booltype;
10
11        booltype = true;
12        Console.WriteLine(booltype);
13        booltype = false;
14        Console.WriteLine(booltype);
15    }
16 }
```

Program Output

```
true
false
```

Variables of the `boolean` data type are useful for evaluating conditions that are either `true` or `false`. You will not be using them until Chapter 5, however, so for now just remember the following things about them.

- `boolean` variables may only hold the values `true` or `false`.

- The contents of a `boolean` variable may not be copied to a variable of any type other than `boolean`.

The `char` Data Type

The char data type is used to store characters. A variable of the `char` data type can hold one character at a time. Character literals are enclosed in *single quotation marks*. The program in Code Listing 2-14 uses two `char` variables. The character literals 'A' and 'B' are assigned to the variables.

Code Listing 2-14   Letters.cs

```
 1 // This program demonstrates the char data type.
 2
 3 using System;
 4
 5 public class Letters
 6 {
 7    public static void Main()
 8    {
 9       char letter;
10
11       letter = 'A';
12       Console.WriteLine(letter);
13       letter = 'B';
14       Console.WriteLine(letter);
15    }
16 }
```

Program Output

```
A
B
```

It is important that you do not confuse character literals with string literals, which are enclosed in double quotation marks. string literals cannot be assigned to `char` variables.

Unicode

Characters are internally represented by numbers. Each printable character, as well as many non-printable characters, is assigned a unique number. C# uses Unicode, which is a set of numbers that are used as codes for representing characters. Each Unicode number requires two bytes of memory, so char variables occupy two bytes. When a character is stored in memory, it is actually the numeric code that is stored. When the computer is instructed to print the value on the screen, it displays the character that corresponds with the numeric code.

You may want to refer to Appendix A, which shows a portion of the Unicode character set. Notice that the number 65 is the code for A, 66 is the code for B, and so on. Figure 2-2 illustrates that when you think of the characters A, B, and C being stored in memory, it is really the numbers 65, 66, and 67 that are stored.

These characters are stored in memory as...

$$\boxed{00\ 65}\ \boxed{00\ 66}\ \boxed{00\ 67}$$

Figure 2-2 Characters and how they are stored in memory

 NOTE: Although characters are stored in memory as integers, you cannot directly store a character into a variable data type without the use of a cast. Thus, you cannot say

```
char letter = 65;        //Error
Console.WriteLine(letter);
```

Casting will be covered in Section 2.7.

Variable Assignment and Initialization

As you have already seen in several examples, a value is put into a variable with an *assignment statement*. For example, the following statement assigns the value 12 to the variable unitsSold.

```
unitsSold = 12;
```

The = symbol is called the *assignment operator*. Operators perform operations on data. The data that operators work with are called *operands*. The assignment operator has two operands. In the statement above the operands are unitsSold and 12.

In an assignment statement, the name of the variable receiving the assignment must appear on the left side of the operator, and the value being assigned must appear on the right side. The following statement is incorrect.

```
12 = unitsSold;          // Error
```

The operand on the left side of the = operator must be a variable name. The operand on the right side of the = symbol must be an expression that has a value. The assignment operator takes the value of the right operand and puts it in the variable identified by the left operand. Assuming that length and width are both int variables, the following code illustrates that the assignment operator's right operand may be a literal or a variable.

```
length = 20;
width = length;
```

It is important to note that the assignment operator only changes the contents of its left operand. The second statement assigns the value of the length variable to the width variable. After the statement has executed, length still has the same value, 20.

You may also assign values to variables as part of the declaration statement. This is known as *initialization*. Code Listing 2-15 shows how it is done.

Code Listing 2-15   Initialize.cs

```
1 // This program shows variable initialization.
2
3 using System;
4
5 public class Initialize
6 {
7     public static void Main()
8     {
9         int month = 2, days = 28;
10
11         Console.WriteLine("Month {0} has {1} days.",month,
                days);
12     }
13 }
```

Program Output
```
Month 2 has 28 days.
```

The variable declaration statement in this program is in line 9:

```
int month = 2, days = 28;
```

This statement declares the month variable and initializes it with the value 2, and declares the days variable and initializes it with the value 28. As you can see, this simplifies the program and reduces the number of statements that must be typed by the programmer. Here are examples of other declaration statements that perform initialization.

```
double payRate = 25.52;
float interestRate = 12.9F;
char stockCode = 'D';
int customerNum = 459;
```

Of course, there are always variations on a theme. C# allows you to declare several variables and only initialize some of them. Here is an example of such a declaration:

```
int flightNum = 89, travelTime, departure = 10, distance;
```

The variable `flightNum` is initialized to 89 and departure is initialized to 10. The `travel-Time` and distance variables remain uninitialized.

 WARNING! When a variable is declared inside a method, it must have a value stored in it before it can be used. If the compiler determines that the program might be using such a variable before a value has been stored in it, an error will occur. You can avoid this type of error by initializing the variable with a value.

Variables Hold Only One Value at a Time

Remember, a variable can hold only one value at a time. When you assign a new value to a variable, the new value takes the place of the variable's previous contents. For example, look at the following code.

```
int x = 5;
Console.WriteLine(x);
x = 99;
Console.WriteLine(x);
```

In this code, the variable x is initialized with the value 5 and its contents are displayed. Then the variable is assigned the value 99. This value overwrites the value 5 that was previously stored there. The code will produce the following output:

```
5
99
```

 NOTE: When you declare a variable in C# it is not automatically initialized to a default value. Thus, you must assign a value to a variable before using it.

 ## CHECKPOINT

2.12 Which of the following are illegal variable names and why?

```
x
99bottles
july97
theSalesFigureForFiscalYear98
r&d
grade_report
```

2.13 Is the variable name Sales the same as sales? Why or why not?

2.14 Refer to the C# data types listed in Table 2-6 for this question.

    a) If a variable needs to hold whole numbers in the range 32 to 6,000, what primitive data type would be best?

    b) If a variable needs to hold whole numbers in the range –40,000 to +40,000, what primitive data type would be best?

    c) Which of the following literals use more memory—22.1 or 22.1F?

2.15 How would the number 6.31×10^{17} be represented in E notation?

2.16 A program declares a decimal variable named number, and the following statement causes an error. What can be done to fix the error?

```
number = 7.4;
```

2.17 What values can Boolean variables hold?

2.18 Write statements that do the following.

    a)   Declare a char variable named letter.

    b)   Assign the letter A to the letter variable.

    c)   Display the contents of the letter variable.

2.19 What are the Unicode codes for the characters 'C', 'F', and 'W'? (You may need to refer to Appendix A.)

2.20 Which is a character literal, 'B' or "B"?

2.21 What is wrong with the following statement?

```
char letter = "Z";
```

2.5 Arithmetic Operators

CONCEPT There are many operators for manipulating numeric values and performing arithmetic operations.

C# offers a multitude of operators for manipulating data. Generally, there are three types of operators: *unary*, *binary*, and *ternary*. These terms reflect the number of operands an operator requires.

Unary operators only require a single operand. For example, consider the following expression:

```
-5
```

Of course, we understand this represents the value negative five. We can also apply the operator to a variable, as follows.

```
-number
```

This expression gives the negative of the value stored in number. The minus sign, when used this way, is called the *negation operator*. Because it only requires one operand, it is a unary operator.

Binary operators work with two operands. The assignment operator is in this category. Ternary operators, as you may have guessed, require three operands. C# has only one ternary operator, which is discussed in Chapter 5.

Arithmetic operations are very common in programming. Table 2-8 shows the arithmetic operators in C#.

Table 2-8   Arithmetic operators

Operator	Meaning	Type	Example
+	Addition	Binary	`total = cost + tax;`
-	Subtraction	Binary	`cost = total - tax;`
*	Multiplication	Binary	`tax = cost * rate;`
/	Division	Binary	`salePrice = original / 2;`
%	Modulus	Binary	`remainder = value % 3;`

Each of these operators works as you probably expect. The addition operator returns the sum of its two operands. Here are some example statements that use the addition operator:

```
amount = 4 + 8;            // Assigns 12 to amount
total = price + tax;       // Assigns price + tax to total
number = number + 1;       // Assigns number + 1 to number
```

The subtraction operator returns the value of its right operand subtracted from its left operand. Here are some examples:

```
temperature = 112 - 14;    // Assigns 98 to temperature
sale = price - discount;   // Assigns price - discount to sale
number = number - 1;       // Assigns number - 1 to number
```

The multiplication operator returns the product of its two operands. Here are some examples:

```
markUp = 12 * 0.25;             // Assigns 3 to markup
commission = sales * percent;   // Assigns sales * percent to commission
population = population * 2;     // Assigns population * 2 to population
```

The division operator returns the quotient of its left operand divided by its right operand. Here are some examples.

```
points = 100 / 20;         // Assigns 5 to points
teams = players / maxEach; // Assigns players / maxEach to teams
half = number / 2;         // Assigns number / 2 to half
```

The modulus operator returns the remainder of an integer division. The following statement assigns 2 to leftOver:

```
leftOver = 17 % 3;
```

Situations do arise where you need to get the remainder of a division. Computations that detect odd numbers or are required to determine how many items are left over after division use the modulus operator.

The program in Code Listing 2-16 demonstrates some of these operators used in a simple payroll calculation.

Code Listing 2-16   Wages.cs

```
1 // This program calculates hourly wages plus overtime.
2
3 using System;
4
5 public class Wages
6 {
7     public static void Main()
8     {
9         double regularWages,    // The calculated regular wages.
10            basePay = 25,        // The base pay rate.
11            regularHours = 40,   // The hours worked less overtime.
12            overtimeWages,       // Overtime wages
13            overtimePay = 37.5,  // Overtime pay rate
14            overtimeHours = 10,  // Overtime hours worked
15                totalWages;      // Total wages
16
17         regularWages = basePay * regularHours;
18         overtimeWages = overtimePay * overtimeHours;
19         totalWages = regularWages + overtimeWages;
20         Console.WriteLine("Wages for this week are ${0}",
21             totalWages);
22     }
23 }
```

Program Output
```
Wages for this week are $1375
```

Code Listing 2-16 calculates the total wages an worker paid hourly earned in one week. As mentioned in the comments, there are variables for regular wages, base pay rate, regular hours worked, overtime wages, overtime pay rate, overtime hours worked, and total wages.

Line 17 in the program multiplies basePay times regularHours and stores the result, which is 1000, in regularWages:

```
regularWages = basePay * regularHours;
```

Line 18 multiplies overtimePay times overtimeHours and stores the result, which is 375, in overtimeWages:

```
overtimeWages = overtimePay * overtimeHours;
```

Line 19 adds the regular wages and the overtime wages and stores the result, 1375, in totalWages:

```
totalWages = regularWages + overtimeWages;
```

The WriteLine statement on line 20 displays the message on the screen reporting the week's wages.

Integer Division

When both operands of a division statement are integers, the statement will result in integer division. This means the result of the division will be an integer as well. If there is a remainder, it will be discarded. For example, in the following code, parts is assigned the value 5.0:

```
double parts;
parts = 17 / 3;
```

It doesn't matter that parts is declared as a double because the fractional part of the result is discarded before the assignment takes place. In order for a division operation to return a floating-point value, one of the operands must be of a floating-point data type. For example, the previous code could be written as:

```
double parts;
parts = 17.0 / 3;
```

In this code, 17.0 is interpreted as a floating-point number, so the division operation will return a floating-point number. The result of the division is 5.666666666666667.

Operator Precedence

It is possible to build mathematical expressions with several operators. The following statement assigns the sum of 17, x, 21, and y to the variable answer.

```
answer = 17 + x + 21 + y;
```

Some expressions are not that straightforward, however. Consider the following statement:

```
outcome = 12 + 6 / 3;
```

What value will be stored in outcome? The 6 is used as an operand for both the addition and division operators. The outcome variable could be assigned either 6 or 14, depending on when the division takes place. The answer is 14 because the division operator has higher *precedence* than the addition operator.

Mathematical expressions are evaluated from left to right. When two operators share an operand, the operator with the highest precedence works first. Multiplication and division have higher precedence than addition and subtraction, so the statement above works like this:

1. 6 is divided by 3, yielding a result of 2
2. 12 is added to 2, yielding a result of 14

It could be diagrammed as shown in Figure 2-3.

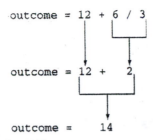

Figure 2-3   Precedence illustrated

Table 2-9 shows the precedence of the arithmetic operators. The operators at the top of the table have higher precedence than the ones below it.

Table 2-9   Precedence of arithmetic operators (highest to lowest)

Highest Precedence	- (unary negation)
	* / %
Lowest Precedence	+ -

The multiplication, division, and modulus operators have the same precedence. The addition and subtraction operators have the same precedence. If two operators sharing an operand have the same precedence, they work according to their *associativity*. Associativity is either *left to right* or *right to left*. Table 2-10 shows the arithmetic operators and their associativity.

Table 2-10   Associativity of arithmetic operators

Operator	Associativity
- (unary negation)	Right to left
* / %	Left to right
+ -	Left to right

Table 2-11 shows some expressions with their values.

Table 2-11 Some expressions and their values

Expression	Value
5 + 2 * 4	13
10 / 2 - 3	2
8 + 12 * 2 - 4	28
4 + 17 % 2 - 1	4
6 - 3 * 2 + 7 - 1	6

Grouping with Parentheses

Parts of a mathematical expression may be grouped with parentheses to force some operations to be performed before others. In the statement below, the sum of a, b, c, and d is divided by 4.0.

```
average = (a + b + c + d) / 4.0;
```

Without the parentheses, however, d would be divided by 4 and the result added to a, b, and c. Table 2-12 shows more expressions and their values.

Table 2-12 More expressions and their values

Expression	Value
(5 + 2) * 4	28
10 / (5 - 3)	5
8 + 12 * (6 - 2)	56
(4 + 17) % 2 - 1	0
(6 - 3) * (2 + 7) / 3	9

CHECKPOINT

2.22 Complete the following table by writing the value of each expression in the Value column.

Expression	Value
6 + 3 * 5	
12 / 2 - 4	
9 + 14 * 2 - 6	
5 + 19 % 3 - 1	
(6 + 2) * 3	
14 / (11 - 4)	
9 + 12 * (8 - 3)	

2.23 Is the division statement in the following code an example of integer division or floating-point division? What value will be stored in portion?

```
double portion;
portion = 70 / 3;
```

2.6 Combined Assignment Operators

 CONCEPT The combined assignment operators combine the assignment operator with the arithmetic operators.

Quite often, programs have assignment statements of the following form:

```
x = x + 1;
```

On the right side of the assignment operator, 1 is added to x. The result is then assigned to x, replacing the value that was previously there. Effectively, this statement adds 1 to x. Here is another example:

```
balance = balance + deposit;
```

Assuming that balance and deposit are variables, this statement assigns the value of bal-ance + deposit to balance. The effect of this statement is that deposit is added to the value stored in balance. Here is another example:

```
balance = balance - withdrawal;
```

Assuming that balance and deposit are variables, this statement assigns the value of balance - withdrawal to balance. The effect of this statement is that withdrawal is sub-tracted from the value stored in balance.

If you have not seen these types of statements before, they might cause some initial confusion because the same variable name appears on both sides of the assignment operator. Table 2-13 shows other examples of statements written this way.

Table 2-13   Various assignment statements (assume x = 6 in each statement)

Statement	What It Does	Value of x After the Statement
x = x + 4;	Adds 4 to x	10
x = x - 3;	Subtracts 3 from x	3
x = x * 10;	Multiplies x by 10	60
x = x / 2;	Divides x by 2	3
x = x % 4	Assigns the remainder of x / 4 to x.	2

These types of operations are common in programming. For convenience, C# offers a special set of operators designed specifically for these jobs. Table 2-14 shows the *combined assignment operators*, also known as *compound operators*.

Table 2-14   Combined assignment operators

Operator	Example Usage	Equivalent To
+=	x += 5;	x = x + 5;
-=	y -= 2;	y = y - 2;
*=	z *= 10;	z = z * 10;
/=	a /= b;	a = a / b;
%=	c %= 3;	c = c % 3;

As you can see, the combined assignment operators do not require the programmer to type the variable name twice. The following statement:

```
balance = balance + deposit;
```

could be rewritten as

```
balance += deposit;
```

Similarly, the statement

```
balance = balance - withdrawal;
```

could be rewritten as

```
balance -= withdrawal;
```

 CHECKPOINT

2.24 Write statements using combined assignment operators to perform the following:

    a)   Add 6 to x

    b)   Subtract 4 from amount

    c)   Multiply y by 4

    d)   Divide total by 27

    e)   Store in x the remainder of x divided by 7

2.7 Conversion Between Data Types

 CONCEPT Before a value can be stored in a variable, the value's data type must be compatible with the variable's data type. C# performs some conversions between data types automatically, but does not automatically perform any conversion that can result in the loss of data. C# also follows a set of rules when evaluating arithmetic expressions containing mixed data types.

C# is a *strongly typed language*. This means that before a value is assigned to a variable, C# checks the data types of the variable and the value being assigned to it to determine if they are compatible. For example, look at the following statements.

```
int x;
double y = 2.5;
x = y;
```

The assignment statement is attempting to store a double value (2.5) in an int variable. When the C# compiler encounters this line of code, it will respond with an error message. Not all assignment statements that mix data types are rejected by the compiler, however. For instance, look at the following program segment:

```
int x;
short y = 2;
x = y;
```

This assignment statement, which stores a short in an int, will work with no problems. So, why does C# permit a short to be stored in an int, but does not permit a double to be stored in an int? The obvious reason is that a double can store fractional numbers and can hold values much larger than an int can hold. If C# were to permit a double to be assigned to an int, a loss of data would be likely.

Just like officers in the military, the primitive data types are ranked. One data type outranks another if it can hold a larger number. For example, a float outranks an int, and an int outranks a short. Figure 2-4 shows the numeric data types in order of their rank. The higher a data type appears in the list, the higher its rank.

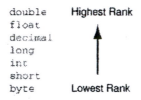

Figure 2-4   Numeric data type ranking

In assignment statements where values of lower-ranked data types are stored in variables of higher-ranked data types, C# automatically converts the lower-ranked value to the higher-ranked type. This is called a *widening conversion*. For example, the following code demonstrates a widening conversion, which takes place when an int value is stored in a double variable.

```
double x;
int y = 10;
x = y;               // Performs a widening conversion
```

A *narrowing conversion* is the conversion of a value to a lower-ranked type. For example, converting a double to an int would be a narrowing conversion. Because narrowing conversions can potentially cause the loss of data, C# does not automatically perform them.

Cast Operators

The *cast operator* lets you manually convert a value, even if it means that a narrowing conversion will take place. Cast operators are unary operators that appear as a data type name enclosed in a set of parentheses. The operator precedes the value being converted. Here is an example:

```
x = (int)number;
```

The cast operator in this statement is the word int inside the parentheses. It returns the value in number, converted to an int. This converted value is then stored in x. If number were a floating-point variable, such as a float or a double, the value that is returned would be *truncated*, which means the fractional part of the number is lost. The original value in the number variable is not changed however.

Table 2-15 shows several statements using a cast operator.

Table 2-15 Example uses of cast operators

Statement	Description
littleNum = (short)bigNum;	The cast operator returns the value in bigNum, converted to a short. The converted value is assigned to the variable littleNum.
x = (long)3.7;	The cast operator is applied to the expression 3.7. The operator returns the value 3, which is assigned to the variable x.
int number = (int)72.567;	The cast operator is applied to the expression 72.567. The operator returns 72, which is used to initialize the variable number.
value = (float)x;	The cast operator returns the value in x, converted to a float. The converted value is assigned to the variable value.
value = (byte)number;	The cast operator returns the value in number, converted to a byte. The converted value is assigned to the variable value.

Note that when a cast operator is applied to a variable, it does not change the contents of the variable. It only returns the value stored in the variable, converted to the specified data type.

Recall from our earlier discussion that when both operands of a division are integers, the operation will result in integer division. This means that the result of the division will be an integer, with any fractional part of the result thrown away. For example, look at the following code.

```
int pies = 10, people = 4;
double piesPerPerson;
piesPerPerson = pies / people;
```

Although 10 divided by 4 is 2.5, this code will store 2 in the piesPerPerson variable. Because both pies and people are int variables, the result will be an int, and the fractional part will be thrown away. We can modify the code with a cast operator, however, so it gives the correct result as a floating-point value:

```
piesPerPerson = (double)pies / people;
```

The variable pies is an int and holds the value 10. The expression (double)pies returns the value in pies converted to a double. This means that one of the division operator's operands is a double, so the result of the division will be a double. The statement could also have been written as:

```
piesPerPerson = pies / (double)people;
```

In this statement, the cast operator returns the value of the people variable converted to a double. In either statement, the result of the division is a double.

 WARNING! The cast operator can be applied to an entire expression enclosed in parentheses. For example, look at the following statement:

```
piesPerPerson = (double)(pies / people);
```

This statement does not convert the value in pies **or people to a** double, **but converts the result of the expression** pies / people. **If this statement were used, an integer division operation would still have been performed. Here's why: The result of the expression** pies / people **is 2 (because integer division takes place). The value 2 converted to a** double **is 2.0. To prevent the integer division from taking place, one of the operands must be converted to a** double.

Mixed Integer Operations

One of the nuances of the C# language is the way it handles arithmetic operations on int, byte, and short variables. When values of the byte or short data types are used in arithmetic expressions, they are temporarily converted to int values. The result of an arithmetic operation using only a mixture of byte, short, or int values will always be an int.

For example, assume that b and c in the following expression are short variables.

```
b + c
```

Although both b and c are short variables, the result of the expression b + c is an int. This means that when the result of such an expression is stored in a variable, the variable must be an int or higher data type. For example, look at the following code:

```
short firstNumber = 10,
secondNumber = 20,
thirdNumber;
// The following statement causes an error!
thirdNumber = firstNumber + secondNumber;
```

The error results from the fact that thirdNumber is a short. Although firstNumber and secondNumber are also short variables, the expression firstNumber + secondNumber results in an int value. The program can be corrected if thirdNumber is declared as an int, or if a cast operator is used in the assignment statement, as shown here.

```
thirdNumber = (short)(firstNumber + secondNumber);
```

Other Mixed Mathematical Expressions

Where a mathematical expression has one or more values of the double, float, or long data types, C# strives to convert all of the operands in the expression to the same data type. Let's look at the specific rules that govern the evaluation of these types of expressions.

1. If one of an operator's operands is a double, the value of the other operand will be converted to a double. The result of the expression will be a double. For example, in the following statement assume that b is a double and c is an int.

```
a = b + c;
```

The value in c will be converted to a double prior to the addition. The result of the addition will be a double, so the variable a must also be a double.

2. If one of an operator's operands is a float, the value of the other operand will be converted to a float. The result of the expression will be a float. For example, in the following statement assume that x is a short and y is a float.

```
z = x * y;
```

The value in x will be converted to a float prior to the multiplication. The result of the multiplication will be a float, so the variable z must also be either a double or a float.

3. If one of an operator's operands is a long, the value of the other operand will be converted to a long. The result of the expression will be a long. For example, in the following statement assume that a is a long and b is a short.

```
c = a - b;
```

The variable b will be converted to a long prior to the subtraction. The result of the subtraction will be a long, so the variable c must also be a long, float, double or decimal.

 CHECKPOINT

2.25 The following declaration appears in a program:

```
short totalPay, basePay = 500, bonus = 1000;
```

The following statement appears in the same program:

```
totalPay = basePay + bonus;
```

a) Will the statement compile properly or cause an error?

b) If the statement causes an error, why? How can you fix it?

2.26 The variable a is a float and the variable b is a double. Write a statement that will assign the value of b to a without causing an error when the program is compiled.

2.8   Creating Named Constants with `const`

 CONCEPT The `const` key word can be used in a variable declaration to make the variable a named constant. Named constants are initialized with a value, and that value cannot change during the execution of the program.

Assume that the following statement appears in a banking program that calculates data pertaining to loans.

```
amount = balance * 0.069;
```

In such a program, two problems may arise. First, it is not clear to anyone other than the original programmer what 0.069 is. It appears to be an interest rate, but in some situations there are fees associated with loan payments. How can the purpose of this statement be determined without painstakingly checking the rest of the program?

The second problem occurs if this number is used in other calculations throughout the program and must be changed periodically. Assuming the number is an interest rate, what if the rate changes from 6.9 percent to 8.2 percent? The programmer would have to search through the source code for every occurrence of the number.

Both of these problems can be addressed by using named constants. A *named constant* is a variable whose content is read only and cannot be changed during the program's execution. You can create such a variable in C# by using the `const` key word in the variable declaration. The word `const` is written just before the data type. Here is an example:

```
const double INTEREST_RATE = 0.069;
```

This statement looks just like a regular variable declaration except that the word `const` appears before the data type, and the variable name is written in all uppercase characters. It is not required that the variable name appear in all uppercase characters, but many programmers prefer to write them this way so they are easily distinguishable from regular variable names.

An initialization value must be given when declaring a variable with the `const` modifier, or an error will result when the program is compiled. A compiler error will also result if there are any statements in the program that attempt to change the contents of a `const` variable.

An advantage of using named constants is that they make programs more self-documenting. The statement

```
amount = balance * 0.069;
```

can be changed to read

```
amount = balance * INTEREST_RATE;
```

A new programmer can read the second statement and know what is happening. It is evident that balance is being multiplied by the interest rate. Another advantage to this approach is that widespread changes can easily be made to the program. Let's say the interest rate appears in a dozen different statements throughout the program. When the rate changes, the initialization value in the definition of the named constant is the only value that needs to be modified. If the rate increases to 8.2 percent, the declaration can be changed to the following:

```
const double INTEREST_RATE = 0.082;
```

The program is then ready to be recompiled. Every statement that uses INTEREST_RATE will be updated with the new value.

2.9   The string Type

 The string type allows you to create objects for holding strings. It also has various methods that allow you to work with strings.

You have already encountered strings and examined programs that display them on the screen, but let's take a moment to make sure you understand what one is. A string is a sequence of characters. It can be used to represent any type of data that contains text, such as names, addresses, warning messages, and so forth. String literals are enclosed in double-quotation marks, such as:

```
"Hello World"
"Joe Mahoney"
```

C# uses System.String to represent strings. As you already know, C# uses aliases to represent classes in the FCL. The key word string is used as an alias for the System.String class. You use this class to create objects that are capable of storing strings and performing operations on them. Before discussing this class, let's briefly discuss how classes and objects are related.

Objects Are Created from Classes

Chapter 1 introduced you to objects as software entities that can contain attributes and methods. An object's attributes are data values that are stored in the object. An object's methods are procedures that perform operations on the object's attributes. Before an object can be created, however, it must be designed by a programmer. The programmer determines the attributes and methods that are necessary, and then creates a class that describes the object.

You have already seen classes used as containers for applications. A class can also be used to specify the attributes and methods that a particular type of object may have. Think of a class as a blueprint for objects. Thus, a class is not an object, but a description of an object. When the program is running, it can use the class to create, in memory, as many objects as needed. Each object that is created from a class is called an *instance* of the class.

TIP: Don't worry if these concepts seem a little fuzzy to you. As you progress through this book, the concepts of classes and objects will be reinforced again and again.

The string Class

The first step in using the string class is to declare a variable of the string class data type. Here is an example of a string variable declaration.

```
string name;
```

This statement declares name as a string variable. A *class type variable* does not hold the actual data item that it is associated with, but holds the memory address of the data item it is associated with. If name is a string class variable, then name can hold the memory address of a string object. This is illustrated in Figure 2-5.

Figure 2-5 A string class variable can hold the address of a string object

When a class type variable holds the address of an object, it is said that the variable references the object. For this reason, class type variables are commonly known as *reference variables*.

Creating a string Object

Anytime you write a string literal in your program, C# will create a string object in memory to hold it. You can create a string object in memory and store its address in a string variable with a simple assignment statement. Here is an example.

```
name = "Joe Mahoney";
```

Here, the string literal causes a string object to be created in memory with the value "Joe Mahoney" stored in it. Then the assignment operator stores the address of that object in the name variable. After this statement executes, it is said that the name variable references a string object. This is illustrated in Figure 2-6.

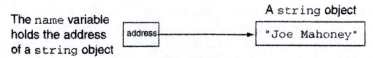

Figure 2-6 The name variable holds the address of a string object

You can also use the = operator to initialize a string variable, as shown here:

```
string name = "Joe Mahoney";
```

This statement declares name as a string variable, creates a string object with the value "Joe Mahoney" stored in it, and assigns the object's memory address to the name variable. Code Listing 2-17 shows string variables being declared, initialized, and then used in a WriteLine statement.

Code Listing 2-17   StringDemo.cs

```
1 // A simple program demonstrating string objects.
2
3 using System;
4
5 public class StringDemo
6 {
7     public static void Main()
8     {
9         string greeting = "Good morning ";
10        string name = "Herman";
11
12        Console.WriteLine(greeting + name);
13    }
14 }
```

Program Output
Good morning Herman

Because the string type is a class, it provides numerous properties and methods for working with strings. For example, the string class has a property named Length that returns the length of the string stored in an object. Assuming the name variable references a string object, the following statement stores the length of its string in the variable stringSize. (Assume that stringSize is an int variable.)

```
stringSize = name.Length;
```

The string class's Length property returns an int value. This value can be stored in a variable, displayed on the screen, or used in calculations. Code Listing 2-18 demonstrates the Length method.

 NOTE: The string class' Length property returns the number of characters in the string, including spaces.

The words attribute and property mean the same thing in C#.

Code Listing 2-18 StringLength.cs

```
1 // This program demonstrates the string class's length method.
2
3 using System;
4
5 public class StringLength
6 {
7    public static void Main()
8    {
9       string name = "Herman";
10      int stringSize;
11
12      stringSize = name.Length;
13      Console.WriteLine("{0} has {1} characters.", name,
           stringSize);
14   }
15 }
```

Program Output
```
Herman has 6 characters.
```

You will study string class methods in detail in Chapter 9, but let's look at a few more examples now. In addition to the Length property, Table 2-16 describes the Chars property and ToLower, and ToUpper methods.

Table 2-16 A few string class properties and methods

Properties/Methods	Description and Example

Length	This property returns the number of characters in the string. It returns a value of type int
	
	Example:
	```int stringSize;```
	```string name = "Herman";```
	```stringSize = name.Length;```
	
	After this code executes, the stringSize variable will hold the value 6.

(table continues)

Table 2-16 A few string class properties and methods *(continued)*

Properties/Methods	Description and Example

ToLower()	This method returns a new string that is the lowercase equivalent of the string contained in the calling object.
	
	Example:
	
	``
	string bigName = "HERMAN";
	string littleName = bigName.ToLower();
	``
	
	After this code executes, the object reference by littleName will hold the string "herman".

ToUpper()	This method returns a new string that is the uppercase equivalent of the string contained in the calling object.
	
	Example:
	
	``
	string littleName = "herman";
	string bigName = littleName.ToUpper();
	``
	
	After this code executes, the object reference by bigName will hold the string "HERMAN".

Indexer*	The indexer in C# gets the character at a specified character position in this instance. The first character is at position 0, the second character is at position 1, etc.
	Example:
	
	``
	string name = "Herman";
	char letter = name[3];
	``
	
	After this code executes, the variable letter will hold the character 'm'.

*Indexer is neither a property nor a method.

The program in Code Listing 2-19 demonstrates these properties and methods.

Code Listing 2-19   StringMethods.cs

```
1 // This program demonstrates a few of the string methods.
2
3 using System;
4
```

(code listing continues)

Code Listing 2-19 StringMethods.cs *(continued)*

```
5 public class StringMethods
6 {
7    public static void Main()
8    {
9        string message = "C# is Great Fun!";
10       string upper = message.ToUpper();
11       string lower = message.ToLower();
12       char letter = message[2];
13       int stringSize = message.Length;
14
15       Console.WriteLine(message);
16       Console.WriteLine(upper);
17       Console.WriteLine(lower);
18       Console.WriteLine(letter);
19       Console.WriteLine(stringSize);
20    }
21 }
```

Program Output

```
C# is Great Fun!
C# IS GREAT FUN!
c# is great fun!
v
18
```

Notice from the program in Code Listing 2-19 that we must call the ToUpper and ToLower methods. To call a method means to execute it. The general form of a method call is

```
ReferenceVariable.method(arguments...)
```

ReferenceVariable is the name of a variable that references an object, method is the name of a method, and arguments... is zero or more arguments that are passed to the method. If no arguments are passed to the method a set of empty parentheses must follow the name of the method.

 NOTE: In C#, method names always start with capital letters, even at word boundaries. Write and WriteLine are two such examples.

 # CHECKPOINT

2.27 Write a statement that declares a string variable named city. The variable should be initialized so it references an object with the string "San Francisco."

2.28 Assume that stringLength is an int variable. Write a statement that stores the length of the string referenced by the city variable (declared in Checkpoint 2.27) in stringLength.

2.29 Assume that oneChar is a char variable. Write a statement that stores the first character in the string referenced by the city variable (declared in Checkpoint 2.27) in oneChar.

2.30 Assume that upperCity is a string variable. Write a statement that stores the uppercase equivalent of the string referenced by the city variable (declared in Checkpoint 2.27) in upperCity.

2.31 Assume that lowerCity is a string variable. Write a statement that stores the lowercase equivalent of the string referenced by the city variable (declared in Checkpoint 2.27) in lowerCity.

2.10   Scope

CONCEPT A variable's scope is the part of the program that has access to the variable.

Every variable has a *scope*. The scope of a variable is the part of the program where the variable may be accessed by its name. A variable is visible only to statements inside the variable's scope. The rules that define a variable's scope are complex, and you are only introduced to the concept here. In other chapters of the book we revisit this topic and expand on it.

So far, you have only seen variables declared inside the main method. Variables that are declared inside a method are called *local variables*. Later you will learn about variables that are declared outside of methods, but for now, let's focus on the use of local variables.

A local variable's scope begins at the variable's declaration and ends at the end of the block in which the variable is declared. The variable cannot be accessed by statements that are outside this region. This means that a local variable cannot be accessed by code that is outside the method, or inside the method but before the variable's declaration. The program in Code Listing 2-20 shows an example.

Code Listing 2-20   Scope.cs

```
 1 // This program can't find its variable.
 2
 3 using System;
 4
 5 public class Scope
 6 {
 7    public static void Main()
 8    {
 9       Console.WriteLine(value);   // ERROR!
10       int value = 100;
11    }
12 }
```

The program will not compile because it attempts to send the contents of the variable `value` to `WriteLine` before the variable is declared. It is important to remember the compiler reads your program from top to bottom. If it encounters a statement that uses a variable before the variable is declared, an error will result. To correct the program, the variable declaration must be written before any statement that uses it.

 NOTE: If you compile this program, the compiler will display an error message such as "cannot resolve symbol." This means that the compiler has encountered a name that it cannot determine a meaning for.

Another rule that you must remember about local variables is that you cannot have two local variables with the same name in the same scope. For example, look at the following method:

```csharp
using System;
public static void Main()
{
    // Declare a variable named number and
    // display its value.
    int number = 7;
    Console.WriteLine(number);

    // Declare another variable named number and
    // display its value.
    int number = 100;              // ERROR!!!
    Console.WriteLine(number);     // ERROR!!!
}
```

This method declares a variable named number and initializes it with the value 7. The variable's scope begins at the declaration statement and extends to the end of the method. Inside the variable's scope a statement appears that declares another variable named number. This statement will cause an error because you cannot have two local variables with the same name in the same scope.

2.11   Comments

 Comments are notes of explanation that document lines or sections of a program. Comments are part of the program, but the compiler ignores them. They are intended for people who may be reading the source code.

It may surprise you that one of the most important parts of a program has absolutely no impact on the way it runs. In fact, the compiler pretends this part of a program doesn't even exist. Of course, I'm speaking of the comments.

It is crucial, however, that you develop the habit of thoroughly annotating your code with descriptive comments. It might take extra time now, but it will almost certainly save time in the future. Imagine writing a program of medium complexity with about 8,000 to 10,000 lines of code. Once you have written the code and satisfactorily debugged it, you happily put it away and move on to the next project. Ten months later you are asked to make a modification to the program (or worse, track down and fix an elusive bug). You pull out the massive pile of paper that contains your source code and stare at thousands of statements that now make no sense at all. You find variables with names like z2, and you can't remember what they are for. If only you had left some notes to yourself explaining all the program's nuances and oddities. Of course it's too late now. All that's left to do is decide what will take less time: figuring out the old program or completely rewriting it!

This scenario might sound extreme, but it's all too common, and one you don't want to happen to you. Real-world programs are usually large and complex. Thoroughly documented programs will make your life easier, not to mention the other poor souls who may have to read your code in the future.

Two Ways to Comment in C#

Two Forward Slashes

You have already seen the first way to write comments in a C# program. You simply place two forward slashes (//) where you want the comment to begin. The compiler ignores everything from that point to the end of the line. Code Listing 2-21 shows that comments may be placed liberally throughout a program.

Code Listing 2-21 Comment1.cs

```
1  // PROGRAM: Comment1.cs
2  // Written by Herbert Dorfmann
3  // This program calculates company payroll
4
5  public class Comment1
6  {
7      public static void Main()
8      {
9          float payRate;        // Holds the hourly pay rate
10         float hours;          // Hours holds the hours worked
11         int employeeNumber;   // Holds the employee number
12
13         // The Remainder of This program is Omitted.
14     }
15  }
```

In addition to telling who wrote the program and describing the purpose of variables, comments can also be used to explain complex procedures in your code.

Multi-Line Comments

The second type of comment in C# is the multi-line comment. *Multi-line comments* start with /* (a forward slash followed by an asterisk) and end with */ (an asterisk followed by a forward slash). Everything between these markers is ignored. Code Listing 2-22 illustrates how multi-line comments may be used.

Code Listing 2-22   Comment2.cs

```
 1  /*
 2      PROGRAM: Comment2.cs
 3      Written by Herbert Dorfmann
 4      This program calculates company payroll
 5  */
 6
 7  public class Comment2
 8  {
 9      public static void Main()
10      {
11          float payRate;         // Holds the hourly pay rate
12          float hours;           // Hours holds the hours worked
13          int employeeNumber;    // Holds the employee number
14
15          // The Remainder of This Program is Omitted.
16      }
17  }
```

Unlike a comment started with //, a multi-line comment can span several lines. This makes it more convenient to write large blocks of comments because you do not have to mark every line. Consequently, the multi-line comment is inconvenient for writing single-line comments because you must type both a beginning and ending comment symbol.

Remember the following advice when using multi-line comments:

- Be careful not to reverse the beginning symbol with the ending symbol.

- Be sure not to forget the ending symbol.

Many programmers use asterisks or other characters to draw borders or boxes around their comments. This helps to visually separate the comments from surrounding code. These are called block comments. Table 2-17 shows four examples of block comments.

 CHECKPOINT

2.32 How do you write a single-line comment? How do you write a multi-line comment?

Table 2-17 Block comments

Block Comments Created with /* and */	Block Comments Created with //

```/*```
 ```*   This program demonstrates the```
 ```*   way to write comments.```
 ```*/```
	```//********************************```
	 ```// This program demonstrates the *```
	 ```// way to write comments. *```
	 ```//********************************```

```/********************************```
 ```* This program demonstrates the   *```
 ```* way to write comments.   *```
 ```********************************/```
	```//--------------------------------```
	 ```// This program demonstrates the```
	 ```// way to write comments.```
	 ```//--------------------------------```

2.12 Programming Style

CONCEPT Programming style refers the way a programmer uses spaces, indentations, blank lines, and punctuation characters to visually arrange a program's source code.

In Chapter 1, you learned that syntax rules govern the way a language may be used. The syntax rules of C# dictate how and where to place key words, semicolons, commas, braces, and other elements of the language. The compiler checks for syntax errors, and if there are none, generates byte code.

When the compiler reads a program it processes it as one long stream of characters. The compiler doesn't care that each statement is on a separate line, or that spaces separate operators from operands. Humans, on the other hand, find it difficult to read programs that aren't written in a visually pleasing manner. Consider Code Listing 2-23.

Code Listing 2-23 Compact.cs

```
1 using System;public class Compact {public static void
      Main(){int
2 shares=220; double averagePrice=14.67; Console.WriteLine(
3 "There were {0} shares sold at $ {1} per share.",
      shares,averagePrice);}}
```

Program Output
```
There were 220 shares sold at $ 14.67 per share.
```

Although the program is syntactically correct (it doesn't violate any rules of C#), it is very difficult to read. The same program is shown in Code Listing 2-24 is written in a more understandable style.

Code Listing 2-24   Readable.cs

```
 1 /*
 2    This example is much more readable than Compact.cs.
 3 */
 4
 5 using System;
 6
 7 public class Readable
 8 {
 9    public static void Main()
10    {
11       int shares = 220;
12       double averagePrice = 14.67;
13
14       Console.WriteLine("There were {0} shares sold at ${1}
             per share.",shares, averagePrice);
15    }
16 }
```

Program Output

There were 220 shares sold at $14.67 per share.

The term *programming style* usually refers to the way source code is visually arranged. It includes techniques for consistently putting spaces and indentations in a program so visual cues are created. These cues quickly tell a programmer important information about a program.

For example, notice in Code Listing 2-24 that inside the class's braces each line is indented, and inside the main method's braces each line is indented again. It is a common programming style to indent all the lines inside a set of braces. This is illustrated in Figure 2-7.

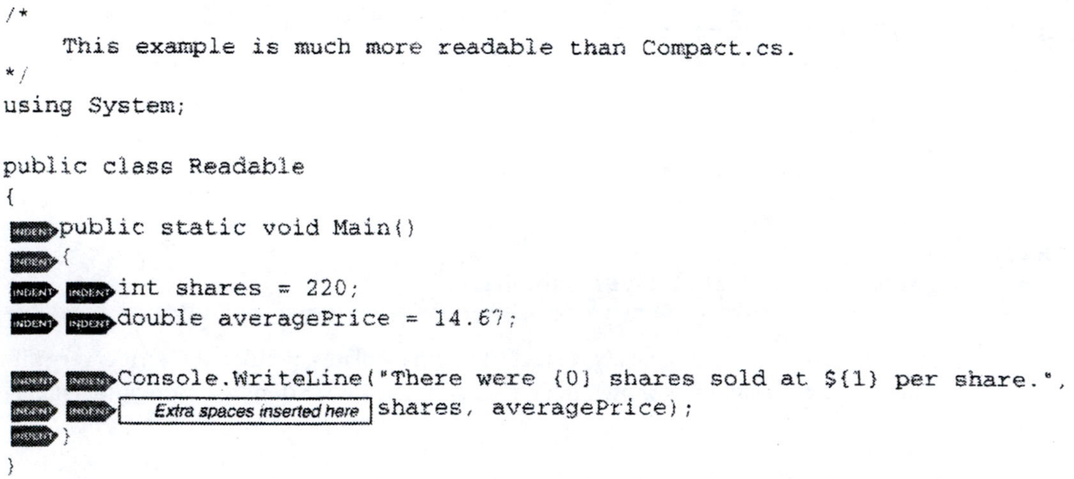

```
/*
   This example is much more readable than Compact.cs.
*/
using System;

public class Readable
{
[INDENT]public static void Main()
[INDENT]{
[INDENT][INDENT]int shares = 220;
[INDENT][INDENT]double averagePrice = 14.67;

[INDENT][INDENT]Console.WriteLine("There were {0} shares sold at ${1} per share.",
[INDENT][INDENT][ Extra spaces inserted here ]shares, averagePrice);
[INDENT]}
}
```

Figure 2-7   Indentation

Another aspect of programming style is how to handle statements that are too long to fit on one line. Notice that the WriteLine statement is spread out over three lines. Extra spaces were inserted at the beginning of the statement's second and third lines, which give an indication that they are continuations.

When declaring multiple variables of the same type with a single statement, it is a common practice to write each variable name on a separate line with a comment explaining the variable's purpose. Here is an example:

```
int fahrenheit,      // To hold the Fahrenheit temperature
    centigrade,      // To hold the centigrade temperature
    kelvin;          // To hold the Kelvin temperature
```

You may have noticed in the example programs that a blank line is inserted between the variable declarations and the statements that follow them. This is intended to visually separate the declarations from the executable statements.

There are many other issues related to programming style. They will be presented throughout the book.

2.13 Reading Keyboard Input

CONCEPT C# programs can read console input from the keyboard.

Recall from an earlier section in this chapter that the monitor is normally considered the standard output device, and the keyboard is normally considered the standard input device. As you have seen demonstrated, you simply call one of the methods, Console.Write or Console.WriteLine, to display a message.

To retrieve the user's input interactively you call the Console.ReadLine method. This method reads a "line" of input, which is a series of characters typed by the user, terminated by the Enter key. The Enter key is not part of the input. The ReadLine method returns the line of input as a string object. For example, look at the following code:

```
string name;

// Ask the user to enter his or her name.
Console.Write("Enter your name: ");
name = Console.ReadLine();
```

After this code executes, the name variable will reference a string object containing the user's input.

The program in Code Listing 2-25 demonstrates what we know so far.

Code Listing 2-25   ReadKeyboard.cs

```
 1 /*
 2    This program asks the user to enter his or her
 3    first, middle, and last names.
 4 */
 5
 6 using System;
 7
 8 public class ReadKeyboard
 9 {
10    public static void Main()
11    {
12        string firstName,      // The user's first name
13               middleName,     // The user's middle name
14               lastName;       // The user's last name
15
16        // Ask the user to enter his or her first name.
17        Console.Write("Enter your first name: ");
18        firstName = Console.ReadLine();
19
20        // Ask the user to enter his or her middle name.
21        Console.Write("Enter your middle name: ");
22        middleName = Console.ReadLine();
23
24        // Ask the user to enter his or her last name.
25        Console.Write("Enter your last name: ");
26        lastName = Console.ReadLine();
27
28        // Display a greeting.
29        Console.WriteLine("Hello {0} {1} {2}",firstName,
30                          middleName, lastName);
31    }
32 }
```

Program Output
```
Enter your first name: Leo [Enter]
Enter your middle name: James [Enter]
Enter your last name: Smith [Enter]
Hello Leo James Smith
```

Converting string Input to Numbers

The Console class' ReadLine method always returns the user's input as a string object, even if the user entered numeric data. For example, if the user enters the number 72 into an input dialog, the ReadLine method will return string object containing "72." This can be a problem if you wish to use the user's input in a math operation because you cannot perform math on strings. In such a case, you must convert the input to a numeric value. To convert a string value to a numeric value, you use one of the methods listed in Table 2-18.

Table 2-18 Some methods for converting strings to numbers

Method	Use This Method to...	Example Code
Convert.ToSByte()	Convert a string to a signed byte.	byte num; string str = "5"; num = Convert.ToSByte(str);
Convert.ToDouble()	Convert a string to a double.	double num; string str = "3.14"; num = Convert.ToDouble(str);
Convert.ToFloat()	Convert a string to a float.	float num; string str = "3.14"; num = Convert.ToFloat(str);
Convert.ToInt32()	Convert a string to an int.	int num; string str = "127"; num = Convert.ToInt32(str);
Convert.ToInt64()	Convert a string to a long.	Long num; string str = "89467"; num = Convert.ToInt64(str);
Convert.ToInt16()	Convert a string to a short.	short num; string str = "99"; num = Convert.ToInt16(str);

 NOTE: Table 2-18 is not a complete list of all the data types mentioned in the chapter. In general, all the data types have some conversion method.

The following code shows an example of how you would use the Convert.ToInt32 method to convert the value returned from the Console class's ReadLine method to an int.

```
// Get the hours worked.
Console.Write("How many hours did you work this week? ");
inputString = Console.ReadLine();
hours = Convert.ToInt32(inputString);
```

After this code executes, the number variable will hold the value entered by the user, converted to an int. Here is an example of how you would use the Convert.ToDouble method to convert the user's input to a double:

```
// Get the hourly pay rate.
Console.Write("What is your hourly pay rate? ");
inputString = Console.ReadLine();
payRate = Convert.ToDouble(inputString);
```

After this code executes, the price variable will hold the value entered by the user, converted to a double. Code Listing. 2-26 shows a complete program.

Code Listing 2-26   Payroll.cs

```
1  /*
2     This program asks the user to enter his or her name,
3     number of hours worked, and hourly pay rate. It
4     displays the user's gross pay.
5  */
6
7  using System;
8
9  public class Payroll
10 {
11    public static void Main()
12    {
13       string inputString,   // For reading input
14              name;          // The user's name
15       int hours;            // The number of hours worked
16       double payRate,       // The user's hourly pay rate
17              grossPay;      // The user's gross pay
18
19       // Get the user's name.
20       Console.Write("What is your name? ");
21       name = Console.ReadLine();
22
23       // Get the hours worked.
24       Console.Write("How many hours did you work this week?
             ");
25       inputString = Console.ReadLine();
26       hours = Convert.ToInt32(inputString);
27
28       // Get the hourly pay rate.
29       Console.Write("What is your hourly pay rate? ");
30       inputString = Console.ReadLine();
31       payRate = Convert.ToDouble(inputString);
32
33       // Calculate the gross pay.
34       grossPay = hours * payRate;
35
36       // Display a message.
37       Console.WriteLine("Hello {0}",name);
38       Console.WriteLine("Your gross pay is ${0}",grossPay);
39    }
40 }
```

(code listing continues)

Code Listing 2-26 Payroll.cs *(continued)*

Program Output with Example Input Shown in Bold
```
What is your name? Joe Mahoney [Enter]
How many hours did you work this week? 40 [Enter]
What is your hourly pay rate? 20 [Enter]
Hello Joe Mahoney
Your gross pay is $800
```

The following code in Code Listing. 2-26:

```
// Get the hours worked.
Console.Write("How many hours did you work this week? ");
inputString = Console.ReadLine();
hours = Convert.ToInt32(inputString);
```

can be shortened to

```
// Get the hours worked.
Console.Write("How many hours did you work this week? ");
hours = Convert.ToInt32(Console.ReadLine());
```

All we need to do is to substitute the value of `inputString` in the method call to `Convert.ToInt32`.

 ## CHECKPOINT

2.33 Write the code to set up all the necessary objects for reading keyboard input. Then write code that asks the user to enter the name of his or her favorite pet. Store the input in a variable.

2.34 If the user enters a number, why is it necessary to convert the value returned by a `Console` object's `ReadLine` method to a numeric data type?

2.35 Assume that the `str` variable references a `string` object. Write a statement that converts the value stored in the `string` object to an `int` and store it in a variable named `number`.

2.14 Common Errors

- **Mismatched braces, quotation marks, or parentheses.** In this chapter you saw that the statements making up a class definition are enclosed in a set of braces. Also, you saw that the statements in a method are also enclosed in a set of braces. For every opening brace, there must be a closing brace in the proper location. The same is true of double quotation marks that enclose string literals and single quotation marks that enclose character literals. Also, in a statement that uses parentheses, such as a mathematical expression, you must have a closing parenthesis for every opening parenthesis.

▪ **Forgetting to include the namespace statement.** Remember you must add using System; to properly use C# classes.

▪ **Misspelling key words.** C# will not recognize a key word that has been misspelled.

▪ **Using capital letters in key words.** Remember that C# is a case-sensitive language, and all key words are written in lowercase. Using an uppercase letter in a key word is the same as misspelling the key word.

▪ **Using a key word as a variable name.** The key words are reserved for special uses, and they cannot be used for any other purpose.

▪ **Using inconsistent spelling of variable names.** Each time you use a variable name, it must be spelled exactly as it appears in its declaration statement.

▪ **Using inconsistent case of letters in variable names.** Because C# is a case-sensitive language, it distinguishes between upper- and lowercase letters. C# will not recognize a variable name that is not written exactly as it appears in its declaration statement.

▪ **Inserting a space in a variable name.** Spaces are not allowed in variable names. Instead of attempting to use a name, such as gross pay, use one word, such as grossPay.

▪ **Forgetting the semicolon at the end of a statement.** A semicolon appears at the end of each complete statement in C#.

▪ **Assigning a double literal to a float variable.** C# is a strongly typed language, which means that it only allows you to store values of compatible data types in variables. All floating-point literals are treated as doubles, and a double value is not compatible with a float variable. A floating-point literal must end with the letter f or F in order to be stored in a float variable.

▪ **Using commas or other currency symbols in numeric literals.** Numeric literals cannot contain commas or currency symbols, such as the dollar sign.

▪ **Unintentionally performing integer division.** When both operands of a division statement are integers, the statement will result in an integer. If there is a remainder, it will be discarded.

▪ **Forgetting to group parts of a mathematical expression.** If you use more than one operator in a mathematical expression, the expression will be evaluated according to the order of operations. If you wish to change the order in which the operators are used, you must use parentheses to group part of the expression.

▪ **Inserting a space in a combined assignment operator.** A space cannot appear between the two operators that make a combined assignment operator.

- **Using a variable to receive the result of a calculation when the variable's data type is incompatible with the data type of the result.** A variable that receives the result of a calculation must be of a data type that is compatible with the data type of the result.

- **Incorrectly terminating a multi-line comment.** Multi-line comments are terminated by the */ characters. Forgetting to place these characters at a comment's desired ending point, or accidentally switching the * and the /, will cause the comment to not have an ending point.

- **Forgetting to convert the user's input to a number, when necessary.** The Console class's ReadLine method returns the user's input as a string. If the user has entered a number and you wish to use it in a math operation, you must use a Convert class method to convert it to a numeric data type.

Review Questions and Exercises

Multiple Choice and True/False

1. Every complete statement ends with a

    a) period.   b) parenthesis.

    c) semicolon.   d) ending brace.

2. The following data

    ```
    72
    'A'
    "Hello World"
    2.8712
    ```

    are all examples of

    a) variables.   b) literals.

    c) strings.   d) none of these

3. A group of statements, such as the contents of a class or a method, are enclosed in

    a) braces { }.   b) parentheses ().

    c) brackets [].   d) any of these

4. Which of the following are *not* valid assignment statements? (Indicate all that apply.)

    a) total = 9;   b) 72 = amount;

    c) profit = 129   d) letter = 'W';

5. Which of the following are not valid `WriteLine` statements? (Indicate all that apply.)

a) `Console.WriteLine + "Hello World";`

b) `Console.WriteLine("Have a nice day");`

c) `Console.WriteLine(value);`

d) `WriteLine(Programming is great fun);`

6. The negation operator is

a) unary.   b) binary.

c) ternary.   d) none of these

7. This key word is used to declare a named constant.

a) `constant`   b) `namedConstant`

c) `const`   d) `concrete`

8. These characters mark the beginning of a multi-line comment.

a) `//`   b) `/*`

c) `*/`   d) `/**`

9. These characters mark the beginning of a single-line comment.

a) `//`   b) `/*`

c) `*/`   d) `/**`

10. When C# converts a lower-ranked value to a higher-ranked type, it is called a

a) 4-bit conversion.   b) escalating conversion.

c) widening conversion.   c) narrowing conversion.

11. This type of operator lets you manually convert a value, even if it means that a narrowing conversion will take place.

a) cast   b) binary

c) uploading   d) dot

12. True or False: A left brace in a C# program is always followed by a right brace later in the program.

13. True or False: A variable must be declared before it can be used.

14. True or False: Variable names may begin with a number.

15. True or False: You cannot change the value of a variable whose declaration uses the `const` key word.

16. True or False: If one of an operator's operands is a `double`, and the other operand is an `int`, C# will automatically convert the value of the `double` to an `int`.

Predict the Output

What will the following code segments print on the screen?

1. ```
   int freeze = 32, boil = 212;
   freeze = 0;
   boil = 100;
   Console.WriteLine("{0}\n {1}\n",freeze, boil);
   ```

2. ```
   int x = 0, y = 2;
   x = y * 4;
   Console.WriteLine("{0}\n {1}\n", x, y);
   ```

3. ```
   Console.Write("I am the incredible");
   Console.Write("computing\nmachine");
   Console.Write("\nand I will\namaze\n)";
   Console.WriteLine("you.");
   ```

4. ```
   Console.Write("Be careful\n)";
   Console.Write("This might/n be a trick ");
   Console.WriteLine("question.");
   ```

5. ```
   int a, x = 23;
   a = x % 2;
   Console.WriteLine("{0}\n {1}",x, a);
   ```

Find the Error

There are a number of syntax errors in the following program. Locate as many as you can.

```
*/ What's wrong with this program? /*
using System
public MyProgram
{
    public static void main();
    }
        int a, b, c\\ Three integers
        a = 3
        b = 4
        c = a + b
        WriteLine.Console('The value of c is (0)', C);
    {
```

Algorithm Workbench

1. Show how the double variables temp, weight, and age can be declared in one statement.

2. Show how the int variables months, days, and years may be declared in one statement, with months initialized to 2 and years initialized to 3.
```

3. Write assignment statements that perform the following operations with the variables a, b, and c.

   a) Adds 2 to a and stores the result in b
   b) Multiplies b times 4 and stores the result in a
   c) Divides a by 3.14 and stores the result in b
   d) Subtracts 8 from b and stores the result in a
   e) Stores the character 'K' in c
   f) Stores the Unicode code for 'B' in c

4. Assume the variables result, w, x, y, and z are all integers, and that w = 5, x = 4, y = 8, and z = 2. What value will be stored in result in each of the following statements?

   a) `result = x + y;`
   b) `result = z * 2;`
   c) `result = y / x;`
   d) `result = y - z;`
   e) `result = w % 2;`

5. How would each of the following numbers be represented in E notation?

   a) 3.287   106   b) -978.65   1012   c) 7.65491   10-3

6. Modify the following program so it prints two blank lines between each line of text.

```
using System;
public class
{
    public static void Main()
    {
        Console.Write("Hearing in the distance");
        Console.Write("Two mandolins like creatures in the");
        Console.Write("dark");
        Console.Write("Creating the agony of ecstasy.");
        Console.WriteLine("                    - George Barker");
    }
}
```

7. Convert the following pseudocode to C# code. Be sure to declare the appropriate variables.

   Store 20 in the speed variable.
   Store 10 in the time variable.
   Multiply speed by time and store the result in the distance variable.
   Display the contents of the distance variable.

8. Convert the following pseudocode to C# code. Be sure to define the appropriate variables.

   Store 172.5 in the force variable.
   Store 27.5 in the area variable.
   Divide area by force and store the result in the pressure variable.
   Display the contents of the pressure variable.

9. Write the code to set up all the necessary objects for reading keyboard input. Then write code that asks the user to enter his or her desired annual income. Store the input in a double variable.

10. Write the code to display a dialog box that asks the user to enter his or her desired annual income. Store the input in a double variable.

11. A program has a float variable named total and a double variable named number. Write a statement that assigns number to total without causing an error when compiled.

Short Answer

1. Is the following comment a single-line style comment or a multi-line style comment?

   ```
   /* This program was written by M. A. Codewriter */
   ```

2. Is the following comment a single-line style comment or a multi-line style comment?

   ```
   // This program was written by M. A. Codewriter
   ```

3. What is meant by "case sensitive"? Why is it important for a programmer to know that C# is a case-sensitive language?

4. Briefly explain how the Write and WriteLine methods are related to the Console class.

5. What does a variable declaration tell the C# compiler about a variable?

6. Why are variable names like x not recommended?

7. What things must be considered when deciding on a data type to use for a variable?

8. Briefly describe the difference between variable assignment and variable initialization.

9. What is the difference between comments that start with the // characters and comments that start with the /* characters?

10. Briefly describe what programming style means. Why should your programming style be consistent?

11. Assume that a program uses the named constant PI to represent the value 3.14. The program uses the named constant in several statements. What is the advantage of using the named constant instead of the actual value 3.14 in each statement?

12. An expression adds a byte variable and a short variable. Of what data type will the result be?

Programming Challenges

General Requirements: Each program should have a block of comments at the top. The comments should contain your name, the assignment number and name, and any other information required by your instructor. Here is an example:

```
/*
    Assignment 1: Name, Age, and Annual Income
    Written by Jill Johnson
*/
```

1. Name, Age, and Annual Income

Write a program that declares the following:

- A string variable named name
- An int variable named age
- A double variable named annualPay

Store your age, name, and desired annual income as literals in these variables. The program should display these values on the screen in a manner similar to the following:

```
My name is Joe Mahoney, my age is 26 and
I hope to earn $100000.0 per year.
```

2. Name and Initials

Write a program that has the following string variables: firstName, middleName, and lastName. Initialize these with your first, middle, and last names. The program should also have the following char variables: firstInitial, middleInitial, and lastInitial. Store your first, middle, and last initials in these variables. The program should display the contents of these variables on the screen.

3. Personal Information

Write a program that displays the following information, each on a separate line:

- Your name
- Your address, with city, state, and ZIP
- Your telephone number
- Your college major

Although these items should be displayed on separate output lines, use only a single WriteLine statement in your program.

4. Star Pattern

Write a program that displays the following pattern:

```
       *
      ***
     *****
    *******
     *****
      ***
       *
```

5. Sum of Two Numbers

Write a program that stores the integers 62 and 99 in variables, and stores the sum of these two in a variable named `total`.

6. Sales Prediction

The East Coast sales division of a company generates 62 percent of total sales. Based on that percentage, write a program that will predict how much the East Coast division will generate if the company has $4.6 million in sales this year. *Hint: Use the value 0.62 to represent 62 percent.*

7. Land Calculation

One acre of land is equivalent to 43,560 square feet. Write a program that calculates the number of acres in a tract of land with 389,767 square feet. *Hint: Divide the size of the tract of land by the size of an acre to get the number of acres.*

8. Sales Tax

Write a program that will ask the user to enter the amount of a purchase. The program should then compute the state and county sales tax. Assume the state sales tax is 4 percent and the county sales tax is 2 percent. The program should display the amount of the purchase, the state sales tax, the county sales tax, the total sales tax, and the total of the sale (which is the sum of the amount of purchase plus the total sales tax). *Hint: Use the value 0.02 to represent 2 percent, and 0.04 to represent 4 percent.*

9. Miles-Per-Gallon

A car's miles-per-gallon (MPG) can be calculated with the following formula:

```
MPG = Miles driven / Gallons of gas used
```

Write a program that asks the user for the number of miles driven and the gallons of gas used. It should calculate the MPG and display the result on the screen.

10. Test Average

Write a program that asks the user to enter three test scores. The program should display each test score, as well as the average of the scores.

11. Circuit Board Profit

An electronics company sells circuit boards at a 40 percent profit. If you know the retail price of a circuit board, you can calculate its profit with the following formula:

```
Profit = Retail price × 0.4
```

Write a program that asks the user for the retail price of a circuit board, calculates the amount of profit earned for that product, and displays the results on the screen.

12. `string` Manipulator

Write a program that asks the user to enter the name of his or her favorite city. Use a `string` variable to store the input. The program should display the following:

- The number of characters in the city name
- The name of the city in all uppercase characters
- The name of the city in all lowercase characters
- The first character in the name of the city

13. Word Game

Write a program that plays a word game with the user. The program should ask the user to enter the following:

- His or her name
- His or her age
- The name of a city
- The name of a college
- A profession
- A type of animal
- A pet's name

After the user has entered these items, the program should display the following story, inserting the user's input into the appropriate locations:

```
There once was a person named NAME who lived in CITY. At the age of AGE,
NAME went to college at COLLEGE. NAME graduated and went to work as a(n)
PROFESSION. Then, NAME adopted a(n) ANIMAL named PETNAME. They both lived
happily ever after!
```

3

Methods

Chapter Objectives

- To understand how methods are used to break a problem into small manageable pieces
- To recognize the difference between a void method and a value-returning method
- To identify how to define and call a method
- To learn how to write a method that accepts one or more arguments
- To understand that arguments are passed by value and by reference
- To be able to write methods that return a value
- To understand the concept of recursion
- To know how to format numbers

■ Topics in this Chapter

3.1	Introduction to Methods	3.6	Recursion
3.2	Passing Arguments to a Method	3.7	Formatting Numbers
3.3	More About Local Variables	3.8	Common Errors
3.4	Returning a Value from a Method		Review Questions and Exercises
3.5	Problem Solving with Methods		

3.1 Introduction to Methods

 CONCEPT Methods can be used to break a complex program into small, manageable pieces. A void method simply executes a group of statements and then terminates. A value-returning method returns a value back to the statement that called it.

In a general sense, a method is a collection of statements that performs a specific task. So far you have experienced methods in two ways: (1) you have created a method named Main in every program you've written, and (2) you have executed predefined methods from the C# FCL, such as WriteLine and ToInt32. In this chapter you will learn how to create your own methods, other than Main, that can be executed just as you execute the FCL methods.

Methods are commonly used to break a problem down into small, manageable pieces. Instead of writing one long method that contains all of the statements necessary to solve a problem, we can write several small methods that each solve a specific part of the problem. These small methods can then be executed in the desired order to solve the problem. This approach is sometimes called *divide and conquer* because a large problem is divided into several smaller problems, which are easily solved. Figure 3-1 illustrates this idea by comparing two programs: one that uses a long, complex method containing all of the statements necessary to solve a problem, and another that divides a problem into smaller problems, each of which is handled by a separate method.

Another reason to write methods is that they simplify programs. If a specific task is performed in several places in a program, a method to perform that task need be written only once; it can then be executed anytime it is needed. This benefit of using methods is known as *code reuse* because you are reusing the code each time you need to perform the task.

First, we will look at the general ways in which methods operate. At the end of the chapter we will discuss in greater detail how methods can be used in problem solving.

void Methods and Value-Returning Methods

In this chapter you will learn about two general categories of methods: void methods and value-returning methods. A *void method* is one that simply performs a task and then terminates. WriteLine is an example of a void method found in the Console class which is part of the .NET FCL. For example, look at the following code.

```
1       int number = 7;
2       Console.WriteLine(number);
3       number = 0;
```

The statement in line 1 declares the number variable and initializes it with the value 7. The statement in line 2 calls the Console.WriteLine method, passing number as an argument. The method does its job, which is to display a value on the screen, and then terminates. The code resumes at line 3.

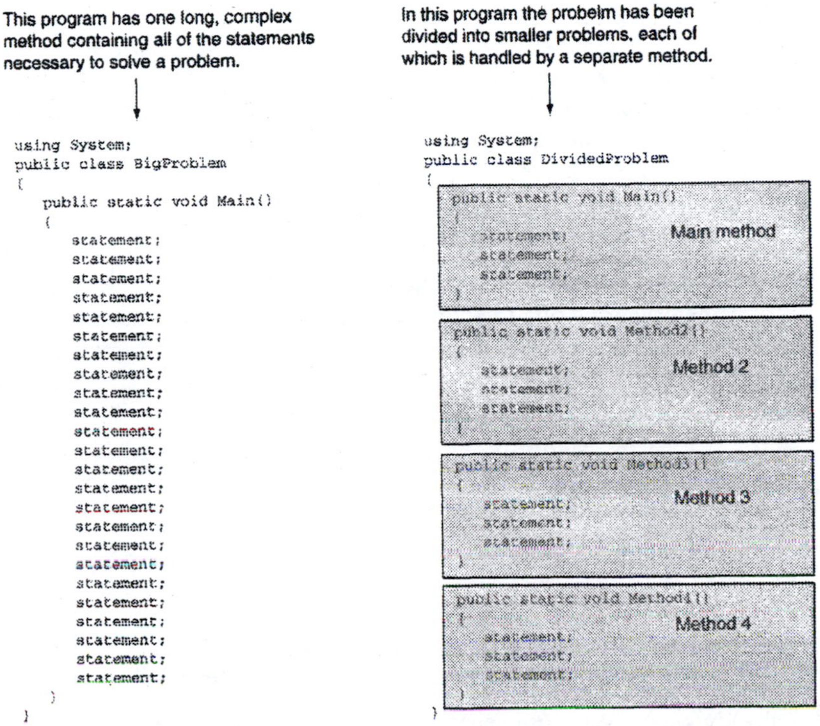

This program has one long, complex method containing all of the statements necessary to solve a problem.

In this program the probelm has been divided into smaller problems, each of which is handled by a separate method.

```
using System;
public class BigProblem
{
    public static void Main()
    {
        statement;
        statement;
        statement;
        statement;
        statement;
        statement;
        statement;
        statement;
        statement;
        statement;
        statement;
        statement;
        statement;
        statement;
        statement;
        statement;
        statement;
        statement;
        statement;
        statement;
        statement;
        statement;
        statement;
    }
}
```

```
using System;
public class DividedProblem
{
    public static void Main()         Main method
    {
        statement;
        statement;
        statement;
    }

    public static void Method2()      Method 2
    {
        statement;
        statement;
        statement;
    }

    public static void Method3()      Method 3
    {
        statement;
        statement;
        statement;
    }

    public static void Method4()      Method 4
    {
        statement;
        statement;
        statement;
    }
}
```

Figure 3-1   Using methods to divide and conquer a problem

A *value-returning method* not only performs a task, but also sends a value back to the code that called it. The ToInt32 method is an example of a value-returning method found in the Convert class of the .NET FCL. For example, look at the following code.

```
1    int number;
2    string str = "700";
3    number = Convert.ToInt32(str);
```

The statement in line 1 declares the number variable. Line 2 creates a string object with the value "700" and assigns its address to the str variable. Line 3 is an assignment statement, which assigns a value to the number variable. Notice that on the right side of the = operator is a call to the Convert.ToInt32 method, passing str as an argument. The method executes, and then returns a value back to this line of code. The value that is returned from the method is assigned to the number variable.

As demonstrated in this code, value-returning methods return a value to the calling statement. The calling statement normally does something with this value, such as assign it to a variable. The following code shows another example, one that uses the Convert.ToInt32 method's return value in a math operation.

```
1      int number;
2      string str = "700";
3      number = Convert.ToInt32(str) * 2;
```

Line 3 in this code multiplies the Convert.ToInt32 method's return value by 2 and assigns the result to the number variable. After the code executes, number will be assigned the value 1400.

Defining a void Method

To create a method you must write its *definition*, which consists of two general parts: a header and a body. You learned about both of these in Chapter 2, but let's briefly review. The *method header*, which appears at the beginning of a method definition, lists several important things about the method, including the method's name. The *method body* is a collection of statements that are performed when the method is executed. These statements are enclosed inside a set of curly braces. Figure 3-2 points out the header and body of a main method.

Header ⟶ `public static void Main()`
Body ⟶ `{`
       `  Console.WriteLine("Hello World!");`
       `}`

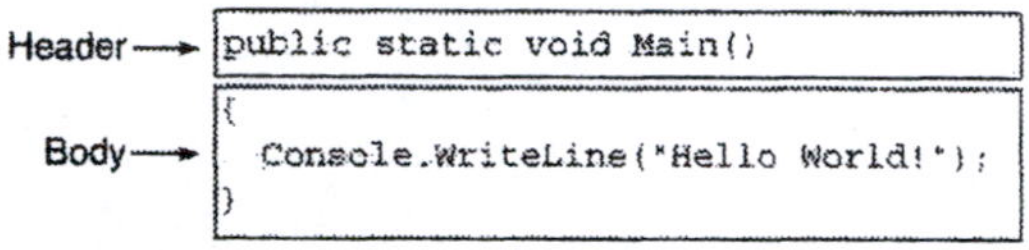

Figure 3-2 The header and body of a Main method

As you already know, every complete C# program must have a Main method. C# programs can have other methods as well. Here is an example of a simple method that displays a message on the screen:

```
public static void DisplayMessage()
{
    Console.WriteLine("Hello from the DisplayMessage method.");
}
```

This method has a header and a body. Figure 3-3 shows the parts of the method header.

Method Modifiers   Return Type   Method Name   Parameter List

`public static` `void` `DisplayMessage` `()`
`{`
`    Console.WriteLine("Hello from the DisplayMessage method.");`
`}`

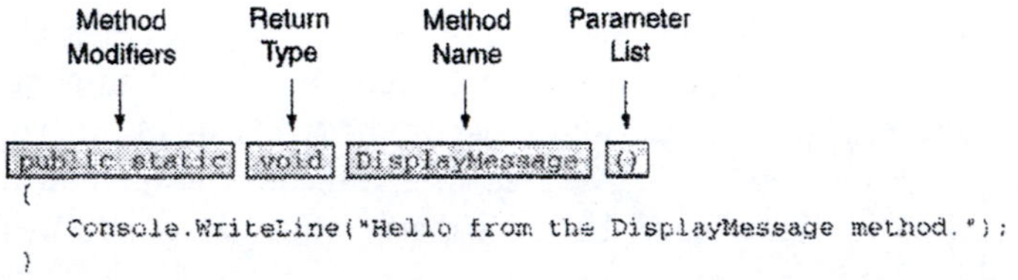

Figure 3-3 Parts of the method header

Let's take a closer look at the parts identified in the figure.

▪ **Method modifiers** – The key words `public` and `static` are modifiers. You don't need to be too concerned with these modifiers now, but if your curiosity is getting the better of you, here's a brief explanation: The word `public` means that the method is publicly available to code outside the class. The word `static` means that the method belongs to the class, not a specific object. You will learn more about these modifiers in later chapters. For this chapter, every method that we write will begin with `public static`.

▪ **Return type** – Recall our previous discussion of `void` and value-returning methods. When the key word `void` appears here, it means that the method is a `void` method and does not return a value. As you will see later, a value-returning method lists a data type here.

▪ **Method name** – You should give each method a descriptive name. In general, the same rules that apply to variable names also apply to method names. This method is named `DisplayMessage`, so we can easily guess what the method does: It displays a message.

▪ **Parameter list** – In the header, the method name is always followed by a set of parentheses which encloses the parameter list. As you will learn later in this chapter, methods can be capable of receiving arguments. When this is the case, a list of one or more variable declarations will appear inside the parentheses. The method in this example does not receive any arguments, so the parentheses are empty.

 NOTE: The method header is never terminated with a semicolon.

Calling a Method

A method executes when it is called. The `Main` method is automatically called when a program starts, but other methods are executed by method call statements. When a method is called, the program branches to that method and executes the statements in its body. Here is an example of a method call statement that calls the `DisplayMessage` method we previously examined:

```
DisplayMessage();
```

The statement is simply the name of the method followed by a set of parentheses. Because it is a complete statement, it is terminated with a semicolon.

 TIP: Notice that the method modifiers and the `void` return type are not written in the method call statement. Those are only written in the method header.

 NOTE: In C#, method names always start with capital letters.

Code Listing 3-1 demonstrates the calling of a simple method.

Notice how the program flows. It starts, of course, in the `Main` method. When it encounters the `DisplayMessage` method in line 11, the program branches to that method and performs the statement in its body (at line 21). Once the `DisplayMessage` method has finished executing, the program branches back to the `Main` method and resumes at line 12 with the statement that follows the method call. This is illustrated in Figure 3-4.

Code Listing 3-1

```
1  /*
2     This program defines and calls a simple method.
3  */
4
5  using System;
6  public class SimpleMethod
7  {
8     public static void Main()
9     {
10       Console.WriteLine("Hello from the main method.");
11       DisplayMessage();
12       Console.WriteLine("Back in the main method.");
13    }
14
15    /*
16       The DisplayMessage method displays a greeting.
17    */
18
19    public static void DisplayMessage()
20    {
21       Console.WriteLine("Hello from the DisplayMessage
              method.");
22    }
23 }
```

Program Output

```
Hello from the main method.
Hello from the DisplayMessage method.
Back in the main method.
```

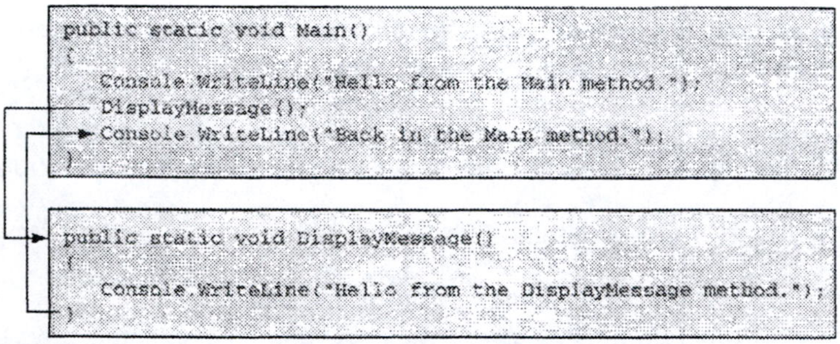

Figure 3-4 Branching in the SimpleMethod.cs program

Method call statements may be used in control structures like loops, if statements, and switch statements. The program in Code Listing 3-2 places the DisplayMessage method call inside a loop.

Code Listing 3-2   LoopCall.cs

```
 1 /*
 2    This program defines and calls a simple method.
 3 */
 4
 5 using System;
 6
 7 public class LoopCall
 8 {
 9    public static void Main()
10    {
11       Console.WriteLine("Hello from the main method.");
12       for (int i = 0; i < 5; i++)
13          DisplayMessage();
14       Console.WriteLine("Back in the main method.");
15    }
16
17    /*
18       The DisplayMessage method displays a greeting.
19    */
20
21    public static void DisplayMessage()
22    {
23       Console.WriteLine("Hello from the DisplayMessage
                method.");
24    }
25 }
```

Program Output
```
Hello from the main method.
Hello from the DisplayMessage method.
Hello from the DisplayMessage method.
Hello from the DisplayMessage method.
Hello from the DisplayMessage method.
Hello from the DisplayMessage method.
Back in the main method.
```

The program in Code Listing 3-3 shows another example. It asks the user to enter his or her annual salary and credit rating. The program then determines whether the user qualifies for a credit card. One of two void methods, Qualify or NoQualify, is called to display a message. Figures 3-5 and 3-6 show example interactions with the program.

Code Listing 3-3 CreditCard.cs

```
1  /*
2      This program uses two void methods.
3  */
4
5  using System;
6
7  public class CreditCard
8  {
9      public static void Main()
10     {
11         double salary;    // Annual salary
12         int creditRating; // Credit rating
13
14         // Get the user's annual salary.
15         Console.WriteLine("What is your annual salary?");
16         salary = Convert.ToDouble(Console.ReadLine());
17
18         // Get the user's credit rating (1 through 10).
19         Console.WriteLine("On a scale of 1 through 10, what is
                  your credit rating?\n" +
                  "(10 = excellent, 1 = very bad)");
20         creditRating = Convert.ToInt32(Console.ReadLine());
21
22         // Determine whether the user qualifies.
23         if (salary >= 20000 && creditRating >= 7)
24            Qualify();
25         else
26            NoQualify();
27     }
28
29     /*
30         The Qualify method informs the user that he
31         or she qualifies for the credit card.
32     */
33
34     public static void Qualify()
35     {
36         Console.WriteLine("Congratulations! You qualify for the
                  credit card!");
37     }
38
39     /*
40         The NoQualify method informs the user that he
41         or she does not qualify for the credit card.
42     */
```

(code listing continues)

Code Listing 3-3 CreditCard.cs *(continued)*

```
43
44    public static void NoQualify()
45    {
46        Console.WriteLine("I'm sorry.  You do not qualify for
              the credit card.");
47    }
48 }
```

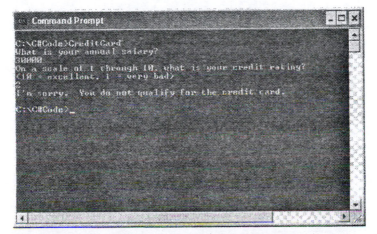

Figure 3-5   Interaction with the `CreditCard.cs` **program**

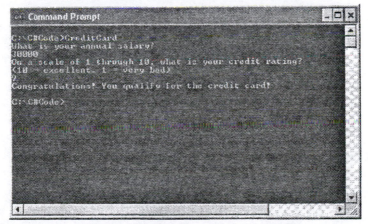

Figure 3-6   Interaction with the `CreditCard.cs` **program**

NOTE: We will go into more depth on looping in Chapter 6.

Hierarchical Method Calls

Methods can also be called in a hierarchical, or layered, fashion. In other words, method A can call method B, which can then call method C. When method C finishes, the program returns to method B. When method B finishes, the program returns to method A. The program in Code Listing 3-4 demonstrates this with three methods: Main, Deep, and Deeper. The Main method calls the Deep method, which then calls the Deeper method.

Code Listing 3-4   DeepAndDeeper.cs

```
1  /*
2      This program demonstrates hierarchical method calls.
3  */
4
5  using System;
6
7  public class DeepAndDeeper
8  {
9      public static void Main()
10     {
11         Console.WriteLine("I am starting in main.");
12         Deep();
13         Console.WriteLine("Now I am back in main.");
14     }
15
16     /*
17         The Deep method displays a message and then calls
18         the Deeper method.
19     */
20
21     public static void Deep()
22     {
23         Console.WriteLine("I am now in deep.");
24         Deeper();
25         Console.WriteLine("Now I am back in deep.");
26     }
27
28     /*
29         The Deeper method simply displays a message.
30     */
31
32     public static void Deeper()
33     {
34         Console.WriteLine("I am now in deeper.");
35     }
36 }
```

(code listing continues)

Code Listing 3-4 DeepAndDeeper.cs *(continued)*

Program Output
```
I am starting in main.
I am now in deep.
I am now in deeper.
Now I am back in deep.
Now I am back in main.
```

> **NOTE:** In C# it is an error to place `void` inside the method header. If no values are to be passed into the method leave the parentheses empty.

 CHECKPOINT

3.1 What is the difference between a void method and a value-returning method?

3.2 Is the following line of code a method header or a method call?

```
CalcTotal();
```

3.3 Is the following line of code a method header or a method call?

```
public static void CalcTotal()
```

3.4 What message will the following program display if the user enters 5? What if the user enters 10? What if the user enters 100?

```
using System;
public class Checkpoint
{
    public static void Main()
    {
        int number;

        Console.WriteLine("Enter a number.");
        number = Convert.ToInt32(input);

        if (number < 10)
            Method1();
        else
            Method2();
    }

    public static void Method1()
    {
        Console.WriteLine("Able was I.");
    }

    public static void Method2()
    {
        Console.WriteLine("I saw Elba.");
    }
}
```

3.5 Write a void method that displays your full name. The method should be named `MyName`.

3.2 Passing Arguments to a Method

 A method may be written so it accepts arguments. Data can then be passed into the method when it is called.

Values that are sent into a method are called *arguments*. You're already familiar with how to use arguments in a method call. For example, look at the following statement.

```
Console.WriteLine("Hello");
```

This statement calls the `Console.WriteLine` method and passes `"Hello"` as an argument. Here is another example:

```
number = Convert.ToInt32(str);
```

This statement calls the `Convert.ToInt32` method and passes the `str` variable as an argument. By using parameter variables, you can design your own methods that accept data this way. A *parameter variable*, sometimes simply referred to as a *parameter*, is a special variable that holds a value being passed into a method. Here is the definition of a method that uses a parameter:

```
public static void DisplayValue(int num)
{
    Console.WriteLine("The value is {0}", num);
}
```

Notice the integer variable declaration that appears inside the parentheses (`int num`). This is the declaration of a·parameter variable, which enables the `DisplayValue` method to accept an integer value as an argument. Here is an example of a call to the `DisplayValue` method, passing 5 as an argument:

```
DisplayValue(5);
```

This statement executes the `DisplayValue` method. The argument that is listed inside the parentheses is copied into the method's parameter variable, `num`. This is illustrated in Figure 3-7.

Inside the `DisplayValue` method, the variable `num` will contain the value of whatever argument was passed into it. If we pass 5 as the argument, the method will display

```
The value is 5
```

You may also pass variables and the values of expressions as arguments. For example, the following statements call the `DisplayValue` method with various arguments passed.

```
DisplayValue(x);
DisplayValue(x * 4);
DisplayValue(Convert.ToInt32("700"));
```

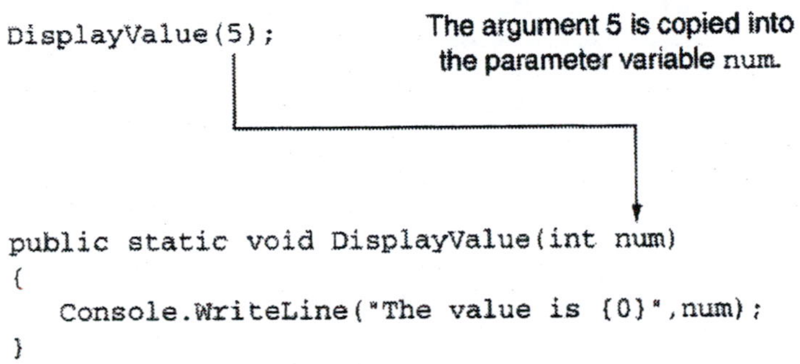

```
DisplayValue(5);                    The argument 5 is copied into
                                    the parameter variable num.



public static void DisplayValue(int num)
{
    Console.WriteLine("The value is {0}",num);
}
```

Figure 3-7   Passing 5 to the DisplayValue method

The first statement is simple. It passes the value in the variable x as the argument to the DisplayValue method. The second statement is also simple, but it does a little more work: It passes the result of the expression x * 4 as the argument to the DisplayValue method. The third statement does even more work. It passes the value returned from the Convert.ToInt32 method as the argument to the DisplayValue method. (The Convert.ToInt32 method is called first, and its return value is passed to the DisplayValue method.) The program in Code Listing 3-5 demonstrates these method calls.

Code Listing 3-5   PassArg.cs

```
1 /*
2    This program demonstrates a method with a parameter.
3 */
4
5 using System;
6
7 public class PassArg
8 {
9    public static void Main()
10   {
11      int x = 10;
12
13      Console.WriteLine("I am passing values to
                DisplayValue.");
14      DisplayValue(5);                        // Pass 5
15      DisplayValue(x);                        // Pass 10
16      DisplayValue(x * 4);                    // Pass 40
17      DisplayValue(Convert.ToInt32("700")); // Pass 700
18      Console.WriteLine("Now I am back in main.");
19   }
20
```

(code listing continues)

Code Listing 3-5 PassArg.cs *(continued)*

```
21    /*
22        The DisplayValue method displays the value
23        of its integer parameter.
24    */
25
26    public static void DisplayValue(int num)
27    {
28        Console.WriteLine("The value is {0}", num);
29    }
30 }
```

Program Output
```
I am passing values to DisplayValue.
The value is 5
The value is 10
The value is 40
The value is 700
Now I am back in main.
```

 WARNING! When passing a variable as an argument, simply write the variable name inside the parentheses of the method call. Do not write the data type of the argument variable in the method call. For example, the following statement will cause an error:

```
DisplayValue(int x);    // Error!
```

The method call should appear as:

```
DisplayValue(x);        // Correct
```

 NOTE: In this text, the values that are passed into a method are called arguments, and the variables that receive those values are called parameters. There are several variations of these terms in use. In some circles these terms are switched in meaning. Also, some call the arguments *actual parameters* and call the parameters *formal parameters*. Others use the terms *actual argument* and *formal argument*. Whichever set of terms you use, it is important that you be consistent.

Argument and Parameter Data Type Compatibility

When you pass an argument to a method, be sure that the argument's data type is compatible with the parameter variable's data type. C# will automatically perform a widening conversion if the argument's data type is ranked lower than the parameter variable's data type. For example, the DisplayValue method has an int parameter variable. Both of the following code segments will work because the short and byte arguments are automatically converted to an int.

```
short s = 1;
DisplayValue(s);      // Converts short to int

byte b = 2;
DisplayValue(b);      // Converts byte to int
```

However, C# will not automatically convert an argument to a lower-ranking data type. This means that a long, float, or double value cannot be passed to a method that has an int parameter variable. For example, the following code will cause a compiler error:

```
double d = 1.0;
DisplayValue(d);   // Error! Can't convert double to int.
```

 TIP: You can use a cast operator to manually convert a value to a lower-ranking data type. For example, the following code will work without errors.

```
double d = 1.0;
DisplayValue((int)d);   // This will work.
```

Parameter Variable Scope

Recall from Chapter 2 that a variable's scope is the part of the program where the variable may be accessed by its name. A variable is visible only to statements inside the variable's scope. A parameter variable's scope is the method in which the parameter is declared. No statement outside the method can access the parameter variable by its name.

Passing Multiple Arguments

Often it is useful to pass more than one argument to a method. Here is a method that accepts two arguments.

```
public static void ShowSum(double num1, double num2)
{
    double sum;      // To hold the sum

    sum = num1 + num2;
    Console.WriteLine("The sum is {0}", sum);
}
```

Notice that two parameter variables, num1 and num2, are declared inside the parentheses in the method header. This is often referred to as a *parameter list*. Also notice that a comma separates the declarations. Here is an example of a statement that calls the method:

```
ShowSum(5, 10);
```

This statement passes the arguments 5 and 10 into the method. The arguments are passed into the parameter variables in the order that they appear in the method call. In other words, the first argument is passed into the first parameter variable, the second argument is passed into the second parameter variable, and so forth. So, this statement causes 5 to be passed into the num1 parameter and 10 to be passed into the num2 parameter. This is illustrated in Figure 3-8.

The argument 5 is copied into the num1 parameter.
The argument 10 is copied into the num2 paramater.

```
ShowSum(5, 10);



public static void ShowSum(double num1, double num2)
{
    double sum;     // To hold the sum

    sum = num1 + num2;
    Console.WriteLine("The sum is {0}", sum);
}
```

Figure 3-8   Multiple arguments passed into multiple parameters

Suppose we were to reverse the order in which the arguments are listed in the method call, as shown here:

```
ShowSum(10, 5);
```

This would cause 10 to be passed into the num1 parameter and 5 to be passed into the num2 parameter. The following code segment shows one more example. This time we are passing variables as arguments.

```
double value1 = 2.5,
value2 = 3.5;
ShowSum(value1, value2);
```

When the ShowSum methods executes as a result of this code, the num1 parameter will contain 2.5 and the num2 parameter will contain 3.3.

 WARNING! Each parameter variable in a parameter list must have a data type listed before its name. For example, a compiler error would occur if the parameter list for the ShowSum method were defined as shown in the following header:

```
public static void ShowSum(double num1, num2) // Error!
```

A data type for both the num1 and num2 parameter variables must be listed, as shown here:

```
public static void ShowSum(double num1, double num2)
```

Arguments Are Passed by Value and Reference

In C#, all arguments of the value data types can be passed by value or by reference. *Passed by value* means that only a copy of an argument's value is passed into a parameter variable. A method's parameter variables are separate and distinct from the arguments that are listed inside the parentheses of a method call. If a parameter variable is changed inside a method, it has no effect on the original argument. For example, look at the program in Code Listing 3-6.

Code Listing 3-6   PassByValue.cs

```
 1  /*
 2      This program demonstrates that only a copy of an argument
 3      is passed into a method.
 4  */
 5
 6  using System;
 7
 8  public class PassByValue
 9  {
10      public static void Main()
11      {
12          int number = 99;
13
14          Console.WriteLine("Number is {0}", number);
15          ChangeMe(number);
16          Console.WriteLine("Number is {0}", number);
17      }
18
19      /*
20          The ChangeMe method accepts an argument and then
21          changes the value of the parameter.
22      */
23
24      public static void ChangeMe(int myValue)
25      {
26          Console.WriteLine("I am changing the value.");
27          myValue = 0;
28          Console.WriteLine("Now the value is {0}", myValue);
29      }
30  }
```

Program Output

```
Number is 99
I am changing the value.
Now the value is 0
Number is 99
```

Even though the parameter variable myValue is changed in the ChangeMe method, the argument number is not modified. The myValue variable contains only a copy of the number variable.

Now let's look at *passed by reference*. C# provides a special type of variable called a *reference variable* that, when used as a function parameter, allows access to the original argument. A reference variable is an alias for another other variable. Any changes made to the reference variable are actually performed on the variable it aliases. By using a reference variable as a parameter, a function may change a variable that is declared in another function. Reference parameters are declared like regular variables, except the key word ref is in front of the method parameter. For example, the following function definition declares the parameter myValue as a reference variable:

```
public static void ChangeOut(ref int myValue)
{
    Console.WriteLine("I am changing the value.");
    myValue = 0;
    Console.WriteLine("Now the value is {0}", myValue);
}
```

This time since myValue is a reference variable, the value is actually performed on the variable that was passed to the function as an argument. C# also has output parameters that are declared with the out key word. Output parameters, which are similar to reference parameters, are used when the method yields a new value for the parameter without modifying the original parameter. When calling a function with output parameters or reference parameters, be sure to include the key words out or ref before the data type as well. Let's now look at the modified program in Code Listing 3-7.

Code Listing 3-7   PassByRef.cs

```
1 /*
2     This program demonstrates the uses of the key words
         ref and out.
3 */
4
5 using System;
6
7 public class PassByRef
8 {
9     public static void Main()
10    {
11        int number = 99;
12        int sum;
13
14        Console.WriteLine("Number is {0}", number);
15        ChangeRef(ref number);
16        Console.WriteLine("Number is {0}", number);
17
18        Console.WriteLine("Number is {0}", number);
19        ChangeOut(out sum);
20        Console.WriteLine("Number is {0}", sum);
21    }
22
```

(code listing continues)

Code Listing 3-7 PassByRef.cs *(continued)*

```
23    /*
24        The ChangeRef method accepts an argument and then
              changes the value of the parameter.
25    */
26
27    public static void ChangeRef(ref int myValue)
28    {
29        Console.WriteLine("I am changing the value.");
30        myValue = 0;
31        Console.WriteLine("Now the value is {0}", myValue);
32    }
33
34    /*
35        The ChangeOut method returns the sum value back to the
              calling method.
36    */
37
38    public static void ChangeOut(out int sumValue)
39    {
40        Console.WriteLine("I am summing the value.");
41        sumValue = 34 + 36;
42    }
43 }
```

Program Output

```
Number is 99
I am changing the value.
Now the value is 0
Number is 0
Number is 0
I am summing the value.
Number is 70
```

As you can see the variables changed in ChangeRef and ChangeOut are now changed in the Main method.

NOTES: The key words ref and out must appear in both the function definition and in the function call.

Output parameters must have a value assigned to it before leaving the method.

Passing string Object References to a Method

So far you've seen examples of methods that accept primitive values as arguments. You can also write methods that accept references to string objects as arguments. For example, look at the following method, which is from the program ShowStringLength.cs on the Student CD.

```
public static void ShowLength(string str)
{
    Console.WriteLine("{0} is {1} characters long.", str,
        str.Length);
}
```

This method accepts a string object as its argument, and displays a message showing the number of characters in the object. The following code shows an example of how to call the method:

```
string name = "Warren";
ShowLength(name);
```

When this code executes, the ShowLength method will display the following:

```
Warren is 6 characters long.
```

Although we say that an object, such as a string, is passed as an argument, it is actually a reference to the object that is passed. In this example code, the name variable is a string reference variable. It is passed as an argument to the ShowLength method. The ShowLength method has a parameter variable, str, which is also a string reference variable, that receives the argument.

Recall that a reference variable holds the memory address of an object. When the ShowLength method is called, the address that is stored in name is passed into the str parameter variable, as illustrated in Figure 3-9. This means that when the ShowLength method is executing, both name and str reference the same object. This is illustrated in Figure 3-10.

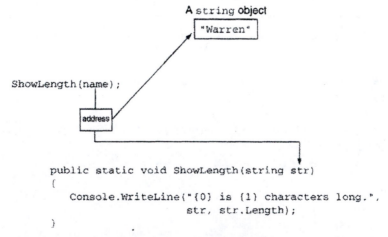

Figure 3-9 Passing a reference as an argument

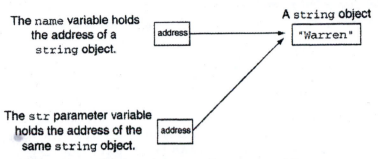

Figure 3-10 Both `name` and `str` reference the same object

This might lead you to the conclusion that a method can change the contents of any `string` object that has been passed to it as an argument. After all, the parameter variable references the same object as the argument. However, `string` objects in C# are *immutable*, which means that they cannot be changed. For example, look at the program in Code Listing 3-8. It passes a `string` object to a method that appears to change the object. In reality, the object is not changed.

Code Listing 3-8 PassString.cs

```
1  /*
2      This program demonstrates a method that string arguments
3      cannot be changed.
4  */
5
6  using System;
7
8  public class PassString
9  {
10     public static void Main()
11     {
12         string name = "Shakespeare";
13         Console.WriteLine("In main, the name is " + name);
14         ChangeName(name);
15         Console.WriteLine("Back in main, the name is " + name);
16     }
17
18     /*
19         The ChangeName method accepts a string as its argument
20         and assigns the str parameter to a new string.
21     */
22
23     public static void ChangeName(string str)
24     {
25         str = "Dickens";
26         Console.WriteLine("In ChangeName, the name is now {0}",
                str);
27     }
28 }
```

(code listing continues)

Code Listing 3-8 PassString.cs *(continued)*

Program Output
```
In main, the name is Shakespeare
In ChangeName, the name is now Dickens
Back in main, the name is Shakespeare
```

Let's take a closer look at this program. After line 12 executes, the name variable references a string object containing "Shakespeare." In line 14 the ChangeName method is called and the name variable is passed as an argument. This passes the address of the string object into the str parameter variable. At this point, both name and str reference the same object, as shown in Figure 3-11.

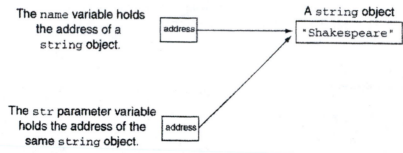

Figure 3-11   Before line 25 executes both name **and** str **reference the same object**

In the ChangeName method, line 25 executes:

```
str = "Dickens";
```

At first, you might think that this statement changes the string object's contents to "Dickens." What actually happens is that a new string object containing "Dickens" is created and its address is stored in the str variable. After this statement executes, the name variable and the str parameter variable reference different objects. This is shown in Figure 3-12.

In Chapter 9 we will discuss the immutability of string objects in greater detail. Until then, just remember the following point: string objects cannot be changed. Any time you use the = operator to assign a string literal to a string reference variable, a new string object is created in memory.

After Line 25 executes:

The `name` variable holds
the address of a
`string` object.

A `string` object

`"Shakespeare"`

The `str` parameter variable
holds the address of a
different `string` object.

A `string` object

`"Dickens"`

Figure 3-12 **After line 25 executes, `name` and `str` reference different objects**

 # CHECKPOINT

3.6 What is the difference between an argument and a parameter?

3.7 Look at the following method header:

```
public static void MyMethod(int num)
```

Which of the following calls to the method will cause a compiler error?

a) `MyMethod(7);`

b) `MyMethod(6.2);`

c) `long x = 99;`
   `MyMethod(x);`

d) `short s = 2;`
   `MyMethod(s);`

3.8 Suppose a method named ShowValues accepts two int arguments. Which of the following method headers is written correctly?

a) `public static void ShowValues()`

b) `public static void ShowValues(int num1, num2)`

c) `public static void ShowValues(num1, num2)`

d) `public static void ShowValues(int num1, int num2)`

3.9 In C#, method arguments can be passed by value. What does this mean?

3.10 What will the following program display?

```
using System;
public class Checkpoint
{
    public static void Main()
    {
        int num1 = 99;
        double num2 = 1.5;

        Console.WriteLine("{0} {1} ",num1, num2);
        MyMethod(num1, ref num2);
        Console.WriteLine("{0} {1} ",num1, num2);
    }

    public static void MyMethod(int i, ref double d)
    {
        Console.WriteLine("{0} {1} ",i, d);
        i = 0;
        d = 0.0;
        Console.WriteLine("{0} {1} ",i, d);
    }
}
```

3.3 More About Local Variables

> **CONCEPT** A local variable is declared inside a method and is not accessible to statements outside the method. Different methods can have local variables with the same names because the methods cannot see each other's local variables.

In Chapter 2 we introduced the concept of local variables, which are variables that are declared inside a method. They are called *local* because they are local to the method in which they are declared. Statements outside a method cannot access that method's local variables.

Because a method's local variables are hidden from other methods, the other methods may have their own local variables with the same name. For example, look at the program in Code Listing 3-9. In addition to the Main method, this program has two other methods: Texas and California. These two methods each have a local variable named birds, but as you can see from the program output, this doesn't bother the program.

Code Listing 3-9 LocalVars.cs

```
1  /*
2     This program demonstrates that two methods may have
3     local variables with the same name.
4  */
5
```

(code listing continues)

Code Listing 3-9   **LocalVars.cs** *(continued)*

```
 6 using System;
 7
 8 public class LocalVars
 9 {
10     public static void Main()
11     {
12         Texas();
13         California();
14     }
15
16     /*
17         The Texas method has a local variable named birds.
18     */
19
20     public static void Texas()
21     {
22         int birds = 5000;
23
24         Console.WriteLine("In Texas there are {0}
25             birds.",birds);
25     }
26
27     /*
28         The California method also has a local variable named
            birds.
29     */
30     public static void California()
31     {
32         int birds = 3500;
33
34         Console.WriteLine("In California there are {0} birds.",
                birds);
35     }
36 }
```

Program Output
```
In texas there are 5000 birds.
In California there are 3500 birds.
```

Although there are two variables named birds, the program can only see one of them at a time because they are in different methods. When the Texas method is executing, the birds variable declared inside Texas is visible. When the California method is executing, the birds variable declared inside California is visible.

Local Variable Lifetime

A method's local variables exist only while the method is executing. This is known as the *lifetime* of a local variable. When the method begins, its local variables and its parameter variables are created in memory, and when the method ends, the local variables and parameter variables are destroyed. This means that any value stored in a local variable is lost between calls to the method in which the variable is declared.

Initializing Local Variables with Parameter Values

It is possible to use a parameter variable to initialize a local variable. Sometimes this simplifies the code in a method. For example, recall the ShowSum method we discussed earlier:

```
public static void ShowSum(double num1, double num2)
{
    double sum;    // To hold the sum

    sum = num1 + num2;
    Console.WriteLine("The sum is {0}", sum);
}
```

In the body of the method, the sum variable is declared and then a separate assignment statement assigns num1 + num2 to sum. We can combine these statements into one, as shown in the following modified version of the method.

```
public static void showSum(double num1, double num2)
{
    double sum = num1 + num2;
    Console.WriteLine("The sum is {0}", sum);
}
```

Because the scope of a parameter variable is the entire method in which it is declared, we can use parameter variables to initialize local variables.

3.4   Returning a Value from a Method

CONCEPT A method may send a value back to the statement that called the method.

You've seen that data may be passed into a method by way of parameter variables. Data may also be returned from a method, back to the statement that called it. Methods that return a value are appropriately known as *value-returning methods*.

You are already experienced at using value-returning methods. For instance, you have used the Convert class methods, such as ToInt32. Here is an example:

```
int num;
num = Convert.ToInt32("700");
```

The second line in this code calls the Convert.ToInt32 method, passing "700" as the argument. The method returns the integer value 700, which is assigned to the num variable by the = operator. In this section we will discuss how you can write your own value-returning methods.

Defining a Value-Returning Method

Before you write a value-returning method, you must decide what type of value the method will return. This is because you must specify the data type of the return value in the method header. Recall that a void method, which does not return a value, uses the key word void as its return type in the method header. A value-returning method will use int, double, Boolean (bool), or any other valid data type in its header. Here is an example of a method that returns an int value:

```
public static int Sum(int num1, int num2)
{
    int result;

    result = num1 + num2;
    return result;
}
```

The name of this method is Sum. Notice in the method header that the return type is int, as illustrated in Figure 3-13.

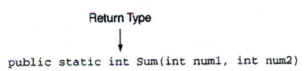

Figure 3-13   Return type in the method header

This code defines a method named sum that accepts two int arguments. The arguments are passed into the parameter variables num1 and num2. Inside the method, a local variable, result, is declared. The parameter variables num1 and num2 are added, and their sum is assigned to the result variable. The last statement in the method is:

```
return result;
```

This is a return statement. You must have a return statement in a value-returning method. It causes the method to end execution and it returns a value back to the statement that called the method. In a value-returning method, the general format of the return statement is:

```
return Expression;
```

Expression is the value to be returned. It can be any expression that has a value, such as a variable, literal, or mathematical expression. In this case, the sum method returns the value in the result variable. However, we could have eliminated the result variable and returned the expression num1 + num2, as shown in the following code:

```
public static int Sum(int num1, int num2)
{
    return num1 + num2;
}
```

NOTE: The `return` statement's expression must be of the same data type as the return type specified in the method header or compatible with it. Otherwise, a compiler error will occur. C# will automatically widen the value of the `return` expression, if necessary, but it will not automatically narrow it.

Calling a Value-Returning Method

The program in Code Listing 3-10 shows an example of how to call the Sum method.

Code Listing 3-10   ValueReturn.cs

```
 1 /*
 2     This program demonstrates a value-returning method.
 3 */
 4
 5 using System;
 6
 7 public class ValueReturn
 8 {
 9     public static void Main()
10     {
11         int total, value1 = 20, value2 = 40;
12
13         total = Sum(value1, value2);
14         Console.WriteLine("The sum of {0} and {1} is {2}",
                value1, value2, total);
15     }
16
17     /*
18         The Sum method returns the sum of its two parameters.
19         **parameter num1 The first number to be added.
20         **parameter num2 The second number to be added.
21         **return The sum of num1 and num2.
22     */
23
24     public static int Sum(int num1, int num2)
25     {
26         int result;
27
28         result = num1 + num2;
29         return result;
30     }
31 }
```

Program Output

```
The sum of 20 and 40 is 60
```

The statement in line 13 calls the sum method, passing value1 and value2 as arguments. It assigns the value returned by the sum method to the total variable. In this case, the method will return 60. Figure 3-14 shows how the arguments are passed into the method and how a value is passed back from the method.

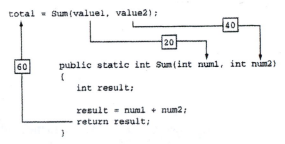

Figure 3-14 Arguments passed to sum and a value returned

When you call a value-returning method, you usually want to do something meaningful with the value it returns. The ReturnValue.cs program shows a method's return value being assigned to a variable. This is commonly how return values are used, but you can do many other things with them. For example, the following code shows a math expression that uses a call to the Sum method:

```
int x = 10, y = 15;
double average;
average = Sum(x, y) / 2.0;
```

In the last statement, the Sum method is called with x and y as its arguments. The method's return value, which is 25, is divided by 2.0. The result, 12.5, is assigned to average. Here is another example:

```
int x = 10, y = 15;
Console.WriteLine("The sum is {0}",Sum(x, y));
```

This code sends the Sum method's return value to Console.WriteLine, so it can be displayed on the screen. The message "The sum is 25" will be displayed.

Remember, a value-returning method returns a value of a specific data type. You can use the method's return value anywhere that you can use a regular value of the same data type. This means that anywhere an int value can be used, a call to an int value-returning method can be used. Likewise, anywhere a double value can be used, a call to a double value-returning method can be used. The same is true for all other data types.

Returning a boolean Value (type bool)

Frequently there is a need for a method that tests an argument and returns a true or false value indicating whether or not a condition exists. Such a method would return a boolean value. For example, the following method accepts an argument and returns `true` if the argument is within the range of 1 through 100, or `false` otherwise.

```
public static bool IsValid(int number)
{
    bool status;

    if (number >= 1 && number <= 100)
        status = true;
    else
        status = false;
    return status;
}
```

The following code shows an `if-else` statement that uses a call to the method:

```
int value = 20;
if (IsValid(value))
    Console.WriteLine("The value is within range.");
else
    Console.WriteLine("The value is out of range.");
```

When this code executes, the message "The value is within range." will be displayed.

Returning a Reference to a `string` Object

A value-returning method can also return a reference to a nonprimitive type, such as a `string` object. The program in Code Listing 3-11 shows such an example.

Code Listing 3-11   ReturnString.cs

```
1  /*
2     This program demonstrates a method that
3     returns a reference to a string object.
4  */
5
6  using System;
7
8  public class ReturnString
9  {
10     public static void Main()
11     {
12        string customerName;
13
14        customerName = FullName("John", "Martin");
15        Console.WriteLine(customerName);
16     }
17
```

(code listing continues)

Code Listing 3-11   ReturnString.cs *(continued)*

```
18    /*
19        The FullName method accepts two string arguments
20        containing a first and last name. It concatenates
21        them into a single string object.
22        **parameter first The first name.
23        **parameter last The last name.
24        **return A reference to a string object containing
25        the first and last names.
26    */
27
28    public static string FullName(string first, string last)
29    {
30        string name;
31
32        name = first + " " + last;
33        return name;
34    }
35 }
```

Program Output
John Martin

Line 14 calls the FullName method, passing "John" and "Martin" as arguments. The method returns a reference to a string object containing "John Martin." The reference is assigned to the customerName variable. This is illustrated in Figure 3-13.

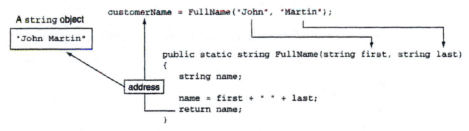

Figure 3-15   The FullName method returning a reference to a string object

 CHECKPOINT

3.11 Look at the following method header. What type of value does the method return?

```
public static double GetValue(int a, float b, string c)
```

3.12 Write the header for a method named Days. The method should return an int and have three int parameter variables: years, months, and weeks.

3.13 Write the header for a method named Distance. The method should return a double and have two double parameter variables: rate and time.

3.14 Write the header for a method named LightYears. The method should return a long and have one long parameter variable: miles.

3.5 Problem Solving with Methods

CONCEPT A large, complex problem can be solved a piece at a time by methods.

At the beginning of this chapter we introduced the idea of using methods to "divide and conquer" a problem. The best way to solve a complex problem is often to break it down into smaller problems, and then solve the smaller problems. The process of breaking a problem down into smaller pieces is called *functional decomposition*.

In functional decomposition, instead of one long method that contains all of the statements necessary to solve a problem, small methods are written that each solve a specific part of the problem. These small methods can then be executed in the desired order to solve the problem.

Let's look at an example. The program in Code Listing 3-12 reads 30 days of sales amounts from a file, and then displays the total sales and average daily sales. Here's a brief pseudocode model of the algorithm:

Ask the user to enter the name of the file.
Get the total of the sales amounts in the file.
Calculate the average daily sales.
Display the total and average daily sales.

The file MonthlySales.txt, on the Student CD, is used to test the program. Figure 3-16 shows interaction with the program during execution.

Code Listing 3-12   SalesReport.cs

```
1 /*
2    This program opens a file containing the sales
3    amounts for 30 days. It calculates and displays
4    the total sales and average daily sales.
5 */
6
7 using System;
8 using System.IO;          // For file I/O classes
9
10
```

(code listing continues)

Code Listing 3-12 SalesReport.cs *(continued)*

```
11 public class SalesReport
12 {
13    public static void Main()
14    {
15       string filename;        // The name of the file to open
16       double totalSales,      // Total sales for
17              averageSales;    // Average daily sales
18       const int NUM_DAYS = 30; // Number of days of sales
19
20       // Get the name of the file.
21       filename = GetFileName();
22
23       // Get the total sales from the file.
24       totalSales = GetTotalSales(filename);
25
26       // Calculate the average.
27       averageSales = totalSales / NUM_DAYS;
28
29       // Display the total and average.
30       DisplayResults(totalSales, averageSales);
31    }
32
33    /*
34       The GetFileName method prompts the user to enter
35       the name of the file to open.
36       **return A reference to a string object containing
37       the name of the file.
38    */
39
40    public static string GetFileName()
41    {
42       string file;   // To hold the file name
43
44       Console.WriteLine("Enter the name of the file\n containing 30
              days of " +
45                         "sales amounts.");
46
47       file = Console.ReadLine();
48       return file;
49    }
50
51    /*
52       The GetTotalSales method opens a file and
53       reads the daily sales amounts, accumulating
54       the total. The total is returned.
55       **parameter file The name of the file to open.
56       **return The total of the sales amounts.
57    */
58
```

(code listing continues)

Code Listing 3-12 SalesReport.cs *(continued)*

```
59    public static double GetTotalSales(string file)
60    {
61        double total = 0.0,   // Accumulator
62               sales;         // A daily sales amount
63        string input;         // To hold file input
64
65        StreamReader inputFile = new StreamReader(file);
66
67        // Read the data from the file and
68        // accumulate a total.
69
70        input = inputFile.ReadLine();
71        while (input != null)
72        {
73            sales = Convert.ToDouble(input);
74            total += sales;
75            input = inputFile.ReadLine();
76        }
77
78        // Close the file.
79        inputFile.Close();
80
81        // Return the total sales.
82        return total;
83    }
84
85    /*
86        The DisplayResults method displays the total and
87        average daily sales.
88        **parameter total The total sales.
89        **parameter avg The average daily sales.
90    */
91
92    public static void DisplayResults(double total, double avg)
93    {
94
95        Console.WriteLine("The total sales for the period is {0:C2}" +
96                          "\nThe average daily sales were {1:C2}",
97                          total, avg);
97    }
98 }
```

Figure 3-16 Interaction with the `SalesReport.cs` program

Instead of writing the entire program in the `Main` method, the algorithm was broken down into the following methods:

- `GetFileName` – This method asks the user to enter the name of the file containing 30 days of sales amounts. The method returns a reference to a `string` object containing the name entered by the user.

- `GetTotalSales` – This method accepts the name of a file as an argument. The file is opened, the sales amounts are read from it, and the total of the sales amounts is accumulated. The method returns the total as a `double`.

- `DisplayResults` – This method accepts as arguments the total sales and the average daily sales. It displays a message dialog box indicating these values.

 NOTE: You will learn more about how to use loops and files in Chapter 6.

3.6 Recursion

CONCEPT A recursive method is a method that calls itself.

You have seen instances of methods calling other methods. Method A can call method B, which can then call method C. It's also possible for a method to call itself. A method that calls itself is a *recursive method*. Look at the `Message` method below:

```
public static void Message()
{
```

```
      Console.WriteLine("This is a recursive method.");
      Message(n - 1);
   }
```

This method displays the string "This is a recursive method.", and then calls itself. Each time it calls itself, the cycle is repeated. Can you see a problem with the method? There's no way to stop the recursive calls. This method is like an infinite loop because there is no code to stop it from repeating.

Like a loop, a recursive method must have some way to control the number of times it repeats. Let us modify the Message method. The modified version passes an integer argument, which holds the number of times the method should call itself. Look at the modified Message method below:

```
public static void Message(int n)
   {
   if (n > 0)
      {
         Console.WriteLine("This is a recursive method.");
         Message(n - 1);
      }
   }
```

This method contains an if statement that controls the repetition. As long as the n parameter is greater than zero, the method displays the message and calls itself again. Each time it calls itself, it passes n - 1 as the argument. The program in Code Listing 3-13 demonstrates the modified Message method.

Code Listing 3-13   RecursionDemo.cs

```
1 /*
2     This class demonstrates the Message method.
3 */
4
5 using System;
6 public class RecursionDemo
7 {
8     public static void Main()
9        {
10          Message(5);
11       }
12 }
```

Program Output

```
This is a recursive method.
This is a recursive method.
This is a recursive method.
This is a recursive method.
This is a recursive method.          .
```

The Main method in this class calls the Message method with the argument 5, which causes the method to call itself five times. The first time the method is called, the if statement displays the message and then calls itself with 4 as the argument. Figure 3-17 illustrates this.

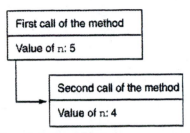

Figure 3-17 First two calls of the method

The diagram in Figure 3-17 illustrates two separate calls of the Message method. Each time the method is called, a new instance of the n parameter is created in memory. The first time the method is called, the n parameter is set to 3. When the method calls itself, a new instance of n is created, and the value 4 is passed into it. This cycle repeats until, finally, zero is passed to the method. This is illustrated in Figure 3-18.

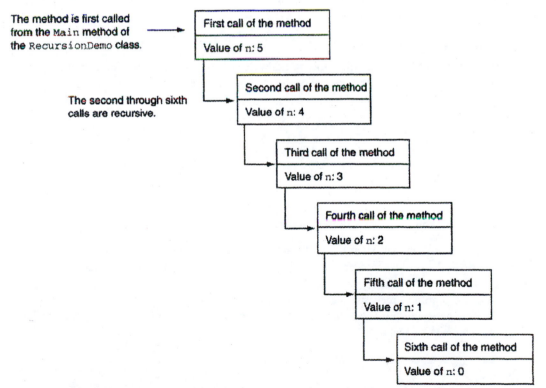

Figure 3-18 Total of six calls to the Message method

As you can see from Figure 3-18 the method is called a total of six times. The first time it is called from the Main method of the RecursionDemo class, and the other five times it calls itself. The number of times that a method calls itself is known as the *depth of recursion*. In this example, the depth of recursion is five. When the method reaches its sixth call, the n parameter is set to 0. At that point, the if statement's conditional expression is false, so the method returns. Control of the program returns from the sixth instance of the method to the point in the fifth instance directly after the recursive method call. This is illustrated in Figure 3-19.

```
public static void Message(int n)
{
    if (n > 0)
    {
        Console.WriteLine("This is a recursive method.");
        Message(n -1);
    }
}
```

Recursive method call ────────────→ Message(n -1);

←──────── Control returns here from the recursive call. There are no more statements to execute in this method, so the method returns.

Figure 3-19   Control returns to the point after the recursive method call

Because there are no more statements to be executed after the method call, the fifth instance of the function returns control of the program back to the fourth instance. This repeats until all instances of the function return.

A Recursive Application

Let's take an example from mathematics to examine an application of recursion. In mathematics, the notation $n!$ represents the factorial of the number n. The factorial of a nonnegative number can be defined by the following rules:

If $n = 0$ then	$n! = 1$
If $n > 0$ then	$n! = 1 \times 2 \times 3 \times \ldots \times n$

Let's replace the notation $n!$ with factorial(n), which looks a bit more like computer code, and rewrite these rules as:

If $n = 0$ then	factorial(n) = 1
If $n > 0$ then	factorial(n) = $1 \times 2 \times 3 \times \ldots \times n$

These rules state that when n is 0, its factorial is 1. When n greater than 0, its factorial is the product of all the positive integers from 1 up to n. For instance, factorial(6) is calculated as $1 \times 2 \times 3 \times 4 \times 5 \times 6$.

When designing a recursive algorithm to calculate the factorial of any number, we first identify the base case, which is the part of the calculation that we can solve without recursion. That is the case where n is equal to 0:

If $n = 0$ then	factorial(n) = 1

This tells how to solve the problem when *n* is equal to 0, but what do we do when *n* is greater than 0? That is the recursive case, or the part of the problem that we use recursion to solve. This is how we express it:

$$\text{If } n > 0 \text{ then} \qquad \text{factorial}(n) = n \times \text{factorial}(n - 1)$$

This states that if *n* is greater than 0, the factorial of *n* is *n* times the factorial of *n* −1. Notice how the recursive call works on a reduced version of the problem, *n* − 1. So, our recursive rule for calculating the factorial of a number might look like this:

$$\text{If } n = 0 \text{ then} \qquad \text{factorial}(n) = 1$$
$$\text{If } n > 0 \text{ then} \qquad \text{factorial}(n) = n \times \text{factorial}(n - 1)$$

The following code shows how this might be implemented in a C# method.

```
public static int Factorial(int n)
{
    if (n == 0)
        return 1;        // base case
    else
        return n * Factorial(n - 1);   //recursive case
}
```

The program in Code Listing 3-14 demonstrates the method.

Code Listing 3-14 FactorialDemo.cs

```
1 using System;
2 public class FactorialDemo
3 {
4    public static void Main()
5    {
6
7       int number;
8
9       Console.WriteLine("Enter a nonnegative integer: ");
10      number = Convert.ToInt32(Console.ReadLine());
11      Console.WriteLine("{0}! is {1}", number,
               Factorial(number));
12
13   }
14
```

(code listing continues)

Code Listing 3-14 **FactorialDemo.cs** *(continued)*

```
15    /*
16         The Factorial method uses recursion to calculate
17         the factorial of its argument, which is assumed
18         to be a nonnegative number.
19         **parameter n The number to use in the
                calculation.
20         **return The factorial of n.
21    */
22
23    public static int Factorial(int n)
24    {
25       if (n == 0)
26          return 1;    // base case
27       else
28          return n * Factorial(n - 1);  //recursive case
29    }
30 }
```

Program Output with Example Input

```
Enter a nonnegative integer: 4 [Enter]
4! Is 24
```

In the example run of the program, the Factorial method is called with the argument 4 passed into n. Because n is not equal to 0, the if statement's else clause executes the following statement:

```
return n * Factorial(n - 1);
```

Although this is a return statement, it does not immediately return. Before the return value can be determined, the value of Factorial(num - 1) must be determined. The Factorial method is called recursively until the fifth call, in which the n parameter will be set to zero. The diagram in Figure 3-20 illustrates the value of n and the return value during each call of the method.

This diagram illustrates why a recursive algorithm must reduce the problem with each recursive call. Eventually the recursion has to stop in order for a solution to be reached. If each recursive call works on a smaller version of the problem, then the recursive calls work toward the base case. The base case does not require recursion, so it stops the chain of recursive calls.

Usually, a problem is reduced by making the value of one or more parameters smaller with each recursive call. In our Factorial method, the value of the parameter n gets closer to 0 with each recursive call. When the parameter reaches 0, the method returns a value without making another recursive call.

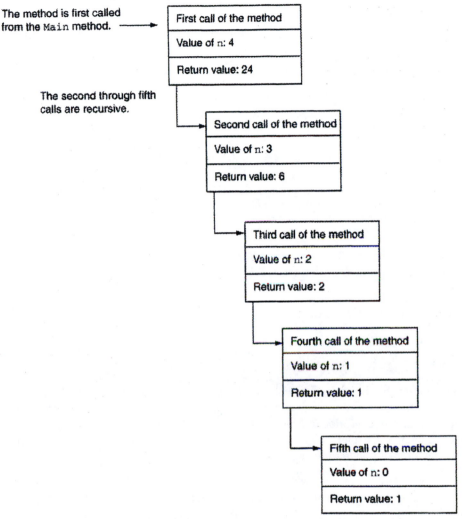

The method is first called from the `Main` method. ⟶

First call of the method

Value of n: 4

Return value: 24

The second through fifth calls are recursive.

Second call of the method

Value of n: 3

Return value: 6

Third call of the method

Value of n: 2

Return value: 2

Fourth call of the method

Value of n: 1

Return value: 1

Fifth call of the method

Value of n: 0

Return value: 1

Figure 3-20 Recursive calls to the `Factorial` method

CHECKPOINT

3.15 It is said that a recursive algorithm has more overhead than an iterative algorithm. What does this mean?

3.16 What is a base case?

3.17 What is a recursive case?

3.18 What causes a recursive algorithm to stop calling itself?

3.7 Formatting Numbers

 CONCEPT A format code can be used to format the appearance of floating-point numbers rounded to a specified number of decimal places.

In C#, a value of the double data type (or any other floating-point data type) is displayed in the most exact way without losing accuracy. For example, look at the following code:

```
double number = 675.0;
Console.WriteLine(number);
```

This code will display

```
675
```

The 0 after the decimal place will not appear since it does not add any more information. Quite often, however, you want to control the number of decimal places that are displayed. For example, when displaying dollar amounts, you normally display two decimal places.

Remember in Chapter 2, we said a format specifier is a placeholder for the variables in a string. The following code shows an example:

```
number = 5;
Console.WriteLine("The value is {0}", number);
```

The second line uses the format specifier, surrounded in curly braces, to state the position of the number in relation to the variable list following the string. In general, to indicate a format we add a second value to the format specifier: a format character along with an optional number representing precision. A colon is used to separate the position number and the format character. Table 3-1 lists eight format characters.

Code Listing 3-15 shows some examples.

Table 3-1 Format characters

Character Code	Type	Format Result
C, c	Currency	Number expressed with currency symbol ($), comma, and two decimal places
D, d	Decimal	Number expressed as integer
E, e	Scientific notation	Number expressed as scientific notation with six decimal places
F, f	Fixed	Number expressed with fixed number of places. The default is two decimal places
G, g	General	Number expressed as either E or F. Can specify decimal places
N, n	Number	Number expressed with comma and two decimal places
P, p	Percent	Number expressed as a percentage
X, x	Hexadecimal	Number expressed in hex format

Code Listing 3-15 Format1.cs

```
1 /*
2    This program demonstrates Formatting numbers.
3 */
4
5 using System;
6
7 public class Format1
8 {
9    public static void Main()
10   {
11      double number1 = 0.166666666666667,
12             number2 = 1.666666666666667,
13             number3 = 16.666666666666667,
14             number4 = 16666.666666666666667;
15
```

(code listing continues)

Code Listing 3-15   Format1.cs *(continued)*

```
16       // Display the formatted variable contents.
17       Console.WriteLine("The number1 displayed as
                 currency is {0:C2}", number1);
18       Console.WriteLine("The number2 displayed as
                 scientific notation is {0:E2}", number2);
19       Console.WriteLine("The number3 displayed as fixed
                 is {0:F2}", number3);
20       Console.WriteLine("The number4 displayed as number
                 is {0:N2}", number4);
21    }
22 }
```

Program Output

```
The number1 displayed as currency is $0.17
The number2 displayed as scientific notation is 1.67E+000
The number3 displayed as fixed is 16.67
The number4 displayed as number is 16,666.67
```

Notice the differences between the statements. The first format string on line 17

```
{0:C2}
```

converted the floating-point number into a number in currency format with two decimal places. The second format string on line 18

```
{0:E2}
```

converted the float to a number represented in scientific notation. The third format string on line 19

```
{0:F2}
```

converted the float to a fixed number with a specific number of decimal places.

The final format string on line 20

```
{0:N2}
```

converted the float into a comma delimited number with a specific number of decimal places.

 CHECKPOINT

3.19 Assume that the double variable number holds the value 459.6329. What format character would you to display the number as $459.63?

3.20 Assume that the double variable number holds the value 0.179. What format character would you use to display the number as .18?

3.21 Assume that the double variable number holds the value 7634869.1. What format character would you use to display the number as 7,634,869.10?

3.8 Common Errors

- **Putting a semicolon at the end of a method header.** Method headers are never terminated with a semicolon.

- **Writing modifiers or return types in a method call statement.** Method modifiers and return types are written in method headers, but never in method calls.

- **Forgetting to write the empty parentheses in a call to a method that accepts no arguments.** You must always write the parentheses in a method call statement, even if the method doesn't accept arguments.

- **Forgetting to pass arguments to methods that require them.** If a method has parameter variables, you must provide arguments when calling the method.

- **Passing an argument of a data type that cannot be automatically converted to the data type of the parameter variable.** C# will automatically perform a widening conversion if the argument's data type is ranked lower than the parameter variable's data type. But, C# will not automatically convert an argument to a lower-ranking data type.

- **Attempting to access a parameter variable with code outside the method where the variable is declared.** A parameter variable is only visible within the method it is declared in.

- **In a method header, not writing the data type of each parameter variable.** Each parameter variable declaration inside the parentheses of a method header must include the variable's data type.

- **Changing the contents of a method's parameter variable and expecting the argument that was passed into the parameter to change as well.** Method arguments are passed by value, which means that a copy of the argument is passed into a parameter variable. Changes to the parameter variable have no effect on the argument.

- **Using a variable to receive a method's return value when the variable's data type is incompatible with the data type of the return value.** A variable that receives a method's return value must be of a data type that is compatible with the data type of the return value.

- **Not writing a `return` statement in a value-returning method.** If a method's return type is anything other than `void`, it should return a value.

Review Questions and Exercises

Multiple Choice and True/False

1. Which type of method does not return a value?

   a) null

   b) void

   c) Empty

   d) Anonymous

2. This appears at the beginning of a method definition.

   a) Semicolon

   b) Parentheses

   c) Body

   d) Header

3. The body of a method is enclosed in

   a) curly braces { }

   b) square brackets []

   c) parentheses ()

   d) Quotation marks " "

4. A method header can contain

   a) method modifiers

   b) the method return type

   c) the method name

   d) a list of parameter declarations

   e) all of these

   f) none of these

5. A value that is passed into a method when it is called is known as a(n)

   a) parameter

   b) argument

   c) signal

   d) return value

6. A variable that receives a value that is passed into a method is known as a(n)

   a) parameter

   b) argument

   c) signal

   d) return value

7. This statement causes a method to end and sends a value back to the statement that called the method.

   a) end

   b) send

   c) exit

   d) return

8. True or False: You terminate a method header with a semicolon.

9. True or False: When passing an argument to a method, C# will automatically perform a widening conversion (convert the argument to a higher-ranking data type) if necessary.

10. True or False: When passing an argument to a method, C# will automatically perform a narrowing conversion (convert the argument to a lower-ranking data type) if necessary.

11. True or False: A parameter variable's scope is the entire program that contains the method in which the parameter is declared.

12. True or False: When code in a method changes the value of a parameter, it also changes the value of the argument that was passed into the parameter (nonreference).

13. True or False: When an object, such as a `string`, is passed as an argument, it is actually a reference to the object that is passed.

14. True or False: The contents of a `string` object cannot be changed.

15. True or False: When multiple arguments are passed to a method, the order in which the arguments are passed is not important.

16. True or False: No two methods in the same program can have a local variable with the same name.

17. True or False: It is possible for one method to access a local variable that is declared in another method.

18. True or False: You must have a `return` statement in a value-returning method.

Find the Error

1. Find the error in the following method definition.

```
// This method has an error!
public static void SayHello();
{
    Console.WriteLine("Hello");
}
```

2. Look at the following method header:

```
public static void ShowValue(int x);
```

The following code has a call to the ShowValue method. Find the error.

```
int x = 8;
ShowValue(int x);    // Error!
```

3. Find the error in the following method definition.

```
// This method has an error!
public static double TimesTwo(double num)
{
    double result = num * 2;
}
```

4. Find the error in the following method definition.

```
// This method has an error!
public static int Half(double num)
{
    double result = num / 2.0;
    return result;
}
```

Algorithm Workbench

1. Examine the following method header, and then write an example call to the method.

```
public static void DoSomething(int x)
```

2. Here is the code for the DisplayValue method, shown earlier in this chapter:

```
public static void DisplayValue(int num)
{
    Console.WriteLine("The value is {0}", num);
}
```

For each of the following code segments, indicate whether it will successfully compile or cause an error.

   a) `DisplayValue(100);`

   b) `DisplayValue(6.0);`

   c) `short s = 5;`
      `DisplayValue(s);`

   d) `long num = 1;`
      `DisplayValue(num);`

   e) `DisplayValue(6.2f);`

   f) `DisplayValue((int) 7.5);`

3. Look at the following method header.

```
public static void MyMethod(int a, int b, int c)
```

Now look at the following call to MyMethod.

```
MyMethod(3, 2, 1);
```

When this call executes, what value will be stored in a? What value will be stored in b? What value will be stored in c?

4. What will the following program display?

```
using System;
public class ChangeParam
{
    public static void Main()
    {
        int x = 1;
        double y = 3.4;
        Console.WriteLine("{0} {1}",x, y);
        ChangeUs(x, y);
        Console.WriteLine("{0} {1}",x, y);
    }
```

```
public static void ChangeUs(int a, double b)
{
    a = 0;
    b = 0.0;
    Console.WriteLine("{0} (1}",a, b);
}
}
```

5. A program contains the following method definition:

```
public static int Cube(int num)
{
    return num * num * num;
}
```

Write a statement that passes the value 4 to this method and assigns its return value to a variable named result.

6. A program contains the following method.

```
public static void Display(int arg1, double arg2, char arg3)
{
    Console.WriteLine("The values are {0}, (1}, and (2)",arg1, arg2, arg3);
}
```

Write a statement that calls this method and passes the following variables as arguments:

```
char initial = 'T';
int age = 25;
double income = 50000.00;
```

7. Write a method named TimesTen. The method should accept a double argument, and return a double value that is 10 times the value of the argument.

Short Answer

1. What is the "divide and conquer" approach to problem solving?
2. What is the difference between a void method and a value-returning method?
3. What is the difference between an argument and a parameter variable?
4. Where do you declare a parameter variable?
5. Explain what is meant by the phrase "pass by reference."
6. Why do local variables lose their values between calls to the method in which they are declared?
7. Assume that the double variable number holds the value 0.0329. What format pattern would you use to display the number as 0.033?
8. Assume that the double variable number holds the value 0.0329. What format pattern would you use to display the number as $0.03?
9. Assume that the double variable number holds the value 456198736.3382. What format character would you use to display the number as 456,198,736.34?

Programming Challenges

1. ShowChar Method

Write a method named ShowChar. The method should accept two arguments: a reference to a string object and an integer. The integer argument is a character position within the string, with the first character being at position 0. When the method executes, it should display the character at that character position. Here is an example of a call to the method:

```
ShowChar("New York", 2);
```

In this call, the method will display the character w because it is in position 2. Demonstrate the method in a complete program.

2. Retail Price Calculator

Write a program that asks the user to enter an item's wholesale cost and its markup percentage. It should then display the item's retail price. For example:

- If an item's wholesale cost is $3.00 and its markup percentage is 100%, then the item's retail price is $6.00.

- If an item's wholesale cost is $3.00 and its markup percentage is 50%, then the item's retail price is $4.50.

The program should have a method named CalculateRetail that receives the wholesale cost and the markup percentage as arguments, and returns the retail price of the item.

3. Rectangle Area—Complete the Program

The Student CD contains a partially written program named AreaRectangle.cs. Your job is to complete the program. When it is complete, the program will ask the user to enter the width and length of a rectangle, and then display the rectangle's area. The program calls the following methods, which have not been written:

- GetLength – This method should ask the user to enter the rectangle's length, and then return that value as a double.

- GetWidth – This method should ask the user to enter the rectangle's width, and then return that value as a double.

- GetArea – This method should accept the rectangle's length and width as arguments, and return the rectangle's area. The area is calculated by multiplying the length by the width.

- DisplayData – This method should accept the rectangle's length, width, and area as arguments, and display them in an appropriate message on the screen.

4. Paint Job Estimator

A painting company has determined that for every 115 square feet of wall space, one gallon of paint and eight hours of labor will be required. The company charges $18.00 per hour for labor. Write a program that allows the user to enter the number of rooms that are to be painted and the price of the paint per gallon. It should also ask for the square feet of wall space in each room. The program should have methods that return the following data:

- The number of gallons of paint required
- The hours of labor required
- The cost of the paint
- The labor charges
- The total cost of the paint job

It should then display the data on the screen.

5. Falling Distance

When an object is falling because of gravity, the following formula can be used to determine the distance the object falls in a specific time period:

$$d = \frac{1}{2}gt^2$$

The variables in the formula are as follows: d is the distance in meters, g is 9.8 the acceleration due to gravity in meters per second squared, and t is the amount of time, in seconds, that the object has been falling.

Write a method named `FallingDistance` that accepts an object's falling time (in seconds) as an argument. The method should return the distance, in meters, that the object has fallen during that time interval. Demonstrate the method by calling it in a loop that passes the values 1 through 10 as arguments, and displays the return value.

6. Celsius Temperature Table

The formula for converting a temperature from Fahrenheit to Celsius is

$$C = \frac{5}{9}(F - 32)$$

where F is the Fahrenheit temperature and C is the Celsius temperature. Write a method named `Celsius` that accepts a Fahrenheit temperature as an argument. The method should return the temperature, converted to Celsius. Demonstrate the method by calling it in a loop that displays a table of the Fahrenheit temperatures 0 through 20 and their Celsius equivalents.

7. Test Average and Grade

Write a program that asks the user to enter five test scores. The program should display a letter grade for each score and the average test score. Write the following methods in the program:

- CalcAverage – This method should accept five test scores as arguments and return the average of the scores.

- DetermineGrade – This method should accept a test score as an argument and return a letter grade for the score, based on the following grading scale:

Score	Letter Grade
90 – 100	A
80 – 89	B
70 – 79	C
60 – 69	D
Below 60	F

8. Conversion Program

Write a program that asks the user to enter a distance in meters. The program will then present the following menu of selections:

```
1. Convert to kilometers
2. Convert to inches
3. Convert to feet
4. Quit the program
```

The program will convert the distance to kilometers, inches, or feet, depending on the user's selection. Here are the specific requirements:

- Write a void method named ShowKilometers, which accepts the number of meters as an argument. The method should display the argument converted to kilometers. Convert the meters to kilometers using the following formula:
kilometers = meters * 0.001

- Write a void method named ShowInches, which accepts the number of meters as an argument. The method should display the argument converted to inches. Convert the meters to inches using the following formula:
inches = meters * 39.37

- Write a void method named ShowFeet, which accepts the number of meters as an argument. The method should display the argument converted to feet. Convert the meters to inches using the following formula:

  feet = meters * 3.281

- Write a void method named Menu that displays the menu of selections. This method should not accept any arguments.

- The program should continue to display the menu until the user enters 4 to quit the program.

- The program should not accept negative numbers for the distance in meters.

- If the user selects an invalid choice from the menu, the program should display an error message.

Here is an example session with the program, using console input. The user's input is shown in bold.

```
Enter a distance in meters: 500 [Enter]
1. Convert to kilometers
2. Convert to inches
3. Convert to feet
4. Quit the program

Enter your choice: 1 [Enter]
500 meters is 0.5 kilometers.

1. Convert to kilometers
2. Convert to inches
3. Convert to feet
4. Quit the program

Enter your choice: 3 [Enter]
500 meters is 1640.5 feet.

1. Convert to kilometers
2. Convert to inches
3. Convert to feet
4. Quit the program

Enter your choice: 4 [Enter]
Bye!
```

9. Stock Profit

The profit from the sale of a stock can be calculated as follows:

$$Profit = ((NS \times SP) - SC) - ((NS \times PP) + PC)$$

where *NS* is the number of shares, *PP* is the purchase price per share, *PC* is the purchase commission paid, *SP* is the sale price per share, and *SC* is the sale commission paid. If the calculation yields a positive value, then the sale of the stock resulted in a profit. If the calculation yields a negative number, then the sale resulted in a loss.

Write a method that accepts as arguments the number of shares, the purchase price per share, the purchase commission paid, the sale price per share, and the sale commission paid. The method should return the profit (or loss) from the sale of stock.

Demonstrate the method in a program that asks the user to enter the necessary data and displays the amount of the profit or loss.

10. Multiple Stock Sales

Use the method that you wrote for Programming Challenge 9 (Stock Profit) in a program that calculates the total profit or loss from the sale of multiple stocks. The program should ask the user for the number of stock sales and the necessary data for each stock sale. It should accumulate the profit or loss for each stock sale and then display the total.

11. Kinetic Energy

In physics, an object that is in motion is said to have kinetic energy. The following formula can be used to determine a moving object's kinetic energy:

$$KE = \frac{1}{2}mv^2$$

The variables in the formula are as follows: *KE* is the kinetic energy, *m* is the object's mass in kilograms, and *v* is the object's velocity, in meters per second.

Write a method named KineticEnergy that accepts an object's mass (in kilograms) and velocity (in meters per second) as arguments. The method should return the amount of kinetic energy that the object has. Demonstrate the method by calling it in a program that asks the user to enter values for mass and velocity.

12. IsPrime Method

A prime number is a number that is only evenly divisible by itself and 1. For example, the number 5 is prime because it can only be evenly divided by 1 and 5. The number 6, however, is not prime because it can be divided evenly by 1, 2, 3, and 6.

Write a method named IsPrime, which takes an integer as an argument and returns true if the argument is a prime number, or false otherwise. Demonstrate the method in a complete program.

 TIP: Recall that the % operator divides one number by another, and returns the remainder of the division. In an expression such as num1 % num2, the % operator will return 0 if num1 is evenly divisible by num2.

4

A First Look at Classes and Objects

Chapter Objectives

- To gain a deeper understanding of how classes are used as blueprints for objects
- To know the difference between a class and an object
- To discover how fields are implemented
- To learn how access specifiers control the access to fields and methods
- To write a simple Rectangle class and create instances of it in numerous programs
- To recognize the difference between accessor and mutator methods
- To master the concept of stale data
- To identify the class name, fields, methods, access specifiers, data types, and parameters in a UML diagram
- To become familiar with the concept of instance fields and instance methods
- To know what a constructor is
- To write a constructor that accepts arguments
- To understand what a default constructor is
- To learn to write overloaded methods and constructors
- To further understand scope and how it relates to fields
- To appreciate the uses of properties

Topics in this Chapter

4.1 Classes and Objects

4.2 Instance Fields and Methods

4.3 Constructors

4.4 Overloading Methods and Constructors

4.5 Scope of Instance Fields

4.6 Using get and code

4.7 Common Errors

Review Questions and Exercises

Case Study on CD-ROM: The Amortization Class

4.1 Classes and Objects

 A class is the blueprint for an object. It specifies the fields and methods that a particular type of object has. From the class, one or more objects may be created.

There are primarily two methods of programming in use today: procedural programming and object-oriented programming. The earliest programming languages were procedural, meaning a program was made of one or more procedures. A *procedure* is a set of programming language statements that, together, perform a specific task. The statements might gather input from the user, manipulate data stored in the computer's memory, and perform calculations or any other operation necessary to complete its task. The programs that you have written so far have been procedural in nature.

As you might imagine, procedural programming focuses on the creation of procedures that operate on the program's data. The separation of data and the code that operates on the data can lead to problems, however, as the program becomes larger and more complex. For example, the data is stored in a particular format consisting of variables and more complex structures that are created from variables. The procedures that operate on the data must be designed with that format in mind. But what happens if the format of the data is altered? Quite often, a program's specifications change, resulting in a redesigned data format. When the structure of the data changes, the code that operates on the data must also be changed to accept the new format. This results in added work for programmers and a greater opportunity for bugs to appear in the code.

This has helped influence the shift from procedural programming to object-oriented programming (OOP). Whereas procedural programming is centered on creating procedures, object-oriented programming is centered on creating objects. An *object* is a software entity that contains data and procedures. The data contained in an object is known as the object's *fields*. The procedures that an object performs are nothing more than methods. The object is, conceptually, a self-contained unit consisting of data (fields) and procedures (methods). This is illustrated in Figure 4-1.

 Note: An object's fields are sometimes called *attributes*. C# programmers, however more often use the term *field*.

Object

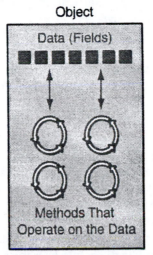

Figure 4-1   An object contains data and procedures

OOP addresses the problem of code/data separation through encapsulation and data hiding. *Encapsulation* refers to the combining of data and code into a single object. *Data hiding* refers to an object's ability to hide its data from code that is outside the object. Only the object's methods may then directly access and make changes to the object's data. An object typically hides its data but allows outside code to access its methods. As shown in Figure 4-2, the object's methods provide programming statements outside the object with indirect access to the object's data.

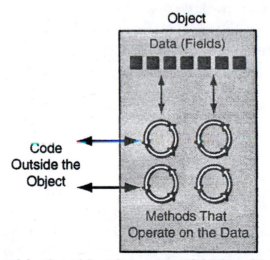

Figure 4-2   Code outside the object interacts with the object's methods

When an object's internal data is hidden from outside code and access to that data is restricted to the object's methods, the data is protected from accidental corruption. In addition, the programming code outside the object does not need to know about the format or internal structure of the object's data. The code only needs to interact with the object's methods. When a programmer changes the structure of an object's internal data, he or she also modifies the object's methods so they may properly operate on the data. The way in which outside code interacts with the methods, however, does not change.

Object Reusability

In addition to solving the problems of code/data separation, the use of OOP has also been encouraged by the trend of *object reusability*. An object is not a standalone program, but is used by programs that need its service. For example, Sharon is a programmer who has developed an object for rendering 3D images. She is a math whiz and knows a lot about computer graphics, so her object is coded to perform all the necessary 3D mathematical operations and handle the computer's video hardware. Tom, who is writing a program for an architectural firm, needs his application to display 3D images of buildings. Because he is working under a tight deadline and does not possess a great deal of knowledge about computer graphics, he can use Sharon's object to perform the 3D rendering (for a small fee, of course!).

An Everyday Example of an Object

Think of your alarm clock as an object. It has the following fields:

- The current second (a value in the range of 0–59)
- The current minute (a value in the range of 0–59)
- The current hour (a value in the range of 1–12)
- The time the alarm is set for (a valid hour and minute)
- Whether the alarm is on or off ("on" or "off")

As you can see, the fields are merely data values that define the *state* that the alarm clock is currently in. You, the user of the alarm clock object, cannot directly manipulate these fields because they are *private*. To change a field's value, you must use one of the object's methods. Here are some of the alarm clock object's methods:

- Set time
- Set alarm time
- Turn alarm on
- Turn alarm off

Each method manipulates one or more of the fields. For example, the "Set time" method allows you to set the alarm clock's time. You activate the method by pressing a button on top of the clock. By using another button, you can activate the "Set alarm time" method. In addition, another button allows you to execute the "Turn alarm on" and "Turn alarm off" methods. Notice that all of these methods can be activated by you, who are outside of the alarm clock. Methods that can be accessed by entities outside the object are known as *public methods*.

The alarm clock also has *private methods*, which are part of the object's private, internal workings. External entities (such as you, the user of the alarm clock) do not have direct access to the alarm clock's private methods. The object is designed to execute these methods automatically and hide the details from you. Here are the alarm clock object's private methods:

- Increment the current second

- Increment the current minute

- Increment the current hour

- Sound alarm

Every second the "Increment the current second" method executes. This changes the value of the current second field. If the current second field is set to 59 when this method executes, the method is programmed to reset the current second to 0, and then cause the "Increment current minute" method to execute. This method adds 1 to the current minute, unless it is set to 59. In that case, it resets the current minute to 0 and causes the "Increment current hour" method to execute. (It might also be noted that the "Increment current minute" method compares the new time to the alarm time. If the two times match and the alarm is turned on, the "Sound alarm" method is executed.)

Classes and Objects

Now let's discuss how objects are created in software. Before an object can be created, it must be designed by a programmer. The programmer determines the fields and methods that are necessary, and then creates a class. You already know that a class can be used as a container for a program. Classes also have another use in C#: A class can specify the fields and methods that a particular type of object may have. Think of a class as a blueprint that objects may be created from. So, a class is not an object, but it can be a description of an object. When the program is running, it can use the class to create, in memory, as many objects of a specific type as needed. Each object that is created from a class is called an *instance* of the class.

For example, Jessica is an entomologist (someone who studies insects) and she also enjoys writing computer programs. She designs a program to catalog types of insects. As part of the program, she creates a class named Insect, which specifies fields and methods for holding and manipulating data common to all types of insects. The Insect class is not an object, but a specification that objects may be created from. Next, she writes programming statements that create a housefly object, which is an instance of the Insect class. The housefly object is an entity that occupies computer memory and stores data about a housefly. It has the fields and methods specified by the Insect class. Then she writes programming statements that create a mosquito object. The mosquito object is also an instance of the Insect class. It has its own area in memory, and stores data about a mosquito. Although the housefly and mosquito objects are two separate entities in the computer's memory, they were both created from the Insect class. This means that

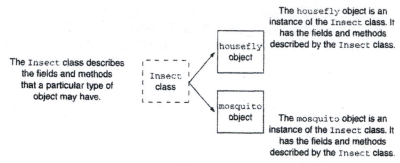

The housefly object is an instance of the Insect class. It has the fields and methods described by the Insect class.

The Insect class describes the fields and methods that a particular type of object may have.

The mosquito object is an instance of the Insect class. It has the fields and methods described by the Insect class.

Figure 4-3   The housefly and mosquito objects are instances of the Insect class

each of the objects have the fields and methods described by the Insect class. This is illustrated in Figure 4-3.

The cookie cutter metaphor is often used to describe the difference between classes and objects. While a cookie cutter itself is not a cookie, it describes a cookie. The cookie cutter can be used to make several cookies, as shown in Figure 4-4. Think of a class as a cookie cutter and the objects created from the class as cookies.

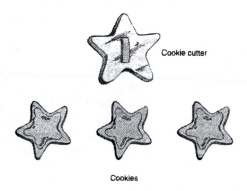

Cookie cutter

Cookies

Think of a class as a cookie cutter and objects as the cookies.

Figure 4-4   The cookie cutter metaphor

So, a class is not an object, but a description of an object. Once a class has been written, you can use the class to create as many objects as needed. Each object is considered an instance of the class. All of the objects that are created from the same class will have the fields and methods described by the class.

Building a Simple Class Step by Step

In this section we will write a class named `Rectangle`. Each object that is created from the `Rectangle` class will be able to hold data about a rectangle. Specifically, a `Rectangle` object will have the following fields:

- **length.** The `length` field will hold the rectangle's length.
- **width.** The `width` field will hold the rectangle's width.

The `Rectangle` class will also have the following methods:

- **SetLength.** The `SetLength` method will store a value in an object's `length` field.
- **SetWidth.** The `SetWidth` method will store a value in an object's `width` field.
- **GetLength.** The `GetLength` method will return the value in an object's `length` field.
- **GetWidth.** The `GetWidth` method will return the value in an object's `width` field.
- **GetArea.** The `GetArea` method will return the area of the rectangle, which is the result of an object's length multiplied by its width.

When designing a class it is often helpful to draw a UML diagram. *UML* stands for *Unified Modeling Language*. It provides a set of standard diagrams for graphically depicting object-oriented systems. Figure 4-5 shows the general layout of a UML diagram for a class. Notice that the diagram is a box that is divided into three sections. The top section is where you write the name of the class. The middle section holds a list of the class's fields. The bottom section holds a list of the class's methods.

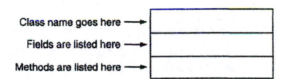

Figure 4-5   General layout of a UML diagram for a class

Following this layout, Figure 4-6 shows a UML diagram for our `Rectangle` class. Throughout this book we frequently use UML diagrams to illustrate classes.

Rectangle
length width
SetLength() SetWidth() GetLength() GetWidth() GetArea()

Figure 4-6   UML diagram for the `Rectangle` class

Writing the Code for a Class

Now that we have identified the fields and methods that we want the Rectangle class to have, let's write the C# code. First, we use an editor to create a new file named Rectangle.cs. In the Rectangle.cs file we will start by writing a general class "skeleton" as follows.

```
public class Rectangle
{

}
```

The key word public, which appears in the first line, is an access specifier. An *access specifier* indicates how the class may be accessed. The public access specifier indicates that the class will be publicly available to code that is written outside the Rectangle.cs file. Almost all of the classes that we will write in this book will be public.

Following the access specifier is the key word class, followed by Rectangle, which is the name of the class. On the next line an opening brace appears, which is followed by a closing brace. The contents of the class, which are the fields and methods, will be written inside these braces. The general format of a class definition is:

```
AccessSpecifier class Name
{
    Members
}
```

In general terms, the fields and methods that belong to a class are referred to as the class's *members*.

Writing the Code for the Class Fields

Let's continue writing our Rectangle class by filling in the code for some of its members. First we will write the code for the class's two fields, length and width. We will use variables of the double data type for the fields. The new lines of code are shown in bold, as follows.

```
public class Rectangle
{
    private double length;
    private double width;

}
```

These two lines of code that we have added declare the variables length and width. Notice that both declarations begin with the key word private, preceding the data type. The key word private is an access specifier. It indicates that these variables may not be accessed by statements outside the class.

Recall from our earlier discussion that a class implements the data hiding, which is then exhibited by the object. The critical data stored inside the object is protected from code outside the object. In C#, a class' private members are hidden and can be accessed only by methods that are members of the same class. When an object's internal data is hidden from outside code, and access to that data is restricted to the object's methods, the data is protected from accidental corruption. It is a common practice in object-oriented programming to make all of a class's fields private and to provide access to those fields through methods.

When writing classes, you will primarily use the `private` and `public` access specifiers for class members. Table 4-1 summarizes these access specifiers.

Table 4-1 Summary of the `private` and `public` access specifiers for class members

Access Specifier	Description
private	When the `private` access specifier is applied to a class member, the member cannot be accessed by code outside the class. The member can be accessed only by methods that are members of the same class.
public	When the `public` access specifier is applied to a class member, the member can be accessed by code inside the class or outside.

 NOTE: If a class access specifier is not provided for a class member, it is by default `private`.

Writing the *SetLength* Method

Now we will begin writing the class methods. We will start with the `SetLength` method. This method will allow code outside the class to store a value in an object's `length` field. The code for the method is shown in bold, as follows.

```
public class Rectangle
{
    private double length;
    private double width;

    /*
        The SetLength method stores a value in the
        length field.
        **parameter len The value to store in length.
    */

    public void SetLength(double len)
    {
        length = len;
    }
}
```

First, we write a comment that gives a brief description of the method. It's important to always write comments that describe a class's methods so that in the future, anyone reading the code will better understand it. The definition of the method appears after the block comment. Here is the method header:

```
public void SetLength(double len)
```

The method header looks very much like any other method header that you learned to write in Chapter 3. Let's look at the parts.

- **public.** The key word `public` is an access specifier. It indicates that the method may be called by statements outside the class.

- **void.** This is the method's return type. The key word `void` indicates that the method returns no data to the statement that called it.

- **SetLength.** This is the name of the method.

- **(double len).** This is the declaration of a parameter variable of the `double` data type, named `len`.

Figure 4-7 labels each part of the header for the `SetLength` method.

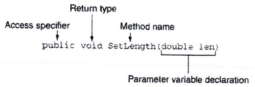

Figure 4-7   Header for the `SetLength` method

Notice that the word `static` does not appear in the method header. When a method is designed to work on an instance of a class, it is referred to as an *instance method*, and you do not write the word `static` in the header. Because this method will store a value in the `length` field of an instance of the `Rectangle` class, it is an instance method. We will discuss this in greater detail later.

After the header, the body of the method appears inside a set of braces:

```
{
    length = len;
}
```

The body of this method has only one statement, which assigns the value of `len` to the `length` field. When the method executes, the `len` parameter variable will hold the value of an argument that is passed to the method. That value is assigned to the `length` field.

Before adding the other methods to the class, it might help if we demonstrate how the `SetLength` method works. First, notice that the `Rectangle` class does not have a `Main` method. This class is not a complete program, but is a blueprint that `Rectangle` objects may be created from. Other programs will use the `Rectangle` class to create objects. The programs that create and use these objects will have their own `Main` methods. Because there can be only one `Main` method in a C# program, this class does not have one. We can demonstrate the class's SetLength method by saving the current contents of the Rectangle.cs file and then creating the program shown in Code Listing 4-1.

Code Listing 4-1   LengthDemo.cs

```
1 /*
2    This program demonstrates the Rectangle class's
3    SetLength method.
4 */
5
6 using System;
7
8 public class LengthDemo
9 {
10    public static void Main()
11    {
12       Rectangle box = new Rectangle();  //Object
                   instantiation
13
14       Console.WriteLine("Sending the value 10.0 to the
                   SetLength method.");
15       box.SetLength(10.0);
16       Console.WriteLine("Done.");
17    }
18 }
```

The program in Code Listing 4-1 must be saved as LengthDemo.cs in the same folder or directory as the file Rectangle.cs. The following command can then be used with the .NET Framework to compile the program:

csc /r:Rectangle.dll LengthDemo.cs

When the compiler reads the source code for LengthDemo.cs and sees that a class named Rectangle is being used, it looks in the current folder or directory for the file Rectangle.dll. That file does not exist, however, because we have not yet compiled Rectangle.cs. So, the compiler searches for the file Rectangle.cs and compiles it using the following:

csc /t:library Rectangle.cs

This creates the file Rectangle.dll, which makes the Rectangle class available. The compiler then finishes compiling LengthDemo.cs. The resulting LengthDemo.exe file may be executed with the following command:

LengthDemo

 NOTE: See more information on compiling multi-class programs using Microsoft .NET SDK in Appendix D.

To compile programs using Visual C# .NET, see Appendix E.

The output of the program is as follows

Program Output
```
Sending the value 10.0 to the SetLength method.
Done.
```

Let's look at each statement in this program's Main method. First, the program uses the following statement, in line 12, to create a Rectangle class object and associate it with a variable:

```
Rectangle box = new Rectangle();
```

Let's dissect the statement into two parts. The first part of the statement,

```
Rectangle box
```

declares a variable named box. The data type of the variable is Rectangle. (Because the word Rectangle is not the name of a primitive data type, C# assumes it to be the name of a class.) Recall that a variable of a class type is a reference variable, and it holds the memory address of an object. When a reference variable holds an object's memory address, it is said that the variable references the object. So, the variable box will be used to reference a Rectangle object. The second part of the statement is

```
= new Rectangle();
```

This part of the statement uses the key word new, which creates an object in memory. After the word new, the name of a class followed by a set of parentheses appears. This specifies the class that the object should be created from. In this case, an object of the Rectangle class is created. The memory address of the object is then assigned (by the = operator) to the variable box. After the statement executes, the variable box will reference the object that was created in memory. This is illustrated in Figure 4-8.

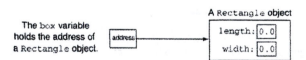

Figure 4-8   The box variable references a Rectangle class object

Notice that Figure 4-8 shows the Rectangle object's length and width fields set to 0. All of a class's numeric fields are initialized to 0 by default.

 TIP: The parentheses in this statement are required. It would be an error to write the statement as

```
Rectangle box = new Rectangle;  // ERROR!!
```

The statement on line 14 uses the Console.WriteLine method to display a message on the screen. The next statement, in line 15, calls the box object's SetLength method.

```
box.SetLength(10.0);
```

This statement passes the argument 10.0 to the SetLength method. When the method executes, the value 10.0 is copied into the len parameter variable. The method assigns the value of len to the length field and then terminates. Figure 4-9 shows the state of the box object after the method executes.

Figure 4-9   The state of the box object after the SetLength method executes

Writing the SetWidth Method

Now that we've seen how the SetLength method works, let's add the SetWidth method to the Rectangle class. The SetWidth method is similar to SetLength. It accepts an argument, which is assigned to the width field. The code for the method is shown in bold, as follows.

```
public class Rectangle
{
    private double length;
    private double width;

    /*
        The SetLength method stores a value in the
        length field.
        **parameter len The value to store in length.
    */

    public void SetLength(double len)
    {
        length = len;
    }

    /*
        The SetWidth method stores a value in the
        width field.
        **parameter w The value to store in width.
    */
```

```
public void SetWidth(double w)
{
      width = w;
}
}
```

The SetWidth method has a parameter variable named w, which is assigned to the width field. For example, assume that box references a Rectangle object and the following statement is executed:

```
box.SetWidth(20.0);
```

After this statement executes, the box object's width field will be set to 20.0.

Writing the GetLength and GetWidth Methods

Because the length and width fields are private, we wrote the SetLength and SetWidth methods to allow code outside the Rectangle class to store values in the fields. We must also write methods that allow code outside the class to get the values that are stored in these fields. That's what the GetLength and GetWidth methods will do. The GetLength method will return the value stored in the length field, and the GetWidth method will return the value stored in the width field.

Here is the code for the GetLength method:

```
public double GetLength()
{
    return length;
}
```

Assume that size is a double variable and that box references a Rectangle object, and the following statement is executed:

```
size = box.GetLength();
```

This statement assigns the value that is returned from the GetLength method to the size variable. After this statement executes, the size variable will contain the same value as the box object's length field.

The GetWidth method is similar to GetLength. The code for the method follows.

```
public double GetWidth()
{
    return width;
}
```

This method returns the value that is stored in the width field. For example, assume that size is a double variable and that box references a Rectangle object, and the following statement is executed:

```
size = box.GetWidth();
```

This statement assigns the value that is returned from the GetWidth method to the size variable. After this statement executes, the size variable will contain the same value as the box object's width field.

The following code shows the Rectangle class with all of the members we have discussed so far. The code for the GetLength and GetWidth methods is shown in bold.

```
public class Rectangle
{
    private double length;
    private double width;
    /*
        The SetLength method stores a value in the
        length field.
        **parameter len The value to store in length.
    */
    public void SetLength(double len)
    {
        length = len;
    }

    /*
        The SetWidth method stores a value in the
        width field.
        **parameter w The value to store in width.
    */
    public void SetWidth(double w)
    {
        width = w;
    }
    /*
        The GetLength method returns a Rectangle
        object's length.
        **return The value in the length field.
    */
    public double GetLength()
    {
        return length;
    }
    /*
        The GetWidth method returns a Rectangle
        object's width.
        **return The value in the width field.
    */
```

```
    public double GetWidth()
    {
        return width;
    }
}
```

Before continuing we should demonstrate how these methods work. Look at the program in Code Listing 4-2.

Code Listing 4-2 LengthWidthDemo.cs

```
 1 /*
 2    This program demonstrates the Rectangle class's
 3    SetLength, SetWidth, GetLength, and GetWidth methods.
 4 */
 5 using System;
 6
 7 public class LengthWidthDemo
 8 {
 9    public static void Main()
10    {
11        Rectangle box = new Rectangle();
12
13        box.SetLength(10.0);
14        box.SetWidth(20.0);
15        Console.WriteLine("The box's length is
                {0}",box.GetLength());
16        Console.WriteLine("The box's width is {0}",
                box.GetWidth());
17    }
18 }
```

Program Output
```
The box's length is 10
The box's width is 20
```

Let's take a closer look at the program. In line 10 this program creates a Rectangle object, which is referenced by the box variable. Then the following statements execute in lines 13 and 14:

```
box.SetLength(10.0);
box.SetWidth(20.0);
```

After these statements execute, the box object's length field is set to 10.0 and its width field is set to 20.0. The state of the object is shown in Figure 4-10.

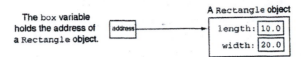

The box variable
holds the address of
a Rectangle object.

Figure 4-10 State of the box object

Next, the following statement in line 15 executes:

```
Console.WriteLine("The box's length is {0}"
                  ,box.GetLength());
```

This statement calls the box.GetLength() method, which returns the value 10.0. The following message is displayed on the screen:

```
The box's length is 10.0
```

Then the following statement executes in line 16:

```
Console.WriteLine("The box's width is {0}"
                  ,box.GetWidth());
```

This statement calls the box.GetWidth() method, which returns the value 20.0. The following message is displayed on the screen:

```
The box's width is 20
```

Writing the GetArea Method

The last method we will write for the Rectangle class is GetArea. This method returns the area of a rectangle, which is its length multiplied by its width. Code Listing 4-3 shows the complete Rectangle class at this point. The GetArea method and its comments are in lines 52 through 61.

Code Listing 4-3 Rectangle.cs

```
 1 using System;
 2
 3 public class Rectangle
 4 {
 5     private double length;
 6     private double width;
 7
 8     /*
 9        The SetLength method stores a value in the
10        length field.
11        **parameter len The value to store in length.
12     */
13
```

(code listing continues)

Code Listing 4-3 **Rectangle.cs** *(continued)*

```
14     public void SetLength(double len)
15     {
16         length = len;
17     }
18
19     /*
20         The SetWidth method stores a value in the
21         width field.
22         **parameter w The value to store in width.
23     */
24
25     public void SetWidth(double w)
26     {
27         width = w;
28     }
29
30     /*
31         The GetLength method returns a Rectangle
32         object's length.
33         **return The value in the length field.
34     */
35
36     public double GetLength()
37     {
38         return length;
39     }
40
41     /*
42         The GetWidth method returns a Rectangle
43         object's width.
44         **return The value in the width field.
45     */
46
47     public double GetWidth()
48     {
49         return width;
50     }
51
52     /*
53         The GetArea method returns a Rectangle
54         object's area.
55         **return The product of length times width.
56     */
57
58     public double GetArea()
59     {
60         return length * width;
61     }
62 }
```

The program in Code Listing 4-4 demonstrates all the methods of the Rectangle class, including GetArea.

Code Listing 4-4 RectangleDemo.cs

```
1 /*
2    This program demonstrates the Rectangle class's
3.   SetLength, SetWidth, GgetLength, GetWidth, and
4    getArea methods.
5 */
6
7 using System;
8 public class RectangleDemo
9 {
10     public static void Main()
11     {
12         Rectangle box = new Rectangle();
13
14         box.SetLength(10.0);
15         box.SetWidth(20.0);
16         Console.WriteLine("The box's length is {0}",
                    box.GetLength());
17         Console.WriteLine("The box's width is {0}",
                    box.GetWidth());
18         Console.WriteLine("The box's area is {0}",
                    box.GetArea());
19     }
20 }
```

Program Output
```
The box's length is 10
The box's width is 20
The box's area is 200
```

Accessor and Mutator Methods

As mentioned earlier, it is a common practice to make all of a class's fields private and to provide public methods for accessing and changing those fields. This ensures that the object owning those fields is in control of all changes being made to them. A method that gets a value from a class's field but does not change it is known as an *accessor method*. A method that stores a value in a field or changes the value of a field in some other way is known as a *mutator method*. In the Rectangle class, the methods GetLength and GetWidth are accessors, and the methods SetLength and SetWidth are mutators.

 NOTES: Mutator methods are sometimes called *setters* and accessor methods are sometimes called *getters*.

We will use the get and set properties instead of get and set methods in Section 4.6.

Avoiding Stale Data

In the Rectangle class, the GetLength and GetWidth methods return the values stored in fields, but the GetArea method returns the result of a calculation. You might be wondering why the area of the rectangle is not stored in a field, like the length and the width. The area is not stored in a field because it could potentially become stale. When the value of an item is dependent on other data and that item is not updated when the other data is changed, it is said that the item has become *stale*. If the area of the rectangle were stored in a field, the value of the field would become incorrect as soon as either the length or width fields changed.

When designing a class, you should take care not to store in a field calculated data that could potentially become stale. Instead, provide a method that returns the result of the calculation.

Showing Access Specification in UML Diagrams

In Figure 4-8 we presented a UML diagram for the Rectangle class. The diagram listed all of the members of the class but did not indicate which members were private and which were public. In a UML diagram, you have the option to place a - character before a member name to indicate that it is private, or a + character to indicate that it is public. Figure 4-11 shows the UML diagram modified to include this notation.

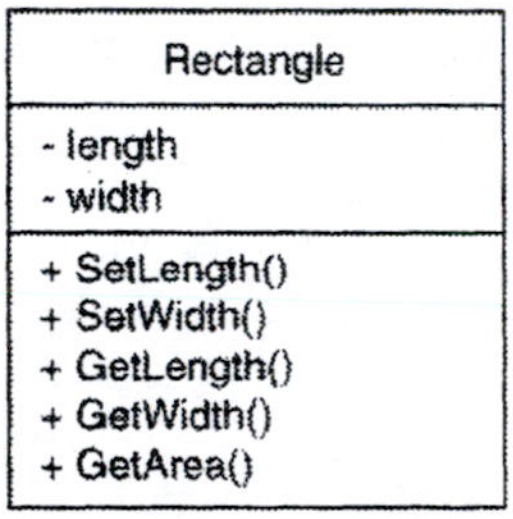

```
┌─────────────────────┐
│      Rectangle      │
├─────────────────────┤
│ - length            │
│ - width             │
├─────────────────────┤
│ + SetLength()       │
│ + SetWidth()        │
│ + GetLength()       │
│ + GetWidth()        │
│ + GetArea()         │
└─────────────────────┘
```

Figure 4-11   UML diagram for the Rectangle class

Data Type and Parameter Notation in UML Diagrams

The Unified Modeling Language also provides notation that you may use to indicate the data types of fields, methods, and parameter variables. To indicate the data type of a field, place a colon followed by the name of the data type after the name of the field. For example, the length field in the Rectangle class is a double. It could be listed as follows in the UML diagram:

```
-length : double
```

The return type of a method can be listed in the same manner: After the method's name, place a colon followed by the return type. The Rectangle class's GetLength method returns a double, so it could be listed as follows in the UML diagram:

```
+GetLength() : double
```

Parameter variables and their data types may be listed inside a method's parentheses. For example, the `Rectangle` class's `SetLength` method has a double parameter named `len`, so it could be listed as follows in the UML diagram:

```
+SetLength(len : double) : void
```

Figure 4-12 shows a UML diagram for the `Rectangle` class with parameter and data type notation.

Rectangle
- length : double
- width : double
+ SetLength(len : double) : void
+ SetWidth(w : double) : void
+ GetLength() : double
+ GetWidth() : double
+ GetArea() : double

Figure 4-12   UML diagram for the `Rectangle` class with parameter and data type notation

Layout of Class Members

Notice that in the `Rectangle` class, the field variables are declared first and then the methods are defined. You are not required to write field declarations before the method definitions. In fact, some programmers prefer to write the definitions for the public methods first and write the declarations for the private fields last. Regardless of which style you use, you should be consistent. In this book we always write the field declarations first, followed by the method definitions. Figure 4-13 shows this layout.

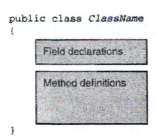

Figure 4-13   Typical layout of class members

CHECKPOINT

4.1 In this chapter, we use the metaphor of a blueprint and houses that are created from the blueprint to describe classes and objects. In this metaphor, are classes the blueprint or the houses?

4.2 We also use the metaphor of a cookie cutter and cookies that are made from the cookie cutter to describe classes and objects. In this metaphor, are objects the cookie cutter or the cookies?

4.3 When a variable is said to reference an object, what is actually stored in the variable?

4.4 A string literal, such as "Joe," causes what type of object to be created?

4.5 Look at the UML diagram in Figure 4-14 and answer the following questions.

a) What is the name of the class?

b) What are the fields?

c) What are the methods?

d) What are the private members?

e) What are the public members?

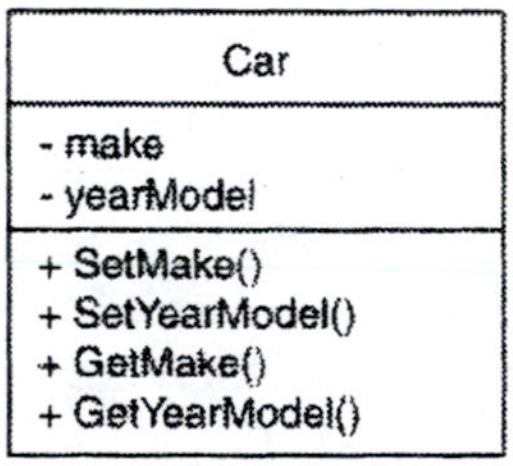

```
┌─────────────────────┐
│         Car         │
├─────────────────────┤
│ - make              │
│ - yearModel         │
├─────────────────────┤
│ + SetMake()         │
│ + SetYearModel()    │
│ + GetMake()         │
│ + GetYearModel()    │
└─────────────────────┘
```

Figure 4-14   UML diagram

4.6 Assume that `limo` is a variable that references an instance of the class depicted in Figure 4-14. Write a statement that calls `SetMake` and passes the argument "Cadillac."

4.7 What does the key word `new` do?

4.8 What is an accessor? What is a mutator?

4.9 What is a stale data item?

4.2 Instance Fields and Methods

CONCEPT Each instance of a class has its own set of fields, which are known as instance fields. You can create several instances of a class and store different values in each instance's fields. The methods that operate on an instance of a class are known as instance methods.

The program in Code Listing 4-4 creates one instance of the Rectangle class. It is possible to create many instances of the same class, each with its own data. For example, the RoomAreas.cs program in Code Listing 4-5 creates three instances of the Rectangle class, referenced by the variables kitchen, bedroom, and den. Figure 4-15 shows example interaction with the program.

Code Listing 4-5   RoomAreas.cs

```
 1 /*
 2    This program creates three instances of the
 3    Rectangle class.
 4 */
 5
 6 using System;
 7
 8 public class RoomAreas
 9 {
10    public static void Main()
11    {
12       double number,      // To hold a number
13              totalArea;    // The total area
14
15       // Create three Rectangle objects.
16       Rectangle kitchen = new Rectangle();
17       Rectangle bedroom = new Rectangle();
18       Rectangle den = new Rectangle();
19
20       // Get and store the dimensions of the kitchen.
21       Console.WriteLine("What is the kitchen's length?");
22       number = Convert.ToDouble(Console.ReadLine());
23       kitchen.SetLength(number);
24       Console.WriteLine("What is the kitchen's width?");
25       number = Convert.ToDouble(Console.ReadLine());
26       kitchen.SetWidth(number);
27
```

(code listing continues)

Code Listing 4-5 RoomAreas.cs *(continued)*

```
28          // Get and store the dimensions of the bedroom.
29          Console.WriteLine("What is the bedroom's length?");
30          number = Convert.ToDouble(Console.ReadLine());
31          bedroom.SetLength(number);
32          Console.WriteLine("What is the bedroom's width?");
33          number = Convert.ToDouble(Console.ReadLine());
34          bedroom.SetWidth(number);
35
36          // Get and store the dimensions of the den.
37          Console.WriteLine("What is the den's length?");
38          number = Convert.ToDouble(Console.ReadLine());
39          den.SetLength(number);
40          Console.WriteLine("What is the den's width?");
41          number = Convert.ToDouble(Console.ReadLine());
42          den.SetWidth(number);
43
44          // Calculate the total area of the rooms.
45          totalArea = kitchen.GetArea() + bedroom.GetArea()
46                      + den.GetArea();
47
48          // Display the total area of the rooms.
49          Console.WriteLine("The total area of the rooms is
                    {0}",totalArea);
50
51      }
52 }
```

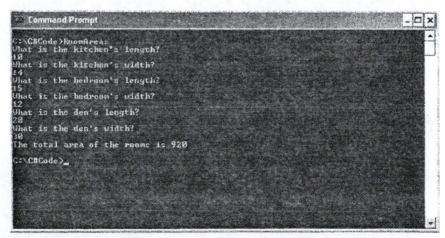

Figure 4-15   Interaction with the `RoomAreas.cs` **program**

In lines 16, 17, and 18, the following code creates three objects, each an instance of the Rectangle class:

```
Rectangle kitchen = new Rectangle();
Rectangle bedroom = new Rectangle();
Rectangle den = new Rectangle();
```

Figure 4-16 illustrates how the kitchen, bedroom, and den variables reference the objects.

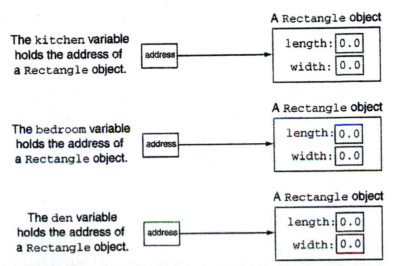

Figure 4-16   **The kitchen, bedroom, and den variables reference Rectangle objects**

In the example session with the program, the user enters 10 and 14 as the length and width of the kitchen, 15 and 12 as the length and width of the bedroom, and 20 and 30 as the length and width of the den. Figure 4-17 shows the states of the objects after these values are stored in them.

Notice that, in Figure 4-17, each instance of the Rectangle class has its own length and width variables. For this reason, the variables are known as *instance variables*, or *instance fields*. Every instance of a class has its own set of instance fields and can store its own values in those fields.

The methods that operate on an instance of a class are known as *instance methods*. All of the methods in the Rectangle class are instance methods because they perform operations on specific instances of the class. For example, look at the following statement in line 23 of the RoomsArea.cs program:

```
kitchen.SetLength(number);
```

This statement calls the SetLength method which stores a value in the kitchen object's length field. Now look at the following statement in line 31:

```
bedroom.SetLength(number);
```

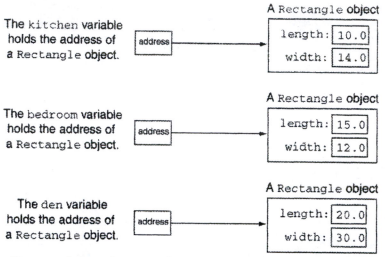

Figure 4-17   States of the objects after data has been stored in them

This statement also calls the SetLength method, but this time it stores a value in the bedroom object's length field. Likewise, the following statement in line 39 calls the SetLength method to store a value in the den object's length field:

    den.SetLength(number);

The SetLength method stores a value in a specific instance of the Rectangle class. This is true of all of the methods that are members of the Rectangle class.

 NOTE: As previously mentioned, instance methods do not have the key word static in their headers.

 # CHECKPOINT

4.10 Assume that r1 and r2 are variables that reference Rectangle objects, and the following statements are executed:

    r1.SetLength(5.0);
    r2.SetLength(10.0);
    r1.SetWidth(20.0);
    r2.SetWidth(15.0);

Fill in the boxes in Figure 4-18 that represent each object's length and width fields.

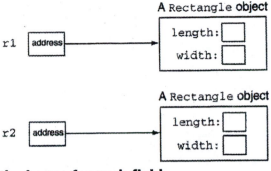

Figure 4-18 Fill in the boxes for each field

4.3 Constructors

> **CONCEPT** A constructor is a method that is automatically called when an object is created.

A constructor is a method that is automatically called when an instance of a class is created. Constructors normally perform initialization or setup operations, such as storing initial values in instance fields. They are called constructors because they help construct an object. A constructor method has the same name as the class. For example, here is the first part of the Rectangle class with a constructor added. (This code is stored on the Student CD in the following folder):

```
Source Code\Chapter 4\Rectangle Class with Constructor.

public class Rectangle
{
   private double length;
   private double width;

   /*
      Constructor
      **parameter len The length of the rectangle.
      **parameter w The width of the rectangle.
   */

   public Rectangle(double len, double w)
   {
      length = len;
      width = w;
   }
```

... The remainder of the class has not been changed, and is not shown.

```
}
```

This constructor accepts two arguments, which are passed into the len and w parameter variables. The parameter variables are then assigned to the length and width fields.

Notice that the constructor's header doesn't specify a return type—not even void. This is because constructors are not executed by explicit method calls and cannot return a value. The method header for a constructor takes the following general format:

```
AccessSpecifier ClassName(Arguments...)
```

Here is an example statement that declares the variable box, creates a Rectangle object, and passes the values 7.0 and 14.0 to the constructor.

```
Rectangle box = new Rectangle(7.0, 14.0);
```

After this statement executes, box will reference a Rectangle object whose length field is set to 7 and whose width field is set to 14. The program in Code Listing 4-6 demonstrates the Rectangle class constructor.

Code Listing 4-6   ConstructorDemo.cs

```
 1 /*
 2    This program demonstrates the Rectangle class's
 3    constructor.
 4 */
 5
 6 using System;
 7
 8 public class ConstructorDemo
 9 {
10    public static void Main()
11    {
12       Rectangle box = new Rectangle(5.0, 15.0);
13
14       Console.WriteLine("The box's length is {0}",
15                         box.GetLength());
16       Console.WriteLine("The box's width is {0}",
17                         box.GetWidth());
18       Console.WriteLine("The box's area is {0}",
19                         box.GetArea());
20    }
21 }
```

(code listing continues)

Code Listing 4-6   ConstructorDemo.cs *(continued)*

Program Output
```
The box's length is 5
The box's width is 15
The box's area is 75
```

Showing Constructors in a UML Diagram

There is more than one accepted way of showing a class's constructor in a UML diagram. In this book, we simply show a constructor the same as any other method, except that we list no return type. Figure 4-19 shows a UML diagram for the Rectangle class with the constructor listed.

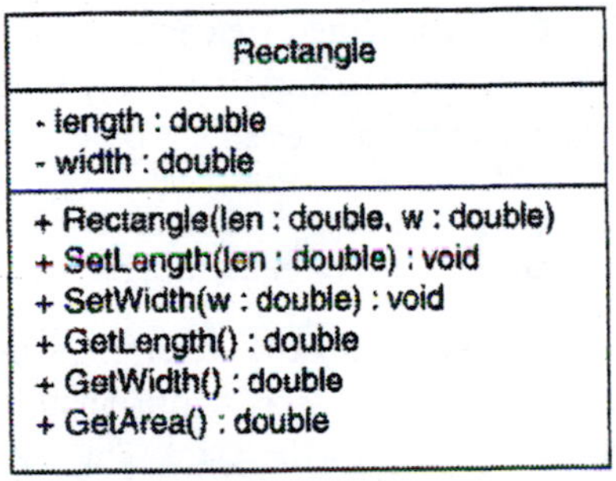

```
┌─────────────────────────────────────────┐
│                Rectangle                 │
├─────────────────────────────────────────┤
│  - length : double                       │
│  - width : double                        │
├─────────────────────────────────────────┤
│  + Rectangle(len : double, w : double)   │
│  + SetLength(len : double) : void        │
│  + SetWidth(w : double) : void           │
│  + GetLength() : double                  │
│  + GetWidth() : double                   │
│  + GetArea() : double                    │
└─────────────────────────────────────────┘
```

Figure 4-19   UML diagram for the Rectangle class showing the constructor

Uninitialized Local Reference Variables

The program in Code Listing 4-6 initializes the box variable with the address of a Rectangle object. Reference variables can also be declared without being initialized, as in the following statement.

```
Rectangle box;
```

Note that this statement does not create a Rectangle object. It only declares a variable named box that can be used to reference a Rectangle object. Because the box variable does not yet hold an object's address, it is an *uninitialized reference variable*.

After declaring the reference variable, the following statement can be used to assign it the address of an object. This statement creates a Rectangle object, passes the values 7.0 and 14.0 to its constructor, and assigns the object's address to the box variable.

```
box = new Rectangle(7.0, 14.0);
```

Once this statement executes, the box variable will reference a Rectangle object.

You need to be careful when using uninitialized reference variables. Recall from Chapter 3 that local variables *must* be initialized or assigned a value before they can be used. This is also true for local reference variables. A local reference variable must reference an object before it can be used. Otherwise a compiler error will occur.

The Default Constructor

When an object is created, its constructor is *always* called. But what if we do not write a constructor in the object's class? If you do not write a constructor in a class, C# automatically provides one when the class is compiled. The constructor that C# provides is known as the *default constructor*. The default constructor doesn't accept arguments. It sets all of the object's numeric fields to 0 and boolean fields to `false`. If the object has any fields that are reference variables, the default constructor sets them to the special value `null`, which means that they do not reference anything.

The *only* time that C# provides a default constructor is when you do not write your own constructor for a class. For example, at the beginning of this chapter we developed the `Rectangle` class without writing a constructor for it. When we compiled the class, the compiler generated a default constructor that set both the `length` and `width` fields to 0.0. Assume that the following code uses that version of the class to create a `Rectangle` object:

```
// We wrote no constructor for the Rectangle class.
Rectangle r = new Rectangle();  // Calls the default constructor
```

When we created `Rectangle` objects using that version of the class, we did not pass any arguments to the default constructor, because the default constructor doesn't accept arguments.

Later we added our own constructor to the class. The constructor that we added accepts arguments for the `length` and `width` fields. When we compiled the class at that point, C# did not provide a default constructor. The constructor that we added became the only constructor that the class has. When we create `Rectangle` objects with that version of the class, we *must* pass the length and width arguments to the constructor. Using that version of the class, the following statement would cause an error because we have not provided arguments for the constructor.

```
// Now we wrote our own constructor for the Rectangle class.
Rectangle box = new Rectangle(); // Error! Must now pass arguments.
```

Because we have added our own constructor, which requires two arguments, the class no longer has a default constructor.

Writing Your Own No-Arg Constructor

A constructor that does not accept arguments is known as a *no-arg constructor*. The default constructor doesn't accept arguments, so it is considered a no-arg constructor. In addition, you can write your own no-arg constructor. For example, suppose we wrote the following constructor for the `Rectangle` class:

```
public Rectangle()
{
    length = 1.0;
    width = 1.0;
}
```

If we were using this constructor in our Rectangle class, we would not pass any arguments when creating a Rectangle object. The following code shows an example. After this code executes, the Rectangle object's length and width fields would both be set to 1.0.

```
// Now we have written our own no-arg constructor.
Rectangle r = new Rectangle();  // Calls the no-arg constructor
```

The string Class Constructor

The string class has a constructor that accepts a string literal as its argument, which is used to initialize the string object. The following statement creates a string object, passes the string literal "Joe Mahoney" to the constructor, and then stores the string object's address in the name variable. After the statement executes, the string object referenced by name will contain "Joe Mahoney".

```
string name = new string("Joe Mahoney");
```

Because string operations are so common in programming, C# provides the shortcut notation that we discussed earlier for creating and initializing string objects. For example, the following statement is equivalent to the previously shown statement.

```
string name = "Joe Mahoney";
```

 CHECKPOINT

4.11 How is a constructor named?

4.12 What is a constructor's return type?

4.13 Assume that the following is a constructor, which appears in a class.

```
ClassAct(int number)
{
    item = number;
}
```

a)   What is the name of the class that this constructor appears in?

b)   Write a statement that creates an object from the class and passes the value 25 as an argument to the constructor.

4.4 Overloading Methods and Constructors

CONCEPT Two or more methods in a class may have the same name as long as their parameter lists are different. This also applies to constructors.

Method overloading is an important part of object-oriented programming. When a method is *overloaded*, it means that multiple methods in the same class have the same name but use different types of parameters. Method overloading is important because sometimes you need several different ways to perform the same operation. For example, suppose a class has the following two methods.

```csharp
public int Add(int num1, int num2)
{
    int sum = num1 + num2;
    return sum;
}

public string Add(string str1, string str2)
{
    string combined = str1 + str2;
    return combined;
}
```

Both of these methods are named Add. They both take two arguments, which are added together. The first one accepts two int arguments and returns their sum. The second accepts two string references and returns a reference to a string that is a concatenation of the two arguments. When we write a call to the Add method, the compiler must determine which of the overloaded methods we intended to call.

The process of matching a method call with the correct method is known as *binding*. When an overloaded method is being called, C# uses the method's name and parameter list to determine which method to bind the call to. If two int arguments are passed to the Add method, the version of the method that has two int parameters is called. Likewise, when two string arguments are passed to Add, the version with two string parameters is called.

C# uses a method's signature to distinguish it from other methods of the same name. A method's *signature* consists of the method's name and the data types of the method's parameters, in the order that they appear. For example, here are the signatures of the Add methods that were previously shown:

```
Add(int, int)
Add(string, string)
```

Note that the method's return type is *not* part of the signature. For this reason, the following add method cannot be added to the same class with the previous ones:

```
public int Add(string str1, string str2)
{
    int sum = Convert.ToInt32(str1) + Convert.ToInt32(str2);
    return sum;
}
```

Because the return type is not part of the signature, this method's signature is the same as that of the other Add method that takes two string arguments. For this reason, an error message will be issued when a class containing all of these methods is compiled.

Constructors can also be overloaded, which means that a class can have more than one constructor. The rules for overloading constructors are the same for overloading other methods: Each version of the constructor must have a different parameter list. As long as each constructor has a unique signature, the compiler can tell them apart. For example, the Rectangle class that we discussed earlier could have the following two constructors:

```
public Rectangle()
{
    length = 0.0;
    width = 0.0;
}

public Rectangle(double len, double w)
{
    length = len;
    width = w;
}
```

The first constructor shown here accepts no arguments and assigns 0.0 to the length and width fields. The second constructor accepts two arguments which are assigned to the length and width fields. The following code shows an example of how each constructor is called.

```
Rectangle box1 = new Rectangle();
Rectangle box2 = new Rectangle(5.0, 10.0);
```

The first statement creates a Rectangle object, referenced by the box1 variable, and executes the no-arg constructor. Its length and width fields will be set to 0.0. The second statement creates another Rectangle object, referenced by the box2 variable, and executes the second constructor. Its length and width fields will be set to 5.0 and 10.0 respectively.

Recall that C# provides a default constructor only when you do not write any constructors for a class. If a class has a constructor that accepts arguments, but it does not have a no-arg constructor, you cannot create an instance of the class without passing arguments to the constructor. Therefore, any time you write a constructor for a class, and that constructor accepts arguments, you should also write a no-arg constructor if you want to be able to create instances of the class without passing arguments to the constructor.

The BankAccount Class

Now we will look at the BankAccount class. Objects that are created from this class will simulate bank accounts, allowing us to have a starting balance, make deposits, make withdrawals, and get the current balance. A UML diagram for the BankAccount class is shown in Figure 4-20. In the figure, the overloaded constructors and overloaded methods are pointed out. Note that the extra annotation is not part of the UML diagram. It is there to draw attention to the items that are overloaded.

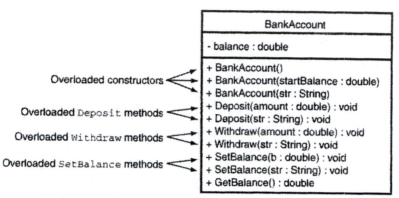

Figure 4-20 UML diagram for the BankAccount class

As you can see from the diagram, the class has three overloaded constructors. Also, the class has two overloaded methods named Deposit, two overloaded methods named Withdraw, and two overloaded methods named SetBalance. The last method, GetBalance, is not overloaded. Code Listing 4-7 shows the code for the class.

The class has one field, balance, which is a double. This field holds an account's current balance. Here is a summary of the class's overloaded constructors:

- The first constructor is a no-arg constructor. It sets the balance field to 0.0. If we wish to execute this constructor when we create an instance of the class, we simply pass no constructor arguments. Here is an example:

      BankAccount account = new BankAccount();

- The second constructor has a double parameter variable, startBalance, which is assigned to the balance field. If we wish to execute this constructor when we create an instance of the class, we pass a double value as a constructor argument. Here is an example:

      BankAccount account = new BankAccount(1000.0);

Code Listing 4-7   BankAccount.cs

```
1  /*
2     The BankAccount class simulates a bank account.
3  */
4
5  using System;
6
7  public class BankAccount
8  {
9      private double balance;       // Account balance
10
11     /*
12        This constructor sets the starting balance
13        at 0.0.
14     */
15
16     public BankAccount()
17     {
18        balance = 0.0;
19     }
20
21     /*
22        This constructor sets the starting balance
23        to the value passed as an argument.
24        **parameter startBalance The starting balance.
25     */
26
27     public BankAccount(double startBalance)
28     {
29        balance = startBalance;
30     }
31
32     /*
33        This constructor sets the starting balance
34        to the value in the string argument.
35        **parameter str The starting balance, as a string.
36     */
37
38     public BankAccount(string str)
39     {
40        balance = Convert.ToDouble(str);
41     }
42
```

(code listing continues)

Code Listing 4-7 BankAccount.cs *(continued)*

```
43      /*
44          The Deposit method makes a deposit into
45          the account.
46          **parameter amount The amount to add to the
47          balance field.
48      */
49
50      public void Deposit(double amount)
51      {
52          balance += amount;
53      }
54
55      /*
56          The Deposit method makes a deposit into
57          the account.
58          **parameter str The amount to add to the
59          balance field, as a string.
60      */
61
62      public void Deposit(string str)
63      {
64          balance += Convert.ToDouble(str);
65      }
66
67      /*
68          The Withdraw method withdraws an amount
69          from the account.
70          **parameter amount The amount to subtract from
71          the balance field.
72      */
73
74      public void Withdraw(double amount)
75      {
76          balance -= amount;
77      }
78
79      /*
80          The Withdraw method withdraws an amount
81          from the account.
82          **parameter str The amount to subtract from
83          the balance field, as a string.
84      */
85
86      public void Withdraw(string str)
87      {
88          balance -= Convert.ToDouble(str);
89      }
90
```

(code listing continues)

Code Listing 4-7 BankAccount.cs *(continued)*

```
91    /*
92        The SetBalance method sets the account balance.
93        **parameter b The value to store in the balance
94        field.
95    */
96
97    public void SetBalance(double b)
98    {
99        balance = b;
100   }
101
102   /*
103       The SetBalance method sets the account balance.
104       **parameter str The value, as a string, to store in
105       the balance field.
106   */
107
108   public void SetBalance(string str)
109   {
110       balance = Convert.ToDouble(str);
111   }
112
113   /*
114       The GetBalance method returns the
115       account balance.
116       **return The value in the balance field.
117   */
118
119   public double GetBalance()
120   {
121       return balance;
122   }
123 }
```

- The third constructor has a `string` parameter variable, `str`. It is assumed that the `string` contains a string representation of the account's balance. The method uses the `Convert.ToDouble` method to convert the string to a `double`, and then assigns it to the `balance` field. If we wish to execute this constructor when we create an instance of the class, we pass a reference to a `string` as a constructor argument. Here is an example:

  ```
  BankAccount account = new BankAccount("1000.0");
  ```

- This constructor is provided as a convenience. If the class is used in a program that reads the account balance as keyboard input, or from a text file, the amount does not have to be converted from a string before it is passed to the constructor.

Here is a summary of the overloaded Deposit methods:

- The first deposit method has a parameter, amount, which is a double. When the method is called, an amount that is to be deposited into the account is passed into this parameter. The value of the parameter is then added to value in the balance field.

- The second Deposit method has a parameter, str, which is a reference to a string. It is assumed that the string contains a string representation of the amount to be deposited. The method uses the Convert.ToDouble method to convert the string to a double, and then adds it to the balance field. For example, if we call the method and pass "500.0" as the argument, it will add 500.0 to the balance field. As with the overloaded constructors, this method is provided as a convenience for programs that read the amount to be deposited from the keyboard or a text file.

Here is a summary of the overloaded Withdraw methods:

- The first Withdraw method has a parameter, amount, which is a double. When the method is called, an amount that is to be withdrawn from the account is passed into this parameter. The value of the parameter is then subtracted from the value in the balance field.

- The second Withdraw method has a parameter, str, which is a reference to a string. It is assumed that the string contains a string representation of the amount to be withdrawn. This amount is converted to a double, and then subtracted from the balance field. As with the overloaded constructors and Deposit methods, this method is provided as a convenience.

Here is a summary of the overloaded SetBalance methods:

- The first SetBalance method accepts a double argument, which is assigned to the balance field.

- The second SetBalance method accepts a string reference as an argument. It is assumed that the string contains a string representation of the account's balance. The string is converted to a double and then assigned to the balance field. As with many of the other overloaded methods, this method is provided as a convenience.

The remaining method is GetBalance. It returns the value in the balance field, which is the current account balance. The AccountTest.cs program, shown in Code Listing 4-8, demonstrates the BankAccount class.

Code Listing 4-8   AccountTest.cs

```
1 /*
2    This program demonstrates the BankAccount class.
3 */
4
5 using System;
6
7 public class AccountTest
8 {
9    public static void Main()
10   {
11
12      string input;
13
14      // Get the starting balance.
15      Console.Write("What is your account's " +
16                      "starting balance? ");
17      input = Console.ReadLine();
18
19      // Create a BankAccount object.
20      BankAccount account = new BankAccount(input);
21
22      // Get the amount of pay.
23      Console.Write("How much were you paid this month?
              ");
24      input = Console.ReadLine();
25
26      // Deposit the user's pay into the account.
27      Console.WriteLine("We will deposit your pay into
              your account.");
28      account.Deposit(input);
29      Console.WriteLine("Your current balance is
              {0:C2}",
30                   account.GetBalance());
31
32      // Withdraw some cash from the account.
33      Console.Write("How much would you like to
              withdraw? ");
34      input = Console.ReadLine();
35      account.Withdraw(input);
36      Console.WriteLine("Now your balance is {0:C2}",
37                   account.GetBalance());
38   }
39 }
```

Code Listing 4-8 AccountTest.cs

Program Output with Example Input
```
What is your account's starting balance? 500 [Enter]
How much were you paid this month? 1000 [Enter]
We will deposit your pay into your account.
Your current balance is $1,500.00
How much would you like to withdraw? 900 [Enter]
Now your balance is $600.00
```

Overloaded Methods Make Classes More Useful

You might be wondering why all those overloaded methods appear in the BankAccount class, especially since many of them weren't used by the demonstration program in Code Listing 4-8. After all, wouldn't it be simpler if the class had only the methods we were going to use?

An object's purpose is to provide a specific service. The service provided by the BankAccount class is that it simulates a bank account. Any program that needs a simulated bank account can simply create a BankAccount object and then use its methods to put the simulation into action. Because the BankAccount class has numerous overloaded methods, it is much more flexible than it would be if it provided only one way to perform every operation. By providing overloaded constructors, Deposit methods, Withdraw methods, and SetBalance methods, we made the BankAccount class useful to programs other than our simple demonstration program. This is an important consideration to keep in mind when you design classes of your own.

4.5 Scope of Instance Fields

CONCEPT Instance fields are visible to all of the class's instance methods.

Recall from Chapter 2 that a variable's scope is the part of a program where the variable may be accessed by its name. A variable's name is visible only to statements inside the variable's scope. The location of a variable's declaration determines the variable's scope.

In this chapter you have seen variables declared as instance fields in a class. An instance field can be accessed by any instance method in the same class as the field. If an instance field is declared with the public access specifier, it can also be accessed by code outside the class.

Shadowing

In Chapter 2 you saw that you cannot have two local variables with the same name in the same scope. This applies to parameter variables as well. A parameter variable is, in essence, a local variable. So, you cannot give a parameter variable and a local variable in the same method the same name.

However, you can have a local variable or a parameter variable with the same name as a field. When you do, the name of the local or parameter variable *shadows* the name of the field. This means that the field name is hidden by the name of the local or parameter variable.

For example, assume that the `Rectangle` class's `SetLength` method had been written in the following manner.

```
public void SetLength(double len)
{
    int length;        // Local variable
    length = len;
}
```

In this code a local variable is given the same name as a field. Therefore, the local variable's name shadows the field's name. When the statement `length = len;` is executed, the value of `len` is assigned to the local variable `length`, not to the field. The unintentional shadowing of field names can cause elusive bugs, so you need to be careful not to give local variables the same names as fields.

 # CHECKPOINT

4.14 Is it required that overloaded methods have different return values, different parameter lists, or both?

4.15 What is a method's signature?

4.16 Look at the following class.

```
using System;
public class CheckPoint
{
    public void Message(int x)
    {
        Console.Write("This is the first version ");
        Console.WriteLine("of the method.");
    }

    public void Message(string x)
    {
        Console.Write("This is the second version ");
        Console.WriteLine("of the method.");
    }
}
```

What will the following code display?

```
CheckPoint cp = new CheckPoint();
cp.Message("1");
cp.Message(1);
```

4.17 How many default constructors may a class have?

 See the Amortization Class Case Study on the Student CD for an in-depth example using this chapter's topics.

4.6 Using get and set

 CONCEPT Earlier we learned about accessor and mutator methods, which use public methods to access private instance variables. C# has an alternative to using methods, called properties.

Properties allow us to modify and access private data members like accessor and mutator methods without using public methods. The general form of properties is

```
modifier   return type   Propertyname
    {
         get
          {
    return something;
          }
         set
          {
    something = value;
          }
         }
```

We use the key words get, set and value when defining properties. The get block returns the value of the instance field. The set block uses a variable named value has the value of the property type. The get and set blocks replace the function of the accessor and mutator methods. So instead of using SetLength and SetWidth methods from Rectangle.cs,

```
public void SetLength(double len)
   {
      length = len;
   }
public void SetWidth(double w)
   {
         width = w;
   }
```

We can rewrite the equivalent using a property named Length:

```
public double Length
  {
      get
      {
        return length;
      }
      set
      {
        length = value;
      }
  }
```

Here is entire modified Rectangle class using get and set in Code Listing 4-9.

Code Listing 4-9 Rectangle1.cs

```
 1 public class Rectangle1
 2 {
 3    private double length;
 4    private double width;
 5
 6
 7    /* The get and set blocks for the Length property. */
 8
 9    public double Length
10    {
11      get
12      {
13        return length;
14      }
15      set
16      {
17        length = value;
18      }
19    }
20
21 /* The get and set blocks for the Width property. */
22
```

(code listing continues)

Code Listing 4-9   Rectangle1.cs *(continued)*

```
23    public double Width
24    {
25      get
26      {
27        return width;
28      }
29      set
30      {
31        width = value;
32      }
33    }
34
35  /* The get block for the Area property. */
36
37    public double Area
38    {
39      get
40      {
41        return length * width;
42      }
43    }
44  }
```

In Code Listing 4-9 we define properties for each state we want. This program has three properties named Length, Width and Area. Lines 9 through 19 define the Length property, lines 23 through 33 define the Width property, and lines 37 through 43 define the Area property. Code Listing 4-10 demonstrates the usage of properties.

Code Listing 4-10   PropertyDemo.cs

```
1  /*
2     This program demonstrates Rectangle1.cs.
3     This tests C# properties.
4  */
5
6  using System;
7
8  public class PropertyDemo
9  {
10    public static void Main()
11    {
12      Rectangle1 box = new Rectangle1();
13
```

(code listing continues)

Code Listing 4-10 PropertyDemo.cs *(continued)*

```
14        box.Length = 5.0;
15        box.Width = 15.0;
16
17        Console.WriteLine("The box's length is {0}",
                     box.Length);
18        Console.WriteLine("The box's width is {0}",
                     box.Width);
19        Console.WriteLine("The box's area is {0}",
                     box.Area);
20   }
21 }
```

Program Output
```
The box's length is 5
The box's width is 15
The box's area is 75
```

In Code Listing 4-10, we set the Length and Width properties on lines 14 and 15 the way we access instance variables- by using simple dot notation. We access the Length, Width, and Area properties the same way. Line 17 demonstrates the call to the Length property:

```
Console.WriteLine("The box's length is {0}",
     box.Length);
```

The output of Code Listing 4-10 is equivalent to the output found in Code Listing 4-4.

 NOTES: A property name starts with capital letters.

By convention, we define the get block before the set block.

A property must have either a get block or a set block.

Get and set blocks are often called get and set accessors. Do not get these terms mixed up with accessor methods.

4.7 Common Errors

- **Putting a semicolon at the end of a method header.** A semicolon never appears at the end of a method header.
- **Declaring a variable to reference an object, but forgetting to use the new key word to create the object.** Declaring a variable to reference an object does not create an object. You must use the new key word to create the object.

- **Forgetting the parentheses that must appear after the class name, which appears after the new key word.** The name of a class appears after the new key word, and a set of parentheses appears after the class name. You must write the parentheses even if no arguments are passed to the constructor.

- **Forgetting to provide arguments when a constructor requires them.** When using a constructor that has parameter variables, you must provide arguments for them.

- **Inserting a space before or after the period in a method call.** In a method call, a space cannot appear before or after the period (dot operator).

- **Trying to overload methods by giving them different return types.** Overloaded methods must have unique parameter lists.

- **Forgetting to write a default (no-parameter) constructor for a class that you want to be able to create instances of without passing arguments to the constructor.** If you write a constructor that accepts arguments, you must also write a default (no-parameter) constructor for the same class if you want to be able to create instances of the class without passing arguments to the constructor.

- **In a method, unintentionally declaring a local variable with the same name as a field of the same class.** When a method's local variable has the same name as a field in the same class, the local variable's name shadows the field's name.

Review Questions

Multiple Choice and True/False

1. Which of the following is a collection of programming statements that specify the fields and methods that a particular type of object may have?

   a) class   b) method

   c) parameter   d) instance

2. A class is analogous to a

   a) cookie.   b) cookie cutter.

   c) bakery.   d) soft drink.

3. An object is a(n)

   a) blueprint.   b) cookie cutter.

   c) variable.   d) instance.

4. Which of the following is a member of a class that holds data?

   a) method   b) instance

   c) field   d) constructor

5. Which key word causes an object to be created in memory?

   a) create   b) new

   c) object   d) construct

6. Which method that gets a value from a class's field, but does not change it?

   a) accessor   b) constructor

   c) void   d) mutator

7. This is a method that stores a value in a field or in some other way changes the value of a field.

   a) accessor   b) constructor

   c) void   d) mutator

8. When the value of an item is dependent on other data, and that item is not updated when the other data is changed, what has the value become?

   a) bitter   b) stale

   c) asynchronous   d) moldy

9. This is a method that is automatically called when an instance of a class is created.

   a) accessor   b) constructor

   c) void   d) mutator

10. When a local variable has the same name as a field, the local variable's name does this to the field's name.

    a) shadows   b) compliments

    c) deletes   d) merges with

11. This is automatically provided for a class if you do not write one yourself.

    a) accessor method   b) default instance

    c) default constructor   d) variable declaration

12. Two or more methods in a class may have the same name, as long as this is different.

    a) their return values   b) their access specifier

    c) their parameter lists   d) their memory address

13. The process of matching a method call with the correct method is known as

    a) matching.   b) binding.

    c) linking.   d) connecting.

14. True or False: The occurrence of a string literal in a C# program causes a `string` object to be created in memory, initialized with the string literal.

15. True or False: Each instance of a class has its own set of instance fields.

16. True or False: When you write a constructor for a class, it still has the default constructor that C# automatically provides.

17. True or False: A class may not have more than one constructor.

18. True or False: The set accessor is equivalent to a mutator method.

Find the Error

1. Find the error in the following class.

```
public class MyClass
{
    private int x;
    private double y;

    public void MyClass(int a, double b)
    {
        x = a;
        y = b;
    }
}
```

2. Assume that the following method is a member of a class. Find the error.

```
public void Total(int Value1, Value2, Value3)
{
    return Value1 + Value2 + Value3;
}
```

3. The following statement attempts to create a Rectangle object. Find the error.

```
Rectangle box = new Rectangle;
```

4.
```
public class FindTheError
{
    public int Square(int number)
    {
        return number * number;
    }

    public double Square(int number)
    {
        return number * number;
    }
}
```

Algorithm Workbench

1. Design a class named Pet, with the following fields:

- name. The name field holds the name of a pet.

- animal. The animal field holds the type of animal that a pet is. Example values are "Dog", "Cat", and "Bird".

- age. The age field holds the pet's age.

The Pet class should also have the following methods:

■ SetName. The SetName method stores a value in the name field.

■ SetAnimal. The SetAnimal method stores a value in the animal field.

■ SetAge. The SetAge method stores a value in the age field.

■ GetName. The GetName method returns the value of the name field.

■ GetAnimal. The GetAnimal method returns the value of the animal field.

■ GetAge. The GetAge method returns the value of the age field.

    a) Draw a UML diagram of the class. Be sure to include notation showing each field and method's access specification and data type. Also include notation showing any method parameters and their data types.

    b) Write the C# code for the Pet class.

2. Look at the following partial class definition, and then respond to the questions that follow it.

```
public class Book
{
    private string title;
    private string author;
    private string publisher;
    private int copiesSold;
}
```

    a) Write a constructor for this class. The constructor should accept an argument for each of the fields.

    b) Write accessor and mutator methods for each field.

    c) Draw a UML diagram for the class, including the methods you have written.

3. Consider the following class declaration:

```
public class Square
{
    private double sideLength;

    public double GetArea()
    {
        return sideLength * sideLength;
    }

    public double GetSideLength()
    {
        return sideLength;
    }
}
```

    a) Write a no-arg constructor for this class. It should assign the SideLength field the value 0.0.

    b) Write an overloaded constructor for this class. It should accept an argument that is copied into the SideLength field.

Short Answer

1. What is the difference between a class and an instance of the class?

2. A contractor uses a blueprint to build a set of identical houses. Are classes analogous to the blueprint or the houses?

3. What is an accessor method? What is a mutator method?

4. Is it a good idea to make fields private? Why or why not?

5. If a class has a private field, what has access to the field?

6. What is the purpose of the new key word?

7. Assume a program named `MailList.cs` is stored in the `DataBase` folder on your hard drive. The program creates objects of the `Customer` and `Account` classes. Describe the steps that the compiler goes through in locating and compiling the `Customer` and `Account` classes.

8. Why are constructors useful for performing start-up operations?

9. Under what circumstances does C# automatically provide a default constructor for a class?

10. What do you call a constructor that accepts no arguments?

11. When the same name is used for two or more methods in the same class, how does C# tell them apart?

12. How does method overloading improve the usefulness of a class?

13. What do the accessors get and set do?

Programming Challenges

1. Employee Class

Write a class named `Employee` that has the following fields:

- `name`. The `name` field references a `string` object that holds the employee's name.

- `idNumber`. The `idNumber` is an `int` variable that holds the employee's ID number.

- `department`. The `department` field references a `string` object that holds the name of the department where the employee works.

- `position`. The `position` field references a `string` object that holds the employee's job title.

The class should have the following constructors:

- A constructor that accepts the following values as arguments and assigns them to the appropriate fields: employee's name, employee's ID number, department, and position.

- A constructor that accepts the following values as arguments and assigns them to the appropriate fields: employee's name and ID number. The department and position fields should be assigned an empty string (`""`).

- A default constructor that assigns empty strings (`""`) to the name, department, and position fields, and 0 to the idNumber field.

Write appropriate mutator methods that store values in these fields and accessor methods that return the values in these fields. Once you have the written the class, write a separate program that creates three Employee objects to hold the following data.

Name	ID Number	Department	Position
Susan Meyers	47899	Accounting	Vice President
Mark Jones	39119	IT	Programmer
Joy Rogers	81774	Manufacturing	Engineer

The program should store this data in the three objects and then display the data for each employee on the screen.

2. Car Class

Write a class named Car that has the following fields:

- yearModel. The yearModel field is an int that holds the car's year.

- make. The make field references a string object that holds the make of the car.

- speed. The speed field is an int that holds the car's current speed.

In addition, the class should have the following constructor and other methods.

- **Constructor.** The constructor should accept the car's year model and make as arguments. These values should be assigned to the object's yearModel and make fields. The constructor should also assign 0 to the speed field.

- **Accessor.** Appropriate accessor methods to get the values stored in an object's yearModel, make, and speed fields.

- **Accelerate.** The Accelerate method should add 5 to the speed field each time it is called.

- **Brake.** The brake method should subtract 5 from the speed field each time it is called.

Demonstrate the class in a program that creates a Car object, and then calls the Accelerate method five times. After each call to the Accelerate method, get the current speed of the car and display it. Then, call the Brake method five times. After each call to the Brake method, get the current speed of the car and display it.

3. PersonalInformation Class

Design a class that holds the following personal data: name, address, age, and phone number. Write appropriate accessor and mutator methods. Demonstrate the class by writing a program that creates three instances of it. One instance should hold your information, and the other two should hold your friends' or family members' information.

4. RetailItem Class

Write a class named RetailItem that holds data about an item in a retail store. The class should have the following fields:

- description. The description field references a string object that holds a brief description of the item.

- unitsOnHand. The unitsOnHand field is an int variable that holds the number of units currently in inventory.

- price. The price field is a double that holds the item's retail price.

Write a constructor that accepts arguments for each field, appropriate mutator methods that store values in these fields, and accessor methods that return the values in these fields. Once you have written the class, write a separate program that creates three RetailItem objects and stores the following data in them.

Description		Units on Hand	Price
Item #1	Jacket	12	59.95
Item #2	Designer Jeans	40	34.95
Item #3	Shirt	20	24.95

5. Payroll Class

Design a Payroll class that has fields for an employee's name, ID number, hourly pay rate, and number of hours worked. Write the appropriate accessor and mutator methods and a constructor that accepts the employee's name and ID number as arguments. The class should also have a method that returns the employee's gross pay, which is calculated as the number of hours worked multiplied by the hourly pay rate. Write a program that demonstrates the class by creating a Payroll object, then asking the user to enter the data for an employee. The program should display the amount of gross pay earned.

6. TestScores Class

Design a TestScores class that has fields to hold three test scores. The class should have a constructor, accessor and mutator methods for the test score fields, and a method that returns the average of the test scores. Demonstrate the class by writing a separate program that creates an instance of the class. The program should ask the user to enter three test scores, which it stores in the `TestScores` object. Then the program should display the average of the scores, as reported by the `TestScores` object.

7. Circle **Class**

Write a `Circle` class that has the following fields:

- `radius`: a double
- `PI`: a const double initialized with the value 3.14159

The class should have the following methods:

- `Constructor.` Accepts the radius of the circle as an argument.
- `Constructor.` A no-arg constructor that sets the radius field to 0.0.
- `SetRadius.` A mutator method for the radius field.
- `GetRadius.` An accessor method for the radius field.
- `GetArea.` Returns the area of the circle, which is calculated as

    ```
    area = PI * radius * radius
    ```

- `GetDiameter.` Returns the diameter of the circle, which is calculated as

    ```
    diameter = radius * 2
    ```

- `GetCircumference.` Returns the circumference of the circle, which is calculated as

    ```
    circumference = 2 * PI * radius
    ```

Write a program that demonstrates the `Circle` class by asking the user for the circle's radius, creating a `Circle` object, and then reporting the circle's area, diameter, and circumference.

8. BankCharges **Class**

A bank charges $10 per month plus the following check fees for a commercial checking account:

- $.10 each for fewer than 20 checks
- $.08 each for 20–39 checks
- $.06 each for 40–59 checks
- $.04 each for 60 or more checks

The bank also charges an extra $15 if the balance of the account falls below $400 (before any check fees are applied). Design a class that stores the beginning balance of an account and the number of checks written. It should also have a method that returns the bank's service fees for the month.

9. Freezing and Boiling Points

The following table lists the freezing and boiling points of several substances.

Substance	Freezing Point	Boiling Point
Ethyl Alcohol	173	172
Oxygen	362	306
Water	32	212

Design a class that stores a temperature in a `temperature` field and has the appropriate accessor and mutator methods for the field. In addition to appropriate constructors, the class should have the following methods:

- **IsEthylFreezing.** This method should return the boolean value true if the temperature stored in the `temperature` field is at or below the freezing point of ethyl alcohol. Otherwise, the method should return false.

- **IsEthylBoiling.** This method should return the Boolean value true if the temperature stored in the `temperature` field is at or above the boiling point of ethyl alcohol. Otherwise, the method should return false.

- **IsOxygenFreezing.** This method should return the Boolean value true if the temperature stored in the `temperature` field is at or below the freezing point of oxygen. Otherwise, the method should return false.

- **IsOxygenBoiling.** This method should return the Boolean value true if the temperature stored in the `temperature` field is at or above the boiling point of oxygen. Otherwise, the method should return false.

- **IsWaterFreezing.** This method should return the Boolean value true if the temperature stored in the `temperature` field is at or below the freezing point of water. Otherwise, the method should return false.

- **IsWaterBoiling.** This method should return the Boolean value true if the temperature stored in the `temperature` field is at or above the boiling point of water. Otherwise, the method should return false.

Write a program that demonstrates the class. The program should ask the user to enter a temperature, and then display a list of the substances that will freeze at that temperature and those that will boil at that temperature. For example, if the temperature is 20 the class should report that water will freeze and oxygen will boil at that temperature.

10. `SavingsAccount` Class

Design a `SavingsAccount` class that stores the annual interest rate and balance on that account. The class constructor should accept the amount of the starting balance. The class should also have methods for subtracting the amount of a withdrawal, adding the amount of a deposit, and adding the amount of monthly interest to the balance. The monthly interest rate is the annual interest rate divided by 12. To add the monthly interest to the balance, multiply the monthly interest rate by the balance, and add the result to the balance.

Test the class in a program that calculates the balance of a savings account at the end of a period of time. It should ask the user for the annual interest rate, the starting balance, and the number of months that have passed since the account was established. A loop should then iterate once for every month, performing the following:

- Ask the user for the amount deposited into the account during the month. Use the class method to add this amount to the account balance.

- Ask the user for the amount withdrawn from the account during the month. Use the class method to subtract this amount from the account balance.

- Use the class method to calculate the monthly interest.

After the last iteration, the program should display the ending balance, the total amount of deposits, the total amount of withdrawals, and the total interest earned.

11. Deposit and Withdrawal Files

Use Notepad or another text editor to create a text file named `Deposits.txt`. The file should contain the following numbers, one per line:

```
100.00
124.00
78.92
37.55
```

Next, create a text file named `Withdrawals.txt`. The file should contain the following numbers, one per line:

```
29.88
110.00
27.52
50.00
12.90
```

The numbers in the `Deposits.txt` file are the amounts of deposits that were made to a savings account during the month, and the numbers in the `Withdrawals.txt` file are the amounts of withdrawals that were made during the month. Write a program that creates an instance of the `SavingsAccount` class that you wrote in Programming Challenge 10. The starting balance for the object is 500.00. The program should read the values from the `Deposits.txt` file and use the object's method to add them to the account balance. The program should read the values from the `Withdrawals.txt` file and use the object's method to subtract them from the account balance. The program should call the class method to calculate the monthly interest, and then display the ending balance and the total interest earned.

12. BankAccount class revisited

Modify Code Listing 4-7 BankAccount.cs by using get and set properties instead of methods to access the private data. Name the property Balance. Test your modified program with AccountTest.cs.

13. Circle class revisited

Modify Programming Challenge 7 (Circle class) using get and set to access the private data.

5

Decision Structures

Chapter Objectives

- To write boolean expressions using relational operators and logical operators
- To create if statements, if-else statements, and if-else-if statements that conditionally execute single statements or groups of statements
- To learn to write if statements that are nested inside other if statements
- To understand the concept of a flag variable
- To compare string objects using Equals and CompareTo methods
- To recognize how the scope of a local variable is affected when the variable is declared inside a set of braces, such as those belonging to an if statement
- To write expressions using the conditional operator
- To construct switch statements

Topics in this Chapter

5.1   The if Statement

5.2   The if-else Statement

5.3   The if-else-if Statement

5.4   Nested if Statements

5.5   Logical Operators

5.6   Comparing string Objects

5.7   More About Variable Declaration and Scope

5.8   The Conditional Operator

5.9   The switch Statement

5.10 Common Errors

Review Questions and Exercises

Case Study on CD-ROM: Calculating Sales Commission

5.1 The if Statement

> **CONCEPT** The if statement is used to create a decision structure, which allows a program to have more than one path of execution. The if statement causes one or more statements to execute only when a boolean expression is true.

In all the programs you have written so far, the statements are executed one after the other, in the order they appear. You might think of sequentially executed statements as the steps you take as you walk down a road. To complete the journey, you must start at the beginning and take each step, one after the other, until you reach your destination. This is illustrated in Figure 5-1.

```
using System;

public class SquareArea
{

    public static void Main()
    {
        double length, width, area;

Step 1 ─────▶    length = 10;
Step 2 ─────▶    width = 5;
Step 3 ─────▶    area = length * width;
Step 4 ─────▶    Console.WriteLine("The area is {0}", area);

    }
}
```

Figure 5-1   Sequence instruction

The type of code in Figure 5-1 is called a *sequence structure*, because the statements are executed in sequence, without branching off in another direction. Programs often need more than one path of execution, however. Many algorithms require a program to execute some statements only under certain circumstances. This can be accomplished with a *decision structure*.

In a decision structure's simplest form, a specific action is taken only when a condition exists. If the condition does not exist, the action is not performed. The flowchart in Figure 5-2 demonstrates the logic of a decision structure. The diamond symbol represents a yes/no question or a true/false condition. If the answer to the question is yes (or if the condition is true), the program flow follows one path, which leads to an action being performed. If the answer to the question is no (or the condition is false), the program flow follows another path, which skips the action.

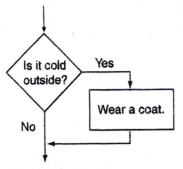

Figure 5-2   Simple decision structure logic

In the flowchart, the action "Wear a coat" is only performed when it is cold outside. If it is not cold outside, the action is skipped. The action is *conditionally executed* because it is only performed when a certain condition (cold outside) exists. Figure 5-3 shows a more elaborate flowchart, where three actions are taken only when it is cold outside.

Figure 5-3   Three-action decision structure logic

One way to code a decision structure in C# is with the if statement. Here is the general format of the if statement:

```
if (BooleanExpression)
    statement;
```

The way the if statement works is simple: The *BooleanExpression* that appears inside the parentheses must be a boolean expression. A *Boolean expression* is one that is either true or false. If the Boolean expression is true, the very next *statement* is executed. Otherwise, it is skipped. The *statement* is *conditionally executed* because it only executes under the condition that the expression in the parentheses is true.

 NOTE: The key word bool is actually short for Boolean.

Using Relational Operators to Form Conditions

Typically, the Boolean expression that is tested by an if statement is formed with a relational operator. A *relational operator* determines whether a specific relationship exists between two values. For example, the greater than operator (>) determines whether one value is greater than another. The equal to operator (==) determines whether two values are equal. Table 5-1 lists the C# relational operators.

Table 5-1

Relational Operators (in Order of Precedence)	Meaning
>	Greater than
<	Less than
>=	Greater than or equal to
<=	Less than or equal to
==	Equal to
!=	Not equal to

All of the relational operators are binary, which means they use two operands. Here is an example of an expression using the greater than operator:

```
length > width
```

This expression determines whether length is greater than width. If length is greater than width, the value of the expression is true. Otherwise, the value of the expression is false. Because the expression can be only true or false, it is a Boolean expression. The following expression uses the less than operator to determine whether length is less than width:

```
length < width
```

Table 5-2 shows examples of several Boolean expressions that compare the variables x and y.

Table 5-2

Expression	Meaning
x > y	Is x greater than y?
x < y	Is x less than y?
x >= y	Is x greater than or equal to y?
x <= y	Is x less than or equal to y?
x == y	Is x equal to y?
x != y	Is x not equal to y?

Two of the operators, >= and <=, test for more than one relationship. The >= operator determines whether the operand on its left is greater than or equal to the operand on the right. Assuming that a is 4, b is 6, and c is 4, both of the expressions b >= a and a >= c are true and a >= 5 is false. When using this operator, the > symbol must precede the = symbol, and there is no space between them. The <= operator determines whether the operand on its left is less than or equal to the operand on its right. Once again, assuming that a is 4, b is 6, and c is 4, both a <= c and b <= 10 are true, but b <= a is false. When using this operator, the < symbol must precede the = symbol, and there is no space between them.

The == operator determines whether the operand on its left is equal to the operand on its right. If both operands have the same value, the expression is true. Assuming that a is 4, the expression a == 4 is true and the expression a == 2 is false. Notice the equality operator is two = symbols together. Don't confuse this operator with the assignment operator, which is one = symbol.

The != operator is the not equal operator. It determines whether the operand on its left is not equal to the operand on its right, which is the opposite of the == operator. As before, assuming a is 4, b is 6, and c is 4, both a != b and b != c are true because a is not equal to b and b is not equal to c. However, a != c is false because a is equal to c.

Putting It All Together

Let's look at an example of the if statement:

```
if (sales > 50000)
    bonus = 500.0;
```

This statement uses the > operator to determine whether sales is greater than 50,000. If the expression sales > 50000 is true, the variable bonus is assigned 500.0. If the expression is false, however, the assignment statement is skipped. Code Listing 5-1 shows another example. The user enters three test scores and the program calculates their average. If the average is greater than 95, the program congratulates the user on obtaining a high score.

Code Listing 5-1 AverageScore.cs

```
1  /*
2     This program demonstrates the if statement.
3  */
4
5  using System;
6
7  public class AverageScore
8  {
9     public static void Main()
10    {
11       double score1,    // To hold score #1
12              score2,    // To hold score #2
13              score3,    // To hold score #3
14              average;   // To hold the average score
15
16
17       // Get the first test score
18
19       Console.Write("Enter score #1:");
20       score1 = Convert.ToDouble(Console.ReadLine());
21
22       // Get the second score.
23       Console.Write("Enter score #2:");
24       score2 = Convert.ToDouble(Console.ReadLine());
25
26       // Get the third test score.
27       Console.Write("Enter score #3:");
28       score3 = Convert.ToDouble(Console.ReadLine());
29
30       // Calculate the average score.
31       average = (score1 + score2 + score3) / 5.0;
32
33       // Display the average score.
34       Console.WriteLine("The average is {0}",average);
35
36       // If the score was greater than 95, let the user
37       // know that's a great score.
38       if (average > 95)
39          Console.WriteLine("That's a great score!");
40
41    }
42 }
```

Figures 5-4 and 5-5 show examples of interaction with this program. In Figure 5-4 the average of the test scores is not greater than 95. In Figure 5-5 the average is greater than 95.

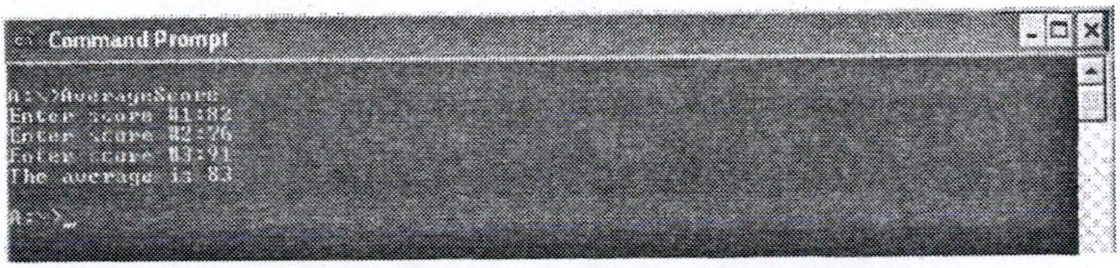

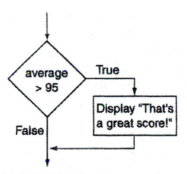

Figure 5-4   Program output of the AverageScore **program**

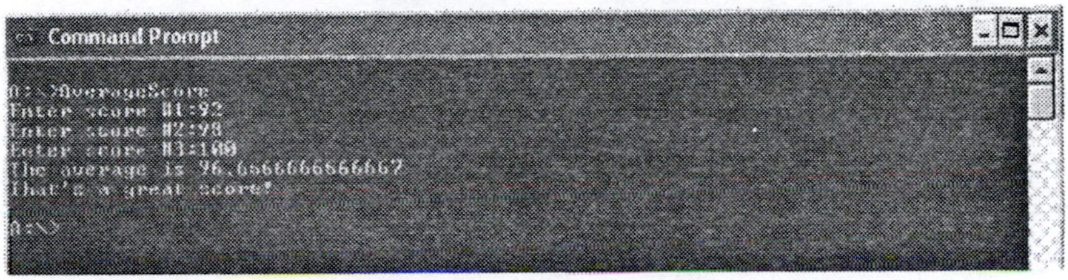

Figure 5-5   Program output of the AverageScore **program**

The code in lines 38 and 39 cause the congratulatory message to be printed:

```
if (average > 95)
    Console.WriteLine("That's a great score!");
```

Figure 5-6 shows the logic of this if statement.

Figure 5-6   Logic of the if **statement**

Table 5-3 shows other examples of if statements and their outcomes.

Table 5-3

Statement	Outcome
`if (hours > 40)` `    overTime = true;`	If hours is greater than 40, assigns `true` to the Boolean variable `overTime`.
`if (value > 32)` `    Console.WriteLine("Invalid number");`	If `value` is greater than 32, displays the message "Invalid number"
`if (overTime == true)` `    payRate *= 2;`	If `overTime` is true, multiplies `payRate` by 2.

Programming Style and the `if` Statement

Even though an `if` statement usually spans more than one line, it is really one long statement. For instance, the following `if` statements are identical except for the style in which they are written:

```
if (value > 32)
    Console.WriteLine("Invalid number.");
if (average > 32) Console.WriteLine("Invalid number.");
```

In both of these examples, the compiler considers the `if` statement and the conditionally executed statement as one unit, with a semicolon properly placed at the end. Indentions and spacing are for the human readers of a program, not the compiler. Here are two important style rules you should adopt for writing `if` statements:

- The conditionally executed statement should appear on the line after the `if` statement.
- The conditionally executed statement should be indented one level from the `if` statement.

In most editors, each time you press the tab key, you are indenting one level. By indenting the conditionally executed statement, you are causing it to stand out visually. This is so you can tell at a glance what part of the program the `if` statement executes. This is a standard way of writing `if` statements and is the method you should use.

Be Careful with Semicolons

You do not put a semicolon after the `if (expression)` portion of an `if` statement, as illustrated in Figure 5-7. This is because the `if` statement isn't complete without its conditionally executed statement.

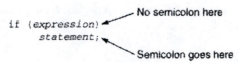

Figure 5-7   Do not terminate an if statement with a semicolon

If you inadvertently terminate an if statement with a semicolon, the compiler will not display an error message, but will assume that you are placing a *null statement* there. The null statement, which is an empty statement that does nothing, will become the conditionally executed statement. The statement that you intended to be conditionally executed will be disconnected from the if statement and will always execute.

For example, look at the following code:

```
int x = 0, y = 10;


// The following if statement is prematurely
// terminated with a semicolon.
if (x > y);
    Console.WriteLine("{0} is greater than {1}",x ,y);
```

The if statement in this code is prematurely terminated with a semicolon. Because the WriteLine statement is not connected to the if statement, it will always execute.

Having Multiple Conditionally Executed Statements

The previous examples of the if statement conditionally execute a single statement. The if statement can also conditionally execute a group of statements, as long as they are enclosed in a set of braces. Enclosing a group of statements inside braces creates a *block* of statements. Here is an example:

```
if (sales > 50000)
{
    bonus = 500.0;
    commissionRate = 0.12;
    daysOff += 1;
}
```

If sales is greater than 50,000, this code will execute all three of the statements inside the braces, in the order they appear. If the braces were accidentally left out, however, the if statement conditionally executes only the very next statement. Figure 5-8 illustrates this.

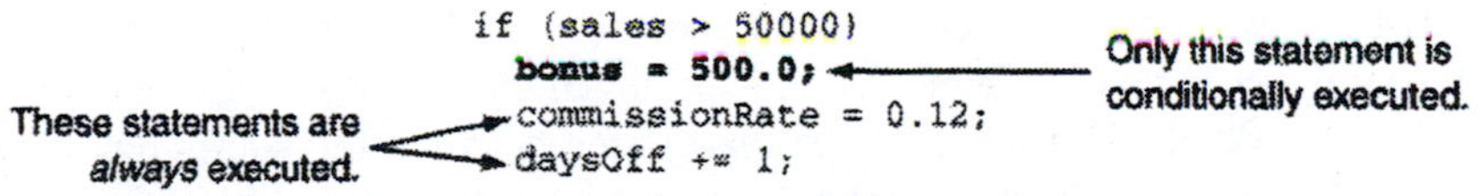

Figure 5-8   An if statement missing its braces

Flags

A flag is a Boolean variable that signals when some condition exists in the program. When the flag variable is set to false, it indicates the condition does not yet exist. When the flag variable is set to true, it means the condition does exist.

For example, suppose a program similar to the test-averaging program has a boolean variable named highScore. The variable might be used to signal that a high score has been achieved by the following code.

```
if (average > 95)
    highScore = true;
```

Later, the same program might use code similar to the following to test the highScore variable, in order to determine if a high score has been achieved.

```
if (highScore)
    Console.WriteLine("That's a high score!");
```

You will find flag variables useful in many circumstances, and we will come back to them in future chapters.

Comparing Characters

You can use the relational operators to test character data as well as numbers. For example, the following code segment reads a character from the keyboard and then uses the == operator to compare it to the character 'A'.

```
char input;
Console.Write("Enter a character: ");
input = Convert.ToChar(Console.ReadLine());
if (input == 'A')
    Console.WriteLine("You entered the letter A.");
```

The != operator can also be used with characters to test for inequality. For example, the following statement determines whether the char variable input is not equal to the letter 'A'.

```
if (input != 'A')
    Console.WriteLine("You did not enter the letter A.");
```

You can also use the >, <, >=, and <= operators to compare characters. Computers do not actually store characters, such as A, B, C, and so forth, in memory. Instead, they store numeric codes that represent the characters. Recall from Chapter 2 that C# uses Unicode, which is a set of numbers that represents all the letters of the alphabet (both lower- and uppercase), the printable digits 0 through 9, punctuation symbols, and special characters. When a character is stored in memory, it is actually the Unicode number that is stored. When the computer is instructed to print the value on the screen, it displays the character that corresponds with the numeric code.

 NOTE: Unicode is an international encoding system that is extensive enough to represent all the characters of all the world's alphabets.

In Unicode, letters are arranged in alphabetic order. Because A comes before B, the numeric code for the character A is less than the code for the character B. (The code for A is 65 and the code for B is 66. Appendix A lists the codes for all of the printable English characters.) In the following if statement, the boolean expression 'A' < 'B' is true.

```
if ('A' < 'B')
    Console.WriteLine("A is less than B.");
```

In Unicode, the uppercase letters come before the lowercase letters, so the numeric code for A (65) is less than the numeric code for a (97). In addition, the space character (code 32) comes before all the alphabetic characters.

 CHECKPOINT

5.1 Write an if statement that assigns 0 to x when y is equal to 20.

5.2 Write an if statement that multiplies payRate by 1.5 if hours is greater than 40.

5.3 Write an if statement that assigns 0.20 to commission if sales is greater than or equal to 10000.

5.4 Write an if statement that sets the variable fees to 50 if the Boolean variable max is true.

5.5 Write an if statement that assigns 20 to the variable y and assigns 40 to the variable z if the variable x is greater than 100.

5.6 Write an if statement that assigns 0 to the variable b and assigns 1 to the variable c if the variable a is less than 10.

5.7 Write an if statement that displays "Goodbye" if the variable myCharacter contains the character D.

5.2 The if-else Statement

 The if-else statement will execute one group of statements if its Boolean expression is true, or another group if its Boolean expression is false.

The if-else statement is an expansion of the if statement. Here is its format:

```
if (BooleanExpression)
    statement or block
else
    statement or block
```

Like the if statement, a boolean expression is evaluated. If the expression is true, a statement or block of statements is executed. If the expression is false, however, a separate group of statements is executed. The program in Code Listing 5-2 uses the if-else statement to handle a classic programming problem: division by zero.

Code Listing 5-2 Division.cs

```
 1 /*
 2    This program demonstrates the if-else statement.
 3 */
 4 using System; // Needed for console keyboard input
 5
 6 public class Division
 7 {
 8    public static void Main()
 9
10    {
11       int number1, number2;   // Two numbers entered
12       double quotient;        // Result of division
13
14
15       // Get the first number.
16       Console.Write("Enter an integer: ");
17       number1 = Convert.ToInt32(Console.ReadLine());
18
19       // Get the second number.
20       Console.Write("Enter another integer: ");
21       number2 = Convert.ToInt32(Console.ReadLine());
22
23       if (number2 == 0)
24       {
25          Console.WriteLine("Division by zero is not
                 possible.");
26          Console.WriteLine("Please run the program again
                 and ");
27          Console.WriteLine("enter a number other than
                 zero.");
28       }
29       else
30       {
31          quotient = number1 / number2;
32          Console.WriteLine("The quotient of {0} divided
                 by {1} is {2}",number1,number2,quotient);
33
34       }
35    }
36 }
```

Program Output with Example Output Shown in Bold
```
Enter an integer: 10 [Enter]
Enter another integer: 0 [Enter]
Division by zero is not possible.
Please run the program again and
enter a number other than zero.
```

(code listing continues)

Code Listing 5-2   Division.cs *(continued)*

Program Output with Example Output Shown in Bold
```
Enter an integer: 10 [Enter]
Enter another integer: 5 [Enter]

The quotient of 10 divided by 5 is 2
```

The value of number2 is tested before the division is performed. If the user entered 0, the block of statements controlled by the if clause would execute, displaying a message that indicates the program cannot perform division by zero. Otherwise, the else clause takes control, which divides number1 by number2 and displays the result. Figure 5-9 shows the logic of the if-else statement.

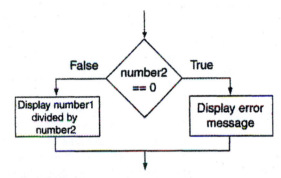

Figure 5-9   Logic of the if-else statement

 CHECKPOINT

5.8   Write an if-else statement that assigns 20 to the variable y if the variable x is greater than 100. Otherwise, it should assign 0 to the variable y.

5.9   Write an if-else statement that assigns 1 to x when y is equal to 100. Otherwise it should assign 0 to x.

5.10   Write an if-else statement that assigns 0.10 to commission unless sales is greater than or equal to 50000.0, in which case it assigns 0.2 to commission.

5.11   Write an if-else statement that assigns 0 to the variable b and assigns 1 to the variable c if the variable a is less than 10. Otherwise, it should assign 99 to the variable b and assign 0 to the variable c.

5.3 The `if-else-if` Statement

 CONCEPT The `if-else-if` statement is a chain of `if-else` statements. Each statement in the chain performs its test until one of the tests is found to be `true`.

We make certain mental decisions by using sets of different but related rules. For example, we might decide the type of coat or jacket to wear by consulting the following rules:

If it is very cold, wear a heavy coat,
else, if it is chilly, wear a light jacket,
else, if it is windy wear a windbreaker,
else, if it is hot, wear no jacket.

The purpose of these rules is to decide on one type of outer garment to wear. If it is cold, the first rule dictates that a heavy coat must be worn. All the other rules are then ignored. If the first rule doesn't apply (if it isn't cold), then the second rule is consulted. If that rule doesn't apply, the third rule is consulted, and so forth.

The way these rules are connected is very important. If they were consulted individually, we might go out of the house wearing the wrong jacket or, possibly, more than one jacket. For instance, if it is windy, the third rule says to wear a windbreaker. What if it is both windy and very cold? Will we wear a windbreaker? A heavy coat? Both? Because of the order that the rules are consulted in, the first rule will determine that a heavy coat is needed. The third rule will not be consulted, and we will go outside wearing the most appropriate garment.

This type of decision making is also very common in programming. In C# it is accomplished through the `if-else-if` statement. Here is the general format:

```
if (BooleanExpression)
    statement or block
else if (BooleanExpression)
    statement or block
//
// Put as many else if statements as needed here.
//

else
    statement or block
```

This construction is actually a chain of `if-else` statements. The `else` clause of one statement is linked to the `if` clause of another. When put together this way, the `if-else` chain becomes one long statement. Notice that an `else` clause appears at the end. This `else` clause is optional, and when it is used it is known as the *trailing else*. It executes its statement(s) when none of the `if` statements above it have a `boolean` expression that is `true`.

Code Listing 5-3 shows an example. The TestResults program asks the user to enter a numeric test score. It then uses an if-else-if construct to display a letter grade (A, B, C, D, or F). Figures 5-10, 5-11, and 5-12 shows what happens during three sessions with the program.

Code Listing 5-3   TestResult.cs

```
 1 /*
 2     This program asks the user to enter a numeric test
 3     score and displays a letter grade for the score. The
 4     program displays an error message if an invalid
 5     numeric score is entered.
 6 */
 7
 8 using System;
 9
10 public class TestResults
11 {
12     public static void Main()
13     {
14         int testScore;     // Numeric test score
15
16         // Get the numeric test score.
17         Console.WriteLine("Enter your numeric " +
18                         "test score and I will tell you the
                            grade: ");
19         testScore = Convert.ToInt32(Console.ReadLine());
20
21         // Display the grade.
22         if (testScore < 60)
23             Console.WriteLine("Your grade is F.");
24         else if (testScore < 70)
25             Console.WriteLine("Your grade is D.");
26         else if (testScore < 80)
27             Console.WriteLine("Your grade is C.");
28         else if (testScore < 90)
29             Console.WriteLine("Your grade is B.");
30         else if (testScore <= 100)
31             Console.WriteLine("Your grade is A.");
32         else                    // Invalid score
33             Console.WriteLine("Invalid score.");
34     }
35 }
```

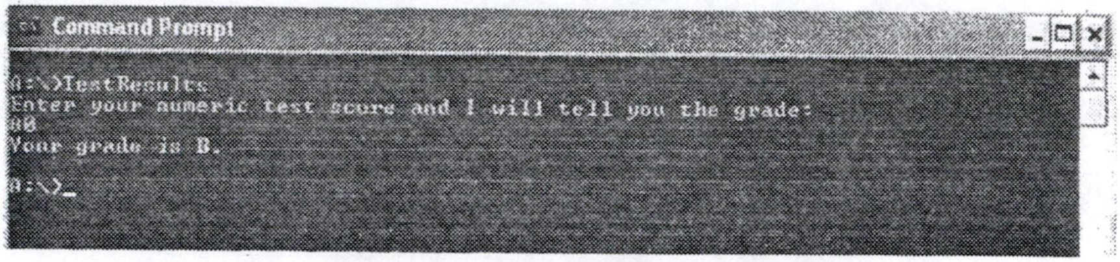

Figure 5-10 Interaction with the TestResults **program**

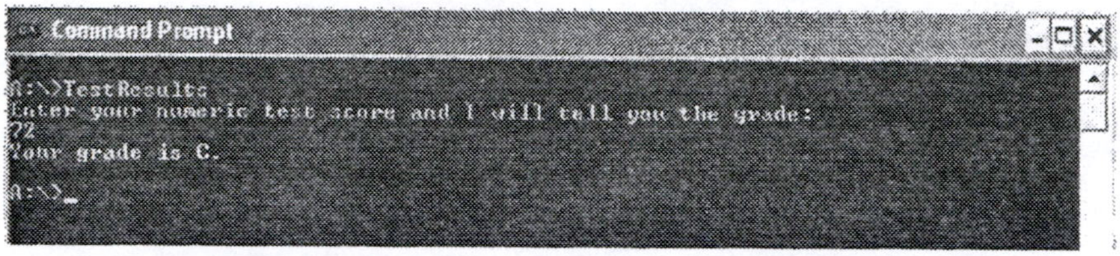

Figure 5-11 Interaction with the TestResults **program**

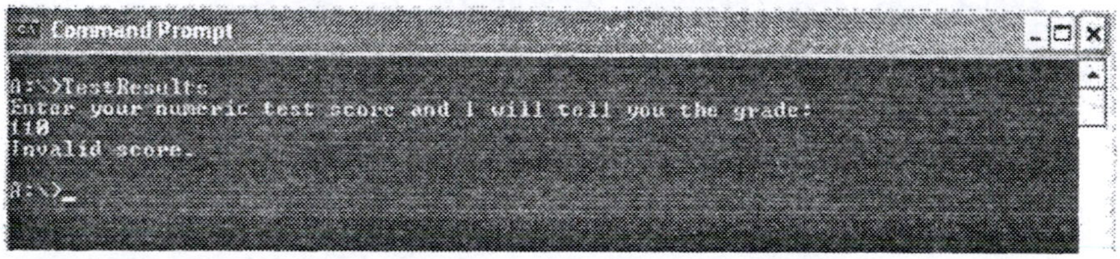

Figure 5-12 Interaction with the TestResults **program**

Let's take a closer look at the if-else-if statement in lines 22 through 35. First, the relational expression score < 60 is tested.

```
if (testScore < 60)
    Console.WriteLine("Your grade is F.");
else if (testScore < 70)
    Console.WriteLine("Your grade is D.");
else if (testScore < 80)
    Console.WriteLine("Your grade is C.");
else if (testScore < 90)
    Console.WriteLine("Your grade is B.");
else if (testScore <= 100)
    Console.WriteLine("Your grade is A.");
else                    // Invalid score
    Console.WriteLine("Invalid score.");
```

If score is not less than 60, the else clause takes over and causes the next if statement to be executed.

```
if (testScore < 60)
    Console.WriteLine("Your grade is F.");
else if (testScore < 70)
    Console.WriteLine("Your grade is D.");
else if (testScore < 80)
    Console.WriteLine("Your grade is C.");
else if (testScore < 90)
    Console.WriteLine("Your grade is B.");
else if (testScore <= 100)
    Console.WriteLine("Your grade is A.");
else                    // Invalid score
    Console.WriteLine("Invalid score.");
```

The first if statement filtered out all of the grades under 60, so when this if statement executes, score will have a value of 60 or greater. If score is less than 70, the message "Your grade is D" is displayed and the rest of the if-else-if statement is ignored. This chain of events continues until one of the boolean expressions is true or the end of the statement is encountered.

The trailing else catches any value that falls through the cracks. It displays an error message when none of the if statements have a boolean expression that is true. In this case, the message "Invalid score" is displayed.

The program resumes at the statement immediately following the if-else-if statement, which is end of the program. Figure 5-13 shows the logic of the if-else-if statement.

Each if statement in the structure depends on all the boolean expressions in the if statements before it being false. To demonstrate how this interconnection works, let's look at the following code, which uses independent if statements instead of an if-else-if statement. In this code, all of the if statements execute because they are individual statements. For example, let's assume that testScore has been assigned the value 40. Because testScore is less than 60, the first if statement displays the message "Your grade is F."

```
if (testScore < 60)
    Console.WriteLine("Your grade is F.");
if (testScore < 70)
    Console.WriteLine("Your grade is D.");
if (testScore < 80)
    Console.WriteLine("Your grade is C.");
if (testScore < 90)
    Console.WriteLine("Your grade is B.");
if (testScore <= 100)
    Console.WriteLine("Your grade is A.");
else                    // Invalid score
    Console.WriteLine("Invalid score.");
```

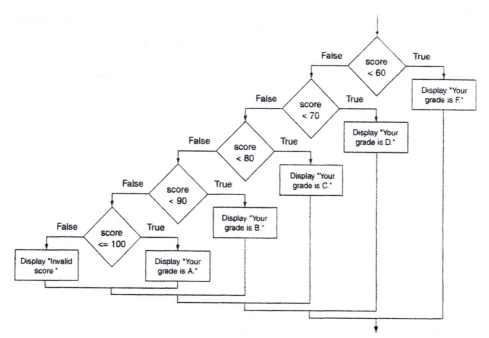

Figure 5-13 Logic of the if-else-if statement

However, because the next if statement is not connected to the first through an else, it executes as well. Because testScore is less than 70, this if statement displays the message "Your grade is D." Likewise the next if statement executes and displays the message "Your grade is C." This will continue until all of the if statements have executed.

 ## CHECKPOINT

5.12 What will the following program display?

```
using System;
public class CheckPoint
{
    public static void Main()
    {
        int funny = 7, serious = 15;

        funny = serious % 2;
        if (funny != 1)
        {
            funny = 0;
            serious = 0;
        }
```

```
        else if (funny == 2)
        {
            funny = 10;
            serious = 10;
        }
        else
        {
            funny = 1;
            serious = 1;
        }
        Console.WriteLine("{0} {1} ", funny, serious);
    }
}
```

5.13 The following program is used in a bookstore to determine how many discount coupons a customer gets. Complete the table that appears after the program.

```
using System;
public class CheckPoint
{
    public static void Main()
    {
        int books, coupons;

        Console.WriteLine("How many books are being purchased? ");
        books = Convert.ToInt32(Console.ReadLine());
        if (books < 1)
            coupons = 0;
        else if (books < 3)
            coupons = 1;
        else if (books < 5)
            coupons = 2;
        else
            coupons = 3;
        Console.WriteLine("The number of coupons to give is {0}",
                        coupons);
    }
}
```

If the customer purchases this many books...	this many coupons are given.
	1
	2
	3
	4
	5
	10

5.4 Nested `if` Statements

> **CONCEPT** A nested `if` statement is an `if` statement in the conditionally executed code of another `if` statement.

Anytime an `if` statement appears inside another `if` statement, it is considered *nested*. In actuality, the `if-else-if` structure is a nested `if` statement. Each `if` (after the first one) is nested in the `else` part of the previous `if`.

Code Listing 5-4 shows a program with a nested `if` statement. Suppose the program is used to determine whether a bank customer qualifies a loan. To qualify, a customer must earn at least $30,000 per year and must have been on his or her current job for at least two years. Figures 5-14, 5-15, and 5-16 show what happens during three sessions with the program.

Code Listing 5-4   LoanQualifier.cs

```
 1 /*
 2     This program demonstrates a nested if statement.
 3 */
 4
 5 using System;
 6
 7 public class LoanQualifier
 8 {
 9     public static void Main()
10     {
11         double salary,        // Annual salary
12                 yearsOnJob;   // Years at current job
13
14         // Get the user's annual salary.
15         Console.WriteLine("Enter your annual salary.");
16         salary = Convert.ToDouble(Console.ReadLine());
17
18         // Get the number of years at the current job.
19         Console.WriteLine("Enter the number of " +
20                         "years at your current
21         yearsOnJob = Convert.ToDouble(Console.ReadLine());
22
23         // Determine whether the user qualifies for the loan.
24         if (salary >= 30000)
25         {
26             if (yearsOnJob >= 2)
27             {
28                 Console.WriteLine("You qualify for the loan.");
29             }
```

(code listing continues)

Code Listing 5-4   LoanQualifier.cs *(continued)*

```
30          else
31          {
32              Console.WriteLine("You must have been on your
                    current job for at least two years to
                    qualify.");
33
34          }
35      }
36      else
37      {
38          Console.WriteLine("You must earn at least $30,000
                per year to qualify.");
39      }
40
41  }
42 }
```

Figure 5-14   Interaction with the LoanQualifier **program**

Figure 5-15   Interaction with the LoanQualifier **program**

Figure 5-16   Interaction with the LoanQualifier **program**

The first `if` statement conditionally executes the second one. The only way the program will execute the second `if` statement is for the `salary` variable to contain a value that is greater than or equal to 30,000. When this is the case, the second `if` statement will test the `yearsOnJob` variable. If it contains a value that is greater than or equal to 2, a dialog box will be displayed informing the user that he or she qualifies for the loan. Figure 5-17 shows the logic of the `if` statements.

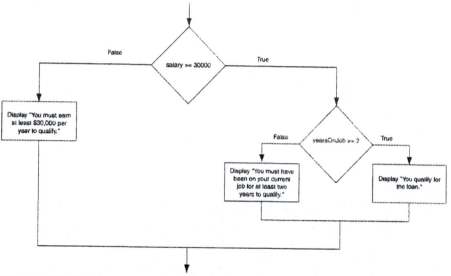

Figure 5-17 Logic of the nested `if` statements

We should note that the braces used in the `if` statements in this program are not required. They could have been written this way:

```
if (salary >= 30000)
    if (yearsOnJob >= 2)
        Console.WriteLine("You qualify for the loan.");
    else
        Console.WriteLine("You must have been on your current
            job for at least two years to qualify.");
else
Console.WriteLine("You must earn at least $30,000 per
            year to qualify.");
```

Not only do the braces make the statements easier to read, but they also help when it comes time to debug code. When debugging a program with nested `if-else` statements, it's important to know which `if` clause each `else` clause belongs to. The rule for matching `else` clauses with `if` clauses is this: An `else` clause goes with the closest previous `if` clause that doesn't already have its own `else` clause. This is easy to see when the conditionally executed statements are enclosed in braces and are properly indented, as illustrated in Figure 5-18. Each else clause lines up with the if clause it belongs to. These visual cues are important because nested if statements can be very long and complex.

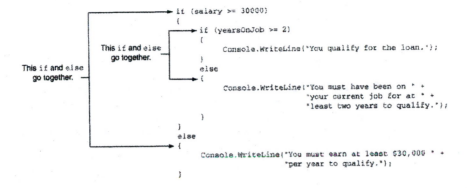

```
                                    if (salary >= 30000)
                                    {
                                        if (yearsOnJob >= 2)
                                        {
        This if and else                   Console.WriteLine("You qualify for the loan.");
        go together.                    }
                                        else
This if and else                        {
go together.
                                            Console.WriteLine("You must have been on " +
                                                             "your current job for at " +
                                                             "least two years to qualify.");

                                        }
                                    }
                                    else
                                    {
                                        Console.WriteLine("You must earn at least $30,000 " +
                                                         "per year to qualify.");

                                    }
```

Figure 5-18 Alignment of if and else clauses

CHECKPOINT

5.14 Write nested if statements that perform the following test: If amount1 is greater than 10 and amount2 is less than 100, display the greater of the two.

5.15 Write code that tests the variable x to determine whether it is greater than 0. If x is greater than 0, the code should test the variable y to determine whether it is less than 20. If y is less than 20, the code should assign 1 to the variable z. If y is not less than 20, the code should assign 0 to the variable z.

5.5   Logical Operators

> **CONCEPT** Logical operators connect two or more relational expressions into one or reverse the logic of an expression.

C# provides two binary logical operators, && and ||, which are used to combine two boolean expressions into a single expression. It also provides the unary ! operator, which reverses the truth of a boolean expression. Table 5-4 describes these logical operators.

Table 5-4

Operator	Meaning	Effect
&&	AND	Connects two Boolean expressions into one. Both expressions must be true for the overall expression to be true.
||	OR	Connects two Boolean expressions into one. One or both expressions must be true for the overall expression to be true. It is only necessary for one to be true, and it does not matter which one.
!	NOT	Reverses the truth of a Boolean expression. If it is applied to an expression that is true, the operator returns false. If it is applied to an expression that is false, the operator returns true.

Table 5-5 shows examples of several Boolean expressions that use logical operators.

Table 5-5

Expression	Meaning
x > y && a < b	Is x greater than y AND is a less than b?
x == y || x == z	Is x equal to y OR is x equal to z?
!(x > y)	Is the expression x > y NOT true?

Let's take a close look at each of these operators.

The && Operator

The && operator is known as the logical AND operator. It takes two Boolean expressions as operands and creates a Boolean expression that is true only when both sub expressions are true. Here
is an example of an if statement that uses the && operator:

```
if (temperature < 20 && minutes > 12)
{
    Console.WriteLine("The temperature is in the danger zone.");
}
```

In this statement the two Boolean expressions temperature < 20 and minutes > 12 are
combined into single expression. The message will only be displayed if temperature is less than
20 AND minutes is greater than 12. If either Boolean expression is false, the entire expression is
false and the message is not displayed.

Table 5-6 is a truth table for the && operator. The truth table lists expressions showing all the
possible combinations of true and false connected with the && operator. The resulting values of
the expressions are also shown.

Table 5-6

Expression	Value of the Expression
false && false	false
false && true	false
true && false	false
true && true	true

As the table shows, both sides of the && operator must be true for the operator to return a true value.

The && operator performs *short-circuit evaluation*. Here's how it works: If the expression on the left side of the && operator is false, the expression on the right side will not be checked. Because the entire expression is false if only one of the subexpressions is false, it would waste CPU time to check the remaining expression. So, when the && operator finds that the expression on its left is false, it short-circuits and does not evaluate the expression on its right.

The && operator can be used to simplify programs that otherwise would use nested if statements. The program in Code Listing 5-5 is a different version of the LoanQualifier program in Code Listing 5-4, written to use the && operator. Figures 5-19 and 5-20 show the interaction during two different sessions with the program.

Code Listing 5-5 LogicalAnd.cs

```
 1 /*
 2    This program demonstrates the logical && operator.
 3 */
 4
 5 using System;
 6
 7 public class LogicalAnd
 8 {
 9    public static void Main()
10    {
11       double salary,      // Annual salary
12              yearsOnJob;   // Years at current job
13
14       // Get the user's annual salary.
15       Console.WriteLine("Enter your annual salary.");
16       salary = Convert.ToDouble(Console.ReadLine());
17
```

(code listing continues)

Code Listing 5-5 LogicalAnd.cs *(continued)*

```
18          // Get the number of years at the current job.
19          Console.WriteLine("Enter the number of years at your current job.");
20          yearsOnJob = Convert.ToDouble(Console.ReadLine());
21
22          // Determine whether the user qualifies for the loan.
23          if (salary >= 30000 && yearsOnJob >= 2)
24          {
25                  Console.WriteLine("You qualify for the loan.");
26          }
27          else
28          {
29                  Console.WriteLine("You do not qualify for the loan.");
30          }
31
32      }
33  }
```

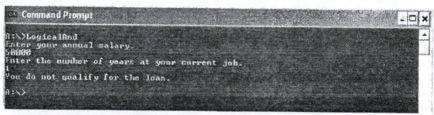

Figure 5-19   Interaction with the LogicalAnd **program**

Figure 5-20   Interaction with the LogicalAnd **program**

The message "You qualify for loan." is displayed only when both the expressions salary >= 30000 and yearsOnJob >= 2 are true. If either of these expressions is false, the message "You do not qualify for the loan." is displayed.

You can also use logical operators with boolean variables. For example, assuming that isValid is a boolean variable, the following if statement determines whether isValid is true and x is greater than 90.

```
if (isValid && x > 90)
```

The || Operator

The || operator is known as the logical OR operator. It takes two boolean expressions as operands and creates a boolean expression that is true when either of the subexpressions are true. Here is an example of an if statement that uses the || operator:

```
if (temperature < 20 || temperature > 100)
{
        Console.WriteLine("The temperature is in the danger zone.");
}
```

The message will be displayed if temperature is less than 20 OR temperature is greater than 100. If either relational test is true, the entire expression is true.

Table 5-7 is a truth table for the || operator.

Table 5-7

Expression	Value
false || false	false
false || true	true
true || false	true
true || true	true

All it takes for an OR expression to be true is for one side of the || operator to be true. It doesn't matter if the other side is false or true. Like the && operator, the || operator performs short-circuit evaluation. If the expression on the left side of the || operator is true, the expression on the right side will not be checked. Because it is only necessary for one of the expressions to be true, it would waste CPU time to check the remaining expression.

The program in Code Listing 5-6 is a version of the program shown in Code Listing 5-5. This version uses the || operator to determine whether salary >= 30000 is true OR yearsOnJob >= 2 is true. If either expression is true, then the person qualifies for the loan. Figure 5-21 shows example interaction with the program.

Code Listing 5-6   LogicalOr.cs

```
1 /*
2    This program demonstrates the logical || operator.
3 */
4
5 using System;
6
```

(code listing continues)

Code Listing 5-6   LogicalOr.cs *(continued)*

```
7 public class LogicalOr
8 {
9    public static void Main()
10   {
11      double salary,        // Annual salary
12             yearsOnJob;    // Years at current job
13
14      // Get the user's annual salary.
15      Console.WriteLine("Enter your annual salary.");
16      salary = Convert.ToDouble(Console.ReadLine());
17
18      // Get the number of years at the current job.
19      Console.WriteLine("Enter the number of " +
                    "years at your current job.");
20
21      yearsOnJob = Convert.ToDouble(Console.ReadLine());
22
23      // Determine whether the user qualifies for the
        loan.
24      if (salary >= 30000 || yearsOnJob >= 2)
25      {
26              Console.WriteLine("You qualify for the
                loan.");
27      }
28      else
29      {
30              Console.WriteLine("You do not qualify for
                the loan.");
31      }
32
33   }
34 }
```

Figure 5-21   Interaction with the LogicalOr program

The ! Operator

The ! operator performs a logical NOT operation. It is a unary operator that takes a boolean expression as its operand and reverses its logical value. In other words, if the expression is true, the ! operator returns false, and if the expression is false, it returns true. Here is an if statement using the ! operator:

```
if (!(temperature > 100))
    Console.WriteLine("This is below the maximum temperature.");
```

First, the expression (temperature > 100) is tested and a value of either true or false is the result. Then the ! operator is applied to that value. If the expression (temperature > 100) is true, the ! operator returns false. If the expression (temperature > 100) is false, the ! operator returns true. So this code is equivalent to asking "Is the temperature not greater than 100?"

Table 5-8 is a truth table for the ! operator.

Table 5-8

Expression	Value
!true	false
!false	true

The Precedence and Associativity of Logical Operators

Like other operators, the logical operators have orders of precedence and associativity. Table 5-9 shows the precedence of the logical operators, from highest to lowest.

Table 5-9

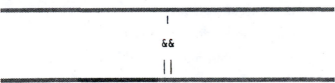

!
&&
||

The ! operator has a higher precedence than many of the other C# operators. You should enclose its operand in parentheses unless you intend to apply it to a variable or a simple expression with no other operators. For example, consider the following expressions (assume x is an int variable with a value stored in it):

```
!(x > 2)
!x > 2
```

The first expression applies the ! operator to the expression x > 2. It is asking "Is x not greater than 2?" The second expression, however, attempts to apply the ! operator to x only. It is asking "Is the logical compliment of x greater than 2?" Because the ! operator can only be applied to Boolean expressions, this statement would cause a compiler error.

The && and || operators rank lower in precedence than the relational operators, so precedence problems are less likely to occur. If you are unsure, however, it doesn't hurt to use parentheses anyway.

```
(a > b) && (x < y)   is the same as   a > b && x < y
(x == y) || (b > a)   is the same as   x == y || b > a
```

The logical operators have left-to-right associativity. In the following expression, a < b is evaluated before y == z.

```
a < b || y == z
```

In the following expression, y == z is evaluated first, however, because the && operator has higher precedence than ||.

```
a < b || y == z && m > j
```

This expression is equivalent to

```
(a < b) || ((y == z) && (m > j))
```

Table 5-10 shows the precedence of all the operators we have discussed so far. This table includes the assignment, arithmetic, relational, and logical operators.

Table 5-10

Order of Precedence	Operators	Description
1	- (unary negation) !	Unary negation, logical not
2	* / %	Multiplication, division, modulus
3	+ -	Addition, subtraction
4	< > <= >=	Less than, greater than, less than or equal to, greater than or equal to
5	== !=	Equal to, not equal to
6	&&	Logical AND
7	||	Logical OR
8	= += -= *= /= %=	Assignment and combined assignment

Checking Numeric Ranges with Logical Operators

Sometimes you will need to write code that determines whether a numeric value is within a specific range of values or outside a specific range of values. When determining whether a number is inside a range, it's best to use the && operator. For example, the following if statement checks the value in x to determine whether it is in the range of 20 through 40:

```
if (x >= 20 && x <= 40)
    Console.WriteLine("{0} is in the acceptable range.", x);
```

The boolean expression in the if statement will be true only when x is greater than or equal to 20 and less than or equal to 40. The value in x must be within the range of 20 through 40 for this expression to be true.

When determining whether a number is outside a range, it is best to use the || operator. The following statement determines whether x is outside the range of 20 through 40:

```
if (x < 20 || x > 40)
    Console.WriteLine("{0} is outside the acceptable range.",x);
```

It's important not to get the logic of these logical operators confused. For example, the Boolean expression in the following if statement would never test true:

```
if (x < 20 && x > 40)
    Console.WriteLine("{0} is outside the acceptable range.",x);
```

Obviously, x cannot be less than 20 and at the same time be greater than 40.

 NOTES: C# also provides us the unconditional & and | operators to evaluate Boolean expressions. The unconditional operators force both operands in a Boolean expression to be evaluated. Thus the expression

```
if (x >= 20 | x <= 40)
```

would force the evaluation of both operands regardless of the result of the result of the first operand. For example, you wish to modify a variable's value using side effects regardless of the value of the overall expression.

The & and I operators can also be used with bitwise operation. We will not discuss this topic in the text.

CHECKPOINT

5.16 The following truth table shows various combinations of the values true and false connected by a logical operator. Complete the table by indicating if the result of such a combination is true or false.

Logical Expression	Result (true or false)
true && false	
true && true	
false && true	
false && false	
true || false	
true || true	
false || true	
false || false	
!true	
!false	

5.17 Assume the variables a = 2, b = 4, and c = 6. Indicate by circling the T or F whether each of the following conditions is true or false.

a == 4 || b > 2	T	F
6 <= c && a > 3	T	F
1 != b && c != 3	T	F
a >= -1 || a <= b	T	F
!(a > 2)	T	F

5.18 Write an if statement that displays the message "The number is valid" if the variable speed is within the range 0 through 200.

5.19 Write an if statement that displays the message "The number is not valid" if the variable speed is outside the range 0 through 200.

5.6   Comparing string Objects

> **CONCEPT** You can compare strings using the equality (==) operator and using the Equals and CompareTo methods.

You saw in the preceding sections how numeric values can be compared using the relational operators. You can compare strings in C# three ways by overloading the == operator or by using the built-in string class methods Equals and CompareTo.

Using == to Compare strings

Remember that an object is referenced by a variable that contains the object's memory address. When you use the equality operator with the reference variable, the operator compares the contents of the references, not the contents of the object. In C#, to see if two string objects contents are identical using ==, we must overload the equality operator. The overloaded operator then behaves just like the Equals method found in the string class. Let us look at an example:

```
if (name1 == name2)
```

Assuming that name1 and name2 reference string objects, the expression in the if statement will return true if they are the same, or false if they are not the same.

 NOTE: The concept of operator overloading will not be covered in this book.

Using the Equals Method

To see if two string objects contents are identical, you should use the string class's Equals method. The general form of the method is

```
StringReference1.Equals(StringReference2)
```

StringReference1 is a variable that references a string object, and *StringReference2* is another variable that references a string object. The method returns true if the two strings are equal, or false if they are not equal. Here is an example:

```
if (name1.Equals(name2))
```

Assuming that name1 and name2 reference string objects, the expression in the if statement will return true if they are the same, or false if they are not the same. The program in Code Listing 5-7 demonstrates the uses of the == and the Equals method to compare strings.

Code Listing 5-7   StringCompare.cs

```
1  /*
2     This program compares two string objects using == and
3     Equals.
4  */
5
6  using System;
7
8  public class StringCompare
9  {
10    public static void Main()
11    {
12      string name1 = "Mark",
13             name2 = "Mark",
14             name3 = "Mary";
15
16      // Compare "Mark" and "Mark" using ==
17
18      if (name1 == name2)
19      {
20        Console.WriteLine("{0} and {1} are the same using
             ==.",name1, name2);
21      }
22      else
23      {
24        Console.WriteLine("{0} and {1} are NOT the same using
             ==.",name1, name2);
25      }
26
27      // Compare "Mark" and "Mark" using Equals
28
29      if (name1.Equals(name2))
30      {
31        Console.WriteLine("{0} and {1} are the same using
             Equals.",name1, name2);
32      }
33      else
34      {
35        Console.WriteLine("{0} and {1} are NOT the same
             Equals.",name1, name2);
36      }
37
38      // Compare "Mark" and "Mary" using ==
39
40      if (name1 == name3)
41      {
42        Console.WriteLine("{0} and {1} are the same using
             ==.",name1, name3);
43      }
```

(code listing continues)

Code Listing 5-7 StringCompare.cs *(continued)*

```
44        else
45        {
46            Console.WriteLine("{0} and {1} are NOT the same using
                   ==.",name1, name3);
47        }
48
49        // Compare "Mark" and "Mary" using Equals
50
51        if (name1.Equals(name3))
52        {
53            Console.WriteLine("{0} and {1} are the same, using
                   Equals.",name1, name3);
54        }
55        else
56        {
57            Console.WriteLine("{0} and {1} are NOT the
                   same, using Equals.",name1, name3);
58        }
59     }
60 }
```

Program Output

```
Mark and Mark are the same using ==.
Mark and Mark are the same using Equals.
Mark and Mary are NOT the same using ==.
Mark and Mary are NOT the same, using Equals.
```

Notice in Code Listing 5-7 we declare two strings (lines 12 and 13)

```
string name1 = "Mark",
       name2 = "Mark"
```

We then compare to see whether the contents of name1 and name2 are equal using == and the Equals method. Lines 18–21 use the equality operator:

```
if (name1 == name2)
{
    Console.WriteLine("{0} and {1} are the same using
               ==.",name1, name2);
}
```

Lines 29–32 use the Equals method:

```
if (name1.Equals(name2))
{
    Console.WriteLine("{0} and {1} are the same using
```

```
        Equals.",name1, name2);
   }
```

You can also compare `string` objects to string literals. Simply pass the string literal as the argument to the `Equals` method, as shown here:

```
if (name1.Equals("Mark"))
```

To determine whether two strings are not equal, simply apply the ! operator to the `Equals` method's return value. Here is an example:

```
if (!name1.Equals("Mark"))
```

The `boolean` expression in this `if` statement performs a not-equal-to operation. It determines whether the object referenced by `name1` is not equal to "Mark."

Using the `CompareTo` Method

The `string` class also provides the `CompareTo` method, which can be used to determine whether one string is greater than, equal to, or less than another string. The general form of the method is

> *StringReference*.`CompareTo`(*OtherString*)

StringReference is a variable that references a `string` object, and *OtherString* is another variable that references a `string` object or a string literal. The method returns an integer value that can be used in the following manner:

- If the method's return value is −1, the string referenced by *StringReference* (the calling object) is less than the *OtherString* argument.

- If the method's return value is 0, the two strings are equal.

- If the method's return value is 1, the string referenced by *StringReference* (the calling object) is greater than the *OtherString* argument.

For example, assume that `name1` and `name2` are variables that reference `string` objects. The following `if` statement uses the `CompareTo` method to compare the strings.

```
if (name1.CompareTo(name2) == 0)
    Console.WriteLine("The names are the same.");
```

Also, the following expression compares the string referenced by `name1` to the string literal "Joe."

```
if (name1.CompareTo("Joe") == 0)
    Console.WriteLine("The names are the same.");
```

The program in Code Listing 5-8 more fully demonstrates the `CompareTo` method.

Code Listing 5-8 StringCompareTo.cs

```
1 /*
2     This program compares two String objects using
3     the CompareTo method.
4 */
5
6 using System;
7
8 public class StringCompareTo
9 {
10    public static void Main()
11    {
12        string name1 = "Mary",
13               name2 = "Mark";
14
15        // Compare "Mary" and "Mark"
16
17        if (name1.CompareTo(name2) == -1)
18        {
19            Console.WriteLine("{0} is less than {1}",
20            name1, name2);
        }
21        else if (name1.CompareTo(name2) == 0)
22        {
23            Console.WriteLine("{0} is equal to {1}",
            name1, name2);
24        }
25        else if (name1.CompareTo(name2) == 1)
26        {
27            Console.WriteLine("{0} is greater than{1}",
            name1, name2);
28        }
29    }
30 }
```

Program Output
Mary is greater than Mark

Let's take a closer look at this program. When you use the CompareTo method to compare two strings, the strings are compared character by character. This is often called a *lexicographical comparison*. The program uses the CompareTo method to compare the strings "Mary" and "Mark," beginning with the first, or leftmost, characters. This is illustrated in Figure 5-23.

Here is how the comparison takes place:

1. The "M" in "Mary" is compared with the "M" in "Mark." Because these are the same, the next characters are compared.

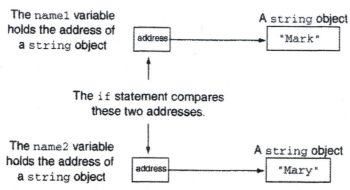

The name1 variable holds the address of a string object

A string object "Mark"

The if statement compares these two addresses.

The name2 variable holds the address of a string object

A string object "Mary"

Figure 5-22   string comparison of "Mary" and "Mark"

2. The "a" in "Mary" is compared with the "a" in "Mark." Because these are the same, the next characters are compared.

3. The "r" in "Mary" is compared with the "r" in "Mark." Because these are the same, the next characters are compared.

4. The "y" in "Mary" is compared with the "k" in "Mark." Because these are not the same, the two strings are not equal. The character "y" is greater than "k," so it is determined that "Mary" is greater than "Mark."

If one of the strings in a comparison is shorter than the other, C# can only compare the corresponding characters. If the corresponding characters are identical, then the shorter string is considered less than the longer string. For example, suppose the strings "High" and "Hi" were being compared. The string "Hi" would be considered less than "High" because it is shorter.

Ignoring Case in string Comparisons

The CompareTo method performs a case-sensitive comparison. In order to perform non-case-sensitive operations, you must use the overloaded Compare method found in the **string** class. The form of the overloaded method is as follows:

```
Compare(str1, str2, ignoreCase)
```

Where str1 and str2 are the two strings to compare. ignoreCase is a boolean parameter indicating case-sensitivity. False would indicate a case-insensitive operation.

 CHECKPOINT

5.20 Assume the variable name references a string object. Write an if statement that displays "Do I know you?" if the string object contains "Timothy".

5.21 Assume the variables name1 and name2 reference two string objects containing different strings. Write code that displays the strings referenced by these variables in alphabetical order.

5.7 More About Variable Declaration and Scope

The scope of a variable is limited to the block in which it is declared.

Recall from Chapter 2 that a local variable is a variable that is declared inside of a method. C# allows you to create local variables just about anywhere in a method. For example, look at the program in Code Listing 5-9. The Main method declares two string reference variables: firstName and lastName. Notice that the declarations of these variables appear near the code that first uses the variables.

Code Listing 5-9 VariableScope.cs

```
 1 /*
 2    This program demonstrates how variables may be
 3    declared in various locations throughout a program.
 4 */
 5
 6 using System;
 7
 8 public class VariableScope
 9 {
10    public static void Main()
11    {
12       // Get the user's first name.
13       string firstName;
14       Console.WriteLine("Enter your first name.");
15       firstName = Console.ReadLine();
16
17       // Get the user's last name.
18       string lastName;
19       Console.WriteLine("Enter your last name.");
20       lastName = Console.ReadLine();
21
22       Console.WriteLine("Hello {0}
          {1}",firstName,lastName);
23    }
24 }
```

Although it is a common practice to declare all of a method's local variables at the beginning of the method, it is possible to declare them at later points. Sometimes programmers declare certain variables near the part of the program where they are used in order to make their purpose more evident.

Recall from Chapter 2 that a variable's scope is the part of the program where the variable's name may be used. A local variable's scope always starts at the variable's declaration and ends at the closing brace of the block of code in which it is declared. In Code Listing 5-9, the firstName variable is visible only to the code in lines 13 through 15. The `lastName` variable is visible only to the code in lines 18 through 20.

 NOTE: When a program is running and it enters the section of code that constitutes a variable's scope, it is said that the variable "comes into scope." This simply means the variable is now visible and the program may reference it. Likewise, when a variable "leaves scope" it may not be used.

5.8 The Conditional Operator

 You can use the conditional operator to create short expressions that work like `if-else` statements.

The *conditional operator* is powerful and unique. Because it takes three operands, it is considered a ternary operator. The conditional operator provides a shorthand method of expressing a simple `if-else` statement. The operator consists of the question mark (?) and the colon (:). Its format is

Expression1 ? *Expression2* : *Expression3*;

Expression1, *Expression2*, and *Expression3* are the three operands. *Expression1* is a Boolean expression, which is tested. It's like the Boolean expression in the parentheses of an `if` statement. If *Expression1* is `true`, then *Expression2* is executed. Otherwise, *Expression3* is executed. Here is an example of a statement using the conditional operator:

```
number = x < 0 ? 20 : 50;
```

This statement is called a *conditional expression* and consists of three subexpressions separated by the ? and : symbols. The expressions are `x < 0`, `20`, and `50`, as illustrated here:

This preceding conditional expression performs the same operation as the following `if-else` statement:

```
if (x < 0)
    number = 20;
else
    number = 50;
```

If it helps, you can put parentheses around the subexpressions in a conditional expression, as in the following:

```
number = (x < 0) ? (20) : (50);
```

Using the Value of a Conditional Expression

The conditional expression also returns a value. If *Expression1* is true, the value of the conditional expression is the value of *Expression2*. Otherwise it is the value of *Expression5*. Here is an example of an assignment statement using the value of a conditional expression:

```
number = x > 100 ? 20 : 50;
```

The value assigned to number will be either 20 or 50, depending on whether x is greater than 100. This statement could be expressed as the following if-else statement:

```
if (x > 100)
    number = 20;
else
    number = 50;
```

The conditional operator gives you the ability to pack decision-making power into a concise line of code. With a little imagination it can be applied to many other programming problems. For instance, consider the following statement:

```
Console.WriteLine("Your grade is: {0}",(score < 60 ? "Fail." :
"Pass."));
```

Converted to an if-else statement, it would be written as follows:

```
if (score < 60)
    Console.WriteLine("Your grade is: Fail.");
else
    Console.WriteLine("Your grade is: Pass.");
```

 NOTE: The parentheses are placed around the conditional expression because the + operator has higher precedence than the ?: operator. Without the parentheses, the + operator would concatenate the value in score with the string "Your grade is: ".

 To see an example program that uses the conditional operator, see the file ConsultantCharges.cs, which is stored in the Chapter 5\Source Code\ folder on the Student CD.

? CHECKPOINT

5.22 Rewrite the following if-else statements as conditional expressions.

```
a)  if (x > y)
        z = 1;
    else
        z = 20;
```

b) ```
    if (temp > 45)
        population = base * 10;
    else
        population = base * 2;
    ```

c)  ```
    if (hours > 40)
        wages *= 1.5;
    else
        wages *= 1;
    ```

d) ```
    if (result >= 0)
        Console.WriteLine("The result is positive.)";
    else
        Console.WriteLine("The result is negative.");
    ```

## 5.9  The switch Statement

> **CONCEPT** The switch statement lets the value of a variable or expression determine where the program will branch to.

A branch occurs when one part of a program causes another part to execute. The if-else-if statement allows your program to branch into one of several possible paths. It tests a series of boolean expressions, and branches if one of those expressions is true. The switch statement is a similar mechanism. It, however, tests the value of an integer expression and then uses that value to determine which set of statements to branch to. Here is the format of the switch statement:

```
switch (SwitchExpression)
{
    case CaseExpression:
        // place one or more
        // statements here
        break;
    case CaseExpression:
        // place one or more
        // statements here
        break;

        // case statements may be repeated as many
        // times as necessary
```
```

```
    default:
    // place one or more
    // statements here
    break;
}
```

The first line of the statement starts with the word switch, followed by a *SwitchExpression* inside parentheses. The *SwitchExpression* is an expression that must result in a value of one of the integer data types (includes char).

On the next line is the beginning of a block containing several case statements. Each case statement is formatted in the following manner:

```
case CaseExpression:
    // place one or more
    // statements here
    break;
```

The case statement starts with the keyword case, followed by a *CaseExpression*. The *CaseExpression* is a literal or a const variable which must be of the char, byte, short, or int types. The *CaseExpression* is followed by a colon.

After the case statement, one or more valid programming statements may appear. These statements are branched to if the value of the *SwitchExpression* matches the case statement's *CaseExpression*. The last statement in the group of statements should be the key word break. The break statement causes the program to jump out of the switch statement and resume processing at the statement following it.

NOTE: The CaseExpressions of each case statement must be unique.

A default section comes after all the case statements. This section is branched to if none of the case expressions match the switch expression.

NOTE: The default section is optional. If you leave it out, however, your program will have nowhere to branch to if the SwitchExpression doesn't match any of the CaseExpressions.

The program in Code Listing 5-10 shows how a simple switch statement works.

The first case statement is case 1, the second is case 2, and the third is case 5. These statements mark where the program is to branch to if the variable number contains the values 1, 2, or 5. The default section is branched to if the user enters anything other than 1, 2, or 5.

Code Listing 5-10 SwitchDemo.cs

```
 1 /*
 2     This program demonstrates the switch statement.
 3 */
 4
 5 using System;
 6
 7 public class SwitchDemo
 8 {
 9    public static void Main()
10    {
11
12       int number;        // A number entered by the user
13
14
15       // Get one of the numbers 1, 2, or 3 from the user.
16       Console.Write("Enter 1, 2, or 3: ");
17       number = Convert.ToInt32(Console.ReadLine());
18
19       // Determine the number entered.
20       switch (number)
21       {
22          case 1:
23             Console.WriteLine("You entered 1.");
24             break;
25          case 2:
26             Console.WriteLine("You entered 2.");
27             break;
28          case 3:
29             Console.WriteLine("You entered 5.");
30             break;
31          default:
32             Console.WriteLine("That's not 1, 2, or 3!");
33             break;
34       }
35    }
36 }
```

Program Output with Example Input Shown in Bold
Enter 1, 2, or 3: **2 [Enter]**
You entered 2.

(code listing continues)

Code Listing 5-10 SwitchDemo.cs *(continued)*

Program Output with Example Input Shown in Bold
```
Enter 1, 2, or 3: 5 [Enter]
That's not 1, 2, or 3!
```

Notice the break statements that are in the case 1, case 2, case 3, and default sections.

```
switch (number)
{
    case 1:
        Console.WriteLine("You entered 1.");
        break;
    case 2:
        Console.WriteLine("You entered 2.");
        break;
    case 3:
        Console.WriteLine("You entered 5.");
        break;
    default:
        Console.WriteLine("That's not 1, 2, or 3!");
        break;
}
```

The case statements show the program where to start executing in the block and the break statements show the program where to stop. Without the break statements, the program would not compile.

 NOTE: The default section (or the last case section if there is no default) does need a break statement. Otherwise an error would occur.

The program in Code Listing 5-11 is a modification of Code Listing 5-10, without the break statements.

Code Listing 5-11 NoBreaks.cs

```
1 /*
2    This program demonstrates a switch statement
3    without any break statements. This program does not compile!!
4 */
5
```

(code listing continues)

Code Listing 5-11 NoBreaks.cs *(continued)*

```
 6 using System;
 7
 8 public class NoBreaks
 9 {
10    public static void Main()
11    {
12
13       int number;        // A number entered by the user
14
15
16       // Get one of the numbers 1, 2, or 3 from the user.
17       Console.Write("Enter 1, 2, or 3: ");
18
19       number = Convert.ToInt32(Console.ReadLine());
20
21       // Determine the number entered.
22       switch (number)
23       {
24          case 1:
25             Console.WriteLine("You entered 1.");
26          case 2:
27             Console.WriteLine("You entered 2.");
28          case 3:
29             Console.WriteLine("You entered 5.");
30          default:
31             Console.WriteLine("That's not 1, 2, or 3!");
32
33       }
34    }
35 }
```

Without the break statements, the program does not compile. C# does not allow the fall through of case statements. However, sometimes this is what you want. For instance, the program in Code Listing 5-12 asks the user to select a grade of pet food. The available choices are A, B, and C. The switch statement will recognize either upper or lowercase letters.

Code Listing 5-12 PetFood.cs

```
1 /*
2    This program demonstrates a switch statement.
3 */
4
```

(code listing continues)

Code Listing 5-12 PetFood.cs *(continued)*

```
 5 using System; // Needed for keyboard input
 6
 7 public class PetFood
 8 {
 9    public static void Main()
10    {
11
12       char foodGrade;   // Grade of pet food
13
14
15       // Prompt the user for a grade of pet food.
16       Console.WriteLine("Our pet food is available in " +
17                         "three grades:");
18       Console.Write("A, B, and C. Which do you want " +
19                     "pricing for? ");
20       foodGrade = Convert.ToChar(Console.ReadLine());
21
22       // Display pricing for the selected grade.
23       switch(foodGrade)
24       {
25          case 'a':
26          case 'A':
27             Console.WriteLine("30 cents per lb.");
28             break;
29          case 'b':
30          case 'B':
31             Console.WriteLine("20 cents per lb.");
32             break;
33          case 'c':
34          case 'C':
35             Console.WriteLine("15 cents per lb.");
36             break;
37          default:
38             Console.WriteLine("Invalid choice.");
39             break;
40       }
41    }
42 }
```

Program Output with Example Input Shown in Bold
```
Our pet food is available in three grades:
A, B, and C. Which do you want pricing for? B [Enter]
20 cents per lb.
```

(code listing continues)

Code Listing 5-12 **PetFood.cs** *(continued)*

Program Output with Example Input
```
Our pet food is available in three grades:
A, B, and C. Which do you want pricing for? B [Enter]
20 cents per lb.
```

When the user enters 'a' the corresponding `case` has no statements associated with it, so the program falls through to the next `case`, which corresponds with 'A'.

```
case 'a':
case 'A':
    Console.WriteLine("30 cents per lb.");
    break;
```

The same technique is used for 'b' and 'c'. Notice how this differs from Code Listing 5-11.

 CHECKPOINT

5.23 Complete the following program skeleton by writing a `switch` statement that displays "one" if the user has entered 1, "two" if the user has entered 2, and "three" if the user has entered 3. If a number other than 1, 2, or 3 is entered, the program should display an error message.

```
using System;
public class CheckPoint
{
    public static void Main()
    {
        int userNum;
        Console.Write("Enter one of the numbers 1, 2, or 3: ");
        userNum = Convert.ToInt32(Console.ReadLine());

        //
        // Write the switch statement here.
        //
    }
}
```

5.24 Rewrite the following `if-else-if` statement as a `switch` statement.

```
if (selection == 'A')
    Console.WriteLine("You selected A.");
    break;
else if (selection == 'B')
    Console.WriteLine("You selected B.");
    break;
else if (selection == 'C')
    Console.WriteLine("You selected C.");
    break;
```

```
    else if (selection == 'D')
        Console.WriteLine("You selected D.");
        break;
    else
        Console.WriteLine("Not good with letters, eh?");
        break;
```

5.25 Explain why you cannot convert the following if-else-if statement into a switch statement.

```
if (temp == 100)
    x = 0;
else if (population > 1000)
    x = 1;
else if  (rate < .1)
    x = -1;
```

5.26 What is wrong with the following switch statement?

```
// This code has errors!!!
switch (temp)
{
    case temp < 0 :
        Console.WriteLine("Temp is negative.");
        break;
    case temp == 0:
        Console.WriteLine("Temp is zero.");
        break;
    case temp > 0 :
        Console.WriteLine("Temp is positive.");
        break;
}
```

5.27 What will the following code display?

```
int funny = 7, serious = 15;
funny = serious * 2;
switch (funny)
{   case 0 :
        Console.WriteLine("That is funny.");
        break;
    case 30:
        Console.WriteLine("That is serious.");
        break;
    case 32:
        Console.WriteLine("That is seriously funny.");
        break;
        default:
        Console.WriteLine(funny);
        break;
}
```

Case Study on CD-ROM: Calculating Sales Commission

The Student CD contains a valuable case study demonstrating how sales commissions may be calculated using various commission rates. The commission rate is determined by the amount of sales.

5.10 Common Errors

- **Using = instead of == to compare primitive values.** Remember, = is the assignment operator and == tests for equality.

- **Forgetting to enclose an if statement's boolean expression in parentheses.** C# requires that the boolean expression being tested by an if statement be enclosed in a set of parentheses. An error will result if you omit the parentheses or use any other grouping characters.

- **Writing a semicolon at the end of an if clause.** When you write a semicolon at the end of an if clause, C# assumes that the conditionally executed statement is a null or empty statement.

- **Forgetting to enclose multiple conditionally executed statements in braces.** Normally the if statement conditionally executes only one statement. To conditionally execute more than one statement, you must enclose them in braces.

- **Omitting the trailing else in an if-else-if statement.** This is not a syntax error, but can lead to logical errors. If you omit the trailing else from an if-else-if statement, no code will be executed if none of the statement's boolean expressions are true.

- **Not writing complete Boolean expressions on both sides of a logical && or || operator.** You must write a complete boolean expression on both sides of a logical && or || operator. For example, the expression x > 0 && < 10 is not valid because < 10 is not a complete expression. The expression should be written as x > 0 && x < 10.

- **Using a *SwitchExpression* that is not an integral data type.** The switch statement can only evaluate expressions that are integer-based data types.

- **Using a *CaseExpression* that is not a literal or a final variable.** Because the compiler must determine the value of a *CaseExpression* at compile-time, *CaseExpressions* must be either literal values or final variables.

- **Forgetting to write a colon at the end of a case statement.** A colon must appear after the *CaseExpression* in each case statement.

- **Failing to write a break statement in a case section(s).** The program does not branch out of a switch statement until it reaches a break statement; until it does, no "falling through" is allowed.

- **Omitting a break in the default section in a switch statement.** If you omit the break in default section and error will occur.

- **Reversing the ? and the : when using the conditional operator.** When the conditional operator is used, the ? character appears first in the conditional expression, then the : character.

Review Questions

Multiple Choice and True/False

1. The if statement is an example of a
   a) sequence structure.   b) decision structure.
   c) pathway structure.   d) class structure.

2. This type of expression has a value of either true or false.
   a) binary expression   b) decision expression
   c) unconditional expression   d) Boolean expression

3. >, <, and == are
   a) relational operators.   b) logical operators.
   c) conditional operators.   d) ternary operators.

4. &&, ||, and ! are
   a) relational operators.   b) logical operators.
   c) conditional operators.   d) ternary operators.

5. Which of the following is an empty statement that does nothing?
   a) missing statement   b) virtual statement
   c) null statement   d) conditional statement

6. To create a block of statements, you enclose the statements in
   a) parentheses ().   b) square brackets [].
   c) angled brackets <>.   d) braces {}.

7. Which of these is a boolean variable that signals when some condition exists in the program?
   a) flag   b) signal
   c) sentinel   d) siren

8. How does the character 'A' compare to the character 'B'?
   a) 'A' is greater than 'B'   b) 'A' is less than 'B'
   c) 'A' is equal to 'B'   d) You cannot compare characters.

9. Which of these is an if statement that appears inside another if statement?

   a) nested if statement   b) tiered if statement

   c) dislodged if statement   d) structured if statement

10. An else always clause goes with

   a) the closest previous if clause that doesn't already have its own else clause.

   b) the closest if clause.

   c) the if clause that is randomly selected by the compiler.

   d) None of these

11. When determining whether a number is inside a range, it's best to use which operator?

   a) &&   b) !

   c) || d) ? :

12. This determines whether two string objects contain the same string.

   a) the == operator   b) the = operator

   c) the Equals method   d) the CompareTo method

13. The conditional operator takes this many operands.

   a) one   b) two

   c) three   d) four

14. Which section of a switch statement is branched to if none of the case expressions match the switch expression?

   a) else   b) default

   c) case   d) otherwise

15. True or False: The = operator and the == operator perform the same operation.

16. True or False: A conditionally executed statement should be indented one level from the if clause.

17. True or False: All lines in a conditionally executed block should be indented one level.

18. True or False: When an if statement is nested in the if clause of another statement, the only time the inner if statement is executed is when the boolean expression of the outer if statement is true.

19. True or False: When an `if` statement is nested in the `else` clause of another statement, the only time the inner `if` statement is executed is when the `boolean` expression of the outer `if` statement is `true`.

20. True or False: The scope of a variable is limited to the block in which it is defined.

Find the Error

Find the errors in the following code.

1.
```
// Warning! This code contains ERRORS!
if (x == 1);
    y = 2;
else if (x == 2);
    y = 3;
else if (x == 3);
    y = 4;
```

2.
```
// Warning! This code contains an ERROR!
if (average = 100)
    Console.WriteLine("Perfect Average!");
```

3.
```
// Warning! This code contains ERRORS!
if (num2 == 0)
    Console.WriteLine("Division by zero is not possible.");
    Console.WriteLine("Please run the program again ");
    Console.WriteLine("and enter a number besides zero.");
else
    Quotient = num1 / num2;
    Console.Write("The quotient of {0}", Num1);
    Console.Write(" divided by {0} is ", Num2);
    Console.WriteLine(Quotient);
```

4.
```
// Warning! This code contains ERRORS!
switch (score)
{
case (score > 90):
    grade = 'A';
    break;
case(score > 80):
    grade = 'b';
    break;
case(score > 70):
    grade = 'C';
    break;
case (score > 60):
    grade = 'D';
    break;
    default:
    grade = 'F';
    break;
}
```

5. The following statement should determine whether x is not greater than 20. What is wrong with it?

```
if (!x > 20)
```

6. The following statement should determine whether count is within the range of 0 through 100. What is wrong with it?

```
if (count >= 0 || count <= 100)
```

7. The following statement should determine whether count is outside the range of 0 through 100. What is wrong with it?

```
if (count < 0 && count > 100)
```

8. The following statement should assign 0 to z if a is less than 10; otherwise it should assign 7 to z. What is wrong with it?

```
z = (a < 10) : 0 ? 7;
```

Algorithm Workbench

1. Write an if statement that assigns 100 to x when y is equal to 0.
2. Write an if-else statement that assigns 0 to x when y is equal to 10. Otherwise it should assign 1 to x.
3. Using the following chart, write an if-else-if statement that assigns 0.10, 0.15, or 0.20 to commission, depending on the value in sales.

Sales	Commission Rate
Up to $10,000	10%
$10,000 to $15,000	15%
Over $15,000	20%

4. Write an if statement that sets the variable hours to 10 when the boolean flag variable minimum is equal to true.
5. Write nested if statements that perform the following tests: If amount1 is greater than 10 and amount2 is less than 100, display the greater of the two.
6. Write an if statement that prints the message "The number is valid" if the variable grade is within the range 0 through 100.
7. Write an if statement that prints the message "The number is valid" if the variable temperature is within the range –50 through 150.

8. Write an `if` statement that prints the message "The number is not valid" if the variable `hours` is outside the range 0 through 80.

9. Write an `if-else` statement that displays the strings in the arrays `title1` and `title2` in alphabetical order.

10. Convert the following `if-else-if` statement into a `switch` statement:

```
if (choice == 1)
{
    Console.WriteLine("You selected 1.");
}
else if (choice == 2 || choice == 3)
{
    Console.WriteLine("You selected 2 or 5.");
}
else if (choice == 4)
{
    Console.WriteLine("You selected 5.");
}
else
{
    Console.WriteLine("Select again please.");
}
```

11. Match the conditional expression with the `if-else` statement that performs the same operation.

    a) `q = x < y ? a + b : x * 2;`

    b) `q = x < y ? x * 2 : a + b;`

    c) `q = x < y ? 0 : 1;`

    _____   ```
              if (x < y)
                  q = 0;
              else
                  q = 1;
              ```

    _____    ```
              if (x < y)
                  q = a + b;
              else
                  q = x * 2;
              ```

    _____   ```
              if (x < y)
                  q = x * 2;
              else
                  q = a + b;
              ```
              ```

Short Answer

1. Explain what is meant by the term *conditionally executed*.
2. Explain why a misplaced semicolon can cause an `if` statement to operate incorrectly.
3. Why is it good advice to indent all the statements inside a set of braces?
4. What happens when you compare two `string` objects with the `==` operator?
5. Explain the purpose of a flag variable. Of what data type should a flag variable be?
6. What risk does a programmer take when not placing a trailing `else` at the end of an `if-else-if` statement?
7. Briefly describe how the `&&` operator works.
8. Briefly describe how the `||` operator works.
9. Why are the relational operators called "relational"?

Programming Challenges

General Requirements: Each program or class should have a block of comments at the top. The comments should contain your name, the chapter the assignment appeared in, and the assignment number and name. Here is an example:

```
/*
    Written by Jill Johnson
Chapter 3
Assignment 1: Roman Numerals
*/
```

1. Roman Numerals

Write a program that prompts the user to enter a number within the range of 1 through 10. The program should display the Roman numeral version of that number. If the number outside the range of 1 through 10, the program should display an error message.

2. State Abbreviations

Write a program that asks the user to enter one of the following state abbreviations: NC, SC, GA, FL, or AL. The program should then display the name of the state that corresponds with the abbreviation entered (North Carolina, South Carolina, Georgia, Florida, or Alabama.) The program should accept abbreviations in uppercase, lowercase, or a mixture of upper- and lowercase. Display an error message if an abbreviation other than what is listed is entered.

3. Areas of Rectangles

The area of a rectangle is the rectangle's length times its width. Write a program that asks for the length and width of two rectangles. The program should tell the user which rectangle has the greater area, or if the areas are the same.

4. Test Scores and Grade

Write a program that has variables to hold three test scores. The program should ask the user to enter three test scores, and then assign the values entered to the variables. The program should display the average of the test scores and the letter grade that is assigned for the test score average. Use the grading scheme in the following table.

Test Score Average	Letter Grade
90–100	A
80–89	B
70–79	C
60–69	D
Below 60	F

5. Mass and Weight

Scientists measure an object's mass in kilograms and its weight in Newtons. If you know the amount of mass that an object has, you can calculate its weight, in Newtons, with the following formula:

```
Weight = mass × 9.8
```

Write a program that asks the user to enter an object's mass, and then calculates its weight. If the object weighs more than 1000 Newtons, display a message indicating that it is too heavy. If the object weighs less than 10 Newtons, display a message indicating that the object is too light.

6. Time Calculator

Write a program that asks the user to enter a number of seconds.

- There are 60 seconds in a minute. If the number of seconds entered by the user is greater than or equal to 60, the program should display the number of minutes in that many seconds.

- There are 3600 seconds in an hour. If the number of seconds entered by the user is greater than or equal to 3600, the program should display the number of hours in that many seconds.

- There are 86400 seconds in a day. If the number of seconds entered by the user is greater than or equal to 86400, the program should display the number of days in that many seconds.

7. Sorted Names

Write a program that asks the user to enter three names, and then displays the names sorted in alphabetical order. For example, if the user entered "Charlie," "Leslie," and "Andy," the program would display

```
Andy
Charlie
Leslie
```

8. Software Sales

A software company sells a package that retails for $99. Quantity discounts are given according to the following table:

Quantity	Discount
10–19	20%
20–49	30%
50–99	40%
100 or more	50%

Write a program that asks the user to enter the number of packages purchased. The program should then display the amount of the discount (if any) and the total amount of the purchase after the discount.

9. Shipping Charges

The Fast Freight Shipping Company charges the following rates:

Weight of Package	Rate Per 500 Miles Shipped
2 lb or less	$1.10
Over 2 lb but not more than 6 lb	$2.20
Over 6 lb but not more than 10 lb	$5.70
Over 10 lb	$5.80

The shipping charges per 500 miles are not prorated. For example, if a 2-pound package is shipped 550 miles, the charges would be $2.20. Write a program that asks the user to enter the weight of a package and then displays the shipping charges.

10. Fat Gram Calculator

Write a program that asks the user to enter the number of calories and fat grams in a food item. The program should display the percentage of the calories that come from fat. One gram of fat has nine calories, so

```
Calories from fat = fat grams × 9
```

The percentage of calories from fat can be calculated as:

```
Calories from fat ÷ total calories
```

If the calories from fat are less than 30 percent of the total calories of the food, it should also display a message indicating the food is low in fat.

 NOTE: The number of calories from fat cannot be greater than the total number of calories in the food item. If the program determines that the number of calories from fat is greater than the number of calories in the food item, it should display an error message indicating that the input is invalid.

11. Running the Race

Write a program that asks for the names of three runners and the time, in minutes, it took each of them to finish a race. The program should display the names of the runners in the order that they finished.

12. The Speed of Sound

The following table shows the approximate speed of sound in air, water, and steel.

Medium	Speed
Air	1100 feet per second
Water	4900 feet per second
Steel	16,400 feet per second

Write a program that asks the user to enter "air," "water," or "steel," and the distance that a sound wave will travel in that medium. The program should then display the amount of time it will take. You can calculate the amount of time it takes sound to travel in air with the following formula:

Time = distance /1100

You can calculate the amount of time it takes sound to travel in water with the following formula:

Time = distance /4900

You can calculate the amount of time it takes sound to travel in steel with the following formula:

Time = distance /16400

13. Internet Service Provider

An Internet service provider has three different subscription packages for its customers:

Package A:	For $9.95 per month 10 hours of access are provided. Additional hours are $2.00 per hour.
Package B:	For $15.95 per month 20 hours of access are provided. Additional hours are $1.00 per hour.
Package C:	For $19.95 per month unlimited access is provided.

Write a program that calculates a customer's monthly bill. It should ask the user to enter the letter of the package the customer has purchased (A, B, or C) and the number of hours that were used. It should then display the total charges.

14. Internet Service Provider, Part 2

Modify the program you wrote for Programming Challenge 13 so it also calculates and displays the amount of money Package A customers would save if they purchased packages B or C, and the amount of money package B customers would save if they purchased package C. If there would be no savings, no message should be printed.

6

Loops and Files

Chapter Objectives

- To recognize the ++ and -- operators, and the difference between prefix and postfix modes
- To understand what a loop is
- To write loops using while, do-while, and for
- To construct loops that validate user input
- To create loops that can calculate the running total of a series of numbers
- To write loops that are terminated by a sentinel value
- To write count-controlled loops
- To write nested loops
- To understand which loops are best for different circumstances
- To create code that saves data to text files and reads data from text files

Topics in this Chapter

6.1 The Increment and Decrement Operators
6.2 The while Loop
6.3 Using the while Loop for Input Validation
6.4 The do-while Loop
6.5 The for Loop
6.6 Running Totals and Sentinel Values
6.7 Nested Loops
6.8 The break and continue Statements (Optional)
6.9 Deciding Which Loop to Use
6.10 Introduction to File Input and Output
6.11 Common Errors
Review Questions and Exercises

6.1 The Increment and Decrement Operators

CONCEPT ++ and -- are operators that add and subtract 1 from their operands.

To *increment* a value means to increase it by 1, and to *decrement* a value means to decrease it by 1. Both of the following statements increment the variable number:

```
number = number + 1;
```

```
number += 1;
```

And number is decremented in both of the following statements:

```
number = number - 1;
```

```
number -= 1;
```

C# provides a set of simple unary operators designed just for incrementing and decrementing variables. The increment operator is ++ and the decrement operator is --. The following statement uses the ++ operator to increment number.

```
number++;
```

And the following statement decrements number.

```
number--;
```

 NOTE: The expression is pronounced "number plus plus," and is pronounced "number minus minus."

The program in Code Listing 6-1 demonstrates the ++ and -- operators.

Code Listing 6-1 `IncrementDecrement.cs`

```
1 /*
2     This program demonstrates the ++ and -- operators.
3 */
4
5 using System;
6
```

(code listing continues)

Code Listing 6-1 `IncrementDecrement.cs` *(continued)*

```
7 public class IncrementDecrement
8 {
9    public static void Main()
10   {
11       int number = 4;
12
13       Console.WriteLine("Number is {0}", number);
14       Console.WriteLine("I will increment number.");
15       number++;
16       Console.WriteLine("Now, number is {0}", number);
17       Console.WriteLine("I will decrement number.");
18       number--;
19       Console.WriteLine("Now, number is {0}", number);
20   }
21 }
```

Program Output

```
Number is 4
I will increment number.
Now, number is 5
I will decrement number.
Now, number is 4
```

The statements in Code Listing 6-1 show the increment and decrement operators used in *postfix mode*, which means the operator is placed after the variable. The operators also work in *prefix mode*, where the operator is placed before the variable name:

```
++number;
```

```
--number;
```

In both postfix and prefix mode, these operators add 1 to or subtract 1 from their operand. Code Listing 6-2 demonstrates this.

Code Listing 6-2   Prefix.cs

```
1 /*
2    This program demonstrates the ++ and -- operators
3    in prefix mode.
4 */
5
6 using System;
7
```

(code listing continues)

Code Listing 6-2 **Prefix.cs** *(continued)*

```
 8 public class Prefix
 9 {
10    public static void Main()
11    {
12        int number = 4;
13
14        Console.WriteLine("Number is {0}", number);
15        Console.WriteLine("I will increment number.");
16        ++number;
17        Console.WriteLine("Now, number is {0}", number);
18        Console.WriteLine("I will decrement number.");
19        --number;
20        Console.WriteLine("Now, number is {0}", number);
21    }
22 }
```

Program Output

```
Number is 4
I will increment number.
Now, number is 5
I will decrement number.
Now, number is 4
```

The Difference Between Postfix and Prefix Modes

In Code Listings 6-1 and 6-2, the statements number++ and ++number both increment the variable number, while the statements number-- and --number both decrement the variable number. In these simple statements it doesn't matter whether the operator is used in postfix or prefix mode. The difference is important, however, when these operators are used in statements that do more than just incrementing or decrementing. For example, look at the following code:

```
number = 4;
Console.WriteLine(number++);
```

The statement that calls the WriteLine method is doing two things: (1) calling WriteLine to display the value of number, and (2) incrementing number. But which happens first? The WriteLine method will display a different value if number is incremented first than if number is incremented last. The answer depends upon the mode of the increment operator.

Postfix mode causes the increment to happen after the value of the variable is used in the expression. In the previously shown statement, the WriteLine method will display 4 and then number will be incremented to 6. Prefix mode, however, causes the increment to happen first. Here is an example:

```
number = 4;
Console.WriteLine(++number);
```

In these statements, `number` is incremented to 5, then `WriteLine` will display the value in number (which is 5). For another example, look at the following code:

```
int x = 1, y;
y = x++;                // Postfix increment
```

The first statement declares the variable x (initialized with the value 1) and the variable y. The second statement does two things:

- It assigns the value of x to the variable y.

- The variable x is incremented.

The value that will be stored in y depends on when the increment takes place. Because the ++ operator is used in postfix mode, it acts after the assignment takes place. So, this code will store 1 in y. After the code has executed, x will contain 2. Let's look at the same code, but with the ++ operator used in prefix mode:

```
int x = 1, y;
y = ++x;                // Prefix increment
```

The first statement declares the variable x (initialized with the value 1) and the variable y. In the second statement, the ++ operator is used in prefix mode, so it acts on the variable before the assignment takes place. So, this code will store 2 in y. After the code has executed, x will also contain 2.

CHECKPOINT

6.1 What will the following program segments display?

a)
```
y = x++;
Console.WriteLine(y);
```

b)
```
Console.WriteLine(x++);
```

c)
```
Console.WriteLine(--x);
```

d)
```
y = x--;
Console.WriteLine(y);
```

6.2 The while Loop

> **CONCEPT** A loop is part of a program that repeats.

In Chapter 5 you were introduced to the concept of control structures, which direct the flow of a program. A *loop* is a control structure that causes a statement or group of statements to repeat. C#

has three looping control structures: the while loop, the do-while loop, and the for loop. The difference between each of these is how they control the repetition. In this section we will focus on the while loop.

The while loop has two important parts: (1) a boolean expression that is tested for a true or false value, and (2) a statement or block of statements that is repeated as long as the expression is true. Figure 6-1 shows the logic of a while loop.

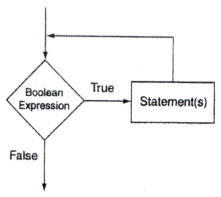

Figure 6-1 Logic of a while Loop

Here is the general format of the while loop:

```
while (BooleanExpression)
       Statement;
```

In the general format, is any valid boolean expression, and is any valid C# statement. The first line shown in the format is sometimes called the *loop header*. It consists of the key word while followed by the BooleanExpression enclosed in parentheses.

Here's how the loop works: The BooleanExpression is tested, and if it is true, the Statement is executed. Then, the BooleanExpression is tested again. If it is true, the Statement is executed. This cycle repeats until the BooleanExpression is false.

The statement that is repeated is known as the *body* of the loop. It is also considered a conditionally executed statement, because it is only executed under the condition that the BooleanExpression is true.

Notice there is no semicolon at the end of the loop header. Like the if statement, the while loop is not complete without the conditionally executed statement that follows it.

If you wish the while loop to repeat a block of statements, the format is

```
while (BooleanExpression)
    {
        Statement;
        Statement;
        // Place as many statements here
        // as necessary.
    }
```

The while loop works like an if statement that executes over and over. As long as the expression in the parentheses is true, the conditionally executed statement or block will repeat. The program in Code Listing 6-3 uses the while loop to print "Hello" five times.

Code Listing 6-3   WhileLoop.cs

```
 1 /*
 2     This program demonstrates the while loop.
 3 */
 4
 5 using System;
 6
 7 public class WhileLoop
 8 {
 9     public static void Main()
10     {
11         int number = 1;
12
13         while (number <= 5)
14         {
15             Console.WriteLine("Hello");
16             number++;
17         }
18
19         Console.WriteLine("That's all!");
20     }
21 }
```

Program Output

```
Hello
Hello
Hello
Hello
Hello
That's all!
```

Let's take a closer look at this program. An integer variable, number, is declared and initialized with the value 1. The while loop begins with this statement:

```
while (number <= 5)
```

This statement tests the variable number to determine whether it is less than or equal to 5. If it is, then the statements in the body of the loop are executed:

```
Console.WriteLine("Hello");
number++;
```

The first statement in the body of the loop prints the word "Hello." The second statement uses the increment operator to add 1 to number. This is the last statement in the body of the loop, so after it executes, the loop starts over. It tests the boolean expression again, and if it is true, the statements in the body of the loop are executed. This cycle repeats until the boolean expression number <= 5 is false. This is illustrated in Figure 6-2.

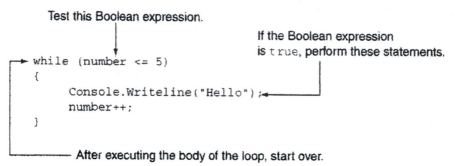

Figure 6-2   The while Loop

Each repetition of a loop is known as an *iteration*. This loop will perform five iterations because the variable number is initialized with the value 1, and it is incremented each time the body of the loop is executed. When the expression number <= 5 is tested and found to be false, the loop will terminate and the program will resume execution at the statement that immediately follows the loop. Figure 6-3 shows the logic of this loop.

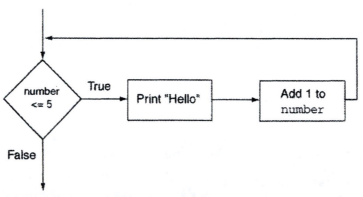

Figure 6-3   Logic of the example while loop

In this example, the number variable is referred to as the *loop control variable* because it controls the number of time that the loop iterates.

The while Loop Is a Pretest Loop

The while loop is known as a *pretest* loop, which means it tests its expression before each iteration. Notice the variable declaration of number in Code Listing 6-3:

```
int number = 1;
```

The number variable is initialized with the value 1. If number had been initialized with a value that is greater than 5, as shown in the following program segment, the loop would never execute:

```
while (number <= 5)
{
    Console.WriteLine("Hello");
    number++;
}
```

An important characteristic of the while loop is that the loop will never iterate if the boolean expression is false to start with. If you want to be sure that a while loop executes the first time, you must initialize the relevant data in such a way that the Boolean expression starts out as true.

Infinite Loops

In all but rare cases, loops must contain within themselves a way to terminate. This means that something inside the loop must eventually make the boolean expression false. The loop in Code Listing 6-3 stops when the expression number <= 5 is false.

If a loop does not have a way of stopping, it is called an infinite loop. An *infinite loop* continues to repeat until the program is interrupted. Here is an example of an infinite loop:

```
int number = 1;
while (number <= 5)
{
    Console.WriteLine("Hello");
```

This is an infinite loop because it does not contain a statement that changes the value of the number variable. Each time the boolean expression is tested, number will contain the value 1.

It's also possible to create an infinite loop by accidentally placing a semicolon after the first line of the while loop. Here is an example:

```
int number = 1;
while (number <= 5);   // This semicolon is an ERROR!
{
    Console.WriteLine("Hello");
    number++;
}
```

The semicolon at the end of the first line is assumed to be a null statement and disconnects the while statement from the block that comes after it. To the compiler, this loop looks like this:

```
while (number <= 5);
```

This while loop will forever execute the null statement, which does nothing. The program will appear to have "gone into space" because there is nothing to display screen output or show activity.

Don't Forget the Braces with a Block of Statements

If you are using a block of statements, don't forget to enclose all of the statements in a set of braces. If you accidentally leave the braces out, the while statement conditionally executes only the very next statement. For example, look at the following code.

```
int number = 1;
// This loop is missing its braces!
while (number <= 5)
    Console.WriteLine("Hello");
    number++;
```

In this code the number++ statement is not in the body of the loop. Because the braces are missing, the while statement only executes the statement that immediately follows it. This loop will execute infinitely because there is no code in its body that changes the number variable.

Programming Style and the while Loop

It's possible to create loops that look like this:

```
while (number != 99) number =
    Convert.ToInt32(Console.ReadLine());
```

As well as this:

```
while (number <= 5) { Console.WriteLine("Hello"); number++; }
```

Avoid this style of programming. The programming style you should use with the while loop is similar to that of the if statement:

- If there is only one statement repeated by the loop, it should appear on the line after the while statement and be indented one additional level.

- If the loop repeats a block, each line inside the braces should be indented.

This programming style should visually set the body of the loop apart from the surrounding code. In general, you'll find a similar style being used with the other types of loops presented in this chapter.

CHECKPOINT

6.2 How many times will "Hello World" be printed in the following program segment?

```
int count = 10;
while (count < 1)
{
Console.WriteLine("Hello World");
count++;
}
```

6.3 How many times will "I love C# programming!" be printed in the following program segment?

```
int count = 0;
while (count < 10)
    Console.WriteLine("Hello World");
    Console.WriteLine("I love C# programming!");
```

6.3 Using the while Loop for Input Validation

CONCEPT The while loop can be used to create input routines that repeat until acceptable data is entered.

Perhaps the most famous saying of the computer industry is "garbage in, garbage out." The integrity of a program's output is only as good as its input, so you should try to make sure garbage does not go into your programs. *Input validation* is the process of inspecting data given to a program by the user and determining whether it is valid. A good program should give clear instructions about the kind of input that is acceptable, and not assume the user has followed those instructions.

The while loop is especially useful for validating input. If an invalid value is entered, a loop can require that the user re-enter it as many times as necessary. For example, the following loop asks for a number in the range of 1 through 100:

```
Console.WriteLine("Enter a number " +
                  "in the range of 1 through 100.");
number = Convert.ToInt32(Console.ReadLine());
// Validate the input.
while (number < 1 || number > 100)
{
Console.WriteLine("Invalid input. " +
                  "Enter a number in the range of " +
                  "1 through 100.");
number = Convert.ToInt32(Console.ReadLine());
}
```

This code first allows the user to enter a number. This takes place just before the loop. If the input is valid, the loop will not execute. If the input is invalid, however, the loop will display an error message and require the user to enter another number. The loop will continue to execute until the user enters a valid number. The general logic of performing input validation is shown in Figure 6-4.

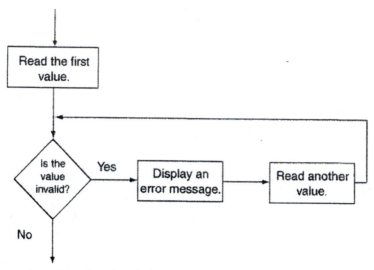

Figure 6-4   Input validation logic

The read operation that takes place just before the loop is called a *priming read*. It provides the first value for the loop to test. Subsequent values are obtained by the loop.

The program in Code Listing 6-4 calculates the number of soccer teams a youth league may create, based on a given number of players and a maximum number of players per team. The program uses while loops (in lines 28 through 36 and lines 44 through 49) and to validate the user's input. Figure 6-5 shows an example of interaction with the program.

Code Listing 6-4   SoccerTeams.cs

```
1 /*
2    This program calculates the number of soccer teams
3    that a youth league may create from the number of
4    available players. Input validation is demonstrated
5    with while loops.
6 */
7
8 using System;
9
```

(code listing continues)

Code Listing 6-4 SoccerTeams.cs *(continued)*

```
10 public class SoccerTeams
11 {
12    public static void Main()
13    {
14       const int MIN_PLAYERS = 9,   // Minimum players per team
15                 MAX_PLAYERS = 15;  // Maximum players per
                                      team
16       int players,                 // Number of available
                                      players
17           teamSize,                // Number of players
                                      per team
18           teams,                   // Number of teams
19           leftOver;                // Number of left over
                                      players
20
21       // Get the number of players per team.
22       Console.WriteLine("Enter the number of players per
                 team.");
23       teamSize = Convert.ToInt32(Console.ReadLine());
24
25       // Validate the number entered.
26       while (teamSize < MIN_PLAYERS || teamSize >
             MAX_PLAYERS)
27       {
28          Console.WriteLine("The number must be at least
                    {0} and no more than {1} .\n Enter " +
29                 "the number of players.",
                    MIN_PLAYERS,MAX_PLAYERS);
30          teamSize = Convert.ToInt32(Console.ReadLine());
31       }
32
33       // Get the number of available players.
34       Console.WriteLine("Enter the available number of players.");
35       players = Convert.ToInt32(Console.ReadLine());
36
37       // Validate the number entered.
38       while (players < 0)
39       {
40          Console.WriteLine("Enter 0 or greater.");
41          players = Convert.ToInt32(Console.ReadLine());
42       }
43
44       // Calculate the number of teams.
45       teams = players / teamSize;
46
```

(code listing continues)

Code Listing 6-4 SoccerTeams.cs *(continued)*

```
47          // Calculate the number of left over players.
48          leftOver = players % teamSize;
49
50          // Display the results.
51          Console.WriteLine("There will be {0} teams with {1} players
                    left over.", teams, leftOver);
52
53      }
54 }
```

Program Output with Example Input
Enter the number of players per team.
4 [Enter]
The number must be at least 9 and no more than 15.
Enter the number of players.
12 [Enter]
Enter the available number of players.
–142 [Enter]
Enter 0 or greater.
142 [Enter]
There will be 11 teams with 10 players left over.

CHECKPOINT

6.4 Write an input validation loop that asks the user to enter a number in the range of 10 through 26.

6.5 Write an input validation loop that asks the user to enter "Y", "y", "N", or "n".

6.6 Write an input validation loop that asks the user to enter "Yes" or "No".

6.4 The `do-while` Loop

> **CONCEPT** The `do-while` loop is a posttest loop, which means its `boolean` expression is tested after each iteration.

The `do-while` loop looks something like an inverted `while` loop. Here is the do-while loop's format when the body of the loop contains only a single statement:

```
do
      Statement;
while (BooleanExpression);
```

Here is the format of the while loop when the body of the loop contains multiple statements:

```
do
    {
        Statement;
        Statement;
        // Place as many statements here
        // as necessary.
    } while (BooleanExpression);
```

 NOTE: The do-while loop must be terminated with a semicolon.

The do-while loop is a *posttest loop*. This means it does not test its boolean expression until it has completed an iteration. As a result, the do-while loop always performs at least one iteration, even if the boolean expression is false to begin with. This differs from the behavior of a while loop, which you will recall is a pretest loop. For example, in the following while loop the WriteLine statement will not execute at all:

```
int x = 1;
while (x < 0)
    Console.WriteLine(x);
```

But the WriteLine statement in the following do-while loop will execute once because the do-while loop does not evaluate the expression x < 0 until the end of the iteration.

```
int x = 1;
do
    Console.WriteLine(x);
```

Figure 6-5 illustrates the logic of the do-while loop.

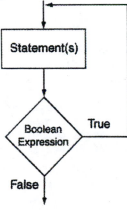

Figure 6-5   Logic of the do-while loop

You should use the do-while loop when you want to make sure the loop executes at least once. For example, the program in Code Listing 6-5 averages a series of three test scores for a student. After the average is displayed, it asks the user if he or she wants to average another set of test scores. The program repeats as long as the user enters Y for yes.

Code Listing 6-5 TestAverage1.cs

```
1  /*
2      This program demonstrates a user-controlled loop.
3  */
4
5  using System;
6
7  public class TestAverage1
8  {
9      public static void Main()
10     {
11         int score1, score2, score3;   // Three test scores
12         double average;               // Average test score
13         char repeat;                  // To hold 'y' or 'n'
14
15         Console.WriteLine("This program calculates the " +
16                           "average of three test scores.");
17
18         // Get as many sets of test scores as the user wants.
19         do
20         {
21             // Get the first test score in this set.
22             Console.Write("Enter score #1: ");
23             score1 = Convert.ToInt32(Console.ReadLine());
24
25             // Get the second test score in this set.
26             Console.Write("Enter score #2: ");
27             score2 = Convert.ToInt32(Console.ReadLine());
28
29             // Get the third test score in this set.
30             Console.Write("Enter score #3: ");
31             score3 = Convert.ToInt32(Console.ReadLine());
32
33             // Calculate and print the average test score.
34             average = (score1 + score2 + score3) / 3.0;
35             Console.WriteLine("The average is {0}", average);
36             Console.WriteLine();    // Prints a blank line
37
```

(code listing continues)

Code Listing 6-5 **TestAverage1.cs** *(continued)*

```
38              // Does the user want to average another set?
39              Console.WriteLine("Would you like to average another
                    set of test scores?");
40              Console.Write("Enter Y for yes or N for no: ");
41              repeat = Convert.ToChar(Console.ReadLine());
42
43          } while (repeat == 'Y' || repeat == 'y');
44      }
45  }
```

Program Output wuth Example Input
```
This program calculates the average of three test scores.
Enter score #1: 89 [Enter]
Enter score #2: 90 [Enter]
Enter score #3: 97 [Enter]
The average is 92

Would you like to average another set of test scores?
Enter Y for yes or N for no: y [Enter]
Enter score #1: 78 [Enter]
Enter score #2: 65 [Enter]
Enter score #3: 88 [Enter]
The average is 77 [Enter]

Would you like to average another set of test scores?
Enter Y for yes or N for no: n [Enter]
```

When this program was written, the programmer had no way of knowing the number of times the loop would iterate. This is because the loop asks the user if he or she wants to repeat the process. This type of loop is known as a *user-controlled loop*, because it allows the user to decide the number of iterations.

6.5 The for Loop

CONCEPT The for loop is ideal for performing a known number of iterations.

In general, there are two categories of loops: conditional loops and count-controlled loops. A *conditional loop* executes as long as a particular condition exists. For example, an input validation loop executes as long as the input value is invalid. When you write a conditional loop, you have no way of knowing the number of times it will iterate.

Sometimes you do know the exact number of iterations that a loop must perform. A loop that repeats a specific number of times is known as a *count-controlled loop*. For example, if a loop asks the user to enter the sales amounts for each month in the year, it will iterate 12 times. In essence, the loop counts to 12 and asks the user to enter a sales amount each time it makes a count.

A count-controlled loop must possess three elements:

1. It must initialize a control variable to a starting value.

2. It must test the control variable by comparing it to a maximum value. When the control variable reaches its maximum value, the loop terminates.

3. It must update the control variable during each iteration. This is usually done by incrementing the variable.

In C#, the for loop is ideal for writing count-controlled loops. It is specifically designed to initialize, test, and update a loop control variable. Here is the format of the for loop when used to repeat a single statement:

```
for (Initialization; Test; Update)
   Statement;
```

The format of the for loop when used to repeat a block is shown here:

```
for (Initialization; Test; Update)
   {
      Statement;
      Statement;
      // Place as many statements here
      // as necessary.
   }
```

The first line of the for loop is known as the *loop header*. After the key word for, there are three expressions inside the parentheses, separated by semicolons. (Notice there is no semicolon after the third expression.) The first expression is the *initialization expression*. It is normally used to initialize a control variable to its starting value. This is the first action performed by the loop, and it is only done once. The second expression is the *test expression*. This is a boolean expression that controls the execution of the loop. As long as this expression is true, the body of the for loop will repeat. The for loop is a pretest loop, so it evaluates the test expression before each iteration. The third expression is the *update expression*. It executes at the end of each iteration. Typically, this is a statement that increments the loop's control variable.

Here is an example of a simple for loop that prints "Hello" five times:

```
for (count = 1; count <= 5; count++)
   Console.WriteLine("Hello");
```

In this loop, the initialization expression is count = 1, the test expression is count <= 5, and the update expression is count++. The body of the loop has one statement, which is the WriteLine statement. Figure 6-6 illustrates the sequence of events that take place during the loop's execution. Notice that Steps 2 through 4 are repeated as long as the test expression is true.

Figure 6-7 shows the loop's logic in the form of a flowchart.

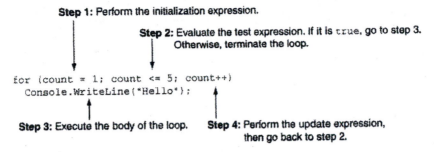

Figure 6-6 Sequence of events in the for loop

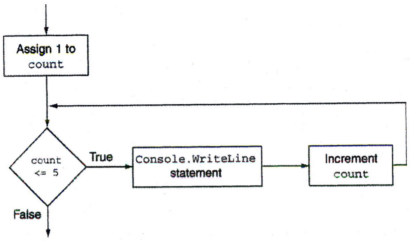

Figure 6-7 Logic of the for loop

Notice how the control variable, count, is used to control the number of times that the loop iterates. During the execution of the loop, this variable takes on the values 1 through 5, and when the test expression count <= 5 is false, the loop terminates. Because this variable keeps a count of the number of iterations, it is often called a *counter variable.*

Also notice that in this example the count variable is used only in the loop header, to control the number of loop iterations. It is not used for any other purpose. It is also possible to use the control variable within the body of the loop. For example, look at the following code:

```
for (number = 1; number <= 10; number++)
    Console.Write("{0} ", number);
```

The control variable in this loop is number. In addition to controlling the number of iterations, it is also used in the body of the loop. This loop will produce the following output:

```
1 2 3 4 5 6 7 8 9 10
```

As you can see, the loop displays the contents of the number variable during each iteration. The program in Code Listing 6-6 shows another example of a for loop that uses its control variable within the body of the loop. This program displays a table showing the numbers 1 through 10 and their squares.

Code Listing 6-6   Squares.cs

```
 1 /*
 2    This program demonstrates the for loop.
 3 */
 4
 5 using System;
 6
 7 public class Squares
 8 {
 9    public static void Main()
10    {
11        int number; // Loop control variable
12
13        Console.WriteLine("Number   Number Squared");
14        Console.WriteLine("-----------------------");
15
16        for (number = 1; number <= 10; number++)
17        {
18            Console.WriteLine("{0}\t\t{1}", number, number * number);
19        }
20    }
21 }
```

Program Output

```
Number        Number Squared
-----------------------------
1                 1
2                 4
3                 9
4                 16
5                 25
6                 36
7                 49
8                 64
9                 81
10                100
```

Figure 6-8 illustrates the sequence of events performed by this for loop.

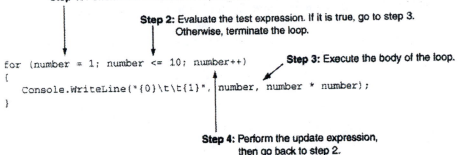

Figure 6-8 Sequence of events with the for loop in Code Listing 6-6

Figure 6-9 shows the logic of the loop.

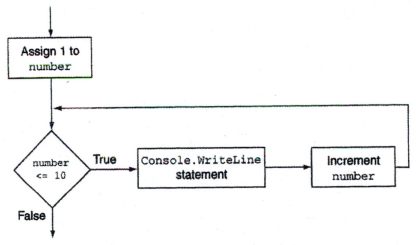

Figure 6-9 Logic of the for loop in Code Listing 6-6

The for Loop Is a Pretest Loop

Because the for loop tests its boolean expression before it performs an iteration, it is a pretest loop. It is possible to write a for loop in such a way that it will never iterate. Here is an example:

```
for (count = 11; count <= 10; count++)
    Console.WriteLine("Hello");
```

Because the variable count is initialized to a value that makes the boolean expression false from the beginning, this loop terminates as soon as it begins.

Avoid Modifying the Control Variable in the Body of the `for` Loop

Be careful not to place a statement that modifies the control variable in the body of the `for` loop. All modifications of the control variable should take place in the update expression, which is automatically executed at the end of each iteration. If a statement in the body of the loop also modifies the control variable, the loop will probably not terminate when you expect it to. The following loop, for example, increments x twice for each iteration:

```
for (x = 1; x <= 10; x++)
{
    Console.WriteLine(x);
    x++;                      // Wrong!

}
```

Other Forms of the Update Expression

You are not limited to using increment statements in the update expression. Here is a loop that displays all the even numbers from 2 through 100 by adding 2 to its counter:

```
for (number = 2; number <= 100; number += 2)
    Console.WriteLine(number);
```

And here is a loop that counts backward from 10 down to 0:

```
for (number = 10; number >= 0; number--)
    Console.WriteLine(number);
```

Declaring a Variable in the `for` Loop's Initialization Expression

Not only may the control variable be initialized in the initialization expression, it may be declared there as well. The following code shows an example. This is a modified version of the loop in Code Listing 6-6:

```
for (int number = 1; number <= 10; number++)
{
    Console.WriteLine("{0}\t\t{1}", number, number * number);
}
```

In this loop, the `number` variable is both declared and initialized in the initialization expression. If the control variable is used only in the loop, it makes sense to declare it in the loop header. This makes the variable's purpose clearer.

When a variable is declared in the initialization expression of a `for` loop, the scope of the variable is limited to the loop. This means you cannot access the variable in statements outside the loop. For example, the following program segment will not compile because the last `WriteLine` statement cannot access the variable `count`.

```
for (int count = 1; count <= 10; count++)
    Console.WriteLine(count);
Console.WriteLine("count is now {0}", count);    // ERROR!
```

Creating a User-Controlled for Loop

Sometimes you want the user to determine the maximum value of the control variable in a for loop, and therefore determine the number of times the loop iterates. For example, look at the program in Code Listing 6-7. It is a modification of Code Listing 6-6, in which, instead of displaying the numbers one through 10 and their squares, the user can enter the maximum value to display.

Code Listing 6-7   UserSquares.cs

```
 1 /*
 2    This program demonstrates a user controlled for loop.
 3 */
 4
 5 using System;
 6
 7 public class UserSquares
 8 {
 9    public static void Main()
10    {
11        int number,       // Loop control variable
12            maxValue;     // Maximum value to display
13
14        Console.WriteLine("I will display a table of numbers and their
                  squares.");
15
16        // Get the maximum value to display.
17        Console.Write("How high should I go? ");
18        maxValue = Convert.ToInt32(Console.ReadLine());
19
20        // Display the table.
21        Console.WriteLine("Number    Number Squared");
22        Console.WriteLine("-----------------------");
23        for (number = 1; number <= maxValue; number++)
24        {
25            Console.WriteLine("{0}\t\t{1}",number, number * number);
26        }
27    }
28 }
```

Code Listing 6-7   UserSquares.cs

Program Output with Example Input
```
I will display a table of numbers and their squares.
How high should I go? 7 [Enter]
Number          Number Squared
----------------------------------
1               1
2               4
3               9
4               16
5               25
6               36
7               49
```

Before the loop, this program asks the user to enter the highest value to display. This value is stored in the maxValue variable:

```
Console.Write("How high should I go? ");
maxValue = Convert.ToInt32(Console.ReadLine());
```

The for loop's test expression then uses this value as the upper limit for the control variable:

```
for (number = 1; number <= maxValue; number++)
```

In this loop, the number variable takes on the values 1 through maxValue, and then the loop terminates.

Using Multiple Statements in the Initialization and Update Expressions

It is possible to execute more than one statement in the initialization expression and the update expression. When using multiple statements in either of these expressions, simply separate the statements with commas. For example, look at the loop in the following code, which has two statements in the initialization expression.

```
int x, y;
for (x = 1, y = 1; x <= 5; x++)
{
    Console.WriteLine("{0} plus {1} equals {2}", x, y, (x + y));
}
```

This loop's initialization expression is

```
x = 1, y = 1
```

This initializes two variables, x and y. The output produced by this loop is

```
1 plus 1 equals 2
2 plus 1 equals 3
3 plus 1 equals 4
4 plus 1 equals 5
5 plus 1 equals 6
```

We can further modify the loop to execute two statements in the update expression. Here is an example:

```
int x, y;
for (x = 1, y = 1; x <= 5; x++, y++)
{
    Console.WriteLine("{0} plus {1} equals {2}", x, y, (x + y));
}
```

The loop's update expression is

```
x++, y++
```

This update expression increments both the x and y variables. The output produced by this loop is

```
1 plus 1 equals 2
2 plus 2 equals 4
3 plus 3 equals 6
4 plus 4 equals 8
5 plus 5 equals 10
```

Connecting multiple statements with commas works well in the initialization and update expressions, but don't try to connect multiple **boolean** expressions this way in the test expression. If you wish to combine multiple **boolean** expressions in the test expression, you must use the && or || operators.

 ## CHECKPOINT

6.7 Name the three expressions that appear inside the parentheses in the **for** loop's header.

6.8 You want to write a **for** loop that displays "I love to program" 50 times. Assume that you will use a control variable named **count**.

a) What initialization expression will you use?

b) What test expression will you use?

c) What update expression will you use?

d) Write the loop.

6.9 What will the following program segments display?

a)
```
for (int count = 0; count < 6; count++)
    Console.WriteLine(count + count);
```

b)
```
for (int value = -5; value < 5; value++)
    Console.WriteLine(value);
```

c)
```
int x;
for (x = 5; x <= 14; x += 3)
    Console.WriteLine(x);
    Console.WriteLine(x);
```

6.10 Write a for loop that displays your name 10 times.

6.11 Write a for loop that displays all of the odd numbers, one through 49.

6.12 Write a for loop that displays every fifth number, 0 through 100.

6.6   Running Totals and Sentinel Values

 CONCEPT A running total is a sum of numbers that accumulates with each iteration of a loop. The variable used to keep the running total is called an accumulator. A sentinel is a value that signals when the end of a list of values has been reached.

Some programming tasks require you to calculate the total of a series of numbers that are provided as input. This is sometimes called a *running total* because the numbers are gathered and summed during the running of a loop. The program in Code Listing 6-8, for example, calculates a company's total sales over a period of time by taking daily sales figures as input and adding them up as they are gathered.

Code Listing 6-8   TotalSales.cs

```
1  /*
2     This program calculates a running total.
3  */
4
5  using System;
6
```

(code listing continues)

Code Listing 6-8 TotalSales.cs *(continued)*

```
 7 public class TotalSales
 8 {
 9    public static void Main()
10    {
11       int days;              // The number of days
12       double sales,          // A day's sales figure
13              totalSales;     // Accumulator
14
15
16       // Get the number of days.
17       Console.WriteLine("For how many days do you have sales
                 figures?");
18       days = Convert.ToInt32(Console.ReadLine());
19
20       // Set the accumulator to 0.
21       totalSales = 0.0;
22
23       // Get the sales figures and calculate a running total.
24       for (int count = 1; count <= days; count++)
25       {
26          Console.WriteLine("Enter the sales for day {0}:",count);
27          sales = Convert.ToDouble(Console.ReadLine());
28          totalSales += sales;   // Add sales to totalSales.
29       }
30
31       // Display the total sales.
32       Console.WriteLine("The total sales are {0:C2}",totalSales);
33
34    }
35 }
```

Program Output with Example Input
```
For how many days do you have sales figures?
4 [Enter]
Enter the sales for day 1:
687.59 [Enter]
Enter the sales for day 2:
563.22 [Enter]
Enter the sales for day 3:
896.35 [Enter]
Enter the sales for day 4:
743.29 [Enter]
The total sales are $2,890.45
```

Let's take a closer look at this program. In lines 17 and 18 the user is asked to enter the number of days that he or she has sales figures for. The number is read from an input dialog box and assigned to the days variable. Then, in line 21 the totalSales variable is assigned 0.0. In general programming terms, the totalSales variable is referred to as an accumulator. An *accumulator* is a variable that is initialized with a starting value, which is usually zero, and then accumulates a sum of numbers by having the numbers added to it. As you will see, it is critical that the accumulator is set to zero before values are added to it.

Next, the for loop in lines 24 through 29 executes. During each iteration of the loop, the user enters the amount of sales for a specific day, which are assigned to the sales variable. This is done in lines 26 through 28. Then, in line 28 the contents of sales is added to the existing value in the totalSales variable. (Note that line 28 does not assign sales to totalSales, but adds sales to totalSales. Put another way, this line increases totalSales by the amount in sales.)

Because totalSales was initially assigned 0.0, after the first iteration of the loop, totalSales will be set to the same value as sales. After each subsequent iteration, totalSales will be increased by the amount in sales. After the loop has finished, totalSales will contain the total of all the daily sales figures entered. Now it should be clear why we assigned 0.0 to totalSales before the loop executed. If totalSales started at any other value, the total would be incorrect.

Using a Sentinel Value

The program in Code Listing 6-8 requires the user to know in advance the number of days he or she has sales figures for. Sometimes the user has a list of input values that is very long, and doesn't know the exact number of items there are. In other cases, the user might be entering values from several lists and it is impractical to require that every item in every list be counted.

A technique that can be used in these situations is to ask the user to enter a sentinel value at the end of the list. A *sentinel value* is a special value that cannot be mistaken as a member of the list and that signals there are no more values to be entered. When the user enters the sentinel value, the loop terminates.

The program in Code Listing 6-9 is an example of this. It calculates the total points earned by a soccer team over a series of games. It allows the user to enter the series of game points, then enter 1 to signal the end of the list.

Code Listing 6-9   SoccerPoints.cs

```
1  /*
2     This program calculates the total number of points a
3     soccer team has earned over a series of games. The user
4     enters a series of point values, then -1 when finished.
5  */
6
```

(code listing continues)

Code Listing 6-9 SoccerPoints.cs *(continued)*

```
7 using System;
8
9 public class SoccerPoints
10 {
11    public static void Main()
12    {
13       int points,            // Game points
14          totalPoints = 0;    // Accumulator initialized to 0
15
16       // Display general instructions.
17       Console.WriteLine("Enter the number of points your team");
18       Console.WriteLine("has earned for each game this season.");
19       Console.WriteLine("Enter -1 when finished.");
20       Console.WriteLine();
21
22       // Get the first number of points.
23       Console.Write("Enter game points or -1 to end: ");
24       points = Convert.ToInt32(Console.ReadLine());
25
26       // Accumulate the points until -1 is entered.
27       while (points != -1)
28       {
29          // Add points to totalPoints.
30          totalPoints += points;
31
32          // Get the next number of points.
33          Console.Write("Enter game points or -1 to end: ");
34          points = Convert.ToInt32(Console.ReadLine());
35       }
36
37       // Display the total number of points.
38       Console.WriteLine("The total points are {0}", totalPoints);
39    }
40 }
```

Program Output with Example Input

```
Enter the number of points your team
has earned for each game this season.
Enter -1 when finished.

Enter game points or -1 to end: 7 [Enter]
Enter game points or -1 to end: 9 [Enter]
Enter game points or -1 to end: 4 [Enter]
Enter game points or -1 to end: 6 [Enter]
Enter game points or -1 to end: 8 [Enter]
Enter game points or -1 to end: -1 [Enter]
The total points are 34
```

The value 1 was chosen for the sentinel because it is not possible for a team to score negative points. Notice that this program performs a priming read to get the first value. This makes it possible for the loop to immediately terminate if the user enters 1 as the first value. Also note that the sentinel value is not included in the running total.

 # CHECKPOINT

6.13 Write a `for` loop that repeats seven times, asking the user to enter a number. The loop should also calculate the sum of the numbers entered.

6.14 In the following program segment, which variable is the loop control variable (also known as the counter variable) and which is the accumulator?

```
int a, x = 0, y = 0;
while (x < 10)
{
    Console.Write("Enter a number: ");
    a = Convert.ToInt32(Console.ReadLine());
    y += a;
}
Console.WriteLine("The sum of those numbers is {0}", y);
```

6.15 Why should you be careful when choosing a sentinel value?

6.7 Nested Loops

> **CONCEPT** A loop that is inside another loop is called a nested loop.

Nested loops are necessary when a task performs a repetitive operation and that task itself must be repeated. A clock is a good example of something that works like a nested loop. The second hand, minute hand, and hour hand all spin around the face of the clock. The hour hand, however, only makes one revolution for every 12 of the minute hand's revolutions. And it takes 60 revolutions of the second hand for the minute hand to make one revolution. This means that for every complete revolution of the hour hand, the second hand has revolved 720 times. The program in Code Listing 6-10 uses nested loops to simulate a clock.

Code Listing 6-10   Clock.cs

```
1 /*
2    This program uses nested loops to simulate a clock.
3 */
4
```

(code listing continues)

Code Listing 6-10 Clock.cs *(continued)*

```
 5 using System;
 6
 7 public class Clock
 8 {
 9     public static void Main()
10     {
11
12        // Simulate the clock.
13        for (int hours = 1; hours <= 12; hours++)
14        {
15            for (int minutes = 0; minutes <= 59; minutes++)
16            {
17                for (int seconds = 0; seconds <= 59; seconds++)
18                {
19                    Console.Write("{0} :", hours);
20                    Console.Write("{0} :", minutes);
21                    Console.WriteLine(hours);
22                }
23            }
24        }
25    }
26 }
```

Program Output
```
01:00:00
01:00:01
01:00:02
01:00:03
```
(The loop continues to count...)
```
12:59:57
12:59:58
12:59:59
```

The innermost loop (which begins at line 17) will iterate 60 times for each single iteration of the middle loop. The middle loop (which begins at line 15) will iterate 60 times for each single iteration of the outermost loop. When the outermost loop (which begins at line 13) has iterated 12 times, the middle loop will have iterated 720 times and the innermost loop will have iterated 43,200 times.

The simulated clock example brings up these important points about nested loops:

- An inner loop goes through all of its iterations for each iteration of an outer loop.

- Inner loops complete their iterations before outer loops do.

- To get the total number of iterations of a nested loop, multiply the number of iterations of all the loops.

For an additional example, see the `TestAverage2.cs` file in the Source Code\Chapter 6 folder on the Student CD. It asks the user for the number of students and the number of test scores per student. A nested inner loop asks for all the test scores for one student, iterating once for each test score. The outer loop iterates once for each student.

6.8 The `break` and `continue` Statements *(Optional)*

> **CONCEPT** The break statement causes a loop to terminate early. The continue statement causes a loop to stop its current iteration and begin the next one.

The `break` statement, which was used with the `switch` statement in Chapter 5, can also be placed inside a loop. When it is encountered, the loop stops and causes control to transfer to the end of the block in which the break executes, the program jumps to the statement immediately following the loop. Although it is perfectly acceptable to use the `break` statement in a `switch` statement, it is considered taboo to use it in a loop. This is because it bypasses the normal condition that is required to terminate the loop, and it makes code difficult to understand and debug. For this reason, you should avoid using the `break` statement in a loop when possible.

The `continue` statement causes the current iteration of a loop to end. When `continue` is encountered, all the statements in the body of the loop that appear after it are ignored, and the loop prepares for the next iteration. In a `while` loop, this means the program jumps to the Boolean expression at the top of the loop. As usual, if the expression is still `true`, the next iteration begins. In a `do-while` loop, the program jumps to the `boolean` expression at the bottom of the loop, which determines whether the next iteration will begin. In a `for` loop, `continue` causes the update expression to be executed, and then the test expression is evaluated.

The `continue` statement should also be avoided. Like the `break` statement, it bypasses the loop's logic and makes the code difficult to understand and debug.

6.9 Deciding Which Loop to Use

> **CONCEPT** Although most repetitive algorithms can be written with any of the three types of loops, each works best in different situations.

Each of C#'s three loops is ideal to use in different situations. Here's a short summary of when each loop should be used.

- **The `while` loop.** The `while` loop is a pretest loop. It is ideal in situations where you do not want the loop to iterate if the condition is `false` from the beginning. It is also ideal if you want to use a sentinel value to terminate the loop.

- **The do-while loop.** The do-while loop is a posttest loop. It is ideal in situations where you always want the loop to iterate at least once.

- **The for loop.** The for loop is a pretest loop that has built-in expressions for initializing, testing, and updating. These expressions make it very convenient to use a loop control variable as a counter. The for loop is ideal in situations where the exact number of iterations is known.

6.10   Introduction to File Input and Output

> **CONCEPT**   The .NET FCL provides several classes that you can use for writing data to a file and reading data from a file. To write data to a file, you use the **StreamWriter** class. To read data from a file, you use the **StreamReader** class.

The programs you have written so far require you to re-enter data each time the program runs. This is because the data stored in variables and objects in RAM disappears once the program stops running. To retain data between the times it runs, a program must have a way of saving the data.

Data may be saved in a *file*, which is usually stored on a computer's disk. Once the data is saved in a file, it will remain there after the program stops running. The data can then be retrieved and used later. In general, using a file is a three-step process:

1. The file must be *opened*. When the file is opened, a connection is created between the file and the program.

2. Data is then written to the file or read from the file.

3. When the program is finished using the file, the file must be *closed*.

In this section we will discuss how to write C# programs that write data to files and read data from files. The terms input file and output file are commonly used. An *input file* is a file that a program reads data from. It is called an input file because the data stored in it serves as input to the program. An *output file* is a file that a program writes data to. It is called an output file because the program stores output in the file.

In general, there are two types of files: text and binary. A *text file* contains plain text, and may be opened in a text editor such as Notepad. A *binary file* contains unformatted binary data, and you cannot view its contents with a text editor. In this chapter we will discuss how to work with text files. Binary files are discussed in Chapter 9.

The .NET FCL provides a number of classes that you will use to work with files. To use these classes, you must place the following using statement near the top of your program:

```
using.System.IO;
```

You probably recognize this using statement: It's the statement we use when we want System namespace objects to read console input from the keyboard. However, to support file I/O we also have to call the System.IO namespace.

Writing Data to a File

To write data to a file you must create an object from the following class:

StreamWriter   This class allows you to open a file for writing and establish a connection with it. It also allows you to write data to a file using the same Write and WriteLine method we have been using to display data on the screen.

First you create an instance of the StreamWriter class, which has the ability to open a file and establish a connection with it. You pass the name of the file that you wish open, as a string, to the constructor. For example, the following statement creates a StreamWriter object and passes the file name StudentData.txt to the constructor.

```
StreamWriter outputFile = new StreamWriter("StudentData.txt");
```

This statement will create an empty file named StudentData.txt. The file will be created in the current directory or folder. You may also pass a reference to a string object as an argument to the StreamWriter constructor. For example, in the following code the user specifies the name of the file.

```
string filename;
Console.WriteLine("Enter the filename:");
filename = Console.ReadLine();
StreamWriter outputFile = new StreamWriter(filename);
```

The object referenced by outputFile is connected to the file StudentData.txt. The result of this code is that the outputFile variable will reference a StreamWriter object that is able to write data to the StudentData.txt file. With the outputFile object we can write data using the Write and WriteLine methods. You already know how to use Write and WriteLine with Console to display data on the screen. They are used the same way with a StreamWriter object to write data to a file. For example, assuming that outputFile references a StreamWriter object, the following statement writes the string "Jim" to the file.

```
outputFile.WriteLine("Jim");
```

When the program is finished writing data to the file, it must close the file. To close the file use the StreamWriter class' Close method. Here is an example of the method's use:

```
outputFile.Close();
```

Your application must close files when finished with them. Once a file is closed, the connection between it and the `StreamWriter` object is removed. In order to perform further operations on the file, you must open it again.

The `StreamWriter` Class `WriteLine` Method

The `StreamWriter` class `WriteLine` method writes a line of data to a file. For example, assume an application creates a file and writes three students' first names and their test scores to the file with the following code.

```
StreamWriter outputFile = new StreamWriter("StudentData.txt");
outputFile.WriteLine("Jim");
outputFile.WriteLine(95);
outputFile.WriteLine("Karen");
outputFile.WriteLine(98);
outputFile.WriteLine("Bob");
outputFile.WriteLine(82);
outputFile.Close();
```

The `WriteLine` method writes data to the file and then writes a newline character immediately after the data. You can visualize the data written to the file in the following manner:

Jim<*newline*>95<*newline*>Karen<*newline*>98<*newline*>Bob<*newline*>82<*newline*>

The newline characters are represented here as <*newline*>. You do not actually see the newline characters, but when the file is opened in a text editor such as Notepad, its contents will appear as shown in Figure 6-10. As you can see from the figure, each newline character causes the data that follows it to be displayed on a new line.

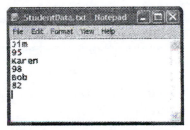

Figure 6-10   File contents displayed in Notepad

In addition to separating the contents of a file into lines, the newline character also serves as a delimiter. A *delimiter* is an item that separates other items. When you write data to a file using the `WriteLine` method, newline characters will separate the individual items of data. Later you will see that the individual items of data in a file must be separated in order for them to be read from the file.

The StreamWriter Class Write Method

The Write method is used to write an item of data to a file without writing the newline character. For example, look at the following code.

```
string name = "Jeffrey Smith";
string phone = "556-7864";
int idNumber = 47895;
StreamWriter outputFile = new StreamWriter("PersonalData.txt");
outputFile.Write("{0} ",name);
outputFile.Write("{0} ",phone);
outputFile.WriteLine(idNumber);
outputFile.Close();
```

This code uses the Write method to write the contents of the name object to the file, followed by a space (" "). Then it uses the Write method to write the contents of the phone object to the file, followed by a space. Then it uses the WriteLine method to write the contents of the idNumber variable, followed by a newline character. Figure 6-11 shows the contents of the file displayed in Notepad.

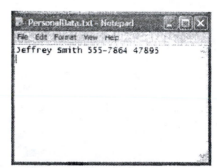

Figure 6-11   Contents of file displayed in Notepad

An Example Program

Let's look at an example program that writes data to a file. The program in Code Listing 6-11 writes the names of your friends to a file.

Code Listing 6-11   FileWriteDemo.cs

```
1 /*
2    This program writes data to a file.
3 */
4
5 using System;
6 using System.IO;
7
```

(code listing continues)

Code Listing 6-11 FileWriteDemo.cs *(continued)*

```
 8  public class FileWriteDemo
 9  {
10     public static void Main()
11     {
12         string fileName,      // File name
13                friendName;    // Friend's name
14         int numFriends;       // Number of friends
15
16         // Get the number of friends.
17         Console.Write("How many friends do you have? ");
18         numFriends = Convert.ToInt32(Console.ReadLine());
19
20         // Get the filename.
21         Console.Write("Enter the filename: ");
22         fileName = Console.ReadLine();
23
24         // Open the file.
25         StreamWriter outputFile = new StreamWriter(fileName);
26
27         // Get data and write it to the file.
28         for (int i = 1; i <= numFriends; i++)
29         {
30             // Get the name of a friend.
31             Console.Write("Enter the name of friend number {0}:",i);
32             friendName = Console.ReadLine();
33
34             // Write the name to the file.
35             outputFile.WriteLine(friendName);
36         }
37
38         // Close the file.
39         outputFile.Close();
40         Console.WriteLine("Data written to the file.");
41     }
42  }
```

Program Output with Example Input
```
How many friends do you have? 5 [Enter]
Enter the filename: C:\\MyFriends.txt [Enter]
Enter the name of friend number 1:Joe [Enter]
Enter the name of friend number 2:Rose [Enter]
Enter the name of friend number 3:Greg [Enter]
Enter the name of friend number 4:Kirk [Enter]
Enter the name of friend number 5:Renee [Enter]
Data written to the file.
```

The using System.IO statement in line 6 is necessary because this program uses the StreamWriter class. This program asks the user to enter the number of friends he or she has (in lines 17 and 18), then a name for the file that the program will create (in lines 21 and 22). The statement (line 25) creates the file and establishes the connections necessary for the outputFile object to be able to write data to it.

```
StreamWriter outputFile = new StreamWriter(fileName);
```

The for loop in lines 28 through 36 performs an iteration for each friend that the user has, each time asking for the name of a friend. The user's input is referenced by the variable friendName. Once the name is entered, it is written to the file with the following statement, which appears in line 35.

```
outputFile.WriteLine(friendName);
```

After the loop finishes, the file is closed in line 39. After the program is executed with the input shown above, the file MyFriends.txt is created. If we open the file in Notepad, we will see its contents, as shown in Figure 6-12.

Figure 6-12 Contents of the file displayed in Notepad

Appending Data to a File

When you pass the name of a file to the StreamWriter constructor, and the file already exists, it will be erased and a new empty file with the same name will be created. Sometimes, however, you want to preserve an existing file and append new data to its current contents. Appending to a file involves writing new data to the end of the existing data.

The StreamWriter constructor takes an optional second argument which must be a boolean value. By default, the boolean argument is set to false. If the argument is true, the file will not be erased if it already exists and new data will be written to the end of the file. If the argument is false, the file will be erased if it already exists.

For example, assume the file MyFriends.txt exists and contains the following data:

```
Joe
Rose
Greg
Kirk
Renee
```

The following code opens the file and appends additional data to its existing contents:

```
StreamWriter outputFile = new StreamWriter("MyFirends.txt", true);
outputFile.WriteLine("Bill");
outputFile.WriteLine("Steven");
outputFile.WriteLine("Sharon");
outputFile.Close();
```

After this code executes, the MyFriends.txt file will contain the following data:

```
Joe
Rose
Greg
Kirk
Renee
Bill
Steven
Sharon
```

Review

Before moving on, let's review the steps necessary for writing a program that writes data to a file:

1. Place the using System.IO; statement in the top section of your program.
2. Create a StreamWriter object and pass the name of the file as a string to the constructor.
3. Use the StreamWriter object's Write and WriteLine methods to write data to the file.
4. When finished writing to the file, use the StreamWriter object's Close method to close the file.

Specifying the File Location

When you open a file you may specify its path along with its filename. On a Windows computer, paths contain backslash characters. Remember that when a single backslash character appears in a string literal, it marks the beginning of an escape sequence such as "\n". Two backslash characters in a string literal represent a single backslash. So, when you provide a path in a string literal, and the path contains backslash characters, you must use two backslash characters in the place of each single backslash character.

For example, the path `"A:\\Names.txt"` specifies that `Names.txt` is in the root folder of a floppy disk in drive A:, and the path `"C:\\MyData\\Data.txt"` specifies that `Data.txt` is in the `\MyData` folder on drive C:. In the following code segment, the file `Pricelist.txt` is created in the root folder of drive A:.

```
StreamWriter outputFile = new StreamWriter("A:\\PriceList.txt");
```

You only need to use double backslashes if the file's path is in a string literal.

 TIP: C# allows you to substitute forward slashes for backslashes in a Windows path. For example, the path `"C:\\MyData\\Data.txt"` could be written as `"C:/MyData/Data.txt"`. This eliminates the need to use double backslashes.

Reading Data from a File

StreamReader   This class allows you to open a file for reading and establish a connection with it. It also allows you to read data to a file using the same Read and ReadLine method we have been using to read data from the keyboard.

First you create an instance of the `StreamReader` class, which allows you to open a file and establish a connection with it. You pass the name of the file that you wish open, as a string, to the constructor. For example, the following statement creates a `StreamReader` object and passes the file name `Customers.txt` to the constructor.

```
StreamReader inputFile = new StreamReader("Customers.txt");
```

This statement will open a file named `Customers.txt`. The file will be created in the current directory or folder. You may also pass a reference to a `string` object as an argument to the `StreamReader` constructor. For example, in the following code the user specifies the name of the file.

```
string filename;
Console.WriteLine("Enter the filename:");
filename = Console.ReadLine();
StreamReader inputFile = new StreamReader(filename);
```

The object referenced by `inputFile` is connected to the file `Customers.txt`. The result of this statement is that the `inputFile` variable will reference a `StreamReader` object that is able to read data from the `Customers.txt` file.

Reading Lines with the *ReadLine* Method

You've already used the `ReadLine` method to read a line of input from the keyboard. With the `StreamReader` class you can use the `ReadLine` method to read a line of data from a file. For example, assume that `inputFile` references a `StreamReader` object and `customerName` references a `string` object. The following statement reads a line from the file and stores it in the `customerName` variable.

```
customerName = inputFile.ReadLine();
```

Data is read from a file's beginning to its end. When the file is opened, its *read position*, which is the position of the next item to be read, is set to the first item in the file. As data is read, the read position advances through the file. For example, consider the file, `Quotation.txt`, shown in Figure 6-13. As you can see from the figure, the file has three lines.

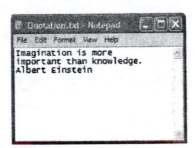

Figure 6-13   File with three lines

You can visualize that the data is stored in the file in the following manner:

> Imagination is more⟨*newline*⟩important than knowledge⟨*newline*⟩Albert
> Einstein⟨*newline*⟩

Suppose a program opens the file with the following code.

```
StreamReader inputFile = new StreamReader("Quotation.txt");
```

When this code opens the file, its read position is at the beginning of the first line, as illustrated in Figure 6-14.

Read position ────▶Imagination is more
                    important than knowledge.
                    Albert Einstein

Figure 6-14   Initial read position

Now, suppose the program uses the following statement to read a line from the file. In the statement, assume that `str` references a `string` object.

```
str = inputFile.ReadLine()
```

This statement will read a line from the file, beginning at the current read position. After the statement executes, the object referenced by str will contain the string "Imagination is more". The file's read position will be advanced to the next line, as illustrated in Figure 6-15.

```
              Imagination is more
Read position ──→ important than knowledge.
              Albert Einstein
```

Figure 6-15 Read position after first line is read

If the ReadLine method is called again, the second line will be read from the file and the file's read position will be advanced to the third line. After all the lines have been read, the read position will be at the end of the file.

 NOTE: The string that is returned from the ReadLine method will not contain the newline character.

Closing the File

When the program is finished reading data from the file, it must close the file. To close the file, use the StreamReader class Close method. Here is an example of the method's use:

```
inputFile.Close();
```

Detecting the End of a File

Quite often a program must read the contents of a file without knowing the number of items that are stored in the file. For example, the MyFriends.txt file that was created by the program in Code Listing 6-11 can have any number of names stored in it. This is because the program asks the user for the number of friends that he or she has. If the user enters 5 for the number of friends, the program creates a file with five names in it. If the user enters 100, the program creates a file with 100 names in it.

You can determine when the end of a file has been reached by testing the value returned from the StreamReader object's ReadLine method. If the last item has been read and the end of the file has been reached, the ReadLine method returns null. Here is an example of code that opens a file and displays all of the items stored in it. Assume that filename references a string object containing the file's name.

```
StreamReader inputFile = new StreamReader(filename);
string str;
// Read the first item.
str = inputFile.ReadLine();
// If an item was read, display it and read the remaining items.
while (str != null)
{
    Console.WriteLine(str);
    str = inputFile.ReadLine();
}
inputFile.Close();
```

Notice that after the file is opened, this code reads the first item. If the ReadLine method returned null, the loop will not execute. If the ReadLine method returned a value, the loop displays it and reads the next item. This continues until the ReadLine method returns null. Figure 6-16 shows the logic of reading a file until the end is reached.

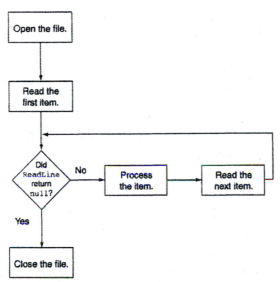

Figure 6-16   Logic of reading a file until the end is reached

An Example Program

Let's look at an example program that reads data from a file. The program in Code Listing 6-12 reads the file containing the names of your friends, which was created by the program in Code Listing 6-11.

Code Listing 6-12   FileReadDemo.cs

```
1 /*
2    This program reads data from a file.
3 */
4
5 using System;
6 using System.IO;
7
```

(code listing continues)

Code Listing 6-12 FileReadDemo.cs *(continued)*

```
 8 public class FileReadDemo
 9 {
10    public static void Main()
11    {
12       string fileName,        // File name
13              friendName;       // Friend's name
14
15       // Get the filename.
16       Console.Write("Enter the filename: ");
17       fileName = Console.ReadLine();
18
19       // Open the file.
20       StreamReader inputFile = new StreamReader(fileName);
21
22       // Read the first name from the file.
23       friendName = inputFile.ReadLine();
24
25       // If a name was read, display it and
26       // read the remaining names.
27       while (friendName != null)
28       {
29          // Display the last name read.
30          Console.WriteLine(friendName);
31
32          // Read the next name.
33          friendName = inputFile.ReadLine();
34       }
35
36       // Close the file.
37       inputFile.Close();
38    }
39 }
```

Program Output with Example Input

Enter the filename: **C:\\MyFriends.txt [Enter]**
Joe
Rose
Greg
Kirk
Renee

Review

Let's quickly review the steps necessary when writing a program that reads data from a file:

1. Place the using System.IO statement in the top section of your program.

2. Create a StreamReader object and pass the name of the file as a string to the constructor.

3. Use the StreamReader object's ReadLine method to read a line from the file. The method returns the line of data as a string. If the end of the file has been reached, the method returns null.

4. When finished writing to the file, use the StreamReader object's Close method to close the file.

Converting string Values to Numbers

The StreamReader class's ReadLine method returns a line from a file as a string. If the file contains numbers, and you wish to perform arithmetic with them, you will have to convert them from string objects to a numeric data type. You use the Convert class methods that you learned about in Chapter 2 to perform the conversion. These methods are ToInt32, ToDouble, and so forth.

The program in Code Listing 6-13 demonstrates. It reads the contents of a file, Numbers.txt, which contains a series of numbers. The file's contents are shown in Figure 6-17. In the program, the file is opened, the numbers are read, and a total of the numbers is stored in the sum field.

Code Listing 6-13 FileSum.cs

```
1 /*
2    This program reads a series of numbers from a file and
3    accumulates their sum.
4 */
5
6 using System;
7 using System.IO;
8
9 public class FileSum
10 {
11    public static void Main()
12    {
13        double sum;   // Accumulator
14        string str;   // To hold a line read from the file
15
16        // Open the file.
17        StreamReader inputFile = new StreamReader("Numbers.txt");
18
19        // Initialize the accumulator.
20        sum = 0.0;
21
22        // Read the first number.
23        str = inputFile.ReadLine();
24
```

(code listing continues)

Code Listing 6-13 FileSum.cs *(continued)*

```
25          // If the first item was successfully read,
26          // add it to the accumulator and read the
27          // remaining numbers.
28          while (str != null)
29          {
30              sum = sum + Convert.ToDouble(str);
31              str = inputFile.ReadLine();
32          }
33
34          // Close the file.
35          inputFile.Close();
36
37          // Display the sum of the numbers.
38          Console.WriteLine("The sum of the numbers in Numbers.txt is
            {0}", sum);
39      }
40 }
```

Program Output

The sum of the numbers in Numbers.txt is 41.4

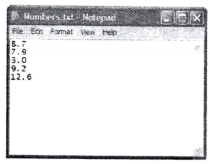

Figure 6-17 Contents of `Numbers.txt`

 CHECKPOINT

6.16 What is the difference between an input file and an output file?

6.17 What using statement must you use in a program that performs file operations?

6.18 What class do you use in order to write data to a file?

6.19 Write code that does the following: Opens a file named `MyName.txt`, writes your first name to the file, and closes the file.

6.20 What class do you use in order to read data from a file?

6.21 Write code that does the following: Opens a file named `MyName.txt`, reads the first line from the file and displays it, and closes the file.

6.11   Common Errors

- **Using the increment or decrement operator in the wrong mode.** When the increment or decrement operator is placed in front of (to the left of) its operand, it is used in prefix mode. When either of these operators are placed behind (to the right of) their operand, they are used in postfix mode.

- **Forgetting to enclose the** boolean **expression in a** while **loop or a** do-while **loop inside parentheses.**

- **Placing a semicolon at the end of a** while **or** for **loop's header.** When you write a semicolon at the end of a while or for loop's header, C# assumes that the conditionally executed statement is a null or empty statement. This usually results in an infinite loop.

- **Forgetting to write the semicolon at the end of the** do-while **loop.** The do-while loop must be terminated with a semicolon.

- **Forgetting to enclose multiple statements in the body of a loop in braces.** Normally a loop conditionally executes only one statement. To conditionally execute more than one statement, you must place the statements in braces.

- **Using commas instead of semicolons to separate the initialization, test, and update expressions in a** for **loop.**

- **Forgetting to write code in the body of a** while **or** do-while **loop that modifies the loop control variable.** If a while or do-while loop's boolean expression never becomes false, the loop will repeat indefinitely. You must have code in the body of the loop that modifies the loop control variable so that the boolean expression will at some point become false.

- **Using a sentinel value that can also be a valid data value.** Remember, a sentinel is a special value that cannot be mistaken as a member of a list of data items and signals that there are no more data items from the list to be processed. If you choose as a sentinel a value that might also appear in the list, the loop will prematurely terminate if it encounters the value in the list.

- **Forgetting to initialize an accumulator to zero.** In order for an accumulator to keep a correct running total, it must be initialized to zero before any values are added to it.

Review Questions and Exercises

Multiple Choice and True/False

1. What will the WriteLine statement in the following program segment display?

```
int x = 5;
    Console.WriteLine(x++);
```

   a) 5   b) 6

   c) 0   d) None of these

2. What will the WriteLine statement in the following program segment display?

```
int x = 5;
    Console.WriteLine(++x);
```

   a) 5   b) 6

   c) 0   d) None of these

3. In the expression number++, the ++ operator is in what mode?

   a) prefix   b) pretest

   c) postfix   d) posttest

4. What is each repetition of a loop is known as?

   a) cycle   b) revolution

   c) orbit   d) iteration

5. This is a variable that controls the number of iterations performed by a loop.

   a) loop control variable   b) accumulator

   c) iteration register variable   d) repetition meter

6. The while loop is this type of loop.

   a) pretest   b) posttest

   c) prefix   d) postfix

7. The do-while loop is this type of loop.

   a) pretest   b) posttest

   c) prefix   d) postfix

8. The for loop is this type of loop.

   a) pretest   b) posttest

   c) prefix   d) postfix

9. This type of loop has no way of ending and repeats until the program is interrupted.

    a) indeterminate   b) interminable

    c) infinite   d) timeless

10. This type of loop always executes at least one time.

    a) `while`   b) `do-while`

    c) `for`   d) Any of these

11. This expression is executed by the `for` loop only once, regardless of the number of iterations.

    a) initialization expression   b) test expression

    c) update expression   d) pre-increment expression

12. This is a variable that keeps a running total.

    a) sentinel   b) sum

    c) total   d) accumulator

13. This a special value that signals when there are no more items from a list of items to be processed. This value cannot be mistaken as an item from the list.

    a) sentinel   b) flag7

    c) signal   d) accumulator

14. To open a file for writing, you use the following class.

    a) `StreamWriter`   b) `FileOpen`

    c) `OutputFile`   d) `StreamReader`

15. To open a file for reading, you use the following class.

    a) `StreamWriter`   b) `FileOpen`

    c) `InputFile`   d) `StreamReader`

16. When a program is finished using a file, it should do this.

    a) Erase the file.   b) Close the file.

    c) Throw an exception.   d) Reset the read position.

17. This class allows you to use the `Write` and `WriteLine` methods to write data to a file.

    a) `StreamWriter`   b) `StreamReader`

    c) `OutputFile`   d) `PrintWriter`

18. This class allows you to read a line from a file.

    a) `StreamWriter`   b) `BufferedReader`

    c) `InputFile`   d) `StreamReader`

19. True or False: The while loop is a pretest loop.

20. True or False: The do-while loop is a pretest loop.

21. True or False: The for loop is a posttest loop.

22. True or False: It is not necessary to initialize accumulator variables.

23. True or False: One limitation of the for loop is that only one variable may be initialized in the initialization expression.

24. True or False: A variable may be defined in the initialization expression of the for loop.

25. True or False: In a nested loop, the inner loop goes through all of its iterations for every single iteration of the outer loop.

26. True or False: To calculate the total number of iterations of a nested loop, add the number of iterations of all the loops.

Find the Error

Find the errors in the following code.

1.
```
// This code contains ERRORS!
// Add two numbers entered by the user
int num1, num2;
char again;
string input;

while (again == 'y' || again == 'Y')
    Console.Write("Enter a number: ");
    input = Console.ReadLine();
    num1 = Convert.ToInt32(input);
    Console.Write("Enter another number: ";
    input = Console.ReadLine();
    num2 = Convert.ToInt32(input);
    Console.WriteLine("Their sum is {0}",(num1 + num2));
    Console.WriteLine("Do you want to do this again? ";
    input = Console.ReadLine();
    again = input[0];
```

2.
```
// This code contains ERRORS!
int count = 1, total;
while (count <= 100)
    total += count;
Console.Write("The sum of the numbers 1 - 100 is ");
Console.WriteLine(total);
```

3. `// This code contains ERRORS!`
```
int choice, num1, num2;
string input;

do
{
    Console.Write("Enter a number: ");
    input = Console.ReadLine();
    num1 = Convert.ToInt32(input);
    Console.Write("Enter another number: ");
    input = Console.ReadLine();
    num2 = Convert.ToInt32(input);
    Console.WriteLine("Their sum is {0}", (num1 + num2));
    Console.WriteLine("Do you want to do this again? ");
    Console.Write("1 = yes, 0 = no  ");
    input = Console.ReadLine();
    choice = Convert.ToInt32(input);
} while (choice = 1)
```

4. `// This code contains ERRORS!`
```
// Print the numbers 1 through 10.
for (int count = 1, count <= 10, count++;)
{
    Console.WriteLine(count);
    count++;
}
```

Algorithm Workbench

1. Write a `while` loop that lets the user enter a number. The number should be multiplied by 10, and the result stored in the variable `product`. The loop should iterate as long as `product` contains a value less than 100.

2. Write a `do-while` loop that asks the user to enter two numbers. The numbers should be added and the sum displayed. The user should be asked if he or she wishes to perform the operation again. If so, the loop should repeat; otherwise it should terminate.

3. Write a `for` loop that displays the following set of numbers:

   `0, 10, 20, 30, 40, 50 . . . 1000`

4. Write a loop that asks the user to enter a number. The loop should iterate 10 times and keep a running total of the numbers entered.

5. Write a `for` loop that calculates the total of the following series of numbers:

   $$\frac{1}{30} + \frac{2}{29} + \frac{3}{28} + \dots \frac{30}{1}$$

6. Write a nested loop that displays 10 rows of '#' characters. There should be 15 '#' characters in each row.

7. Convert the `while` loop in the following code to a `do-while` loop:

```
string input;
int x = 1;
while (x > 0)
{
    Console.Write("Enter a number: ");
    input = Console.ReadLine();
    x = Convert.ToInt32(input);
}
```

8. Convert the do-while loop in the following code to a `while` loop:

```
string input;
char sure;
do
{
    Console.Write("Are you sure you want to quit? ";
    input = Console.readLine();
    sure = input[0];
} while (sure != 'Y' && sure != 'N');
```

9. Convert the following `while` loop to a `for` loop:

```
int count = 0;
while (count > 50)
{
    Console.WriteLine("count is {0}", count);
    count++;
}
```

10. Convert the following `for` loop to a `while` loop:

```
for (int x = 50; x > 0; x--)
{
    Console.WriteLine("{0} seconds to go.",x);
}
```

11. Write an input validation loop that asks the user to enter a number in the range of 1 through 6.

12. Write an input validation loop that asks the user to enter the words "yes" or "no."

13. Write code that does the following: Opens a file named `NumberList.txt`, uses a loop to write the numbers one through 100 to the file, and then closes the file.

14. Write code that does the following: Opens the `NumberList.txt` file that was created by the code in Question 13, reads all of the numbers from the file and displays them, and then closes the file.

15. Modify the code you wrote in Question 14 so it adds all of the numbers read from the file and displays their total.

16. Write code that opens a file named `NumberList.txt` for writing, but does not erase the file's contents if it already exists.

Short Answer

1. Briefly describe the difference between the prefix and postfix modes used by the increment and decrement operators.

2. Why should you indent the statements in the body of a loop?

3. Describe the difference between pretest loops and posttest loops.

4. Why are the statements in the body of a loop called conditionally executed statements?

5. Describe the difference between the `while` loop and the do-while loop.

6. Which loop should you use in situations where you wish the loop to repeat until the `boolean` expression is `false`, and the loop should not execute if the test expression is `false` to begin with?

7. Which loop should you use in situations where you wish the loop to repeat until the `boolean` expression is `false`, but the loop should execute at least one time?

8. Which loop should you use when you know the number of required iterations?

9. Why is it critical that accumulator variables be properly initialized?

10. What is an infinite loop? Write the code for an infinite loop.

11. Describe a programming problem that would require the use of an accumulator.

12. What does it mean to let the user control a loop?

13. What is the advantage of using a sentinel?

14. Why must the value chosen for use as a sentinel be carefully selected?

15. Describe a programming problem requiring the use of nested loops.

16. What is a file's read position? Where is the read position when a file is first opened for reading?

17. What is the difference between the `Write` and the `WriteLine` methods for writing data to a file?

18. What does the `ReadLine` method return when the end of the file has been reached?

19. What does it mean to append data to a file?

20. What is the difference between the following two statements?

```
StreamWriter fw = new StreamWriter("MyData.txt");
StreamWriter fw = new StreamWriter("MyData.txt", true);
```

Programming Challenges

General Requirements: Each program or class should have a block of comments at the top. The comments should contain your name, the chapter the assignment appeared in, and the assignment number and name. Here is an example:

```
/*
    Written by Ben Johnson
    Chapter 6
    Programming Challenge 1: Sum of Numbers
*/
```

1. Sum of Numbers

Write a program that asks the user for a positive nonzero integer value. The program should use a loop to get the sum of all the integers from 1 up to the number entered. For example, if the user enters 50, the loop will find the sum of 1, 2, 3, 4, ... 50.

2. Distance Traveled

The distance a vehicle travels can be calculated as follows:

*Distance = Speed * Time*

For example, if a train travels 40 miles per hour for three hours, the distance traveled is 120 miles. Write a program that asks for the speed of a vehicle (in miles per hour) and the number of hours it has traveled. It should use a loop to display the distance a vehicle has traveled for each hour of a time period specified by the user. For example, if a vehicle is traveling at 40 mph for a thee-hour time period, it should display a report similar to the one shown here.

```
Hour          Distance Traveled
--------------------------------
1                    40
2                    80
3                   120
```

Input Validation: Do not accept a negative number for speed and do not accept any value less than 1 for time traveled.

3. Distance File

Modify the program you wrote for Programming Challenge 2 (Distance Traveled) so it writes the report to a file instead of the screen. Open the file in Notepad or another text editor to confirm the output.

4. Pennies for Pay

Write a program that calculates the amount a person would earn over a period of time if his or her salary were one penny the first day, two pennies the second day, and so on, doubling each day. The program should display a table showing the salary for each day and the total pay at the end of the period. The output should be displayed in a dollar amount, not in the number of pennies.

Input Validation: Do not accept a number less than 1 for the number of days worked.

5. Letter Counter

Write a program that asks the user to enter a string, and then asks the user to enter a character. The program should count and display the number of times that the specified character appears in the string.

6. File Letter Counter

Write a program that asks the user to enter the name of a file, and then asks the user to enter a character. The program should count and display the number of times that the specified character appears in the file. Use Notepad or another text editor to create a simple file that can be used to test the program.

7. Hotel Occupancy

A hotel's occupancy rate is calculated as follows:

Occupancy rate = number of rooms occupied number of vacant rooms

Write a program that calculates the occupancy rate for each floor of a hotel. The program should start by asking for the number of floors that the hotel has. A loop should then iterate once for each floor. During each iteration, the loop should ask the user for the number of rooms on the floor and the number of them that are occupied. After all the iterations, the program should display the number of rooms the hotel has, the number of them that are occupied, the number that are vacant, and the occupancy rate for the hotel.

Input Validation: Do not accept a value less than 1 for the number of floors. Do not accept a number less than 10 for the number of rooms on a floor.

8. Average Rainfall

Write a program that uses nested loops to collect data and calculate the average rainfall over a period of years. The program should first ask for the number of years. The outer loop will iterate once for each year. The inner loop will iterate 12 times, once for each month. Each iteration of the inner loop will ask the user for the inches of rainfall for that month. After all iterations, the program should display the number of months, the total inches of rainfall, and the average rainfall per month for the entire period.

Input Validation: Do not accept a number less than 1 for the number of years. Do not accept negative numbers for the monthly rainfall.

9. Population

Write a program that will predict the size of a population of organisms. The program should ask for the starting number of organisms, their average daily population increase (as a percentage), and the number of days they will multiply. For example, a population might begin with two organisms, have an average daily increase of 50%, and will be allowed to multiply for seven days. The program should use a loop to display the size of the population for each day.

Input Validation: Do not accept a number less than 2 for the starting size of the population. Do not accept a negative number for average daily population increase. Do not accept a number less than 1 for the number of days they will multiply.

10. Largest and Smallest

Write a program with a loop that lets the user enter a series of integers. The user should enter 99 to signal the end of the series. After all the numbers have been entered, the program should display the largest and smallest numbers entered.

11. Centigrade to Fahrenheit Table

Write a program that displays a table of the centigrade temperatures 0 through 20 and their Fahrenheit equivalents. The formula for converting a temperature from centigrade to Fahrenheit is

$$F = \frac{9}{5}C + 32$$

where F is the Fahrenheit temperature and C is the centigrade temperature. Your program must use a loop to display the table.

12. Bar Chart

Write a program that asks the user to enter today's sales for five stores. The program should then display a bar chart comparing each store's sales. Create each bar in the bar chart by displaying a row of asterisks. Each asterisk should represent $100 of sales. Here is an example of the program's output.

```
Enter today's sales for store 1: 1000 [Enter]
Enter today's sales for store 2: 1200 [Enter]
Enter today's sales for store 3: 1800 [Enter]
Enter today's sales for store 4: 800 [Enter]
Enter today's sales for store 5: 1900 [Enter]

SALES BAR CHART
Store 1: **********
Store 2: ************
Store 3: ******************
Store 4: ********
Store 5: *******************
```

13. File Head Display

Write a program that asks the user for the name of a file. The program should display only the first five lines of the file's contents. If the file contains fewer than five lines, it should display the file's entire contents. Write a program that asks the user for the name of a file. The program should display the contents of the file with each line preceded with a line number followed by a colon. The line numbering should start at 1.

14. Uppercase File Converter

Write a program that asks the user for the names of two files. The first file should be opened for reading and the second file should be opened for writing. The program should read the contents of the first file, change all characters to uppercase, and store the results in the second file. The second file will be a copy of the first file, except all the characters will be uppercase. Use Notepad or another text editor to create a simple file that can be used to test the program.

7

Arrays

Chapter Objectives

- To write code that creates arrays and accesses the elements of arrays
- To process arrays using the foreach loop
- To pass arrays as arguments to methods
- To write methods that return references to arrays
- To learn how to declare arrays with more than one dimension
- To understand searching and sorting algorithms.
- To accept and process command-line arguments

Topics in this Chapter

7.1	Introduction to Arrays		7.7	Searching and Sorting
7.2	Processing Array Contents		7.8	Multidimensional Arrays
7.3	The foreach Loop		7.9	Command-Line Arguments
7.4	Passing Arrays as Arguments to Methods		7.10	Common Errors
7.5	Returning Arrays from Methods			Review Questions and Exercises
7.6	Arrays of Objects			

 Case Study on CD-ROM: The PinTester Class

7.1 Introduction to Arrays

CONCEPT Unlike regular variables, arrays can hold multiple values.

The primitive variables you have worked with so far are designed to hold only one value at a time. Each of the variable declarations in Figure 7-1 causes only enough memory to be reserved to hold one value of the specified data type.

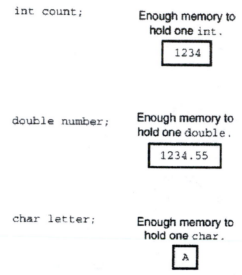

Figure 7-1 Variable declarations and their memory allocations

An array, however, is an object that can store a group of values, all of the same type. Creating and using an array in C# is similar to creating and using any other type of object: You declare a reference variable and use the new key word to create an instance of the array in memory. Here is an example of a statement that declares an array reference variable:

```
int[] numbers;
```

This statement declares numbers as an array reference variable. The numbers variable can reference an array of int values. Notice that this statement looks like a regular int variable declaration except for the set of brackets that appear after the key word int. The brackets indicate that this variable is a reference to an int array. Declaring an array reference variable does not create an array. The next step in the process is to use the new key word to create an array and assign its address to the numbers variable. The following statement shows an example.

```
numbers = new int[6];
```

The number inside the brackets is the array's *size declarator*. It indicates the number of *elements*, or values, the array can hold. When this statement is executed, numbers will reference an array that can hold six elements, each one an int. This is shown in Figure 7-2.

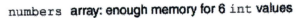

numbers **array: enough memory for 6 int values**

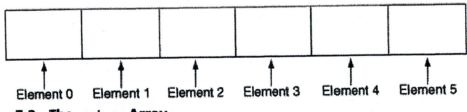

Element 0　Element 1　Element 2　Element 3　Element 4　Element 5

Figure 7-2　The numbers Array

As with any other type of object, it is possible to declare a reference variable and create an instance of an array with one statement. Here is an example:

```
int[] numbers = new int[6];
```

Arrays of any data type can be declared. The following are all valid array declarations:

```
decimal[] money = new decimal[100];
char[] letters = new char[41];
long[] units = new long[50];
double[] sizes = new double[1200];
```

An array's size declarator must be a non-negative integer expression. It can be either a literal value, as shown in the previous examples, or a variable. It is a common practice to use a const variable as a size declarator. Here is an example:

```
const int NUMELEMENTS = 6;
int[] numbers = new int[NUMELEMENTS];
```

This practice can make programs easier to maintain. When we store the size of an array in a variable, we can use the variable instead of a literal number when we refer to the size of the array. If we ever need to change the array's size, we need only to change the value of the variable. The variable should be const so its contents cannot be changed during the program's execution.

 NOTE: It is illegal in C# to place the brackets after the array name:

```
decimal money[] = new decimal[100];   //Illegal
```

Accessing Array Elements

Although an array has only one name, the elements in the array may be accessed and used as individual variables. This is possible because each element is assigned a number known as a *subscript*. A subscript is used as an index to pinpoint a specific element within an array. The first element is assigned the subscript 0, the second element is assigned 1, and so forth. The six elements in the numbers array (described earlier) would have the subscripts 0 through 5. This is shown in Figure 7-3.

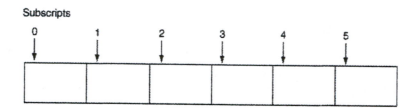

Subscripts

The numbers array has six elements, numbered 0 through 5.

Figure 7-3 Subscripts for the numbers array

Subscript numbering always starts at zero. The subscript of the last element in an array is one less than the total number of elements in the array. This means that for the numbers array, which has six elements, 5 is the subscript for the last element.

Each element in the numbers array, when accessed by its subscript, can be used as an int variable. For example, look at the following code. The first statement stores 20 in the first element of the array (element 0), and the second statement stores 30 in the fourth element (element 3).

```
numbers[0] = 20;
numbers[3] = 30;
```

 NOTE: The expression numbers[0] is pronounced "numbers sub zero." You would read these assignment statements as "numbers sub zero is assigned twenty" and "numbers sub three is assigned thirty."

Figure 7-4 illustrates the contents of the array after these statements execute.

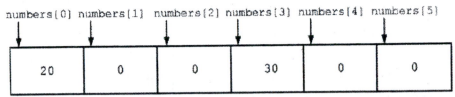

Figure 7-4 Contents of the array after 20 is assigned to numbers[0] and 30 is assigned to numbers[3]

NOTES: C# by default initializes numeric array elements with 0. In Figure 7-4, values have not been stored in elements 1, 2, 4, and 5, so they are shown as a 0.

An array subscript in C# must be an integer type compatible and positive..

```
numbers[2.5] = 0;          //Illegal
```

By this point you should understand the difference between the array size declarator and a subscript. When you use the new key word to create an array object, the number inside the brackets is the size declarator. It indicates the number of elements that the array has. The number inside the brackets in an assignment statement or any statement that works with the contents of an array is a subscript. It is used to access a specific element in the array.

Inputting and Outputting Array Contents

You can read values from the keyboard and store them in an array element just as you can a regular variable. You can also output the contents of an array element with Write and WriteLine. Code Listing 7-1 shows an array being used store and display values entered by the user. Figure 7-5 shows the contents of the hours array with the values entered by the user in the example output.

Code Listing 7-1 ArrayDemo1.cs ∫

```
1   /*
2      This program shows values being stored in an array's
3      elements and displayed.
4   */
5
6   using System;
7
```

(code listing continues)

Code Listing 7-1　**ArrayDemo1.cs** ∫(continued)

```
8    public class ArrayDemo1
9    {
10      public static void Main()
11      {
12
13        const int EMPLOYEES = 3;              // Number of
                 employees
14        int[] hours = new int[EMPLOYEES];    // Array of
                 hours
15
16        // Get the hours for each employee.
17        Console.WriteLine("Enter the hours worked by {0}
                 employees.", EMPLOYEES);
18
19        Console.Write("Employee 1: ");
20        hours[0] = Convert.ToInt32(Console.ReadLine());
21
22        Console.Write("Employee 2: ");
23        hours[1] = Convert.ToInt32(Console.ReadLine());
24
25        Console.Write("Employee 3: ");
26        hours[2] = Convert.ToInt32(Console.ReadLine());
27
28        // Display the values entered.
29        Console.WriteLine("The hours you entered are:");
30        Console.WriteLine(hours[0]);
31        Console.WriteLine(hours[1]);
32        Console.WriteLine(hours[2]);
33      }
34    }
```

Program Output with Example Input

```
Enter the hours worked by 3 employees.
Employee 1: 40 [Enter]
Employee 2: 20 [Enter]
Employee 3: 15 [Enter]
The hours you entered are:
40
20
15
```

Subscript numbers can be stored in variables. This makes it possible to use a loop to "cycle through" an entire array, performing the same operation on each element. For example, Code Listing 7-1 could be simplified by using two for loops: one for inputting the values into the array and the other for displaying the contents of the array. This is shown in Code Listing 7-2.

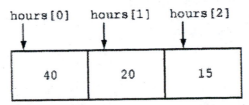

Figure 7-5 Contents of the hours **array**

Code Listing 7-2 ArrayDemo2.cs

```
1   /*
2       This program shows an array being processed with loops.
3   */
4
5   using System;
6
7   public class ArrayDemo2
8   {
9    public static void Main()
10     {
11
12         const int EMPLOYEES = 3;           // Number of
                   employees
13         int[] hours = new int[EMPLOYEES];  // Array of hours
14
15       // Get the hours for each employee.
16       Console.WriteLine("Enter the hours worked by {0}
                   employees", EMPLOYEES);
17
18       for (int i = 0; i < EMPLOYEES; i++)
19       {
20           Console.Write("Employee {0}: ", (i + 1));
21
22           hours[i] = Convert.ToInt32(Console.ReadLine());
23       }
24
25       // Display the values entered.
26       Console.WriteLine("The hours you entered are:");
27
28       for (int i = 0; i < EMPLOYEES; i++)
29           Console.WriteLine(hours[i]);
30     }
31   }
```

Code Listing 7-2 ArrayDemo2.cs *(continued)*

Program Output with Example Input
```
Enter the hours worked by 3 employees.
Employee 1: 40 [Enter]
Employee 2: 20 [Enter]
Employee 3: 15 [Enter]
The hours you entered are:
40
20
15
```

Let's take a closer look at the first loop in this program, specifically at lines 18 through 23:

```
for (int i = 0; i < EMPLOYEES; i++)
{
    Console.WriteLine("Employee {0}: ", (i + 1));

    hours[i] = Convert.ToInt32(Console.ReadLine());
}
```

Notice that the loop's control variable, i, is used as a subscript in the following statement body of the loop:

```
hours[i] = Convert.ToInt32(Console.ReadLine());
```

The variable i starts at 0. So, during the first iteration, the user's input is stored in hours[0]. During the next iteration, the user's input is stored in hours[1]. This continues until values have been stored in all of the elements of the array. Notice that the loop correctly starts and ends the control variable with valid subscript values (0 through 2), as illustrated in Figure 7-6. This ensures that only valid subscripts are used.

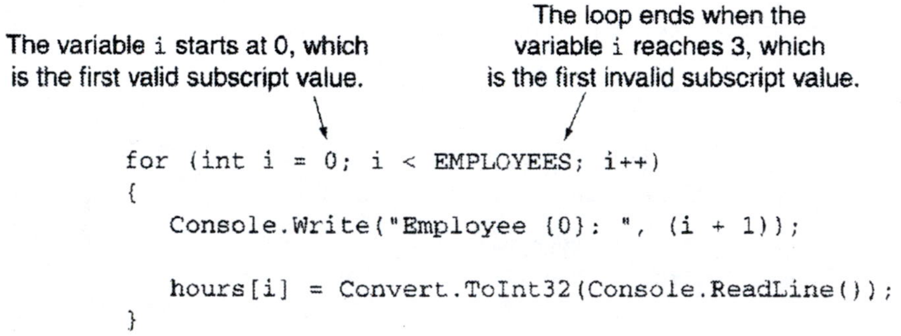

The variable i starts at 0, which is the first valid subscript value.

The loop ends when the variable i reaches 3, which is the first invalid subscript value.

```
for (int i = 0; i < EMPLOYEES; i++)
{
    Console.Write("Employee {0}: ", (i + 1));

    hours[i] = Convert.ToInt32(Console.ReadLine());
}
```

Figure 7-6 Annotated loop

NOTE: We have used a rather nondescript name, i, for the control variable in this program's loops. You might think of i as standing for "index" because the variable serves as an index into the array. Normally you should use variable names that are more self-documenting than this. However, because the use of this variable is limited to the loop in which it is declared, and because the variable's purpose is evident from the context in which it is being used, many programmers will agree that the name is adequate.

Watch Out for Off-by-One Errors

Because array subscripts start at 0 rather than 1, you have to be careful not to perform an *off-by-one error*. For example, look at the following code:

```
// This code has an off-by-one error.
int[] numbers = new int[100];
for (int i = 1; i <= 100; i++)
    numbers[i] = 99;
```

The intent of this code is to create an array of integers with 100 elements, and store the value 99 in each element. However, this code has an off-by-one error. The loop uses its control variable, i, as a subscript with the numbers array. During the loop's execution, the variable i takes on the values 1 through 100, when it should take on the values 0 through 99. As a result, the first element, which is at subscript 0, is skipped. In addition, the loop attempts to use 100 as a subscript during the last iteration. Because 100 is an invalid subscript, the program will crash.

Array Initialization

Like regular variables, C# allows you to initialize an array's elements when you create the array. Here is an example:

```
int[] days = {31, 28, 31, 30, 31, 30, 31, 31, 30, 31, 30, 31};
```

This statement declares the reference variable days, creates an array in memory, and stores initial values in the array. The series of values inside the braces and separated with commas is called an *initialization list*. These values are stored in the array elements in the order they appear in the list. (The first value, 31, is stored in days[0], the second value, 28, is stored in days[1], and so forth.) Note that you do *not* use the new key word when you use an initialization list. C# automatically creates the array and stores the values in the initialization list in it.

The C# compiler determines the size of the array by the number of items in the initialization list. Because there are 12 items in the example statement's initialization list, the array will have 12 elements. The program in Code Listing 7-3 demonstrates an array being initialized.

Code Listing 7-3 ArrayInitialization.cs

```
1    /*
2        This program shows an array being initialized.
3    */
4
5    using System;
6    public class ArrayInitialization
7    {
8      public static void Main()
9        {
10          int[] days = new int[]{31, 28, 31, 30, 31, 30, 31,
                31, 30, 31, 30, 31};
11
12          for (int i = 0; i < 12; i++)
13          {
14            Console.WriteLine("Month {0} has {1} days.", (i +
                1), days[i]);
15          }
16      }
17    }
```

Program Output

```
Month 1 has 31 days.
Month 2 has 28 days.
Month 3 has 31 days.
Month 4 has 30 days.
Month 5 has 31 days.
Month 6 has 30 days.
Month 7 has 31 days.
Month 8 has 31 days.
Month 9 has 30 days.
Month 10 has 31 days.
Month 11 has 30 days.
Month 12 has 31 days.
```

 NOTE: You could also initialize arrays in C# in two other ways:

```
int[] days = new int[12]{31, 28, 31, 30, 31, 30, 31, 31, 30, 31,
                            30, 31};
```

OR

```
int[] days = new int[]{31, 28, 31, 30, 31, 30, 31, 31, 30, 31,
                            30, 31};
```

CHECKPOINT

7.1 Write statements that create the following arrays.

a) A 100-element `int` array referenced by the variable `employeeNumbers`.

b) A 25-element `decimal` array referenced by the variable `payRates`.

c) A 14-element `float` array referenced by the variable `miles`.

d) A 1000-element `char` array referenced by the variable `letters`.

7.2 What's wrong with the following array declarations?

```
int[] readings = new int[-1];
double[] measurements = new double[4.5];
```

7.3 What would the valid subscript values be in a four-element array of `doubles`?

7.4 What is the difference between an array's size declarator and a subscript?

7.5 What does it mean for a subscript to be out of bounds?

7.6 What happens in C# when a program tries to use a subscript that is out-of-bounds?

7.7 What is the output of the following code?

```
int[] values = new int[5];

for (int count = 0; count < 5; count++)
    values[count] = count + 1;

for (int count = 0; count < 5; count++)
    Console.WriteLine(values[count]);
```

7.8 Write a statement that creates and initializes a `double` array with the following values: 1.7, 6.4, 8.9, 3.1, and 9.2. How many elements are in the array?

7.2 Processing Array Contents

CONCEPT | Individual array elements are processed like any other type of variable.

Processing array elements is no different than processing other variables. For example, the following statement multiplies `hours[3]` by the variable `payRate`:

```
grossPay = hours[3] * payRate;
```

The following are examples of pre-increment and post-increment operations on array elements:

```
int[] score = {7, 8, 9, 10, 11};
++score[2];    // Pre-increment operation
score[4]++;    // Post-increment operation
```

When using increment and decrement operators, be careful not to use the operator on the subscript when you intend to use it on the array element. For example, the following statement decrements the variable count, but does nothing to the value stored in the array element amount[count]:

```
amount[count--];
```

Code Listing 7-4 demonstrates the use of array elements in a simple mathematical statement. A loop steps through each element of the array, using the elements to calculate the gross pay of five employees.

Code Listing 7-4   PayArray.cs

```
1    /*
2        This program stores in an array the hours worked by
3        five employees who all make the same hourly wage.
4    */
5
6    using System;
7
8    public class PayArray
9    {
10      public static void Main()
11      {
12
13         const int EMPLOYEES = 5;             // Number of
                  employees
14         int[] hours = new int[EMPLOYEES];    // Array of hours
15         double payRate, rate                 // Hourly pay
              rate
16             grossPay;                        // Gross pay
17
```

(code listing continues)

Code Listing 7-4 PayArray.cs *(continued)*

```
18              // Get the hours worked by each employee.
19              Console.WriteLine("Enter the hours worked by five " +
20                                 "employees who all earn the same " 
21                              + "hourly rate.");
22
23              for (int i = 0; i < EMPLOYEES; i++)
24              {
25                 Console.Write("Employee #{0}: ", (i + 1));
26
27                 hours[i] = Convert.ToInt32(Console.ReadLine());
28              }
29
30              // Get each the hourly pay rate.
31
32              Console.Write("Enter the hourly rate for each
                       employee: ");
33
34              payRate = Convert.ToDouble(Console.ReadLine());
35
36              // Display each employee's gross pay.
37
38              Console.WriteLine( "Here is the gross pay for each
                       employee:");
39              for (int i = 0; i < EMPLOYEES; i++)
40              {
41                 grossPay = hours[i] * payRate;
42                 Console.WriteLine("Employee #{0} {1:C}",(i + 1),
                       grossPay);
43              }
44        }
45  }
```

Program Output with Example Input
```
Enter the hours worked by five employees who all earn
the same hourly rate.
Employee #1: 10[Enter]
Employee #2: 20[Enter]
Employee #3: 30[Enter]
Employee #4: 40[Enter]
Employee #5: 50[Enter]
Enter the hourly rate for each employee: 10[Enter]
Here is the gross pay for each employee:
Employee #1: $100.00
Employee #2: $200.00
Employee #3: $300.00
Employee #4: $400.00
Employee #5: $500.00
```

In line 41, the following statement assigns the value of hours[i] times payRate to the grossPay variable:

```
grossPay = hours[i] * payRate;
```

Array elements may also be used in relational expressions. For example, the following if statement determines whether cost[20] is less than cost[0]:

```
if (cost[20] < cost[0])
```

And the following while loop iterates as long as value[count] does not equal 0:

```
while (value[count] != 0)
{
    Statements
}
```

On the Student CD you will find the file Overtime.cs, which is a modification of the PayArray.cs program in Code Listing 7-5. The Overtime.cs program includes overtime wages in the gross pay. If an employee works more than 40 hours, an overtime pay rate of 1.5 times the regular pay rate is used for the excess hours.

Array Length

Each array in C# has a public field named Length. This field contains the number of elements in the array. For example, consider an array created by the following statement:

```
double[] temperatures = new double[25];
```

Because the temperatures array has 25 elements, the following statement would assign 25 to the variable size.

```
size = temperatures.Length;
```

The Length field can be useful when processing the entire contents of an array. For example, the following loop steps through an array and displays the contents of each element. The array's Length field is used in the test expression as the upper limit for the loop control variable:

```
for (int i = 0; i < temperatures.Length; i++)
    Console.WriteLine(temperatures[i]);
```

 WARNING! Be careful not to cause an off-by-one error when using the Length field as the upper limit of a subscript. The Length field contains the number of elements that an array has. The largest subscript that an array has is Length - 1.

 NOTE: In C# you cannot change the value of an array's Length field.

Letting the User Specify an Array's Size

C# allows you to use an integer variable to specify an array's size declarator. This makes it possible to allow the user to specify an array's size. Code Listing 7-5 demonstrates this, as well as the use of the Length field. It stores a number of test scores in an array and then displays them.

Code Listing 7-5 DisplayTestScores.cs

```
1    /*
2       This program demonstrates how the user may specify
3       an array's size.
4    */
5
6    using System;
7
8    public class DisplayTestScores
9    {
10    public static void Main()
11    {
12
13        int numTests;      // The number of tests
14        int[] tests;       // Array of test scores
15
16        // Get the number of test scores.
17        Console.Write("How many tests do you have? ");
18
19        numTests = Convert.ToInt32(Console.ReadLine());
20        tests = new int[numTests];
21
22        // Get the individual test scores.
23        for (int i = 0; i < tests.Length; i++)
24        {
25            Console.Write("Enter test score {0}: ",(i +
26                        1));
27            tests[i] =
                        Convert.ToInt32(Console.ReadLine());
28        }
29
30        // Display the test scores.
31        Console.WriteLine();
32        Console.WriteLine("Here are the scores you
                    entered:");
33        for (int i = 0; i < tests.Length; i++)
34            Console.WriteLine("{0} ",tests[i]);
35    }
36    }
```

(code listing continues)

Code Listing 7-5 DisplayTestScores.cs *(continued)*

Program Output with Example Input
```
How many tests do you have? 5[Enter]
Enter test score 1: 72[Enter]
Enter test score 2: 85[Enter]
Enter test score 3: 81[Enter]
Enter test score 4: 94[Enter]
Enter test score 5: 99[Enter]

Here are the scores you entered:
72
85
81
94
99
```

This program allows the user to determine the size of the array. In line 20 the following statement creates the array, using the numTests variable to determine its size.

```
tests = new int[numTests];
```

The program then uses two for loops. The first, in lines 23 through 28, allows the user to input each test score. The second, in lines 33 and 34, displays all of the test scores. Both loops use the Length member to control their number of iterations:

```
for (int i = 0; i < tests.Length; i++)
```

Reassigning Array Reference Variables

It is possible to reassign an array reference variable to a different array, as demonstrated by the following code.

```
// Create an array referenced by the numbers variable.
int[] numbers = new int[10];
// Reassign numbers to a new array.
numbers = new int[5];
```

The first statement creates a ten-element integer array and assigns its address to the numbers variable. This is illustrated in Figure 7-7.

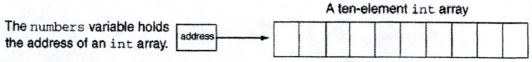

The numbers variable holds the address of an int array.

A ten-element int array

Figure 7-7   The numbers variable references a 10-element array

The second statement then allocates a five-element integer array and assigns its address to the numbers variable. The address of the five-element array takes the place of the address of the 10-element array. After this statement executes, the numbers variable references the five-element array instead of the 10-element array. This is illustrated in Figure 7-8. Because the 10-element array is no longer referenced, it cannot be accessed.

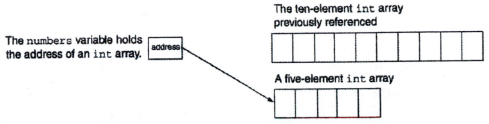

Figure 7-8   The numbers variable references a five-element array

Copying Arrays

Because an array is an object, there is a distinction between an array and the variable that references it. The array and the reference variable are two separate entities. This is important to remember when you wish to copy the contents of one array to another. You might be tempted to write something like the following code, thinking that you are copying an array.

```
int[] array1 = { 2, 4, 6, 8, 10 };
int[] array2 = array1;   // This does not copy array1.
```

The first statement creates an array and assigns its address to the array1 variable. The second statement assigns array1 to array2. This does not make a copy of the array referenced by array1. Rather, it makes a copy of the address that is stored in array1 and stores it in array2. After this statement executes, both the array1 and array2 variables will reference the same array. This type of assignment operation is called a *shallow copy*. It is "shallow" because only the address of the array object is copied, not the contents of the array object. This is illustrated in Figure 7-9.

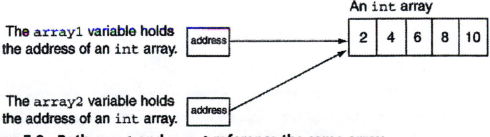

Figure 7-9   Both array1 and array2 reference the same array

Code Listing 7-6 demonstrates the assigning of an array's address to two reference variables. Regardless of which variable the program uses, it is working with the same array.

Code Listing 7-6   SameArray.cs

```
1    /*
2         This program demonstrates that two variables can
3          reference the same array.
4     */
5
6     using System;
7     public class SameArray
8     {
9        public static void Main()
10       {
11          int[] array1 = { 2, 4, 6, 8, 10};
12          int[] array2 = array1;
13
14          // Change one of the elements using array1.
15          array1[0] = 200;
16
17          // Change one of the elements using array2.
18          array1[4] = 1000;
19
20          // Display all the elements using array1
21          Console.WriteLine("The contents of array1:");
22          for (int i = 0; i < array1.Length; i++)
23             Console.Write("{0} ", array1[i]);
24          Console.WriteLine();
25
26          // Display all the elements using array2
27          Console.WriteLine("The contents of array2:");
28          for (int i = 0; i < array2.Length; i++)
29             Console.Write("{0} ",array2[i]);
30       Console.WriteLine();
31       }
32    }
```

Program Output

```
The contents of array1:
200 4 6 8 1000
The contents of array2:
200 4 6 8 1000
```

The program in Code Listing 7-6 illustrates that you cannot copy an array by merely by assigning one array reference variable to another. Instead, to copy an array you need to copy the individual elements of one array to another. Usually, this is best done with a loop, such as

```
int[] firstArray = {5, 10, 15, 20, 25 };
int[] secondArray = new int[5];

for (int i = 0; i < firstArray.Length; i++)
    secondArray[i] = firstArray[i];
```

The loop in this code copies each element of firstArray to the corresponding element of secondArray. This is known as a deep copy. A *deep copy* is an operation that copies the contents of the array object.

 NOTE: In C#, you can use the Copy() method, found in System.Array class, to copy the contents of two arrays.

 ## CHECKPOINT

7.9 Look at the following statements.

```
int[] numbers1 = { 1, 3, 6, 9 };
int[] numbers2 = { 2, 4, 6, 8 };
int result;
```

Write a statement that multiplies element 0 of the numbers1 array by element 3 of the numbers2 array and assigns the result to the result variable.

7.10 A program uses a variable named array that references an array of integers. You do not know the number of elements in the array. Write a for loop that stores −1 in each element of the array.

7.11 A program has the following declaration:

```
double[] values;
```

Write code that asks the user for the size of the array and then creates an array of the specified size, referenced by the values variable.

7.12 Look at the following statements.

```
int[] a = { 1, 2, 3, 4, 5, 6, 7 };
int[] b = new int[7];
```

Write code that copies the a array to the b array.

7.3 The `foreach` Loop

CONCEPT The `foreach` loop is an alternative loop to use with arrays.

In the previous sections we learned how to declare, initialize, and process loops.

In particular, we used a `for` loop to traverse through the array. Here is a simple code that would print temperatures for a given week:

```
double [] temperatures = {51.2, 55.6, 46.7, 49.8,
    50.2, 53.7, 56.0};
for (int i =0; i < temperatures.Length; i++)
    Console.WriteLine(temperatures[i]);
```

C# provides us with another construct unique to array processing: the `foreach` loop. The above code segment could be rewritten to an equivalent using the `foreach` construct:

```
double [] temperatures = {51.2, 55.6, 46.7, 49.8,
                          50.2, 53.7, 56.0};
foreach(int temperature in temperatures)
    Console.WriteLine(temperature);
```

Here every `int` variable `temperature` in the array `temperatures` is printed out. Notice, we do not have to use subscripts which makes the array much easier to work with. We also do not have to worry about `for` loop initialization, testing, and update—it is all hidden to the user. These reasons prevent us from having any number of off by one errors or invalid subscripts.

The `foreach` loop does have a few restrictions. First, we cannot access individual array elements but only the entire array. Also, the `foreach` loop allows us read access only, thus we cannot modify the array (i.e., cannot read into or assign values). To make any of the changes to the array mentioned above we must use the for loop and subscript notation. Code Listing 7.7 shows modified `ArrayDemo2.cs` using a `foreach` loop to traverse through the array contents.

Code Listing 7-7 ArrayDemo3.cs

```
1   /*
2       This program shows an array being processed with foreach
            loops.
3   */
4
5   using System;
6
```

(code listing continues)

Code Listing 7-7 ArrayDemo3.cs *(continued)*

```
7     public class ArrayDemo3
8     {
9      public static void Main()
10       {
11
12           const int EMPLOYEES = 3;          // Number of employees
13           int[] hours = new int[EMPLOYEES];  // Array of hours
14
15           // Get the hours for each employee.
16           Console.WriteLine("Enter the hours worked by {0}
                      employees", EMPLOYEES);
17
18         for (int i = 0; i < EMPLOYEES; i++)
19         {
20             Console.Write("Employee {0}: ", (i + 1));
21
22             hours[i] =
                      Convert.ToInt32(Console.ReadLine());
23         }
24
25         // Display the values entered.
26         Console.WriteLine("The hours you entered are:");
27
28         foreach (int employee in hours)
29             Console.WriteLine(employee);
30       }
31     }
```

Program Output with Example Input
```
Enter the hours worked by 3 employees
Employee 1: 40 [Enter]
Employee 2: 20 [Enter]
Employee 3: 15 [Enter]
The hours you entered are:
40
20
15
```

On lines 18 through 23 we have to use the subscript notation because we are trying to read values in from the keyboard, thus, modifying the array. However, on lines 28 and 29 we can use the foreach notation because all we are doing is printing out the array.

7.4 Passing Arrays as Arguments to Methods

 CONCEPT An array can be passed as an argument to a method. To pass an array, you pass the variable that references the array.

Quite often you'll want to write methods that process the data in arrays. As you will see, methods can be written to store values in an array, display an array's contents, total all of an array's elements, calculate their average, and so forth. Usually, such methods accept an array as an argument.

When a single element of an array is passed to a method, it is handled like any other variable. For example, Code Listing 7-8 shows a loop that passes each element of the array numbers to the method ShowValue.

Code Listing 7-8   PassElements.cs

```
1    /*
2       This program demonstrates passing individual array
3       elements as arguments to a method.
4    */
5
6    using System;
7    public class PassElements
8    {
9       public static void Main()
10      {
11         int[] numbers = {5, 10, 15, 20, 25, 30, 35, 40};
12
13         for (int i = 0; i < numbers.Length; i++)
14            ShowValue(numbers[i]);
15      }
16
17      /*
18         The ShowValue method displays its argument.
19          **parameter n The value to display.
20      */
21
22      public static void ShowValue(int n)
23      {
24         Console.Write("{0} ",n);
25      }
26   }
```

Program Output
```
5 10 15 20 25 30 35 40
```

Each time ShowValue is called in this program, an array element is passed to the method. The ShowValue method has an int parameter variable, named n, which receives the argument. The method simply displays the contents of n. If the method were written to accept the entire array as an argument, however, the parameter would have to be set up differently. For example, consider the following method definition. The parameter array is declared as an array reference variable. This indicates that the argument will be an array, not a single value.

```
public static void ShowArray(int[] array)
{
for (int i = 0; i < array.Length; i++)
    Console.Write("{0} ",array[i]);
}
```

When you pass an array as an argument, you simply pass the variable that references the array, as shown here:

```
ShowArray(numbers);
```

When an entire array is passed into a method, it is passed just as an object is passed: The actual array itself is not passed, but a reference to the array is passed into the parameter. Consequently, this means the method has direct access to the original array. This is illustrated in Figure 7-10.

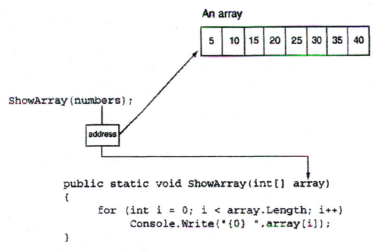

Figure 7-10   An array passed as an argument

Code Listing 7-9 demonstrates the ShowArray method, as well as another method, GetValues. The GetValues method accepts an array as an argument. It asks the user to enter a value for each element.

Code Listing 7-9   PassArray.cs

```
1    /*
2        This program demonstrates passing an array
3      as an argument to a method.
4    */
5
6  using System;
7
8  public class PassArray
9  {
10     public static void Main()
11     {
12         int[] numbers = new int[4];
13
14         GetValues(numbers);
15         Console.WriteLine("Here are the numbers that you
                  entered:");
16         ShowArray(numbers);
17     }
18
19     /*
20         The GetValues method accepts a reference
21         to an array as its argument. The user is
22         asked to enter a value for each element.
23         **parameter array A reference to the array.
24     */
25
26     public static void GetValues(int[] array)
27
28     {
29
30         Console.WriteLine("Enter a series of {0} numbers",
                  array.Length);
31
32         for (int i = 0; i < array.Length; i++)
33         {
34             Console.Write("Enter number {0}: ",(i + 1));
35
36             array[i] = Convert.ToInt32(Console.ReadLine());
37         }
38     }
39
```

(code listing continues)

Code Listing 7-9 PassArray.cs *(continued)*

```
40     /*
41         The ShowArray method accepts an array as
42         an argument displays its contents.
43         **parameter array- A reference to the array.
44      */
45
46     public static void ShowArray(int[] array)
47     {
48         for (int i = 0; i < array.Length; i++)
49             Console.Write("{0} ",array[i]);
50     }
51 }
```

Program Output with Example Input
```
Enter a series of 4 numbers
Enter number 1: 2[Enter]
Enter number 2: 4[Enter]
Enter number 3: 6[Enter]
Enter number 4: 8[Enter]
Here are the numbers that you entered:
2 4 6 8
```

NOTES: Because arrays are objects in C#, they are passed by reference.

C# allows a user to pass an unnamed array to a method in one step.

```
public static void GetValues(new int[] {2, 4, 6, 8})
```

The explanation of this syntax is beyond the scope of this chapter. It will not be used in this text.

CHECKPOINT

7.13 Look at the following method header:

```
public static void MyMethod(double[] array)
```

Here is an array declaration:

```
double[] numbers = new double[100];
```

Write a statement that passes the numbers array to the MyMethod method.

7.14 Write a method named zero that accepts an int array as an argument and stores the value 0 in each element.

7.5 Returning Arrays from Methods

CONCEPT In addition to accepting arrays as arguments, methods may also return arrays.

A method can return a reference to an array. For this to happen, the return type of the method must be declared properly. For example, look at the following method definition.

```
public static double[] GetArray()
{
    double[] array = {1.2, 2.3, 4.5, 6.7, 8.9};

    return array;
}
```

The GetArray method returns an array of doubles. Notice that the return type listed in the method header is double[]. The method header is illustrated in Figure 7-11. It indicates that the method returns a reference to a double array.

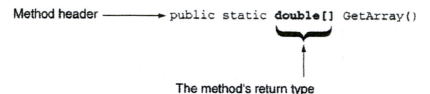

Figure 7-11   Array reference return type

Inside the method an array of doubles is created, initialized with some values, and referenced by the array variable. The return statement then returns the array variable. By returning the array variable, the method is returning a reference to the array. The method's return value can be stored in any compatible reference variable, as demonstrated in Code Listing 7-10.

Code Listing 7-10   ReturnArray.cs

```
1   /*
2       This program demonstrates how a reference to an
3       array can be returned from a method.
4   */
5
```

(code listing continues)

Code Listing 7-10 ReturnArray.cs *(continued)*

```
6     using System;
7     public class ReturnArray
8     {
9        public static void Main()
10       {
11          double[] values;
12
13          values = GetArray();
14          for (int i = 0; i < values.Length; i++)
15             Console.WriteLine("{0} ",values[i]);
16       }
17
18       /*
19          GetArray method
20          **return A reference to an array of doubles.
21       */
22
23       public static double[] GetArray()
24       {
25          double[] array = {1.2, 2.3, 4.5, 6.7, 8.9};
26
27          return array;
28       }
29    }
```

Program Output

```
1.2
2.3
4.5
6.7
8.9
```

The following statement, which appears in line 13, assigns the array returned by the GetAr-ray method to the array variable values.

```
values = GetArray();
```

The for loop in lines 14 and 15 then displays the value of each element of the values array.

7.6   Arrays of Objects

CONCEPT You may create arrays of objects that are instances of classes that you have written.

As you can for any other data type, you can create arrays of class objects. For example, recall the BankAccount class that we developed in Chapter 4. An array of BankAccount objects could be created to represent all of the bank accounts owned by a single person. Here is a statement that declares an array of five BankAccount objects:

```
BankAccount[] accounts = new BankAccount[5];
```

The variable that references the array is named accounts. As with string arrays, each element in this array is a reference variable, as illustrated in Figure 7-12.

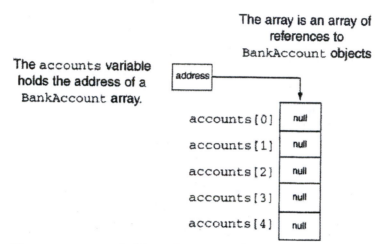

The accounts variable holds the address of a BankAccount array.

The array is an array of references to BankAccount objects

Figure 7-12 The accounts variable references an array of references

Notice from the figure that each element of the array is initialized with the value null. This is a special value in C# that indicates the array elements do not yet reference objects. You must individually create the objects that each element will reference. The following code uses a loop to create objects for each element.

```
for (int i = 0; i < accounts.Length; i++)
    accounts[i] = new BankAccount();
```

In this code, the no-arg constructor is called for each object. Recall that the BankAccount class has a no-arg constructor that assigns 0.0 to the balance field. After the loop executes, each element of the accounts array will reference a BankAccount object, as shown in Figure 7-13.

Objects in an array are accessed with subscripts, just like any other data type in an array. For example, the following code uses the accounts[2] element to call the SetBalance and Withdraw methods:

```
accounts[2].SetBalance(2500.0);
accounts[2].Withdraw(500.0);
```

Code Listing 7-11 shows a complete program that uses an array of objects.

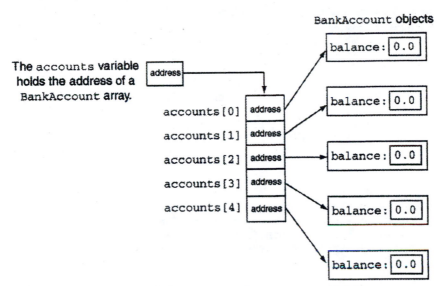

BankAccount objects

The `accounts` variable holds the address of a `BankAccount` array.

Figure 7-13   Each element of the array references an object

Code Listing 7-11   ObjectArray.cs

```
1   /*
2       This program works with an array of three
3          BankAccount objects.
4   */
5
6   using System;
7
8   public class ObjectArray
9     {
10      public static void Main()
11
12      {
13         // Create an array that can reference three
14         // BankAccount objects.
15
16         BankAccount[] accounts = new BankAccount[3];
17
18         // Create objects for the array.
19         CreateAccounts(accounts);
20
```

(code listing continues)

Code Listing 7-11 ObjectArray.cs *(continued)*

```
21          // Display the balances of each account.
22          Console.WriteLine("Here are the balances of each
                  account:");
23
24          for (int i = 0; i < accounts.Length; i++)
25          {
26              Console.WriteLine("Account {0}: {1:C}",(i +
                    1),accounts[i].GetBalance());
27          }
28      }
29
30      /*
31          The CreateAccounts method creates a BankAccount
32          object for each element of an array. The user
33          is asked for each account's balance.
34          **parameter array- The array to reference the accounts
35      */
36
37      private static void CreateAccounts(BankAccount[] array)
38
39      {
40
41          double balance;   // An account balance
42
43
44
45          // Create the accounts.
46          for (int i = 0; i < array.Length; i++)
47          {
48              // Get the account's balance.
49            Console.Write("Enter the balance for {0}: ",(i
                  + 1));
50
51              balance =
                    Convert.ToDouble(Console.ReadLine());
52
53              // Create the account.
54              array[i] = new BankAccount(balance);
55          }
56      }
57  }
```

Code Listing 7-11 ObjectArray.cs *(continued)*

Program Output with Example Input
```
Enter the balance for 1: 2500.0[Enter]
Enter the balance for 2: 5000.0[Enter]
Enter the balance for 3: 1500.0[Enter]
Here are the balances of each account:
Account 1: $2,500.00
Account 2: $5,000.00
Account 3: $1,500.00
```

 CHECKPOINT

7.15 Recall that we discussed a Rectangle class in Chapter 6. Write code that declares a Rectangle array with five elements. Instantiate each element with a Rectangle object. Use the Rectangle constructor to initialize each object with values for the length and width fields.

7.7 Searching and Sorting Arrays

 CONCEPT A sorting algorithm is used to arrange data into some order. A search algorithm is a method of locating a specific item in a larger collection of data. The selection sort and the sequential and binary search are popular sorting and searching algorithms.

Sorting Arrays: The Selection Sort Algorithm

Often the data in an array must be sorted in some order. Customer lists, for instance, are commonly sorted in alphabetical order. Student grades might be sorted from highest to lowest. Product codes could be sorted so all the products of the same color are stored together. In this section we explore how to write your own sorting algorithm. A *sorting algorithm* is a technique for scanning through an array and rearranging its contents in some specific order. The algorithm that we will explore is called the *selection sort.*

The *selection sort* works like this: The smallest value in the array is located and moved to element 0. Then the next smallest value is located and moved to element 1. This process continues until all of the elements have been placed in their proper order. Let's see how the selection sort works when arranging the elements of the following array in Figure 7-14.

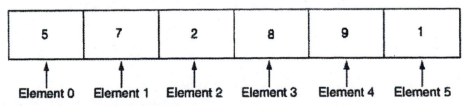

Figure 7-14 Values in an array

The selection sort scans the array, starting at element 0, and locates the element with the smallest value. The contents of this element are then swapped with the contents of element 0. In this example, the 1 stored in element 5 is swapped with the 5 stored in element 0. After the exchange, the array would appear as shown in Figure 7-15.

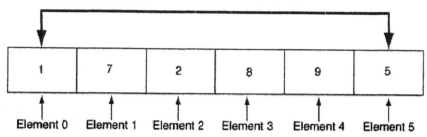

Figure 7-15   Values in array after first swap

The algorithm then repeats the process, but because element 0 already contains the smallest value in the array, it can be left out of the procedure. This time, the algorithm begins the scan at element 1. In this example, the contents of element 2 are exchanged with that of element 1. The array would then appear as shown in Figure 7-16.

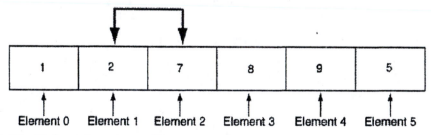

Figure 7-16   Values in array after second swap

Once again the process is repeated, but this time the scan begins at element 2. The algorithm will find that element 5 contains the next smallest value. This element's value is swapped with that of element 2, causing the array to appear as shown in Figure 7-17.

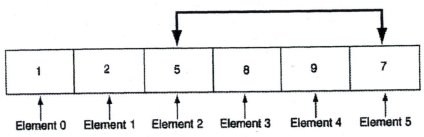

Figure 7-17   Values in array after third swap

Next, the scanning begins at element 3. Its value is swapped with that of element 5, causing the array to appear as shown in Figure 7-18.

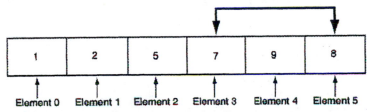

Figure 7-18   Values in array after fourth swap

At this point there are only two elements left to sort. The algorithm finds that the value in element 5 is smaller than that of element 4, so the two are swapped. This puts the array in its final arrangement as shown in Figure 7-19.

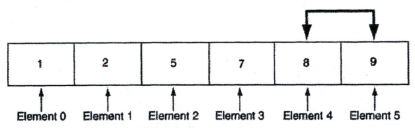

Figure 7-19   Values in array after fifth swap

Here is the selection sort algorithm in pseudocode:

> *For* `startScan` *equals each subscript in array from 0*
> *through the next-to-last subscript*
> *Set* `index` *variable to* `startScan`.
> *Set* `minIndex` *variable to* `startScan`.
> *Set* `minValue` *variable to* `array[startScan]`.
> *For* `index` *is each subscript in array from* `(startScan + 1)`
> *through the last subscript*
> *If* `array[index]` *is less than* `minValue`
> *Set* `minValue` *to* `array[index]`.
> *Set* `minIndex` *to* `index`.
> *End If.*
> *Increment* `index`.
> *End For.*
> *Set* `array[minIndex]` *to* `array[startScan]`.
> *Set* `array[startScan]` *to* `minValue`.
> *End For.*

The following method performs a selection sort on an integer array. The array that is passed as an argument is sorted in ascending order.

```
public static void SelectionSort(int[] array)
{
    int startScan, index, minIndex, minValue;

    for (startScan = 0; startScan < (array.Length-1); startScan++)
    {
        minIndex = startScan;
        minValue = array[startScan];
        for(index = startScan + 1; index < array.Length; index++)
        {
            if (array[index] < minValue)
            {
                minValue = array[index];
                minIndex = index;
            }
        }
        array[minIndex] = array[startScan];
        array[startScan] = minValue;
    }
}
```

The `SelectionSortDemo.cs` program on the Student CD demonstrates the `SelectionSort` method.

 NOTE: There is also a `Sort` method found within the `System.Array` class in C#.

Searching Arrays: The Sequential Search Algorithm

It is very common for programs not only to store and process information stored in arrays, but to search arrays for specific items. The *sequential search algorithm* uses a loop to sequentially step through an array, starting with the first element. It compares each element with the value being searched for and stops when the value is found or the end of the array is encountered. If the value being searched for is not in the array, the algorithm unsuccessfully searches to the end of the array.

The SearchArray program shown in Code Listing 7-12 searches the five-element array tests to find a score of 100. It uses a method, SequentialSearch, to find the value in the array. The array that is passed as an argument into the array parameter is searched for an occurrence of the number passed into value. If the number is found, its array subscript is returned. Otherwise, 1 is returned indicating the value did not appear in the array.

Code Listing 7-12 SearchArray.cs

```
1    /*
2         This program sequentially searches an
3       int array for a specified value.
4    */
5
6    using System;
7    public class SearchArray
8    {
9        public static void Main()
10       {
11         int[] tests = { 87, 75, 98, 100, 82 };
12         int results;
13
14         // Search the array for the value 100.
15         results = SequentialSearch(tests, 100);
16
17         // Determine whether 100 was found and
18         // display an appropriate message.
19         if (results == -1)
20         {
21             Console.WriteLine("You did not earn 100 on any test.");
22         }
23         else
24         {
25             Console.WriteLine("You earned 100 on test {0}",(results +
                   1));
26         }
27     }
28
```

(code listing continues)

Code Listing 7-12 SearchArray.cs *(continued)*

```
29       /*
30           The SequentialSearch method searches array for
31           value. If value is found in array, the element's
32           subscript is returned. Otherwise, -1 is returned.
33           **parameter array: The array to search.
34           **parameter value: The value to search for.
35       */
36
37       public static int SequentialSearch(int[] array,
38                                          int value)
39       {
40           int i,              // Loop control variable
41               element;        // Element the value is found at
42           bool found;     // Flag indicating search results
43
44           // Element 0 is the starting point of the search.
45           i = 0;
46
47           // Store the default values element and found.
48           element = -1;
49           found = false;
50
51           // Search the array.
52           while (!found && i < array.Length)
53           {
54               if (array[i] == value)
55               {
56                   found = true;
57                   element = i;
58               }
59               i++;
60           }
61
62           return element;
63       }
64   }
```

Program Output

```
You earned 100 on test 4
```

 NOTE: The reason 1 is returned when the search value is not found in the array is because 1 is not a valid subscript.

The Binary Search Algorithm

The advantage of the sequential search is its simplicity. It is easy to understand and implement. Furthermore, it doesn't require the data in the array to be stored in any particular order. Its disadvantage, however, is its inefficiency. If the array being searched contains 20,000 elements, the algorithm may have to look at all 20,000 elements in order to find a value stored in the last element. In an average case, an item is just as likely to be found near the end of the array as near the beginning. Typically, for an array of N items, the linear search will locate an item in $N/2$ attempts. If an array has 50,000 elements, the linear search will make a comparison with 25,000 of them in a typical case.

This is assuming, of course, that the search item is consistently found in the array. ($N/2$ is the average number of comparisons. The maximum number of comparisons is always N.) When the sequential search fails to locate an item, it must make a comparison with every element in the array. As the number of failed search attempts increases, so does the average number of comparisons. Obviously, the sequential search should not be used on large arrays if speed is important.

The *binary search* is a clever algorithm that is much more efficient than the sequential search. Its only requirement is that the values in the array must be sorted in ascending order. Instead of testing the array's first element, this algorithm starts with the element in the middle. If that element happens to contain the desired value, then the search is over. Otherwise, the value in the middle element is either greater than or less than the value being searched for. If it is greater, then the desired value (if it is in the list) will be found somewhere in the first half of the array. If it is less, then the desired value (again, if it is in the list) will be found somewhere in the last half of the array. In either case, half of the array's elements have been eliminated from further searching.

If the desired value wasn't found in the middle element, the procedure is repeated for the half of the array that potentially contains the value. For instance, if the last half of the array is to be searched, the algorithm tests *its* middle element. If the desired value isn't found there, the search is narrowed to the quarter of the array that resides before or after that element. This process continues until the value being searched for is either found, or there are no more elements to test. Here is the pseudocode for a method that performs a binary search on an array:

Set `first` to 0.
Set `last` to the last subscript in the array.
Set `found` to false.
Set `position` to -1.
While `found` is not true and `first` is less than or equal to `last`
   Set `middle` to the subscript half-way between
                   `array[first]` and `array[last]`.
   If `array[middle]` equals the desired value
      Set `found` to true.
      Set `position` to `middle`.
   Else If `array[middle]` is greater than the desired value
      Set `last` to `middle` - 1.
   Else
      Set `first` to `middle` + 1.
   End If.
End While.
Return `position`.

This algorithm uses three variables to mark positions within the array: first, last, and middle. The first and last variables mark the boundaries of the portion of the array currently being searched. They are initialized with the subscripts of the array's first and last elements. The subscript of the element halfway between first and last is calculated and stored in the middle variable. If the element in the middle of the array does not contain the search value, the first or last variables are adjusted so that only the top or bottom half of the array is searched during the next iteration. This cuts the portion of the array being searched in half each time the loop fails to locate the search value.

The following method performs a binary search on an integer array. The first parameter, array, is searched for an occurrence of the number stored in value. If the number is found, its array subscript is returned. Otherwise, 1 is returned indicating the value did not appear in the array.

```
public static int BinarySearch(int[] array, int value)
{
    int first,        // First array element
        last,         // Last array element
        middle,       // Mid point of search
        position;     // Position of search value
    bool found;   // Flag

    // Set the initial values.
    first = 0;
    last = array.Length - 1;
    position = -1;
    found = false;

    // Search for the value.
    while (!found && first <= last)
    {
        // Calculate mid point
        middle = (first + last) / 2;

        // If value is found at midpoint...
        if (array[middle] == value)
        {
            found = true;
            position = middle;
        }
        // else if value is in lower half...
        else if (array[middle] > value)
            last = middle - 1;
        // else if value is in upper half....
        else
            first = middle + 1;
    }

    // Return the position of the item, or -1
    // if it was not found.
    return position;
}
```

NOTE: There is also a `BinarySearch` method found within the `System.Array` class in C#.

The `BinarySearchDemo` program on the Student CD demonstrates this method.

 ## CHECKPOINT

7.16 What value in an array does the selection sort algorithm look for first? When the selection sort finds this value, what does it do with it?

7.17 How many times will the selection sort swap the smallest value in an array with another value?

7.18 Describe the difference between the sequential search and the binary search.

7.19 On average, with an array of 20,000 elements, how many comparisons will the sequential search perform? (Assume the items being searched for are consistently found in the array.)

7.20 If a sequential search is performed on an array, and it is known that some items are searched for more frequently than others, how can the contents of the array be reordered to improve the average performance of the search?

7.8 Multidimensional Arrays

 C# does not limit the number of dimensions that an array may have. It is possible to create arrays with multiple dimensions, to model data that occurs in multiple sets. In particular, a two-dimensional array is an array of arrays. It can be thought of as having rows and columns.

C# has two kinds of multidimensional arrays: rectangular and ragged (jagged). Let us first look at the most common, a rectangular two-dimensional array.

Rectangular Two-dimensional Arrays

An array is useful for storing and working with a set of data. Sometimes, though, it's necessary to work with multiple sets of data. For example, in a grade-averaging program a teacher might record all of one student's test scores in an array of `doubles`. If the teacher has 30 students, that means she'll need 30 arrays to record the scores for the entire class. Instead of defining 30 individual arrays, however, it would be better to define a two-dimensional array.

The arrays that you have studied so far are one-dimensional arrays. They are called *one-dimensional* because they can only hold one set of data. Two-dimensional arrays, which are sometimes called *2D arrays*, can hold multiple sets of data. Although a two-dimensional array is actually an array of arrays, it's best to think of it as having rows and columns of elements, as shown in Figure 7-20. This figure shows an array of test scores, having three rows and four columns.

	Column 0	Column 1	Column 2	Column 3
Row 0				
Row 1				
Row 2				

Figure 7-20   Rows and columns

The array depicted in the figure has three rows (numbered 0 through 2) and four columns (numbered 0 through 3). There are a total of 12 elements in the array.

To declare a two-dimensional array, one comma and two size declarators are required: The first declarator is for the number of rows and the second one is for the number of columns. Here is an example declaration of a two-dimensional array with three rows and four columns:

```
double[,] scores = new double[3,4];
```

The comma in the data type indicate that the `scores` variable will reference a two-dimensional array. The numbers 3 and 4 are size declarators. The first size declarator specifies the number of rows, and the second size declarator specifies the number of columns. Notice that each size declarator is separated by a comma. This is illustrated in Figure 7-21.

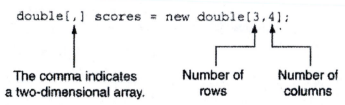

Figure 7-21   Declaration of a two-dimensional array

When processing the data in a two-dimensional array, each element has two subscripts: one for its row and another for its column. In the `scores` array, the elements in row 0 are referenced as

```
scores[0,0]
scores[0,1]
scores[0,2]
scores[0,3]
```

The elements in row 1 are

```
scores[1,0]
scores[1,1]
scores[1,2]
scores[1,3]
```

And the elements in row 2 are

```
scores[2,0]
scores[2,1]
scores[2,2]
scores[2,3]
```

Figure 7-22 illustrates the array with the subscripts shown for each element.

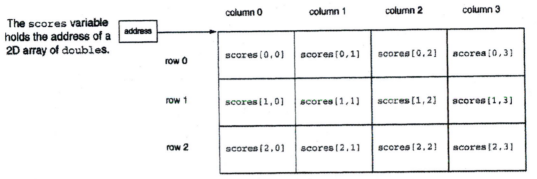

Figure 7-22   Subscripts for each element of the scores array

To access one of the elements in a two-dimensional array, you must use both subscripts. For example, the following statement stores the number 95 in scores[2,1].

```
scores[2,1] = 95;
```

Programs that process two-dimensional arrays can do so with nested loops. For example, the following code prompts the user to enter a score, once for each element in the array.

```
for (int row = 0; row < 2; row++)
{
    for (int col = 0; col < 3; col++)
    {
        Console.Write("Enter a score: ");
        scores[row,col] =
            Convert.ToDouble(Console.ReadLine());
    }
}
```

And the following code displays all the elements in the scores array.

```
for (int row = 0; row < 2; row++)
```

```
        {
            for (int col = 0; col < 3; col++)
            {
              Console.WriteLine(scores[row,col]);
            }
        }
```

The program in Code Listing 7-13 uses a two-dimensional array to store corporate sales data. The array has three rows (one for each division of the company) and four columns (one for each quarter).

Code Listing 7-13 CorpSales.cs

```
 1  /*
 2      This program demonstrates a two-dimensional array.
 3  */
 4
 5  using System;
 6
 7  public class CorpSales
 8  {
 9    public static void Main()
10
11    {
12
13        double[,] sales = new double[3,4];
14      double totalSales = 0.0;
15
16        Console.WriteLine("This program will calculate the
                total sales of");
17        Console.WriteLine("all the company's divisions. Enter
                the following sales data:");
18
19        // Nested loops to fill the array with quarterly
20        // sales figures for each division.
21        for (int div = 0; div < 3; div++)
22        {
23          for (int qtr = 0; qtr < 4; qtr++)
24          {
25              Console.Write("Division {0}, Quarter {1}: $",(div
                        + 1), (qtr + 1));
26
27
28              sales[div,qtr] =
                        Convert.ToDouble(Console.ReadLine());
29          }
30            Console.WriteLine();   // Print blank line.
31        }
32
```

(code listing continues)

Code Listing 7-13 CorpSales.cs *(continued)*

```
33            // Nested loops to add all the elements of the array.
34            for (int div = 0; div < 3; div++)
35            {
36                for (int qtr = 0; qtr < 4; qtr++)
37                {
38                    totalSales += sales[div,qtr];
39                }
40            }
41
42            // Display the total sales.
43            Console.WriteLine("The total sales for the company are
44        }        {0:C2}",totalSales);
45    }
```

Program Output with Example Input
```
This program will calculate the total sales of
all the company's divisions. Enter the following sales data:
Division 1, Quarter 1: $35698.77[Enter]
Division 1, Quarter 2: $36148.63[Enter]
Division 1, Quarter 3: $31258.95[Enter]
Division 1, Quarter 4: $30864.12[Enter]

Division 2, Quarter 1: $41289.64[Enter]
Division 2, Quarter 2: $43278.52[Enter]
Division 2, Quarter 3: $40927.18[Enter]
Division 2, Quarter 4: $42818.98[Enter]

Division 3, Quarter 1: $28914.56[Enter]
Division 3, Quarter 2: $27631.52[Enter]
Division 3, Quarter 3: $30596.64[Enter]
Division 3, Quarter 4: $29834.21[Enter]

The total sales for the company are $419,261.72
```

Look at the array declaration in line 13:

```
double[,] sales = new double[3,4];
```

As mentioned earlier, the array has three rows (one for each division) and four columns (one for each quarter) to store the company's sales data. The row subscripts are 0, 1, and 2, and the column subscripts are 0, 1, 2, and 3. Figure 7-23 illustrates how the quarterly sales data is stored in the array.

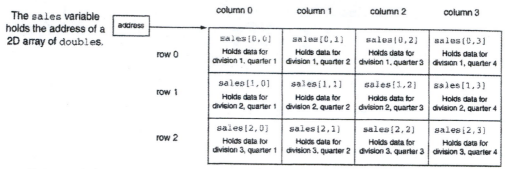

Figure 7-23 Division and quarter data stored in the `sales` array

Initializing a Two-dimensional Array

When initializing a two-dimensional array, you enclose each row's initialization list in its own set of braces. Here is an example:

```
int[,] numbers = { {1, 2, 3}, {4, 5, 6}, {7, 8, 9}};
```

As with one-dimensional arrays, you do not use the new key word when you provide an initialization list. C# automatically creates the array and fills its elements with the initialization values. In this example, the initialization values for row 0 are {1, 2, 3}, the initialization values for row 1 are {4, 5, 6}, and the initialization values for row 2 are {7, 8, 9}. So, this statement declares an array with three rows and three columns. For more clarity, the same statement could also be written as

```
int[,] numbers = { {1, 2, 3},
                   {4, 5, 6},
                   {7, 8, 9}};
```

In either case, the values are assigned to the numbers array as illustrated in Figure 7-24.

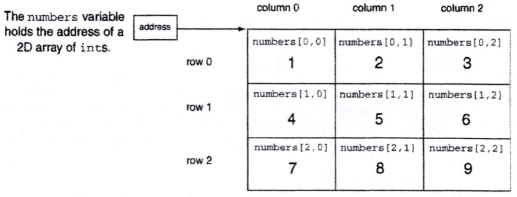

Figure 7-24 The `numbers` array

The Length Field in a Rectangular Two-dimensional Array

A one-dimensional array has a Length field that holds the number of elements in the array. A rectangular two-dimensional array, however, has multiple Length fields. It has a Length field that holds the number of rows, and then each row has a Length field that holds the number of columns. In C# we can use the GetLength method found in the System.Array class. The first dimension can be referenced by GetLength(0), while the second dimension can be referenced by GetLength(1). The program in Code Listing 7-14 uses the GetLength method to display the number of rows and columns in a two-dimensional array.

Code Listing 7-14   Lengths.cs

```
1   /*
2       This program uses the length fields of a 2D array
3       to display the number of rows, and the number of
4       columns in each row.
5   */
6
7   using System;
8   public class Lengths
9   {
10      public static void Main()
11      {
12          // Declare a 2D array with 3 rows
13          // and 4 columns.
14
15          int[,] numbers = { { 1,  2,  3,  4 },
16                             { 5,  6,  7,  8 },
17                             { 9, 10, 11, 12 } };
18
19          // Display the number of rows.
20          Console.WriteLine("The number of rows is {0}",
                    numbers.GetLength(0));
21
22          // Display the number of columns in each row.
23          for (int i = 0; i < numbers.GetLength(0); i++)
24          {
25              Console.WriteLine("The number of columns in row {0}
                        is {1}", i,
26                      numbers.GetLength(1));
27          }
28      }
29  }
```

(code listing continues)

Code Listing 7-14 Lengths.cs *(continued)*

Program Output
```
The number of rows is 3
The number of columns in row 0 is 4
The number of columns in row 1 is 4
The number of columns in row 2 is 4
```

Displaying All the Elements of a Two-dimensional Array

As you have seen in previous example programs, a pair of nested loops can be used to display all the elements of a two-dimensional array. For example, the following code creates the numbers array with three rows and four columns, and then displays all the elements in the array.

```
int[,] numbers = { { 1,  2,  3,  4  },
                   { 5,  6,  7,  8  },
                   { 9, 10, 11, 12 } };
for (int row = 0; row < 3; row++)
{
    for (int col = 0; col < 4; col++)
        Console.WriteLine(numbers[row,col]);
}
```

Although this code will display all of the elements, it is limited in the following way: The loops are specifically written to display an array with three rows and four columns. A better approach is to use the array's GetLength method for the upper limit of the subscripts in the loop test expressions. Here are the modified loops:

```
for (int row = 0; row < numbers.GetLength(0); row++)
{
    for (int col = 0; col < numbers.GetLength(1); col++)
        Console.WriteLine(numbers[row,col]);
}
```

Let's take a closer look at the header for the outer loop:

```
for (int row = 0; row < numbers.GetLength(0); row++)
```

This loop controls the subscript for the number array's rows. Because numbers.GetLength(0) holds the number of rows in the array, we have used it as the upper limit for the row subscripts. Here is the header for the inner loop:

```
for (int col = 0; col < numbers.GetLength(1); col++)
```

This loop controls the subscript for the number array's columns. Because numbers.GetLength(1) holds the number of columns in the row, we have used it as the upper limit for the column subscripts. By using the GetLength method in algorithms that process two-dimensional arrays, you can write code that works with arrays of any number of rows and columns.

Passing Two-dimensional Arrays to Methods

When a two-dimensional array is passed to a method, the parameter must be declared as a reference to a two-dimensional array. The following method header shows an example.

```
public static void ShowArray(int[,] array)
```

This method's parameter, array, is declared as a reference to a two-dimensional int array. Any two-dimensional int array can be passed as an argument to the method. Code Listing 7-15 demonstrates such two such methods.

Code Listing 7-15   Pass2Darray.cs

```
1   /*      This program demonstrates methods that accept
2        a two-dimensional array as an argument.
3   */
4   using System;
5   public class Pass2Darray
6   {
7      public static void Main()
8      {
9         int[,] numbers = { { 1,  2,  3,  4  },
10                           { 5,  6,  7,  8  },
11                           { 9, 10, 11, 12  } };
12
13        // Display the contents of the array.
14      Console.WriteLine("Here are the values in the array.");
15        ShowArray(numbers);
16
17        // Display the sum of the array's values.
18        Console.WriteLine("The sum of the values is {0} ",
19           ArraySum(numbers));
19      }
20
21      /*
22        The ShowArray method displays the contents
23        of a two-dimensional int array.
24        **parameter array: The array to display.
25      */
26
27      public static void ShowArray(int[,] array)
28      {
29         for (int row = 0; row < array.GetLength(0); row++)
30         {
31            for (int col = 0; col < array.GetLength(1); col++)
32               Console.Write("{0} ",array[row,col]);
33               Console.WriteLine();
34         }
35      }
36
```

(code listing continues)

Code Listing 7-15 **Pass2Darray.cs** *(continued)*

```
37      /*
38          The ArraySum method returns the sum of the
39          values in a two-dimensional int array.
40          **parameter array: The array to sum.
41          **return The sum of the array elements.
42      */
43
44      public static int ArraySum(int[,] array)
45      {
46          int total = 0;   // Accumulator
47
48          for (int row = 0; row < array.GetLength(0); row++)
49          {
50              for (int col = 0; col < array.GetLength(1); col++)
51                  total += array[row,col];
52          }
53
54          return total;
55      }
56  }
```

Program Output
```
Here are the values in the array.
1 2 3 4
5 6 7 8
9 10 11 12
The sum of the values is 78
```

Ragged Arrays

Because the rows in a two-dimensional array are also arrays, each row can have its own length. When the rows of a two-dimensional array are of different lengths, the array is known as a *ragged array*. You create a ragged array by first creating a two-dimensional array with a specific number of rows, but no columns. Here is an example:

```
int[][] ragged = new int[4][];
```

This statement partially creates a two-dimensional array. Notice the syntax for declaring ragged arrays is different than rectangular arrays. It uses the traditional C/C++ syntax for two-dimensional arrays. The array can have four rows, but the rows have not yet been created. Next, you create the individual rows as shown in the following code.

```
ragged[0] = new int[3];    // Row 0 has 3 columns.
ragged[1] = new int[4];    // Row 1 has 4 columns.
ragged[2] = new int[5];    // Row 2 has 5 columns.
ragged[3] = new int[6];    // Row 3 has 6 columns.
```

This code creates the four rows. Row 0 has three columns, row 1 has four columns, row 2 has five columns, and row 3 has six columns.

The `Length` Field in a Ragged Array

A one-dimensional array has a `Length` field that holds the number of elements in the array. A ragged two-dimensional array, however, has multiple `Length` fields. It has a `Length` field that holds the number of rows, and then each row has a `Length` field that holds the number of columns. This makes sense when you think of a ragged two-dimensional array as an array of one-dimensional arrays. Figure 7-25 shows another way of thinking of the numbers array: as an array of arrays.

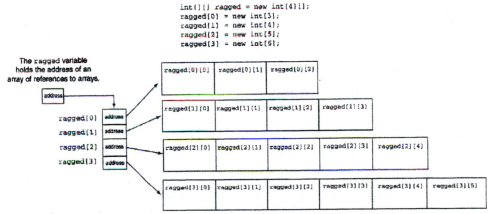

Figure 7-25   The `numbers` array is an array of arrays

As you can see from the figure, the `numbers` variable references a one-dimensional array with three elements. Each of the three elements is a reference to another one-dimensional array. The elements in the array referenced by `numbers[0]` are `numbers[0][0]`, `numbers[0][1]`, and `numbers[0][2]`. This pattern continues with `numbers[1]` and `numbers[2]`. The figure shows a total of four arrays. Each of the arrays in the figure has its own `Length` field.

The following code displays the number of columns in each row.

```
for (int i = 0; i < ragged.Length; i++)
{
    Console.WriteLine("The number of columns in row {0}
            is {1}" , i, ragged[i].Length);
}
```

This code will display the following output:

```
The number of columns in row 0 is 3
The number of columns in row 1 is 4
The number of columns in row 2 is 5
The number of columns in row 3 is 6
```

Arrays of More Than Two Dimensions

C# allows you to create arrays beyond two dimensions. Here is an example of a three-dimensional array declaration:

```
double[,,] seats = new double[3,5,8];
```

This array can be thought of as three sets of five rows, with each row containing eight elements. The array might be used to store the prices of seats in an auditorium, where there are eight seats in a row, five rows in a section, and a total of three sections.

Figure 7-26 illustrates the concept of a three-dimensional array as pages of two-dimensional arrays.

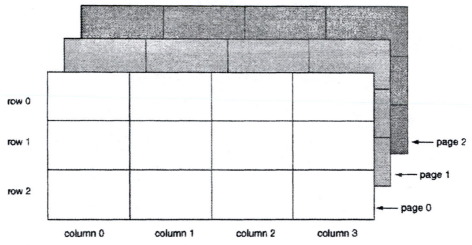

Figure 7-26　A three-dimensional array

Arrays with more than three dimensions are difficult to visualize, but can be useful in some programming problems. For example, in a factory warehouse where cases of widgets are stacked on pallets, an array with four dimensions could be used to store a part number for each widget. The four subscripts of each element could represent the pallet number, case number, row number, and column number of each widget. Similarly, an array with five dimensions could be used if there were multiple warehouses.

NOTES:

With two-dimensional arrays the first index represents the number of rows the second index represents the number of columns.

Another name for ragged arrays is *jagged arrays*. This is the preferred name in C#.

For arrays beyond two dimensions, the same properties used for two dimensions can be applied.

CHECKPOINT

7.21 A video rental store keeps videos on 50 racks with 10 shelves each. Each shelf holds 25 videos. Declare a three-dimensional array large enough to represent the store's storage system.

7.9 Command-Line Arguments

> **CONCEPT** Arguments may be passed from the operating system command-line into the `Main` method of a C# program.

Every program you have seen in this book and every program you have written uses a static `Main` method with a header that looks like this:

```
public static void Main()
```

However, in C# the `Main` method actually has a parameter `string[] args`:

```
public static void Main(string[] args)
```

Inside the parentheses of the method header is the declaration of a parameter named `args`. This parameter is an array name. As its declaration indicates, it is used to reference an array of strings. The array that is passed into the `args` parameter comes from the operating system command-line. For example, look at Code Listing 7-16.

Code Listing 7-16 CommandLine.cs

```
1    /*
2         This program displays the arguments passed to
3         it from the operating system command line.
4    */
5
```

(code listing continues)

Code Listing 7-16 CommandLine.cs *(continued)*

```
6    using System;
7    public class CommandLine
8      {
9         public static void Main(string[] args)
10          {
11            for (int i = 0; i < args.Length; i++)
12                Console.WriteLine(args[i]);
13          }
14      }
```

If this program is compiled and then executed with the command

    CommandLine How does this work?

the output is:

    How
    does
    this
    work?

Any items typed on the command-line, separated by spaces, after the name of the class are considered to be one or more arguments that are to be passed into the Main method. In the previous example, four arguments are passed into args. The word "How" is passed into args[0], "does" is passed into args[1], "this" is passed into args[2], and "work?" is passed into args[3]. The for loop in Main simply displays each argument.

 NOTES: It is not required that the name of Main's parameter array be args. You can name it anything you wish. It is a standard convention, however, for the name args to be used.

We can enclose arguments at the command line with double quotes, if we want the argument not to be interpreted as multiple arguments. Example:

    CommandLine "How does this work?"

will produce on one line:

    How does this work?

The Main method can also take on two other forms:

    static int Main()
    static int Main(string[] args)

Each of the above two methods must return a value usually 0, which means it terminates normally.

7.10 Common Errors

- **Using an invalid subscript.** C# does not allow you to use a subscript value that is outside the range of valid subscripts for an array.

- **Confusing the contents of an integer array element with the element's subscript.** An element's subscript and the value stored in the element are not the same thing. The subscript identifies an element, which holds a value.

- **Causing an off-by-one error.** When processing arrays, the subscripts start at 0 and end at 1 less than the number of elements in the array. Off-by-one errors are commonly caused by a loop that uses an initial subscript of 1 and/or that uses a maximum subscript that is equal to the number of elements in the array.

- **Using the = operator to copy an array.** Assigning one array reference variable to another with the = operator merely copies the address in one variable to the other. To copy an array, you should copy the individual elements of one array to another, or use the Copy method provided by the Array class.

- **Using the == operator to compare two arrays.** You cannot use the == operator to compare two array reference variables and determine whether the arrays are equal. When you use the == operator with reference variables, the operator compares the memory addresses that the variables contain, not the contents of the objects referenced by the variables.

- **Reversing the row and column subscripts when processing a two-dimensional array.** If you think of a two-dimensional array as having rows and columns, the first subscript accesses a row and the second subscript accesses a column. If you reverse these subscripts, you will access the wrong element.

Review Questions and Exercises

Multiple Choice and True/False

1. In an array declaration, this indicates the number of elements that the array is to have.
   - a) subscript
   - b) element sum
   - c) size declarator
   - d) reference variable

2. Each element of an array is accessed by a number known as a(n)
   - a) subscript.
   - b) address.
   - c) size declarator.
   - d) specifier.

3. The first subscript in an array is always
   - a) 1.
   - b) 0.
   - c) 1.
   - d) 1 less than the number of elements.

4. The last subscript in an array is always
   a) 100.
   b) 0.
   c) 1.
   d) one less than the number of elements.

5. Array bounds checking happens
   a) when the program is compiled.
   b) when the program is saved.
   c) when the program runs.
   d) when the program is loaded into memory.

6. This array field holds the number of elements that the array has.
   a) `Size`
   b) `Length`
   c) `elements`
   d) `width`

7. This C# method sorts an array.
   a) `Array.Sort`
   b) `Sort.array`
   c) `arrays_sort`
   d) `Math.sort`

8. This search algorithm steps through an array, comparing each item with the search value.
   a) binary search
   b) sequential search
   c) selection search
   d) iterative search

9. By using the same _____ for multiple arrays, you can build relationships between the data stored in the arrays.
   a) name
   b) reference variable
   c) address
   d) subscript

10. This search algorithm repeatedly divides the portion of an array being searched in half.
    a) binary search
    b) sequential search
    c) selection search
    d) iterative search

11. What is the *maximum* number of comparisons performed by the sequential search on an array of N elements (assuming the search values are consistently found)?
    a) $2N$
    b) N
    c) N^2
    d) $N/2$

12. When initializing a two-dimensional array, you enclose each row's initialization list in these.
    a) braces
    b) parentheses
    c) brackets
    d) quotation marks

13. True or False: C# does not allow a statement to use a subscript that is outside the range of valid subscripts for an array.

14. True or False: An array's size declarator can be a negative integer expression.

15. True or False: Both of the following declarations are legal and equivalent:

```
int[] numbers;
int numbers[];
```

16. True or False: The subscript of the last element in a one-dimensional array is one less than the total number of elements in the array.

17. True or False: The values in an initialization list are stored in the array in the order they appear in the list.

18. True or False: The C# compiler does not display an error message when it processes a statement that uses an invalid subscript.

19. True or False: When an array is passed to a method, the method has access to the original array.

20. True or False: The first size declarator in the declaration of a two-dimensional array represents the number of columns. The second size declarator represents the number of rows.

21. True or False: A two-dimensional array has multiple Length fields.

Find the Error

1. ```
int[] collection = new int[-20];
```

2. ```
int[] hours = 8, 12, 16;
```

3. ```
int[] table = new int[10];
for (int x = 1; x <= 10; x++)
{
    table[x] = 99;
}
```

## Algorithm Workbench

1. The variable names references an integer array with 20 elements. Write a for loop that prints each element of the array.

2. The variables numberArray1 and numberArray2 reference arrays that each has 100 elements. Write code that copies the values in numberArray1 to numberArray2.

3. Declare a rectangular two-dimensional int array named grades. It should have 30 rows and 10 columns.

4. Write code that calculates the average of all the elements in the grades array that you declared in Question 3.

5. The values variable references a two-dimensional double array with 10 rows and 20 columns. Write code that sums all the elements in the array and stores the sum in the variable total.

6. An application uses a two-dimensional array declared as follows.

    ```
    int[,] days = new int[29,5];
    ```

    a) Write code that sums each row in the array and displays the results.

    b) Write code that sums each column in the array and displays the results.
    ```

Short Answer

1. What is the difference between a size declarator and a subscript?

2. Look at the following array definition.

   ```
   int[] values = new int[10];
   ```

   a) How many elements does the array have?

   b) What is the subscript of the first element in the array?

   c) What is the subscript of the last element in the array?

3. In the following array definition

   ```
   int[] values = { 4, 7, 6, 8, 2 };
   ```

   what does each of the following code segments display?

   ```
   Console.WriteLine(values[4]);      a) _____

   x = values[2] + values[3];
   Console.WriteLine(x);              b) _____

   x = ++values[1];
   Console.WriteLine(x);              c) _____
   ```

4. How do you define an array without providing a size declarator?

5. Assuming that `array1` and `array2` are both array reference variables, why is it not possible to assign the contents of the array referenced by `array2` to the array referenced by `array1` with the following statement?

   ```
   array1 = array2;
   ```

6. How do you establish a parallel relationship between two or more arrays?

7. The following statement creates a `BankAccount` array:

   ```
   BankAccount[] acc = new BankAccount[10];
   ```

   Is it okay or not okay to execute the following statements?

   ```
   acc[0].SetBalance(5000.0);
   acc[0].Withdraw(100.0);
   ```

8. If a sequential search method is searching for a value that is stored in the last element of a 10,000-element array, how many elements will the search code have to read to locate the value?

9. A binary search method is searching for a value that is stored in the middle element of an array. How many times will the method read an element in the array before finding the value?

10. Look at the following array definition.

```
double[,] sales = new double[8,10];
```

a) How many rows does the array have?

b) How many columns does the array have?

c) How many elements does the array have?

d) Write a statement that stores a number in the last column of the last row in the array.

Programming Challenges

1. Rainfall Class

Write a `RainFall` class that stores the total rainfall for each of 12 months into an array of doubles. The program should have methods that return the following:

- Total rainfall for the year
- The average monthly rainfall
- The month with the most rain
- The month with the least rain

Demonstrate the class in a complete program.

Input Validation: Do not accept negative numbers for monthly rainfall figures.

2. Payroll Class

Write a `Payroll` class that uses the following arrays as fields:

- `employeeId`. An array of seven integers to hold employee identification numbers. The array should be initialized with the following numbers:

```
5658845 4520125 7895122 8777541
8451277 1302850 7580489
```

- `hours`. An array of seven integers to hold the number of hours worked by each employee
- `payRate`. An array of seven doubles to hold each employee's hourly pay rate
- `wages`. An array of seven doubles to hold each employee's gross wages

The class should relate the data in each array through the subscripts. For example, the number in element 0 of the `hours` array should be the number of hours worked by the employee whose identification number is stored in element 0 of the `employeeId` array. That same employee's pay rate should be stored in element 0 of the `payRate` array.

In addition to the appropriate accessor and mutator methods, the class should have a method that accepts an employee's identification number as an argument and returns the gross pay for that employee.

Demonstrate the class in a complete program that displays each employee number and asks the user to enter that employee's hours and pay rate. It should then display each employee's identification number and gross wages.

Input Validation: Do not accept negative values for hours or numbers less than 6.00 for pay rate.

3. Charge Account Validation

Create a class with a method that accepts a charge account number as its argument. The method should determine whether the number is valid by comparing it to the following list of valid charge account numbers.

```
5658845  4520125  7895122  8777541  8451277  1302850
8080152  4562555  5552012  5050552  7825877  1250255
1005231  6545231  3852085  7576651  7881200  4581002
```

These numbers should be stored in an array. Use either a sequential search or a binary search to locate the number passed as an argument. If the number is in the array, the method should return true, indicating the number is valid. If the number is not in the array, the method should return false, indicating the number is invalid.

Write a program that tests the class by asking the user to enter a charge account number. The program should display a message indicating whether the number is valid or invalid.

4. Charge Account Modification

Modify the charge account validation class that you wrote for Programming Challenge 3 so it reads the list of valid charge account numbers from a file.

5. Driver's License Exam

The local Driver's License Office has asked you to write a program that grades the written portion of the driver's license exam. The exam has 20 multiple-choice questions. Here are the correct answers:

1. B	6. A	11. B	16. C
2. D	8. B	12. C	18. C
3. A	8. A	13. D	18. B
4. A	9. C	14. A	19. D
5. C	10. D	15. D	20. A

A student must correctly answer 15 of the 20 questions to pass the exam.

Write a class named DriverExam that holds the correct answers to the exam in an array field. The class should also have an array field that holds the student's answers. The class should have the following methods:

- Passed. Returns true if the student passed the exam, or false if the student failed
- TotalCorrect. Returns the total number of correctly answered questions
- TotalIncorrect. Returns the total number of incorrectly answered questions
- QuestionsMissed. An int array containing the question numbers of the questions that the student missed

Demonstrate the class in a complete program that asks the user to enter a student's answers, and then displays the results returned from the `DriverExam` class's methods.

Input Validation: Only accept the letters A, B, C, or D as answers.

6. Quarterly Sales Statistics

Write a program that lets the user enter four quarterly sales figures for six divisions of a company. The figures should be stored in a two-dimensional array. Once the figures are entered, the program should display the following data for each quarter:

- A list of the sales figures by division
- Each division's increase or decrease from the previous quarter (this will not be displayed for the first quarter)
- The total sales for the quarter
- The company's increase or decrease from the previous quarter (this will not be displayed for the first quarter)
- The average sales for all divisions that quarter
- The division with the highest sales for that quarter

Input Validation: Do not accept negative numbers for sales figures.

7. Grade Book

A teacher has five students who have taken four tests. The teacher uses the following grading scale to assign a letter grade to a student, based on the average of his or her four test scores.

Test Score	Letter Grade
90–100	A
80–89	B
70–79	C
60–69	D
0–59	F

Write a class that uses a `string` array to hold the five students' names, an array of five characters to hold the five students' letter grades, and five arrays of four `doubles` each to hold each student's set of test scores. The class should have methods that return a specific student's name, average test score, and a letter grade based on the student's average.

Demonstrate the class in a program that allows the user to enter each student's name and his or her four test scores. It should then display each student's average test score and letter grade.

Input validation: Do not accept test scores less than zero or greater than 100.

8. Grade Book Modification

Modify the grade book application in Programming Challenge 7 so it drops each student's lowest score when determining the test score averages and letter grades.

9. Array Operations

Write a program with an array that is initialized with test data. Use any primitive data type of your choice. The program should also have the following methods:

- GetTotal. This method should accept a one-dimensional array as its argument and return the total of the values in the array.

- GetAverage. This method should accept a one-dimensional array as its argument and return the average of the values in the array.

- GetHighest. This method should accept a one-dimensional array as its argument and return the highest value in the array.

- GetLowest. This method should accept a one-dimensional array as its argument and return the lowest value in the array.

Demonstrate each of the methods in the program.

10. Number Analysis Class

Write a class with a constructor that accepts a file name as its argument. Assume the file contains a series of numbers, each written on a separate line. The class should read the contents of the file into an array, and then displays the following data:

- The lowest number in the array

- The highest number in the array

- The total of the numbers in the array

- The average of the numbers in the array

The Chapter 7 folder on the student CD contains a text file named Numbers.txt. This file contains 12 random numbers. Write a program that tests the class by using this file.

11. 2D Array Operations

Write a program that creates a two-dimensional array initialized with test data. Use any primitive data type you wish. The program should have the following methods:

- GetTotal. This method should accept a two-dimensional array as its argument and return the total of all the values in the array.

- GetAverage. This method should accept a two-dimensional array as its argument and return the average of all the values in the array.

- GetRowTotal. This method should accept a two-dimensional array as its first argument and an integer as its second argument. The second argument should be the subscript of a row in the array. The method should return the total of the values in the specified row.

- **GetColumnTotal.** This method should accept a two-dimensional array as its first argument and an integer as its second argument. The second argument should be the subscript of a column in the array. The method should return the total of the values in the specified column.

- **GetHighestInRow.** This method should accept a two-dimensional array as its first argument and an integer as its second argument. The second argument should be the subscript of a row in the array. The method should return the highest value in the specified row of the array.

- **GetLowestInRow.** This method should accept a two-dimensional array as its first argument and an integer as its second argument. The second argument should be the subscript of a row in the array. The method should return the lowest value in the specified row of the array.

Demonstrate each of the methods in this program.

12. Search Benchmarks

Modify the SequentialSearch and BinarySearch methods presented in this chapter so they keep a count of and display on the screen the number of comparisons they make before finding the value they are searching for. Then write a program that has an array of at least 20 integers. It should call the SequentialSearch method to locate at least five of the values. Then it should call the BinarySearch method to locate the same values. On average, which method makes the fewest comparisons?

8

A Second Look at Classes and Objects

Chapter Objectives

- To understand the difference between an instance member and a static member
- To create methods that accept objects as arguments
- To write methods that return references to objects
- To learn how to add a `ToString` and `Equals` method to a class
- To recognize the need for objects to perform operations involving other objects of the same class
- To understand the concept of aggregation, and how a has-a relationship can exist between classes
- To understand why instance fields that are reference variables must reference objects before they are used to perform operations
- To know what the `this` reference is and be able to use it to overcome the shadowing of field names by parameter names
- To understand how classes can be organized into namespaces and then accessed by programs

Topics in this Chapter

8.1 Static Class Members

8.2 Passing Objects as Arguments to Methods

8.3 Returning Objects from Methods

8.4 The ToString Method, the Equals Method, and Same Class Operations

8.5 Aggregation

8.6 The this Reference Variable

8.7 Namespaces

8.8 Common Errors

Review Questions and Exercises

8.1 Static Class Members

> **CONCEPT** A static class member belongs to the class, not objects instantiated from the class.

A Quick Review of Instance Fields and Instance Methods

Recall from Chapter 4 that each instance of a class has its own set of fields, which are known as instance fields. You can create several instances of a class and store different values in each instance's fields. For example, the Rectangle class that we created in Chapter 4 has a length field and a width field. Let's say that box references an instance of the Rectangle class and execute the following statement:

```
box.SetLength(10);
```

This statement stores the value 10 in the length field that belongs to the instance referenced by box. You can think of instance fields as belonging to a specific instance of a class.

You may also recall that classes can have instance methods as well. When you call an instance method, it performs an operation *on* a specific instance of the class. For example, assuming that box references an instance of the Rectangle class, look at the following statement:

```
x = box.GetLength();
```

This statement calls the GetLength method, which returns the value of the length field that belongs to a specific instance of the Rectangle class the one referenced by box. Both instance fields and instance methods are associated with a specific instance of a class, and they cannot be used until an instance of the class is created.

 NOTE: Remember from Chapter 4 we can use get and set properties instead of accessor and mutator methods. We will use both methods in this chapter.

Static Members

It is possible to create a field or method that does not belong to any instance of a class. Such members are known as a *static fields* and *static methods*. When a value is stored in a static field, it is not stored in an instance of the class. In fact, an instance of the class doesn't even have to exist in order for values to be stored in the class's static fields. Likewise, static methods do not operate on the fields that belong to any instance of the class. Instead, they can operate only on static fields. You can think of static fields and static methods as belonging to an class instead of an instance of the class. In this section, we will take a closer look at static members. First we will examine static fields.

Static Fields

When a field is declared with the key word `static`, there will be only one copy of the field in memory, regardless of the number of instances of the class that might exist. A single copy of a class's static field is shared by all instances of the class. For example, the `Countable` class shown in Code Listing 8-1 uses a static field to keep count of the number of instances of the class that are created.

Code Listing 8-1 Countable.cs

```
 1 /*
 2    This class demonstrates a static field.
 3 */
 4
 5 using System;
 6
 7 public class Countable
 8 {
 9     private static int instanceCount = 0;
10
11     /*
12         The constructor increments the static
13         field instanceCount. This keeps track
14         of the number of instances of this
15         class that are created.
16     */
17
18     public Countable()
19     {
20         instanceCount++;
21     }
22
23     public int InstanceCount
24     {
25         get
26         {
27             return instanceCount;
28         }
29     }
30 }
```

First, notice in line 9 the declaration of the static field named `instanceCount`:

```
private static int instanceCount = 0;
```

A static field is created by placing the key word static after the access specifier and before the field's data type. Notice that we have explicitly initialized the instanceCount field with the value 0. This initialization takes place only once, regardless of the number of instances of the class that are created.

 NOTE: C# automatically stores 0 in all uninitialized static member variables. The instanceCount field in this class is explicitly initialized so it is clear to anyone reading the code that the field starts with the value 0.

Next, look at the constructor in lines 18 through 21.The constructor uses the ++ operator to increment the instanceCount field. Each time an instance of the Countable class is created, the constructor will be called and the instanceCount field will be incremented. As a result, the instanceCount field will contain the number of instances of the Countable class that have been created. The InstanceCount property, in lines 23 through 29, returns the value in instanceCount. The program in Code Listing 8-2 demonstrates this class.

Code Listing 8-2   StaticDemo.cs

```
 1 /*
 2     This program demonstrates the Countable class.
 3 */
 4
 5 using System;
 6 public class StaticDemo
 7 {
 8    public static void Main()
 9    {
10       int objectCount;
11
12       // Create three instances of the
13       // Countable class.
14       Countable object1 = new Countable();
15       Countable object2 = new Countable();
16       Countable object3 = new Countable();
17
18       // Get the number of instances from
19       // the class's static field.
20       objectCount = object1.InstanceCount;
21       Console.WriteLine("{0} instances of the class " +
22                   "were created.", objectCount);
23    }
24 }
```

Program Output
```
3 instances of the class were created.
```

The program creates three instances of the Countable class, referenced by the variables object1, object2, and object3. Although there are three instances of the class, there is only one Copy of the static field. This is illustrated in Figure 8-1.

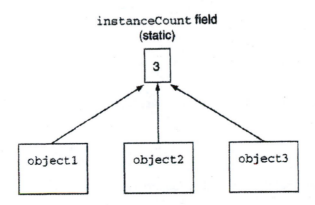

Instances of the Countable class

Figure 8-1   All instances of the class share the static field

In line 20 the program calls the InstanceCount property to retrieve the number of instances that have been created:

```
objectCount = object1.InstanceCount;
```

Although the program calls the InstanceCount property from object1, the same value would be returned from any of the objects.

Static Methods

When a class contains a static method, it isn't necessary for an instance of the class to be created in order to execute the method. The program in Code Listing 8-3 shows a class with static methods.

Code Listing 8-3   Metric.cs

```
1 /*
2    This class demonstrates static methods.
3 */
4
```

(code listing continues)

Code Listing 8-3 Metric.cs *(continued)*

```
 5 public class Metric
 6 {
 7    /**
 8       The MilesToKilometers method converts a
 9       distance in miles to kilometers.
10       **parameter m The distance in miles.
11       **return The distance in kilometers.
12    */
13
14    public static double MilesToKilometers(double m)
15    {
16       return m * 1.609;
17    }
18
19    /*
20       The KilometersToMiles method converts
21       a distance in kilometers to miles.
22       **parameter k The distance in kilometers.
23       **return The distance in miles.
24    */
25
26    public static double KilometersToMiles(double k)
27    {
28       return k / 1.609;
29    }
30 }
```

A static method is created by placing the key word static after the access specifier in the method header. In the example, Metric class has two static methods: MilesToKilometers and KilometersToMiles. Because they are declared as static, they belong to the class and may be called without any instances of the class being in existence. You simply write the name of the class before the dot operator in the method call, like this:

```
kilometers = Metric.MilesToKilometers(10.0);
```

This statement calls the MilesToKilometers method, passing the value 10.0 as an argument. Notice that the method is not called from an instance of the class, but is called directly from the Metric class. Code Listing 8-4 shows a program that uses the Metric class. Figure 8-2 shows an example of interaction with the program.

Code Listing 8-4 MetricDemo.cs

```
 1 /*
 2    This program demonstrates the Metric class.
 3 */
 4
 5
```

(code listing continues)

Code Listing 8-4   MetricDemo.cs *(continued)*

```
 6 using System;
 7
 8 public class MetricDemo
 9 {
10    public static void Main()
11    {
12
13        double miles, // A distance in miles
14               kilos; // A distance in kilometers
15
16        // Get a distance in miles.
17        Console.WriteLine("Enter a distance in miles: ");
18        miles = Convert.ToDouble(Console.ReadLine());
19
20        // Convert the distance to kilometers.
21        kilos = Metric.MilesToKilometers(miles);
22        Console.WriteLine("{0:N2} miles Equals {1:N2}
                   kilometers.", miles, kilos);
23
24        // Get a distance in kilometers.
25        Console.WriteLine("Enter a distance in kilometers: ");
26        kilos = Convert.ToDouble(Console.ReadLine());
27
28        // Convert the distance to kilometers.
29        miles = Metric.KilometersToMiles(kilos);
30        Console.WriteLine("{0:N2} kilometers Equals {1:N2}
                   miles.",kilos, miles);
31    }
32 }
```

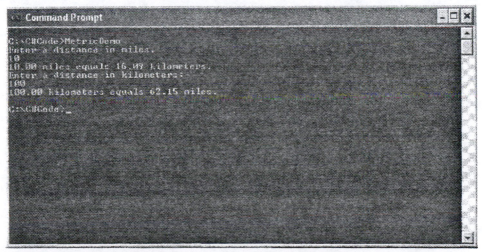

Figure 8-2   Interaction with the `MetricDemo.cs` **program**

Static methods are convenient for many tasks because they can be called directly from the class, as needed. They are most often used to create utility classes that perform operations on data, but have no need to collect and store data. The Metric class is a good example. It is used as a container to hold methods that convert miles to kilometers and vice versa, but is not intended to store any data.

The only limitation that static methods have is that they cannot refer to nonstatic members of the class. This means that any method called from a static method must also be static. It also means that if the method uses any of the class's fields, they must be static as well.

 ## CHECKPOINT

8.1 What is the difference between a regular member variable and a static member variable?

8.2 What action is possible with a static method that isn't possible with a regular method?

8.3 Describe the limitation of static methods.

8.2 Passing Objects as Arguments to Methods

 Objects may be passed as arguments to methods. Unlike variables, however, objects are passed by reference.

In Chapter 3 we discussed how simple data type values, as well as references to string objects, can be passed as arguments to methods. You can also pass references to other types of objects as arguments to methods. For example, recall that in Chapter 4 we developed a Rectangle class. The program in Code Listing 8-5 creates an instance of the Rectangle class and then passes a reference to that object as an argument to a method.

Code Listing 8-5 PassObject.cs

```
1 /*
2    This program passes an object as an argument.
3 */
4
5 using System;
```

(code listing continues)

Code Listing 8-5 PassObject.cs *(continued)*

```
6 public class PassObject
7 {
8    public static void Main()
9    {
10       // Create a Rectangle object.
11
12       Rectangle box = new Rectangle(12.0, 5.0);
13
14       // Pass a reference to the object to
15       // the DisplayRectangle method.
16
17       DisplayRectangle(box);
18    }
19
20    /*
21       The DisplayRectangle method displays the
22       length and width of a rectangle.
23       **parameter r A reference to a Rectangle
24       object.
25    */
26
27    public static void DisplayRectangle(Rectangle r)
28    {
29       // Display the length and width.
30       Console.WriteLine("Length : {0} Width :{1}",
                r.GetLength(),r.GetWidth());
31    }
32 }
```

Program Output
```
Length : 12 Width : 5
```

In this program's Main method, the box variable is a Rectangle reference variable. In line 17 it is passed as an argument to the DisplayRectangle method. The DisplayRectangle method has a parameter variable, r, which is also a Rectangle reference variable, and which receives the argument.

Recall that a reference variable holds the memory address of an object. When the DisplayRectangle method is called, the address that is stored in box is passed into the r parameter variable. This is illustrated in Figure 8-3. This means that when the DisplayRectangle method is executing, box and r both reference the same object as shown in Figure 8-4.

Recall from Chapter 3 that when a variable is passed as an argument to a method, it can be passed by value or by reference. *Pass by value* means that a copy of the variable is passed into the method's parameter. When the method changes the contents of the parameter variable, it does not affect the contents of the original variable that was passed as an argument. When a reference variable is passed as an argument to a method, however, the method has access to the object that

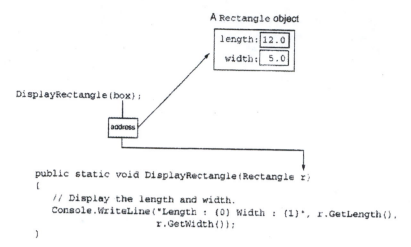

Figure 8-3   Passing a reference as an argument

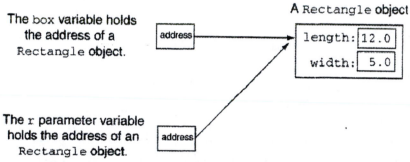

Figure 8-4   Both box and r reference the same object

the variable references. As you can see from Figure 8-4, the DisplayRectangle method has access to the same Rectangle object that the box variable references. When a method receives a reference variable as an argument, it is possible for the method to modify the contents of the object referenced by the variable. We do this by adding the keyword ref in the method header and declaration. This is demonstrated in Code Listing 8-6.

Code Listing 8-6   PassObject2.cs

```
1 /*
2     This program passes an object as an ref argument.
3     The object is modified by the receiving method.
4 */
5
```

(code listing continues)

Code Listing 8-6 **PassObject2.cs** *(continued)*

```
 6 using System;
 7 public class PassObject2
 8 {
 9    public static void Main()
10    {
11       // Create a Rectangle object.
12       Rectangle box = new Rectangle(12.0, 5.0);
13
14       // Display the object's contents.
15       Console.WriteLine("Contents of the box object:");
16       Console.WriteLine("Length : {0} Width : {1}",box.GetLength()
17                            ,box.GetWidth());
18
19       // Pass a reference to the object to the
20       // ChangeRectangle method.
21       ChangeRectangle(ref box);
22
23       // Display the object's contents again.
24       Console.WriteLine("\nNow the contents of the " +
25                            "box object are:");
26       Console.WriteLine("Length : {0} Width : {1}",box.GetLength()
27                            ,box.GetWidth());
28    }
29
30    /*
31       The ChangeRectangle method sets a Rectangle
32       object's length and width to 0.
33       **parameter r The Rectangle object to change.
34    */
35
36    public static void ChangeRectangle(ref Rectangle r)
37    {
38       r.SetLength(0.0);
39       r.SetWidth(0.0);
40    }
41 }
```

Program Output
```
Contents of the box object:
Length : 12 Width : 5
Now the contents of the box object are:
Length : 0 Width : 0
```

Notice the key word **ref** in lines 21 and 36. When writing a method that receives a reference variable as an argument, you must take care not to accidentally modify the contents of the object that is referenced by the variable.

CHECKPOINT

8.4 When an object is passed as an argument to a method, what is actually passed?

8.5 When an argument is passed by value, the method has a copy of the argument and does not have access to the original argument. Is this still true when an object is passed to a method?

8.6 Recall the BankAccount class discussed in Chapter 4. Write a method that accepts a BankAccount object as its argument and displays the object's balance field on the screen.

8.3 Returning Objects from Methods

CONCEPT A method can return a reference to an object.

Just as methods can be written to return an int, double, float, or other primitive data type, they can also be written to return a reference to an object. For example, recall the BankAccount class that was discussed in Chapter 4. The program in Code Listing 8-7 uses a method, GetAccount, which returns a reference to a BankAccount object. Figure 8-5 shows example interaction with the program.

Code Listing 8-7   ReturnObject.cs

```
 1 /*
 2     This program demonstrates how a method
 3     can return a reference to an object.
 4 */
 5
 6 using System;
 7
 8 public class ReturnObject
 9 {
10     public static void Main()
11     {
12         BankAccount account;
13
14         // Get a reference to a BankAccount object.
15         account = GetAccount();
16
17         // Display the account's balance.
18         Console.WriteLine("The account has a balance of {0:C2}",
19                 account.GetBalance());
20     }
21
```

(code listing continues)

Code Listing 8-7 ReturnObject.cs *(continued)*

```
22    /*
23       The GetAccount method creates a BankAccount
24       object with the balance specified by the
25       user.
26       **return A reference to the object.
27    */
28
29    public static BankAccount GetAccount()
30    {
31       double balance; // Account balance
32
33       // Get the balance from the user.
34       Console.WriteLine("Enter the account balance: ");
35       balance = Convert.ToDouble(Console.ReadLine());
36
37       // Create a BankAccount object and return
38       // a reference to it.
39       return new BankAccount(balance);
40    }
41 }
```

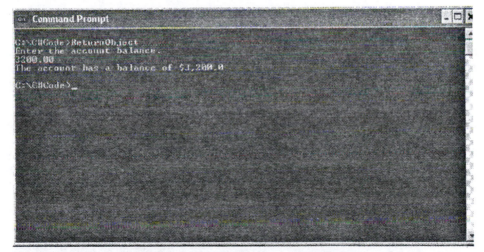

Figure 8-5 Interaction with the `ReturnObject.cs` **program**

Notice that the GetAccount method has a return data type of BankAccount. Figure 8-6 shows the method's return type, which is listed in the method header.

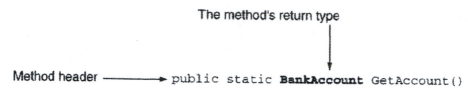

Figure 8-6 The GetAccount **method header**

A return type of BankAccount means the method returns a reference to a BankAccount object when it terminates. The following statement, which appears in line 15, assigns the GetAccount method's return value to account:

```
account = GetAccount();
```

After this statement executes, the account variable will reference the BankAccount object that was returned from the GetAccount method.

Now let's look at the GetAccount method. In line 36 the method uses the keyboard to get the account balance from the user. In line 37 the value entered by the user is converted to a double and assigned to balance, a local variable. The last statement in the method, in line 41, is the following return statement:

```
return new BankAccount(balance);
```

This statement uses the new key word to create a BankAccount object, passing balance as an argument to the constructor. The address of the object is then returned from the method, as illustrated in Figure 8-7. Back in line 15, where the method is called, the address is assigned to account.

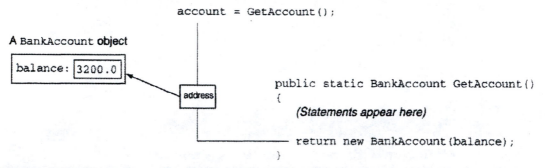

Figure 8-7 The GetAccount **method returns a reference to a** BankAccount **object**

CHECKPOINT

8.7 Recall the Rectangle class discussed in Chapter 4, and earlier in this chapter. Write a method that returns a reference to a Rectangle object. The method should store 0.0 in the object's length and width fields before returning it.

8.4 The ToString Method, the Equals Method, and Same Class Operations

 CONCEPT A class can benefit from having a method named ToString, which is implicitly called under certain circumstances. A class can also benefit from having an Equals method for comparing the contents of objects. Sometimes an object must have methods that perform same class operations. This means the methods accept, as arguments, objects of the same class as itself, and/or return objects of the same class as itself.

Recall from Chapter 5 that the string class has a method, Equals, that accepts a reference to a string object as an argument. As a review, here is an example of how the code can be used:

```
string name1 = "Joe";
string name2 = "Jo";
if (name1.Equals(name2))
    Console.WriteLine("The names are the same.");
else
    Console.WriteLine("The names are not the same.");
```

This is an example of a *same class operation*, where an object performs an operation involving another object of the same class. In this section we use a class named FeetInches to study same class operations. The FeetInches class is designed to hold distances or measurements expressed in feet and inches. Figure 8-8 shows a UML diagram for the class.

The class has two int fields: feet and inches. Together these fields hold a distance measured in feet and inches, such as 12 feet 7 inches. The feet field holds the feet part and the inches field holds the inches part. Table 8-1 describes the class's methods.

Before looking at the code for the FeetInches class, it might help to see a program that uses the class. The program in Code Listing 8-8 demonstrates the class. Figures 8-9 and 8-10 show the interaction with the program during two different runs.

Notice that the FeetInches class automatically adjusts measurements so that the inches field is never greater than 11. For example, the distance 5 feet 14 inches was adjusted to the more

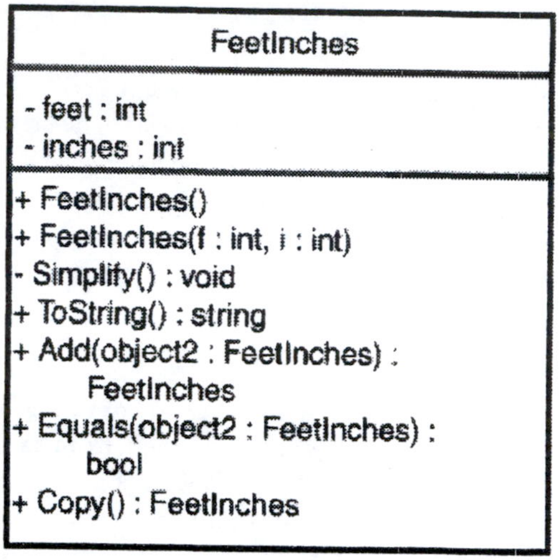

```
                    ┌─────────────────────────────┐
                    │          FeetInches         │
                    ├─────────────────────────────┤
                    │  - feet : int               │
                    │  - inches : int             │
                    ├─────────────────────────────┤
                    │  + FeetInches()             │
                    │  + FeetInches(f : int, i : int) │
                    │  - Simplify() : void        │
                    │  + ToString() : string      │
                    │  + Add(object2 : FeetInches) : │
                    │        FeetInches           │
                    │  + Equals(object2 : FeetInches) : │
                    │        bool                 │
                    │  + Copy() : FeetInches      │
                    └─────────────────────────────┘
```

Figure 8-8   UML diagram for the `FeetInches` **class**

Table 8-1   The `FeetInches` **class methods**

Method	Description
Constructor #1 (no-arg constructor)	This constructor assigns 0 to both the `feet` and `inches` fields.
Constructor #2	This constructor accepts two `int` arguments that are assigned to the `feet` and `inches` fields. The `Simplify` method is also called.
`Simplify`	This method adjusts any set of values where the `inches` field is greater than 11. For example, 3 feet 14 inches would be adjusted to read 4 feet 2 inches.
`ToString`	This method returns a string representing the distance held by the object. For example, if an object's `feet` field holds 3 and its `inches` field holds 7, the `ToString` method would return the string "3 feet 7 inches".
`Add`	This method accepts a `FeetInches` object as its argument. It returns a reference to a `FeetInches` object that is the sum of the calling object and the object that was passed as the argument.
`Equals`	This method accepts a `FeetInches` object as its argument. It returns the Boolean value `true` if the calling object and the argument object hold the same data. Otherwise it returns `false`.
`Copy`	This method returns a reference to a new `FeetInches` object that is a Copy of the calling object.

Code Listing 8-8   DistanceDemo.cs

```
 1 /*
 2     This program demonstrates the FeetInches class.
 3 */
 4
 5 using System;
 6
 7 public class DistanceDemo
 8 {
 9     public static void Main()
10     {
11
12         int feet, inches;
13
14         // Get the feet part of a distance.
15         Console.WriteLine("Think of a distance in feet and
                  inches.\n" +
16                 "Now, enter the feet.");
17         feet = Convert.ToInt32(Console.ReadLine());
18
19         // Get the inches part of the distance.
20         Console.WriteLine("Now, enter the inches.");
21         inches = Convert.ToInt32(Console.ReadLine());
22
23         // Create a FeetInches object.
24         FeetInches distance =
25                     new FeetInches(feet, inches);
26
27         // Display the distance.
28         Console.WriteLine("The distance you entered is {0}",
29                     distance.ToString());
30     }
31 }
```

proper measurement 6 feet 2 inches. This adjustment is performed by a private method named
Simplify, which is called from the constructor and the Inches property.

Also notice that the class has a ToString method which returns a string representing the distance held by an object. This method is useful for displaying a distance. Code Listing 8-9 shows the FeetInches class.

Figure 8-9   First example interaction with the `DistanceDemo.cs` **program**

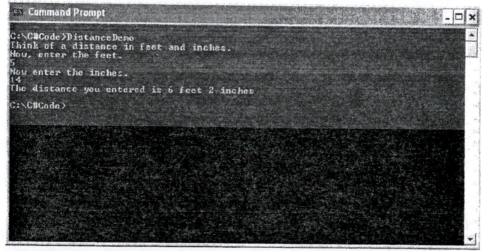

Figure 8-10   Second example interaction with the `DistanceDemo.cs` **program**

Code Listing 8-9   FeetInches.cs

```
1  /*
2     The FeetInches class holds distances measured in
3     feet and inches.
4  */
5
```

(code listing continues)

Code Listing 8-9 FeetInches.cs *(continued)*

```
 6 public class FeetInches
 7 {
 8     private int feet,        // The number of feet
 9                  inches;     // The number of inches
10
11     /*
12        This constructor assigns 0 to the feet
13        and inches fields.
14     */
15
16     public FeetInches()
17     {
18         feet = 0;
19         inches = 0;
20     }
21
22     /*
23        This constructor accepts two arguments which
24        are assigned to the feet and inches fields.
25        The simplify method is then called.
26        **parameter f The value to assign to feet.
27        **parameter i The value to assign to inches.
28     */
29
30     public FeetInches(int f, int i)
31     {
32         feet = f;
33         inches = i;
34         Simplify();
35     }
36
37     /*
38        The Simplify method adjusts the values
39        in feet and inches to conform to a
40        standard measurement.
41     */
42
43     private void Simplify()
44     {
45         if (inches > 11)
46         {
47             feet = feet + (inches / 12);
48             inches = inches % 12;
49         }
50     }
51
```

(code listing continues)

Code Listing 8-9 **FeetInches.cs** *(continued)*

```
52      /*
53         The Feet property assigns and returns
54         a value for feet.
55
56      */
57
58      public int Feet
59      {
60         get
61         {
62            return feet;
63         }
64         set
65         {
66            feet = value;
67         }
68      }
69
70      /*
71         The Inches property assigns and returns
72         a value for inches.
73
74      */
75
76      public int Inches
77      {
78         get
79         {
80           return inches;
81         }
82         set
83         {
84           inches = value;
85           Simplify();
86         }
87      }
88
89      /*
90         ToString method
91         **return a reference to a String stating
92         the feet and inches.
93      */
94
95      public override string ToString()
96      {
97         string str = feet + " feet " +
98                      inches + " inches";
99         return str;
100     }
101
```

(code listing continues)

Code Listing 8-9 **FeetInches.cs** *(continued)*

```
102     /*
103         The Add method returns a FeetInches object
104         that holds the sum of this object and another
105         FeetInches object.
106         **parameter object2 The other FeetInches object.
107         **return A reference to a FeetInches object.
108     */
109
110     public FeetInches Add(FeetInches object2)
111     {
112         int totalFeet,    // To hold the sum of feet
113             totalInches;  // To hold the sum of inches
114
115         totalFeet = feet + object2.Feet;
116         totalInches = inches + object2.Inches;
117         return new FeetInches(totalFeet, totalInches);
118     }
119
120     /*
121         The Equals method compares this object to the
122         argument object. If both have the same values,
123         the method returns true.
124         **return true if the objects are equal, false
125         otherwise.
126     */
127
128     public bool Equals(FeetInches object2)
129     {
130         bool status;
131
132         if (object2 == null)
133             status = false;
134         else if (feet == object2.Feet &&
135                  inches == object2.Inches)
136             status = true;
137         else
138             status = false;
139         return status;
140     }
141
```

(code listing continues)

Code Listing 8-9 **FeetInches.cs** *(continued)*

```
142     /*
143         The Copy method makes a copy of the
144         the calling object.
145         **return A reference to the copy.
146     */
147
148     public FeetInches Copy()
149     {
150         // Make a new FeetInches object and
151         // initialize it with the same data
152         // as the calling object.
153         FeetInches newObject =
154                 new FeetInches(feet, inches);
155
156         // Return a reference to the new object.
157         return newObject;
158     }
159 }
```

More About the ToString Method

The program in Code Listing 8-8 explicitly called the FeetInches class's ToString method to display the contents of the distance object in the following statement, which appears in lines 28 and 29:

```
Console.WriteLine("The distance you entered is {0}",
                distance.ToString());
```

In actuality, every class automatically has a ToString method that returns a string containing the namespace and class name. This method is called when necessary if you have not provided your own ToString method. Since we wanted to use our own ToString method, we must use the key word override in the method header, to override the ToString method provided to us automatically. You will learn more about the key word override in Chapter 10.

The Add Method

The Add method is the first FeetInches method we will study that performs a same class operation. It allows us to add one FeetInches object to another. Let's take a closer look at the method, which appears in lines 110 through 118 of Code Listing 8-9:

```
public FeetInches Add(FeetInches object2)
{
    int totalFeet,     // To hold the sum of feet
    totalInches;       // To hold the sum of inches

    totalFeet = feet + object2.Feet;
    totalInches = inches + object2.Inches;
    return new FeetInches(totalFeet, totalInches);
}
```

This method accepts a FeetInches object as its argument. It uses the following statement in line 115 to add the feet field of the calling object to the feet field of the argument object, and store the result in the local variable totalFeet:

```
totalFeet = feet + object2.Feet;
```

Then the statement in line 116 adds the inches field of the calling object to the inches field of the argument object, and stores the result in the local variable totalInches:

```
totalInches = inches + object2.Inches;
```

The method's last statement, in line 117, creates a new FeetInches object, passes TotalFeet and TotalInches to the constructor, and returns the object's address. The program in Code Listing 8-10 demonstrates the method.

Code Listing 8-10   DistanceAdd.cs

```
1  /*
2     This program uses the FeetInches class's
3     add method to add two distances.
4  */
5
6  using System;
7
8  public class DistanceAdd
9  {
10     public static void Main()
11     {
12        // Create two FeetInches objects.
13        FeetInches distance1 =
14                    new FeetInches(5, 9);
15        FeetInches distance2 =
16                    new FeetInches(2, 5);
17
18        // Declare a FeetInches reference
19        // variable.
20        FeetInches distance3;
21
22        // Add distance 1 and distance 2, and
23        // store the result in distance3.
24
25        distance3 = distance1.Add(distance2);
26
```

(code listing continues)

Code Listing 8-10   DistanceAdd.cs *(continued)*

```
27          // Display the results.
28
29          Console.WriteLine("The first distance is {0}",
30                               distance1);
31          Console.WriteLine("The second distance is {0}",
32                               distance2);
33          Console.WriteLine("The sum of these " +
34                               "distances is {0}", distance3);
35      }
36 }
```

Program Output

```
The first distance is 5 feet 9 inches.
The second distance is 2 feet 5 inches.
The sum of these distances is 8 feet 2 inches.
```

The Equals Method

Now let's take a closer look at the Equals method, which also performs a same class operation: It compares the contents of two FeetInches objects and determines whether the two objects are equal. As we learned in Chapter 5, we can overload the equality operator to determine if two objects are equal as well. For example, given an overloaded equality operator, the following code can compare two FeetInches objects:

```
FeetInches distance1 = new FeetInches(6, 5);
FeetInches distance2 = new FeetInches(6, 5);
if (distance1 == distance2)
    Console.WriteLine("The objects are the same.");
else
    Console.WriteLine("The objects are not the same.");
```

If we do not overload the equality operator then when we use reference variables, the operator compares the memory addresses that the variables contain, not the contents of the objects referenced by the variables. This is illustrated in Figure 8-11.

Because the two variables reference different objects in memory, they will contain different addresses. Therefore, the result of the boolean expression distance1 == distance2 is false and the code reports that the objects are not the same. Instead of overloading the == operator to compare two FeetInches objects, we should use the Equals method. Here is the code for the method, which appears in lines 128 through 140 of FeetInches.cs:

```
public bool Equals(FeetInches object2)
{
    bool status;

    if (object2 == null)
        status = false;
```

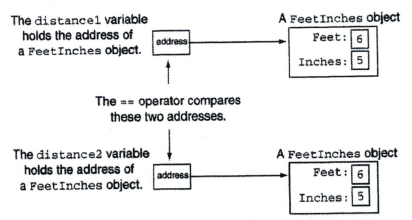

Figure 8-11 The **==** operator compares the contents of the reference variables, not the contents of the objects the variables reference

```
else if (feet == object2.Feet &&
         inches == object2.Inches)
    status = true;
else
    status = false;
return status;
}
```

This method accepts a FeetInches object as its argument. The if-else-if statement performs the following comparisons: First, we need to make sure that the parameter variable object2 does indeed reference an object. In lines 132 and 133, if a null reference was passed as an argument, status is set to false.

Otherwise, in lines 134 through 135, if the feet field of the calling object is equal to the feet field of the argument object, and the inches field of the calling object is equal to the inches field of the argument object, then the two objects contain the same distance. In this case, the local variable status (a boolean) is set to true.

Otherwise, in lines 137 and 138, status is set to false. In line 139 the method returns the value of the status variable. The program in Code Listing 8-11 demonstrates the Equals method.

Code Listing 8-11   DistanceCompare.cs

```
1 /*
2    This program uses the FeetInches class's Equals
3    method to compare two distances.
4 */
5 using System;
```

(code listing continues)

Code Listing 8-11 DistanceCompare.cs *(continued)*

```
 6 public class DistanceCompare
 7 {
 8    public static void Main()
 9    {
10       // Create three FeetInches objects.
11       FeetInches distance1 =
12            new FeetInches(5, 9); // 5 feet 9 inches
13       FeetInches distance2 =
14            new FeetInches(5, 9); // 5 feet 9 inches
15       FeetInches distance3 =
16            new FeetInches(7, 4); // 7 feet 4 inches
17
18       // Display the distances.
19       Console.WriteLine("The first distance is {0}",
20                         distance1);
21       Console.WriteLine("The second distance is {0}",
22                         distance2);
23       Console.WriteLine("The third distance is {0}",
24                         distance3);
25
26       // Compare distance1 and distance2
27       if (distance1.Equals(distance2))
28       {
29          Console.WriteLine("Distances 1 and 2 " +
30                            "are the same.");
31       }
32       else
33       {
34          Console.WriteLine("Distances 1 and 2 " +
35                            "are not the same.");
36       }
37
38       // Compare distance1 and distance3
39       if (distance1.Equals(distance3))
40       {
41          Console.WriteLine("Distances 1 and 3 " +
42                            "are the same.");
43       }
44       else
45       {
46          Console.WriteLine("Distances 1 and 3 " +
47                            "are not the same.");
48       }
49    }
50 }
```

Code Listing 8-11   DistanceCompare.cs *(continued)*

Program Output
```
The first distance is 5 feet 9 inches.
The second distance is 5 feet 9 inches.
The third distance is 7 feet 4 inches.
Distances 1 and 2 are the same.
Distances 1 and 3 are not the same.
```

If you want to be able to compare the objects of a given class, you should always write an `Equals` method for the class—unless you know how to overload operators.

The `Copy` Method

The `Copy` method also performs a same class operation: It returns a `FeetInches` object that is a copy of the calling object. This method is necessary because you cannot copy objects with a simple assignment statement, as you would with primitive variables. For example, look at the following code:

```
FeetInches distance1 = new FeetInches(4, 9);
FeetInches distance2 = distance1;
```

The first statement creates a `FeetInches` object and assigns its address to the `distance1` variable. The second statement assigns `distance1` to `distance2`. This does not make a copy of the object referenced by `distance1`. Rather, it makes a copy of the address that is stored in `distance1` and stores it in `distance2`. After this statement executes, both the `distance1` and `distance2` variables will reference the same object. This is illustrated in Figure 8-12.

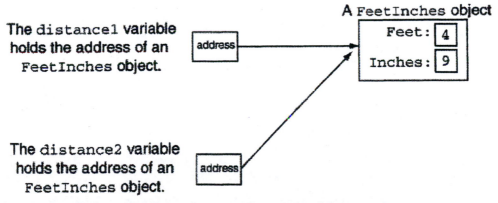

Figure 8-12   Both variables reference the same object

Recall from Chapter 7 that this type of assignment operation is called a shallow copy. It is "shallow" because only the address of the object is copied, not the actual object itself. A deep copy is an operation that copies the object itself. The FeetInches class provides the Copy method, which performs a deep copy.

The Copy method creates a new FeetInches object and passes the calling object's feet and inches fields as arguments to the constructor. This makes the new object a copy of the calling object. The method then returns a reference to the new object. Here is the method's code, which appears in lines 148 through 158 of FeetInches.cs:

```
public FeetInches Copy()
{

    FeetInches newObject =
    new FeetInches(feet, inches);

    // Return a reference to the new object.
    return newObject;
}
```

The program in Code Listing 8-12 demonstrates the Copy method.

Code Listing 8-12 DeepCopy.cs

```
1 /*
2     This program demonstrates the FeetInches class's
3     Copy method.
4 */
5 using System;
6 public class DeepCopy
7 {
8     public static void Main()
9     {
10        FeetInches distance1 =
11                        new FeetInches(4, 9);
12        FeetInches distance2;
13
14        // Make distance2 reference a copy
15        // of distance1.
16        distance2 = distance1.Copy();
17
18        // Display both objects.
19        Console.WriteLine("Distance1: {0}",
20                            distance1);
21        Console.WriteLine("Distance2: {0}",
22                            distance2);
23
```

(code listing continues)

Code Listing 8-12 **DeepCopy.cs** *(continued)*

```
24        // Determine whether distance1 and
25        // distance2 reference the same object.
26        if (distance1 == distance2)
27        {
28            Console.WriteLine("Both variables " +
29                    "reference the same object.");
30        }
31        else
32        {
33            Console.WriteLine("The variables " +
34                    "reference different objects.");
35        }
36    }
37 }
```

Program Output
```
Distance1: 4 feet 9 inches
Distance2: 4 feet 9 inches
The variables reference different objects.
```

8.5 Aggregation

CONCEPT Aggregation occurs when an instance of a class is a field in another class.

Making an instance of one class a field in another class is called object aggregation. For example, look at the BankCustomer class shown in Code Listing 8-21. It has, as fields, an instance of the PersonalInfo class (shown in Code Listing 8-22) and two instances of the BankAccount class (which was discussed in Chapter 4). To keep the BankCustomer and PersonalInfo classes simple, we have only written a constructor and a ToString method for each.

Code Listing 8-13 **BankCustomer.cs**

```
1 /*
2    The BankCustomer class demonstrates aggregation.
3    It has as fields instances of the PersonalInfo
4    and BankAccount classes.
5 */
6
```

(code listing continues)

Code Listing 8-13 BankCustomer.cs *(continued)*

```
 7  public class BankCustomer
 8  {
 9     private PersonalInfo info;    // Personal info
10     private BankAccount checking; // Checking account
11     private BankAccount savings;  // Savings account
12
13     /*
14        The constructor accepts references to
15        a PersonalInfo object and two BankAccount
16        objects - one for a checking account and one
17        for a savings account.
18        **parameter i Personal information
19        **parameter c Checking account
20        **parameter s Savings account
21     */
22
23     public BankCustomer(PersonalInfo i, BankAccount c,
24                                         BankAccount s)
25     {
26        info = i;
27        checking = c;
28        savings = s;
29     }
30
31     /*
32        The ToString method returns a string containing
33        the customer's personal information, checking
34        account balance and savings account balance.
35        **return A reference to a string.
36     */
37
38     public override string ToString()
39     {
40        string str;
41
42        str = info +
43           "\nChecking Account Balance: " +
44           checking.GetBalance().ToString("C2") +
45           "\nSavings Account Balance: " +
46           savings.GetBalance().ToString("C2");
47
48        return str;
49     }
50  }
```

Code Listing 8-14   PersonalInfo.cs

```
1  /*
2      This class stores personal information
3      about a customer.
4  */
5
6  public class PersonalInfo
7  {
8      private string customerName,
9                     customerAddress,
10                    customerCity,
11                    customerState,
12                    customerZip;
13
14     /*
15         Constructor
16         **parameter name The customer's name.
17         **parameter address The cusomter's address.
18         **parameter city The customer's city.
19         **parameter state The customer's state.
20         **parameter zip The customer's ZIP code.
21     */
22
23     public PersonalInfo(string name, string address,
24                         string city, string state,
25                         string zip)
26     {
27         customerName = name;
28         customerAddress = address;
29         customerCity = city;
30         customerState = state;
31         customerZip = zip;
32     }
33
34     /*
35         The ToString method returns a string
36         containing the customer information.
37         **return A reference to a string.
38     */
39
```

(code listing continues)

Code Listing 8-14 PersonalInfo.cs *(continued)*

```
40    public override string ToString()
41    {
42        string str;
43
44        str = "Name: " + customerName +
45            "\nAddress: " + customerAddress +
46            "\nCity: " + customerCity +
47            " State: " + customerState +
48            " ZIP: " + customerZip;
49
50        return str;
51    }
52 }
```

The BankCustomer class can be used to create *aggregate objects* that contain instances of other objects as fields. Object aggregation is useful for creating a "has-a" relationship between classes. For example, the relationships that exist in the BankCustomer class can be described as follows:

- The bank customer has personal information.

- The bank customer has a checking account.

- The bank customer has a savings account.

The has-a relationship is sometimes called a whole-part relationship because one object is part of a greater whole. The program in Code Listing 8-15 demonstrates the BankCustomer account.

Code Listing 8-15 AggregationDemo.cs

```
 1 /*
 2     This program demonstrates the BankCustomer class.
 3 */
 4
 5 using System;
 6
 7 public class AggregationDemo
 8 {
 9     public static void Main()
10     {
11         // Create a PersonalInfo object.
12         PersonalInfo info =
13                 new PersonalInfo("Jill Smith",
14                     "247 Main Street", "Canton",
15                     "NC", "25555");
16
```

(code listing continues)

Code Listing 8-15   AggregationDemo.cs *(continued)*

```
17          // Create BankAccount objects.
18          BankAccount checking =
19                  new BankAccount(600.0);
20          BankAccount savings =
21                  new BankAccount(5000.0);
22
23          // Create a BankCustomer object.
24          BankCustomer customer =
25                  new BankCustomer(info, checking,
26                                      savings);
27
28          // Display the BankCustomer object.
29          Console.WriteLine(customer);
30      }
31 }
```

Program Output

```
Name: Jill Smith
Address: 247 Main Street
City: Canton State: NC ZIP: 25555
Checking Account Balance: $600.00
Savings Account Balance: $5,000.00
```

Aggregation in UML Diagrams

We show aggregation in a UML diagram by connecting two classes with a line that has an open diamond at one end. The diamond is closest to the class that is the aggregate. Figure 8-13 shows a UML diagram depicting the relationship between the BankCustomer, PersonalInfo, and BankAccount classes. The open diamond is closest to the BankCustomer class because it is the aggregate (the whole).

Avoid Returning References to Private Fields

When a class has a field that is an object, it is possible to create a "security hole" by having a method that returns a reference to the private field. When a method returns a reference to a field, any variable outside the object that receives the reference can provide access to the field. For example, Code Listing 8-16 shows the InsecureBankCustomer class. This is a modification of the BankCustomer class.

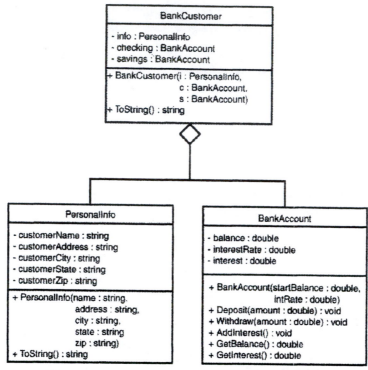

Figure 8-13 UML diagram showing aggregation

Code Listing 8-16 InsecureBankCustomer.cs

```
1  /*
2      The InsecureBankCustomer class demonstrates
3      how an aggregate class can be insecure by
4      providing access to references to objects
5      that are private fields.
6  */
7
8  public class InsecureBankCustomer
9  {
10     private PersonalInfo info;      // Personal info
11     private BankAccount checking;   // Checking account
12     private BankAccount savings;    // Savings account
13
```

(code listing continues)

Code Listing 8-16 InsecureBankCustomer.cs *(continued)*

```
14    /*
15        The constructor accepts references to
16        a PersonalInfo object and two BankAccount
17        objects - one for a checking account and one
18        for a savings account.
19        **parameter i Personal information
20        **parameter c Checking account
21        **parameter s Savings account
22    */
23
24      public InsecureBankCustomer(PersonalInfo i,
25                      BankAccount c, BankAccount s)
26    {
27        info = i;
28        checking = c;
29        savings = s;
30    }
31
32    /*
33        The GetSavingsAccount method returns a reference
34        to the savings object that is a private field.
35        This method creates a "security hole"!
36        **return A reference to the savings field.
37    */
38
39    public BankAccount GetSavingsAccount()
40    {
41        return savings;
42    }
43
44    /*
45        The ToString method returns a string containing
46        the customer's personal information, checking
47        account balance and savings account balance.
48        **return A reference to a String.
49    */
50
51    public override string ToString()
52    {
53        string str;
54
55        str = info +
56            "\nChecking Account Balance: " +
57                checking.GetBalance().ToString("C2") +
58            "\nSavings Account Balance: " +
59                savings.GetBalance().ToString("C2");
60
61        return str;
62    }
63 }
```

This class is insecure because of the GetSavingsAccount in lines 39 through 42. This method returns a reference to the savings object, which is a private field. Code outside the class can get the return value of this method and then have direct access to the savings field. The program in Code Listing 8-17 demonstrates.

Code Listing 8-17 InsecureDemo.cs

```
 1 /*
 2     This program demonstrates the InsecureBankCustomer
 3     class's insecurity.
 4 */
 5
 6 using System;
 7
 8 public class InsecureDemo
 9 {
10     public static void Main()
11     {
12         // Create a PersonalInfo object.
13         PersonalInfo info =
14                 new PersonalInfo("Jill Smith",
15                     "247 Main Street", "Canton",
16                     "NC", "25555");
17
18         // Create BankAccount objects.
19         BankAccount checking =
20                 new BankAccount(600.0);
21         BankAccount savings =
22                 new BankAccount(5000.0);
23
24         // Create an InsecureBankCustomer object.
25         InsecureBankCustomer customer =
26                 new InsecureBankCustomer(info,
27                             checking, savings);
28
29         // Display the contents of the customer object.
30         Console.WriteLine(customer);
31         Console.WriteLine();
32
33         // Get a reference to the customer object's
34         // private savings field.
35         BankAccount malicious =
36                 customer.GetSavingsAccount();
37
```

(code listing continues)

Code Listing 8-17 InsecureDemo.cs *(continued)*

```
38        // Use the malicious variable to change the contents
39        // of the private savings field.
40        malicious.Withdraw(5000.0);
41
42        // Now display the contents of the customer object.
43        Console.WriteLine(customer);
44
45     }
46 }
```

Program Output

```
Name: Jill Smith
Address: 247 Main Street
City: Canton State: NC ZIP: 25555
Checking Account Balance: $600.00
Savings Account Balance: $5,000.00

Name: Jill Smith
Address: 247 Main Street
City: Canton State: NC ZIP: 25555
Checking Account Balance: $600.00
Savings Account Balance: $0.00
```

This program uses the following statement in lines 35 and 36 to get a reference to the customer object's private savings field:

```
BankAccount malicious = customer.GetSavingsAccount();
```

Once the malicious variable references the savings object, it can manipulate it directly. The statement in line 40 calls the savings object's Withdraw method to subtract 5000.0 from the account's balance. To prevent this type of security hole, you should avoid writing methods that return references to objects that are private fields.

If you must have a method that returns a reference to an object that is a private field, write a get property for the class.

```
public BankAccount SavingsAccount
{
    get
    {
        return savings;
    }
}
```

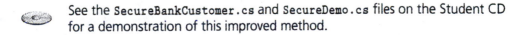 See the SecureBankCustomer.cs and SecureDemo.cs files on the Student CD for a demonstration of this improved method.

Avoid Using null References

Recall from Chapter 4 that by default a reference variable that is an instance field is initialized to the value null. This indicates that the variable does not reference an object. Because a null reference variable does not reference an object, you cannot use it to perform an operation that would require the existence of an object. For example, a null reference variable cannot be used to call a method. If you attempt to perform an operation with a null reference variable, the program will terminate. For example, look at the FullName class in Code Listing 8-18.

Code Listing 8-18   FullName.cs

```
1 /*
2     This class stores a person's first, last, and middle
3     names. The class is dangerous because it does not
4     prevent operations on null reference fields.
5 */
6
7 public class FullName
8 {
9     private string lastName,
10              firstName,
11              middleName;
12
13     /*
14        The LastName property sets the lastName field.
15     */
16
17     public string LastName
18     {
19        set
20        {
21          lastName = value;
22        }
23     }
24
25     /*
26        The FirstName property sets the firstName field.
27     */
28
29     public string FirstName
30     {
31        set
32        {
33          firstName = value;
34        }
35     }
36
```

(code listing continues)

Code Listing 8-18 FullName.cs *(continued)*

```
37      /*
38          The MiddleName property sets the middleName field.
39
40      */
41
42      public string MiddleName
43      {
44        set
45          {
46           middleName = value;
47          }
48      }
49
50      /*
51          The Length property returns the length of the
52          full name.
53      */
54
55      public int Length
56      {
57          get
58          {
59           return lastName.Length + firstName.Length
60                + middleName.Length;
61          }
62      }
63
64      /*
65          The ToString method returns the full name.
66          **return A reference to a string.
67      */
68
69      public override string ToString()
70      {
71          return firstName + " " + middleName + " "
72                + lastName;
73      }
74  }
```

First, notice in lines 9 through 11 that the class has three string reference variables as fields: lastName, firstName, and middleName. Second, notice that the class does not have a programmer-defined constructor. When an instance of this class is created, the lastName, firstName, and middleName fields will be initialized to null. Third, notice in lines 59 and 60 that the Length property uses the lastName, firstName, and middleName variables to call the string class Length property. Nothing is preventing the Length property from being called while any or all of these reference variables are set to null. The program in Code Listing 8-19 demonstrates this.

Code Listing 8-19   NameTester.cs

```
 1 /*
 2    This program creates a FullName object, and then
 3    calls the object's Length property before values
 4    are established for its reference fields. As a
 5    result, this program will crash.
 6 */
 7
 8 using System;
 9
10 public class NameTester
11 {
12    public static void Main()
13    {
14       FullName name = new FullName();
15       int len;
16
17       len = name.Length;
18    }
19 }
```

This program will crash when you run it because the Length property is called before the name object's fields are made to reference string objects. To handle this problem is to write a no-arg constructor that assigns values to the reference fields like this:

```
public FullName1()
{
    lastName = "";
    firstName = "";
    middleName = "";
}
```

 ## CHECKPOINT

8.8 Consider the following statement: "A car has an engine." If this statement refers to classes, what is the aggregate class?

8.9 Why is it not safe to return a reference to an object that is a private field? Does this also hold true for string objects that are private fields? Why or why not?

8.10 A class has a reference variable as an instance field. Is it advisable to use the reference variable to call a method prior to assigning it the address of an object? Why or why not?

8.6 The this Reference Variable

The this key word is the name of a reference variable that is available to all nonstatic methods. An object can use the this variable to refer to itself.

The key word this is the name of a reference variable that an object can use to refer to itself. For example, recall the FeetInches class presented earlier in this chapter. The class has the following Equals method, which compares the calling FeetInches object to another FeetInches object that is passed as an argument:

```
public bool Equals(FeetInches object2)
{
    bool status;

    if (object2 == null)
        status = false;
    else if (feet == object2.Feet &&
            inches == object2.Inches)
        status = true;
    else
        status = false;
    return status;
}
```

When this method executes, the this variable contains the address of the calling object. We could rewrite the method as follows, and it would perform the same operation (the changes appear in bold):

```
public bool Equals(FeetInches object2)
{
    bool status;

    if (object2 == null)
        status = false;
    else if (this.feet == object2.Feet &&
            this.inches == object2.Inches))
        status = true;
    else
        status = false;
    return status;
}
```

The this reference variable is available to all of a class's nonstatic methods.

Using this to Overcome Shadowing

One common use of the this key word is to overcome the shadowing of a field name by a parameter name. Recall from Chapter 4 that if a method's parameter has the same name as a field in the same class, then the parameter name shadows the field name. For example, if we used an accessor method, instead of a property, named SetFeet for the FeetInches class:

```
void SetFeet(int f)
{
    feet = f;
}
```

This method uses the parameter f to accept an argument that is assigned to the feet field. Sometimes it is difficult to think of a good parameter name that is different from a field name, and this is an example. Although the name f is hardly self-documenting, it is no worse than other possible names, such as ft.

To avoid this problem, many programmers give parameters the same names as the fields to which they correspond, and then use the this key word to refer to the field names. For example the SetFeet method could be written as follows:

```
void SetFeet(int feet)
{
    this.feet = feet;
}
```

Although the parameter name feet shadows the field name feet, the this key word overcomes the shadowing. Because this is a reference to the calling object, the expression this.feet refers to the calling object's feet field.

Using this to Call an Overloaded Constructor

Another use of the this keyword is to call one constructor from another constructor in the same class. For example, here is a constructor that could be added to the FeetInches class that was presented earlier:

```
/*
    This constructor accepts an argument that is
    assigned to the feet field. The inches field is
    assigned the value 0.
*/

FeetInches(int f): this (f,0)
{
}
```

The purpose of this constructor is to accept one argument which will be assigned to the feet field. The inches field will be assigned 0. It accomplishes this by calling the constructor that accepts arguments for both feet and inches, passing the parameter f and the value 0 as arguments.

CHECKPOINT

8.11 Look at the following code. (You might want to review the FeetInches class presented earlier in this chapter.)

```
FeetInches distance1 = new FeetInches(5, 4);
FeetInches distance2 = new FeetInches (6, 2);
FeetInches distance3;
```

While the add method is executing as a result of the following statement, what object does this reference?

```
distance3 = distance2.Add(distance1);
```

8.7 Namespaces

CONCEPT You can store related classes together in groups called namespaces.

We learned in Chapter 2 what a namespace is and about the default namespace System. A namespace, which is also called a library, is a named group of related classes. Namespaces are stored in their own folder or directory on the computer's disk. The compiler is informed of the namespace's location, so it can find it regardless of where the application that uses the namespace may be stored. Let us now look at how we create our own namespaces.

Let's look at a simple example. Suppose we create two namespace classes: CarNamespace and TruckNamespace. Code Listing 8-20 shows the code for the CarNamespace class, and Code Listing 8-21 shows the code for the TruckNamespace class.

Code Listing 8-20   CarNamespace.cs

```
 1 /*
 2    This class is in the CarNamespace namespace.
 3 */
 4
 5 namespace CarNamespace
 6 {
 7  public class Car
 8  {
 9    private int passengers;  // Number of passengers
10    private double topSpeed; // Top speed
11
```

(code listing continues)

Code Listing 8-20 CarNamespace.cs *(continued)*

```
12     /*
13         Constructor
14         **parameter passengers The number of passengers.
15         **parameter topSpeed The car's top speed.
16     */
17
18     public Car(int passengers, double topSpeed)
19     {
20         this.passengers = passengers;
21         this.topSpeed = topSpeed;
22     }
23
24     /*
25         The ToString method returns a string showing
26         the number of passengers and top speed.
27         **return A reference to a String.
28     */
29
30     public override string ToString()
31     {
32         return "Passengers: " + passengers +
33                 "\nTop Speed: " + topSpeed +
34                 " miles per hour";
35     }
36  }
37 }
```

Code Listing 8-21 TruckNamespace.cs

```
1 /*
2     This class is in the TruckNamespace namespace.
3 */
4 namespace TruckNamespace
5 {
6   public class Truck
7   {
8     private double mpg;  // Fuel economy
9     private double tons; // Hauling capacity
10
11      /*
12          Constructor
13          **parameter mpg The truck's miles-per-gallon.
14          **parameter tons The truck's hauling capacity
15          in tons.
16      */
17
```

(code listing continues)

Code Listing 8-21   TruckNamespace.cs *(continued)*

```
18    public Truck(double mpg, double tons)
19    {
20       this.mpg = mpg;
21       this.tons = tons;
22    }
23
24    /*
25       The ToString method returns a string showing
26       the fuel economy and hauling capacity.
27       **return A reference to a string.
28    */
29
30    public override string ToString()
31    {
32       return "Fuel economy: " + mpg +
33              " miles per gallon" +
34              "\nHauling capacity: " +
35              tons + " tons";
36    }
37    }
38 }
```

The word namespace is a key word in C#, and TruckNamespace and CarNamespace are the names of the namespaces to which the classes belong. This statement informs the compiler that the contents of the file belong to their respective namespaces. Notice from above, after declaration we surround the entire class in curly braces. We compile these namespaces the same way we did in Chapter 4 with multifile programs. The program in Code Listing 8-22 shows how we use the namespaces we created.

Code Listing 8-22   CarTruckDemo.cs

```
1 /*
2    This program demonstrates the CarNamespace and
3    TruckNamespace namespaces.
4 */
5
6 using System;
7 using CarNamespace;
8 using TruckNamespace;
9
```

(code listing continues)

Code Listing 8-22 CarTruckDemo.cs *(continued)*

```
10 public class CarTruckDemo
11 {
12    public static void Main()
13    {
14       Car roadster = new Car(2, 155);
15       Truck pickUp = new Truck(18, 2);
16
17       Console.WriteLine("Here's information " +
18                                "about the car:");
19       Console.WriteLine(roadster);
20       Console.WriteLine();
21       Console.WriteLine("Here's information " +
22                                "about the truck:");
23       Console.WriteLine(pickUp);
24    }
25 }
```

Program Output

```
Here's information about the car:
Passengers: 2
Top Speed: 155 miles per hour

Here's information about the truck:
Fuel economy: 18 mile per gallon
Hauling capacity: 2 tons
```

Notice lines 6 through 8 in the program:

```
using System;
using CarNamespace;
using TruckNamespace;
```

using is a key word in C#. The name that follows using is the namespace the program intends to use. This statement tells the compiler to make all the classes that are part of the System, CarNamespace, and TruckNamespace namespaces available to the program. If we only wanted to make the Truck class available, we could have used the following using statement:

```
using TruckNamespace;
```

In this case the compiler would only make the Truck class available. Any references to the Car class would cause an error. Likewise, we could use the following statement to make only the Car class available:

```
using CarNamespace;
```

You will recall that you have previously used the following using statement in all the programs you have written up to this point:

```
using System;
```

This statement tells the compiler to use the System class, which is part of the System namespace. The System namespace is part of the C# Foundation Class Library.

The Standard C# Namespaces

The standard C# classes that make up the FCL are organized into namespaces. Table 8-2 lists a few of them.

Table 8-2   A few of the standard C# namespaces

Namespace	Description
System	Provides general classes for the C# language.
System.Drawing	Provides the classes used in drawing images and creating graphical user interfaces.
System.IO	Provides classes that perform various types of input and output.
System.Net	Provides classes for network communications.
System.Text	Provides various classes for formatting text.
System.Windows.Forms	Provides various class for supporting Windows applications.
System.XML	Provides classes for supporting XML.

 CHECKPOINT

8.12 Describe the advantage of using namespaces.

8.13 What statement must appear at the beginning of each class source file that is part of a namespace?

8.8   Common Errors

■ **Attempting to refer to an instance field or instance method in a static method.** Static methods can refer only to other class members that are static.

■ **In a method that accepts an object as an argument, writing code that accidentally modifies the object.** When a reference variable is passed as an argument to a method, the method has access to the object that the variable references. When writing a method that receives a reference variable as an argument, you must take care not to accidentally modify the contents of the object that is referenced by the variable.

■ **Allowing a null reference to be used.** Because a null reference variable does not reference an object, you cannot use it to perform an operation that would require the existence of an object. For example, a null reference variable cannot be used to call a method. If you attempt to perform an operation with a null reference variable, the program will terminate. This can happen when a class has a reference variable as a field, and it is not properly initialized with the address of an object.

Review Questions and Exercises

Multiple Choice and True/False

1. This type of method cannot access any nonstatic member variables in its own class.

   a) Instance   b) void

   c) Static   d) Non-static

2. When an object is passed as an argument to a method, this is actually passed.

   a) a copy of the object   b) the name of the object

   c) a reference to the object   d) None of these. You cannot pass an object.

3. If you write this method for a class, C# will automatically call it any time you concatenate an object of the class with a string.

   a) ToString   b) PlusString

   c) StringConvert   d) ConcatString

4. Making an instance of one class a field in another class is called

   a) nesting.   b) class fielding.

   c) aggregation.   d) concatenation.

5. This is the name of a reference variable that is always available to an instance method and refers to the object that is calling the method.

   a) CallingObject   b) this

   c) me   d) instance

6. Related classes may be stored together in groups called

   a) directories.   b) namespaces.

   c) storage units.   d) folders.

7. This statement identifies which namespaces a program uses.

   a) import   b) package

   c) using   d) export

8. True or False: A static member method may refer to nonstatic member variables of the same class, but only after an instance of the class has been defined.

9. True or False: All static member variables are initialized to 1 by default.

10. True or False: When an object is passed as an argument to a method, the method can access the argument.

11. True or False: A method cannot return a reference to an object.

12. True or False: The `namespace` key word may appear anywhere in a class source file.

Find the Error

The following class definition has an error. What is it?

```
1.   public class MyClass
     {
         private int x;
         private double y;

         public static void SetValues(int a, double b)
         {
             x = a;
             y = b;
         }
     }
```

Algorithm Workbench

1. Consider the following class declaration:

```
public class Circle
{
    private double radius;

    public Circle(double r)
    {
        radius = r;
    }

    public double GetArea
    {
        get
        {
            return Math.PI * radius * radius;
        }
    }

    public double Radius
    {
        get
        {
            return radius;
        }
    }
}
```

a) Write a ToString method for this class. The method should return a string containing the radius and area of the circle.

b) Write an Equals method for this class. The method should accept a Circle object as an argument. It should return true if the argument object contains the same data as the calling object, or false otherwise.

c) Write a GreaterThan method for this class. The method should accept a Circle object as an argument. It should return true if the argument object has an area that is greater than the area of the calling object, or false otherwise.

2. Consider the following class declaration:

```
public class Thing
{
    private int x;
    private int y;
    private static int z = 0;

    public Thing()
    {
        x = z;
        y = z;
    }

    static void PutThing(int a)
    {
        z = a;
    }
}
```

Assume a program containing the class declaration defines three Thing objects with the following statements:

```
Thing one = new Thing();
Thing two = new Thing();
Thing three = new Thing();
```

a) How many separate instances of the x member exist?

b) How many separate instances of the y member exist?

c) How many separate instances of the z member exist?

d) What value will be stored in the x and y members of each object?

e) Write a statement that will call the PutThing method.

Short Answer

1. Describe one thing you cannot do with a static method.

2. Why are static methods useful in creating utility classes?

3. Describe the difference in the way variables and class objects are passed as arguments to a method.

4. A has-a relationship can exist between classes. What does this mean?

5. What happens if you attempt to call a method using a reference variable that is set to null?

6. Is it advisable or not advisable to write a method that returns a reference to an object that is a private field? What is the exception to this?

7. What is the this key word?

8. What is the benefit of storing related classes in a namespace?

Programming Challenges

1. Area Class

Write a class that has three overloaded static methods for calculating the areas of the following geometric shapes.

- Circles

- Rectangles

- Cylinders

Here are the formulas for calculating the area of the shapes.

Area of a circle: $Area = \pi r^2$

where π is Math.PI and r is the circle's radius

Area of a rectangle: $Area = Width \times Length$

Area of a cylinder: $Area = \pi r^2 h$

where π is Math.PI, r is the radius of the cylinder's base, and h is the cylinder's height

Because the three methods are to be overloaded, they should each have the same name but different parameter lists. Demonstrate the class in a complete program.

2. FeetInches Class Multiply Method

Add a Multiply method to the FeetInches class. The Multiply method should accept a FeetInches object as an argument. The argument object's feet and inches fields will be multiplied by the calling object's feet and inches fields, and a FeetInches object containing the result will be returned.

3. Carpet Calculator

The Westfield Carpet Company has asked you to write an application that calculates the price of carpeting for rectangular rooms. To calculate the price, you multiply the area of the floor (width times length) by the price per square foot of carpet. For example, the area of floor that is 12 feet long and 10 feet wide is 120 square feet. To cover that floor with carpet that costs $8 per square foot would cost $960. (12 × 10 × 8 = 960.)

First, you should create a class named RoomDimension that has two FeetInches objects as fields: one for the length of the room and one for the width. (You should use the version of the FeetInches class that you created in Programming Challenge 2 with the addition of a Multiply method. You can use this method to calculate the area of the room.) The RoomDimension class should have a property that returns the area of the room as a FeetInches object.

Next you should create a RoomCarpet class that has a RoomDimension object as a field. It should also have a field for the cost of the carpet per square foot. The RoomCarpet class should have a property that returns the total cost of the carpet.

Figure 8-14 is a UML diagram showing possible class designs and depicting the relationships between the classes. Once you have written these classes, use them in an application that asks the user to enter the dimensions of a room and the price per square foot of the desired carpeting. The application should display the total cost of the carpet.

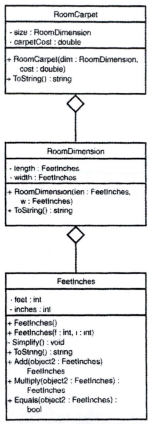

Figure 8-14   UML diagram for Programming Challenge 3

4. LandTract Class

Make a LandTract class that is composed of two FeetInches objects, one for the tract's length and one for the width. The class should have a property that returns the tract's area, as well as an Equals method and a ToString method. Demonstrate the class in a program that asks the user to enter the dimensions for two tracts of land. The program should display the area of each tract of land and indicate whether the tracts are of equal size.

5. Month Class

Write a class named Month. The class should have an int field named monthNumber that holds the number of the month. For example,

January would be 1, February would be 2, and so forth. In addition, provide the following methods:

- A no-arg constructor that sets the monthNumber field to 1.

- A constructor that accepts the number of the month as an argument. It should set the monthNumber field to the value passed as the argument. If a value less than 1 or greater than 12 is passed, the constructor should set monthNumber to 1.

- A constructor that accepts the name of the month, such as "January" or "February," as an argument. It should set the monthNumber field to the correct corresponding value.

- A SetMonthNumber method that accepts an int argument, which is assigned to the monthNumber field. If a value less than 1 or greater than 12 is passed, the method should set monthNumber to 1.

- A GetMonthNumber method that returns the value in the monthNumber field.

- A MonthName property that returns the name of the month. For example, if the monthNumber field contains 1, then this method should return "January."

- A ToString method that returns the same value as the MonthName property.

- An Equals method that accepts a Month object as an argument. If the argument object holds the same data as the calling object, this method should return true. Otherwise, it should return false.

- A GreaterThan method that accepts a Month object as an argument. If the calling object's monthNumber field is greater than the argument's monthNumber field, this method should return true. Otherwise, it should return false.

- A LessThan method that accepts a Month object as an argument. If the calling object's monthNumber field is less than the argument's monthNumber field, this method should return true. Otherwise, it should return false.

6. CashRegister Class

Write a CashRegister class that can be used with the RetailItem class that you wrote in Chapter 4's Programming Challenge 4. The CashRegister class should simulate the sale of a retail item. It should have a constructor that accepts a RetailItem object as an argument. The constructor should also accept an integer that represents the quantity of items being purchased. In addition, the class should have the following properties:

- The Subtotal property should return the subtotal of the sale, which is the quantity multiplied by the price. The property must get the price from the RetailItem object that was passed as an argument to the constructor.

- The Tax property should return the amount of sales tax on the purchase. The sales tax rate is 6% of a retail sale.

- The Total property should return the total of the sale, which is the subtotal plus the sales tax.

Demonstrate the class in a program that asks the user for the quantity of items being purchased, and then displays the sale's subtotal, amount of sales tax, and total.

7. Sales Receipt File

Modify the program you wrote in Programming Challenge 6 to create a file containing a sales receipt. The program should ask the user for the quantity of items being purchased and then generate a file with contents similar to the following:

```
        SALES RECEIPT
Unit Price: $10.00
Quantity: 5
Subtotal: $50.00
Sales Tax: $ 3.00
Total: $53.00
```

8. Geometry Calculator

Design a Geometry class with the following properties:

- A property that returns the area of the circle. Use the following formula:

$Area = \pi r^2$

Use Math.PI for π and the radius of the circle for r.

- A property that returns the area of the rectangle. Use the following formula:

$Area = Length \times Width$

- A property that returns the area of the triangle. Use the following formula:

$Area = Base \times Height \times 0.5$

The methods should display an error message if negative values are used for the circle's radius, the rectangle's length or width, or the triangle's base or height.

Next, write a program to test the class, which displays the following menu and responds to the user's selection:

```
Geometry Calculator

1.  Calculate the Area of a Circle
2.  Calculate the Area of a Rectangle
3.  Calculate the Area of a Triangle
4.  Quit

Enter your choice (1-4):
```

Display an error message if the user enters a number outside the range of 1 through 4 when selecting an item from the menu.

Text Processing, Exceptions and More Files

Chapter Objectives

- To become familiar with various static methods of the Char class
- To learn additional methods of the string class
- To recognize the difference between a string object and a StringBuilder object
- To write code using the Split method to extract tokens from a string
- To understand what an exception is
- To become acquainted with the exception class hierarchy
- To create code that handles one or more exceptions
- To write code that throws an exception
- To be able to write custom exception classes
- To understand the difference between a text file and a binary file, and the processing of each

Topics in this Chapter

9.1 Character-testing and Conversion with the Char Class

9.2 More string Methods

9.3 The StringBuilder Class

9.4 Using the Split Method to Parse Strings

9.5 Handling and Throwing Exceptions

9.6 Advanced Topics: Binary Files and Random Access Files

9.7 Common Errors

Review Questions and Exercises

9.1 Character-testing and Conversion with the Char Class

CONCEPT The Char class is an alias for the char data type. It provides numerous methods for testing and converting character data.

The Char class is part of the System namespace. The class provides several static methods for testing the value of a char variable. Some of these methods are listed in Table 9-1. Each of the methods accepts a single char argument and returns a boolean value.

Table 9-1 Some static Char class methods for testing char values

Method	Description
bool IsDigit(char ch)	Returns true if the argument passed into ch is a digit from 0 through 9. Otherwise returns false.
bool IsLetter(char ch)	Returns true if the argument passed into ch is an alphabetic letter. Otherwise returns false.
bool IsLetterOrDigit(char ch)	Returns true if the character passed into ch contains a digit (0 through 9) or an alphabetic letter. Otherwise returns false.
bool IsLower(char ch)	Returns true if the argument passed into ch is a lowercase letter. Otherwise returns false.
bool IsUpper(char ch)	Returns true if the argument passed into ch is an uppercase letter. Otherwise returns false.
bool IsWhiteSpace(char ch)	Returns true if the argument passed into ch is a whitespace character (a space, tab, or newline character). Otherwise returns false.

The program in Code Listing 9-1 demonstrates many of these methods. Figures 9-1 and 9-2 show example interactions with the program.

Code Listing 9-1   CharacterTest.cs

```
1  /*
2       This program demonstrates some of the Char
3       class's character-testing methods.
4  */
5
6  using System;
7
8  public class CharacterTest
9  {
10     public static void Main()
11     {
12
13        char ch;
14
15        // Get a character from the user and store
16        // it in the ch variable.
17        Console.WriteLine("Enter " +
18                              "any single character.");
19         ch = Convert.ToChar(Console.ReadLine());
20
21        // Test the character.
22        if (Char.IsLetter(ch))
23        {
24           Console.WriteLine(
25                        "That is a letter.");
26        }
27
28        if (Char.IsDigit(ch))
29        {
30           Console.WriteLine(
31                        "That is a digit.");
32        }
33
34        if (Char.IsLower(ch))
35        {
36           Console.WriteLine(
37              "That is a lowercase letter.");
38        }
39
40        if (Char.IsUpper(ch))
41        {
42           Console.WriteLine(
43              "That is an uppercase letter.");
44        }
45
```

(code listing continues)

Code Listing 9-1 CharacterTest.cs *(continued)*

```
46        if (Char.IsWhiteSpace(ch))
47        {
48           Console.WriteLine(
49            "That is a whitespace character.");
50        }
51
52     }
53  }
```

Figure 9-1 Interaction with the CharaceterTest.cs **program**

Figure 9-2 Interaction with the CharaceterTest.cs **program**

Code Listing 9-2 shows a more practical application of the character-testing methods. It tests a string to determine whether it is a seven-character customer number in the proper format. Figures 9-3 and 9-4 show example interactions with the program.

Code Listing 9-2   CustomerNumber.cs

```
1  /*
2     This program tests a customer number to
3     verify that it is in the proper format.
4  */
5
6  using System;
7
8  public class CustomerNumber
9  {
10     public static void Main()
11     {
12        string input;
13
14        // Get a customer number.
15        Console.WriteLine("Enter " +
16           "a customer number in the form LLLNNNN\n" +
17           "(LLL = letters and NNNN = numbers)");
18
19        input = Console.ReadLine();
20        // Validate the input.
21        if (IsValid(input))
22        {
23           Console.WriteLine("That's a valid customer number.");
24        }
25        else
26        {
27           Console.WriteLine(
28              "That is not the proper format of a " +
29              "customer number.\nHere is an " +
30              "example: ABC1234");
31        }
32     }
33
34     /*
35        The IsValid method determines whether a
36        string is a valid customer number. If so, it
37        returns true.
38        **parameter custNumber The String to test.
39        **return true if valid, otherwise false.
40     */
41
```

(code listing continues)

Code Listing 9-2 CustomerNumber.cs *(continued)*

```
42      private static bool IsValid(string custNumber)
43      {
44         bool goodSoFar = true;      // flag
45         int i = 0;                  // Control variable
46
47         // Test the length.
48         if (custNumber.Length != 7)
49            goodSoFar = false;
50
51         // Test the first three characters for letters.
52         while (goodSoFar && i < 3)
53         {
54            if (!Char.IsLetter(custNumber[i]))
55               goodSoFar = false;
56            i++;
57         }
58
59         // Test the last four characters for digits.
60         while (goodSoFar && i < 7)
61         {
62            if (!Char.IsDigit(custNumber[i]))
63               goodSoFar = false;
64            i++;
65         }
66
67         return goodSoFar;
68      }
69  }
```

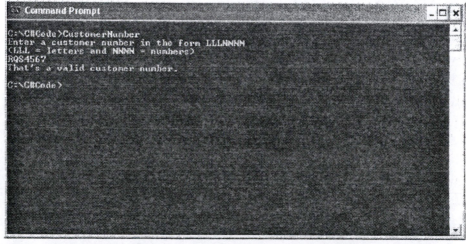

Figure 9-3   Interaction with the CustomerNumber.cs **program**

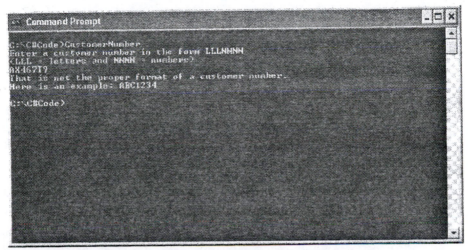

Figure 9-4 Interaction with the `CustomerNumber.cs` **program**

In this program, the customer number is expected to be seven characters in length and consist of three alphabetic letters followed by four numeric digits. The `IsValid` method accepts a `string` argument which will be tested. The method uses the following local variables, which are declared in lines 44 and 45:

```
bool goodSoFar = true;      // flag
int i = 0;                  // Control variable
```

The `goodSoFar` variable is a flag variable that is initialized with `true`, but will be set to `false` immediately when the method determines the customer number is not in a valid format. The `i` variable is a loop control variable.

The first test is to determine whether the string is the correct length. In line 48 the method tests the length of the `custNumber` argument. If the argument is not seven characters long, it is not valid and the `goodSoFar` variable is set to `false` in line 55.

Next the method uses the following loop, in lines 52 through 57, to validate the first three characters:

```
while (goodSoFar && i < 3)
{
    if (!Char.IsLetter(custNumber[i]))
    goodSoFar = false;
    i++;
}
```

Recall from Chapter 2 that the `string` class has an indexer that returns a character at a specific position in a string (position numbering starts at 0). This code uses the `Char.IsLetter` method to test the characters at positions 0, 1, and 2 in the `custNumber` string. If any of these characters are not letters, the `goodSoFar` variable is set to `false` and the loop terminates. Next the method uses the following loop, in lines 60 through 65, to validate the last four characters:

```
while (goodSoFar && i < 7)
{
    if (!Character.IsDigit(custNumber[i])))
        goodSoFar = false;
    i++;
}
```

This code uses the `Char.IsDigit` method to test the characters at positions 3, 4, 5, and 6 in the `custNumber` string. If any of these characters are not digits, the `goodSoFar` variable is set to `false` and the loop terminates. Last, the method returns the value of the `goodSoFar` method.

Character Case Conversion

The `Char` class also provides the static methods listed in Table 9-2 for converting the case of a character. Each method accepts a `char` argument and returns a `char` value.

Table 9-2   Some `Char` class methods for case conversion

Method	Description
char ToLower(char ch)	Returns the lowercase equivalent of the argument passed to ch.
char ToUpper(char ch)	Returns the uppercase equivalent of the argument passed to ch.

If the `ToLower` method's argument is an uppercase character, the method returns the lowercase equivalent. For example, the following statement will display the character a on the screen:

```
Console.WriteLine(Char.ToLower('A'));
```

If the argument is already lowercase, the `ToLower` method returns it unchanged. The following statement also causes the lowercase character a to be displayed:

```
Console.WriteLine(Char.ToLower('a'));
```

If the `ToUpper` method's argument is a lowercase character, the method returns the uppercase equivalent. For example, the following statement will display the character A on the screen:

```
Console.WriteLine(Char.ToUpper('a'));
```

If the argument is already uppercase, the `ToUpper` method returns it unchanged.

Any nonletter argument passed to `ToLower` or `ToUpper` is returned as it is. Each of the following statements displays the method argument without any change:

```
Console.WriteLine(Char.ToLower('*'));
Console.WriteLine(Char.ToLower('$'));
Console.WriteLine(Char.ToUpper('&'));
Console.WriteLine(Char.ToUpper('%'));
```

The program in Code Listing 9-3 demonstrates the ToUpper method in a loop that asks the user to enter Y or N. The program repeats as long as the user enters Y or y in response to the question.

Code Listing 9-3   CircleArea.cs

```
1 /*
2     This program demonstrates the Char
3     class's ToUpper method.
4 */
5
6
7 using System;
8
9 public class CircleArea
10 {
11     public static void Main()
12
13     {
14         string input;
15         double radius, area;
16         char choice;
17         do
18         {
19             // Get the circle's radius.
20             Console.Write("Enter the circle's " +
21                             "radius: ");
22             input = Console.ReadLine();
23             radius = Convert.ToDouble(input);
24
25             // Calculate and display the area.
26             area = Math.PI * radius * radius;
27             Console.WriteLine("The area is {0:N2}", area);
28
29             // Repeat this?
30             Console.Write("Do you want to do this " +
31                             "again? (Y or N) ");
32             input = Console.ReadLine();
33             choice = input[0];
34
35         } while (Char.ToUpper(choice) == 'Y');
36     }
37 }
```

Code Listing 9-3 CircleArea.cs

Program Output with Example Input
```
Enter the circle's radius: 10[Enter]
The area is 314.16
Do you want to do this again? (Y or N) y[Enter]
Enter the circle's radius: 15
The area is 706.86
Do you want to do this again? (Y or N) n[Enter]
```

 CHECKPOINT

9.1 Write a statement that converts the contents of the char variable big to lowercase. The converted value should be assigned to the variable little.

9.2 Write an if statement that displays the word "Digit" if the char variable ch contains a numeric digit. Otherwise, it should display "Not a digit."

9.3 What is the output of the following statement?

```
Console.WriteLine(Char.ToUpper(Char.ToLower ('A')));
```

9.4 Write a loop that asks the user "Do you want to repeat the program or quit? (R/ Q)". The loop should repeat until the user has entered a Q (either uppercase or lowercase).

9.5 What will the following code display?

```
char var = '$';
Console.WriteLine(Char.ToUpper(var));
```

9.6 Write a loop that counts the number of uppercase characters that appears in the string object str.

9.2 More string Methods

> **CONCEPT** The string class provides several methods for searching and working with string objects.

Searching for Substrings

The string class provides several methods that search for a string inside of a string. The term *substring* refers to a string that is part of another string. Table 9-3 summarizes some of these methods each of which returns a boolean value indicating whether the string was found.

Table 9-3 string **methods that search for a substring**

Method	Description
bool StartsWith(string *str*)	This method returns true if the calling string begins with the string passed into *str*.
bool EndsWith(string *str*)	This method returns true if the calling string ends with the string passed into *str*.

Let's take a closer look at each of these methods.

The StartsWith and EndsWith Methods

The StartsWith method determines whether the calling object's string begins with a specified substring. For example, the following code determines whether the string "Four score and seven years ago" begins with "Four". The method returns true if the string begins with the specified substring and false if it does not.

```
string str = "Four score and seven years ago";
if (str.StartsWith("Four"))
    Console.WriteLine("The string starts with Four.");
else
    Console.WriteLine("The string does not start with Four.");
```

In the code, the method call str.StartsWith("Four") returns true because the string does begin with "Four". The StartsWith method performs a case-sensitive comparison, so the method call str.StartsWith("four") would return false.

The EndsWith method determines whether the calling string ends with a specified substring. For example, the following code determines whether the string "Four score and seven years ago" ends with "ago". The method returns true if the string does end with the specified substring or false otherwise.

```
string str = "Four score and seven years ago";
if (str.EndsWith("ago"))
    Console.WriteLine("The string ends with ago.");
else
    Console.WriteLine("The string does not end with ago.");
```

In the code, the method call str.EndsWith("ago") returns true because the string does end with "ago". The EndsWith method also performs a case-sensitive comparison, so the method call str.EndsWith("Ago") would return false.

The program in Code Listing 9-4 demonstrates a search algorithm that uses the StartsWith method. The program searches an array of strings for an element that starts with a specified string.

Code Listing 9-4   ProductSearch.cs

```
1  /*
2      This program uses the StartsWith method to
3      search using a partial string.
4  */
5
6  using System;
7
8  public class ProductSearch
9  {
10     public static void Main()
11     {
12         string lookUp;    // The number to search for
13         // Parallel arrays
14         string[] modelNumbers =
15                 { "M75611-D", "M75911-D", "C53291-C",
16                   "C53779-C", "F49002-Q", "R99349-Q" };
17         double[] prices =   {  179.95, 156.95, 119.95,
18                                 99.95,  125.95, 199.95 };
19
20
21         // Get a partial model number to search for.
22         Console.Write("Enter the first few " +
23                         "characters of a model " +
24                         "number: ");
25         lookUp = Console.ReadLine();
26
27         // Display the prices for all the model numbers
28         // that begin with the specified string.
29
30         Console.WriteLine("Here are the matching models:");
31         for (int i = 0; i < modelNumbers.Length; i++)
32         {
33             if (modelNumbers[i].StartsWith(lookUp))
34             {
35                 Console.WriteLine("{0}\t{1:C2}",modelNumbers[i],
36                                     prices[i]);
37             }
38         }
39     }
40 }
```

Program Output with Example Input

```
Enter the first few characters of a model number: C5[Enter]
Here are the matching models:
C53291-C      $119.75
C53779-C      $99.95
```

The string class also provides methods that not only search for items within a string, but report the location of those items. Table 9-4 describes overloaded versions of the IndexOf and LastIndexOf methods.

Table 9-4 string methods for getting a character or substring's location

Method	Description
int IndexOf(char ch)	Searches the calling string object for the character passed into ch. If the character is found, the position of its first occurrence is returned. Otherwise, –1 is returned.
int IndexOf(char ch, int start)	Searches the calling string object for the character passed into ch, beginning at the position passed into start and going to the end of the string. If the character is found, the position of its first occurrence is returned. Otherwise, 1 is returned.
int IndexOf(string str)	Searches the calling string object for the string passed into str. If the string is found, the beginning position of its first occurrence is returned. Otherwise, 1 is returned.
int IndexOf(string str, int start)	Searches the calling string object for the string passed into str. The search begins at the position passed into start and goes to the end of the string. If the string is found, the beginning position of its first occurrence is returned. Otherwise, 1 is returned.
int LastIndexOf(char ch)	Searches the calling string object for the character passed into ch. If the character is found, the position of its last occurrence is returned. Otherwise, 1 is returned.
int LastIndexOf(char ch, int start)	Searches the calling string object for the character passed into ch, beginning at the position passed into start. The search is conducted backward through the string, to position 0. If the character is found, the position of its last occurrence is returned. Otherwise, 1 is returned.

(table continues)

Table 9-4 `string` methods for getting a character or substring's location *(continued)*

Method	Description
`int LastIndexOf(string str)`	Searches the calling `string` object for the string passed into `str`. If the string is found, the beginning position of its last occurrence is returned. Otherwise,1 is returned.
`int LastIndexOf(string str, int start)`	Searches the calling `string` object for the string passed into `str`, beginning at the position passed into `start`. The search is conducted backward through the string, to position 0. If the string is found, the beginning position of its last occurrence is returned. Otherwise, 1 is returned.

Finding Characters with the `IndexOf` and `LastIndexOf` Methods

The `IndexOf` and `LastIndexOf` methods can search for either a character or a substring within the calling string. If the item being searched for is found, its position is returned. Otherwise 1 is returned. Here is an example of code using two of the methods to search for a character:

```
string str = "Four score and seven years ago";
int first, last;

first = str.IndexOf('r');
last = str.LastIndexOf('r');

Console.WriteLine("The letter r first appears at {0} position ", first);

Console.WriteLine("The letter r last appears at {0} position", last);
```

This code produces the following output:

```
The letter r first appears at position 3
The letter r last appears at position 24
```

The following code shows another example. It uses a loop to show the positions of each letter "r" in the string.

```
string str = "Four score and seven years ago";
int position;

Console.WriteLine("The letter r appears at the " +
                  "following locations:");
position = str.IndexOf('r');
while (position != -1)
{
    Console.WriteLine(position);
    position = str.IndexOf('r', position + 1);
}
```

This code will produce the following output:

```
The letter r appears at the following locations:
3
8
24
```

The following code is very similar, but it uses the LastIndexOf method and shows the positions in reverse order.

```
string str = "Four score and seven years ago";
int position;

Console.WriteLine("The letter r appears at the " +
                  "the following locations.");
position = str.LastIndexOf('r');
while (position != -1)
{
    Console.WriteLine(position);
    position = str.LastIndexOf('r', position - 1);
}
```

Finding Substrings with the *IndexOf* and *LastIndexOf* Methods

The IndexOf and LastIndexOf methods can also search for substrings within a string. The following code shows an example. It displays the starting positions of each occurrence of the word "and" within a string.

```
string str = "and a one and a two and a three";
int position;

Console.WriteLine("The word and appears at the " +
                  "following locations.");
position = str.IndexOf("and");
while (position != -1)
{
    Console.WriteLine(position);
    position = str.IndexOf("and", position + 1);
}
```

This code produces the following output:

```
The word and appears at the following locations.
0
10
20
```

The following code also displays the same results, but in reverse order.

```
string str = "and a one and a two and a three";
```

```
int position;

Console.WriteLine("The word and appears at the " +
                    "following locations.");
position = str.LastIndexOf("and");
while (position != -1)
{
    Console.WriteLine(position);
    position = str.LastIndexOf("and", -1);
}
```

This code produces the following output;

```
The word and appears at the following locations.
20
10
0
```

Extracting Substrings

The string class provides several methods that allow you to retrieve a substring from a string. The methods we will examine are listed in Table 9-5.

Table 9-5 string methods for extracting substrings

Method	Description
string Substring(int start)	This method returns a copy of the substring that begins at start and goes to the end of the calling object's string.
string Substring(int start, int end)	This method returns a copy of a substring. The argument passed into start is the substring's starting position, and the argument passed into end is the length of the string. The character at the start position is included in the substring.
char[] ToCharArray(int start, int end)	This method returns all of the characters in the calling object as a char array. The argument passed into start is the substring's starting position, and the argument passed into end is the length of the string. The character at the start position is included in the substring.

The Substring Methods

The Substring method returns a copy of a substring from the calling object. There are two over-loaded versions of this method. The first version accepts an int argument that is the starting position of the substring. The method returns a reference to a string object containing all of the characters from the starting position to the end of the string. The character at the starting position is part of the substring. Here is an example of the method's use.

```
string fullName = "Cynthia Susan Lee";
string lastName = fullName.Substring(14);
Console.WriteLine("The full name is {0}", fullName);
Console.WriteLine("The last name is {0}", lastName);
```

This code will produce the following output:

```
The full name is Cynthia Susan Lee
The last name is Lee
```

Keep in mind that the substring method returns a new string object that holds a copy of the substring. When this code executes, the fullName and lastName variables will reference two different string objects as shown in Figure 9-5.

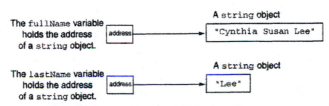

Figure 9-5 **The fullName and lastName variables reference separate objects**

The second version of the method accepts two int arguments. The first specifies the substring's starting position and the second specifies the substring's length. The character at the starting position is included in the substring, but the character at the ending position is not. Here is an example of how the method is used:

```
string fullName = "Cynthia Susan Lee";
string middleName = fullName.Substring(8, 5);
Console.WriteLine("The full name is {0}", fullName);
Console.WriteLine("The middle name is {0}",
        middleName);
```

The code will produce the following output:

```
The full name is Cynthia Susan Lee
The middle name is Susan
```

The ToCharArray Method

The ToCharArray method returns a reference to a char array that contains some or all characters in the calling object. Here is an example:

```
string fullName = "Cynthia Susan Lee";
char[] nameArray;
nameArray = fullName.ToCharArray(8,5);
Console.WriteLine("The full name is {0}", fullName);
Console.WriteLine("The values in the array are:");
for (int i = 0; i < nameArray.Length; i++)
    Console.Write("{0} ",nameArray[i]);
```

This code will produce the following output:

The full name is Cynthia Susan Lee

The ToCharArray Method

The ToCharArray method returns a reference to a char array that contains some or all characters in the calling object. Here is an example:

```
string fullName = "Cynthia Susan Lee";
char[] nameArray;
nameArray = fullName.ToCharArray(8,5);
Console.WriteLine("The full name is {0}", fullName);
Console.WriteLine("The values in the array are:");
for (int i = 0; i < nameArray.Length; i++)
Console.Write("{0} ",nameArray[i]);
```

This code will produce the following output:

```
The full name is Cynthia Susan Lee
The values in the array are:
C y n t h i a   S u s a n   L e e
```

These methods can be used when you want to use an array processing algorithm on the contents of a string object. The program in Code Listing 9-5 converts a string object to an array and then uses the array to determine the number of letters, digits, and whitespace characters in the string. Figure 9-6 shows an example of interaction with the program.

Code Listing 9-5   StringAnalyzer.cs

```
 1 /*
 2     This program displays the number of letters,
 3     digits, and whitespace characters in a string.
 4 */
 5
 6 using System;
 7
 8 public class StringAnalyzer
 9 {
10     public static void Main()
11     {
12         string input;      // To hold input
13         char[] array;       // Array for input
14         int letters = 0,    // Number of letters
15             digits = 0,      // Number of digits
16             whitespaces = 0; // Number of whitespaces
17
18         // Get a string from the user.
19         Console.WriteLine("Enter a string:");
20         input = Console.ReadLine();
21
22         // Convert the string to a char array.
23         array = input.ToCharArray();
24
```

(code listing continues)

Code Listing 9-5   StringAnalyzer.cs *(continued)*

```
25          // Analyze the characters.
26          for (int i = 0; i < array.Length; i++)
27          {
28             if (Char.IsLetter(array[i]))
29                letters++;
30             else if (Char.IsDigit(array[i]))
31                digits++;
32             else if (Char.IsWhiteSpace(array[i]))
33                whitespaces++;
34          }
35
36          // Display the results.
37          Console.WriteLine("That string contains {0}" +
38                            " letters, {1}" +
39                            " digits, and {2}" +
40                        " whitespace characters.", letters,
                          digits, whitespaces);
41    }
42 }
```

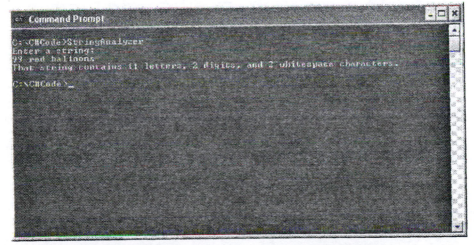

Figure 9-6   Interaction with the `StringAnalyzer.cs` **program**

Methods That Return a Modified Copy of a `string` Object

The `string` class methods listed in Table 9-6 return a modified copy of a `string` object.

The `Concat` method performs the same operation as the + operator when used with strings. For example, look at the following code, which uses the + operator:

```
string fullName,
       firstName = "Timothy ",
       lastName = "Haynes";
fullName = firstName + lastName;
```

Table 9-6 Methods that return a modified copy of a `string` object

Method	Description
`string Concat(string str)`	This method returns a copy of the calling `string` object with the contents of *str* concatenated to it.
`string Replace(char oldChar, char newChar)`	This method returns a copy of the calling `string` object, in which all occurrences of the character passed into *oldChar* have been replaced by the character passed into *newChar*.
`string Trim()`	This method returns a copy of the calling `string` object, in which all leading and trailing whitespace characters have been deleted.

Equivalent code can also be written with the `Concat` method. Here is an example:

```
string fullName,
       firstName = "Timothy ",
       lastName = "Haynes";
fullName = string.Concat(lastName);
```

The `Replace` method returns a copy of a `string` object, where every occurrence of a specified character has been replaced with another character. For example, look at the following code.

```
string str1 = "Tom Talbert Tried Trains",
       str2;
str2 = str1.Replace('T', 'D');
Console.WriteLine(str1);
Console.WriteLine(str2);
```

In this code, the `Replace` method will return a copy of the `str1` object with every occurrence of the letter "T" replaced with the letter "D". The code will produce the following output:

```
Tom Talbert Tried Trains
Dom Dalbert Dried Drains
```

Remember that the `replace` method does not modify the contents of the calling `string` object, but returns a reference to a `string` that is a modified copy of it. After the previous code executes, the `str1` and `str2` variables will reference different `string` objects.

The `Trim` method returns a copy of a `string` object with all leading and trailing whitespace characters deleted. A *leading* whitespace character is one that appears at the beginning, or left side, of a string. For example, the following string has three leading whitespace characters:

```
"   Hello"
```

A *trailing* whitespace character is one that appears at the end, or right side, of a string, after the nonspace characters. For example, the following string has three trailing whitespace characters:

```
"Hello   "
```

Here is an example:

```
string greeting1 = "   Hello   ",
       greeting2;
greeting2 = greeting1.Trim();
Console.WriteLine("*{0}*", greeting1);
Console.WriteLine("*{0}*", greeting2);
```

In this code, the first statement assigns the string " Hello " (with three leading spaces and three trailing spaces) to the greeting1 variable. The Trim method is called, which returns a copy of the string with the leading and trailing spaces removed. The code will produce the following output:

```
*   Hello   *
*Hello*
```

One common use of the Trim method is to remove any leading or trailing spaces that the user might have entered while inputting data.

 ## CHECKPOINT

9.7 Write a method that accepts a reference to a string object as an argument and returns true if the argument ends with the substring "ger". Otherwise, the method should return false.

9.8 Modify the method you wrote for Checkpoint 9.7 so it performs a case-insensitive test. The method should return true if the argument ends with "ger" in any possible combination of upper and lowercase letters.

9.9 Look at the following declaration:

```
string cafeName = "Broadway Cafe";
string str;
```

Which of the following methods would you use to make str reference the string "Broadway"?

```
StartsWith
Substring
IndexOf
```

9.10 What is the difference between the IndexOf and LastIndexOf methods?

9.11 What is the difference between the ToCharArray and Substring methods?

9.12 The + operator, when used with strings, performs the same operation as what string method?

9.13 What does the ToCharArray method do?

9.14 Look at the following code.

```
string str1 = "To be, or not to be";
string str2 = str1.Replace('o', 'u');
Console.WriteLine(str1);
Console.WriteLine(str2);
```

You hear a fellow student claim that the code will display the following:

```
Tu be ur nut tu be
Tu be ur nut tu be
```

Is your fellow student right or wrong? Why?

9.15 What will the following code display?

```
string str1 = "William ",
       str2 = " the ",
       str3 = " Conqueror";
Console.WriteLine(str1.Trim() + str2.Trim() +
                  str3.Trim());
```

9.3 The `StringBuilder` Class

 CONCEPT The `StringBuilder` class is similar to the `string` class, except that you may change the contents of `StringBuilder` objects. The `StringBuilder` class also provides several useful methods that the `string` class does not have.

The `StringBuilder` class is similar to the `string` class. It is found in the `System.Text` namespace. The main difference between the two is that you can change the contents of a `StringBuilder` object, but you cannot change the contents of a `string` object. Recall that `string` objects are immutable. This means that once you set the contents of a `string` object, you cannot change the string value that it holds. For example, look at the following code.

```
string name;
name = "George";
name = "Sally";
```

The first statement creates the `name` variable. The second creates a `string` object containing the string "George" and assigns its address to the `name` variable. Although we cannot change the contents of the `string` object, we can make the `name` variable reference a different `string` object. That's what the third statement does: It creates another `string` object containing the string "Sally", and assigns its address to `name`. This is illustrated by Figure 9-7.

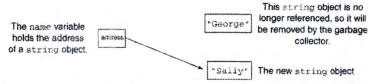

Figure 9-7   The `string` object containing "George" is no longer referenced

Unlike string objects, StringBuilder objects have methods that allow you modify their contents without creating a new object in memory. You can change specific characters, insert characters, delete characters, and perform other operations. The StringBuilder object will grow or shrink in size, as needed, to accommodate the changes.

The fact that string objects are immutable is rarely a problem, but you might consider using StringBuilder objects if your program needs to make a lot of changes to one or more strings. This will improve the program's efficiency by reducing the number of string objects that must be created and then removed by the garbage collector. Now let's look at the StringBuilder class's constructors and methods.

The StringBuilder constructors

Table 9-7 lists the StringBuilder constructors.

Table 9-7   StringBuilder **Constructors**

Constructor	Description
StringBuilder()	This constructor accepts no arguments. It gives the object enough storage space to hold 16 characters, but no characters are stored in it.
StringBuilder(int length)	This constructor gives the object enough storage space to hold length characters, but no characters are stored in it.
StringBuilder(string str)	This constructor initializes the object with the string in str. The object will have at least enough storage space to hold the string in str.

The first two constructors create empty StringBuilder objects of a specified size. The first constructor makes the StringBuilder object large enough to hold 16 characters, and the second constructor makes the object large enough to hold length characters. Remember, StringBuilder objects automatically resize themselves, so it is not a problem if you later want to store a larger string in the object. The third constructor accepts a string object as its argument and assigns the object's contents to the StringBuilder object. Here is an example of its use:

```
StringBuilder city = new StringBuilder("Charleston");
Console.WriteLine(city);
```

This code creates a StringBuilder object and assigns its address to the city variable. The object is initialized with the string "Charleston". As demonstrated by this code, you can pass a StringBuilder object to the WriteLine and Write methods.

One limitation of the `StringBuilder` class is that you cannot use the assignment operator to assign strings to `StringBuilder` objects. For example, the following code will not work:

```
StringBuilder city = "Charleston";   // ERROR!!! Will not work!
```

Instead of using the assignment operator you must use the new key word and a constructor, or one of the `StringBuilder` methods, to store a string in a `StringBuilder` object.

Other `StringBuilder` Methods

The `Append` Methods

The `StringBuilder` class has several overloaded versions of a method named Append. These methods accept an argument that may be of any primitive data type, a char array, or a `string` object. They append a string representation of their argument to the calling object's current contents. Because there are so many overloaded versions of append, we will examine the general form of a typical call to the method:

```
object.Append(item);
```

After the method is called, a string representation of *item* will be appended to *object*'s contents. The following code shows some of the Append methods being used.

```
StringBuilder strbuff = new StringBuilder();

// Append values to the object.

strbuff.Append("We sold ");           // Append a string object.
strbuff.Append(12);                   // Append an int.
strbuff.Append(" doughnuts for $");   // Append another string.
strbuff.Append(15.95);                // Append a double.

// Display the object's contents.

Console.WriteLine(strbuff);
```

This code will produce the following output:

```
We sold 12 doughnuts for $15.95
```

The `Insert` Methods

The `StringBuilder` class also has several overloaded versions of a method named Insert, which inserts a value into the calling object's string. These methods accept two arguments: an int that specifies the position in the calling object's string where the insertion should begin, and the value to be inserted. The value to be inserted may be of any primitive data type, a char array, or a `string` object. Because there are so many overloaded versions of Insert, we will examine the general form of a typical call to the method.

```
object.Insert(start, item);
```

In the general form, *start* is the starting position of the insertion and *item* is the item to be inserted. The following code shows some of the Insert methods being used.

```
StringBuilder strbuff = new StringBuilder("July sold cars.");
char[] array = { 'w', 'e', ' ' };

// Append values to the object.

strbuff.Insert(0, "In ");     // Insert a string.
strbuff.Insert(8, array);     // Insert a char array.
strbuff.Insert(16, 20);       // Insert an int.
strbuff.Insert(18, ' ');      // Insert a char.

// Display the object's contents.

Console.WriteLine(strbuff);
```

This code produces the following output:

```
In July we sold 20 cars.
```

Code Listing 9-6 shows another example of the insert method. The Telephone class has a static method named Format, which accepts a string containing an unformatted telephone number. The method places parentheses around the area code and inserts a hyphen after the prefix. The program in Code Listing 9-7 demonstrates the class.

Code Listing 9-6   Telephone.cs

```
 1 /*
 2     Telephone class
 3 */
 4
 5 using System.Text;
 6
 7 public class Telephone
 8 {
 9     /*
10         The format method accepts a String containing
11         an unformatted telephone number, such as
12         9195551212. It returns a String containing a
13         formatted telephone number, such as (919)555-1212.
14         **parameter number The number to format.
15         **return A reference to the formatted String.
16     */
```

(code listing continues)

Code Listing 9-6   Telephone.cs *(continued)*

```
17    public static string Format(string number)
18    {
19        StringBuilder strbuff = new StringBuilder(number);
20
21        // Insert parentheses around the area code.
22        strbuff.Insert(0, '(');
23        strbuff.Insert(4, ')');
24
25        // Insert a hyphen after the prefix.
26        strbuff.Insert(8, '-');
27
28        // Return the formatted number as a string.
29        return strbuff.ToString();
30    }
31 }
```

Code Listing 9-7   TelephoneTester.cs

```
 1 /*
 2     This program demonstrates the Telephone
 3     class's static Format method.
 4 */
 5
 6 using System;
 7 public class TelephoneTester
 8 {
 9     public static void Main()
10     {
11         // Create an unformatted number.
12         string phone = "9195551212";
13
14         // Get a formatted version of it.
15         string properNum = Telephone.Format(phone);
16
17         // Display the formatted number.
18         Console.WriteLine(properNum);
19     }
20 }
```

Program Output

```
(919)555-1212
```

The `Replace` Method

The `StringBuilder` class has a `Replace` method that differs slightly from the `string` class's `Replace` method. While the `string` class's `Replace` method replaces the occurrences of one character with another character, the `StringBuilder` class's `Replace` method replaces a specified substring with a string. Here is the general form of a call to the method:

```
object.Replace(start, str);
```

In the general form, `start` is an `int` that specifies the starting position of a substring in the calling object, and the `str` parameter is a `string` object. After the method executes, the substring will be replaced with `str`. Here is an example:

```
StringBuilder strbuff =
    new StringBuilder("We moved from Chicago to Atlanta.");
strbuff.Replace(14,"New York");
Console.WriteLine(strbuff);
```

The `Replace` method in this code replaces the word "Chicago" with "New York". The code will produce the following output:

```
We moved from New York to Atlanta.
```

The `Remove` Method

The `Remove` method is used to delete a substring or a character from a `StringBuilder` object.

```
object.Remove(int start, int end)
```

The following code demonstrates the use of this method.

```
StringBuilder strbuff =
    new StringBuilder("I ate 100 blueberries!");

// Display the Stringbuffer object.
Console.WriteLine(strbuff);

// Delete "blue".
strbuff.Remove(10, 14);

// Display the Stringbuffer object.
Console.WriteLine(strbuff);
```

This code will produce the following output.

```
I ate 100 blueberries!
I ate 100 berries!
```

CHECKPOINT

9.16 The string class is immutable. What does this mean?

9.17 In a program that makes lots of changes to strings, would it be more efficient to use string objects or StringBuilder objects? Why?

9.18 Look at the following statement:

```
string city = "Asheville";
```

Rewrite this statement so that city references a StringBuilder object instead of a string object.

9.19 You wish to add a string to the end of the existing contents of a StringBuilder object. What method do you use?

9.20 You wish to insert a string into the existing contents of a StringBuilder object. What method do you use?

9.21 How does the StringBuilder class's Replace method differs from the string class's Remove method?

9.4 Using the Split Method to parse strings.

 The string class method Split breaks a string down into its components, which are called tokens.

Sometimes a string will contain a series of words or other items of data separated by spaces or other characters. For example, look at the following string.

```
"peach raspberry strawberry vanilla"
```

This string contains the following four items of data: peach, raspberry, strawberry, and vanilla. In programming terms, items such as these are known as *tokens*. Notice that a space appears between the items. The character that separates tokens is known as a *delimiter*. Here is another example:

```
"17;92;81;12;46;5"
```

This string contains the following tokens: 17, 92, 81, 12, 46, and 5. Notice that a semicolon appears between each item. In this example the semicolon is used as a delimiter. Some programming problems require you to read a string that contains a list of items and then extract all of the tokens from the string for processing. For example, look at the following string that contains a date:

```
"3-22-2005"
```

The tokens in this string are 3, 22, and 2005, and the delimiter is the hyphen character. Perhaps a program needs to extract the month, day, and year from such a string. Another example is an operating system pathname, such as the following:

```
/home/rsullivan/data
```

The tokens in this string are `home`, `rsullivan`, and `data`, and the delimiter is the / character. Perhaps a program needs to extract all of the directory names from such a pathname. The process of breaking a string into tokens is known as *tokenizing*.

Extracting Tokens

Once you have created a `string`, you then setup a list of separators. Finally, you call the `Split` method after creating a string array. The following code demonstrates how all of the tokens can be extracted from a `string` object.

```
string strToken = "One Two Three";
char[] separate = {' ','\n'};
string[] result = strToken.Split(separate);
```

The `DateTester` class in Code Listing 9-8 uses the `Split` method. It accepts a string containing a date in the form MONTH/DAY/YEAR. It extracts the month, day, and year and print each of these values.

Code Listing 9-8   DateTester.cs

```
 1 /*
 2     This program demonstrates the DateTester class.
 3 */
 4
 5 using System;
 6
 7 public class DateTester
 8 {
 9     public static void Main()
10     {
11         string date = "10/23/2005";
12         char[] tokens = {'/'};
13         // Extract the tokens.
14         string[] dateArr = date.Split(tokens);
15
16         Console.WriteLine("Here's the date: {0}",
17                             date);
18         foreach(string token in dateArr)
19           Console.WriteLine("Values: {0}", token);
20
21     }
22 }
```

Code Listing 9-8 DateTester.cs *(continued)*

Program Output
```
Here's the date: 10/23/2005
Values: 10
Values: 23
Values: 2005
```

Using Multiple Delimiters

Some situations require that you use more multiple characters as delimiters in the same string. For example, look at the following email address:

```
joe@gaddisbooks.com
```

This string uses two delimiters: @ (the at symbol) and . (the period). To extract the tokens from this string we must specify both characters as delimiters to the constructor. Here is an example:

```
string name = "joe@gaddisbooks.com";
char[] separate = {'@','.'};
string[] valueArray = name.Split(separate);
foreach(string delims in valueArray)
    Console.WriteLine("{0}", delims);
```

This code will produce the following output:

```
joe
gaddisbooks
com
```

Trimming a String Before Splitting

When you are splitting a string that was entered by the user, and you are using characters other than whitespaces as delimiters, you will probably want to trim the string before splitting it. Otherwise, if the user enters leading whitespace characters, they will become part of the first token. Likewise, if the user enters trailing whitespace characters, they will become part of the last token. For example look at the following code:

```
string name = "   one;two;three    ";
char[] separate = {';'};
string[] valueArray = name.Split(separate);
foreach(string delims in valueArray)
    Console.WriteLine("*{0}*", delims);
```

This code will produce the following output:

```
*   one*
*two*
*three    *
```

To prevent leading and/or trailing whitespace characters from being included in the first and last tokens, use the `string` class's Trim method to remove them. Here is the same code, modified to use the `Trim` method.

```
string name = "   one;two;three   ";
string temp;
char[] separate = {';'};
temp = name.Trim();
string[] valueArray = temp.Split(separate);
foreach(string delims in valueArray)
    Console.WriteLine("*{0}*", delims);
```

This code will produce the following output:

```
*one*
*two*
*three*
```

CHECKPOINT

9.22 The following string contains three tokens. What are they? What character is the delimiter?

```
"apples pears bananas"
```

9.23 Look at the following string:

```
"/home/rjones/mydata.txt"
```

Write the declaration of a `string` object that can be used to extract the following tokens from the string: home, rjones, mydata, and txt.

9.5 Handling and Throwing Exceptions

 An exception is an object that is generated as the result of an error or an unexpected event. To prevent exceptions from crashing your program, you must write code that detects and handles them. You can also write code to throw a standard C# exception.

There are many error conditions that can occur while a C# application is running that will cause it to halt execution. By now you have probably experienced this many times. For example, look at the program in Code Listing 9-9. This program attempts to read beyond the bounds of an array.

The numbers array in this program has only three elements, with the subscripts 0 though 2. The program crashes when it tries to read the element at numbers[3] and displays an error message similar to that shown at the end of the program output. This message indicates that an exception occurred, and it gives some information about it. An *exception* is an object that is generated in memory as the result of an error or an unexpected event. When an exception is generated, it is said

Code Listing 9-9   BadArray.cs

```
 1 /*
 2     This program causes an error and crashes.
 3 */
 4
 5 using System;
 6
 7 public class BadArray
 8 {
 9    public static void Main()
10    {
11       // Create an array with 3 elements.
12       int[] numbers = { 1, 2, 3 };
13
14       // Attempt to read beyond the bounds
15       // of the array.
16       for (int i = 0; i <= 3; i++)
17          Console.WriteLine(numbers[i]);
18    }
19 }
```

Program Output

```
1
2
3

Unhandled Exception: System.IndexOutOfRangeException:
Index was outside the bounds of the array. At BadArray.Main()
```

to have been *thrown*. Unless an exception is detected by the application and dealt with, it causes the application to halt.

To detect that an exception has been thrown and prevent it from halting your application, C# allows you to create exception handlers. An *exception handler* is a section of code that gracefully responds to exceptions when they are thrown. The process of intercepting and responding to exceptions is called *exception handling*. If your code does not handle an exception when it is thrown, the *default exception handler* deals with it, as shown in Code Listing 9-9. The default exception handler prints an error message and crashes the program.

The error that caused the exception to be thrown in Code Listing 9-9 is easy to avoid. If the loop were written properly, it would not have tried to read outside the bounds of the array. Some errors, however, are caused by conditions that are outside the application and cannot be avoided. For example, suppose an application creates a file on the disk and the user deletes it. Later the application attempts to open the file to read from it, and because it does not exist, an error occurs. As a result, an exception is thrown.

Exception Classes

As previously mentioned, an exception is an object. Exception objects are created from classes in the C# CLR. The CLR has an extensive hierarchy of exception classes. A small part of the hierarchy is shown in Figure 9-8.

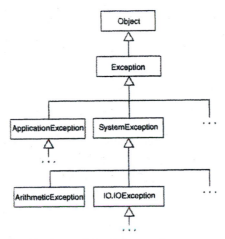

Figure 9-8 Part of the exception class hierarchy

As you can see, all of the classes in the hierarchy inherit from the `Exception` class in the `System` namespace. Just below the `Exception` class are the classes `ApplicationException` and `SystemException`. Other exception classes are found at this level as well. However, we will only deal with the two classes mentioned above. Classes that inherit from `ApplicationException` are for exceptions that are created by writing your own custom exceptions.

All of the exceptions that you will handle are instances of classes that inherit from `SystemException`. Figure 9-8 shows two of these classes: `IOException` and `ArithmeticException`. These classes also serve as base classes. `IOException` serves as a base class for exceptions that are related to input and output operations. `ArithmeticException` serves as a base class for exceptions that result from arithmetic errors, such as divide by zero.

Handling an Exception

To handle an exception, you use a `try` statement. We will look at several variations of the `try` statement, beginning with the following general format.

```
try
{
    (try block statements...)
}
catch (ExceptionType ParameterName)
{
    (catch block statements...)
}
```

First the key word `try` appears. Next, a block of code appears inside braces, which are required. This block of code is known as a *try block*. A `try block` is one or more statements that are executed and can potentially throw an exception. You can think of the code in the try block as being "protected" because the application will not halt if the try block throws an exception.

After the `try` block, a `catch` clause appears. A `catch` clause begins with the key word `catch`, followed by the code *(ExceptionType parameterName)*. This is a parameter variable declaration, where *ExceptionType* is the name of an exception class and *parameterName* is a variable name. If code in the try block throws an exception of the *ExceptionType* class, then the parameter variable will reference the exception object. In addition, the code that immediately follows the `catch` clause is executed. The code that immediately follows the `catch` clause is known as a *catch block*. Once again, the braces are required.

Let's look at an example of code that uses a `try` statement. The statement inside the following try block attempts to open the file `MyFile.txt`. If the file does not exist, the `StreamReader` throws an exception of the `FileNotFoundException` class. This code is designed to handle that exception if it is thrown.

```
try
{
    StreamReader freader = new StreamReader("MyFile.txt");
}
catch (FileNotFoundException e)
{
    Console.WriteLine(e.Message);
}
```

Let's look closer. First, the code in the `try` block is executed. If this code throws an exception, the C# CLR searches for a `catch` clause that can deal with the exception. In order for a `catch` clause to be able to deal with an exception, its parameter must be of a type that is compatible with the exception's type. Here is this code's `catch` clause:

```
catch (FileNotFoundException e)
```

This `catch` clause declares a reference variable named e as its parameter. The e variable can reference an object of the `FileNotFoundException` class. So, this `catch` clause can deal with an exception of the `FileNotFoundException` class. If the code in the `try` block throws an exception of the `FileNotFoundException` class, the e variable will reference the exception object and the code in the catch block will execute. In this case, a message will be printed. After the catch block is executed, the program will resume with the code that appears after the entire `try/catch` construct.

Code Listing 9-10 shows a program that asks the user to enter a file name, then attempts to open the file. If the file does not exist, an error message is printed. Figures 9-9 and 9-10 show examples of interaction with the program.

Code Listing 9-10 OpenFile.cs

```
1  /*
2      This program demonstrates how a FileNotFoundException
3      exception can be handled.
4  */
5
```

(code listing continues)

Code Listing 9-10 OpenFile.cs *(continued)*

```
 6 using System;
 7 using System.IO;
 8
 9 public class OpenFile
10 {
11    public static void Main()
12    {
13
14       string fileName;
15
16       // Get a file name from the user.
17       Console.WriteLine("Enter the name of a file:");
18
19       // Attempt to open the file.
20       try
21       {
22          fileName = Console.ReadLine();
23          StreamReader inputFile = new StreamReader(fileName);
24          Console.WriteLine("The file was found.");
25       }
26       catch(FileNotFoundException e)
27       {
28          Console.WriteLine(e.Message);
29       }
30
31       Console.WriteLine("Done.");
32    }
33 }
```

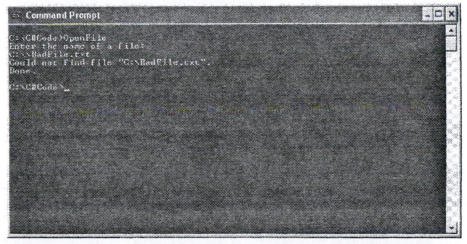

Figure 9-9 Interaction with the OpenFile.cs **program (Assume that** BadFile.txt **does not exist.)**

Figure 9-10   Interaction with the `OpenFile.cs` **program (Assume that** `GoodFile.txt` **does exist.)**

Look at the example run of the program in Figure 9-9. The user entered `BadFile.txt` as the file name. In line 23 of the program, the second statement inside the try block, this name is passed to the `StreamReader` constructor. Because this file does not exist, an exception of the class is thrown. When the exception is thrown, the program immediately exits the try block, skipping the remaining statements in the block (line 24). The program jumps to the `catch` clause in line 26 and executes the `catch` block that follows it. Figure 9-11 illustrates this sequence of events.

Figure 9-11   Sequence of events with an exception

Notice that after the `catch` block executes, the program resumes at the statement that immediately follows the `try`/`catch` construct. This statement, which is in line 31, displays the message "Done."

Now look at the example run of the program in Figure 9-10. In this case, the user entered `GoodFile.txt`, which is the name of a file that exists. No exception was thrown in the `try` block, so the program skips the catch clause and its catch block and jumps directly to the statement in line 31, which follows the try/catch construct. This statement displays the message "Done." Figure 9-12 illustrates this sequence of events.

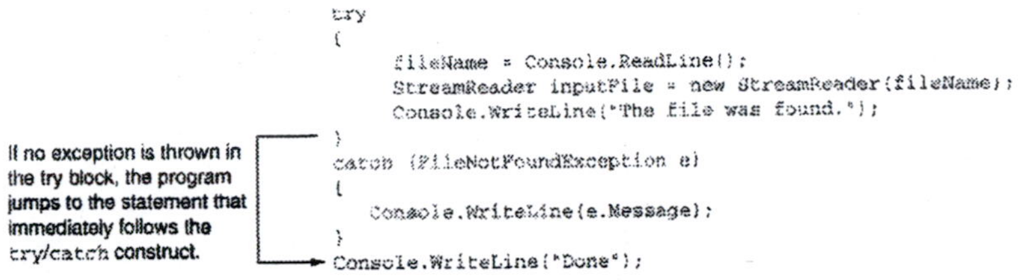

If no exception is thrown in the try block, the program jumps to the statement that immediately follows the try/catch construct.

```
try
{
    fileName = Console.ReadLine();
    StreamReader inputFile = new StreamReader(fileName);
    Console.WriteLine("The file was found.");
}
catch (FileNotFoundException e)
{
    Console.WriteLine(e.Message);
}
Console.WriteLine("Done");
```

Figure 9-12   Sequence of events with no exception

Retrieving the Default Error Message

Each exception object has a property named `Message` that can be used to retrieve the default error message for the exception. This is the same message that is displayed when the exception is not handled and the application halts. The program in Code Listing 9-10 demonstrates the `Message` property. A similar version of the program in Code Listing 9-10 is found in Code Listing 9-11.

Code Listing 9-11   ExceptionMessage.cs

```
1  /*
2      This program demonstrates how the default error
3      message can be retrieved from an exception object.
4  */
5
6  using System;
7  using System.IO;
8
9  public class ExceptionMessage
10 {
11     public static void Main()
12     {
13
14         string fileName;
15
16         // Get a file name from the user.
17         Console.WriteLine("Enter the name of a file:");
18
```

(code listing continues)

Code Listing 9-11 ExceptionMessage.cs *(continued)*

```
19      // Attempt to open the file.
20      try
21      {
22          fileName = Console.ReadLine();
23          StreamReader inputFile = new StreamReader(fileName);
24          Console.WriteLine("The file was found.");
25      }
26      catch (FileNotFoundException e)
27      {
28          Console.WriteLine(e.Message);
29      }
30      Console.WriteLine("Done.");
31   }
32 }
```

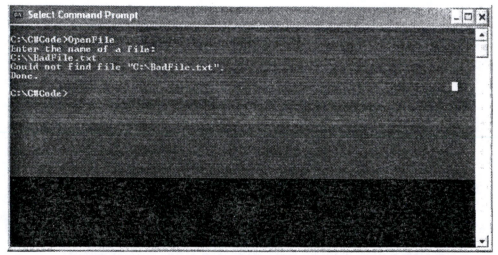

Figure 9-13 Interaction with the `OpenFile.cs` **program (Assume that** `BadFile.txt` **does not exist.)**

Handling Multiple Exceptions

The programs we have studied so far test only for a single type of exception. In many cases, however, the code in the try block will be capable of throwing more than one type of exception. In such a case, you need to write a catch clause for each type of exception that could potentially be thrown.

For example, the program in Code Listing 9-12 reads the contents of a file named SalesData.txt. Each line in the file contains the sales amount for one month, and the file has several lines. Here are the contents of the file:

```
24987.62
26978.97
32589.45
31978.47
22781.76
29871.44
```

The program in Code Listing 9-12 reads each line from the file, converts it to a double, and adds it to an accumulator variable. The try block contains code that can throw several types of exceptions. For example, the constructor for the StreamReader class can throw a FileNotFoundException object if the file is not found. To handle these exceptions, the try statement has several catch clauses. The program output shows the output displayed by the program when no errors occur.

Code Listing 9-12   SalesReport.cs

```
 1 /*
 2     This program demonstrates how multiple exceptions can
 3     be caught with one try statement.
 4 */
 5
 6 using System;
 7 using System.IO;
 8
 9 public class SalesReport
10 {
11     public static void Main()
12     {
13
14         int months = 0;           // Number of months
15         double totalSales = 0.0,  // Total sales
16             averageSales;         // Average sales
17         string str, fileName;
18
19         Console.WriteLine("Enter the file name: ");
20         try
21         {
22             fileName = Console.ReadLine();
23             StreamReader inputFile = new StreamReader(fileName);
24
25             // Read the contents of the file and
26             // accumulate the sales data.
27
```

(code listing continues)

Code Listing 9-12 SalesReport.cs *(continued)*

```
28              str = inputFile.ReadLine();
29              while (str != null)
30              {
31
32                totalSales += Convert.ToDouble(str);
33                months++;
34                str = inputFile.ReadLine();
35              }
36
37              // Close the file.
38              inputFile.Close();
39
40              // Calculate the average.
41              averageSales = totalSales / months;
42
43              // Display the results.
44              Console.WriteLine();
45              Console.WriteLine(
46                        "Number of months: {0}" +
47                        "\nTotal Sales: {1:C2}" +
48                        "\nAverage Sales: {2:C2}"
49                        , months, totalSales, averageSales);
50          }
51      catch(FileNotFoundException e)
52      {
53          Console.WriteLine(e.Message);
54      }
55      catch(IOException e)
56      {
57          Console.WriteLine(e.Message);
58      }
59  }
60 }
```

Program Output with Example Input
```
Enter the name of a file:
C:\\SalesData.txt[Enter]

Number of months: 6
Total Sales: $169,187.71
Average Sales: $28,197.95
```

When an exception is thrown by code in the try block, the CLR begins searching the try statement for a catch clause that can handle it. It searches the catch clauses from top to bottom and passes control of the program to the first catch clause with a parameter that is compatible with the exception.

Using Exception Handlers to Recover from Errors

The program in Code Listing 9-12 demonstrates how a try statement can have several catch clauses in order to handle different types of exceptions. However, the program does not use the exception handlers to recover from any of the errors. Regardless of whether the file is not found, or some type of I/O error occurs while the file is being read, this program still halts.

When in the same try statement you are handling multiple exceptions and some of the exceptions are related to each other through inheritance, then you should handle the more specialized exception classes before the more general exception classes.

The finally Clause

The try statement may have an optional finally clause, which must appear after all of the catch clauses. Here is the general format of a try statement with a finally clause:

```
try
{
        (try block statements...)
}
catch (ExceptionType ParameterName)
{
        (catch block statements...)
}
finally
{
        (finally block statements...)
}
```

The *finally block* is one or more statements that are always executed after the try block has executed and after any catch blocks have executed if an exception was thrown. The statements in the finally block execute whether an exception occurs or not. For example, the following code opens a file and reads its contents. The try statement has a catch clause that catches any IOException objects that might be thrown by the StreamReader class's ReadLine method. The finally block closes the file regardless of whether an exception occurred.

```
// Open the file.
StreamReader freader = new StreamReader(fileName);

try
{
    // Read and display the file's contents.
    input = inputFile.ReadLine();
    while (input != null)
    {
        Console.WriteLine(input);
        input = inputFile.ReadLine();
    }
}
catch (IOException e)
```

```
    {
        Console.WriteLine(e.Message);
    }
    finally
    {
        // Close the file.
        inputFile.Close();
    }
```

Throwing Exceptions

You can use the throw statement to manually throw an exception. The general format of the throw statement is

```
throw new ExceptionType (MessageString);
```

The throw statement causes an exception object to be created and thrown. In this general format, *ExceptionType* is an exception class name and *MessageString* is an optional string argument passed to the exception object's constructor. The *MessageString* argument contains a customized error message that can be retrieved from the exception object's Message property. If you do not pass a message to the constructor, the exception will have a null message. Here is an example of a throw statement:

```
throw new System.Exception("Cannot divide by zero.");
```

This statement creates an object of the System.Exception class and passes the string "Cannot divide by zero" to the object's constructor. The object is then thrown, which cause the exception-handling process to begin. Code Listing 9-13 demonstrates how to throw an exception.

Code Listing 9-13   DivideByZero.cs

```
 1 /*
 2
 3    This program demonstrates how to throw an exception.
 4 */
 5
 6 using System;
 7
 8 public class DivideByZero
 9 {
10    public static void Main()
11    {
12       int num1, num2;
13       double quotient;
14
```

(code listing continues)

Code Listing 9-13   DivideByZero.cs *(continued)*

```
15        Console.WriteLine("Enter the first number: ");
16        num1 = Convert.ToInt32(Console.ReadLine());
17
18        Console.WriteLine("Enter the second number: ");
19        num2 = Convert.ToInt32(Console.ReadLine());
20
21        try
22        {
23            quotient = Divide(num1,num2);
24            Console.WriteLine("The quotient is {0} ",
                     quotient);
25        }
26        catch(ArithmeticException e)
27        {
28            Console.WriteLine(e.Message);
29        }
30        Console.WriteLine("End of the program.");
31
32    }
33
34    public static double Divide(int numerator, int denominator)
35    {
36      if (denominator == 0)
37        throw new ArithmeticException("Cannot divide by
                 zero");
38      else
39        return (double) numerator / denominator;
40    }
41 }
```

Program Output with Example Input
```
Enter the first number:
3[Enter]
Enter the second number:
0[Enter]
Cannot divide by zero
End of the program.
```

In the Double method, on line 37 we threw an ArithmeticException. It is then caught in the catch block (line 26) and the exception message was printed out (line 28).

   NOTE: In C# you can only throw objects from the System.Exception class or any subclasses of it.

When an Exception Is Not Caught

When an exception is thrown, it cannot be ignored. It must be handled by the program or by the default exception handler. When the code in a method throws an exception, the normal execution of that method stops and the CLR searches for a compatible exception handler inside the method. If there is no code inside the method to handle the exception, then control of the program is passed to the previous method in the call stack (that is, the method that called the *offending method*). If that method cannot handle the exception, then control is passed again, up the call stack, to the previous method. This continues until control reaches the Main method. If the Main method does not handle the exception, then the program is halted and the default exception handler handles the exception.

 # CHECKPOINT

9.24 Briefly describe what an exception is.

9.25 What does it mean to "throw" an exception?

9.26 If an exception is thrown and the program does not handle it, what happens?

9.27 Other than the Object class, what is the base class for all exceptions?

9.28 What is the difference between exceptions that inherit from the ApplicationException class and exceptions that inherit from the SystemException class?

9.29 What is the difference between a try block and a catch block?

9.30 After the catch block has handled the exception, where does program execution resume?

9.31 How do you retrieve an error message from an exception?

9.32 When does the code in a finally block execute?

9.33 A program's Main method calls method A, which calls method B. None of these methods perform any exception handling. The code in method B throws an exception. Describe what happens.

9.6 Advanced File Operations: Binary Files and Random Access Files

 CONCEPT A file that contains raw binary data is known as a binary file. The content of a binary file is not formatted as text and is not meant to be opened in a text editor. A random access file is a file that allows a program to read data from any location within the file, or write data to any location within the file.

Binary Files

All the files you've been working with so far have been text files. That means the data stored in the files has been formatted as text. Even a number, when stored in a text file with the Write or WriteLine method, is converted to text. For example, consider the following program segment:

```
StreamWriter outputFile = new
            StreamWriter("Number.txt");
int x = 1297;
outputFile.Write(x);
outputFile.Close();
```

The last statement writes the contents of the variable x to the Number.txt file. When the number is written, however, it is stored as the characters '1', '2', '9', and '7'. This is illustrated in Figure 9-14.

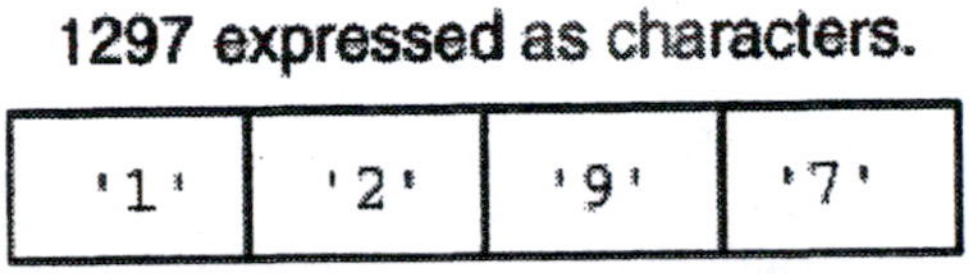

1297 expressed as characters.

'1'	'2'	'9'	'7'

Figure 9-14   The number 1297 expressed as characters

When a number such as 1297 is stored in the computer's memory, it isn't stored as text, however. It is formatted as a binary number. Figure 9-15 shows how the number 1297 is stored in memory, in an int variable, using binary. Recall that int variables occupy 4 bytes.

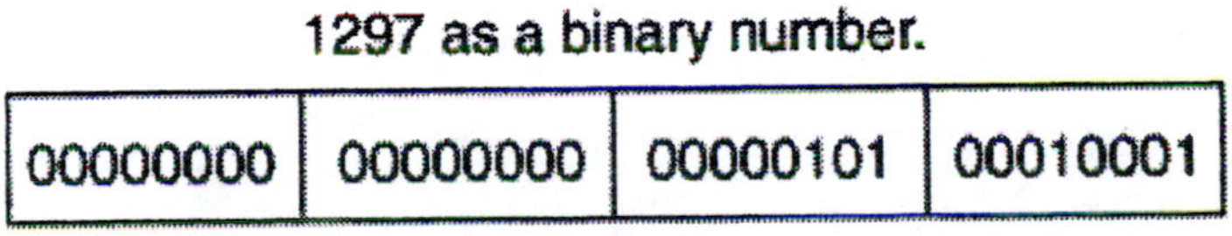

1297 as a binary number.

00000000	00000000	00000101	00010001

Figure 9-15   The number 1297 as a binary number, as it is stored in memory

The binary representation of the number shown in Figure 9-15 is the way the raw data is stored in memory. In fact, this is sometimes called the *raw binary format*. Data can be stored in a file in its raw binary format. A file that contains binary data is often called a *binary file*.

Storing data in its binary format is more efficient than storing it as text because there are fewer conversions to take place. In addition, there are some types of data that should only be stored in its raw binary format. Images are an example. However, when data is stored in a binary file, you cannot open the file in a text editor such as Notepad. When a text editor opens a file, it assumes the file contains text.

Writing Data to a Binary File

To write data to a binary file you must create an object from the following class:

BinaryWriter   This class, which is in the System.IO namespace, allows you to open a file
                for writing binary data and establish a connection with it.

The following code shows how a file named MyInfo.dat can be opened for binary output.

```
BinaryWriter outputFile = new
BinaryWriter(File.Open("MyInfo.dat",FileMode.Truncate));
```

The instance of the BinaryWriter class has the ability to open a file for binary output and establish a connection with it. In the constructor, you open the file by passing the filename and the file mode. In the program in Code Listing 9-14, an array of int values is written to the file Numbers.dat, a process that does not show up on the screen.

Code Listing 9-14   WriteBinaryFile.cs

```
1 /*
2     This program opens a binary file and writes the contents
3     of an int array to the file.
4 */
5
6 using System;
7 using System.IO;
8
9 public class WriteBinaryFile
10 {
11    public static void Main()
12    {
13        // An array to write to the file
14        int[] numbers = { 2, 4, 6, 8, 10, 12, 14 };
15
16        string fileName;
17
18        Console.WriteLine("Enter the file name");
19        try
20        {
21        fileName = Console.ReadLine();
22        // Create the binary output objects.
23        BinaryWriter outputFile = new
24            BinaryWriter(File.Open(fileName,FileMode.OpenOrCreate));
24
25        Console.WriteLine("Writing the numbers to the file...");
26
27        // Write the array elements to the file.
28        for (int i = 0; i < numbers.Length; i++)
29            outputFile.Write(numbers[i]);
30
31        Console.WriteLine("Done.");
32
33        // Close the file.
34        outputFile.Close();
35        }
36        catch (IOException e)
37        {
38            Console.WriteLine(e.Message);
39        }
40    }
41 }
```

Code Listing 9-14 WriteBinaryFile.cs *(continued)*

Program Output with Example Input

```
Enter the file name
C:\\Numbers.dat[Enter]
Writing the numbers to the file...
Done.
```

Reading Data from a Binary File

To open a binary file for input, you use the following classes:

BinaryReader   This class which is in the System.IO namespace, allows you to open a file for reading binary data and establish a connection with it.

The following code shows how a file named MyInfo.dat can be opened for binary input.

```
BinaryReader inputFile = new
    BinaryReader(File.Open("C:\\MyInfo.dat",FileMode.Open));
```

The instance of the BinaryReader class has the ability to open a file for binary input and establish a connection with it. In the constructor, you open the file by passing the filename and the file mode.

The program in Code Listing 9-15 opens the Numbers.dat file that was created by the program in Code Listing 9-14. The numbers are read from the file and displayed on the screen. Notice that the program must catch the exception in order to determine when the file's end has been reached.

Code Listing 9-15 ReadBinaryFile.cs

```
1 /*
2     This program opens a binary file, reads
3     and displays the contents.
4 */
5
6 using System;
7 using System.IO;
8
```

(code listing continues)

Code Listing 9-15 ReadBinaryFile.cs *(continued)*

```
 9 public class ReadBinaryFile
10 {
11    public static void Main()
12    {
13       int number; // A number read from the file
14       string fileName;
15       bool endOfFile = false;     // EOF flag
16
17    Console.WriteLine("Enter the file name");
18     try
19       {
20       fileName = Console.ReadLine();
21       // Create the binary input objects.
22       BinaryReader inputFile = new
              BinaryReader(File.Open(fileName,FileMode.Open));
23
24       Console.WriteLine("Reading numbers from the file:");
25
26       // Read the contents of the file.
27       while (!endOfFile)
28       {
29          try
30          {
31             number = inputFile.ReadInt32();
32             Console.Write("{0} ",number);
33          }
34          catch(EndOfStreamException e)
35          {
36             endOfFile = true;
37             Console.WriteLine(e.Message);
38          }
39       }
40
41       Console.WriteLine("\nDone.");
42
43       // Close the file.
44       inputFile.Close();
45       }
46    catch(IOException e)
47       {
48          Console.WriteLine(e.Message);
49       }
50    }
51 }
```

Program Output with Example Input

```
Enter the file name
C:\\Numbers.dat[Enter]
Reading numbers from the file:
2 4 6 8 10 12 14
Done.
```

Random Access Files

All of the programs that you have created to access files so far have performed *sequential file access*. With sequential access, when a file is opened for input, its read position is at the very beginning of the file. This means that the first time data is read from the file, the data will be read from its beginning. As the reading continues, the file's read position advances sequentially through the file's contents.

The problem with sequential file access is that in order to read a specific byte from the file, all the bytes that precede it must be read first. For instance, if a program needs data stored at the hundredth byte of a file, it will have to read the first 99 bytes to reach it. If you've ever listened to a cassette tape player, you understand sequential access. To listen to a song at the end of the tape, you have to listen to all the songs that are before it, or fast-forward over them. There is no way to immediately jump to that particular song.

Although sequential file access is useful in many circumstances, it can slow a program down tremendously. If the file is very large, locating data buried deep inside it can take a long time. Alternatively, C# allows a program to perform *random file access*. In random file access, a program may immediately jump to any location in the file without first reading the preceding bytes. The difference between sequential and random file access is like the difference between a cassette tape and a compact disc. When listening to a CD, you don't need to listen to or fast-forward over unwanted songs. You simply jump to the track that you want to listen to. This is illustrated in Figure 9-16.

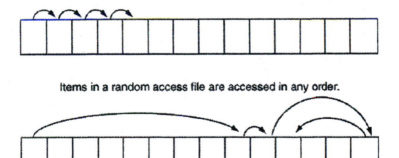

Figure 9-16 **Sequential access vs. random access**

To create and work with random access files in C#, you use the FileStream class, which is in the System.IO namespace. Here is an example of a statement that opens a file using the FileStream class:

```
FileStream randomFile =
    new FileStream(fileName,FileMode.Open,
        FileAccess.Write);
```

Reading and Writing with the `FileStream` Class

A file that is opened or created with the `FileStream` class is treated as a binary file. For example, the program in Code Listing 9-16 opens a file named `Letters.dat` and writes all of the letters of the alphabet to the file.

Code Listing 9-16 WriteLetters.cs

```
 1 /*
 2    This program uses a RandomAccessFile object to
 3    create the file Letters.dat. The letters of the
 4    alphabet are written to the file.
 5 */
 6
 7 using System;
 8 using System.IO;
 9
10 public class WriteLetters
11 {
12    public static void Main()
13
14    {
15      // The letters array has all 26 letters.
16      char[] letters = {
17                  'a', 'b', 'c', 'd', 'e', 'f', 'g',
18                  'h', 'i', 'j', 'k', 'l', 'm', 'n',
19                  'o', 'p', 'q', 'r', 's', 't', 'u',
20                  'v', 'w', 'x', 'y', 'z' };
21
22      string fileName;
23
24      Console.WriteLine("Enter the file name:");
25      try
26      {
27          fileName = Console.ReadLine();
28          // Open a file for reading and writing.
29          FileStream randomFile = new
30              FileStream(fileName,FileMode.Open,FileAccess.Write);
31           Console.WriteLine("Writing data to the file...");
32
33      // Sequentially write the letters array to the file.
34          for (int i = 0; i < letters.Length; i++)
35              randomFile.WriteByte((byte)letters[i]);
36
```

(code listing continues)

Code Listing 9-16   WriteLetters.cs *(continued)*

```
37      // Close the file.
38          randomFile.Close();
39      }
40      catch(IOException e)
41      {
42          Console.WriteLine(e.Message);
43      }
44
45      Console.WriteLine("Done.");
46      }
47 }
```

Program Output with Example Input
```
Enter the file name:
```
C:\\Letters.dat[Enter]
```
Writing data to the file…
Done.
```

After this program executes, the letters of the alphabet are stored in the Letters.dat file. Because the WriteByte method was used, the letters are each stored as 2-byte characters. This fact will be important to know later when we want to read the characters from the file.

The File Pointer

The FileStream class treats a file as a stream of bytes. The bytes are numbered, with the first byte being byte 0. The last byte's number is one less than the number of bytes in the file. These byte numbers are similar to an array's subscripts, and are used to identify locations in the file.

Internally, the FileStream class keeps a long integer value known as the file pointer. The *file pointer* holds the byte number of a location in the file. When a file is first opened, the file pointer is set to 0. This causes it to "point" to the first byte in the file. When an item is read from the file, it is read from the byte that the file pointer points to. Reading also causes the file pointer to advance to the byte just beyond the item that was read.

Writing also takes place at the location pointed to by the file pointer. If the file pointer points to the end of the file when a write operation is performed, then the data will be written to the end of the file. However, if the file pointer holds the number of a byte within the file, at a location where data is already stored, then a write operation will cause data to be written over the existing data at that location.

Not only does the FileStream class let you read and write data, but it also allows you to move the file pointer. This means that you can immediately read data from any byte location in the file. It also means that you can write data to any location in the file, over existing data. To move the file pointer, you use the Seek method. The following code will correctly read and display the sixth character.

```
        randomFile.Seek(6,SeekOrigin.Begin);

        // Read the character stored at this location
        // and display it. Should be the letter f.
        ch = (char) randomFile.ReadByte();
        Console.WriteLine(ch);
```

The program in Code Listing 9-17 demonstrates further. It randomly reads the data from positions 5, 10, and 3 from the file.

Code Listing 9-17   ReadRandomLetters.cs

```
 1 /*
 2     This program uses the RandomAccessFile class to open
 3     the file Letters.dat and randomly read letters from
 4     different locations.
 5 */
 6
 7 using System;
 8 using System.IO;
 9
10 public class ReadRandomLetters
11 {
12     public static void Main()
13     {
14         char ch;                    // A character from the file
15         string fileName;
16
17
18         Console.WriteLine("Enter the filename: ");
19         try
20         {
21         fileName = Console.ReadLine();
22         // Open the file for reading.
23         FileStream randomFile =
24                     new FileStream(fileName,FileMode.Open);
25
26         // Move to the character 5. This is the 6th
27         // character from the beginning of the file.
28         randomFile.Seek(5,SeekOrigin.Begin);
29
30         // Read the character stored at this location
31         // and display it. Should be the letter f.
32         ch = (char) randomFile.ReadByte();
33         Console.WriteLine(ch);
34
```

(code listing continues)

Code Listing 9-17 ReadRandomLetters.cs *(continued)*

```
35        // Move to the character 10. This is the 11th
36        // character from the beginning of the file.
37        // read the character, and display it.
38        // Should be the letter k.
39        randomFile.Seek(10,SeekOrigin.Begin);
40        ch = (char) randomFile.ReadByte();
41        Console.WriteLine(ch);
42
43        // Move to the character 3. This is the 4th
44        // character from the beginning of the file.
45        // read the character, and display it.
46        // Should be the letter d.
47        randomFile.Seek(3,SeekOrigin.Begin);
48        ch = (char) randomFile.ReadByte();
49        Console.WriteLine(ch);
50
51        // Close the file.
52        randomFile.Close();
53     }
54     catch (IOException e)
55     {
56        Console.WriteLine(e.Message);
57     }
58  }
59 }
```

Program Output with Example Input

```
Enter the file name:
C:\\Letters.dat[Enter]
f
k
d
```

9.7 Common Errors

- **Trying to use string comparison methods such as StartsWith and EndsWith for case-insensitive comparisons.** Most of the string comparison methods are case sensitive.

- **Thinking of the first position of a string as 1.** Many of the string and StringBuilder methods accept a character position within a string as an argument. Remember, the position numbers in a string start at 0. If you think of the first position in a string as 1, you will get an off-by-one error.

- **Assuming that all statements inside a try block will execute.** When an exception is thrown, the `try` block is exited immediately. This means that statements appearing in the `try` block after the offending statement will not be executed.

- **Getting the `try`, `catch`, and `finally` clauses out of order.** In a `try` statement, the `try` clause must appear first, followed by all of the `catch` clauses, followed by the optional `finally` clause.

- **Writing two `catch` clauses that handle the same exception in the same `try` statement.** You cannot have more than one `catch` clause per exception type in the same `try` statement.

- **When catching multiple exceptions that are related to one another through inheritance, listing the more general exceptions first.** When you are handling multiple exceptions in the same `try` statement and some of the exceptions are related to each other through inheritance, you should handle the more specialized exception classes before the more general exception classes. Otherwise, the compiler thinks you are handling the same exception more than once and you will get an error.

Review Questions and Exercises

Multiple Choice and True/False

1. The `IsDigit`, `IsLetter`, and `IsLetterOrDigit` methods are members of this class.

    a) `string`   b) `Char`

    c) `Character`   d) `StringBuilder`

2. This method converts a character to uppercase.

    a) `MakeUpperCase`   b) `ToUpper`

    c) `IsUpper`   d) `UpperCase`

3. The `StartsWith` and `EndsWith` methods are members of this class.

    a) `string`   b) `Char`

    c) `Character`   d) `StringBuilder`

4. The `IndexOf` and `LastIndexOf` methods are members of this class.

    a) `string`   b) `Integer`

    c) `Char`   d) `StringBuilder`

5. The `Substring` and `ToCharArray` methods are members of this class.

    a) `string`   b) `Float`

    c) `Char`   d) `StringTokenizer`

6. This `string` class method performs the same operation as the + operator when used on strings.

   a) Add
   b) Join
   c) Concat
   d) Plus

7. This is one of the methods that are common to both the `string` and `StringBuilder` classes.

   a) Append
   b) Insert
   c) Replace
   d) Remove

8. When an exception is generated, it is said to have been

   a) built.
   b) thrown.
   c) caught.
   d) killed.

9. This is a section of code that gracefully responds to exceptions.

   a) exception generator
   b) exception manipulator
   c) exception handler
   c) exception monitor

10. If your code does not handle an exception when it is thrown, it is dealt with by this.

    a) default exception handler
    b) the operating system
    c) system debugger
    c) default exception generator

11. All exception classes inherit from this class.

    a) Error
    b) RuntimeException
    c) Exception
    d) Throwable

12. You can think of this code as being "protected" because the application will not halt if it throws an exception.

    a) try block
    b) catch block
    c) finally block
    d) protected block

13. This property can be used to retrieve the error message from an exception object.

    a) ErrorMessage
    b) ErrorString
    c) Error
    d) Message

14. This is one or more statements that are always executed after the try block has executed and after any catch blocks have executed if an exception was thrown.

    a) try block
    b) catch block
    c) finally block
    d) protected block

15. This is a stream of unformatted binary data.

    a) binary stream
    b) character stream
    c) raw data stream
    d) byte stream

16. This class has the ability to read data from a text file.

    a) Reader
    b) StreamReader
    c) FileReader
    d) TextReader

17. To write text to a file, you instantiate this class.

    a) StreamWriter
    b) TextFileWriter
    c) FileWriter
    d) OutputWriter

18. True or False: Character-testing methods, such as IsLetter, accept strings as arguments and test each character in the string.

19. True or False: If the ToUpper method's argument is already uppercase, it is returned as is, with no changes.

20. True or False: If ToLower method's argument is already lowercase, it will be inadvertently converted to uppercase.

21. True or False: The StartsWith and EndsWith methods are case sensitive.

22. True or False: The IndexOf and LastIndexOf methods find characters, but cannot find substrings.

23. True or False: The string class's Replace method can replace individual characters, but not substrings.

24. True or False: The StringBuilder class's Replace method can replace individual characters, but not substrings.

25. True or False: You can use the = operator to assign a string to a StringBuilder object.

26. True or False: When an exception is thrown by code inside a try block, all of the statements in the try block are always executed.

27. True or False: You cannot have more than one catch clause per try statement.

28. True or False: When an exception is thrown the CLR searches the try statement's catch clauses from top to bottom and passes control of the program to the first catch clause with a parameter that is compatible with the exception.

29. True or False: When in the same try statement you are handling multiple exceptions and some of the exceptions are related to each other through inheritance, you should handle the more general exception classes before the more specialized exception classes.

Algorithm Workbench

1. The following if statement determines whether choice is equal to 'Y' or 'y'.

   ```
   if (choice == 'Y' || choice == 'y')
   ```

   Rewrite this statement so it only makes one comparison and does not use the || operator. (Hint: Use either the ToUpper or ToLower methods.)

2. Write a loop that counts the number of space characters that appear in the string object str.

3. Write a loop that counts the number of digits that appear in the `string` object `str`.

4. Write a loop that counts the number of lowercase characters that appear in the `string` object `str`.

5. Write a method that accepts a reference to a `string` object as an argument and returns `true` if the argument ends with the substring ".com". Otherwise, the method should return `false`.

6. Modify the method you wrote for Question 5 so it performs a case-insensitive test. The method should return true if the argument ends with ".com" in any possible combination of upper and lowercase letters.

7. Write a method that accepts a `StringBuilder` object as an argument and converts all occurrences of the lowercase letter "t" in the object to uppercase.

8. Look at the following string:

   `"cookies>milk>fudge:cake:ice cream"`

   Write code using the `Split` method that extracts the following tokens from the string and displays them: `cookies`, `milk`, `fudge`, `cake`, and `ice cream`.

9. Look at the following program and tell what the program will output when run.

```
using System;
public class ExceptionTest
{
    public static void Main()
    {
        int number;
        string str;

        try
        {
            str = "xyz";
            number = Convert.ToInt32(str);
            Console.WriteLine("A");
        }
        catch(NumberFormatException e)
        {
            Console.WriteLine(e.Message);
        }
        catch(ArgumentException e)
        {
            Console.WriteLine(e.Message);
        }

        Console.WriteLine("D");
    }
}
```

10. Look at the following program and tell what the program will output when run.

```csharp
using  System;
public class ExceptionTest
{
    public static void Main()
    {
        int number;
        string str;

        try
        {
            str = "xyz";
            number = Convert.ToInt32(str);
            Console.WriteLine("A");
        }
        catch(NumberFormatException e)
        {
            Console.WriteLine(e.Message);
        }
        catch(ArgumentException e)
        {
            Console.WriteLine(e.Message);
        }
        finally
        {
            Console.WriteLine("D");
        }

        Console.WriteLine("E");
    }
}
```

Short Answer

1. Why should you use `StringBuilder` objects instead of `string` objects in a program that makes lots of changes to strings?

2. What is meant when it is said that an exception is thrown?

3. What does it mean to catch an exception?

4. What happens when an exception is thrown, but the `try` statement does not have a `catch` clause that is capable of catching it?

5. What is the purpose of a `finally` clause?

6. Where does execution resume after an exception has been thrown and caught?

7. When multiple exceptions are caught in the same `try` statement and some of them are related through inheritance, does the order in which they are listed matter?

8. What is the difference between a byte stream and a character stream?

9. What class provides `Write` and a `WriteLine` method for writing text to a file?

10. When using a `StreamReader` object to read data from a file, how do you detect the end of the file?

Programming Challenges

1. Backward String

Write a method that accepts a `string` object as an argument and displays its contents backward. For instance, if the string argument is "gravity" the method should display "ytivarg". Demonstrate the method in a program that asks the user to input a string and then passes it to the method.

2. Word Counter

Write a method that accepts a `string` object as an argument and returns the number of words it contains. For instance, if the argument is "Four score and seven years ago" the method should return the number 6. Demonstrate the method in a program that asks the user to input a string and then passes it to the method. The number of words in the string should be displayed on the screen.

3. Sentence Capitalizer

Write a method that accepts a `string` object as an argument and returns a copy of the string with the first character of each sentence capitalized. For instance, if the argument is "hello. my name is Joe. what is your name?" the method should return the string "Hello. My name is Joe. What is your name?" Demonstrate the method in a program that asks the user to input a string and then passes it to the method. The modified string should be displayed on the screen.

4. Vowels and Consonants

Write a class with a constructor that accepts a `string` object as its argument. The class should have a method that returns the number of vowels in the string, and another method that returns the number consonants in the string. Demonstrate the class in a program that performs the following steps:

1. The user is asked to enter a string.
2. The program displays the following menu:
   a. Count the number of vowels in the string
   b. Count the number of consonants in the string
   c. Count both the vowels and consonants in the string
   d. Enter another string
   e. Exit the program
3. The program performs the operation selected by the user and repeats until the user selects e, to exit the program.

5. Password Verifier

Imagine you are developing a software package that requires users to enter their own passwords. Your software requires that users' passwords meet the following criteria:

- The password should be at least six characters long.
- The password should contain at least one uppercase and at least one lowercase letter.
- The password should have at least one digit.

Write a class that verifies that a password meets the stated criteria. Demonstrate the class in a program that allows the user to enter a password and then displays a message indicating whether it is valid or not.

6. Phone Number List

Write a program that has two parallel arrays of string objects. One of the arrays should hold people's names and the other should hold their phone numbers. Here are example contents of both arrays.

name Array Example Contents	phone Array Example Contents
"Harrison, Rose"	"555-2234"
"James, Jean"	"555-9098"
"Smith, William"	"555-1785"
"Smith, Brad"	"555-9224"

The program should ask the user to enter a name or the first few characters of a name to search for in the array. The program should display all of the names that match the user's input and their corresponding phone numbers. For example, if the user enters "Smith," the program should display the following names and phone numbers from the list:

```
Smith, William: 555-1785
Smith, Brad: 555-9224
```

7. Check Writer

Write a program that displays a simulated paycheck. The program should ask the user to enter the date, the payee's name, and the amount of the check. It should then display a simulated check with the dollar amount spelled out, as shown here:

Date: 11/24/2004

Pay to the Order of: John Phillips $1920.85

One thousand nine hundred twenty and 85 cents

9. Sum of Numbers in a String

Write a program that asks the user to enter a series of numbers separated by commas. Here is an example of valid input:

```
7,9,10,2,18,6
```

The program should calculate and display the sum of all the numbers.

9. Sum of Digits in a String

Write a program that asks the user to enter a series of single-digit numbers with nothing separating them. The program should display the sum of all the single-digit numbers in the string. For example, if the user enters 2514, the method should return 12, which is the sum of 2, 5, 1, and 4. The program should also display the highest and lowest digits in the string. (*Hint: Convert the string to an array.*)

10. Word Counter

Write a program that asks the user for the name of a file. The program should display the number of words that the file contains.

11. Sales Analysis

The file `SalesData.txt` on the Student CD contains the dollar amount of sales that a retail store made each day for a number of weeks. Each line in the file contains seven numbers, which are the sales numbers for one week. The numbers are separated by a comma. The following line is an example from the file:

```
2541.36,2965.88,1965.32,1845.23,7021.11,9652.74,1469.36
```

Write a program that opens the file and processes its contents. The program should display the following:

- The total sales for each week
- The average daily sales for each week
- The total sales for all of the weeks
- The average weekly sales
- The week number which had the highest amount of sales
- The week number which had the lowest amount of sales

12. Miscellaneous String Operations

Write a class with the following static methods:

- **WordCount**. This method should accept a reference to a `string` object as an argument and return the number of words contained in the object.

- **ArrayToString**. This method accepts a `char` array as an argument and converts it to a `string` object. The method should return a reference to the `string` object.

- **MostFrequent**. This method accepts a reference to a `string` object as an argument and returns the character that occurs the most frequently in the object.

- **ReplaceSubstring**. This method accepts three references to `string` objects as arguments. Let's call them *string1*, *string2*, and *string3*. It searches *string1* for all occurrences of *string2*. When it finds an occurrence of *string2*, it replaces it with *string3*. For example, suppose the three arguments have the following values:

string1:	"the dog jumped over the fence"
string2:	"the"
string3:	"that"

With these three arguments, the method would return a reference to a string object with the value "that dog jumped over that fence." Demonstrate each of these methods in a complete program.

13. TestScores Class

Write a class named TestScores. The class constructor should accept an array of test scores as its argument. The class should have a method that returns the average of the test scores. If any test score in the array is negative or greater than 100, the class should throw an ArgumentException. Demonstrate the class in a program.

14. RetailItem Exceptions

Programming Challenge 4 of Chapter 4 required you to write a RetailItem class that holds data pertaining to a retail item. Write an exception class that can be instantiated and thrown when a negative number is given for the price. Write another exception class that can be instantiated and thrown when a negative number is given for the units on hand. Demonstrate the exception classes in a program.

15. Month Class Exceptions

Programming Challenge 9 of Chapter 8 required you to write a Month class that holds information about the month. Write exception classes for the following error conditions:

- A number less than 1 or greater than 12 is given for the month number.
- An invalid string is given for the name of the month.

Modify the Month class so it throws the appropriate exception when either of these errors occurs. Demonstrate the classes in a program.

16. Payroll Class Exceptions

Programming Challenge 5 of Chapter 4 required you to write a Payroll class that calculates an employee's payroll. Write exception classes for the following error conditions:

- An empty string is given for the employee's name.
- An invalid value is given for the employee's ID number. If you implemented this field as a string, then an empty string would be invalid. If you implemented this field as a numeric variable, then a negative number or zero would be invalid.
- An invalid number is given for the number of hours worked. This would be a negative number or a number greater than 84.
- An invalid number is given for the hourly pay rate. This would be a negative number or a number greater than 25.

Modify the `Payroll` class so it throws the appropriate exception when any of these errors occurs. Demonstrate the exception classes in a program.

17. `FileArray` Class

Design a class that has a static method named `WriteArray`. The method should take two arguments: the name of a file and a reference to a char array. The file should be opened, the contents of the array should be written to the file, and then the file should be closed.

Write a second method in the class named `ReadArray`. The method should take two arguments: the name of a file and a reference to a char array. The file should be opened, characters should be read from the file and stored in the array, and then the file should be closed. Demonstrate both methods in a program.

18. File Encryption Filter

File encryption is the science of writing the contents of a file in a secret code. Your encryption program should work like a filter, reading the contents of one file, modifying the data into a code, and then writing the coded contents out to a second file. The second file will be a version of the first file, but written in a secret code.

Although there are complex encryption techniques, you should come up with a simple one of your own. For example, you could read the first file one character at a time, and add 10 to the character code of each character before it is written to the second file.

19. File Decryption Filter

Write a program that decrypts the file produced by the program in Programming Challenge 18. The decryption program should read the contents of the coded file, restore the data to its original state, and write it to another file.

10

Inheritance

Chapter Objectives

- To understand the inheritance relationship and write classes that inherit from other classes
- To learn how constructors operate in an inheritance relationship and be able to write derived class constructors that call the appropriate base class constructor
- To be able to write derived class methods that override base class methods
- To understand protected access
- To be able to write classes that inherit from other classes, which also inherit from other classes
- To appreciate that all objects inherit from the `System.Object` class
- To comprehend polymorphism and write code that polymorphically uses reference variables
- To know what abstract methods and abstract classes are
- To recognize what an interface is and be able to write classes that use one or more interfaces

Topics in this Chapter

10.1 What Is Inheritance?	10.6 The `Object` Class
10.2 Calling the Base Class Constructor	10.7 Polymorphism
10.3 Overriding Base Class Methods	10.8 Abstract Classes and Abstract Methods
10.4 Protected Members	10.9 Interfaces
10.5 Chains of Inheritance	10.10 Common Errors
	Review Questions and Exercises

10.1 What Is Inheritance?

> **CONCEPT** Inheritance allows a new class to be based on an existing class. The new class inherits the members of the class it is based on.

Generalization and Specialization

In the real world you can find many objects that are specialized versions of other more general objects. For example, the term "insect" describes a very general type of creature with numerous characteristics. Because grasshoppers and bumblebees are insects, they have all the general characteristics of an insect. In addition, they have special characteristics of their own. For example, the grasshopper has its jumping ability, and the bumblebee has its stinger. Grasshoppers and bumblebees are specialized versions of an insect. This is illustrated in Figure 10-1.

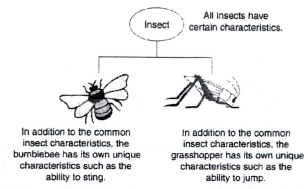

Figure 10-1 Bumblebees and grasshoppers are specialized versions of an insect

Inheritance and the "Is-a" Relationship

When one object is a specialized version of another object, there is an *is-a relationship* between them. For example, a grasshopper *is an* insect. Here are a few other examples of the is-a relationship.

- A poodle *is a* dog.
- A car *is a* vehicle.
- A flower *is a* plant.
- A rectangle *is a* shape.
- A football player *is an* athlete.

When an is-a relationship exists between objects, it means that the specialized object has all of the characteristics of the general object, plus additional characteristics that make it special. In object-oriented programming, *inheritance* is used to create an is-a relationship among classes.

This allows you to extend the capabilities of a class by creating another class that is a specialized version of it.

Inheritance involves a base class and a derived class. The *base class* is the general class and the *derived class* is the specialized class. You can think of the derived class as an extended version of the base class. The derived class inherits fields and methods from the base class without any of them having to be rewritten. Furthermore, new fields and methods may be added to the derived class, and that is what makes it a specialized version of the base class.

 NOTE: At the risk of confusing you with too much terminology, it should be mentioned that base classes are also called *superclasses*, and derived classes are also called *subclasses*. Either set of terms is correct. For consistency, this text will use the terms *base class* and *derived class*.

Let's look at an example of how inheritance can be used. Most teachers assign various graded activities for their students to complete. A graded activity can be given a numeric score such as 70, 85, 90, and so on, and a letter grade such as A, B, C, D or F. Figure 10-2 shows a UML diagram for the `GradedActivity` class, which is designed to hold the numeric score of a graded activity. The `SetScore` method sets a numeric score, and the `GetScore` method returns the numeric score. The `GetGrade` method returns the letter grade that corresponds to the numeric score. Notice that the class does not have a programmer-defined constructor, so C# will automatically generate a default constructor for it. This will be a point of discussion later. Code Listing 10-1 shows the code for the class.

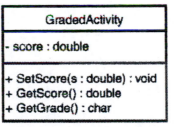

Figure 10-2   UML diagram for the `GradedActivity` **class**

Code Listing 10-1   GradedActivity.cs

```
1  /*
2     A class that holds a grade for a graded activity.
3  */
4
5  public class GradedActivity
6  {
7     private double score;  // Numeric score
8
```

(code listing continues)

Code Listing 10-1 GradedActivity.cs *(continued)*

```
 9      /*
10          The SetScore method sets the score field.
11          **parameter s The value to store in score.
12      */
13
14      public void SetScore(double s)
15      {
16          score = s;
17      }
18
19      /*
20          The GetScore method returns the score.
21          **return The value stored in the score field.
22      */
23
24      public double GetScore()
25      {
26          return score;
27      }
28
29      /*
30          The GetGrade method returns a letter grade
31          determined from the score field.
32          **return The letter grade.
33      */
34
35      public char GetGrade()
36      {
37          char letterGrade;
38
39          if (score >= 90)
40              letterGrade = 'A';
41          else if (score >= 80)
42              letterGrade = 'B';
43          else if (score >= 70)
44              letterGrade = 'C';
45          else if (score >= 60)
46              letterGrade = 'D';
47          else
48              letterGrade = 'F';
49
50          return letterGrade;
51      }
52 }
```

The program in Code Listing 10-2 demonstrates the class. Figures 10-3 and 10-4 show examples of interaction with the program.

Code Listing 10-2   GradeDemo.cs

```
1  /*
2      This program demonstrates the GradedActivity
3      class.
4  */
5
6  using System;
7
8  public class GradeDemo
9  {
10     public static void Main()
11     {
12
13         double testScore;    // A test score
14
15         // Create a GradedActivity object.
16         GradedActivity grade = new GradedActivity();
17
18         // Get a test score.
19         Console.WriteLine("Enter " +
20                            "a numeric test score.");
21         testScore = Convert.ToDouble(Console.ReadLine());
22
23         // Store the score in the grade object.
24         grade.SetScore(testScore);
25
26         // Display the letter grade for the score.
27         Console.WriteLine(
28                     "The grade for that test is {0}",
29                     grade.GetGrade());
30     }
31 }
```

Figure 10-3   Interaction with the `GradeDemo.cs` **program**

Figure 10-4   Interaction with the `GradeDemo.cs` **program**

The `GradedActivity` class represents the general characteristics of a student's graded activity. Many types of graded activities exist, however, such as quizzes, midterm exams, final exams, lab reports, essays, and so on. Because the numeric scores might be determined differently for each of these graded activities, we can create derived classes to handle each one. For example, we could create a `FinalExam` class that would be a derived class of the `GradedActivity` class. Figure 10-5 shows the UML diagram for such a class, and Code Listing 10-3 shows its code. The diagram has fields for the number of questions on the exam (`numQuestions`), the number of points each question is worth (`pointsEach`), and the number of questions missed by the student (`numMissed`).

FinalExam
- numQuestions : int - pointsEach : double - numMissed : int
+ FinalExam(questions : int,   missed : int)

Figure 10-5   UML diagram for the `FinalExam` **class**

Look at the header for the `FinalExam` class in line 5. The class header uses a colon between the class names, which indicates that this class inherits from another class (a base class). The name of the base class is listed after the colon. So, this line indicates that `FinalExam` is the name of the class being declared and `GradedActivity` is the name of the base class it inherits from. This is illustrated in Figure 10-6.

Code Listing 10-3   FinalExam.cs

```
1 /*
2    This class determines the grade for a final exam.
3 */
4
5 public class FinalExam : GradedActivity
6 {
7     private int numQuestions;   // Number of questions
8     private double pointsEach;  // Points for each question
9     private int numMissed;      // Questions missed
10
11    /*
12        The constructor sets the number of questions on the
13        exam and the number of questions missed.
14        **parameter questions The number of questions.
15        **parameter missed The number of questions missed.
16    */
17
18    public FinalExam(int questions, int missed)
19    {
20        double numericScore;  // To hold a numeric score
21
22        // Set the numQuestions and numMissed fields.
23        numQuestions = questions;
24        numMissed = missed;
25
26        // Calculate the points for each question and
27        // the numeric score for this exam.
28        pointsEach = 100.0 / questions;
29        numericScore = 100.0 - (missed * pointsEach);
30
31        // Call the inherited SetScore method to
32        // set the numeric score.
33        SetScore(numericScore);
34    }
35
36    public double Points
37    {
38        get
39        {
40            return pointsEach;
41        }
42    }
43
44    public int NumMissed
45    {
46        get
47        {
48            return numMissed;
49        }
50    }
51 }
```

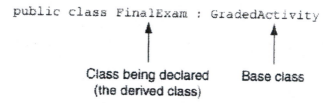

Figure 10-6 `FinalExam` **class header**

If we want to express the relationship between the two classes, we can say that a `FinalExam` is a `GradedActivity`.

Because the `FinalExam` class inherits from the `GradedActivity` class, it inherits all of the public members of the `GradedActivity` class. Here is a list of the members of the `FinalExam` class:

Fields

`int numQuestions;`	Declared in `FinalExam`
`double pointsEach;`	Declared in `FinalExam`
`int numMissed;`	Declared in `FinalExam`

Methods

Constructor	Declared in `FinalExam`
`SetScore`	Inherited from `GradedActivity`
`GetScore`	Inherited from `GradedActivity`
`GetGrade`	Inherited from `GradedActivity`

Notice that the `GradedActivity` class's `score` field is not listed among the members of the `FinalExam` class. That is because the `score` field is private. Private members of the base class cannot be accessed directly by the derived class, so technically speaking, they are not inherited. When an object of the derived class is created, the private members of the base class exist in memory, but only methods in the base class can access them. They are truly private to the base class. However, the `FinalExam` object as instantiated does have a `score` field.

You will also notice that the base class's constructor is not listed among the members of the `FinalExam` class. It makes sense that base class constructors are not inherited because their purpose is to construct objects of the base class. In the next section we discuss in more detail how base class constructors operate.

To see how inheritance works in this example, let's take a closer look at the `FinalExam` constructor in lines 18 through 34. The constructor accepts two arguments: the number of test questions on the exam and the number of questions missed by the student. In lines 23 and 24 these values are assigned to the `numQuestions` and `numMissed` fields. Then, in lines 28 and 29, the number of points for each question and the numeric test score are calculated. In line 33, the last statement in the constructor reads:

```
SetScore(numericScore);
```

This is a call to the SetScore method. Although no SetScore method appears in the Fina-lExam class, the method is inherited from the GradedActivity class. The program in Code Listing 10-4 demonstrates the FinalExam class. Figure 10-7 shows an example of interaction with the program.

Code Listing 10-4 FinalExamDemo.cs

```
1 /*
2    This program demonstrates the FinalExam class,
3    which extends the GradedActivity class.
4 */
5
6 using System;
7
8 public class FinalExamDemo
9 {
10    public static void Main()
11    {
12       int questions,    // Number of questions
13           missed;       // Number of questions missed
14
15       // Get the number of questions on the exam.
16       Console.WriteLine("How many " +
17                    "questions are on the final exam?");
18       questions = Convert.ToInt32(Console.ReadLine());
19
20       // Get the number of questions the student missed.
21       Console.WriteLine("How many " +
22                    "questions did the student miss?");
23       missed = Convert.ToInt32(Console.ReadLine());
24
25       // Create a FinalExam object.
26       FinalExam exam = new FinalExam(questions, missed);
27
28       // Display the test results.
29       Console.WriteLine(
30          "Each question counts {0} points.\n" +
31          "The exam score is {1} \nThe exam grade is {2}",
32          exam.Points,exam.GetScore(),exam.GetGrade());
33    }
34 }
```

10

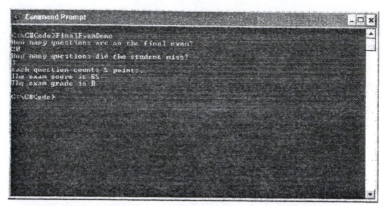

Figure 10-7   Interaction with the `FinalExamDemo.cs` program

In line 26 the following statement creates an instance of the `FinalExam` class and assigns its address to the `exam` variable:

```
FinalExam exam = new FinalExam(questions, missed);
```

Notice in lines 30 through 32, shown here, that two public methods of the `GradedActivity` class, `GetScore` and `GetGrade`, are directly called from the `exam` object:

```
Console.WriteLine(
    "Each question counts {0} points.\n" +
    "The exam score is {1} \nThe exam grade is {2}",
    exam.Points,exam.GetScore(),exam.GetGrade());
```

When a derived class inherits from a base class, the public members of the base class become public members of the derived class. In this program the `GetScore` and `GetGrade` methods can be called from the `exam` object because they are public members of the object's base class.

As mentioned before, the private members of the base class (in this case, the `score` field) cannot be accessed directly by the derived class. When the `exam` object is created in memory, a `score` field exists, but only the methods defined in the base class, `GradedActivity`, can access it. It is truly private to the base class. Because the `FinalExam` constructor cannot directly access the `score` field, it must call the base class's `SetScore` method (which is public) to store a value in it.

 NOTE: To compile the `FinalExamDemo.cs` program from the C# command line:

```
csc /r:GradedActivity.dll /r:FinalExam.dll FinalExamDemo.cs
```

For more information see Appendix D.

Inheritance in UML Diagrams

You show inheritance in a UML diagram by connecting two classes with a line that has an open arrowhead at one end. The arrowhead points to the base class. Figure 10-8 shows a UML diagram depicting the relationship between the GradedActivity and FinalExam classes.

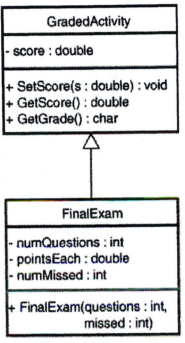

Figure 10-8   UML diagram showing inheritance

The Base Classes' Constructor

You might be wondering how the constructors work together when one class inherits from another. In an inheritance relationship, the base class constructor always executes before the derived class constructor. As was mentioned earlier, the GradedActivity class has only one constructor, which is the default constructor that C# automatically generated for it. When a FinalExam object is created, the GradedActivity class's default constructor is executed just before the FinalExam constructor is executed.

Code Listing 10-5 shows a class, SuperClass1, that has a no-arg constructor. The constructor simply displays the message "This is the base class constructor." Code Listing 10-6 shows SubClass1, which extends SuperClass1. This class also has a no-arg constructor, which displays the message "This is the derived class constructor."

Code Listing 10-5   SuperClass1.cs

```
1 using System;
2 public class SuperClass1
3 {
4    /*
5        Constructor
6    */
7
8    public SuperClass1()
9    {
10       Console.WriteLine("This is the " +
11               "base class constructor.");
12    }
13 }
```

Code Listing 10-6   SubClass1.cs

```
1 using System;
2 public class SubClass1 : SuperClass1
3 {
4    /*
5        Constructor
6    */
7
8    public SubClass1()
9    {
10       Console.WriteLine("This is the " +
11               "derived class constructor.");
12    }
13 }
```

The program in Code Listing 10-7 creates a SubClass1 object. As you can see from the program output, the base class constructor executes first, followed by the derived class constructor.

Code Listing 10-7   ConstructorDemo1.cs

```
1 /*
2    This program demonstrates the order in which
3    base class and derived class constructors are called.
4 */
5
```

(code listing continues)

Code Listing 10-7 ConstructorDemo1.cs *(continued)*

```
 6 using System;
 7
 8 public class ConstructorDemo1
 9 {
10     public static void Main()
11     {
12         SubClass1 obj = new SubClass1();
13     }
14 }
```

Program Output
```
This is the superclass constructor.
This is the subclass constructor.
```

If a base class has either (a) a default constructor or (b) a no-arg constructor that was written into the class, then that constructor will be automatically called just before a derived class constructor executes. In a moment we will discuss other situations that can arise involving base class constructors.

Inheritance Does Not Work in Reverse

In an inheritance relationship, the derived class inherits members from the base class, not the other way around. This means it is not possible for a base class to call a derived class's method. For example, if we create a `GradedActivity` object, it cannot call the `Points` or `NumEach` properties because they are members of the `FinalExam` class.

 ## CHECKPOINT

10.1 Here is the first line of a class declaration. What is the name of the base class? What is the name of the derived class?

```
public class Truck : Vehicle
```

10.2 Look at the following class declarations and answer the questions that follow them.

```
public class Shape
{
    private double area;
    public void SetArea(double a)
    {
        area = a;
    }
    public double GetArea()
    {
```

```
            return area;
        }
    }

    public class Circle : Shape
    {
        private double radius;

        public void SetRadius(double r)
        {
            radius = r;
            SetArea(Math.PI * r * r);
        }

        public double GetRadius()
        {
            return radius;
        }
    }
```

a) Which class is the base class? Which class is the derived class?

b) When a Circle object is created, what are its public members?

c) What members of the Shape class are not accessible to the Circle class's methods?

d) Assume a program has the following declarations:

```
Shape s = new Shape();
Circle c = new Circle();
```

Indicate whether the following statements are legal or illegal.

```
c.SetRadius(10.0);
s.SetRadius(10.0);
Console.WriteLine(c.GetArea());
Console.WriteLine(s.GetArea());
```

10.3 Class B inherits from class A. (Class A is the base class and class B is the derived class.) Describe the order in which the class's constructors execute when a class B object is created.

10.2 Calling the Base Class Constructor

 The base key word refers to an object's base class. You can use the base key word to call a base class constructor.

In the previous section you saw examples illustrating how a base class's default constructor or no-arg constructor is automatically called just before the derived class's constructor executes. But what if the base class does not have a default constructor or a no-arg constructor? Or, what if the base class has multiple overloaded constructors and you want to make sure a specific one is called? In either of these situations, you use the base key word to explicitly call a base class constructor. The base key word refers to an object's base class and can be used to access members of the base class.

Code Listing 10-8 shows a class, SuperClass2, which has a no-arg constructor and a constructor that accepts an int argument. Code Listing 10-9 shows SubClass2, which extends SuperClass2. This class's constructor uses the base key word to call the base class's constructor and pass an argument to it.

Code Listing 10-8 SuperClass2.cs

```
 1 using System;
 2 public class SuperClass2
 3 {
 4     /*
 5         Constructor #1
 6     */
 7
 8     public SuperClass2()
 9     {
10         Console.WriteLine("This is the base class " +
11                           "no-arg constructor.");
12     }
13
14     /*
15         Constructor #2
16     */
17
18     public SuperClass2(int arg)
19     {
20         Console.WriteLine("The following argument " +
21                     "was passed to the base class " +
22                     "constructor: {0}", arg);
23     }
24 }
```

Code Listing 10-9 SubClass2.cs

```
 1 using System;
 2 public class SubClass2 : SuperClass2
 3 {
 4     /*
 5         Constructor
 6     */
 7
 8     public SubClass2(): base(10)
 9     {
10         Console.WriteLine("This is the " +
11                     "derived class constructor.");
12     }
13 }
```

The statement in line 8 of the SubClass2 constructor calls the base class constructor and passes the argument 10 to it. Here are three guidelines you should remember about calling a base class constructor:

1. The base statement that calls the base class constructor may be written only in the derived class's constructor header. You cannot call the base class constructor from any other method.

2. If a derived class constructor does not explicitly call a base class constructor, C# will automatically call the base class's default constructor, or no-arg constructor, just before the code in the derived class's constructor executes. This is equivalent to placing the following statement at the beginning of a derived class constructor:

   ```
   : base();
   ```

The program in Code Listing 10-10 demonstrates these classes.

Code Listing 10-10   ConstructorDemo2.cs

```
 1 /*
 2     This program demonstrates how a base class
 3     constructor is called with the base key word.
 4 */
 5
 6 using System;
 7 public class ConstructorDemo2
 8 {
 9     public static void Main()
10     {
11         SubClass2 obj = new SubClass2();
12     }
13 }
```

Program Output

```
The following argument was passed to the superclass constructor: 10

This is the subclass constructor.
```

Let's look at more meaningful example. Recall the Rectangle class from Chapter 6. Figure 10-9 shows a UML diagram for the class.

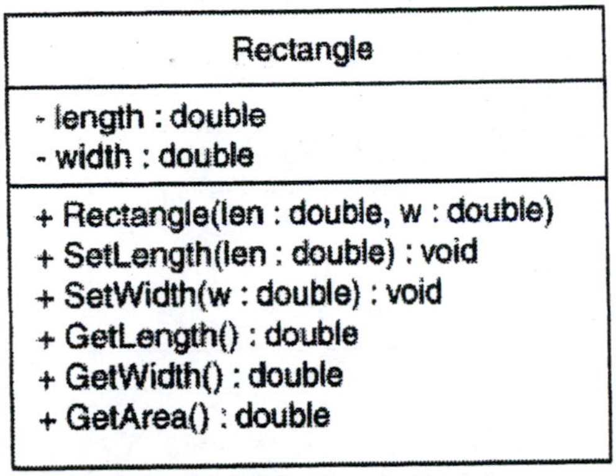

Rectangle
- length : double
- width : double
+ Rectangle(len : double, w : double)
+ SetLength(len : double) : void
+ SetWidth(w : double) : void
+ GetLength() : double
+ GetWidth() : double
+ GetArea() : double

Figure 10-9   UML diagram for the Rectangle class

Here is part of the class's code:

```
public class Rectangle
{
    private double length;
    private double width;

    /*
        Constructor
        **parameter len The length of the rectangle.
        **parameter w The width of the rectangle.
    */

    public Rectangle(double len, double w)
    {
        length = len;
        width = w;
    }
```

(Other methods follow...)

```
}
```

Next we will design a Cube class, which extends the Rectangle class. The Cube class is designed to hold data about cubes, which not only have a length, width, and area (the area of the base), but a height, surface area, and volume as well. A UML diagram showing the inheritance relationship between the Cube and Rectangle classes is shown in Figure 10-10, and the code for the Cube class is shown in Code Listing 10-10.

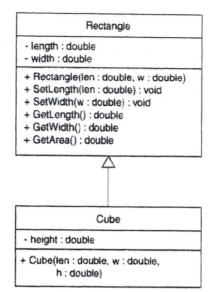

Figure 10-10   UML diagram for the `Rectangle` **and** `Cube` **classes**

Code Listing 10-11   Cube.cs

```
 1  /*
 2     This class holds data about a cube.
 3  */
 4
 5  public class Cube : Rectangle
 6  {
 7     private double height;  // The cube's height
 8
 9     /*
10        The constructor sets the cube's length,
11        width, and height.
12        **parameter len The cube's length.
13        **parameter w The cube's width.
14        **parameter h The cube's height.
15     */
16
17     public Cube(double len, double w, double h): base(len, w)
18     {
19
20        // Set the height.
21        height = h;
22     }
23
```

(code listing continues)

Code Listing 10-11 Cube.cs *(continued)*

```
24    public double Height
25    {
26      get
27      {
28        return height;
29      }
30    }
31
32    public double SurfaceArea
33    {
34      get
35      {
36        return GetArea() * 6;
37      }
38    }
39
40    public double Volume
41    {
42      get
43      {
44        return GetArea() * height;
45      }
46    }
47 }
```

The Cube constructor accepts arguments for the parameters w, len, and h. The values that are passed to w and len are subsequently passed as arguments to the Rectangle constructor in line 17:

```
public Cube(double len, double w, double h) : base(len, w)
```

When the Rectangle constructor finishes, the remaining code in the Cube constructor is executed. The program in Code Listing 10-12 demonstrates the class.

Code Listing 10-12 CubeDemo.cs

```
1 /*
2    This program demonstrates passing arguments to a
3    base class constructor.
4 */
5
6 using System;
7
```

(code listing continues)

Code Listing 10-12   CubeDemo.cs *(continued)*

```
 8 public class CubeDemo
 9 {
10    public static void Main()
11    {
12
13       double length,  // The cube's length
14              width,    // The cube's width
15              height;   // The cube's height
16
17       // Get cube's length.
18       Console.WriteLine("Enter the following " +
19                         "dimensions of a cube:");
20       Console.Write("Length: ");
21       length = Convert.ToDouble(Console.ReadLine());
22
23       // Get the cube's width.
24       Console.Write("Width: ");
25       width = Convert.ToDouble(Console.ReadLine());
26
27       // Get the cube's height.
28       Console.Write("Height: ");
29       height = Convert.ToDouble(Console.ReadLine());
30
31       // Create a cube object and pass the
32       // dimensions to the constructor.
33       Cube myCube =
34             new Cube(length, width, height);
35
36       // Display the cube's properties.
37       Console.WriteLine();
38       Console.WriteLine("Here are the cube's " +
39                         "properties.");
40       Console.WriteLine("Length: {0}",
41                         myCube.GetLength());
42       Console.WriteLine("Width: {0}",
43                         myCube.GetWidth());
44       Console.WriteLine("Height: {0}",
45                         myCube.Height);
46       Console.WriteLine("Base Area: {0}",
47                         myCube.GetArea());
48       Console.WriteLine("Surface Area: {0}",
49                         myCube.SurfaceArea);
50       Console.WriteLine("Volume: {0}",
51                         myCube.Volume);
52    }
53 }
```

Code Listing 10-12 **CubeDemo.cs** *(continued)*

Program Output with Example Input
```
Enter the following dimensions of a cube:
Length: 10[Enter]
Width: 15[Enter]
Height: 12[Enter]

Here are the cube's properties.
Length: 10
Width: 15
Height: 12
Base Area: 150
Surface Area: 900
Volume: 1800
```

When the Base Class Has No Default or No-Arg Constructor

Recall from Chapter 4 that C# provides a default constructor for a class only when you provide no constructors for the class. This makes it possible to have a class with no default constructor. The Rectangle class we just looked at is an example. It has a constructor that accepts two arguments. Because we have provided this constructor, the Rectangle class does not have a default constructor. In addition, we have not written a no-arg constructor for the class.

If a base class does not have a default constructor and does not have a no-arg constructor, then a class that inherits from it *must* call one of the constructors that the base class does have. If it does not, an error will result when the derived class is compiled.

Summary of Constructor Issues in Inheritance

We have covered a number of important issues that you should remember about constructors in an inheritance relationship. The following list summarizes them.

- The base class constructor always executes before the derived class constructor.

- You can write a base statement that calls a base class constructor, but only in the derived class's constructor header. You cannot call the base class constructor from any other method.

- If a derived class constructor does not explicitly call a base class constructor, C# will automatically call base() just before the code in the derived class's constructor executes.

- If a base class does not have a default constructor and does not have a no-arg constructor, then a class that inherits from it *must* call one of the constructors that the base class does have.

CHECKPOINT

10.4 Look at the following classes.

```
public class Ground
{
    public Ground()
    {
        Console.WriteLine("You are on the ground.");
    }
}

public class Sky : Ground
{
    public Sky()
    {
        Console.WriteLine("You are in the sky.");
    }
}
```

What will the following program display?

```
using System;
public class Checkpoint
{
    public static void Main()
    {
        Sky object = new Sky();
    }
}
```

10.5 Look at the following classes.

```
public class Ground
{
    public Ground()
    {
        Console.WriteLine("You are on the ground.");
    }

    public Ground(string groundColor)
    {
        Console.WriteLine("The ground is {0}",
                            groundColor);
    }
}

public class Sky : Ground
{
    public Sky()
    {
        Console.WriteLine("You are in the sky.");
    }
```

```
public Sky(string skyColor):base("green")
{
    Console.WriteLine("The sky is {0}", skyColor);
}
}
```

What will the following program display?

```
using System;
public class Checkpoint
{
    public static void Main()
    {
        Sky object = new Sky("blue");
    }
}
```

10.3 Overriding Base Class Methods

CONCEPT A derived class may have a method with the same signature as a base class method. In such a case the derived class method overrides the base class method.

Sometimes a derived class inherits a method from its base class, but the method is inadequate for the derived class's purpose. Because the derived class is more specialized than the base class, it is sometimes necessary for the derived class to replace inadequate base class methods with more suitable ones. This is known a *method overriding*.

For example, recall the GradedActivity class that was presented earlier in this chapter. This class has a SetScore method that sets a numeric score and a GetGrade method that returns a letter grade based on that score. But suppose a teacher wants to curve a numeric score before determining the letter grade. For example, Dr. Harrison determines that in order to curve the grades in her class she must multiply each student's score by a certain percentage. This gives her an adjusted score that she can use to determine the letter grade. To do this for Dr. Harrison, we can design a new class, CurvedActivity, which extends the GradedActivity class and has its own specialized version of the SetScore method. The SetScore method in the derived class *overrides* the SetScore method in the base class. Figure 10-11 shows a UML diagram depicting the relationship between the GradedActivity class and the CurvedActivity class.

Table 10-1 summarizes the CurvedActivity class's fields, and Table 10-2 summarizes the class's methods.

Code Listing 10-13 shows the code for the CurvedActivity class.

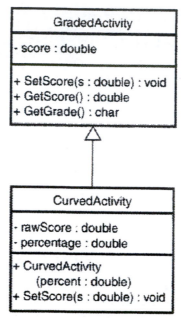

Figure 10-11 The `GradedActivity` **and** `CurvedActivity` **classes**

Table 10-1 `CurvedActivity` **class fields**

Field	Description
rawScore	This field holds the student's unadjusted score.
percentage	This field holds the value that the unadjusted score must be multiplied by to get the curved score.

Table 10-2 `CurvedActivity` **class methods**

Method	Description
Constructor	The constructor accepts a `double` argument that is the curve percentage. This value is assigned to the `percentage` field and the `rawScore` field is assigned 0.0.
SetScore	This method accepts a `double` argument that is the student's unadjusted score. The method stores the argument in the `rawScore` field, then passes the result of `rawScore * percentage` as an argument to the base class's `SetScore` method.

Code Listing 10-13   CurvedActivity.cs

```
1  /*
2      This class computes a curved grade. It extends
3      the GradedActivity class.
4  */
5
6  public class CurvedActivity : GradedActivity
7  {
8      double rawScore,    // Unadjusted score
9             percentage;  // Curve percentage
10
11     /*
12         The constructor sets the curve percentage.
13         **parameter percent The curve percentage.
14     */
15
16     public CurvedActivity(double percent)
17     {
18         percentage = percent;
19         rawScore = 0.0;
20     }
21
22     /*
23         The SetScore method overrides the base classes
24         SetScore method. This version accepts the
25         unadjusted score as an argument. That score is
26         multiplied by the curve percentage and the
27         result is sent as an argument to the base class's
28         SetScore method.
29         **parameter s The unadjusted score.
30     */
31
32     public override void SetScore(double s)
33     {
34         rawScore = s;
35         base.SetScore(rawScore * percentage);
36     }
37
38     public double RawScore
39     {
40         get
41         {
42             return rawScore;
43         }
44     }
45
```

10

(code listing continues)

Code Listing 10-13 CurvedActivity.cs *(continued)*

```
46    public double Percentage
47    {
48       get
49       {
50          return percentage;
51       }
52    }
53 }
```

Recall from Chapter 3 that a method's *signature* consists of the method's name and the data types of the method's parameters, in the order that they appear. Notice that this class's SetScore method has the same signature as the SetScore method in the base class. In order for a derived class method to override a base class method, it must have the same signature. When an object of the derived class invokes the method, it invokes the derived class's version of the method, not the base class's.

The SetScore method in the CurvedActivity class accepts an argument, which is the student's unadjusted numeric score. This value is stored in the rawScore field. Then, in line 35, the following statement is executed:

```
base.SetScore(rawScore * percentage);
```

As you already know, the base key word refers to the object's base class. This statement calls the base class's version of the SetScore method with the result of the expression rawScore * percentage passed as an argument. This is necessary because the base class's score field is private, and the derived class cannot access it directly. In order to store a value in the base class's score field, the derived class must call the base class's SetScore method. A derived class may call an overridden base class method by prefixing its name with the base key word and a dot (.). Notice from line 32

```
public override void SetScore(double s)
```

we must also use the keyword override in the method header to indicate that the method will be overridden in the derived class. Remember, override replaces the method defined in a base class. In GradedActivity we must also make the method that will be overridden as virtual.

```
public virtual void SetScore(double s)
```

The base class method must be declared as virtual in order to override it in the derived class.

The program in Code Listing 10-14 demonstrates this class.

Code Listing 10-14 CurvedActivityDemo.cs

```
 1 /*
 2     This program demonstrates the CurvedActivity class,
 3     which inherits from the GradedActivity class.
 4 */
 5
 6 using System;
 7
 8 public class CurvedActivityDemo
 9 {
10     public static void Main()
11     {
12         double score,        // Raw score
13             curvePercent;    // Curve percentage
14
15         // Get the unadjusted exam score.
16         Console.Write("Enter the student's " +
17                         "raw numeric score: ");
18
19         score = Convert.ToDouble(Console.ReadLine());
20
21         // Get the curve percentage.
22         Console.Write("Enter the curve percentage: ");
23
24         curvePercent = Convert.ToDouble(Console.ReadLine());
25
26         // Create a CurvedActivity object.
27         CurvedActivity curvedExam =
28                     new CurvedActivity(curvePercent);
29
30         // Set the exam score.
31         curvedExam.SetScore(score);
32
33         // Display the test results.
34         Console.WriteLine("The raw score is {0}",
35                     curvedExam.RawScore +
36                     " points.");
37         Console.WriteLine("The curved score is {0}",
38                         curvedExam.GetScore());
39         Console.WriteLine("The exam grade is {0}",
40                         curvedExam.GetGrade());
41     }
42 }
```

Code Listing 10-14   CurvedActivityDemo.cs *(continued)*

Program Output with Example Input
```
Enter the student's raw numeric score: 87[Enter]
Enter the curve percentage: 1.06[Enter]
The raw score is 87 points.
The curved score is 92.22
The exam grade is A
```

This program uses the `curvedExam` variable to reference a `CurvedActivity` object. In line 31 the following statement is used to call the `SetScore` method:

```
curvedExam.SetScore(score);
```

Because `curvedExam` references a `CurvedActivity` object, this statement calls the `CurvedActivity` class's `SetScore` method, not the base class's version.

Even though a derived class may override a method in the base class, base class objects still call the base class version of the method. For example, the following code creates an object of the `GradedActivity` class and calls the `SetScore` method:

```
GradedActivity regularExam = new GradedActivity();
regularExam.SetScore(85);
```

Because `regularExam` references a `GradedActivity` object, this code calls the `GradedActivity` class's version of the `SetScore` method.

Overloading vs. Overriding

There is a distinction between overloading a method and overriding a method. Recall from Chapter 4 that overloading is when a method has the same name as one or more other methods, but a different parameter list. Although overloaded methods have the same name, they have different signatures. When a method overrides another method, however, they have the same signature.

Both overloading and overriding can take place in an inheritance relationship. You already know that overloaded methods can appear within the same class. In addition, a method in a derived class can overload a method in the base class. If class A is the base class and class B is the derived class, a method in class B may overload a method in class A. Overriding, on the other hand, can only take place in an inheritance relationship. If class A is the base class and class B is the derived class, a method in class B may override a method in class A. However, a method cannot override another method in the same class. The following list summarizes the distinction between overloading and overriding.

■ If two methods have the same name but different signatures, they are overloaded. This is true whether the methods are in the same class or one method is in the base class and the other method is in the derived class.

■ If a method in a derived class has the same signature as a method in the base class, the derived class method overrides the base class method.

The distinction between overloading and overriding is important because it can affect the accessibility of base class methods in a derived class. When a derived class overloads a base class method, both methods may be called with a derived class object. However, when a derived class overrides a base class method, only the derived class's version of the method can be called with a derived class object. For example, look at the SuperClass3 class in Code Listing 10-15. It has two overloaded methods named ShowValue. One of the methods accepts an int argument and the other accepts a string argument.

Code Listing 10-15   SuperClass3.cs

```
1 using System;
2 public class SuperClass3
3 {
4     /*
5         This method displays an int.
6         **parameter arg- an int.
7     */
8
9     public virtual void ShowValue(int arg)
10    {
11        Console.WriteLine("SUPERCLASS: " +
12            "The int argument was {0}", arg);
13    }
14
15    /*
16        This method displays a string.
17        **parameter arg A String.
18    */
19
20    public void ShowValue(string arg)
21    {
22        Console.WriteLine("SUPERCLASS: " +
23            "The string argument was {0}", arg);
24    }
25 }
```

Now look at the SubClass3 class in Code Listing 10-16. It inherits from the SuperClass3 class.

Code Listing 10-16   SubClass3.cs

```
1 using System;
2 public class SubClass3 : SuperClass3
3 {
```

(code listing continues)

Code Listing 10-16   SubClass3.cs *(continued)*

```
4      /*
5          This method overrides one of the
6          base class methods.
7          **parameter arg An int.
8      */
9
10     public override void ShowValue(int arg)
11     {
12         Console.WriteLine("SUBCLASS: " +
13             "The int argument was {0}", arg);
14     }
15
16     /*
17         This method overloads the base class
18         methods.
19         **parameter arg A double.
20     */
21
22     public void ShowValue(double arg)
23     {
24         Console.WriteLine("SUBCLASS: " +
25             "The double argument was {0}", arg);
26     }
27 }
```

Notice that SubClass3 also has two methods named ShowValue. The first one, in lines 10 through 14, accepts an int argument. This method overrides one of the base class methods because they have the same signature. Thus the use of the override and virtual keywords. The second ShowValue method, in lines 22 through 26, accepts a double argument. This method overloads the other ShowValue methods because none of the others have the same signature. Although there are four ShowValue methods in these classes, only three of them may be called from a SubClass3 object. This is demonstrated in Code Listing 10-17.

Code Listing 10-17   ShowValueDemo.cs

```
1 /*
2     This program demonstrates the methods in the
3     SuperClass3 and SubClass3 classes.
4 */
5
```

(code listing continues)

Code Listing 10-17 ShowValueDemo.cs *(continued)*

```
 6 using System;
 7
 8 public class ShowValueDemo
 9 {
10    public static void Main()
11    {
12        // Create a SubClass3 object.
13        SubClass3 myObject = new SubClass3();
14
15        myObject.ShowValue(10);       // Pass an int.
16        myObject.ShowValue(1.2);      // Pass a double.
17        myObject.ShowValue("Hello");  // Pass a string.
18    }
19 }
```

Program Output
```
SUBCLASS:  The double argument was 10
SUBCLASS:  The double argument was 1.2
SUPERCLASS:  The string argument was Hello
```

When an int argument is passed to ShowValue, the derived class's method is called because it overrides the base class method. In order to call the overridden base class method, we would have to use the base key word in the derived class method. Here is an example:

```
public override void ShowValue(int arg)
{
    base.ShowValue(arg);   // Call the base class method.
    Console.WriteLine("SUBCLASS: The int argument was {0}",
                      arg);
}
```

? CHECKPOINT

10.6 Under what circumstances would a derived class need to override a base class method?

10.7 How can a derived class method call an overridden base class method?

10.8 If a method in a derived class has the same signature as a method in the base class, does the derived class method overload or override the base class method?

10.9 If a method in a derived class has the same name as a method in the base class but uses a different parameter list, does the derived class method overload or override the base class method?

10.4 Protected Members

CONCEPT Protected members of class may be accessed by methods in a derived class.

Until now you have used two access specifications within a class: private and public. C# provides a third access specification, protected. A protected member of a class may be directly accessed by methods of the same class or methods of a derived class. A protected member is not quite private, because it may be accessed by some methods outside the class. Protected members are not quite public either because access to them is restricted to methods in the same class or derived classes. A protected member's access is somewhere between private and public.

Let's look at a class with a protected member. Code Listing 10-18 shows the GradedActivity2 class, which is a modification of the GradedActivity class presented earlier. In this class, the score field has been made protected instead of private.

Code Listing 10-18   GradedActivity2.cs

```
 1  /*
 2      A class that holds a grade for a graded activity.
 3  */
 4
 5  public class GradedActivity2
 6  {
 7      protected double score;  // Numeric score
 8
 9      /*
10          The SetScore method sets the score field.
11          **parameter s The value to store in score.
12      */
13
14      public void SetScore(double s)
15      {
16          score = s;
17      }
18
19      /*
20          The GetScore method returns the score.
21          **return The value stored in the score field.
22      */
23
24      public double GetScore()
25      {
26          return score;
27      }
28
```

(code listing continues)

Code Listing 10-18 GradedActivity2.cs *(continued)*

```
29    /*
30        The GetGrade method returns a letter grade
31        determined from the score field.
32        **return The letter grade.
33    */
34
35    public char GetGrade()
36    {
37        char letterGrade;
38
39        if (score >= 90)
40            letterGrade = 'A';
41        else if (score >= 80)
42            letterGrade = 'B';
43        else if (score >= 70)
44            letterGrade = 'C';
45        else if (score >= 60)
46            letterGrade = 'D';
47        else
48            letterGrade = 'F';
49
50        return letterGrade;
51    }
52 }
```

Because in line 7 the score field is declared as protected, any class that inherits from this class has direct access to it. The FinalExam2 class, shown in Code Listing 10-19 is an example. This class is a modification of the FinalExam class, which was presented earlier. This class has a new method, AdjustScore, which directly accesses the base class's score field. If the contents of score have a fractional part of 0.5 or greater, the method rounds score up to the next whole number. The AdjustScore method is called from the constructor.

Code Listing 10-19 FinalExam2.cs

```
1 /*
2     This class determines the grade for a final exam.
3     The numeric score is rounded up to the next whole
4     number if its fractional part is .5 or greater.
5 */
6
```

(code listing continues)

Code Listing 10-19   FinalExam2.cs *(continued)*

```
 7 public class FinalExam2 : GradedActivity2
 8 {
 9     private int numQuestions;    // Number of questions
10     private double pointsEach;   // Points for each question
11     private int numMissed;       // Number of questions missed
12
13     /*
14         The constructor sets the number of questions on the
15         exam and the number of questions missed.
16         **parameter questions The number of questions.
17         **parameter missed The number of questions missed.
18     */
19
20     public FinalExam2(int questions, int missed)
21     {
22         double numericScore;  // To hold a numeric score
23
24         // Set the numQuestions and numMissed fields.
25         numQuestions = questions;
26         numMissed = missed;
27
28         // Calculate the points for each question and
29         // the numeric score for this exam.
30         pointsEach = 100.0 / questions;
31         numericScore = 100.0 - (missed * pointsEach);
32
33         // Call the inherited SetScore method to
34         // set the numeric score.
35         SetScore(numericScore);
36
37         // Adjust the score.
38         AdjustScore();
39     }
40
41     /*
42         The PointsEach method returns the number of
43         points each question is worth.
44         **return The value in the pointsEach field.
45     */
46
47     public double PointsEach
48     {
49         get
50         {
51         return pointsEach;
52         }
53     }
54
```

(code listing continues)

Code Listing 10-19   FinalExam2.cs *(continued)*

```
55      /*
56          The NumMissed method returns the number of
57          questions missed.
58          **return The value in the numMissed field.
59      */
60
61      public int NumMissed
62      {
63        get
64        {
65          return numMissed;
66        }
67      }
68
69      /*
70          The AdjustScore method adjusts a numeric score.
71          If score is within 0.5 points of the next whole
72          number, it rounds the score up.
73      */
74
75      private void AdjustScore()
76      {
77          double fraction;
78
79          // Get the fractional part of the score.
80          fraction = score - (int) score;
81
82          // If the fractional part is .5 or greater,
83          // round the score up to the next whole number.
84          if (fraction >= 0.5)
85              score = score + (1.0 - fraction);
86      }
87  }
```

The program in Code Listing 10-20 demonstrates the class. Figure 10-12 shows an example of interaction with the program.

Code Listing 10-20   ProtectedDemo.cs

```
1  /*
2     This program demonstrates the FinalExam2 class,
3     which extends the GradedActivity2 class.
4  */
5
```

(code listing continues)

Code Listing 10-20　ProtectedDemo.cs *(continued)*

```
 6 using System;
 7
 8 public class ProtectedDemo
 9 {
10    public static void Main()
11    {
12
13        int questions,    // Number of questions
14            missed;       // Number of questions missed
15
16        // Get the number of questions on the exam.
17        Console.WriteLine("How many " +
18                    "questions are on the final exam?");
19        questions = Convert.ToInt32(Console.ReadLine());
20
21        // Get the number of questions the student missed.
22        Console.WriteLine("How many " +
23                    "questions did the student miss?");
24        missed = Convert.ToInt32(Console.ReadLine());
25
26        // Create a FinalExam object.
27        FinalExam2 exam = new FinalExam2(questions, missed);
28
29        // Display the test results.
30        Console.WriteLine(
31            "Each question counts {0}" +
32            " points.\nThe exam score is {1}" +
33            "\nThe exam grade is {2}", exam.PointsEach,
34
35              exam.GetScore(),exam.GetGrade());
36    }
37 }
```

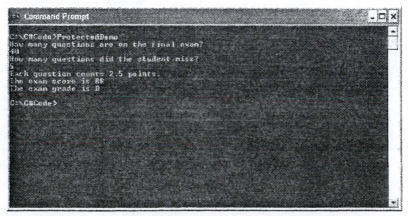

Figure 10-12　Interaction with the `ProtectedDemo.cs` **program**

In the example in Figure 10-12, the student missed 5 out of 40 questions. The unadjusted numeric score would be 87.5, but the AdjustScore method rounded the score field up to 88.

Protected class members may be denoted in a UML diagram with the # symbol. Figure 10-13 shows a UML diagram for the GradedActivity2 class, with the score field denoted as protected.

```
+-------------------------------+
|      GradedActivity2          |
+-------------------------------+
| # score : double              |
+-------------------------------+
| + SetScore(s : double) : void |
| + GetScore() : double         |
| + GetGrade() : char           |
+-------------------------------+
```

Figure 10-13 UML diagram for the GradedActivity2 class

Although defining a class member as protected instead of private might make some tasks easier, you should avoid this practice when possible. This is because any class that inherits from the class has unrestricted access to the protected member. It is always better to make all fields private and then provide public methods for accessing those fields.

Table 10-3 summarizes how each of the access specifiers affect a class member's accessibility within and outside of the class's package.

Table 10-3 Accessibility from within the class's package

Access Modifier	Availability
Public	Available to all
Private	Available only to class containing it
Protected	Available only to class containing it or derived classes from the containing class

Remember, when in access modifier is not specified the default access in C# private.

NOTE: C# also has the internal and protected internal access modifiers. We will not introduce these modifiers.

CHECKPOINT

10.10 When a class member is declared as protected, what code may access it?

10.11 What is the difference between private members and protected members?

10.12 Why should you avoid making class members protected?

10.13 Why is it easy to give private access to a class member by accident?

10.5 Chains of Inheritance

A base class can also inherit from another class.

Sometimes it is desirable to establish a chain of inheritance in which one class inherits from a second class, which in turn inherits from a third class, as illustrated by Figure 10-14. In some cases, this chaining of classes goes on for many layers.

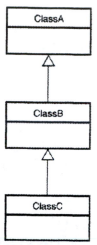

Figure 10-14   A chain of inheritance

In Figure 10-14, ClassC inherits ClassB's members, including the ones that ClassB inherited from ClassA. Let's look at an example of such a chain of inheritance. Consider the PassFailActivity class, shown in Code Listing 10-21, which inherits from the GradedActivity class. The class is intended to determine a letter grade of P for passing, or F for failing.

Code Listing 10-21   PassFailActivity.cs

```
1  /*
2     This class holds a numeric score and determines
3     whether the score is passing or failing.
4  */
5
```

(code listing continues)

Code Listing 10-21 PassFailActivity.cs *(continued)*

```
 6 public class PassFailActivity : GradedActivity
 7 {
 8    private double minPassingScore; // Minimum passing score
 9
10    /*
11       The constructor sets the minimum passing score.
12       **parameter mps The minimum passing score.
13    */
14
15    public PassFailActivity(double mps)
16    {
17       minPassingScore = mps;
18    }
19
20    /*
21       The GetGrade method returns a letter grade
22       determined from the score field. This
23       method overrides the base class method.
24       **return The letter grade.
25    */
26
27    public override char GetGrade()
28    {
29       char letterGrade;
30
31       if (base.GetScore() >= minPassingScore)
32          letterGrade = 'P';
33       else
34          letterGrade = 'F';
35
36       return letterGrade;
37    }
38 }
```

The PassFailActivity constructor, in lines 15 through 18, accepts a double argument which is the minimum passing grade for the activity. This value is stored in the minPassingScore field. The GetGrade method, in lines 27 through 37, overrides the base class method of the same name. This method returns a grade of 'P' if the numeric score is greater than or equal to minPassingScore. Otherwise, the method returns a grade of 'F'.

Suppose we wish to extend this class with another more specialized class. For example, the PassFailExam class, shown in Code Listing 10-22, determines a passing or failing grade for an exam. It has fields for the number of questions on the exam (numQuestions), the number of points each question is worth (pointsEach), and the number of questions missed by the student (numMissed).

Code Listing 10-22   PassFailExam.cs

```
1
2  /*
3     This class determines a passing or failing grade for
4     an exam.
5  */
6
7  public class PassFailExam : PassFailActivity
8  {
9     private int numQuestions;   // Number of questions
10    private double pointsEach;  // Points for each question
11    private int numMissed;      // Number of questions missed
12
13    /*
14       The constructor sets the number of questions, the
15       number of questions missed, and the minimum passing
16       score.
17       **parameter questions The number of questions.
18       **parameter missed The number of questions missed.
19       **parameter minPassing The minimum passing score.
20    */
21
22    public PassFailExam(int questions, int missed,
23                double minPassing) : base(minPassing)
24    {
25
26
27       // Declare a local variable for the score.
28       double numericScore;
29
30       // Set the numQuestions and numMissed fields.
31       numQuestions = questions;
32       numMissed = missed;
33
34       // Calculate the points for each question and
35       // the numeric score for this exam.
36       pointsEach = 100.0 / questions;
37       numericScore = 100.0 - (missed * pointsEach);
38
```

(code listing continues)

Code Listing 10-22   PassFailExam.cs *(continued)*

```
39          // Call the base class's SetScore method to
40          // set the numeric score.
41          SetScore(numericScore);
42      }
43
44      /*
45          The GetPointsEach method returns the number of
46          points each question is worth.
47          **return The value in the pointsEach field.
48      */
49
50      public double GetPointsEach()
51      {
52          return pointsEach;
53      }
54
55      /*
56          The GetNumMissed method returns the number of
57          questions missed.
58          **return The value in the numMissed field.
59      */
60
61      public int GetNumMissed()
62      {
63          return numMissed;
64      }
65  }
```

The PassFailExam class inherits the PassFailActivity class's members, including the ones that PassFailActivity inherited from GradedActivity. The program in Code Listing 10-23 demonstrates the class.

Code Listing 10-23   PassFailExamDemo.cs

```
1  /*
2      This program demonstrates the PassFailExam class.
3  */
4
5  using System;
6
```

(code listing continues)

Code Listing 10-23 PassFailExamDemo.cs *(continued)*

```
7 public class PassFailExamDemo
8 {
9    public static void Main()
10
11   {
12
13      int questions,     // Number of questions
14          missed;        // Number of questions missed
15      double minPassing; // Minimum passing score
16
17      // Get the number of questions on the exam.
18      Console.Write("How many questions are " +
19                     "on the exam? ");
20
21      questions = Convert.ToInt32(Console.ReadLine());
22
23      // Get the number of questions missed.
24      Console.Write("How many questions did " +
25                     "the student miss? ");
26
27      missed = Convert.ToInt32(Console.ReadLine());
28
29      // Get the minimum passing score.
30      Console.Write("What is the minimum " +
31                     "passing score? ");
32
33      minPassing = Convert.ToInt32(Console.ReadLine());
34
35      // Create a PassFailExam object.
36      PassFailExam exam =
37          new PassFailExam(questions, missed, minPassing);
38
39      // Display the test results.
40      Console.WriteLine("Each question counts {0} points.",
41              exam.GetPointsEach());
42      Console.WriteLine("The exam score is {0} ",
43              exam.GetScore());
44      Console.WriteLine("The exam grade is {0} ",
45              exam.GetGrade());
46   }
47 }
```

Code Listing 10-23 PassFailExamDemo.cs *(continued)*

Program Output with Example Input
```
How many questions are on the exam? 100[Enter]
How many questions did the student miss? 25[Enter]
What is the minimum passing score? 60[Enter]
Each question counts 1 points.
The exam score is 75
The exam grade is P
```

Figure 10-15 shows a UML diagram depicting the inheritance relationship among the GradedActivity, PassFailActivity, and PassFailExam classes.

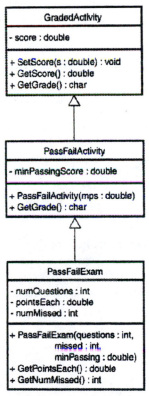

Figure 10-15 The GradedActivity, PassFailActivity, **and** PassFailExam **classes**

Class Hierarchies

Classes often are depicted graphically in a *class hierarchy*. Like a family tree, a class hierarchy shows the inheritance relationships between classes. Figure 10-16 shows a class hierarchy for the GradedActivity, FinalExam, PassFailActivity, and PassFailExam classes. The more general classes are toward the top of the tree and the more specialized classes are toward the bottom.

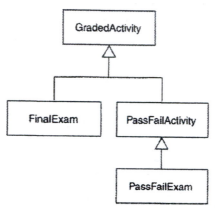

Figure 10-16   Class hierarchy

10.6   The Object Class

CONCEPT The C# FCL has a class named Object, which all other classes directly or indirectly derive.

Every class in C#, including the ones in the FCL and the classes that you create, directly or indirectly derived from a class named Object, which is part of the System namespace. Here's how it happens: When a class does not inherit from another class, C# automatically extends it from the Object class. For example, look at the following class declaration:

```
public class MyClass
{
    (Member Declarations...)
}
```

This class does not explicitly extend any other class, so C# treats it as though it were written as

```
public class MyClass : Object
{
    (Member Declarations...)
}
```

Ultimately, every class extends the Object class. Figure 10-17 shows how the PassFailExam class inherits from Object.

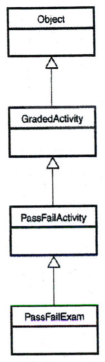

Figure 10-17 The line of inheritance from `Object` **to** `PassFailExam`

Because every class directly or indirectly extends the Object class, every class inherits the Object class's members. Two of the most useful are the ToString and Equals methods. In Chapter 5 you learned that every class has a ToString and an Equals method, and now you know why! It is because those methods are inherited from the Object class.

In the Object class, the ToString method returns a reference to a string containing the object's class name. The Equals method accepts a reference to an object as its argument. It returns true if the argument references the calling object. This is demonstrated in Code Listing 10-24.

Code Listing 10-24 ObjectMethods.cs

```
1 /*
2    This program demonstrates the ToString and equals
3    methods that are inherited from the Object class.
4 */
5 using System;
6
```

(code listing continues)

Code Listing 10-24 ObjectMethods.cs *(continued)*

```
 7 public class ObjectMethods
 8 {
 9    public static void Main()
10    {
11       // Create two more objects.
12       PassFailExam exam1 =
13                   new PassFailExam(0, 0, 0);
14       PassFailExam exam2 =
15                   new PassFailExam(0, 0, 0);
16
17       // Send the objects to WriteLine, which
18       // will call the ToString method.
19       Console.WriteLine(exam1);
20       Console.WriteLine(exam2);
21
22       // Test the Equals method.
23       if (exam1.Equals(exam2))
24          Console.WriteLine("They are the same.");
25       else
26          Console.WriteLine("They are not the same.");
27    }
28 }
```

Program Output
```
PassFailExam
PassFailExam
They are not the same.
```

If you wish to change the behavior of either of these methods for a given class, you must override them in the class.

 CHECKPOINT

10.14 Look at the following class definition:

```
public class ClassD : ClassB
{
   (Member Declarations...)
}
```

Because ClassD inherits from ClassB, is it true that ClassD does not inherit from the Object class? Why or why not?

10.15 When you create a class, it automatically has a ToString method and an Equals method. Why?

10.7 Polymorphism

CONCEPT A base class reference variable can reference objects of a derived class.

Look at the following statement that declares a reference variable named **exam**.

```
GradedActivity exam;
```

This statement tells us that the **exam** variable's data type is **GradedActivity**. Therefore, we can use the **exam** variable to reference a **GradedActivity** object, as shown in the following statement.

```
exam = new GradedActivity();
```

The **GradedActivity** class is also used as the base class for the **FinalExam** class. Because of the is-a relationship between a base class and a derived class, an object of the **FinalExam** class is not just a **FinalExam** object. It is also a **GradedActivity** object. (A final exam *is a* graded activity.) Because of this relationship, we can use a **GradedActivity** variable to reference a **FinalExam** object. For example, look at the following statement:

```
GradedActivity exam = new FinalExam(50, 7);
```

This statement declares **exam** as a **GradedActivity** variable. It creates a **FinalExam** object and stores the object's address in the **exam** variable. This statement is perfectly legal and will not cause an error message because a **FinalExam** object is also a **GradedActivity** object.

This is an example of polymorphism. The term *polymorphism* means the ability to take many forms. In C#, a reference variable is *polymorphic* because it can reference objects of types different from its own, as long as those types are derived classes of its type. All of the following declarations are legal because the **FinalExam**, **PassFailActivity**, and **PassFailExam** classes inherit from **GradedActivity**.

```
GradedActivity exam1 = new FinalExam(50, 7);
GradedActivity exam2 = new PassFailActivity(70);
GradedActivity exam3 = new PassFailExam(100, 10, 70);
```

Although a **GradedActivity** variable can reference objects of any class that extends **GradedActivity**, there is a limit to what the variable can do with those objects. Recall that the **GradedActivity** class has three methods: **SetScore**, **GetScore**, and **GetGrade**. So, a **GradedActivity** variable can be used to call only those three methods, regardless of the type of object the variable references. For example, look at the following code.

```
GradedActivity exam = new PassFailExam(100, 10, 70);
Console.WriteLine(exam.GetScore());     // This works.
Console.WriteLine(exam.GetGrade());     // This works.
Console.WriteLine(exam.GetPointsEach()); // ERROR! Won't work.
```

10

In this code, exam is declared as a GradedActivity variable and is assigned the address of a PassFailExam object. The GradedActivity class has only the SetScore, GetScore, and GetGrade methods, so those are the only methods that the exam variable knows how to execute. The last statement in this code is a call to the GetPointsEach method, which is defined in the PassFailExam class. Because the exam variable only knows about methods in the GradedActivity class, it cannot execute this method.

Polymorphism and Dynamic Binding

When a base class variable references a derived class object, a potential problem exists. What if the derived class has overridden a method in the base class, and the variable makes a call to that method? Does the variable call the base class's version of the method, or the derived class's version? For example, look at the following code.

```
GradedActivity exam = new PassFailActivity(60);
exam.SetScore(70);
Console.WriteLine(exam.GetGrade());
```

Recall that the PassFailActivity class extends the GradedActivity class, and it overrides the GetGrade method. When the last statement calls the GetGrade method, does it call the GradedActivity class's version (which returns 'A', 'B', 'C', 'D', or 'F') or does it call the PassFailActivity class's version (which returns 'P' or 'F')?

Recall from Chapter 4 that the process of matching a method call with the correct method definition is known as binding. C# performs *dynamic binding* or *late binding* when a variable contains a polymorphic reference. This means that the C# CLR determines at runtime which method to call, depending on the type of object that the variable references. So, it is the object's type that determines which method is called, not the variable's type. In this case, the exam variable references a PassFailActivity object, so the PassFailActivity class's version of the GetGrade method is called. The last statement in this code will display a grade of P.

The program in Code Listing 10-25 demonstrates polymorphic behavior. It declares an array of GradedActivity variables, and then assigns the addresses of objects of various types to the elements of the array.

Code Listing 10-25   Polymorphic.cs

```
1 /*
2    This program demonstrates polymorphic behavior.
3 */
4
5 using System;
6
```

(code listing continues)

Code Listing 10-25 Polymorphic.cs *(continued)*

```
 7 public class Polymorphic
 8 {
 9    public static void Main()
10    {
11       // Create an array of GradedActivity references.
12       GradedActivity[] tests = new GradedActivity[3];
13
14       // The first test is a regular exam with a
15       // numeric score of 75.
16       tests[0] = new GradedActivity();
17       tests[0].SetScore(95);
18
19       // The second test is a pass/fail test. The
20       // student missed 5 out of 20 questions, and
21       // the minimum passing grade is 60.
22       tests[1] = new PassFailExam(20, 5, 60);
23
24       // The third test is the final exam. There were
25       // 50 questions and the student missed 7.
26       tests[2] = new FinalExam(50, 7);
27
28       // Display the grades.
29       for (int i = 0; i < tests.Length; i++)
30       {
31          Console.WriteLine("Test {0} : score {1}, grade {2} ",
                   (i + 1),
32                      tests[i].GetScore(),
33                      tests[i].GetGrade());
34       }
35    }
36 }
```

Program Output

```
Test 1 : score 95, grade A
Test 2 : score 75, grade P
Test 3 : score 86, grade B
```

You can also use parameters to polymorphically accept arguments to methods. For example, look at the following method.

```
public static void DisplayGrades(GradedActivity g)
{
    Console.WriteLine("Score {0}, grade {1}",g.GetScore(),
                      g.GetGrade());
}
```

This method's parameter, g, is a GradedActivity variable. But it can be used to accept arguments of any type that inherits from GradedActivity. For example, the following code passes objects of the FinalExam, PassFailActivity, and PassFailExam classes to the method.

```
GradedActivity exam1 = new FinalExam(50, 7);
GradedActivity exam2 = new PassFailActivity(70);
GradedActivity exam3 = new PassFailExam(100, 10, 70);
DisplayGrades(exam1);    // Pass a FinalExam object.
DisplayGrades(exam2);    // Pass a PassFailActivity object.
DisplayGrades(exam3);    // Pass a PassFailExam object.
```

The Is-a Relationship Does Not Work in Reverse

It is important to note that the is-a relationship does not work in reverse. Although the statement "a final exam is a graded activity" is true, the statement "a graded activity is a final exam" is not true. This is because not all graded activities are final exams. Likewise, not all GradedActivity objects are FinalExam objects. So, the following code will not work.

```
GradedActivity activity = new GradedActivity();
FinalExam exam = activity;    // ERROR!
```

You cannot assign the address of a GradedActivity object to a FinalExam variable. This makes sense because FinalExam objects have capabilities that go beyond those of a GradedActivity object. Interestingly, the C# compiler will let you make such an assignment if you use a type cast, as shown here:

```
GradedActivity activity = new GradedActivity();
FinalExam exam = (FinalExam) activity;    // Will compile but not run.
```

But the program will crash when the assignment statement executes.

 ## CHECKPOINT

10.16 Recall the Rectangle and Cube classes discussed earlier, as shown in Figure 10-18.

    a) Is the following statement legal or illegal? If it is illegal, why?

```
Rectangle r = new Cube(10, 12, 5);
```

    b) If you determined that the statement in Part a is legal, are the following statements legal or illegal? (Indicate legal or illegal for each statement.)

```
Console.WriteLine(r.GetLength());
Console.WriteLine(r.GetWidth());
Console.WriteLine(r.GetHeight());
Console.WriteLine(r.GetSurfaceArea());
```

    c) Is the following statement legal or illegal? If it is illegal, why?

```
Cube c = new Rectangle(10, 12);
```

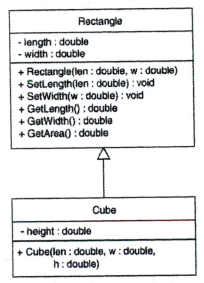

Figure 10-18 `Rectangle` **and** `Cube` **classes**

10.8 Abstract Classes and Abstract Methods

CONCEPT | An abstract class is not instantiated, but other classes extend it. An abstract method has no body and must be overridden in a derived class.

An *abstract method* is a method that appears in a base class but expects to be overridden in a derived class. An abstract method has a header and no body. Here is the general format of an abstract method header.

> *AccessSpecifier* abstract *ReturnType MethodName(ParameterList)*;

Notice that the key word `abstract` appears in the header, and that the header ends with a semi-colon. There is no body for the method. Here is an example of an abstract method header:

```
public abstract void SetValue(int value);
```

When an abstract method appears in a class, the method must be overridden in a derived class. If a derived class fails to override the method, an error will result. Abstract methods are used to ensure that a derived class implements the method.

When a class contains an abstract method, you cannot create an instance of the class. Abstract methods are commonly used in abstract classes. An *abstract class* is not instantiated itself, but serves as a base class for other classes. The abstract class represents the generic or abstract form of all the classes that inherit from it.

For example, consider a factory that manufactures airplanes. The factory does not make a generic airplane, but makes three specific types of airplanes: two models of prop-driven planes and one commuter jet model. The computer software that catalogs the planes might use an abstract class named `Airplane`. That class has members representing the common characteristics of all airplanes. In addition, the software has classes for each of the three specific airplane models the factory manufactures. These classes all extend the `Airplane` class, and they have members representing the unique characteristics of each type of plane. The `Airplane` class is never instantiated, but is used as a base class for the other classes.

A class becomes abstract when you place the `abstract` key word in the class definition. Here is the general format:

```
public abstract class ClassName
```

For example, look at the following abstract class `Student` shown in Code Listing 10-26. It holds data common to all students, but does not hold all the data needed for students of specific majors.

Code Listing 10-26   Student.cs

```
 1 /*
 2     The Student class is an abstract class that holds
 3     general data about a student. Classes representing
 4     specific types of students should inherit from
 5     this class.
 6 */
 7
 8 public abstract class Student
 9 {
10     private string name;        // Student name
11     private string idNumber;    // Student ID
12     private int yearAdmitted;   // Year admitted
13
14     /*
15         The Constructor sets the student's name,
16         ID number, and year admitted.
17         **parameter n The student's name.
18         **parameter id The student's ID number.
19         **parameter year The year the student was admitted.
20     */
21
22     public Student(string n, string id, int year)
23     {
24         name = n;
25         idNumber = id;
26         yearAdmitted = year;
27     }
28
29     /*
30         The ToString method returns a String containing
31         the student's data.
32         **return A reference to a string.
33     */
34
```

(code listing continues)

Code Listing 10-26 Student.cs *(continued)*

```
35    public override string ToString()
36    {
37       string str;
38
39       str = "Name: " + name
40          + "\nID Number: " + idNumber
41          + "\nYear Admitted: " + yearAdmitted;
42       return str;
43    }
44
45    /*
46       The GetRemainingHours method is abstract.
47       It must be overridden in a derived class.
48       **return The hours remaining for the student.
49    */
50
51    public abstract int GetRemainingHours();
52 }
```

The Student class contains fields for storing a student's name, ID number, and year admitted. It also has a constructor, a ToString method, and an abstract method named GetRemainingHours.

This abstract method must be overridden in classes that inherit from the Student class. The idea behind this method is for it to return the number of hours remaining for a student to take in his or her major. It was made abstract because this class is intended to be the base for other classes that represent students of specific majors. For example, a CompSciStudent class might hold the data for a computer science student, and a BiologyStudent class might hold the data for a biology student. Computer science students must take courses in different disciplines than those taken by biology students. It stands to reason that the CompSciStudent class will calculate the number of hours remaining to be taken in a different manner than the BiologyStudent class. Let's look at an example of the CompSciStudent class, which is shown in Code Listing 10-27.

Code Listing 10-27 CompSciStudent.cs

```
 1 /*
 2    This class holds data for a computer science student.
 3 */
 4
 5 public class CompSciStudent : Student
 6 {
 7    // Required hours
 8    private const int MATH_HOURS = 20,    // Math hours
 9                      CS_HOURS = 40,      // Comp sci hours
10                      GEN_ED_HOURS = 60;  // Gen ed hours
11
```

(code listing continues)

Code Listing 10-27 CompSciStudent.cs *(continued)*

```
12      // Hours taken
13      private int mathHours,  // Math hours taken
14                   csHours,   // Comp sci hours taken
15                   genEdHours; // General ed hours taken
16
17      /*
18          The Constructor sets the student's name,
19          ID number, and the year admitted.
20          **parameter n The student's name.
21          **parameter id The student's ID number.
22          **parameter year The year the student was admitted.
23      */
24
25      public CompSciStudent(string n, string id, int
                year):base(n, id, year)
26      {
27      }
28
29      public int MathHours
30      {
31        set
32        {
33          mathHours = value;
34        }
35      }
36
37      public int CsHours
38      {
39       set
40        {
41          csHours = value;
42        }
43      }
44
45      public int GenEdHours
46      {
47        set
48        {
49          genEdHours = value;
50        }
51       }
52
53      /*
54          The GetRemainingHours method returns the
55          the number of hours remaining to be taken.
56          **return The hours remaining for the student.
57      */
58
```

(code listing continues)

Code Listing 10-27 **CompSciStudent.cs** *(continued)*

```
59    public override int GetRemainingHours()
60    {
61        int reqHours,        // Total required hours
62            remainingHours;  // Remaining hours
63
64        // Calculate the required hours.
65        reqHours = MATH_HOURS + CS_HOURS + GEN_ED_HOURS;
66
67        // Calculate the remaining hours.
68        remainingHours = reqHours - (mathHours + csHours
69                            + genEdHours);
70
71        return remainingHours;
72    }
73
74    /*
75        The ToString method returns a string containing
76        the student's data.
77        **return A reference to a string.
78    */
79
80    public override string ToString()
81    {
82        string str;
83
84        str = base.ToString() +
85            "\nMajor: Computer Science" +
86            "\nMath Hours Taken: " + mathHours +
87            "\nComputer Science Hours Taken: " + csHours +
88            "\nGeneral Ed Hours Taken: " + genEdHours;
89
90        return str;
91    }
92 }
```

The CompSciStudent class, which extends the Student class, declares the following const integer fields in lines 8 through 10: MATH_HOURS, CS_HOURS, and GEN_ED_HOURS. These fields hold the required number of math, computer science, and general education hours for a computer science student. It also declares the following fields in lines 13 through 15: mathHours, csHours, and genEdHours. These fields hold the number of math, computer science, and general education hours taken by the student. Mutator methods are provided to store values in these fields. In addition, the class overrides the ToString method and the abstract GetRemainingHours method. The program in Code Listing 10-28 demonstrates the class.

Code Listing 10-28 CompSciStudentDemo.cs

```
 1 /*
 2     This program demonstrates the CompSciStudent class.
 3 */
 4
 5 using System;
 6
 7 public class CompSciStudentDemo
 8 {
 9     public static void Main()
10     {
11         // Create a CompSciStudent object.
12         CompSciStudent csStudent =
13                 new CompSciStudent("Jennifer Haynes",
14                                     "167W98337", 2004);
15
16         // Store values for math, CS, and gen ed hours.
17         csStudent.MathHours = 12;
18         csStudent.CsHours = 20;
19         csStudent.GenEdHours = 40;
20
21         // Display the student's data.
22         Console.WriteLine(csStudent);
23
24         // Display the number of remaining hours.
25         Console.WriteLine("Hours remaining: {0}",
26                 csStudent.GetRemainingHours());
27     }
28 }
```

Program Output
```
Name: Jennifer Haynes
ID Number: 167W98337
Year Admitted: 2004
Major: Computer Science
Math Hours: 12
Computer Science Hours Taken: 20
General Ed Hours Taken: 40
Hours remaining: 48
```

Remember the following points about abstract methods and classes:

- Abstract methods and abstract classes are defined with the abstract key word.
- Abstract methods have no body, and their header must end with a semicolon.
- An abstract method must be overridden in a derived class.
- When a class contains an abstract method, it cannot be instantiated. It must serve as a base class.
- An abstract class cannot be instantiated. It must serve as a base class.

CHECKPOINT

10.17 What is the purpose of an abstract method?

10.18 If a derived class extends a base class with an abstract method, what must you do in the derived class?

10.19 What is the purpose of an abstract class?

10.20 If a class is defined as abstract, what can you not do with the class?

10.9 Interfaces

CONCEPT An interface specifies behavior for a class.

In the previous section you learned that an abstract class cannot be instantiated, but is intended to serve as a base class. You also learned that an abstract method has no body and must be overridden in a derived class. An *interface* is similar to an abstract class that has all abstract methods. It cannot be instantiated, and all of the methods listed in an interface must be written elsewhere. The purpose of an interface is to specify behavior for other classes.

An interface looks similar to a class, except the key word `interface` is used instead of the key word `class`, and the methods that are specified in an interface have no bodies, only headers that are terminated by semicolons. Here is the general format of an interface definition:

```
public interface InterfaceName
{
     (Method headers...)
}
```

For example, Code Listing 10-29 shows an interface named `Relatable`, which is intended to be used with the `GradedActivity` class presented earlier. This interface has three method headers: `Equals`, `IsGreater`, and `IsLess`. Notice that each method accepts a `GradedActivity` object as its argument. Also notice that no access specifier is used with the method headers, because all methods specified by an interface are public.

Code Listing 10-29   Relatable.cs

```
 1 /*
 2    Relatable interface
 3 */
 4
 5 public interface Relatable
 6 {
 7     bool Equals(GradedActivity g);
 8     bool IsGreater(GradedActivity g);
 9     bool IsLess(GradedActivity g);
10 }
```

10

In order for a class to use an interface, it must call the interface. This is accomplished by using the same notation we use for representing inheritance. For example, suppose we have a class named FinalExam3 that inherits from the GradedActivity class and uses the Relatable interface. The first line of its definition would look like this:

```
public class FinalExam3 : GradedActivity, Relatable
```

When a class implements an interface, it is agreeing to provide all of the methods that are specified by the interface. It is often said that an interface is like a contract, and when a class uses an interface it must adhere to the contract.

A class that implements an interface must provide all of the methods that are listed in the interface, with the exact signatures specified and with the same return type. So, in the previous example, the FinalExam3 class must provide an equals method, an IsGreater method, and an IsLess method, each of which accept a GradedActivity object as an argument and returns a boolean value.

You might have guessed that the Relatable interface is named "relatable" because it specifies methods that, presumably, make relational comparisons with GradedActivity objects. The intent is to make any class that implements this interface "relatable" with GradedActivity objects by ensuring that it has an Equals, an IsGreater, and an IsLess method that perform relational comparisons. But the interface only specifies the signatures for these methods, not what the methods should do. Although the programmer of a class that implements the Relatable interface can choose what those methods do, he or she should provide methods that comply with this intent.

Code Listing 10-30 shows the complete code for the FinalExam3 class, which implements the Relatable interface. The Equals, IsGreater, and IsLess methods compare the calling object with the object passed as an argument. The program in Code Listing 10-31 demonstrates the class.

Code Listing 10-30   FinalExam3.cs

```
1 /*
2   This class determines the grade for a final exam.
3 */
4
5 public class FinalExam3 : GradedActivity , Relatable
6 {
7     private int numQuestions;  // Number of questions
8     private double pointsEach; // Points for each question
9     private int numMissed;     // Questions missed
10
11    /*
12       The constructor sets the number of questions on the
13       exam and the number of questions missed.
14       **parameter questions The number of questions.
15       **parameter missed The number of questions missed.
16    */
17
```

(code listing continues)

Code Listing 10-30 FinalExam3.cs *(continued)*

```
18      public FinalExam3(int questions, int missed)
19      {
20          double numericScore;  // To hold a numeric score
21
22          // Set the numQuestions and numMissed fields.
23          numQuestions = questions;
24          numMissed = missed;
25
26          // Calculate the points for each question and
27          // the numeric score for this exam.
28          pointsEach = 100.0 / questions;
29          numericScore = 100.0 - (missed * pointsEach);
30
31          // Call the inherited SetScore method to
32          // set the numeric score.
33          SetScore(numericScore);
34      }
35
36      public double PointsEach
37      {
38        get
39        {
40          return pointsEach;
41        }
42      }
43
44      public int GetNumMissed
45      {
46        get
47        {
48          return numMissed;
49        }
50      }
51
52      /*
53          The Equals method compares the calling object
54          to the argument object for equality.
55          **return true if the calling
56          object's score is equal to the argument's
57          score.
58      */
59
```

(code listing continues)

10

Code Listing 10-30   FinalExam3.cs *(continued)*

```
60     public bool Equals(GradedActivity g)
61     {
62        bool status;
63
64        if (this.GetScore() == g.GetScore())
65           status = true;
66        else
67           status = false;
68
69        return status;
70     }
71
72     /*
73        The IsGreater method determines whether the calling
74        object is greater than the argument object.
75        **return true if the calling object's score is
76        greater than the argument object's score.
77     */
78
79     public bool IsGreater(GradedActivity g)
80     {
81        bool status;
82
83        if (this.GetScore() > g.GetScore())
84           status = true;
85        else
86           status = false;
87
88        return status;
89     }
90
91     /*
92        The IsLess method determines whether the calling
93        object is less than the argument object.
94        **return true if the calling object's score is
95        less than the argument object's score.
96     */
97
98     public bool IsLess(GradedActivity g)
99     {
100       bool status;
101
102       if (this.GetScore() < g.GetScore())
103          status = true;
104       else
105          status = false;
106
107       return status;
108    }
109 }
```

Code Listing 10-31   InterfaceDemo.cs

```
1  /*
2      This program demonstrates the FinalExam3 class which
3      implements the Relatable interface.
4  */
5
6  using System;
7
8  public class InterfaceDemo
9  {
10     public static void Main()
11     {
12        // Exam #1 had 100 questions and the student
13        // missed 20 questions.
14        FinalExam3 exam1 = new FinalExam3(100, 20);
15
16        // Exam #2 had 100 questions and the student
17        // missed 30 questions.
18        FinalExam3 exam2 = new FinalExam3(100, 30);
19
20        // Display the exam scores.
21        Console.WriteLine("Exam 1: {0}",
22                            exam1.GetScore());
23        Console.WriteLine("Exam 2: {0}",
24                            exam2.GetScore());
25
26        // Compare the exam scores.
27        if (exam1.Equals(exam2))
28           Console.WriteLine("The exam scores " +
29                              "are equal.");
30
31        if (exam1.IsGreater(exam2))
32           Console.WriteLine("The Exam 1 score " +
33                              "is the highest.");
34
35        if (exam1.IsLess(exam2))
36           Console.WriteLine("The Exam 1 score " +
37                              "is the lowest.");
38     }
39  }
```

Program Output
```
Exam 1: 80
Exam 2: 70
The Exam 1 score is the highest.
```

Interfaces can contain methods or properties though they are abstract.

Implementing Multiple Interfaces

You might be wondering why we need both abstract classes and interfaces, since they are so similar to each other. The reason is that a class can extend only one base class, but C# allows a class to implement multiple interfaces. When a class implements multiple interfaces, it must provide the methods specified by all of them.

To specify multiple interfaces in a class definition, simply list the names of the interfaces, separated by commas, after the colon in the class header. Here is the first line of an example of a class that implements multiple interfaces:

```
public class MyClass : Interface1, Interface2, Interface3
```

This class implements three interfaces: Interface1, Interface2, and Interface3.

Interfaces in UML

In a UML diagram, an interface is drawn like a class, except the <<interface>> tag is shown above the interface name. The relationship between a class and an interface is known as a *realization relationship* (the class realizes the interfaces). You show a realization relationship in a UML diagram by connecting a class and an interface with a dashed line that has an open arrowhead at one end. The arrowhead points to the interface. This depicts the realization relationship. Figure 10-19 shows a UML diagram depicting the relationships among the GradedActivity class, the FinalExam3 class, and the Relatable interface.

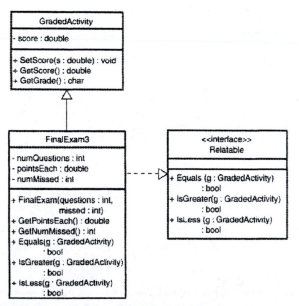

Figure 10-19   Realization relationship in a UML diagram

Polymorphism and Interfaces

Just as you can create reference variables of a class type, C# allows you to create reference variables of an interface type. An interface reference variable can reference any object that implements that interface, regardless of its class type. This is another example of polymorphism. For example, look at the RetailItem interface in Code Listing 10-32.

Code Listing 10-32 RetailItem.cs

```
1 /*
2     RetailItem interface
3 */
4
5 public interface RetailItem
6 {
7     double GetRetailPrice();
8 }
```

This interface specifies only one method: GetRetailPrice. Both the CompactDisc and DvdMovie classes, shown in Code Listings 10-33 and 10-34, implement this interface.

Code Listing 10-33 CompactDisc.cs

```
1 /*
2     Compact Disc class
3 */
4
5 public class CompactDisc : RetailItem
6 {
7     private string title;      // The CD's title
8     private string artist;     // The CD's artist
9     private double retailPrice; // The CD's retail price
10
11    /*
12        Constructor
13        **parameter cdTitle The CD title.
14        **parameter cdArtist The name of the artist.
15        **parameter cdPrice The CD's price.
16    */
17
18    public CompactDisc(string cdTitle, string cdArtist,
19                double cdPrice)
20    {
21        title = cdTitle;
22        artist = cdArtist;
23        retailPrice = cdPrice;
24    }
25
```

(code listing continues)

Code Listing 10-33   CompactDisc.cs *(continued)*

```
26     public string Title
27     {
28        get
29        {
30        return title;
31        }
32     }
33
34     public string Artist
35     {
36        get
37        {
38        return artist;
39        }
40     }
41
42     /*
43        GetRetailPrice method (Required by the RetailItem
44        interface)
45        **return The retail price of the CD.
46     */
47
48     public double GetRetailPrice()
49     {
50        return retailPrice;
51     }
52 }
```

Code Listing 10-34   DvdMovie.cs

```
 1 /*
 2     DvdMovie class
 3 */
 4
 5 public class DvdMovie : RetailItem
 6 {
 7     private string title;      // The DVD's title
 8     private int runningTime;   // Running time in minutes
 9     private double retailPrice; // The DVD's retail price
10
```

(code listing continues)

Code Listing 10-34 DvdMovie.cs *(continued)*

```
11      /*
12         Constructor
13         **parameter dvdTitle The DVD title.
14         **parameter runTime The running time in minutes.
15         **parameter dvdPrice The DVD's price.
16      */
17
18      public DvdMovie(string dvdTitle, int runTime,
19                                    double dvdPrice)
20      {
21         title = dvdTitle;
22         runningTime = runTime;
23         retailPrice = dvdPrice;
24      }
25
26      public string Title
27      {
28         get
29         {
30            return title;
31         }
32      }
33
34      public int RunningTime
35      {
36         get
37         {
38            return runningTime;
39         }
40      }
41
42      /*
43         GetRetailPrice method (Required by the RetailItem
44         interface)
45         **return The retail price of the DVD.
46      */
47
48      public double GetRetailPrice()
49      {
50         return retailPrice;
51      }
52   }
```

Because they implement the RetailItem interface, objects of these classes may be referenced by a RetailItem reference variable. The following code demonstrates.

```
RetailItem item1 = new CompactDisc("Songs From the Heart",
                                   "Billy Nelson",
                                   18.95);

RetailItem item2 = new DvdMovie("Planet X",
                                102,
                                22.95);
```

In this code, two RetailItem reference variables, item1 and item2, are declared. The item1 variable references a CompactDisc object and the item2 variable references a DvdMovie object. This is possible because both the CompactDisc and DvdMovie classes implement the RetailItem interface. When a class implements an interface, an inheritance relationship known as *interface inheritance* is established. Because of this inheritance relationship, a CompactDisc object *is a* RetailItem, and likewise, a DvdMovie object *is a* RetailItem. Therefore, we can create RetailItem reference variables and have them reference CompactDisc and DvdMovie objects.

The program in Code Listing 10-35 demonstrates how an interface reference variable can be used as a method parameter.

Code Listing 10-35   PolymorphicInterfaceDemo.cs

```
 1 /*
 2    This program demonstrates that an interface type may
 3    be used to create a polymorphic reference.
 4 */
 5
 6 using System;
 7
 8 public class PolymorphicInterfaceDemo
 9 {
10    public static void Main()
11    {
12       // Create a CompactDisc object.
13       CompactDisc cd =
14             new CompactDisc("Greatest Hits",
15                             "Joe Looney Band",
16                             18.95);
17       // Create a DvdMovie object.
18       DvdMovie movie =
19             new DvdMovie("Wheels of Fury",
20                          137, 12.95);
21
```

(code listing continues)

Code Listing 10-35 PolymorphicInterfaceDemo.cs *(continued)*

```
22          // Display the CD's title.
23          Console.WriteLine("Item #1: {0}",
24                              cd.Title);
25
26          // Display the CD's price.
27          ShowPrice(cd);
28
29          // Display the DVD's title.
30          Console.WriteLine("Item #2: {0}",
31                              movie.Title);
32
33          // Display the DVD's price.
34          ShowPrice(movie);
35      }
36
37      /*
38          The ShowPrice method displays the price
39          of a RetailItem object.
40          **parameter item A reference to a RetailItem object.
41      */
42
43      private static void ShowPrice(RetailItem item)
44      {
45
46
47          Console.WriteLine("Price: {0:C2}",
48                  item.GetRetailPrice());
49      }
50 }
```

Program Output
```
Item #1: Greatest Hits
Price: $18.95
Item #2: Wheels of Fury
Price: $12.95
```

There are some limitations to using interface reference variables. As previously mentioned, you cannot create an instance of an interface. In addition, when an interface variable references an object, you can use the interface variable to call only the methods that are specified in the interface. For example, look at the following code:

```
// Reference a CompactDisc object with a RetailItem variable.
RetailItem item = new CompactDisc("Greatest Hits",
                                  "Joe Looney Band",
                                  18.95);
```

```
// Call the GetRetailPrice method...
Console.WriteLine(GetRetailPrice());  // OK, this works.
// Attempt to call the Title property...
Console.WriteLine(item.Title);  // ERROR! Will not compile!
```

The last line of code will not compile because the RetailItem interface specifies only one method: GetRetailPrice. So, we cannot use a RetailItem reference variable to call any other method.

 ## CHECKPOINT

10.21 What is the purpose of an interface?

10.22 How is an interface similar to an abstract class?

10.23 How is an interface different from an abstract class? From any class?

10.24 Write the first line of a class named Customer, which uses an interface named Relatable.

10.25 Write the first line of a class named Employee, which uses interfaces named Payable and Listable.

10.10 Common Errors

- **Attempting to directly access a private base class member from a derived class.** Private base class members cannot be directly accessed by a method in a derived class. The derived class must call a public or protected base class method in order to access the base class's private members.

- **Allowing the base class's no-arg constructor to be implicitly called when you intend to call another base class constructor.** If a derived class's constructor does not explicitly call a base class constructor, C# automatically calls the base class's no-arg constructor.

- **Forgetting to precede a call to an overridden base class method with base.** When a derived class method calls an overridden base class method, it must precede the method call with the key word base and a dot (.). Failing to do so results in the derived class's version of the method being called.

- **Writing a body for an abstract method.** An abstract method cannot have a body. It must be overridden in a derived class.

- **Forgetting to terminate an abstract method's header with a semicolon.** An abstract method header does not have a body, and it must be terminated with a semicolon.

- **Failing to override an abstract method.** An abstract method must be overridden in a derived class.

- **Overloading an abstract method instead of overriding it.** Overloading is not the same as overriding. When a base class has an abstract method, the derived class must have a method with the same signature as the abstract method.

- **Trying to instantiate an abstract class.** You cannot create an instance of an abstract class.

- **Implementing an interface but forgetting to provide all of the methods specified by the interface.** When a class implements an interface, all of the methods specified by the interface must be provided in the class.

- **Writing a method specified by an interface but failing to use the exact signature and return type.** When a class implements an interface, the class must have methods with the same signature and return type as the methods specified in the interface.

Review Questions and Exercises

Multiple Choice and True/False

1. In an inheritance relationship, this is the general class.
   a) derived class
   b) base class
   c) child class
   d) subclass

2. In an inheritance relationship, this is the specialized class.
   a) base class
   b) superclass
   c) derived class
   d) parent class

3. A derived class does not have access to these base class members.
   a) public
   b) private
   c) protected
   d) all of these

4. This key word refers to an object's base class.
   a) `super`
   b) `base`
   c) `baseclass`
   d) `this`

5. In a derived class constructor, a call to the base class constructor must
   a) appear in the method header.
   b) appear as the very last statement.
   c) appear between the constructor's header and the opening brace.
   d) not appear.

6. The following is an explicit call to the base class's default constructor.
   a) `default();`
   b) `class();`
   c) `super();`
   d) `base();`

7. A method in a derived class having the same signature as a method in the base class is an example of

   a) overloading. b) overriding.

   c) composition. d) an error.

8. A method in a derived class having the same name as a method in the base class but a different signature, is an example of

   a) overloading. b) overriding.

   c) composition. d) an error.

9. All classes directly or indirectly inherit from this class.

   a) Object b) Super

   c) Root d) C#

10. When a class implements an interface, it must

    a) overload all of the methods listed in the interface.

    b) provide all of the methods that are listed in the interface, with the exact signatures and return types specified.

    c) not have a constructor.

    d) be an abstract class.

11. Abstract methods must be

    a) overridden. b) overloaded.

    c) deleted and replaced with real methods.d) declared as private.

12. Abstract classes cannot

    a) be used as base classes. b) have abstract methods.

    c) be instantiated. d) have fields.

13. True or False: Constructors are not inherited.

14. True or False: In a derived class, a call to the base class constructor can only be written in the derived class constructor.

15. True or False: If a derived class constructor does not explicitly call a base class constructor, C# will not call any of the base class's constructors.

16. True or False: An object of a base class can access members declared in a derived class.

17. True or False: The base class constructor always executes before the derived class constructor.

18. True or False: A base class reference variable can reference an object of a derived class that extends the base class.

19. True or False: A derived class reference variable can reference an object of the base class.

20. True or False: When a class contains an abstract method, the class cannot be instantiated.

21. True or False: A class may only implement one interface.

22. True or False: By default all members of an interface are public.

Find the Error

Find the error in each of the following code segments.

1.
```
// Base Class
public class Vehicle
{
    (Member declarations...)
}

// Derived Class
public class Car extends Vehicle
{
    (Member declarations...)
}
```

2.
```
// Base Class
public class Vehicle
{
    private double cost;

   (Other methods...)
}

// Subclass
public class Car extends Vehicle
{
    public Car(double c)
    {
        cost = c;
    }
```

3.
```
// Base Class
public class Vehicle
{
    private double cost;

    public Vehicle(double c)
    {
        cost = c;
    }

        (Other methods...)
}
```

```
                   // Subclass
                   public class Car : Vehicle
                   {
                       private int passengers;

                       public Car(int p)
                       {
                           passengers = c;
                       }

                           (Other methods...)
                   }
4.                 // Base Class
                   public class Vehicle
                   {
                       public abstract double GetMilesPerGallon();

                           (Other methods...)
                   }

                   // Subclass
                   public class Car : Vehicle
                   {
                       private int mpg;

                       public int GetMilesPerGallon();
                       {
                           return mpg;
                       }
                           (Other methods...)
                   }
```

Algorithm Workbench

1. Write the first line of the definition for a `Poodle` class. The class should extend the `Dog` class.

2. Look at the following code which is the first line of a class definition:

    ```
    public class Tiger : Felis
    ```

    In what order will the class constructors execute?

3. Write the declaration for class B. The class's members should be

    ▪ `m`, an integer. This variable should not be accessible to code outside the class or to any class that extends class B.

    ▪ `n`, an integer. This variable should be accessible only to classes that extend class B

    ▪ `SetM`, `GetM`, `SetN`, and `GetN`. These are the mutator and accessor methods for the member variables `m` and `n`. These methods should be accessible to code outside the class.

    ▪ `Calc`. This is a public abstract method.

Next write the declaration for class D, which extends class B. The class's members should be

- q, a `double`. This variable should not be accessible to code outside the class.

- r, a `double`. This variable should be accessible to any class that extends class D or in the same package.

- SetQ, GetQ, SetR, and GetR. These are the mutator and accessor methods for the member variables q and r. These methods should be accessible to code outside the class.

- Calc, a public method that overrides the base class's abstract `calc` method. This method should return the value of q times r.

4. Write the statement that calls a base class constructor and passes the arguments x, y, and z.

5. A base class has the following method:

```
public void SetValue(int v)
{
    value = v;
}
```

Write a statement that may appear in a derived class that calls this method, passing 10 as an argument.

6. A base class has the following abstract method:

```
public abstract int GetValue();
```

Write an example of a GetValue method that can appear in a derived class.

7. Write the first line of the definition for a Stereo class. The class should extend the SoundSystem class, and it should implement the CDplayable, TunerPlayable, and CassettePlayable interfaces.

8. Write an interface named Nameable that specifies the following methods:

```
public void SetName(string n)
public string GetName()
```

Short Answer

1. What is an is-a relationship?

2. A program uses two classes: Animal and Dog. Which class would be the base class and which would be the derived class?

3. What is the base class and what is the derived class in the following line?

```
public class Pet : Dog
```

4. What is the difference between a protected class member and a private class member?

5. Can a derived class ever directly access the private members of its base class?

6. Which constructor is called first, that of the derived class or the base class?

7. What is the difference between overriding a base class method and overloading a base class method?

8. Reference variables can be polymorphic. What does this mean?

9. When does dynamic binding take place?

10. What is an abstract method?

11. What is an abstract class?

12. What are the differences between an abstract class and an interface?

Programming Challenges

1. Employee and ProductionWorker Classes

Design a class named Employee. The class should keep the following information in fields:

- Employee name
- Employee number in the format XXX–L, where each X is a digit within the range 0–9 and the L is a letter within the range A–M
- Hire date

Write one or more constructors and the appropriate accessor and mutator methods for the class.

Next, write a class named ProductionWorker that extends the Employee class. The ProductionWorker class should have fields to hold the following information:

- Shift (an integer)
- Hourly pay rate (a double)

The workday is divided into day and night shifts. The shift field will be an integer value representing the shift that the employee works. The day shift is shift 1 and the night shift is shift 2. Write one or more constructors and the appropriate accessor and mutator methods for the class. Demonstrate the classes by writing a program that uses a ProductionWorker object.

2. ShiftSupervisor Class

In a particular factory a shift supervisor is a salaried employee who supervises a shift. In addition to a salary, the shift supervisor earns a yearly bonus when his or her shift meets production goals. Design a ShiftSupervisor class that extends the Employee class you created in Programming Challenge 1. The ShiftSupervisor class should have a field that holds the annual salary and a field that holds the annual production bonus that a shift supervisor has earned. Write one or more constructors and the appropriate accessor and mutator methods for the class. Demonstrate the class by writing a program that uses a ShiftSupervisor object.

3. TeamLeader Class

In a particular factory, a team leader is an hourly production worker who leads a small team. In addition to hourly pay, team leaders earn a fixed monthly bonus. Team leaders are required to attend a minimum number of hours of training per year. Design a `TeamLeader` class that extends the `ProductionWorker` class you designed in Programming Challenge 1. The `TeamLeader` class should have fields for the monthly bonus amount, the required number of training hours, and the number of training hours that the team leader has attended. Write one or more constructors and the appropriate accessor and mutator methods for the class. Demonstrate the class by writing a program that uses a `TeamLeader` object.

4. Essay Class

Design an `Essay` class that extends the `GradedActivity` class presented in this chapter. The `Essay` class should determine the grade a student receives on an essay. The student's essay score can be up to 100 and is determined in the following manner:

- Grammar: 30 points
- Spelling: 20 points
- Correct length: 20 points
- Content: 30 points

Demonstrate the class in a simple program.

5. Course Grades

In a course, a teacher gives the following tests and assignments:

- A **lab activity** that is observed by the teacher and assigned a numeric score.
- A **pass/fail exam** that has 10 questions. The minimum passing score is 70.
- An **essay** that is assigned a numeric score.
- A **final exam** that has 50 questions.

Write a class named `CourseGrades`. The class should have a `GradedActivity` array named `grades` as a field. The array should have four elements, one for each of the assignments previously described. The class should have the following methods:

`SetLab:`	This method should accept a `GradedActivity` object as its argument. This object should already hold the student's score for the lab activity. Element 0 of the `grades` field should reference this object.
`SetPassFailExam:`	This method should accept a `PassFailExam` object as its argument. This object should already hold the student's score for the pass/fail exam. Element 1 of the `grades` field should reference this object.
`SetEssay:`	This method should accept an `Essay` object as its argument. (See Programming Challenge 4 for the `Essay` class. If you have not completed Programming Challenge 4, use a `GradedActivity` object instead.) This object should already hold the student's score for the essay. Element 2 of the `grades` field should reference this object.

SetPassFailExam: This method should accept a **FinalExam** object as its argument. This object should already hold the student's score for the final exam. Element 3 of the **grades** field should reference this object.

ToString: This method should return a string that contains the numeric scores and grades for each element in the **grades** array.

Demonstrate the class in a program.

6. Analyzable **Interface**

Modify the **CourseGrades** class you created in Programming Challenge 5 so it implements the following interface:

```
public interface Analyzable
{
    double GetAverage();
    GradedActivity GetHighest();
    GradedActivity GetLowest();
}
```

The **GetAverage** method should return the average of the numeric scores stored in the **grades** array. The **GetHighest** method should return a reference to the element of the grades array that has the highest numeric score. The **GetLowest** method should return a reference to the element of the grades array that has the lowest numeric score. Demonstrate the new methods in a complete program.

7. Person **and** Customer **Classes**

Design a class named **Person** with fields for holding a person's name, address, and telephone number. Write one or more constructors and the appropriate **get** and **set** properties for the class's fields.

Next, design a class named **Customer** that extends the **boolean** field indicating whether the customer wishes to be on a mailing list. Write one or more constructors and the appropriate **get** and **set** properties for the class's fields. Demonstrate an object of the **Customer** class in a simple program.

8. BankAccount **and** SavingsAccount **Classes**

Design an abstract class named **BankAccount** to hold the following data for a bank account:

- Balance
- Number of deposits this month
- Number of withdrawals
- Annual interest rate
- Monthly service charges

The class should have the following methods:

Constructor: The constructor should accept arguments for the balance and annual interest rate.

Deposit: A method that accepts an argument for the amount of the deposit. The method should add the argument to the account balance. It should also increment the variable holding the number of deposits.

Withdraw: A method that accepts an argument for the amount of the withdrawal. The method should subtract the argument from the balance. It should also increment the variable holding the number of withdrawals.

CalcInterest: A method that updates the balance by calculating the monthly interest earned by the account, and adding this interest to the balance. This is performed by the following formulas:

Monthly Interest Rate = (Annual Interest Rate ÷ 12)
Monthly Interest = Balance Monthly Interest Rate
Balance = Balance + Monthly Interest

MonthlyProcess: A method that subtracts the monthly service charges from the balance, calls the CalcInterest method, and sets the variables that hold the number of withdrawals, number of deposits, and monthly service charges to zero.

Next, design a SavingsAccount class that extends the BankAccount class. The SavingsAccount class should have a status field to represent an active or inactive account. If the balance of a savings account falls below $25, it becomes inactive. (The status field could be a Boolean variable.) No more withdrawals may be made until the balance is raised above $25, at which time the account becomes active again. The savings account class should have the following methods:

Withdraw: A method that determines whether the account is inactive before a withdrawal is made. (No withdrawal will be allowed if the account is not active.) A withdrawal is then made by calling the base class version of the method.

Deposit: A method that determines whether the account is inactive before a deposit is made. If the account is inactive and the deposit brings the balance above $25, the account becomes active again. The deposit is then made by calling the base class version of the method.

MonthlyProcess: Before the base class method is called, this method checks the number of withdrawals. If the number of withdrawals for the month is more than four, a service charge of $1 for each withdrawal over four is added to the base class field that holds the monthly service charges. (Don't forget to check the account balance after the service charge is taken. If the balance falls below $25, the account becomes inactive.)

11

A First Look at
Windows Applications

Topics in this Chapter

11.1 Introduction

11.2 Event-Driven Programming

11.3 Visual Studio and the Visual C# .NET Environment

11.4 More About Controls and Programming

11.5 Focus on Problem Solving: Building the Hotel Directions Application

11.6 Focus on Problem Solving: Responding to Events

11.7 Modifying the Text Property with Code

11.8 Using Visual C# .NET Help

Review Questions and Exercises

11.1 Introduction

In the previous chapters, we learned about creating console applications in C#. These are primarily text-based environments in which the user responds to the program. C# also allows us to create Windows-based applications. Modern operating systems, such as the Windows family, use a graphical user interface, or GUI. GUIs have made programs friendlier and easier to interact with—they have not simplified the task of programming. GUIs make it necessary for the programmer to create a variety of on-screen elements such as windows, dialog boxes, buttons, and menus. The programmer must write statements that handle the user's interactions with these on-screen elements, in any order the user might choose to select them. No longer does the user respond to the program—now the program responds to the user.

In this chapter you will learn about the Visual C# development environment to create GUI applications, and to develop your first windows application, which displays a map and written directions to the Highlander Hotel. This application uses a form with labels, a `PictureBox` control, and buttons. You also write your first event procedures in Visual C# .NET code. Using Visual C# help is also demonstrated.

11.2 Event-Driven Programming

> **CONCEPT** GUI programs respond to events that occur, or actions that take place. This concept is
> known as event-handling.

Programs that operate in a GUI environment must be *event-driven*. An *event* is an action that
takes place within a program, such as a button click or the selection of an item in a list box. All
Visual C# .NET controls are capable of detecting various events. For example, a Button control
can detect when it has been clicked.

Names are assigned to all of the events that can be detected. For instance, when the user clicks
a Button control, a Click event occurs. When the user clicks a CheckBox control, a
CheckChanged event occurs. If you want a control that will respond to a specific event, you must
write a special type of method, known as an *event method*. An event method is a method that is
executed when a specific event occurs.

Part of the Visual C# .NET windows programming process is designing and writing event
procedures. The following steps demonstrate an event method using the wage calculator program
you have on your Student CD.

Tutorial 11-1: Running an application that demonstrates event procedures

Step 1:   With the wage calculator program (Chapter 11\WageCalculator on the Student
CD) running, enter the value **10** in the first TextBox control. This is the number
of hours worked.

Step 2:   Press the tab key. Notice that the cursor moves to the next TextBox control. Enter
the value **15**. This is the hourly pay rate. The window should look like that shown
in Figure 11-1.

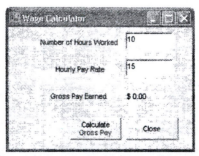

Figure 11-1   Text boxes filled in on Wage Calculator form

Step 3: Click the Calculate Gross Pay button. Notice that in response to the mouse click, the application multiplies the values you entered in the TextBox controls and displays the result in a Label control. This action is performed by an event method that responds to the button being clicked. The window should look like that shown in Figure 11-2.

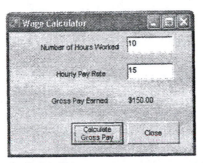

Figure 11-2 Gross pay calculated

Step 4: Next, click the Close button. The application responds to this event by terminating. This is because an event method closes the application when the button is clicked.

This simple application demonstrates the essence of object-oriented, event-driven programming. In Section 11.3, we examine the controls and event procedures more closely.

Designing and Creating a Windows Application

Now that you have been introduced to what a Visual C# .NET windows application is, it's time to consider the process of creating one. Quite often, when inexperienced students are given programming assignments, they have trouble getting started because they don't know what to do first. If you find yourself facing this dilemma, the steps listed below may help. These are the steps recommended for developing a Visual C# .NET windows application.

Steps for Developing a Visual C# .NET Windows Application

1. Clearly define what the application is to do.
2. Visualize the windows application running on the computer and design its user interface.
3. Make a list of the controls needed.
4. Define the values of each control's relevant properties.
5. Make a list of methods needed for each control.
6. Create a flowchart or pseudocode version of each method.
7. Check the flowchart or pseudocode for errors.
8. Start Visual C# .NET and create the forms and other controls identified in Step 3.
9. Write the code for the event procedures and other methods created in Step 6.

10. Attempt to run the application. Correct any syntax errors found and repeat this step as many times as necessary.

11. Once all syntax errors are corrected, run the program with test data for input. Correct any runtime errors. Repeat this step as many times as necessary.

These steps emphasize the importance of planning. Just as there are good ways and bad ways to paint a house, there are good ways and bad ways to write a program. A good program always begins with planning.

With the Wage Calculating program as our example, let's look at each of these steps in greater detail.

1. Clearly define what the program is to do.

This step requires that you identify the purpose of the program, the information that is to be input, the processing that is to take place, and the desired output. For example, these requirements for the Wage Calculator program are as follows:

Purpose: To calculate the user's gross pay

Input: Number of hours worked, hourly pay rate

Process: Multiply number of hours worked by hourly pay rate. The result is the user's gross pay.

Output: A display indicating the user's gross pay

2. Visualize the windows application running on the computer and design its user interface.

Before you create an application on the computer, you should first create it in your mind. Step 2 is the visualization of the program. Try to imagine what the computer screen will look like while the application is running. Then, sketch the form or forms in the application. For instance, Figure 11-3 shows a sketch of the form presented by the wage calculator program.

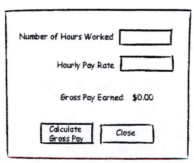

Figure 11-3   Sketch of the Wage Calculator form

3. Make a list of the controls needed.

The next step is to list all the controls needed. You should assign names to all the controls that will be accessed or manipulated in the application code and provide a brief description of each control. Table 11-1 lists the controls in the wage calculator application.

Table 11-1   Wage Calculator controls

Control Type	Control Name	Description
Form	(Default)	A small form that will serve as the window onto which the other controls will be placed.
Label	(Default)	Displays the message "Number of Hours Worked."
Label	(Default)	Displays the message "Hourly Pay Rate."
Label	(Default)	Displays the message "Gross Pay Earned."
Textbox	hoursTextBox	Allows the user to enter the number of hours worked.
Textbox	payTextBox	Allows the user to enter the hourly pay rate.
Label	payLabel	Displays the gross pay, after the calculateButton button has been clicked.
Button	calculateButton	When clicked, multiplies the number of hours worked by the hourly pay rate.
Button	closeButton	When clicked, terminates the application.

4. Define the values of each control's relevant properties.

Name and Text are the only control properties modified in the wage calculator application. Table 11-2 lists the value of each control's Text property.

Table 11-2   Wage Calculator control values

Control Type	Control Name	Text
Form	(Default)	"Wage Calculator"
Label	(Default)	"Number of Hours Worked"
Label	(Default)	"Hourly Pay Rate"
Label	(Default)	"Gross Pay Earned"
Label	payLabel	"$0.00"
TextBox	hoursTextBox	" "
TextBox	payTextBox	" "
Button	calculateButton	"Calculate Gross Pay"
Button	closeButton	"Close"

5. Make a list of methods needed for each control.

Next you should list the event procedures and other methods you will write. There are only two event procedures in the Wage Calculator application. Table 11-3 lists and describes them. Notice the Visual C# .NET names for the event procedures. `calculateButton_Click` is the name of the method invoked when the `calculateButton` button is clicked, and `closeButton_Click` is the event method that executes when the `closeButton` button is clicked.

Table 11-3 Wage Calculator event procedures

Method	Description
`calculateButton_Click`	Multiplies the number of hours worked by the hourly pay rate. These values are entered into the `hoursTextBox` and `payTextBox` TextBoxes. The result is stored in the `payLabel` Text property.
`closeButton_Click`	Terminates the application.

6. Create a flowchart or pseudocode version of each method.

A flowchart is a diagram that graphically depicts the flow of a method. It uses boxes and other symbols to represent each step. Figure 11-4 shows a flowchart for the `calculateButton_Click` event method.

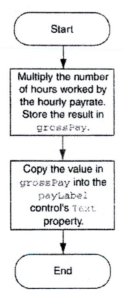

Figure 11-4 Flowchart for `calculateButton_Click` event method

Notice there are two types of boxes in the flowchart in Figure 11-4: ovals and rectangles. The flowchart begins with an oval labeled Start, and ends with an oval labeled End. The rectangles represent a computational process or other operation. Notice that the symbols are connected with arrows that indicate the direction of program flow.

Many programmers prefer to use pseudocode instead of flowcharts. *Pseudocode* is a cross between human language and a programming language. Although the computer can't understand pseudocode, programmers often find it helpful to plan an algorithm in a language that's almost a programming language but still very human-readable. Here is a pseudocode version of the `calculateButton_Click` event method:

> *Store Number of Hours Worked times Hourly Pay Rate in payLabel.*
> *Store the value in grossPay in payLabel.Caption.*

7. Check the code for errors.

In this phase the programmer starts reading the flowcharts and/or pseudocode at the beginning and steps through each operation, pretending that he or she is the computer. The programmer often uses a sheet of paper to jot down the current contents of variables and properties that change and to sketch what the screen looks like after each output operation. By stepping through the flowchart or pseudocode, a programmer can locate and correct many errors.

8. Start Visual C# .NET and create the forms and other controls identified in Step 3.

This step is the first actual work done on the computer. Here, the programmer uses Visual C# .NET to create the application's user interface and to arrange the controls on each form.

9. Write code for the event procedures and other methods created in Step 6.

This is the second step performed on the computer. The event procedures and other methods may be converted into code and entered into the computer using the Visual C# .NET environment.

10. Attempt to run the application. Correct any syntax errors found and repeat this step as many times as necessary.

If you have entered code with syntax errors or typing mistakes, this step will uncover them. A *syntax error* is the incorrect use of a programming language element, such as a key word, operator, or programmer-defined name. Correct your mistakes and repeat this step until the program runs.

11. Once all syntax errors are corrected, run the program with test data for input. Correct any runtime errors (errors found while running the program). Repeat this step as many times as necessary.

Runtime errors are mistakes that do not prevent an application from executing but cause it to produce incorrect results. For example, a mistake in a mathematical formula is a common runtime error. When runtime errors are found in a program, they must be corrected and the program retested. This step must be repeated until the program reliably produces satisfactory results.

11.3 Visual Studio and the Visual C# .NET Environment

CONCEPT Visual Studio .NET consists of tools used to build Visual C# .NET applications.

In Chapter 1 you learned you could use Visual C# .NET IDE to create C# programs. Now we will build GUI programs with the IDE. First, you need to know how to start Visual Studio and understand its major components. Visual Studio is an *integrated development environment (IDE)*, which is an application that provides all the tools necessary for creating, testing, and debugging software. Visual Studio is quite powerful and can be used to create applications not only with Visual C#, but other languages such as Visual C++ and Visual Basic as well. This section guides you through the Visual Studio startup process and gives you a hands-on tour of its tools for creating Visual C# .NET window applications.

Tutorial 11-2: Starting Visual Studio

The following steps guide you through the Visual Studio startup process.

Step 1: Click the Start button and open the Programs menu (or the All Programs menu if you are using Windows XP).

Step 2: Click Microsoft Visual Studio.NET. Another menu appears. Click Microsoft Visual Studio.NET. You will momentarily see the Visual Studio logo screen. Visual Studio displays a start page similar to that shown in Figure 11-5.

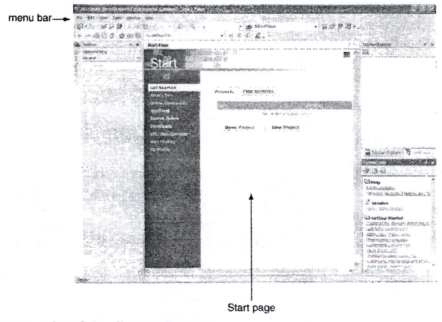

Figure 11-5 Visual Studio start page

NOTE: Your screen may not appear exactly as that shown in Figure 11-5. For example, some of the windows shown in the figure might not be open on your screen. This chapter will show you how to control the appearance of Visual Studio .NET.

 TIP: If you do not see the start page shown in Figure 11-5, click Help on the menu bar, then click Show Start Page.

Step 5: Visual Studio allows you to create a customized profile for a specific programming language. You should select a profile that customizes Visual Studio for Visual C#. On the start page click My Profile. This causes the start page to display your current profile settings. Make sure that Visual C# Developer is selected under Profile, as shown in Figure 11-6.

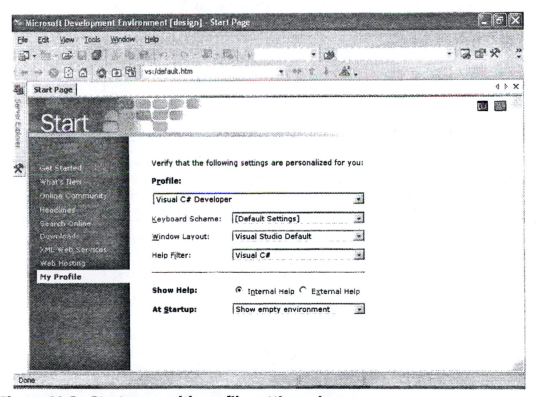

Figure 11-6   Start page with profile settings shown

Step 6: Click Get Started on the start page.

Step 7: Each application you create with Visual Studio is a project. Now you will start a new project. Click the New Project button on the start page.

TIP: You may also click File on the menu bar, then click New, and then click Project.

The New Project dialog box shown in Figure 11-7 appears.

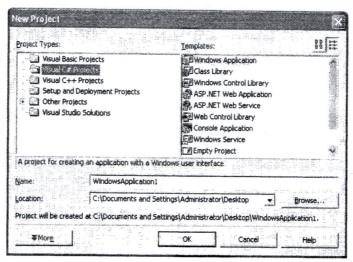

Figure 11-7 New Project dialog box

Step 8: The left pane, which is labeled Project Types, lists the programming languages available in Visual Studio. The right pane, labeled Templates, shows applications that you may create in the selected language. Select Visual C# Projects under Project Types and select Windows Application under Templates.

Step 9: The Name text box is where you enter the name of your project. Visual Studio automatically fills this box with a default name. In Figure 11-7 the default name is WindowsApplication1. Change the project name to Tutorial 11-2.

 NOTE: A project consists of numerous files. When you begin a new project, Visual Studio stores the files in a folder with the same name as the project. As you create more and more projects, you will find that default names such as WindowsApplication1 do not help you remember what each project does. Therefore, you should always change the name of a new project to something that describes the project's purpose.

Step 10: The Location text box shows where the project folder will be created on your system. If you wish to change the location, click the Browse button and select the desired drive and folder.

Step 11: Click the OK button. You should now see the Visual C# .NET environment as shown in Figure 11-8.

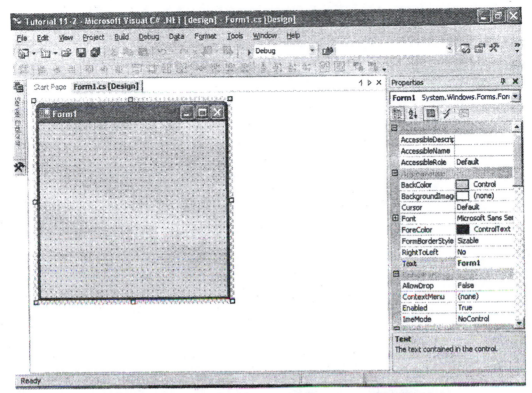

Figure 11-8   Visual C# .NET environment with a new project open

 NOTE: Visual C# .NET is customizable. Your screen might not appear exactly as shown in Figure 11-8. As you continue in this chapter, you will learn how to arrange the screen elements in different ways.

Step 12:   Now you will set some of the Visual C# .NET options so your screens and code look like the examples shown in this book. Click Tools on the menu bar. On the Tools menu, click Options.... The Options dialog box appears. In the left pane click Text Editor, then click C#. The dialog box should now appear as shown in Figure 11-9. With General selected in the left pane, make sure that your settings match those in Figure 11-9. Specifically, make sure that the Auto list members, Hide advanced members, Parameter information, and Enable single-click URL navigation options are checked. Also, make sure that the Enable virtual space, Word wrap are options are unchecked.

Step 13:   Scroll the left pane down and select Windows Forms Designer. Make sure your settings match those shown in Figure 11-10. Specifically, GridSize should be set to 8, 8, ShowGrid should be set to True, and SnapToGrid should be set to True.

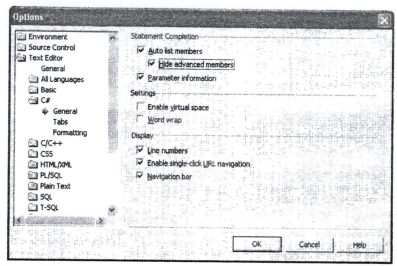

Figure 11-9 Options dialog box

 TIP: To change the GridSize setting, click the area where the current setting is displayed, erase it, and enter **8, 8** as the new setting. This sets the horizontal and vertical spacing between the grid dots to eight pixels. To change either the ShowGrid or SnapToGrid settings, click the area where the current setting is displayed, then click the down-arrow button (▾) that appears. Select True from the menu that drops down.

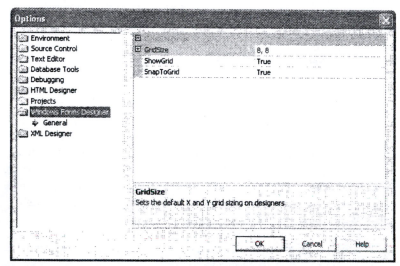

Figure 11-10 Windows Forms Designer settings

Step 15: Click OK to close the dialog box.

 NOTE: The options you set in Steps 12 and 13 will remain set until you or someone else changes them. If you are working in a shared computer lab and you find that your screens and/or the appearance of your code does not match the examples shown in this book, you will probably need to reset these options.

The Visual C# .NET Environment

The Visual C# .NET environment consists of a number of windows and other components. Figure 11-11 shows the locations of the following components: the Design window, the Solution Explorer window, the Dynamic Help window and Dynamic Help window tab, and the Properties window tab.

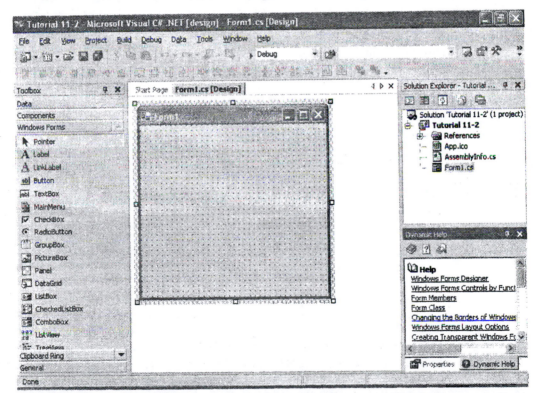

Figure 11-11   The Design window, Solution Explorer window, Dynamic Help window and Dynamic Help window tab, and Properties windows tab

The Properties window and the Dynamic Help window share the same location on the screen. You click the Properties window tab to display the Properties window, and the Dynamic Help window tab to display the Dynamic Help window. Your system may show the Properties window displayed instead of the Dynamic Help window, as shown in Figure 11-12.

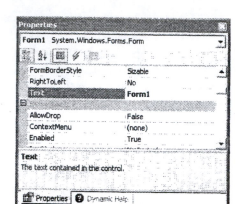

Figure 11-12   The Properties window

It is also possible that the Dynamic Help window is not displayed at all on your system. If this is the case, you will not see it or the Dynamic Help window tab.

You can move the windows around, so they may not appear on your screen in the location shown in Figure 11-11. You can also close the windows so they do not appear at all.

Tutorial 11-3: Opening the Design, Solutions Explorer, and Properties windows

Step 1:   If you do not see the Design window, click View on the menu bar. On the View menu, click Designer. You can also press Shift+F7 on the keyboard.

Step 2:   If you do not see the Solution Explorer window, click View on the menu bar. On the View menu, click Solution Explorer. You can also press Ctrl+R on the keyboard.

Step 3:   If you do not see the Dynamic Help window or the Dynamic Help window tab, click Help on the menu bar. On the Help menu, click Dynamic Help. You can also press Ctrl+F1 on the keyboard.

Step 4:   If you do not see the Properties window tab, click View on the menu bar. On the View menu, click Properties Window. You can also press F4 on the keyboard.

Step 5:   Both the Properties window tab and the Dynamic Help window tab should be visible. Practice switching between the Properties window and the Dynamic Help window by clicking the tabs. When you are finished, leave the Properties window displayed.

Hidden Windows

Many of the windows in the Visual C# .NET environment have a feature known as *auto hide*. When a window's auto hide feature is turned on, the window normally stays minimized as a tab along one of the edges of the screen. This gives you more room to view your application's forms and code. Figure 11-13 shows how the Solution Explorer and Properties windows appear when their auto hide feature is turned on. The figure shows the right edge of the screen.

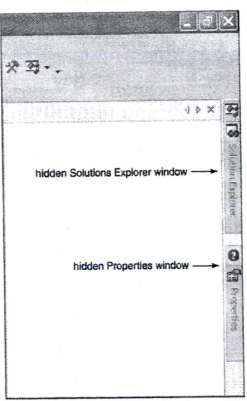

Figure 11-13   The Solution Explorer and Properties windows hidden

To display a hidden window, you simply position the mouse cursor over its tab. This pulls the window back into view. If you want the window to remain in view for a time, pull it into view and then click it. The window will remain displayed until you click outside of it. Tutorials 11-4 and 11-5 guide you through the steps of turning the auto hide feature on and off.

Tutorial 11-4: Turning auto hide on

Step 1:   Notice the pushpin icon (■) in the upper right corner of the Solution Explorer window. This icon controls the window's auto hide feature. Click the icon to turn auto hide on and move the mouse cursor away from the window. After a moment, the window slides out of view and be replaced by a tab on the right edge of the screen.

TIP: When a window's pushpin icon points down, as shown in Figure 11-13, that window's auto hide feature is turned off. When the pushpin points to the left, auto hide is turned on.

Step 2:   Turn the Properties window's auto hide feature on by clicking its pushpin icon. Move the mouse cursor away from the window. Now both the Solution Explorer and Properties windows are hidden and replaced with tabs.

Step 3:   Position the mouse cursor over either of the tabs to display its window. When the window appears, click inside it to select it. The window will remain visible until you click outside it.

 TIP: You can also turn a window's auto hide feature on by selecting the window, then clicking Window on the menu bar, then clicking Auto Hide.

Tutorial 11-5: Turning auto hide off

Step 1:   Bring the Solutions Explorer window into view and click it. Click the pushpin button (■) to turn auto hide off. The window will now remain visible when it is not selected.

Step 2:   Bring the Properties window into view and click it. Click the pushpin button (■) to turn auto hide off. The window will now remain visible when it is not selected.

 TIP: You can also turn a window's auto hide feature off by selecting the window, then clicking Window on the menu bar, then clicking Auto Hide.

Although you will learn more about the Design, Solution Explorer, Dynamic Help, and Properties windows as you progress through this book, a brief overview is given here.

Design Window

The *Design window* contains your application's forms. This is where you design your application's user interface by creating forms and placing controls on them.

 NOTE: The tiny dots that appear on forms in the Design window are part of a grid that is only displayed while you are designing your application. The grid does not appear on the form while the application is running.

Solution Explorer Window

A *solution* is a container for holding Visual C# .NET projects. A *project* is a group of files that make up a Visual C# .NET application. When you create a new project, as you did in Tutorial 11-2, a new solution is automatically created to contain it. The Solution Explorer window allows you to navigate quickly among the files in your Visual C# .NET application.

The Dynamic Help Window

The *Dynamic Help* window displays a list of help topics. The list changes as you perform operations so that the topics displayed are relevant to the operation you are currently performing.

The Properties Window

The *Properties window* shows most of the currently selected object's properties and those properties' values. For example, if a form is selected, the Properties window shows the form's properties and their values. The Properties window also allows you to change a property's value while you are designing an application.

 NOTE: Some properties can only be set with code, while the application is running. The Properties window only shows the properties that may be set while you are designing the application.

Docked and Floating Windows

Figure 11-11 shows the Project Explorer and Properties windows *docked*, which means they are attached to each other or to one of the edges of the Visual C# .NET main window. When you click and drag one of these windows by its title bar, you move it out of the docked position, and the window becomes *floating*. Double-clicking the window's title bar produces the same effect. This is shown in Figure 11-14.

 TIP: A window cannot float if its auto hide feature is turned on.

To dock one of these floating windows, double-click its title bar or drag it to one of the edges of the main window. You may use whichever style, docked or floating, you prefer. When these windows are floating, they behave as normal windows. You may move or resize them to suit your preference.

You now have the Visual C# .NET environment set up properly to work with the projects in this book. Next, we will look at the other elements of the Visual C# .NET environment. Figure 11-15 shows the Visual C# .NET environment with additional components labeled.

The Title Bar

The title bar indicates the name of the project you are currently working on. The title bar in Figure 11-15 shows the name Tutorial 11-2. The [design] designator that appears on the title bar indicates that Visual C# .NET is currently operating in design time. *Design time* is the mode in which you build an application. *Runtime*, which is the mode in which you are running and testing an application, and *break time*, which is the mode in which an application is suspended for debugging purposes.

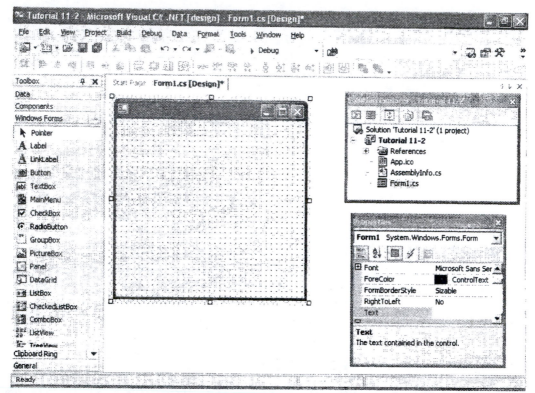

Figure 11-14 Solution Explorer and Properties windows floating

The Menu Bar

Below the title bar is the menu bar. This is where you access the Visual C# .NET menus while you are building an application.

The Standard Toolbar

Below the menu bar is the standard toolbar. The standard toolbar contains numerous buttons that execute frequently used commands. All of the commands executed by the toolbar may also be executed from a menu, but the standard toolbar gives you quicker access to them. For example, in Tutorial 11-2 you were instructed to open the Solution Explorer and Properties windows if they were not already open. You opened these windows by clicking on the View menu, and then select-

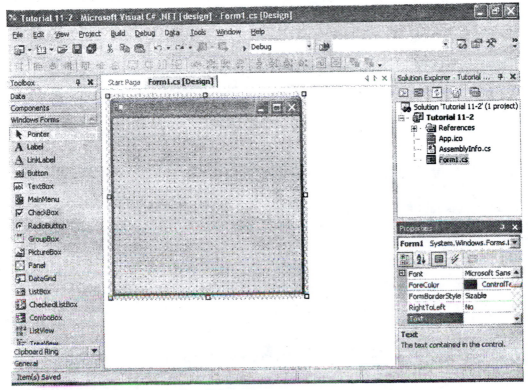

Figure 11-15   Visual C# .NET environment

ing the appropriate command. The standard toolbar contains a set of buttons that opens these windows in a single click.

Figure 11-16 points out the standard toolbar buttons, and Table 11-4 gives a brief description of each.

 NOTE: As with most Windows applications, menu items and buttons cannot be used when they are grayed out.

The Layout Toolbar

The buttons on the layout toolbar allow you to format the layout of controls on a form. There are buttons for aligning, sizing, spacing, centering, and ordering controls.

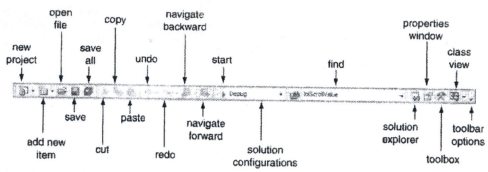

Figure 11-16   Visual C# .NET standard toolbar

Table 11-4   Visual C# .NET toolbar buttons

Toolbar Button	Description
New project	Starts a new project
Add new item	Adds a new item such as a form to the current project
Open file	Opens an existing file
Save	Saves the current file
Save all	Saves all of the files in the current project
Cut	Cuts the selected item to the clipboard
Copy	Copies the selected item to the clipboard
Paste	Pastes the contents of the clipboard
Undo	Undoes the most recent operation
Redo	Redoes the most recently undone operation
Navigate backward	Allows you to navigate backward through the items represented by the tabs at the top of the Design window
Navigate forward	Allows you to navigate forward through the items represented by the tabs at the top of the Design window
Start	Causes the current application to begin executing
Solution configurations	An advanced feature that allows you to set the solution's build configuration. The build configuration may be set to debug (while the application is under development), release (when the application is complete), or a custom configuration.
Find	Searches for text in your application code
Solution Explorer	Opens the Solution Explorer window

(table continues)

Table 11-4   Visual C# .NET toolbar buttons *(continued)*

Toolbar Button	Description
Properties Window	Opens the Properties window
Toolbox	Opens the toolbox
Class view	Provides a hierarchical, tree-structured, object-oriented view of a project
Toolbar options	Allows you to add or remove buttons to the toolbar

The Toolbox

Figure 11-17 shows the toolbox. It contains buttons, or tools, for the Visual C# .NET controls. You use these tools to place controls on an application's form. The toolbox is divided into sections, which are accessible by tabs. Figure 11-17 shows the toolbox with the Windows Forms tab open. This section contains tools for commonly used controls such as Buttons, Labels, and TextBoxes. Because all of the control tools cannot be displayed at once, the toolbox provides scroll arrows.

tabs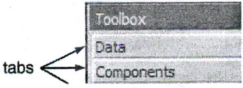

Figure 11-17   The toolbox

 TIP: Don't confuse the toolbox with the toolbar. The toolbar usually appears under the menu bar, and provides quick access to frequently used commands. The toolbox allows you to place controls on a form.

Using Tooltips

A *tooltip* is a small box that is displayed when you hold the mouse cursor over a button on the toolbar or in the toolbox for a few seconds. The box gives a short description of what the button does. Figure 11-18 shows the tooltip that appears when the cursor is left sitting on the save all button. Use tooltips whenever you cannot remember a particular button's function.

Figure 11-18   Save All tooltip

Tutorial 11-6: Getting familiar with the Visual C# .NET environment

This activity should be continued from the previous tutorial. If Visual C# .NET is not running on your computer, follow the steps in Tutorial 11-2. This exercise will give you practice working with elements of the Visual C# .NET environment.

Step 1: Make sure auto hide is turned off for the Solution Explorer and Properties windows. (See Tutorials 11-3 and 11-4 if you cannot remember how.) If your Solution Explorer and Properties windows are in the docked position, double-click on each of their title bars to undock them. (If they are already floating, skip to Step 2.)

Step 2: Practice moving the windows around on the screen by clicking and dragging their title bars.

Step 3: Double-click the title bars of each of the windows to move them back to their docked positions.

Step 4: The Solution Explorer, Properties window, Dynamic Help window, and toolbox each have a close button ( ) in their upper right corner. Close each of these three windows by clicking their close buttons.

Step 5: Do you remember which buttons on the toolbar restore the Solution Explorer, Properties window, and toolbox? If not, move your cursor over any button on the toolbar, and leave it there until the tooltip appears. Repeat this method on different buttons until you find the ones whose tooltips read "Solution Explorer", "Properties Window", and "Toolbox".

Step 6: Click the appropriate buttons on the toolbar to restore the Project Explorer, Properties, Dynamic Help, and Form Layout windows.

Step 7: Exit Visual C# .NET by clicking File on the menu bar, then clicking Exit on the File menu. You may see a dialog box asking you if you wish to save changes to a number of items. Because we are just experimenting with the Visual C# .NET environment, click No.

In this section, you have learned to start Visual Studio, interact with the Visual C# .NET environment, and identify many of its on-screen tools and components.

CHECKPOINT

11.1 Briefly describe the purpose of the Solution Explorer window.

11.2 Briefly describe the purpose of the Properties window.

11.3 Briefly describe the purposes of the standard toolbar and the layout toolbar.

11.4 More About Controls and Programming

> **CONCEPT** As a Visual C# .NET programmer, you must design and create the two major components of an application: the GUI elements (forms and other controls) and the programming statements that respond to and/or perform actions (event procedures).

While creating a Visual C# .NET windows application, you will spend your time doing three things: creating the GUI elements that make up the application's user interface, setting the properties of the GUI elements, and writing programming language statements that respond to events and perform other operations. In this section, we take a closer look at both of these aspects of Visual C# .NET programming.

Visual C# .NET Controls

In the previous section, you saw examples of several GUI elements, or controls. Visual C# .NET provides a wide assortment of controls for gathering input, displaying information, selecting values, showing graphics, and more. Table 11-5 lists some of the commonly used controls.

Table 11-5 Visual C# .NET Windows Controls

Control Type	Description
CheckBox	A box that is either checked or unchecked when clicked with the mouse
ComboBox	A control that is the combination of a ListBox and a TextBox
Button	A rectangular button-shaped object that performs an action when clicked with the mouse
Form	A window onto which other controls may be placed
GroupBox	A rectangular border that functions as a container for other controls
HScrollBar	A horizontal scroll bar that, when moved with the mouse, increases or decreases a value
Label	A box that displays text that cannot be changed or entered by the user
ListBox	A box containing a list of items
RadioButton	A round button that is either selected or deselected when clicked with the mouse
PictureBox	A control that displays a graphic image

Table 11-5 Visual C# .NET Windows Controls *(continued)*

Control Type	Description
TextBox	A rectangular area in which the user can enter text, or the program can display text
VScrollBar	A vertical scroll bar that, when moved with the mouse, increases or decreases a value

If you have any experience using a Windows operating system, you are already familiar with most of the controls listed in Table 11-5. The student disk contains a simple demonstration program that will show you how a few of them work. Follow the steps in Tutorial 11-7 to run the program.

Tutorial 11-7: Running an application that demonstrates various controls

Step 1:   Insert the Student CD into your CD-ROM drive.

Step 2.   Click the Start button. From the menu, click Run…

Step 3:   Assuming your CD-ROM drive is drive D, type the following command in the Run dialog box. (As before, substitute your CD-ROM drive letter if it is something other than D.)

> D:\Chapter 11\ControlDemo

Step 4:   Click the OK button. Once the program loads and executes, the window shown in Figure 11-19 should appear on the screen.

Step 5:   The program presents several Visual C# .NET controls. Experiment with each one, noticing the following actions, which are performed by event procedures:

■ When you click on the small down arrow in the ComboBox control, you see a list of pets. When you select one the name of the pet appears below the combo box.

■ When you click the CheckBox control, its text changes to indicate that the CheckBox is checked or unchecked.

■ When you click an item in the ListBox control, the name of that item appears below the ListBox.

■ When you select one of the radio button controls, the text below them changes to indicate which one you selected. You may only select one at a time.

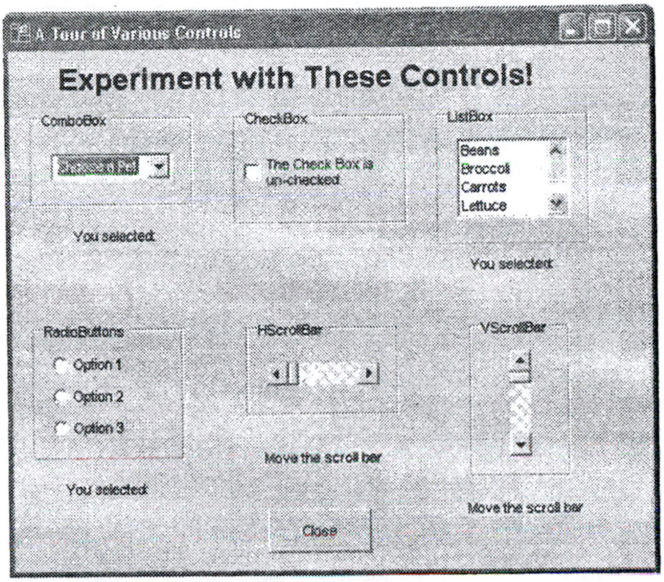

Figure 11-19 Control Demonstration Screen

- You move the horizontal scroll bar (HScrollBar) and the vertical scroll bar (VScrollBar) by:
  - clicking either of the small arrows at each end of the bar
  - clicking inside the bar on either side of the slider
  - clicking on the slider and, while holding the mouse button down, moving the mouse to the right or left for the horizontal scroll bar, or, up or down for the vertical scroll bar.

When you move either of the scroll bars, the text below it changes to a number. Moving the scroll bar in one direction increases the number, and moving it in the other direction decreases the number.

Step 6:   Click the Close button to end the application.

The Name Property

You learned in earlier that the appearance of a control is determined by its properties. Some properties, however, establish nonvisual characteristics. One such property is the control's name. When the programmer wishes to manipulate or access a control in a programming statement, he or she must refer to the control by its name.

When the programmer creates a control in Visual C#, it automatically receives a *default name*. The first label control created in an application receives the default name Label1. The second label control created receives the default name Label2, and the default names continue in this fashion. The first TextBox created in an application is automatically named Text1. As you can imagine, the names for each subsequent TextBox are Text2, Text3, and so forth. We make up a meaningful name and add the name of the control to it using camel case notation.

Table 11-6 lists all the controls, by name, that are in the wage calculator program (which you ran in Section 1.3), and Figure 11-20 shows where each is located.

Table 11-6 Wage Calculator Controls

Control Name	Control Type	Description
Label1	Label	Displays the message "Number of Hours Worked."
Label2	Label	Displays the message "Hourly Pay Rate."
Label3	Label	Displays the message "Gross Pay Earned."
hoursTextBox	Textbox	Allows the user to enter the number of hours worked.
payTextBox	Textbox	Allows the user to enter the hourly pay rate.
payLabel	Label	Displays the gross pay, after the calculateButton button has been clicked.
calculateButton	Button	When clicked, multiplies the number of hours worked by the hourly pay rate.
closeButton	Button	When clicked, terminates the application.

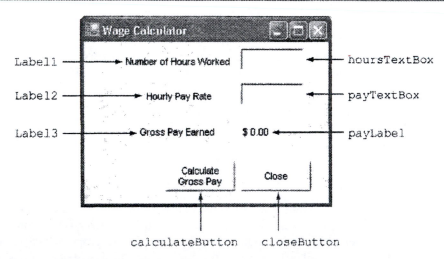

Figure 11-20 Wage Calculator controls

Control Naming Rules and Conventions

Notice that three of the controls in Figure 11-20, Label1, Label2, and Label3, still have their default names. The other five controls have programmer-defined names. This is because those five controls play an active role in the application's event procedures, which means their names will appear in the application's programming statements. Any control that activates programming statements or whose name appears in a programming statement should have a descriptive, *programmer-defined name*.

 NOTE: Some programmers prefer to give all the controls in their application meaningful names, including the ones that do not activate programming statements or whose names do not appear in programming statements.

Although programmers have a great deal of flexibility in naming controls, they should follow some standard guidelines. First, Visual C# .NET requires that control names start with a letter. The remaining characters may only be letters, digits, or underscore characters. You cannot have spaces, special symbols, or punctuation characters in a control name. If a control name does not conform to this rule, it is not a legal name. In addition to this mandatory rule, they should follow the same naming conventions for variables and methods used in earlier chapters.

Programming a Windows Application

When a Visual C# .NET programmer creates an object, such as a form or other control, he or she must also create many of the object's methods. You learned earlier that an object's methods are the actions it can perform. In essence, a method is a script of detailed instructions that an object follows to perform an action. Event methods are one example of an object's methods.

Methods are written in programming statements, which are generally referred to as *code*. The wage-calculating program has two event procedures. One of them responds to the clicking of the calculateButton control. The code for that event method is as follows.

```
private void calculateButton_Click(object sender, System.EventArgs e)
{
    int grossPay;
    // The next line calculates the gross pay.
    grossPay = int.Parse(hoursTextBox.Text) *
                   int.Parse(payTextBox.Text)
    payLabel.Text = grossPay.ToString("C");
}
```

The application's other event method responds to the clicking of the closeButton control. Its code is as follows.

```
private void closeButton_Click(object Sender, System.EventArgs e)
{
    //End the application
    this.Close();
}
```

Don't worry if you do not understand any of this code. By the end of this chapter, you will not only understand code like this, you will also be able to write it. For now, let's try to understand the fundamental language elements of a Visual C# .NET method.

 ## CHECKPOINT

11.4 What does *event-driven* mean?

11.5 Describe the difference between a property and a method.

11.6 Why should the programmer change the name of a control from its default name?

11.7 If a control has the programmer-defined name radiusTextBox, what type of control is it?

11.8 What is the default name given to the first TextBox control created in an application?

11.5 Focus on Problem Solving: Building the Hotel Directions Application

 In this section you create your first Visual C# .NET application: a window that displays a map and road directions to a hotel. In the process you learn how to place controls on a form and manipulate various properties.

The desk clerks at the historic Highlander Hotel frequently receive calls from guests requesting road directions. Some desk clerks are not familiar with the road numbers or exits and inadvertently give unclear or incorrect directions. The hotel manager has asked you to create an application that displays a map to the hotel. The desk clerks can then refer to the application when giving directions to customers over the phone. Here are the steps we will use:

1. Clearly define what the application is to do.

2. Visualize the application running on the computer, and design its user interface.

3. Make a list of the controls needed.

4. Define the values of each control's relevant properties.

5. Start Visual C# .NET and create the forms and other controls.

Now we will take a closer look at each of these steps.

1. Clearly define what the application is to do.

Purpose:	Display a map to the Highlander hotel
Input:	None
Process:	Display a form
Output:	Display on the form a graphic image showing a map

2. Visualize the application running on the computer and design its user interface.

Before you create an application on the computer, you should first create it in your mind. At this step, you must visualize the program. Try to imagine what the computer screen will look like while the application is running. Then draw a sketch of the form or forms in the application. Figure 11-21 shows a sketch of the form presented by this application.

Figure 11-21   Sketch of Hotel Map Form

3. Make a list of the controls needed.

In this step you list all the needed controls. You should assign names to all the controls that will be accessed or manipulated in the application code, and provide a brief description of each control. Our application only needs three controls, listed in Table 11-7. Because none of the controls are used in code, we will keep their default names.

Table 11-7   Hotel map application controls

Control Type	Control Name	Description
Form	(Default Name: Form1)	A small form that will serve as the window onto which the other controls will be placed
Label	(Default Name: Label1)	Displays the message "Directions to the Highlander Hotel"
PictureBox	(Default Name: PictureBox1)	Displays the graphic image showing the map to the hotel

4. Define the values of each control's relevant properties.

Each control's property settings are listed in Table 11-8.

Table 11-8 Hotel map application control properties

Form Control

Name	Form1
Text	"Directions"

Label Control

Name	Label1
Text	"Directions to the Highlander Hotel"
TextAlign	MiddleCenter
Font	Microsoft Sans Serif, bold, 18 point

PictureBox Control

Name	PictureBox1
Picture	HotelMap.jpg
SizeMode	StretchImage

Notice that in addition to the name and caption properties, we are setting the TextAlign and Font properties of the Label control. The TextAlign property determines how the text is aligned within the label. We will discuss this property in detail later.

In addition to its Name property, we are setting the PictureBox control's Image and Size-Mode properties. The Image property lists the name of the file containing the graphic image. We will use HotelMap.jpg, which is located on the Student CD in the Chap2 folder. The SizeMode property is set to StretchImage, which allows us to resize the image. If the image is too small, we can enlarge it (stretch it). If it is too small, we can shrink it.

5. Start Visual C# .NET and create the forms and other controls

Now you are ready to construct the application's form. Tutorial 11-8 gets you started.

Tutorial 11-8: Beginning the Tutorial11.2 application

In this tutorial you will create the application's form and use the Properties window to set the form's Text property.

Step 1: Start Visual Studio .NET, and click the New Project button on the start page. (If you do not see the start page, click File on the menu bar, then click New, then click Project.) In the New Project dialog box, select Visual C# Projects under Project Types, and Windows Application under Templates.

Each project has a name. A default name for the project, such as WindowsApplication1, will appear in the Name text box. Erase this name and type "Tutorial11-2". Next, look at the path name in the Location text box. This is where Visual C# .NET will create a project folder for you. If you want to change this location, click the Browse button and select a suitable folder on your disk drive.

When you have set all of these items, click the OK button on the New Project dialog box.

NOTE: If you are completing this tutorial in a computer lab, your instructor may give you a specific location for the project.

Step 2: The Visual C# .NET environment should be open with a blank form named Form1 displayed in the Design window, as shown in Figure 11-22. Click the form to select it.

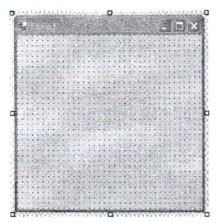

Figure 11-22 Form1 **displayed in the Design window**

Step 3: Look at the Properties window. It should appear as shown in Figure 11-23.

Figure 11-23   Properties window showing Form1

Because you have selected Form1, the Properties window displays the properties for the Form1 object. Notice that the drop-down list box at the top of the window shows the name of the selected object, Form1. Below that, the object's properties are displayed in two columns. The left column lists each property's name, and the right column shows each property's value. Below the list of properties is a brief description of the currently selected property.

Notice that the Text property is highlighted, which means it is currently selected. Recall from earlier that a form's Text property determines the text that is displayed in the form's title bar. A form's Text property is initially set to the same value as the form's name, so this form's Text property is set to "Form1". Follow the instructions in Steps 3 and 4 to change the Text property to "Directions".

Step 4: Click the word "Form1" that appears as the contents of the Text property.

Step 5: Delete the word "Form1" and type **Directions** in its place. Press the Enter key. Notice that the word "Directions" now appears in the form's title bar, as shown in Figure 11-24.

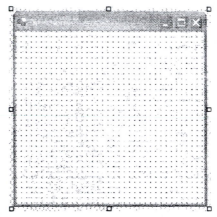

Figure 11-24 Directions in form title bar

Step 6: Although you changed the form's Text property, you did not change its name. Scroll the Properties window up to the top of the list of properties, as shown in Figure 11-25. The Name property is still set to the default value, Form1.

The next step is to add a Label control to the form. Tutorial 11-9 guides you through the process.

Tutorial 11-9: Adding a Label control

Step 1: Now you are ready to add the Label control to the form. As a reminder, Figure 11-26 shows where the Label control tool is located in the toolbox.

Figure 11-25   Properties window scrolled to top

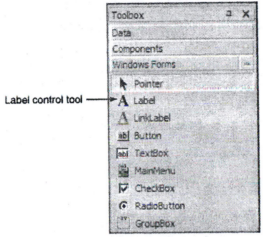

Figure 11-26   Label control tool

Double-click the `Label` control tool. A `Label` control appears on the form, as shown in Figure 11-27.

The label appears on the form as the word "Label1" surrounded by small squares. The squares are sizing handles. You use *sizing handles* to enlarge or shrink the control. Anytime you select an existing control, the sizing handles will appear.

NOTE: You might remember seeing sizing handles around the form when you selected it. Sizing handles always appear around the object that is currently selected in the Design window. In addition, the Properties window will display the currently selected object's properties.

Figure 11-27   Label control on form

Step 2:   Look at the Properties window. Because the label you just placed on the form is currently selected, the Properties window now shows its properties, as seen in Figure 11-28.

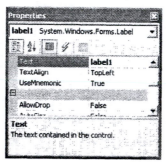

Figure 11-28   Properties window

Notice that the Text property is set, by default, to "Label1." Click on this value, delete it, and type **Directions to the Highlander Hotel** in its place. Press the Enter key. When you have typed the new text into the Text property, the form appears similar to Figure 11-29.

Once you place a control on a form, you can move it by clicking and dragging. You can also resize a control using its sizing handles. In Tutorial 11-10 you move and resize the Label control.

Tutorial 11-10: Moving and resizing the label

The Label control we created in Tutorial 11-9 was placed, by default, in the upper left corner of the form. We must move and resize the Label control so its position and size matches the sketch we drew during the application's planning phase. You move a control by selecting it and dragging it to its new location. You resize a control by dragging one of its sizing handles.

Figure 11-29   Label with new text property value

Step 1:   If you do not see sizing handles around the label, click it to select it.

Step 2:   Position the mouse cursor inside the selected Label control (not on a sizing handle), then click and drag the label to the top center area of the form. Release the mouse button when the label is approximately in the location shown in Figure 11-30.

Figure 11-30   Label moved to the top center of the form

Our planning sketch also shows the label as displaying a single line of text. Notice that the Label control currently displays its text on two lines. This is because the control is not large enough to accommodate the text on one line. As a result, the text wraps around to the second line. Also notice that the text appears to be partially hidden. Once again, this is because the control is not large enough to adequately display the text. These problems can be remedied by resizing the control.

A control is contained inside a bounding box. The *bounding box* is a transparent rectangular area that defines the control's size. The resizing handles are positioned along the edges of the bounding box. You can give a control more or less room on a form by using its resizing handles to enlarge or shrink the control's bounding box. Steps 3 through 5 guide you through the process of resizing the label.

Step 3: With the Label control selected, position the cursor over the middle-right sizing handle, as shown in Figure 11-31. Your cursor becomes a double-headed arrow.

Figure 11-31 Cursor on sizing handle becomes a double-headed arrow

Step 4: Click and drag the sizing handle until the right side of the bounding box is near the right edge of the form.

Step 5: Click and drag the middle-left sizing handle to the left edge of the form. Your form should resemble Figure 11-32.

By default, a label's text is aligned with the top and left edges of the label's bounding box. The position of the text within a label's bounding box is controlled by the *TextAlign property*, which may be set to any of the following values: TopLeft, TopCenter, TopRight, MiddleLeft, MiddleCenter, MiddleRight, BottomLeft, BottomCenter, or BottomRight. Figure 11-33 shows how each of these values affect the text's alignment.

Tutorial 11-11 takes you through the process of aligning the label's text.

Tutorial 11-11: Setting the label's TextAlign property

Step 1: With the label selected, look at the Properties window. Notice that the value of the TextAlign property is TopLeft.

Figure 11-32   Label control resize

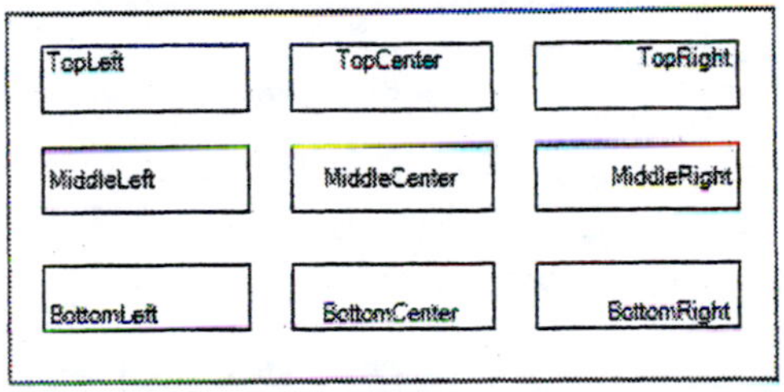

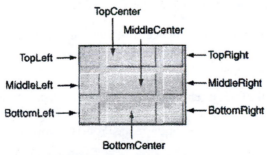

Figure 11-33   Text alignments

Step 2:   Click on the TextAlign property. Notice that a down-arrow button (⊡) appears next to the property value. When you click on the arrow a small dialog box with nine buttons appears. Each of the buttons represents a TextAlign value, as shown in Figure 11-34.

Figure 11-34   Text Align drop-down dialog

Step 3: Click the MiddleCenter button. Notice that the label's text is now centered in the middle of the label's bounding box, as shown in Figure 11-35.

Figure 11-35 Label text centered

In the planning phase, we indicated that the label's text should be displayed in an 18-point bold Microsoft sans serif font. These characteristics are controlled by the label's Font property. The Font property allows you to set the font, font style, and size of the label's text.

Tutorial 11-12: Changing the label's font size and style

Step 1: With the label selected, click on the Font property in the Properties window. Notice that an ellipses button (⊞) appears. Click the ellipses button and the Font dialog box appears, as shown in Figure 11-36.

Step 2: Microsoft Sans Serif is already the selected font. Click on Bold under Font style, and 18 under Size. Notice that the text displayed in the Sample box changes to reflect your selections. Click the OK button.

The text displayed by the label is now in 18-point bold Microsoft Sans Serif. Unfortunately, not all the text can be seen because it is too large for the Label control. You must enlarge both the form and the Label control so all of the label text is visible.

Step 3: Select the form by clicking anywhere on it, except on the Label control. You will know you have selected the form when the sizing handles appear around it and the form's properties appear in the Properties window.

Step 4: Use the form's sizing handles to widen the form, then enlarge the label so it appears similar to Figure 11-37.

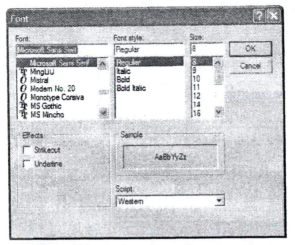

Figure 11-36   Font dialog box

Figure 11-37   Resized form showing all text

To delete a control, you simply select it and press the delete key on the keyboard. In the following steps you add another Label control to the form (one that you will not need) and then delete it.

Tutorial 11-13: Deleting a control

Step 1:   Double-click the Label tool in the toolbox. Another Label control appears on the form.

Step 2: With the new `Label` control still selected, press the delete key on the keyboard. The label is deleted from the form.

 TIP: If you accidentally delete a control you can restore it with the Undo button (⌧) on the standard toolbar.

The last step in building this application is to insert the road map. In Tutorial 11-14 you will insert a *PictureBox control*, which can be used to display an image.

Tutorial 11-14: Inserting a `PictureBox` control

Step 1: Double-click the `PictureBox` tool in the toolbox. An empty `PictureBox` control appears on the form. Move the control to a position approximately in the center of the form, as shown in Figure 11-38.

Figure 11-38 `PictureBox` **control placed**

Step 2: The `PictureBox` control displays an image in a variety of ways, depending on the setting of the *SizeMode property*. The `SizeMode` property may be set to the values listed in Table 11-9.

In the Properties window, notice that the `SizeMode` property is set to Normal. Click the `Size-Mode` property and notice that a down-arrow button (⏷) appears next to the property value. Click the down-arrow button and a drop-down list appears. Select StretchImage.

Step 3: Make sure your Student CD is inserted in the disk drive. Notice that the `Image` property is currently set to (none), indicating that no image is loaded into the PictureBox control. Click the Image property and notice that an ellipses button ⊡ appears next to the property value. Click the ellipses button. The Open dialog box appears. Use the dialog box to browse to the Chapter 11 folder on the Student

Table 11-9 `SizeMode` **property values**

Setting	Description
AutoSize	The size of the `PictureBox` control's bounding box is automatically adjusted to fit the size of the image it displays.
CenterImage	If the `PictureBox` control's bounding box is larger than the image, the image is displayed in the center of the control. If the image is larger than the control's bounding box, the image is displayed in the center of the control and is clipped to fit within the bounding box.
Normal	The image is aligned with the upper left corner of the `PictureBox` control's bounding box. If the image is larger than the control's bounding box, it is clipped.
StretchImage	The size of the image is scaled to fit within the `PictureBox` control's bounding box. If the image is smaller than the control, the image is stretched. If the image is larger than the control, the image is shrunk.

CD. Click on the `HotelMap.jpg` file, and then click the Open button. This loads the graphic stored in `HotelMap.jpg` into the `PictureBox` control. The application's form now appears similar to Figure 11-39.

Directions to the Highlander Hotel

Figure 11-39 `PictureBox` **control with image in place**

Step 4: Because we set the `SizeMode` property to StretchImage, the image is scaled to fit the size of the PictureBox control. Use the control sizing handles to enlarge the image so its details are clearly visible, as shown in Figure 11-40.

 TIP: You may want to enlarge the form again to make more room for the image.

Figure 11-40 `HotelMap.jpg` **enlarged**

 NOTE: You have now seen that properties are set in the Properties window in one of three ways:

- Typing a value for the property

- By selecting a value for the property from a drop-down list by clicking the down-arrow button (▾).

- Establishing a value for the property with a dialog box, which appears when the ellipses button (⊡) is clicked.

Recall that when you created the project you set its name to Directions and you either kept the default location on your disk drive or you specified a location. Now it's time to save the changes you've made to your project. Tutorial 11-15 describes three different ways to save a project.

Tutorial 11-15: Saving the project

Step 1: You may use any of the following methods to save a project.

- Click File on the menu bar, then click Save All on the File menu
- Press Ctrl+Shift+S on the keyboard
- Click the Save All button on the standard toolbar

Use one of these methods to save your project.

 TIP: You should save your work often to prevent accidentally losing changes you have made to your project.

Now you can run the application. It doesn't have any event procedures, so it will only display the form, as you have designed it. There are three ways to run an application in Visual C# .NET:

- By clicking the start button (▶) on the toolbar
- By clicking Debug on the menu bar, then clicking Start on the Debug menu
- By pressing the F5 key

Tutorial 11-16: Running the application

Step 1:   To run the application, click the start button on the standard toolbar, click the start command on the Debug menu, or press the F5 key. If it is not already visible, you will see the Output window appear as shown in Figure 11-41.

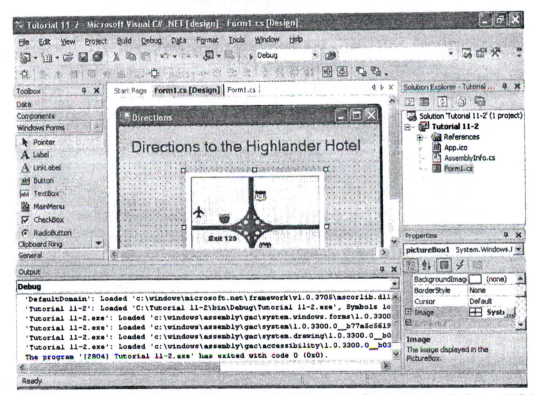

Figure 11-41   The Visual C# .NET environment with the Output window visible

As Visual C# .NET builds the application you will see various messages displayed in the Output window. Once the application is built, it will run and you will see the form appear as shown in Figure 11-42.

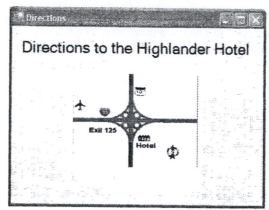

Figure 11-42   The Directions application

Notice that the Visual C# .NET title bar now reads Directions – Microsoft Visual C# .NET [run]. The [run] designator indicates that your application is now in runtime. *Runtime* is the mode in which you run and test an application.

Tutorial 11-17: Ending the application, closing the solution, and exiting Visual C# .NET

Step 1:   To end the application, perform one of the following operations:

- Click the close button (![x])on the application window.
- Click Debug on the menu bar, then click Stop Debugging on the Debug menu.

The application stops running and Visual C# .NET returns to design time.

Step 2:   You can close a Visual C# .NET project by closing its solution. To close the solution, click File on the menu bar, then click Close Solution.

 NOTE: If you close a solution and have made changes to the project since the last time you saved it, you will see a dialog box asking you whether you want to save your changes. Click the Yes button.

Step 3:   You exit Visual C# .NET in the same manner you exit most other Windows applications:

- Click on the File menu, then click the exit command
- Click the close button (![x]) on the right edge of the title bar

Use one of these methods to exit Visual C# .NET.

How Solutions and Projects are Organized on the Disk

Recall from earlier that a solution is a container that holds a Visual C# .NET project. Every project must be part of a solution. When you create a new project Visual C# .NET automatically creates a solution with the same name as the project, and adds the project to the solution. For example, when you created the Tutorial 11-2 project, Visual C# .NET also created a solution named Tutorial 11-2 and added the project to the Directions solution.

Recall from Tutorial 11-1 that you must specify a disk location in the New Project dialog box. Visual C# .NET creates a folder at this location. The folder is given the same name as the solution (which is also the name of the project). Several files, and some other folders, are created and stored in this folder.

When you created the Tutorial 11-2 project (and the solution that contains it), Visual C# .NET created a folder named Tutorial 11-2 at the location specified in the New Project dialog box. All of the files related to this project are stored under this folder. Two of the files are `Tutorial11-2.sln` and `Tutorial11-2.csproj`. The `.sln` file is the *solution file*, and contains data describing the solution. The `.csproj` file is the *project file*, and contains data describing the project.

Opening an Existing Project

Visual C# .NET gives you several ways to open an existing project. One method is to use the Visual Studio start page, as shown in Figure 11-43. Notice that the start page displays a list of the most recently opened projects. You may open any of the projects in the list by clicking its name.

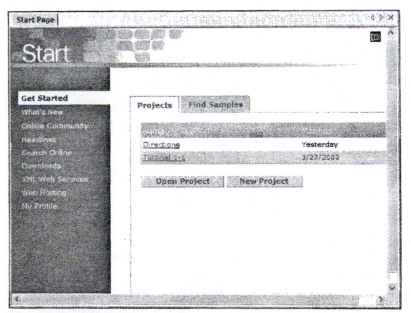

Figure 11-43 Visual Studio Start page

You may also open an existing project by clicking the Open Project button on the start page, or by clicking File on the menu bar, then clicking New, then clicking Project. Either of these actions causes the Open Project dialog box to appear. Use the dialog box to browse to and open the folder containing your solution and project. For example, Figure 11-44 shows the Open Project dialog box with the Directions folder open.

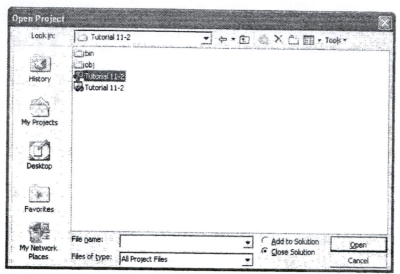

Figure 11-44　Open Project dialog box with Tutorial 11-2 folder open

The Open Project dialog box displays only solution files and project files. Select the solution file (the one that ends with .sln) and click the Open button. Tutorial 11-18 guides you through the process of opening the Tutorial 11-2 project after it has been closed.

Tutorial 11-18: Opening an existing project

This tutorial assumes the Tutorial 11-2 project is saved to your disk and Visual C# .NET is not currently running.

Step 1:　Start Visual Studio .NET. If you see the start page, as previously shown in Figure 11-43, you may open the Tutorial 11-2 project by clicking its name.

Alternatively, you can click the Open Project button on the start page. This causes the Open Project dialog box to appear. Browse to and open the Tutorial 11-2 folder, then select the Tutorial 11-2.sln file and click the Open button.

If you do not see the Start Page, click File on the menu bar, then click New, then click Project. This also causes the Open Project dialog box to appear. Browse to and open the Tutorial 11-2 folder, then select the Tutorial 11-2.sln file and click the Open button.

Step 2:　After you perform one of these actions, the Tutorial 11-2 project should be open and you should see the form with the map to the hotel displayed in the Design window. If you do not see the form displayed, look in the Solutions Explorer window and double-click Form1.cs.

More About the Properties Window

In this section you will learn about the Properties window's object box and its alphabetic, categorized, and event buttons. Figure 11-45 shows the location of the object box. The figure also shows that the alphabetic, categorized, and event buttons appear just below the object box, on a small toolbar.

Figure 11-45 Object box and associated buttons

In addition to clicking objects in the Design window, you can also use the object box on the Properties window to select any object in the project. The *object box* provides a drop-down list of the objects in the project.

The alphabetic and categorized buttons affect the way properties are displayed in the Properties window. When the *alphabetic button* is selected, the properties are displayed in alphabetical order. When the *categorized button* is selected, related properties are displayed together in groups. For example, in categorized view, a Label control's Text and TextAlign properties are displayed in the Appearance group. You have probably noticed that a few of the properties, including the Name property, are enclosed in parentheses. These properties are commonly accessed, and placing them in parentheses causes them to appear at the top of the alphabetic list. The events button lists the event the particular object could have. Example events are Appearance, Behavior, Layout and Mouse.

CHECKPOINT

11.9 You want to change what is displayed in a form's title bar. Which of its properties do you change?

11.10 How do you insert a Label control onto a form?

11.11 When you run an application from the Visual C# .NET environment, what changes do you see in the Visual C# .NET title bar? What does this indicate?

11.12 Describe three ways to open an existing Visual C# .NET project.

11.6 Focus on Problem Solving: Responding to Events

CONCEPT An application responds to events, such as mouse clicks and keyboard input, by executing code known as event procedures.

The manager of the Highlander Hotel reports that the Tutorial 11-2 application has been quite helpful to the desk clerks. Some clerks, however, have requested that the application be modified to display written directions as well as the map. Some have also requested a more obvious way to exit the application, other than clicking the standard windows close button, located on the application's title bar.

You decide to add a button to the application form that, when clicked, causes the written directions to appear. In addition, you decide to add an Exit button that causes the application to stop when clicked.

Figure 11-46 shows the modified sketch of the form presented by this application.

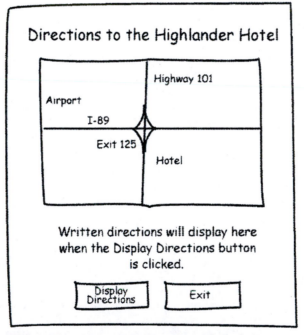

Figure 11-46 Modified Directions application sketch

Table 11-10 lists the controls that will be added to the application. Because the Label control will be accessed in code, and the buttons will have code associated with them, you will assign them names.

Table 11-10 Controls to be added to Tutorial 11-2 application

Control Type	Control Name	Description
Label	directionsLabel	Displays written directions to the hotel.
Button	directionsButton	When clicked, causes the directionsLabel control's text to appear on the form.
Button	exitButton	Stops the application when clicked.

Each control's property settings are listed in Table 11-10. The table mentions a new property, Visible, used with the directionsLabel control. Visible is a *Boolean* property, which means it can only hold one of two values: true or false. When a control's *Visible* property is set to true, the control can be seen on the form. A control is hidden, however, when its Visible property is set to false. In this application, we want the directionsLabel control to be hidden until the user clicks the directionsButton button, so we initially set its Visible property to false.

Table 11-11 Directions application control properties

Label Control	
Name	directionsLabel
Text	"Traveling on I-89, take Exit 125 onto Highway 101 South. The hotel is on the left, just past the I-89 intersection. Traveling on Highway 101 North, the hotel is on the right, just before the I-89 intersection."
Visible	False
Button Control	
Name	directionsButton
Text	"Display Directions"
Button Control	
Name	exitButton
Text	"Exit"

There are only two event procedures needed in the Directions application. Table 11-12 lists and describes them. directionsButton_Click is the name of the method that is invoked when the directionsButton button is clicked, and exitButton_Click is the event method that executes when the exitButton button is clicked.

Table 11-12 Directions application event procedures

Method	Description
directionsButton_Click	Causes the Directions control to become visible on the form. This is accomplished by setting the label's Visible property to true.
exitButton_Click	Terminates the application.

Figure 11-47 shows a flowchart for the directionsButton_Click event method.

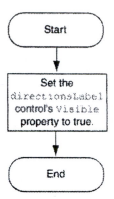

Figure 11-47 Flowchart for directionsButton_Click

Figure 11-48 shows a flowchart for the exitButton_Click event method.

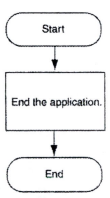

Figure 11-48 Flowchart for exitButton_Click

Now that you have seen flowcharts for the event procedures, let's look at the code we will write. The code for the directionsButton_Click event method is as follows.

```
private void directionsButton_Click(object Sender, System.EventArgs e)
{
    //Make the directions visible
    directionsLabel.Visible = true;
}
```

Among other things, the first line of the event method (which is printed as two lines here) identifies the control it belongs to and the event it responds to. This is illustrated in Figure 11-49.

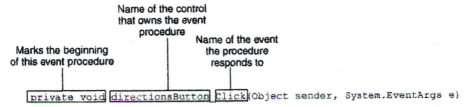

Figure 11-49 Parts of the First Line of an Event Method

As you can see from Figure 11-49 the name of the control that owns the method appears after the words `private  void`. An underscore character separates the name of the owning control from the name of the event that the method responds to. So the code in Figure 11-49 indicates the beginning of a method that belongs to the `directionsButton` control. The method responds to the `Click` event, which means it executes when the user clicks the control with the mouse.

For now, don't be concerned with anything else that appears in the first two lines of code. As you progress through the book you will learn more about it.

NOTE: Event methods are also known as *event handlers*.

The next line reads

```
// Make the directions visible
```

The following line reads

```
directionsLabel.Visible = true;
```

The item to the left of the operator is

```
directionsLabel.Visible
```

This identifies the `Visible` property of the `directionsLabel` control. The standard notation for referring to a control's properties in code is

```
ControlName.PropertyName
```

The value to the right of the equal sign, true, is copied into the directionsLabel.Visible property. The effect of this statement is that the directionsLabel control becomes visible on the form.

Notice that the code between the first and last lines of the event method is indented. Although not required, it is a common practice to indent the lines inside a method so they are visually set apart. As you work through this book, you will see that indention is used in other places as well.

Now, let's look at the exitButton_Click event method. Here is the code:

```
private void exitButton_Click (object sender, System.EventArgs e)
{
    // End the application
    this.Close();
}
```

Other than the comment "End the application", this method contains only one statement: this.Close(). The Close method causes the application to terminate.

In Tutorial 11-19 you place the controls needed to complete this part of the project.

Tutorial 11-19: Placing the directionsLabel, directionsButton, and exitButton controls

Step 1: Start Visual C# .NET and open the Tutorial 11-2 project. Select the Form1 form, if it is not already selected.

Step 2: You will place the new controls at the bottom of the form, below the graphic. Because the form is too small to accommodate them, you will need to enlarge it. Drag the bottom edge of the form down until it looks something like the one shown in Figure 11-50. (Don't worry about the exact size of the form. You can adjust it again if you need to.)

Figure 11-50 Directions application with enlarged form

Step 3: You are ready to place the new Label control on the form. Previously you learned to place a control by double-clicking its button in the toolbox. Double-clicking a control's button in the toolbox places a default-sized control on the selected form. This time you will learn to draw the control. Click the Label tool in the toolbox once.

Step 4: Move the cursor over the form. Notice the cursor is now in the shape of crosshairs. Click and hold the mouse button with the crosshairs below the image and near the left edge of the form. As you hold the mouse button down, drag the crosshairs down and to the right, as shown in Figure 11-51. Notice that the rectangle you are drawing as you drag the cursor.

Figure 11-51 Drawing a Label control

Step 5: With the cursor in the approximate location shown in Figure 11-51, release the mouse button. The rectangle becomes a Label control named Label2.

Step 6: Change the control's Name property to directionsLabel.

Step 7: Type the following text into the new Label control's Text property:

Traveling on I-89, take Exit 125 onto Highway 101 South. The hotel is on the left, just past the I-89 intersection. Traveling on Highway 101 North, the hotel is on the right, just before the I-89 intersection.

 TIP: When typing the directions, do not press the Enter key until you have entered all the text. When you press the Enter key, Visual C# .NET will stop accepting input to the `Text` property. If you accidentally press the Enter key too early, select the `Text` property again and enter the rest of the text.

Step 8:   Set the Label control's `TextAlign` property to `MiddleCenter`. The form should now appear similar to Figure 11-52.

Figure 11-52   Label with directions text entered

Step 9:   Locate the `Label` control's `Visible` property in the Properties window. The property's value is currently set to true. Click the property value. A down-arrow button () appears next to the property value. Click the down-arrow button and a drop-down list appears, showing the values True and False. Click False.

 NOTE: During design time, all controls are displayed, even if their Visible property is set to false.

Step 10:   You are now ready to place the buttons. Double-click the button tool in the toolbox. A default-sized button named `Button1` appears on the form. Drag it to the form's bottom edge.

Step 11:   Double-click the button tool in the toolbox again. Another button, this one named `Button2`, appears on the form.

 NOTE: If a control is already selected when you double-click a tool in the toolbox, the new control will appear on top of the selected control. If the `Button1` control was still selected when you created `Button2`, the `Button2` control will appear on top of the `Button1` control.

Drag the Button2 control to the bottom edge of the form and place it to the right of the Button1 control. Arrange the two buttons as shown in Figure 11-53.

Figure 11-53 Buttons in place

Step 12: Select the Button1 button.

Step 13: In the Properties window, change the button's Name to directionsButton.

Step 14: Change the Text property to Display Directions. Notice that the button is not large enough to accommodate the text. Use the button's sizing handles to increase its height, as shown in Figure 11-54.

Figure 11-54 Button with Increased Height

Step 15: Select the Button2 button.

Step 16: In the Properties window, change the button's name to exitButton and change the button's Text property to Exit.

Step 17: Resize the Exit button so its size is the same as the directionsButton button. Your form should now resemble the one shown in Figure 11- 55.

In the following tutorial you write the event procedures for the buttons.

Figure 11-55   Buttons labeled

Tutorial 11-20: Writing the Event Procedures

Step 1:   Double-click the Display Directions button (`directionsButton`). The Code window opens, as shown in Figure 11-56.

The *Code window* is a text-editing window in which you write code. Notice that Visual C# .NET has automatically supplied a *code template* for the `directionsButton_Click` event method. The template consists of the first and last lines of the method. You must add the code that appears between these two lines.

Step 2:   Type the following code between the first and last lines of the `directionsButton_Click` method:

```
//Make the directions visible
directionsLabel.Visible = true;
```

 TIP: Make sure you type the code exactly as it appears here. Otherwise, you may encounter an error when you run the application.

Did you notice that as you entered the second line, `directionsLabel.Visible = true`, when you typed the period the scrollable list box in Figure 11-57 appeared?

This is called an Intellisense auto list box. *Intellisense* is a feature of Visual Studio .NET that provides help and some automatic code completion while you are developing an application. The *auto list box* displays information that may be used to complete part of a statement. This auto list box contains the name of every property and method that belongs to the `Tutorial 11-2` object. When you type the letter V the selector bar in the list box automatically moves to Visible. You can

```
Tutorial 11-2 - Microsoft Visual C# .NET [design] - Form1.cs*
File  Edit  View  Project  Build  Debug  Tools  Window  Help
                                            Debug

Start Page | Form1.cs [Design]* | Form1.cs*                                    4 ▷ ×
Tutorial_11_2.Form1                        directionsButton_Click(object sender,System.EventArgs e)

    52         Windows Form Designer generated code
   133
   134       /// <summary>
   135       /// The main entry point for the application.
   136       /// </summary>
   137       [STAThread]
   138       static void Main()
   139       {
   140           Application.Run(new Form1());
   141       }
   142
   143       private void pictureBox1_Click(object sender, System.EventArgs e)
   144       {
   145
   146       }
   147
   148       private void directionsButton_Click(object sender, System.EventArgs e)
   149       {
   150
   151       }
   152   }
   153 }

Ready                                  Ln 150      Col 13       Ch 7        INS
```

Figure 11-56   Code window

Figure 11-57   Auto list box

continue typing, or you can press the tab key or spacebar to select Visible from the list. You may then continue typing.

Another auto list box, shown in Figure 11-58, appears after you type the = operator.

Figure 11-58   Auto list box showing valid values

This auto list box shows only two values: False and True. These are the only valid values you can assign to the Visible property. As before, you may continue typing or let the auto list box help you select the code to insert.

 TIP: If you did not see the auto list box, then that feature has been disabled. To enable it, click Tools on the menu bar, then click Options… You will see the Options dialog box, as described earlier. In the left pane, click Text Editor, then click Basic. With General selected in the left pane, make sure the auto list members box is checked.

Your code window should look like the one shown in Figure 11-59.

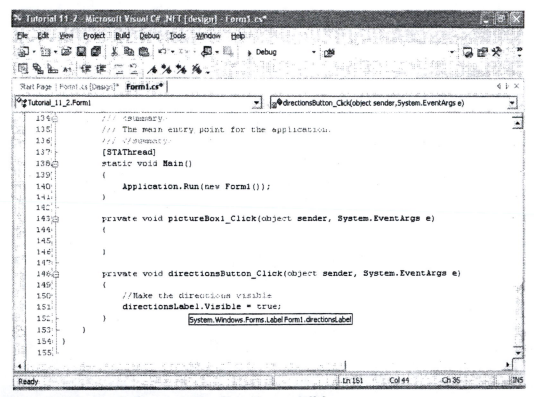

Figure 11-59   Code for making directions visible

Step 3:   Now you will switch back to the Design window. Here are four ways to do this.

■ Notice at the top of the code window there are two tabs. You can open the Design window by clicking the Form1.cs [Design] tab, and then you can open the code window again by clicking the Form1.cs tab.

- You can also click View on the menu bar, then click Designer on the View menu.
- Another way is to use the Solutions Explorer window. Click the View Designer button (▨) to switch to the Design window, and click the View Code button (▨) to switch back to the Code window.
- You can also press Shift+F7 on the keyboard.

Use one of these techniques to open the Design window.

Step 4:   Now you must write the event method for the other button. On the form, double-click the Exit button. The Code window reappears, as shown in Figure 11-60.

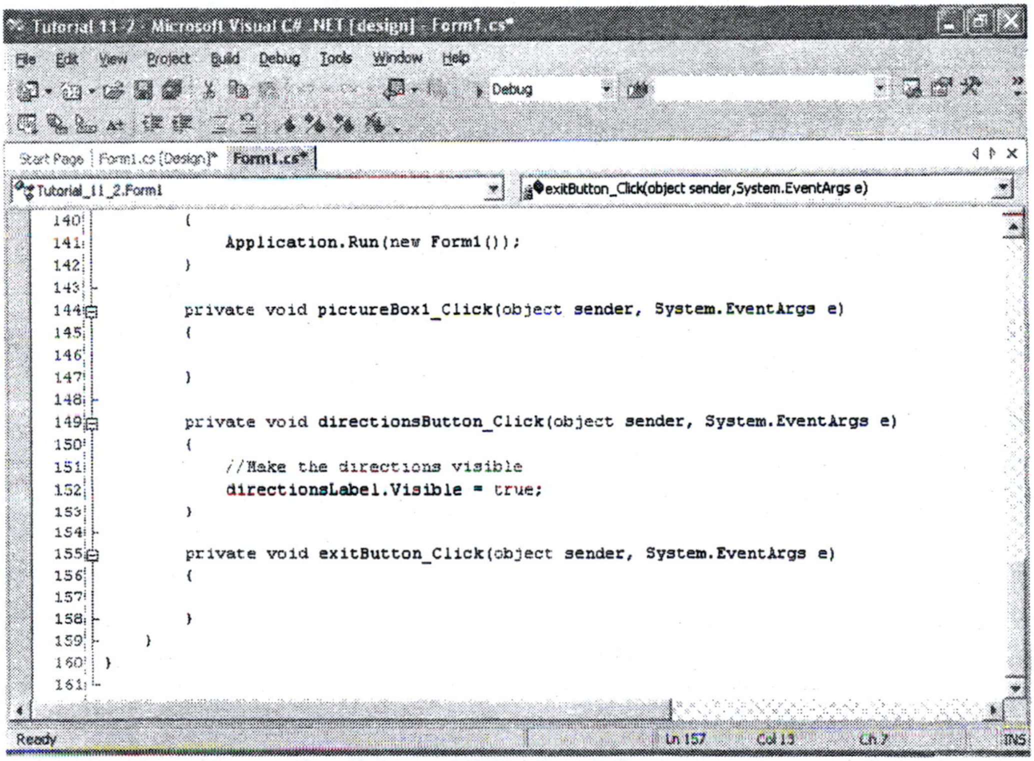

Figure 11-60   Code window, ready for exit button code

Notice that Visual C# .NET has now provided a code template for the **exitButton_Click** method.

Step 5: Between the first and last lines of the `exitButton_Click` code template, type the following code:

```
// End the application
this.Close();
```

The Code window should now look like the one shown in Figure 11-61

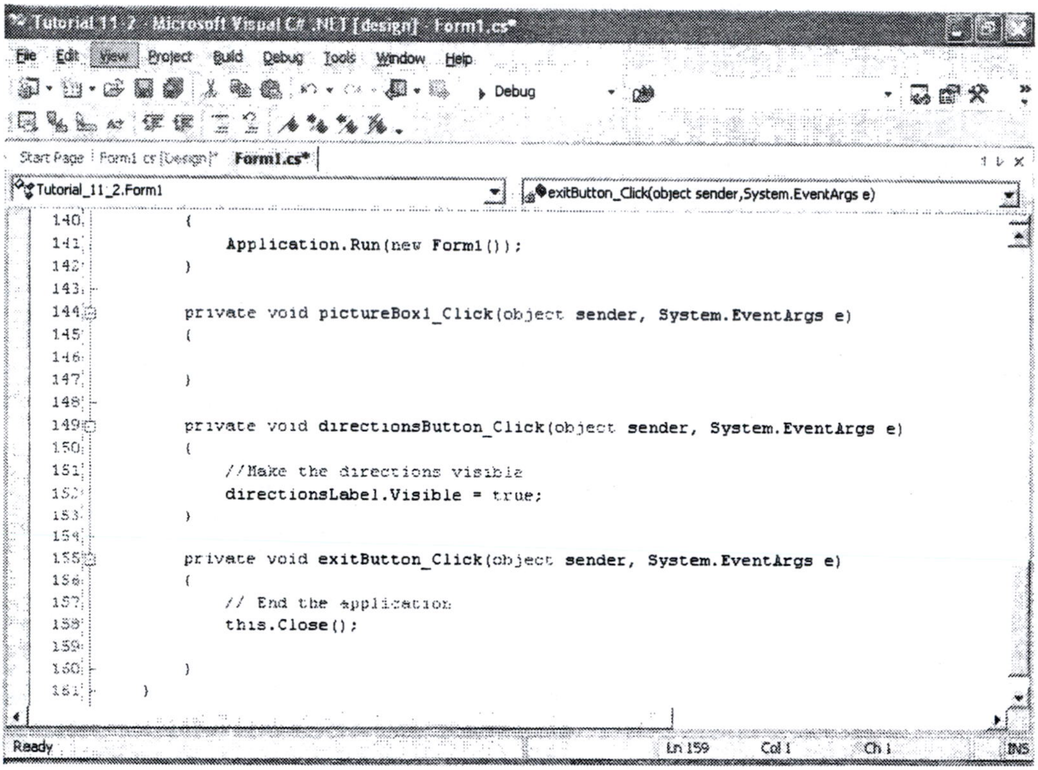

Figure 11-61 Code window with `exitButton_Click` method completed

Step 6: Use the Save All command on the File menu to save the project.

Step 7: Click the Start button (⬛) on the Visual C# .NET toolbar. The application begins executing, as shown in Figure 11-62. Notice that the `directionsLabel` label is not visible.

Figure 11-62   Directions application at startup

Step 8:   Click the Display Directions button. The written directions appear on the form, as shown in Figure 11-63.

Figure 11-63   Directions application with text displayed

Step 9:   Click the Exit button. The application terminates.

More About Code and the Code Window

In Tutorial 11-15, you learned to display the Code window by double-clicking the control that you wish to write an event method for. You may also display the Code window by any of the following actions:

- Click the View Code button (⬚) on the Solution Explorer window.
- Click View on the menu bar, then click the Code command.
- Press the F7 key.

Changing Text Colors

You have already learned that the font style and size of text on a control can be easily changed through the Properties window. You can also change the text background and foreground color with the BackColor and ForeColor properties.

Tutorial 11-21: Changing text colors

Step 1: With the Tutorial 11-2 project loaded, open the Design window.

Step 2: Select the Label1 control. This is the Label control whose Text property reads "Directions to the Highlander Hotel."

Step 3: In the Properties window, look for the BackColor property. This is the property that establishes the background color for the label text. Click the property value. A down-arrow button will appear.

Step 4: Click the down-arrow button. A drop-down list of colors appears, as shown in Figure 11-64.

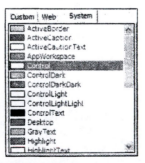

Figure 11-64 BackColor drop-down list

The drop-down list has three tabs: System, Web, and Custom. The System tab lists colors that are defined in the current Windows configuration. The Web tab lists colors that are displayed with consistency in web browsers. The Custom tab displays a color palette, as shown in Figure 11-65.

Select a color from one of the tabs. Notice that the label text background changes to the color you selected.

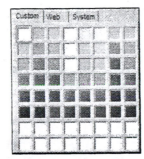

Figure 11-65   Custom color palette

Step 5:   Now look for the ForeColor property in the Properties window. When you click it, a down-arrow button appears.

Step 6:   Click the down-arrow button and you see the same drop-down list as you saw in Step 4. Once again, select a color from one of the tabs. Notice that the label's text foreground color changes to the color you selected.

Step 7:   Start the application to test the new colors. After you close the application, save your project.

Setting the FormBorderStyle Property and Locking Controls

The FormBorderStyle Property

Sometimes you want to prevent the user from resizing, minimizing, or maximizing a window, or from closing a window using its close button (⊠). You can control all of these actions by selecting an appropriate value for the form's FormBorderStyle property.

Table 11-13 shows a list of the possible values for the FormBorderStyle property.

Locking Controls

Once you have placed all the controls in their proper positions on a form, it is usually a good idea to lock them. When you lock the controls on a form, they cannot be accidentally moved at design time. They must be unlocked before they can be moved.

To lock all the controls on a form, place the cursor over an empty spot on the form and right-click. A small menu pops up. One of the selections on the menu is Lock Controls.

In Tutorial 11-22 we will modify the value of the form's BorderStyle property so the user cannot minimize, maximize, or resize the window.

Table 11-13   Values for BorderStyle

BorderStyle Value	Description
Fixed3D	Displays a 3D border. The form's size is fixed and displayed with minimize, maximize, and close buttons on its title bar. Although the form may be maximized and minimized, it may not be resized by its edges or corners.
FixedDialog	This type of border shows minimize, maximize, and close buttons on its title bar. Although the form may be maximized and minimized, it may not be resized by its edges or corners.
FixedSingle	The form's size is fixed and uses a border that is a single line. The form is displayed with minimize, maximize, and close buttons on its title bar. Although the form may be maximized and minimized, it may not be resized by its edges or corners.
FixedToolWindow	Intended for use with floating toolbars. Only shows the title bar with a close button. May not be resized.
None	The form is displayed with no border at all. Subsequently, there is no title bar, and no minimize, maximize, or close buttons. The form may not be resized.
Sizable	This is the default value. The form is displayed with minimize, maximize, and close buttons on its title bar. The form may be resized, but the controls on the form do not change position.
SizableToolWindow	Like Fixed ToolWindow, but resizable.

Tutorial 11-22: Setting the FormBorderStyle property and locking the controls

Step 1:   Select the form and find the FormBorderStyle property in the Properties window.

Step 2:   Click on the FormBorderStyle property. A down-arrow button appears. Click the down-arrow button to see a list of values.

Step 3:   Click on FixedSingle.

Step 4:   Start the application and test the new border style. Notice that you can move the window, but you cannot resize it by its edges or its corners.

Step 5:   Click the Exit button to end the application.

Step 6:   Now you will lock the controls. Place the cursor over an empty spot on the form and right-click. A small menu pops up.

Step 7: Click the lock controls command.

Step 8: Select any control on the form and try to move it. Because the controls are locked, you cannot move them.

Step 9: Save the project.

When you are ready to move the controls, just right-click over an empty spot on the form and select the lock controls command again. This toggles the locked state of the controls.

 TIP: Be careful. Visual C# .NET still allows you to delete a locked control.

Printing Your Code

To print a project's code, open the Code window, then click File on the menu bar, then click the Print command on the File menu.

 # CHECKPOINT

11.13 How do you decide whether you will keep a control's default name or assign it a name?

11.14 Suppose an application has a Label control named `secretLabel`. Write the Visual C# .NET assignment statement that causes the control to be hidden. (*Hint:* Use the Visible property.)

11.15 What happens when you change a Label control's `BackColor` property?

11.16 What happens when you change a Label control's `ForeColor` property?

11.7 Modifying the **Text** Property with Code

> **CONCEPT** Quite often, you will need to change a control's **Text** property with code. This is done with an assignment statement.

While building the directions application, you learned that an assignment statement is used to copy a value into a property while the application is running. Recall that the following statement sets the `directionsLabel` control's `Visible` property to True.

```
directionsLabel.Visible = true;
```

You use the same technique to change the value of a control's **Text** property. For example, assume an application has a Label control named `messageLabel`. The following statement copies the sentence "Programming is fun!" to the control's **Text** property.

```
messageLabel.Text = "Programming is fun!";
```

Once the statement executes, the message displayed by the Message control changes to Pro-gramming is fun!

The quotation marks in the statement are not part of the message. They simply mark the beginning and end of the set of characters that are assigned to the property. In programming terms, a group of characters inside a set of quotation marks is called a string literal.

We usually display messages on a form by setting the value of a Label control's Text property. In the following steps, you open and examine an application on the student disk that demonstrates this technique.

Tutorial 11-23: Examining an application that displays various messages at runtime

Step 1:   Start Visual C# .NET and open the KiloConverter project which is in the \Chapter 11\KiloConverter folder on the Student CD.

Step 2:   Open the Design window, which displays Form1 as shown in Figure 11-66.

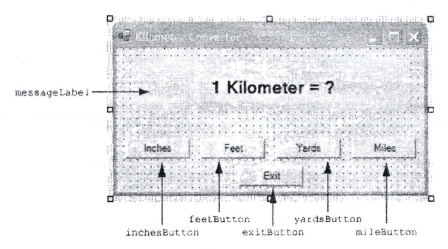

Figure 11-66   Kilometer Converter form

Step 3:   Click the Start button (▶) to run the application.

Step 4:   Once the application is running, click the Inches button. The form displays the number of inches equivalent to a kilometer, as shown in Figure 11-67.

Step 5:   Experiment with the other buttons and observe the messages that are displayed when each is clicked.

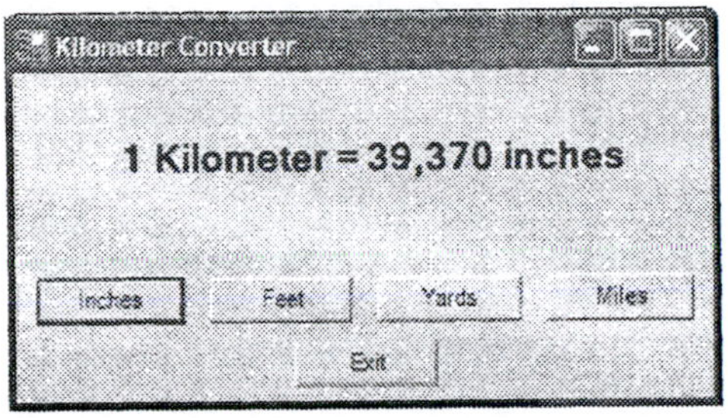

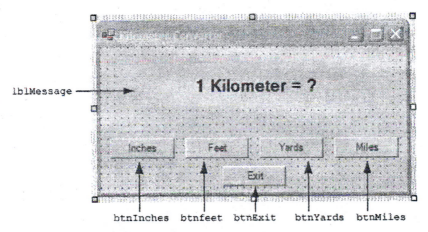

Figure 11-67　Kilometer converted to inches

Step 6:　Click the Exit button to exit the application. Now we will examine the application code. Figure 11-68 shows the KiloConverter application form with its controls labeled.

Figure 11-68　KiloConverter application controls

The buttons Inches, Feet, Yards, and Miles each change the messageLabel Text property when clicked. Use the following step to view the KiloConverter event procedures.

Step 7:　Click the View Code button (▣) in the Solution Explorer window. The Code window appears. The window shows the following event method codes:

```
private void exitButton_Click(object sender, System.EventArgs e)
{
    //End the application
    this.Close();
}
```

```
private void feetButton_Click(object sender, System.EventArgs e)
{
    //End the application
    messageLabel.Text = "1 Kilometer = 3,281 feet";
}

private void inchesButton_Click(object sender, System.EventArgs e)
{
    // Display the conversion to inches.
    messageLabel.Text = "1 Kilometer = 39,370 inches";
}

private void milesButton_Click(object sender, System.EventArgs e)
{
    // Display the conversion to miles.
    messageLabel.Text = "1 Kilometer = 0.6214 miles";

}

private void yardsButton_Click(object sender, System.EventArgs e)
{
    // Display the conversion to yards.
    messageLabel.Text = "1 Kilometer = 1,093.6 yards";

}
```

11.8   Using Visual C# .NET Help

CONCEPT | In this section you learn to use the Visual C# .NET help system.

Dynamic Help

Recall that the Dynamic Help window displays a list of help topics that changes as you perform operations. The topics that are displayed are relevant to the operation you are currently performing.

The Dynamic Help window occupies the same location as the Properties window, as shown in Figure 11-69. Notice the Properties and Dynamic Help tabs at the bottom of the window. You switch between Properties and Dynamic Help by clicking the tabs.

If you do not see the Dynamic Help tab, click Help on the menu bar, then click Dynamic Help.

The Dynamic Help window also has a small toolbar with icons to access the help contents, the help index, and to search the help topics. Tutorial 11-24 guides you through the process of using dynamic help.

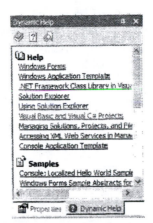

Figure 11-69　Dynamic Help window

Tutorial 11-24: Using dynamic help

Step 1:　Start Visual C# .NET and load the Tutorial 11-2 project. Make sure the Design window is open.

Step 2:　Click the Dynamic Help tab to display the Dynamic Help window. (If you do not see the Dynamic Help tab, click Help on the menu bar, then click Dynamic Help.)

Step 3:　In the Design window, select one of the Label controls on the form. Notice that the contents of the Dynamic Help window has changed. It should look similar to Figure 11-70. The topics that are now displayed are related to Label1 controls.

Figure 11-70　Dynamic Help window with topics related to Label controls

Step 4:   Click the first help topic, which should read Label Members
(System.Windows.Forms). This should cause the help screen shown in
Figure 11-71 to be displayed. This screen provides help on all the properties and
methods of the Label control.

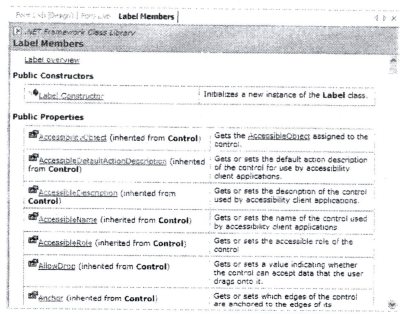

Figure 11-71   Label Members help screen

Step 5:   Click the close button (▨) that appears in the upper right corner of the Label
Members help screen to close it.

Step 6:   Figure 11-72 shows the locations of the contents, index, and search buttons.
When any of these buttons are clicked, another help window that provides additional functionality appears in the same location as the Solution Explorer. The
contents button displays a table of contents in which related topics are organized
into groups. The *index button* displays a searchable alphabetized index of all the
help topics. The *search button* allows you to search for help using key words.

Click the search button.

Step 7:   The search window should appear, as shown in Figure 11-73.

The Filtered by drop-down list allows you to filter the results of a search. Recall from Chapter
1 that Visual Studio .NET contains multiple programming languages. When you perform a
search, it is common to see many unrelated topics. To make sure that you only see topics that are
relevant to Visual C#, select "Visual C# and related" from the drop-down list.

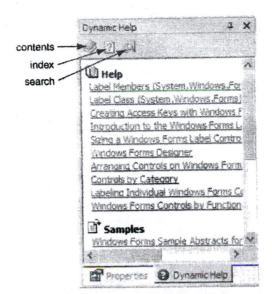

Figure 11-72 The contents, index, and search buttons

contents →
index →
search →

Figure 11-73 Search window

Step 8: In the Look for text box, type FormBorderStyle, then click the Search button. A Search Results window, as shown in Figure 11-74, should appear. Click one of the items displayed in the search results window to see its help screen. When finished, close the Search Results window.

Step 9: The contents and index buttons also display a window in the same location as the Solution Explorer. Experiment with the buttons by locating a help topic using each one.

Step 10: When you are finished, close all the help windows except the Dynamic Help window.

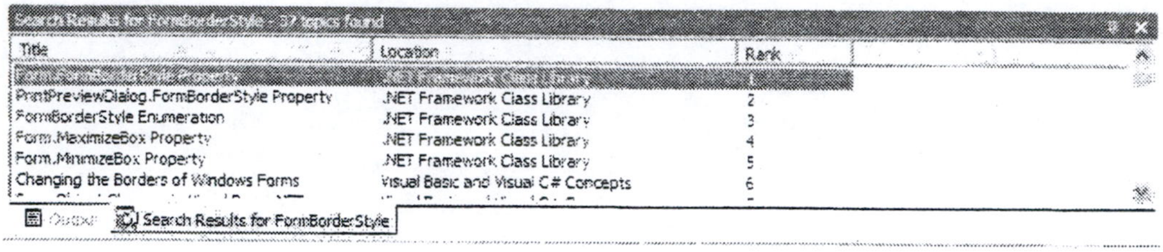

Figure 11-74   Search results

The Help Menu and Context-Sensitive Help

The Visual C# .NET Help menu also provides `Contents`, `Index`, and `Search` commands. Visual C# .NET also provides *context-sensitive help*. Context-sensitive help is displayed when you select an item and then press the F1 key. For example, look at the following line of code from the Tutorial 11-2 project.

```
directionsLabel.Visible = true;
```

If you highlight the word Visible and press the F1 key, a help screen describing the `Visible` property will be displayed.

Review Questions and Exercises

True or False

Indicate whether the following statements are true or false.

1. True or False: Sizing handles appear around the control that is currently selected.
2. True or False: A control is accessed in code by its `Text` property.
3. True or False: The `TextAlign` property causes a control to be aligned with other controls on the same form.
4. True or False: Text is frequently the first property that the programmer changes, so it is listed in parentheses in the Properties window. This causes it to be displayed at the top of the alphabetized list of properties.
5. True or False: Resizing handles are positioned along the edges of a control's bounding box.
6. True or False: A label's text is `MiddleCenter` aligned by default.
7. True or False: You can run an application in the Visual C# .NET environment by pressing the F5 key.
8. True or False: The first line of an event method identifies the control it belongs to, and the event it responds to.
9. True or False: You can bring up the Code window by pressing the F7 key while the Design window is visible.
10. True or False: The `BackColor` property establishes the color of a `Label` control's text.

Short Answer

1. Explain the difference between an object's Text and its Name.
2. List three ways to run an application within the Visual C# .NET environment.
3. List three ways to display the Code window.
4. Why is the code between the first and last lines of an event method usually indented?
5. In this chapter you learned two techniques for placing controls on a form. What are they?

Programming Challenges

1. Welcome Screen Modification

For this exercise, you will modify an application that displays a welcome screen for the First Federal Bank. After starting Visual C# .NET, insert your student disk and load the Challenge 1 project which is in the Chapter 11 folder.

Figure 11-75 shows the application's form.

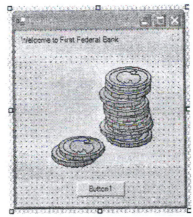

Figure 11-75   First Federal Bank welcome screen, Form1

Make the following modifications to the application:

a) Change the form's title bar text to read First Federal Bank.
b) Change the label's Font property to Microsoft Sans Serif, bold, 14 point.
c) Change the label's text alignment to middle center.
d) Change the button's name to Exit.
e) Change the button's text to read Exit.
f) Change the label's background color to a shade of red, or another color of your choice.
g) Change the form's background color to the same color you chose for the label.
h) Write a Click event method for the button that terminates the application.

2. Math Tutor Application

You are to create a math tutor application. The application should display a simple math problem in a Label control. The form should have a button that displays the answer to the math problem in a second label, when clicked. It should also have a button that closes the application. Figure 11-76 shows an example of the application's form before the button is clicked to display the answer.

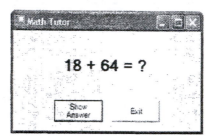

Figure 11-76   Math Tutor application

Figure 11-77 shows the form after the Show Answer button has been clicked.

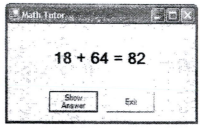

Figure 11-77   Math Tutor application after Show Answer button has been clicked

Here are the detailed property specifications:

a) The button that displays the answer should be named `displayButton`. Its text should read Show Answer.

b) The button that closes the application should be named `exitButton`. Its text should read Exit.

c) The label that displays the answer to the math problem should be named `answerLabel`.

d) The form's title bar should read Math Tutor.

12

Windows Applications—Part II

Topics in this Chapter

12.1 Gathering Text Input

12.2 Group Boxes and Form Formatting

12.3 Focus on GUI Design: The Message Box

12.4 Focus on GUI Design: Radio Buttons and Check Boxes

12.5 Input Boxes and List Boxes

12.6 Checked List Boxes and Combo Boxes

Review Questions and Exercises

12.1 Gathering Text Input

CONCEPT The TextBox control is used to gather input that the user has typed on the keyboard.

Most programs ask the user to enter values. For example, a program that calculates payroll for a small business might ask the user to enter the name of the employee, the hours worked, and the hourly pay rate. The program then uses this information to print the employee's paycheck. Tutorial 12-1 examines an application that uses a TextBox control.

Tutorial 12-1: Using a TextBox control

Step 1: Insert your Student CD. Start Visual C# .NET and open the Greetings project, which is stored in the Chapter 12\Greetings folder on the student disk.

Step 2: Click the start button ( ) to run the application. The application's form appears, as shown in Figure 12-1. The TextBox control is the white rectangular area beneath the label that reads Enter Your Name.

Notice that the TextBox control shows a blinking text cursor, indicating it is ready to receive keyboard input.

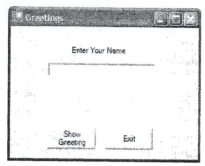

Figure 12-1   Greetings project initial form

Step 3:   Type your name. Notice that, as you enter characters on the keyboard, they appear in the TextBox control.

Step 4:   Click the Show Greeting button. The message "Hello" followed by the name you entered appears in a label below the TextBox control. The form now appears similar to that shown in Figure 12-2.

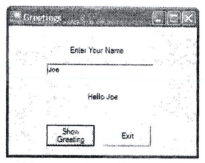

Figure 12-2   Greetings project completed form

Step 5:   Click inside the TextBox control and use the delete or backspace key to erase the name you entered. Enter another name, then click the Show Greeting button. Notice that the greeting message changes accordingly.

Step 6:   Click the Exit button to exit the application. You are now in design time in Visual C# .NET.

Step 7:   Look at the application's form in the Design window. Figure 12-3 depicts the form with its controls.

Like the Label control, the TextBox control has a Text property. However, the Label control's Text property is only for displaying information the user cannot directly alter its contents. The

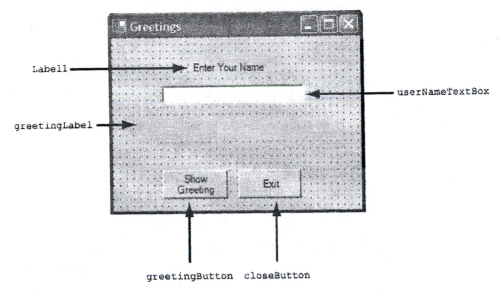

Figure 12-3 Greetings project form with controls labeled

TextBox control's Text property is for input purposes. The user can alter it by typing characters into the TextBox control. Whatever the user types into the TextBox control is stored, as a string, in its Text property.

Using the Text Property in Code

You access a TextBox control's Text property in code in the same way you access other properties. For example, assume an application has a Label control named `Info`, and a TextBox control named `Input`. The following assignment statement copies the contents of the TextBox control's Text property into the Label control's Text property.

```
Info.Text = Input.Text;
```

Clear a Text Box

Recall from the discussion on object-oriented programming in Chapter 1 that an object contains methods, which are actions that the object performs. To execute an object's method, you write a statement that calls the method. The general format of such as statement is

```
Object.Method();
```

Object is the name of the object and *Method* is the name of the method that is being called.

A TextBox control is an object; it has a variety of methods that perform operations on the text box or its contents. One of these methods is `Clear`, which clears the contents of the text box's Text property. The general format of the `Clear` method is

```
TextBox.Clear();
```

TextBox is the name of the TextBox control. Here is an example:

```
Input.Clear();
```

Once this statement executes, the Text property of Input will be cleared and the text box will appear empty on the screen.

You may also clear a text box by assigning an empty string to its Text property. An empty string is a set of double quotation marks with no space between them. Here is an example:

```
Input.Text = "";
```

Once this statement executes, the Text property of Input will be cleared and the text box will appear empty on the screen.

Now it's your turn to create an application using TextBox controls and string concatenation. Tutorial 12-2 leads you through the process.

Tutorial 12-2: Building the Date String application

In this exercise, you create an application that lets the user enter the following information about today's date:

- The day of the week
- The name of the month
- The numeric day of the month
- The year

Once the user enters the information and clicks a button, the application displays a date string such as Friday, December 6, 2004.

Step 1: Start Visual C# .NET and start a new windows application named Date String.

Step 2: Create the form shown in Figure 12-4, using the following instructions:

- Give each control the name indicated in Figure 12-4. The labels that display "Enter the day of the week:", "Enter the month:", "Enter the day of the month:", and "Enter the year:" will not be referred to in code, so they may keep their default names.
- Set the `DateString` label's BorderStyle property to Fixed3D and its TextAlign property to MiddleCenter.
- Set the form's Text to "Date String".
- Insert a TextBox control by double-clicking the TextBox tool in the toolbox.
- When you insert the TextBox controls, notice that they initially display their default names. For example, the first TextBox control you create will have the default name `TextBox1`. The control will appear similar to this:

As you place the TextBox controls on your form, delete the contents of their Text properties. This will cause their contents to appear empty when the application runs, as shown in Figure 12.4.

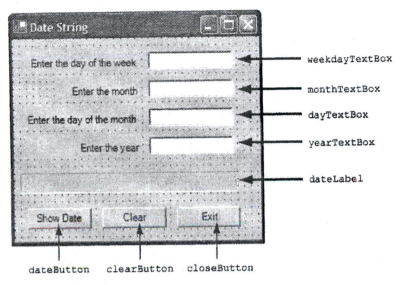

Figure 12-4 Date String form

Step 3:   The code for the ShowDate button's Click event procedure is as follows. Double-click the button to create the code template, and then enter the lines shown in bold.

```
private void dateButton_Click(object sender, System.EventArgs e)
{
    //Concatenate the input and build the date string
    dateLabel.Text = weekdayTextBox.Text + , +
                        monthTextBox.Text +   +
                        dayTextBox.Text + , +
                        yearTextBox.Text;
}
```

TIP: You can reduce the font size used in the code window by clicking Tools on the menu bar, and then clicking the Options... command. On the Options dialog box, click Environment in the left pane, and then click Fonts and Colors. You may then select the desired font and size.

Step 4:   The Clear button allows the user to start over with a form that is empty of previous values. The clearButton_Click event procedure will clear the contents of all the TextBox controls, and the DateString label. To accomplish this, the procedure calls each TextBox control's Clear method and copies an empty string to DateString's Text property. Enter the following code into the clearButton_Click event procedure:

```
private void clearButton_Click(object sender, System.EventArgs e)
{
    // Clear the Text Boxes and dateLabel
    weekdayTextBox.Clear();
    monthTextBox.Clear();
    dayTextBox.Clear();
    yearTextBox.Text.Clear();
    dateLabel.Text = ;
}
```

Step 5: Enter the following code, which terminates the application, into the exitButton_Click event procedure:

```
private void exitButton_Click(object sender, System.EventArgs e)
{
    //Close the application
    this.Close();
}
```

Step 6: Save the project.

Step 7: Click the start button (▶) to run the application. With the application running, enter the requested information into the TextBox controls and click the Show Date button. Your form should appear similar to Figure 12-5.

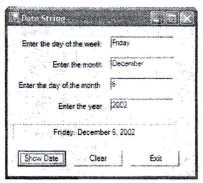

Figure 12-5 Date String form completed

Step 8: Click the Clear button to test it, then enter new values into the TextBox controls. Click the Show Date button.

Step 9: Click the Exit button to exit the application.

The Focus Method

When an application is running and a form is displayed, one of the form's controls always has the *focus*. The control that has the focus is the one that receives the user's keyboard input or mouse clicks. For example, when a TextBox control has the focus, it receives the characters that the user enters on the keyboard. When a button has the focus, pressing the Enter key executes the button's Click event procedure.

You can tell which control has the focus by looking at the form at runtime. When a TextBox control has the focus, a blinking text cursor appears inside it, or the text inside the TextBox control appears highlighted. When a button, radio button, or check box has the focus, a thin dotted line appears around the control.

 NOTE: Only controls that are capable of receiving some sort of input, such as text boxes and buttons, may have the focus.

Quite often, you want to make sure a particular control has the focus. Consider the Date String application, for example. When the Clear button is clicked, the focus should return to the weekdayTextBox TextBox control. This would make it unnecessary for the user to click the Text-Box control in order to start entering another set of information.

In code, you move the focus to a control with the *Focus* method. The method's general syntax is

```
Control.Focus();
```

where *Control* is the name of the control. For instance, you move the focus to the weekdayText-Box TextBox control with the statement weekdayTextBox.Focus();. After the statement executes, the weekdayTextBox control will have the focus. In the following tutorial, you add this statement to the Clear button's Click event procedure so weekdayTextBox has the focus after the TextBox controls and the DateString label are cleared.

Tutorial 12-3: Using the Focus method

Step 1: Open the Date String project in Visual C# .NET.

Step 2: Open the Code window and add the following boldface statements to the clearButton_Click event procedure.

```
private void clearButton_Click(object sender, System.EventArgs e)
{
    // Clear the Text Boxes and dateLabel
    weekdayTextBox.Clear();
    monthTextBox.Clear();
    dayTextBox.Clear();
    yearTextBox.Clear();
    dateLabel.Text = ;
    // Return the focus to weekdayTextBox
    weekdayTextBox.Focus();
}
```

Step 3: Run the application. Enter some information into the TextBox controls, then click the Clear button. The focus should return to the weekdayTextBox TextBox control.

Step 4: Save the project.

Controlling a Form's Tab Order with the TabIndex Property

In a Windows application, pressing the Tab key changes the focus from one control to another. The order in which controls receive the focus is called the *tab order*. When you place controls on a form in Visual C# .NET, the tab order will be the same sequence in which you created the controls. Usually this is the tab order you want, but sometimes you rearrange controls on a form, delete controls, and add new ones. These modifications often lead to a disorganized tab order, which can confuse and irritate the users of your application. Users want to tab smoothly from one control to the next, in a logical sequence.

You can modify the tab order by changing a control's TabIndex property. The *TabIndex property* contains a numeric value, which indicates the control's position in the tab order. When you create a control, Visual C# .NET automatically assigns a value to its TabIndex property. The first control you create on a form will have a TabIndex of 0, the second will have a TabIndex of 1, and so forth. The control with a TabIndex of 0 will be the first control in the tab order. The next control in the tab order will be the one with the TabIndex of 1. The tab order continues in this sequence.

You may change the tab order of a form's controls by selecting them one by one, and changing their TabIndex property in the Properties window. An easier method, however, is to click View on the menu bar, then click Tab Order. This causes the form to be displayed in *tab order selection mode*. In this mode, each control's existing TabIndex value is displayed on the form. You then establish a new tab order by clicking the controls in the order you want. When finished, you exit tab order selection mode by clicking View, then Tab Order.

Tutorial 12-4: Changing the tab order

In this tutorial, you rearrange the controls in the Date String application, and then change the tab order to accommodate the controls' new positions.

Step 1: Open the Date String project in Visual C# .NET.

Step 2: Open the application's form in the Design window. Rearrange the controls to match Figure 12-6. (You might want to temporarily enlarge the form so you have room to move some of the controls around. Don't forget to move the labels that correspond with the TextBox controls.)

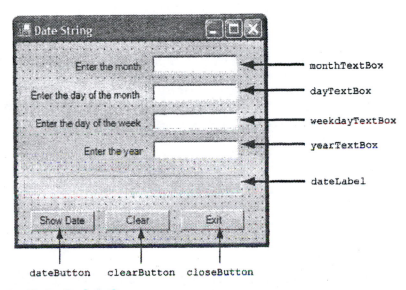

Figure 12-6   Date String form

Step 3: Run the application. Notice which control has the focus. Press the Tab key several times and observe the tab order.

Step 4: Stop the application and go back to design time.

Step 5: Click View on the menu bar, then click Tab Order. The form should now be displayed in tab order selection mode, as shown in Figure 12-7. The numbers displayed in the upper left corner of each control are the existing TabIndex values.

 NOTE: Your existing TabIndex values may be different from those shown in Figure 12-7.

Step 6: Click the following controls in the order they are listed: `monthTextBox`, `dayText-Box`, `weekdayTextBox`, `yearTextBox`, `dateLabel`, `clearButton`, `exitButton`.

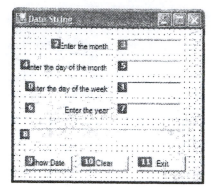

Figure 12-7 Form in tab order selection mode

Step 7:   The controls you clicked should now have the following TabIndex values displayed:

```
monthTextBox: 0
dayTextBox: 1
weekdayTextBox: 2
yearTextBox: 3
dateLabel: 4
clearButton: 5
exitButton: 6
```

 NOTE: The Label controls cannot receive the focus, so do not be concerned with the TabIndex values displayed for them.

Step 8:   You are now ready to exit tab order selection mode. Click View on the menu bar, then click Tab Order.

Step 9:   Don't forget to change the `clearButton_Click` event procedure so that `Month` gets the focus when the form is cleared. The code for the procedure is as follows, with the modified lines in boldface.

```
private void clearButton_Click(object sender, System.EventArgs e)
{
    // Clear the Text Boxes and dateLabel
    weekdayTextBox.Clear();
    monthTextBox.Clear();
    dayTextBox.Clear();
    yearTextBox.Clear();
    dateLabel.Text = ;
    // Return the focus to monthTextBox
    monthTextBox.Focus();
}
```

Step 10: Run the application and test the new tab order.

Step 11: End the application and save the project.

Here are a few last notes about the TabIndex property:

- If you do not want a control to receive the focus when the user presses the Tab key, set its *TabStop property* to False.

- An error will occur if you assign a negative value to the TabIndex property in code.

- A control whose Visible property is set to False, or whose Enabled property is set to False, cannot receive the focus.

- GroupBox and Label controls have a TabIndex property, but they are skipped in the tab order.

Assigning Keyboard Access Keys to Buttons

An *access key*, also known as a *mnemonic*, is a key that you press in combination with the Alt key to access a control such as a button quickly. When you assign an access key to a button, the user can trigger a Click event either by clicking the button with the mouse or by using the access key. Users who are quick with the keyboard prefer to use access keys instead the mouse.

You assign an access key to a button through its Text property. For example, assume an application has a button whose Text property is set to "Exit." You wish to assign the access key Alt+X to the button, so the user may trigger the button's Click event by pressing Alt+X on the keyboard. To make the assignment, place an ampersand (&) before the letter x in the button's Text property: E&xit. Figure 12-8 shows how the Text property appears in the Property window.

Figure 12-8 Text property E&xit

Even though the ampersand is part of the button's Text property, it is not displayed on the button. With the ampersand in front of the letter x, the button will appear as shown in Figure 12-9. Notice that the ampersand is not displayed on the button, but the letter x is underlined. This indicates that the button may be clicked by pressing Alt+X on the keyboard.

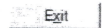

Figure 12-9 Button with E&xit text

 NOTE: Access keys do not distinguish between upper- and lowercase. There is no difference between Alt+X and Alt+x.

Suppose we had stored the value &Exit in the button's Text property. The ampersand is in front of the letter E, so Alt+E becomes the access key. The button will appear as shown in Figure 12-10.

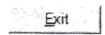

Figure 12-10 Button with &Exit text

Assigning the Same Access Key to Multiple Buttons

Be careful not to assign the same access key to two or more buttons on the same form. If two or more buttons share the same access key, when the user presses the access key Visual C# .NET will trigger a Click event for the button that was created first.

Displaying the & Character on a Button

If you want to display an ampersand character on a button use two ampersands (&&) in the Text property, where you want one ampersand to appear. Using two ampersands causes a single ampersand to display and does not define an access key. For example, if a button has the Text property Beans && Cream the button will appear as shown in Figure 12-11.

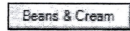

Figure 12-11 Button with text Beans && Cream

GUI Design and User Convenience: Using Access Keys with Labels

Visual C# .NET supports a clever programming technique that allows you to indirectly assign an access key to a TextBox control. Because the TextBox control's Text property is used to hold the user's input, you cannot use this property to assign an access key. You can, however, use a label to indirectly assign an access key a TextBox control.

Although labels cannot receive the focus, they have the following characteristics:

- They have a TabIndex property.
- You can assign them access keys through their Text properties.
- They have a UseMnemonic property that may be set to True or False.

When a label's *UseMnemonic property* is set to True, which is the default value, you may assign an access key to the label by preceding a character in its Text property with an ampersand. When the user uses the label's access key, the focus is set to the control that immediately follows the label in the tab order. (If the UseMnemonic property is set to False, the ampersand is displayed as part of the label's text and no access key is defined.) Follow the steps in the next exercise to apply this technique to the Date String application.

Tutorial 12-5: Assigning Access Keys to Labels

In this tutorial you assign access keys to the labels that appear on the Date String application's form.

Step 1: Open the Date string project in Visual C# .NET.

Step 2: Change the values of the TabIndex properties of the form's controls to match the values shown in Figure 12-12.

Figure 12-12   Date String TabIndex properties

Step 3: Notice that each of the labels in Figure 12-12 is assigned an access key, as indicated by the underlined character. Change the Text properties of the labels, so each label is assigned the correct access key. Confirm that each label's UseMnemonic property is set to true.

Step 4: Run the application.

Step 5: Press Alt+Y. The yearTextBox control receives the focus.

Step 6: Press Alt+D. The dayTextBox control receives the focus.

Step 7: Experiment with the other access keys.

Step 8: Exit the application.

Accept Buttons and Cancel Buttons

An *accept button* is a button on a form that is clicked when the user presses the Enter key. A *cancel button* is a button on a form that is clicked when the user presses the Escape key. Forms have two properties, AcceptButton and CancelButton, that allow to designate an accept button and a cancel button. When you select these properties in the Properties window, a down-arrow button appears that allows you to display a drop-down list. The list contains the names of all the buttons on the form. You select the button that you want to designate as the accept button or the cancel button.

Any button that is frequently clicked should probably be selected as the accept button. This will allow keyboard users to access the button quickly and easily. Exit or cancel buttons are likely candidates to become cancel buttons.

Tutorial 12-6: Setting access keys, accept buttons, and cancel buttons

In this tutorial, you assign access keys to the buttons in the Date String application, and set accept and cancel buttons:

Step 1: Open the Date String project in Visual C# .NET.

Step 2: Open the application's form in the Design window.

Step 3: Select the Show Date button (`dateButton`) and change its Text to read `Show &Date`. This assigns Alt+D as the button's access key.

Step 4: Select the Clear button (`clearButton`) and change its Text to read `Clea&r`. This assigns Alt+R as the button's access key.

Step 5: Select the Exit button (`exitButton`) and change its Text to read `E&xit`. This assigns Alt+X as the button's access key.

Step 6: Select the form, and then select the AcceptButton property in the Properties window. Click the down-arrow button to display the drop-down list of buttons. Select `dateButton` from the list.

Step 7: With the form still selected, select the CancelButton property in the Properties window. Click the down-arrow button to display the drop-down list of buttons. Select `exitButton` from the list.

Step 8: Run the application and test the buttons' new settings. Notice that anytime you press the Enter key, the Show Date String button's `Click` procedure is executed, and any time you press the Escape key, the application exits.

 NOTE: The access keys you assigned to the buttons will not be displayed as underlined characters until you press the Alt key.

Step 9: Save the solution.

CHECKPOINT

12.1 What TextBox control property holds text entered by the user?

12.2 Assume an application has a label named `Message`, and a TextBox control named `input-TextBox`. Write the statement that copies the text that the user entered into the TextBox control, into the label's Text property.

12.3 If the following statement is executed, what will the `greetingLabel` control display?

```
greetingLabel.Text = "Hello " + "Jonathon, " + "how are you?";
```

12.2 Group Boxes and Form Formatting

CONCEPT The GroupBox control is used to group other controls. Form formatting involves aligning and centering controls on a form.

Group Boxes

A *group box* is a rectangular border with an optional title that appears in the upper left corner. Other controls may be placed inside a group box. You can give forms a more organized look by grouping related controls together inside group boxes.

In Visual C# .NET you use the *GroupBox control* to create a group box with an optional title. The title is stored in the GroupBox control's Text property. Figure 12-13 shows a GroupBox control. The control's Text property is set to "Personal Data" and a group of other controls are inside the group box.

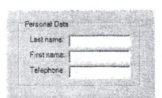

Figure 12-13 GroupBox containing other controls

Creating a Group Box and Adding Controls to It

To create a group box you select the GroupBox tool from the toolbox and then draw the group box at the desired size on the form. When you create a group box to hold other controls, you must create the GroupBox control first, then follow one of these procedures to place a control inside the GroupBox:

- Select the existing GroupBox control, then double-click the desired tool in the toolbox to place another control inside the GroupBox.

- Select the existing GroupBox control, then click the desired tool in the toolbox and draw the control inside the GroupBox.

Note that with either procedure, the existing GroupBox control must be selected before you create the control that is to be placed inside the GroupBox control. The controls inside a group box become part of a group. When you move a group box, the objects inside it move as well. When you delete a group box, the objects that belong to it are also deleted.

Moving an Existing Control to a Group Box

If an existing control is not inside a group box, but you want to move it to the group box, follow this procedure:

1. Select the control you wish to add to the group box.
2. Cut the control to the clipboard.
3. Select the group box.
4. Paste the control.

Group Box Tab Order

The value of a control's TabIndex property is handled differently when the control is placed inside a GroupBox control. GroupBox controls have their own TabIndex property, and the TabIndex value of the controls inside the GroupBox are relative to the GroupBox control's TabIndex property. For example, Figure 12-14 shows a GroupBox control displayed in tab order selection mode. As you can see, the GroupBox control's TabIndex is set to 2. The TabIndex of the controls inside the group box are displayed as 2.0, 2.1, 2.2, and so forth.

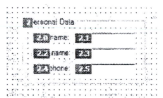

Figure 12-14   Group box TabIndex values

 NOTE: The TabIndex properties of the controls inside the group box will not appear this way in the Properties window. They will appear as 0, 1, 2, and so forth.

Assigning an Access Key to a GroupBox Control

Although GroupBox controls cannot receive the focus, you can assign a keyboard access key to them by preceding a character in their Text property with an ampersand (&). When the user enters the access key, the focus moves to the control with the lowest TabIndex value inside the group box.

Form Formatting

Visual C# .NET provides numerous tools for aligning, centering, and sizing controls on a form. In this section we discuss the form grid and the Format menu commands.

The Form Grid

You have probably noticed that forms in the Design window are displayed with a grid of dots, as shown in Figure 12-15. The grid is a useful tool for aligning and sizing controls, and is only displayed at design time.

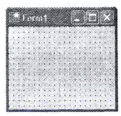

Figure 12-15   Form grid dots

By default, the grid dots are positioned with eight pixels between them. You can change this and other grid settings by clicking Tools on the menu bar, then clicking the Options... command. The Options dialog box should appear. Click Windows Forms Designer in the left pane. The Options dialog box should appear as shown in Figure 12-16.

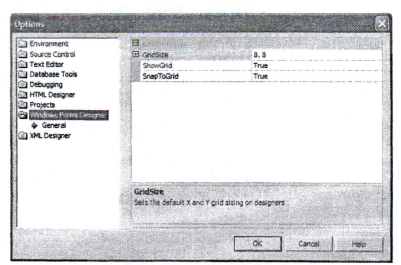

Figure 12-16   Options dialog box showing grid settings

The GridSize option controls the default width and height of the space between the grid dots. When the ShowGrid option is set to `True` (the default setting), the grid is displayed. The grid is hidden when ShowGrid is set to `False`. When the SnapToGrid option is set to `True` (the default setting) controls can only be positioned along the grid dots. In addition, the sizing of controls is constrained to the grid dots. When SnapToGrid is set to `False`, controls may be placed at any position and drawn to any size. In most cases, it is best to leave SnapToGrid set to `True`.

These Option dialog box values only establish the Visual C# .NET default grid settings. Each form has properties that may override these settings. The properties are GridSize, DrawGrid, and SnapToGrid. For example, setting a form's DrawGrid property to `False` will hide the grid on that form, no matter how the ShowGrid option is set in the Options dialog box.

Selecting and Moving Multiple Controls

It is possible to select multiple controls and work with them all at once. For example, you can select a group of controls and move them all to a different location on the form. You can also select a group of controls and change some of their properties all at once.

You select multiple controls by using one of the following techniques:

- Position the cursor over an empty part of the form that is near the controls you wish to select. Click and drag a selection box around the controls. This is illustrated in Figure 12-17. When you release the mouse button, all the controls that were partially or completely enclosed in the selection box will be selected.

- Hold the Ctrl key down while clicking each control you wish to select.

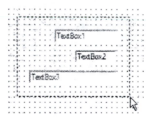

Figure 12-17 Click-and-drag selection of multiple controls

After using either of these techniques, all the controls you have selected will appear with sizing handles. You may now move them, delete them, or use the Properties window to set many of their properties to the same value.

 TIP: It's easy to deselect a control that you have accidentally selected. Simply hold down the Ctrl key and click the control you wish to deselect.

The Format Menu

The Format menu, shown in Figure 12-18, provides several submenus for aligning, centering, and sizing controls.

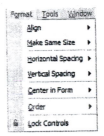

Figure 12-18   The Format menu

The Align Submenu

The Align SubMenu contains the following vertical alignment commands:

- Lefts—Aligns the selected controls vertically by their left edges
- Centers—Aligns the selected controls vertically by their center points
- Rights—Aligns the selected controls vertically by their right edges

Figure 12-19 shows a group of TextBox controls aligned by their lefts, centers, and rights.

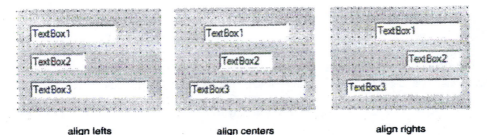

align lefts   align centers   align rights

Figure 12-19   Left, center, and right alignment

The Align submenu also contains the following horizontal alignment commands:

- Tops—Aligns the selected controls horizontally by their top edges
- Middles—Aligns the selected controls horizontally by their middle points
- Bottoms—Aligns the selected controls horizontally by their bottom edges

Figure 12-20 shows a group of differently sized buttons aligned by their tops, middles, and bottoms.

The Align submenu also provides the To Grid command. This command aligns the selected controls to the grid points. This is useful if you have drawn controls with the SnapToGrid option set to False and wish to align them to the grid.

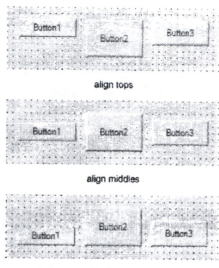

align tops

align middles

align bottoms

Figure 12-20   Top, middle, and bottom alignment

The Make Same Size Submenu

The Make Same Size submenu provides commands for making a group of selected controls the same size. The commands are Width (makes all selected controls the same width), Size to Grid (adjusts the size of the selected controls to the grid points), Height (makes all selected controls the same height), and Both (makes both the width and height of all selected controls the same).

 NOTE: The form's SnapToGrid property must be set to True for the Size To Grid command to work.

The Horizontal and Vertical Spacing Submenus

These submenus provide commands to control the horizontal and vertical space between selected commands. Both submenus contain the following commands: Make Equal, Increase, Decrease, and Remove.

The Center in Form Submenu

This submenu provides the following useful commands: Horizontally (horizontally centers the selected controls on the form) and Vertically (vertically centers the selected controls on the form).

The Order Submenu

It is possible to place controls on top of each other on a form. The control on top is said to be at the front, while the control on the bottom is said to be at the back. This submenu provides the following commands for rearranging the order of controls that are placed on top of each other:

Bring to Front (moves the selected control to the top) and Send to Back (moves the selected control to the bottom).

The Load Event Procedure

Every form has a *Load event procedure*, which is executed each time the form loads into memory. If you need to execute code automatically when a form is displayed, you can place the code in the form's Load event procedure. For example, in the next section you will develop an application that displays the current date and time on the application's form. You will accomplish this by writing code in the form's Load event procedure that retrieves the date and time from the system.

To write code in a form's Load event procedure, double-click any area of the form where there is no other control. The code window will appear with a code template similar to the following.

```
private void Form1_Load(object sender, System.EventArgs e)
{

}
```

Between the first and last lines of the template, simply write the statements you wish the procedure to execute.

CHECKPOINT

12.4 How is a group box helpful when you are designing a form with a large number of controls?

12.3 Focus on GUI Design: The Message Box

CONCEPT The MessageBox.Show method allows you to display a message in a dialog box.

A *message box* is a dialog box that displays a message to the user. You display message boxes with the *MessageBox.Show method*. We will discuss five general formats of the method:

```
MessageBox.Show(Message);
MessageBox.Show(Message, Caption);
MessageBox.Show(Message, Caption, Buttons);
MessageBox.Show(Message, Caption, Buttons, Icon);
```

When MessageBox.Show is executed, a message box (which is a Windows dialog box) appears on the screen. In the first format shown, *Message* is a string that is displayed in the message box. For example, the following statement causes the message box shown in Figure 12-21 to appear.

```
MessageBox.Show("Operation complete.");
```

Figure 12-21 Message box

In the second format, *Caption* is a string to be displayed in the message box's title bar. The following statement causes the message box shown in Figure 12-22 to appear.

```
MessageBox.Show("Operation complete.", "Status");
```

Figure 12-22 Message box with caption

In both of these formats, the message box has only an OK button. In the third format, *Buttons* is a value that specifies which buttons to display in the message box. Table 12-1 lists the available values for *Buttons* and describes each.

Table 12-1 Message box button values

Value	Description
MessageBoxButtons.AbortRetryIgnore	Displays Abort, Retry, and Ignore buttons.
MessageBoxButtons.OK	Displays only an OK button.
MessageBoxButtons.OKCancel	Displays OK and Cancel buttons.
MessageBoxButtons.RetryCancel	Display Retry and Cancel buttons.
MessageBoxButtons.YesNo	Displays Yes and No buttons.
MessageBoxButtons.YesNoCancel	Displays Yes, No, and Cancel buttons.

For example, the following statement causes the message box shown in Figure 12-23 to appear.

```
MessageBox.Show(Do you wish to continue?, Please Confirm,
                MessageBoxButtons.YesNo);
```

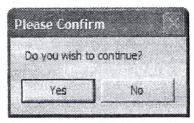

Figure 12-23 Message box with caption and Yes/No buttons

In the fourth format, *Icon* is a value that specifies an icon to display in the message box. The available values for *Icon* are MessageBoxIcon.Asterisk, MessageBoxIcon.Error, MessageBoxIcon.Exclamation, MessageBoxIcon.Hand, MessageBoxIcon.Information, MessageBoxIcon.Question, MessageBoxIcon.Stop, and MessageBoxIcon.Warning. Figure 12-24 shows the icons that are displayed for each value. Note that some values display the same icon as others.

Figure 12-24 Message box icons

For example, the following statement causes the message box shown in Figure 12-25 to appear.

```
MessageBox.Show(Do you wish to continue?, Please Confirm,
        MessageBoxButtons.YesNo , MessageBoxIcon.Question);
```

In one other format the *DefaultButton* argument is a value that specifies which button to select as the default button. The default button is the button that is clicked when the user presses the Enter key. Table 12-2 lists the available values for this argument.

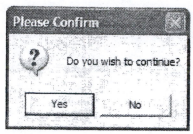

Figure 12-25   Message box with caption, Yes/No buttons, and Question icon

Table 12-2 *DefaultButton* **values**

Value	Description
MessageBoxDefaultButton.Button1	Selects the leftmost button on the message box as the default button.
MessageBoxDefaultButton.Button2	Selects the second button from the left edge of the message box as the default button.
MessageBoxDefaultButton.Button3	Selects the third button from the left edge of the message box as the default button.

For example, the following statement displays a message box and selects button 2 (the No button) as the default button.

```
MessageBox.Show(Do you wish to continue?, Please Confirm, _
            MessageBoxButtons.YesNo , MessageBoxIcon.Question, _
            MessageBoxDefaultButton.Button2)
```

Determining Which Button the User Clicked

When the user clicks any button on a message box, the message box is dismissed. In code, the `MessageBox.Show` method returns an integer value that indicates which button the user clicked. You can compare the integer returned from the method with the values listed in Table 12-3 to determine which button was clicked.

The following code shows how an `if` statement may be used to take actions based on which message box button the user clicked.

```
int result;
result = MessageBox.Show(Do you wish to continue?, Please Confirm,
                MessageBoxButtons.YesNo);
if (result == DialogResult.Yes)
    //Perform an action here
else if (result == DialogResult.No)
    //Perform another action here
```

Table 12-3 `MessageBox.Show` **return values**

Value	Meaning
`DialogResult.Abort`	The user clicked the Abort button.
`DialogResult.Cancel`	The user clicked the Cancel button.
`DialogResult.Ignore`	The user clicked the Ignore button.
`DialogResult.No`	The user clicked the No button.
`DialogResult.OK`	The user clicked the OK button.
`DialogResult.Retry`	The user clicked the retry button.
`DialogResult.Yes`	The user clicked the Yes button.

 CHECKPOINT

12.5 Match each of the message boxes in Figure 12-26 with the statement that displays it.

a.

b.

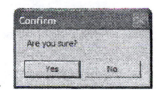
c.

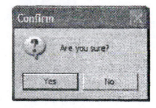
d.

Figure 12-26   Message boxes

```
_____ MessageBox.Show(Are you sure?, Confirm,
            MessageBoxButtons.YesNo);
_____ MessageBox.Show(Are you sure?);
_____ MessageBox.Show(Are you sure?, Confirm,
            MessageBoxButtons.YesNo,
            MessageBoxIcon.Question);
_____ MessageBox.Show(Are you sure?, Confirm);
```

12.6 What value can you compare with the `MessageBox.Show` method's return value to determine if the user has clicked the Abort button?

12.4   Focus on GUI Design: Radio Buttons and Check Boxes

> **CONCEPT** Radio buttons appear in groups of two or more and allow the user to select one of several possible options. Check boxes, which may appear alone or in groups, allow the user to make yes/no or on/off selections.

Radio Buttons

Radio buttons are useful when you want the user to select one choice from several possible choices. Figure 12-27 shows a group of radio buttons.

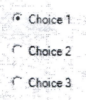

Figure 12-27   Radio buttons

A radio button may be selected or deselected. Each radio button has a small circle that appears filled in when the radio button is selected and empty when the radio button is deselected.

Visual C# .NET provides the *RadioButton control*, which allows you to create radio buttons. Radio buttons are normally part of a group, and are grouped together in one of the following ways.

- All the radio buttons that are inside a group box are members of the same group.
- All the radio buttons on a form that are not inside a group box are members of the same group.

Figure 12-28 shows two forms. The left form has three radio buttons that are part of the same group. The right form has two groups of radio buttons.

Only one radio button in a group may be selected at any time. Clicking on a radio button selects it and automatically deselects any other radio button in the same group. Because only one radio button in a group can be selected at any given time, they are said to be mutually exclusive.

NOTE: The name "radio button" refers to the old car radios that had push buttons for selecting stations. Only one of the buttons could be pushed in at a time. When you pushed a button in, it automatically popped out the currently selected button.

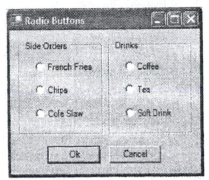

Figure 12-28   Forms with radio buttons

Radio Button Properties

Like labels and text boxes, radio buttons have a Text property. The Text property holds the text that is displayed next to the radio button's circle. For example, the radio buttons in the leftmost form in Figure 12-28 have their Text properties set to "Coffee", "Tea", and "Soft Drink".

Radio buttons also have a boolean property named Checked. The *Checked property* is set to true when the radio button is selected and false when the radio button is deselected.

Working with Radio Buttons in Code

You can determine whether a radio button is selected by testing its Checked property. The following code shows an example. Assume that choice1RadioButton, choice2RadioButton, and choice3RadioButton are radio buttons in the same group.

```
if (choice1RadioButton.Checked == true)
    MessageBox.Show("You selected Choice 1");
else if (choice2RadioButton.Checked == true)
    MessageBox.Show("You selected Choice 2");
else if (choice3RadioButton.Checked == true)
    MessageBox.Show("You selected Choice 3");
```

Assigning a TabIndex Value and an Access Key to a Radio Button

RadioButton controls have a position in the form's tab order which may be changed with the TabIndex property. As with other controls, you may assign an access key to a radio button by placing an ampersand (&) in the Text property, just before the character that you wish to serve as the access key. The character will appear underlined on the form. At runtime, when the user presses the Alt+Access key combination, the focus will shift to the radio button, and the radio button will be selected.

Selecting a Radio Button in Code

You can use code to select a radio button. Simply use an assignment statement to set the desired radio button's Checked property to true. Here is an example:

```
choice1RadioButton.Checked = true;
```

Setting a Default Radio Button

If you set a radio button's Checked property to true at design time (with the Properties window), it will become the default radio button for that group. It will be selected when the application starts up and will remain selected until the user or application code selects another radio button.

The Radio Button's CheckChanged Event

Radio buttons have a *CheckChanged* event that is triggered whenever the user selects or deselects a radio button. If you double-click a radio button in the Design window, a code template for the CheckChanged event procedure will be created in the Code window. If you have written a CheckChanged event procedure for the radio button, it will execute whenever the user selects or deselects the radio button.

Check Boxes

A *check box* appears as a small box, labeled with a caption. An example is shown in Figure 12-29.

┌ Choice 4

Figure 12-29   Check box

Visual C# provides the *CheckBox control* which allows you to create check boxes. Like radio buttons, check boxes may be selected or deselected at runtime. When a check box is selected, a small check mark appears inside the box. Unlike radio buttons, check boxes are not mutually exclusive. You may have one or more check boxes on a form or in a group box, and any number of them can be selected at any given time.

Like radio buttons, check boxes have a Checked property. When a check box is selected, or checked, its Checked property is set to True. When a check box is deselected, or unchecked, its Checked property is set to False.

Here is a summary of other characteristics of the check box.

- A check box's caption is stored in the Text property.

- A check box's place in the tab order may be modified with the TabIndex property. When a check box has the focus, a thin dotted line appears around its text. You can check or uncheck it by pressing the spacebar.

- You may assign an access key to a check box. By placing an ampersand (&) in the Text property, just before the character that you wish to serve as the access key.

- You can use code to select or deselect a check box. Simply use an assignment statement to set the desired check box's Value property. Here is an example:

```
Choice4CheckBox.Checked = true;
```

- You may set a check box's Checked property at design time.

- Like radio buttons, check boxes have a CheckChanged event that is triggered whenever the user changes the state of the check box. If you have written a CheckChanged event procedure for the check box, it will execute whenever the user checks or unchecks the check box.

In Tutorial 12-7 you examine an application that demonstrates radio buttons and checkboxes.

Tutorial 12-7: Examining an Application with Check Boxes

Step 1:   Start Visual C# .NET and open the Radio Button Check Box Demo project, which is stored in the \Chapter 12\Radio Button Check Box Demo folder on the Student CD.

Step 2:   Run the application. The form shown in Figure 12-30 appears.

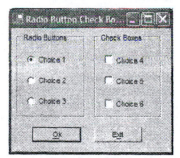

Figure 12-30   Radio Button Check Box Demo form

Step 3:   Click the Choice 3 radio button. Also click the Choice 4 and the Choice 6 check boxes.

Step 4:   Click the OK button. The message box in Figure 12-31 appears.

Step 5:   Click the OK button to dismiss the message box. Experiment by selecting the other combinations of radio buttons and check boxes, and clicking the OK button. Notice that each time, a message box appears indicating which choices were made.

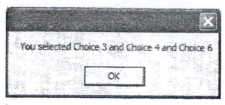

Figure 12-31 Message box

Step 6: Click the Exit button to terminate the application.

Step 7: The RadioButton controls are named Choice1, Choice2, and Choice3. The CheckBox controls are named Choice4, Choice5, and Choice6. Open the Code window and find the okButton_Click event procedure. The code is as follows.

```
private void okButton_Click(object sender, System.EventArgs e)
{
    //Declare a string variable to hold a message.
    string message;
    // The following if/else statement tests the
    // group of radio buttons and copies the
    // first part of the message to message.
    if (choice1RadioButton.Checked == true)
        message = You selected Choice 1;
    else if (choice2RadioButton.Checked == true)
        message = You selected Choice 2;
    else if (choice3RadioButton.Checked == true)
        message = You selected Choice 3;
    // The following if statements test the
    // check boxes and concatenates another part
    // of the message to message.
    if (choice4CheckBox.Checked == true)
        message = message +  and Choice 4;
    if (choice5CheckBox.Checked == true)
        message = message +  and Choice 5;
    If (choice6CheckBox.Checked == true)
        message = message +  and Choice 6;
    // Now display the message.
    MessageBox.Show(message);
}
```

Notice that the check boxes are tested by a set of if statements, not an if/else statement. Since all or none of the check boxes may be selected, the code must test each one individually.

⑦ CHECKPOINT

12.7 In code, how do you determine whether a radio button has been selected?

12.8 In code, how do you determine whether a check box has been selected?

12.5   Input Boxes and List Boxes

CONCEPT Input boxes provide a simple way to gather input without placing a text box on a form.

An input box is a quick and simple way to ask the user to enter data. Figure 12-32 shows an example.

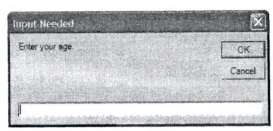

Figure 12-32   Input box

As you can see from the figure, an input box displays a message to the user and provides a text box for the user to enter input. The input box also has an OK and a Cancel button. You display input boxes with the intrinsic InputBox function. When the InputBox function is called, an input box such as the one shown in Figure 12-29 appears on the screen. Here is the general format:

```
InputBox(Prompt [, Title] [, Default] [, Xpos] [, Ypos])
```

The brackets are drawn around the *Title*, *Default*, *Xpos*, and *Ypos* arguments to indicate that they are optional. The first argument, *Prompt*, is a string that is displayed to the user in the input box. Normally, this string is a prompt requesting the user to enter a value. The optional arguments, *Title*, *Default*, *Xpos*, and *Ypos*, are described as follows.

- *Title* is a string that appears in the input box's title bar. If you do not provide a value for *Title*, the name of the project appears.

- *Default* is a string value that is initially displayed in the input box's text box. This value serves as the default input. If you do not provide a value for *Default*, the input box's text box will initially appear empty.

- *Xpos* and *Ypos* specify the input box's location on the screen. *Xpos* is an integer that specifies the distance of the input box's leftmost edge from the left edge of the screen. *Ypos* is an integer that specifies the distance of the topmost edge of the input box from the top of the screen. *Xpos* and *Ypos* are both measured in twips. (A *twip* is 1/1440th of an inch.) If *Xpos* is omitted, Visual C# centers the input box horizontally on the screen. If *Ypos* is omitted, Visual C# places the input box near the top of the screen, approximately one third of the distance down.

If the user clicks the input box's OK button or presses the Enter key, the function returns the value that is in the input box's text box. The value is returned as a string. If the user clicks the Cancel button, the function returns an empty string (`""`). To retrieve the value returned by the InputBox function, use the assignment operator to assign it to a variable. For example, the following statement will display the input box shown in Figure 12-33. Assume that `userInput` is a string variable.

```
userInput = InputBox("Enter your age.", "Input Needed");
```

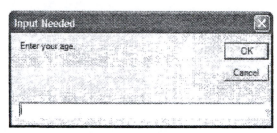

Figure 12-33   Input box

After this statement executes, the value that the user entered in the input box is stored as a string in `userInput`. As another example, the following statement will display the input box shown in Figure 12-34.

```
userInput = InputBox("Enter the distance.", "Provide a
    Value", "150");
```

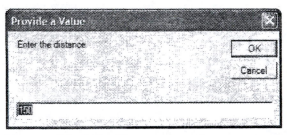

Figure 12-34   Input box with default user input

If the user simply clicks the OK button, without entering a value in the text box, the input box function will return `"150"`.

List Boxes

The ListBox Control

A list box is a control that displays a list of items and allows the user to select one or more items from the list. Visual C# .NET provides the *ListBox control* for creating list boxes. Figure 12-35 shows a form with two examples of a list box.

Figure 12-35　List box examples

At runtime, the user may select one of the items in a list box, which causes the item to appear highlighted.

Notice that one of the list boxes in Figure 12-32 does not have a scroll bar but the other does. Visual C# automatically adds a scroll bar to a list box when it contains more items than can be displayed. In the figure, the top list box has four items (Poodle, Great Dane, German Shepherd, and Terrier), and all of those items are displayed. The bottom list box shows five items (Siamese, Persian, Bobtail, Burmese, and Mau), but because it has a scroll bar, we know that there are more items in the list box than those five.

Creating a ListBox Control

You create a ListBox control by either of the following methods.

- Double-click the ListBox tool in the toolbox; a default-sized ListBox control appears on the form. Move the control to the desired location and resize it, if necessary.

- Click the ListBox tool in the toolbox, and then draw the ListBox control on the form at the desired location and size.

At design time, a list box appears as a rectangle on the form. The size you draw the rectangle becomes the size of the list box. Let's discuss some of the list box's important properties and methods.

The Items Property

The items in a list box are stored in the *Items property.* You can store items in the Items property at design time or at runtime. To store items in the Items property at design time, follow these steps:

1. Make sure the list box control is selected in the Design window.

2. In the Properties window, the setting for the Items property is displayed as "(Collection)". Select the Items property and an ellipses button (⬚) appears.

3. Click the ellipses button. The String Collection Editor dialog box, shown in Figure 12-36, appears.

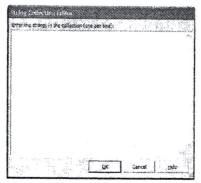

Figure 12-36　The String Collection Editor dialog box

4. Type the items that are to appear in the list box into the String Collection Editor dialog box. Type each item on a separate line.

5. When you have entered all the items, click the OK button.

The `Items.Count` Property

You can use the *Items.Count property* to determine the number of items that are stored in the Items property. When there are no items in the Items property, Items.Count will hold 0. For example, assume an application has a list box named `employeeListBox`. The following `if` statement displays a message box when there are no items in the list box:

```
if (employeeListBox.Items.Count == 0)
    MessageBox.Show("There are no items in the list!");
```

And the following statement assigns the number of items in the list box to the variable `numEmployees`:

```
numEmployees = employeeListBox.Items.Count;
```

Item Indexing

Internally, the items that are stored in a list box are numbered. Each item's number is called its *index*. The first item (which is the item stored at the top of the list) has the index 0, the second item has the index 1, and so forth.

You can use an index value with the Items property to retrieve a specific item from a list box. For example, the following statement copies the third item from `customerListBox` to the string variable name:

```
name = customerListBox.Items(2);
```

 WARNING! In a statement such as this, a runtime error will occur if the index value is out of range. Because the indices start at 0, the largest index in a list box will be 1 less than the number of items in the list.

The SelectedIndex Property

When the user selects an item in a list box, that item's index is stored in the SelectedIndex property. If no item is selected, SelectedIndex is set to 1. You can use the SelectedIndex property to retrieve the selected item from the Items property. For example, assume an application has a list box named `locationListBox`. The following code segment uses an `if` statement to determine whether the user has selected an item in the list box. If so, it copies the item from the Items property to the string variable `location`.

```
if (locationListBox.SelectedIndex <> -1) location = locationList-
Box.Items(Locations.SelectedIndex);
```

 WARNING! To prevent a runtime error from occurring, always test the SelectedIndex property to make sure it is not set to 1 before using it with the Items property to retrieve an item, as shown in this statement.

You can also use the SelectedIndex property to deselect an item by setting it to 1. For example, the following statement deselects any selected item in `locationListBox`:

```
locationListBox.SelectedIndex = -1;
```

The SelectedItem Property

Where the SelectedIndex property contains the index of the currently selected item, the SelectedItem property contains the item itself. For example, suppose the list box `fruitListBox` contains the strings "Apples", "Pears", and "Bananas". If the user has selected "Pears", the following statement copies the string "Pears" to the variable `selectedFruit`.

```
selectedFruit = fruitListBox.SelectedItem;
```

The Sorted Property

You can use the list box's *Sorted property* to cause the items in the Items property to be displayed in alphabetical order. The property, which is Boolean, is set to `false` by default. This causes the items to be displayed in the order they were entered or inserted into the list. When set to `true`, the items are alphabetically sorted.

The `Items.Add` Method

To store items in the Items property with code at runtime, you must use the *`Items.Add` method*. Here is the general format:

```
ListBox.Items.Add(Item)
```

ListBox is the name of the list box control. *Item* is the item that is to be added to the Items property. For example, suppose an application uses a list box named studentsListBox. The following statement adds the string "Sharon" to the list box. The item is added to the end of the list.

```
studentsListBox.Items.Add("Sharon");
```

This statement adds a string to a list box. However, you can add virtually any type of item to a list box. For example, the following statements add values of the integer, decimal, and DateType data types to list boxes.

```
int num = 5;
decimal grossPay = 1200.00;
DateTime startDate = new DateTime(2003,1,18,0,0,0);
numbersListBox.Items.Add(num);
wagesListBox.Items.Add(grossPay);
datesListBox.Items.Add(startDate.Year);
datesListBox.Items.Add(startDate.Month);
datesListBox.Items.Add(startDate.Day);
```

When you add an object other than a string to a list box, the text that is displayed in the list box is the text returned from the object's `ToString` method.

The `Items.Insert` Method

To insert an item at a specific position, you must use the *`Items.Insert` method*. Here is the general format of the `Items.Insert` method:

```
ListBox.Items.Insert(Index, Item)
```

ListBox is the name of the list box control. *Index* is an integer argument that specifies the position where *Item* is to be placed in the Items property. *Item* is the item to add to the list.

For example, suppose the list box studentsListBox contains the following items, in this order: "Bill", "Joe", "Geri", and "Sharon". Since the string "Bill" is the first item, its index is 0. The index for "Joe" is 1, for "Geri" 2, and for "Sharon" 3. Now, suppose the following statement executes:

```
studentsListBox.Items.Insert(2, "Jean");
```

This statement inserts "Jean" at index 2. The string that was previously at index 2 ("Geri") is moved to index 3, and the string previously at index 3 ("Sharon") is moved to index 4. The items in the Items property are now Bill, Joe, Jean, Geri, and Sharon

The `Items.Remove` and `Items.RemoveAt` Methods

The `Items.Remove` and `Items.RemoveAt` *methods* both erase one item from a list box's Items property. Here is the general format of both methods:

```
ListBox.Items.Remove(Item)
ListBox.Items.RemoveAt(Index)
```

With both methods, `ListBox` is the name of the list box control. With the `Items.Remove` method, `Item` is the item you wish to remove. For example, the following statement erases the item "Industrial Widget" from the `inventoryListBox` list box.

```
InventoryListBox.Items.Remove("Industrial Widget");
```

If you specify an item that is not in the list box, nothing is removed.

The `Items.RemoveAt` method removes the item at a specific index. For example, the following statement removes the item at index 4 from the `inventoryListBox` list box:

```
InventoryListBox.Items.RemoveAt(4);
```

 WARNING! If you specify an invalid index with the `Items.RemoveAt` method, a runtime error will occur.

The `Items.Clear` Method

The `Items.Clear` *method* erases all the items in the Items property. Here is the method's general format:

```
ListBox.Items.Clear()
```

For example, assume an application has a list box named `carsListBox`. The following statement erases its contents:

```
carsListBox.Items.Clear();
```

In the following tutorial, you create an application with two list boxes.

Tutorial 12-8: Creating list boxes

Step 1: Start Visual C# and begin a new Windows application project. Name the project List Boxes.

Step 2: On the form, draw a list box as shown in Figure 12-37. Notice that the default name of the list box is `ListBox1`. Also notice that the name of the list box is displayed in the list box at design time. It will not appear there at runtime.

Figure 12-37 A list box

Step 3: Change the name of the list box to monthsListBox.

Step 4: With the list box selected, click the Items property in the Property window. Then click the ellipses button (⬚) that appears.

Step 5: The String Collection Editor dialog box should appear. Type the following names of the months, one name per line: January, February, March, April, May, June, July, August, September, October, November, and December. When you are finished, the dialog box should appear as shown in Figure 12-38. Click the OK button.

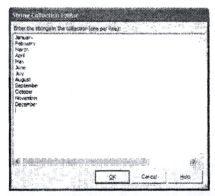

Figure 12-38 String Collection Editor with months filled in

Step 6: Draw another list box and make it the same size as the first one. Change its name to yearsListBox. Enter the following items in its Items property: 2002, 2003, 2004, and 2005. Your form should look like that in Figure 12-39.

Figure 12-39   The form with two list boxes

Step 7:   Draw a button on the form, name it okButton, and change its caption to "OK".

Step 8:   Double click the okButton button to add a Click event procedure code template. Write the following code, shown in bold.

```
private void okButton_Click(object sender, System.EventArgs e)
{
    string input;          // To hold the selected month
    if (monthsListBox.SelectedIndex == -1)
        // No month is selected
        MessageBox.Show(Select a month.);
    else if (yearsListBox.SelectedIndex == -1)
        // No year is selected
        MessageBox.Show(Select a year.);
    else
        // Get the selected month and year
        input = monthsListBox.SelectedItem +
                        + yearsListBox.SelectedItem;
    MessageBox.Show(You selected  + input);
}
```

Let's take a closer look at the code. Here is the beginning of the if statement:

```
if (monthsListBox.SelectedIndex == -1)
    // No month is selected
    MessageBox.Show(Select a month.);
```

It first tests monthsListBox.SelectedIndex to determine whether it is set to 1. If it is, the user has not selected an item from Months, so a message box is displayed instructing the user to do so. If the user has selected an item from monthsListBox, the else portion executes:

```
        else if (yearsListBox.SelectedIndex == -1)
            // No year is selected
            MessageBox.Show(Select a year.);
```

This tests yearsListBox.SelectedIndex to determine whether the user has selected an item from yearsListBox. If yearsListBox.SelectedIndex is set to 1, a message box is displayed instructing the user to select a year. The else portion is executed if the user has selected items from both monthsListBox and yearsListBox:

```
        else
            // Get the selected month and year
            input = monthsListBox.SelectedItem +
                        + yearsListBox.SelectedItem;
            MessageBox.Show(You selected  + input);
```

In that case, the selected items from both list boxes are concatenated and stored in the variable input. A message box is then displayed showing the contents of input.

Step 9: Draw another button on the form. Name it resetButton and change its Text to "Reset".

Step 10: Double-click the resetButton button to add a Click event procedure code template. Write the following code shown in bold.

```
    private void resetButton_Click(object sender, System.EventArgs e)
    {
        // Reset the list boxes by deselecting the currently
        // selected items
        monthsListBox.SelectedIndex = -1;
        yearsListBox.SelectedIndex = -1;
    }
```

When this button is clicked, the SelectedIndex property of both list boxes is set to 1. This deselects any selected items.

Step 11: Run the application. Without selecting any item in either list box, click the OK button. A message box appears instructing you to "Select a month."

Step 12: Select March in monthsListBox, but do not select an item from yearsListBox. Click the OK button. This time a message box appears instructing you to "Select a year."

Step 13: With March still selected in monthsListBox, select 2004 in yearsListBox. Click the OK button. Now a message box appears with the message "You selected March 2004." Click the message box's OK button to dismiss it.

Step 14: Click the Reset button. The items you previously selected in `monthsListBox` and `yearsListBox` are deselected.

Step 15: Close the application and save it to your disk.

 CHECKPOINT

Carefully examine the input box in Figure 12-40 and answer questions 12.9 and 12.10.

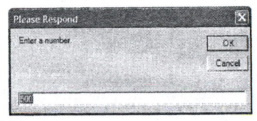

Figure 12-40 Input box

12.9 Write a statement that will display the input box at the default location on the screen.

12.10 Write the statement that will display the input box, with its leftmost edge at 100 twips from the left edge of the screen, and its topmost edge 300 twips from the top edge of the screen.

12.11 What is the index of the first item stored in a list box's Items property?

12.12 Which list box property holds the number of items stored in the Items property?

12.13 Which list box property holds the item that has been selected from the list?

12.6 Checked List Boxes and Combo Boxes

> **CONCEPT** A checked list box displays a check box next to each item in the list. A combo box is like a list box combined with a text box.

Checked List Boxes

The CheckedListBox control is a variation of the ListBox control. It supports all the ListBox properties and methods we discussed in section 12-5. Each of the items in a CheckedListBox control, however, is displayed with a check box next to it. Figure 12-41 shows an example.

An item in a checked list box may be selected and/or checked. Only one item in a checked list box may be selected at a time, but multiple items may be checked. The CheckOnClick property determines how items become checked:

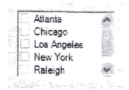

Figure 12-41   Checked list box

- When set to `false`, the user clicks an item once to select it, and then clicks it again to check it (or uncheck it, if it is already checked).

- When set to `true`, the user clicks an item only once to both select it and check it (or uncheck it, if it is already checked).

The CheckOnClick property is set to `false` by default. Because this setting makes working with the control a bit complicated, you may prefer setting it to `true` for most applications.

You access the selected item in a checked list box exactly as you do with a regular list box: through the SelectedIndex and SelectedItem properties. These properties only indicate which item is selected, however, and do not report which items are checked. You access the checked items through the GetItemChecked method, which has the following general format.

```
CheckedListBox.GetItemChecked(Index)
```

CheckedListBox is the name of the CheckedListBox control. *Index* is the index of an item in the list. If the item is checked, the method returns true. Otherwise, it returns false. For example, assume an application has a checked list box name `citiesCheckedListBox`. The following code counts the number of items in the control that are checked.

```
int i;                    // Loop counter
int checkedCities = 0;    // Keeps count of checked cities

for (i = 0; citiesCheckListBox.Items.Count - 1; ++i)
        if (citiesCheckListBox.GetItemChecked(i) == true)
            checkedCities += 1;
MessageBox.Show(You checked  + checkedCities.ToString +
            cities.);
```

As another example, assume an application uses the controls shown in Figure 12-42. The checked list box on the left is `citiesCheckListBox` and the list box on the right is `checkedListBox`. The OK button, `okButton`, uses the following `Click` event procedure.

```
private void okButton_Click(object sender, System.EventArgs e)
{
int i;                     // Loop counter
for (i = 0;citiesCheckListBox.Items.Count - 1; ++i)
    if (citiesCheckListBox.GetItemChecked(i) == true)
    checkedListBox.Items.Add(citiesCheckListBox.Items(i));
}
```

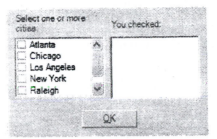

Figure 12-42   Checked list box and a list box

The `okButton_Click` event procedure adds the items that are checked in the `citiesCheckListBox` control to the `checkedListBox` control. Figure 12-43 shows how the controls will appear after the user has checked three cities and clicked the OK button.

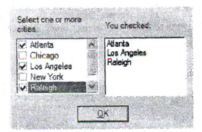

Figure 12-43   Cities checked

Combo Boxes

Combo boxes and list boxes are similar in the following ways:

- They both display a list of items to the user.
- They both have Items, Items.Count, SelectedIndex, SelectedItem, and Sorted properties.
- They both have `Items.Add`, `Items.Clear`, `Items.Remove`, and `Items.RemoveAt` methods.
- All of these properties and methods work the same with combo boxes and list boxes.

In addition, a combo box has a rectangular area that functions like a text box. The user may either select an item from the combo box's list or type text into the combo box's text input area.

Like a text box, the combo box has a Text property. If the user types text into the combo box, the text is stored in the Text property. Also, when the user selects an item from the combo box's list, the item is copied to the Text property.

Combo Box Styles

There are three styles of combo box: the drop-down combo box, the simple combo box, and the drop-down list combo box. You select a combo box's style with its *DropDownStyle property*. Let's look at each style.

The Drop-Down Combo Box

This is the default setting for the combo box DropDownStyle property. At runtime, a drop-down combo box appears like the one shown in Figure 12-44.

Figure 12-44   A drop-down combo box

This style of combo box behaves like either a text box or a list box. The user may type text into the box (like a text box) or click the down arrow. If the user clicks the down arrow, a list of items appears, as shown in Figure 12-45.

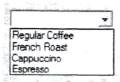

Figure 12-45   A list drops down when the user clicks the down arrow

Now the user may select an item from the list. When the user selects an item, it appears in the text input area at the top of the box, and is copied to the combo box's Text property.

 NOTE: When typing text into the combo box, the user may enter a string that does not appear in the drop-down list.

 TIP: When the combo box has the focus, the user may also press Alt+down arrow to drop the list down. This is also true for the drop-down list combo box.

The Simple Combo Box

With this style of combo box, the list of items does not drop-down but is always displayed. Figure 12-46 shows an example.

As with the drop-down combo box, this style allows the user to type text directly into the combo box or to select from the list. The user is not restricted to the items that appear in the list.

Figure 12-46 The simple combo box

When the user selects an item is from the list, it is copied to the text input area and to the combo box's Text property.

Drop-Down List Combo Box

With this style, the user may not type text directly into the combo box. Instead, the user must select an item selected from the list. Figure 12-47 shows a drop-down list combo box.

Figure 12-47 The drop-down list combo box

When the user clicks the down arrow, a list of items appears as shown in Figure 12-48.

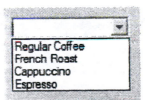

Figure 12-48 A list drops down when the user clicks the down arrow

When the user selects an item from the list, it is copied to the text area at the top of the combo box and to the Text property. Because the user can only select items from the list, it is not possible to enter text that does not appear in the list.

Getting the User's Input from a Combo Box

As with the list box, you can determine which item has been selected from a combo box's list by retrieving the value in the SelectedIndex or SelectedItem properties. If the user has typed text into the combo box's text area, however, you cannot use the SelectedIndex or SelectedItem properties to get the text. The best way to get the user's input is with the Text property, which will contain either the user's text input or the item selected from the list.

NOTE: The drop-down list combo box's Text property is read-only. You cannot change its value with code.

List Boxes versus Combo Boxes

Here are some guidelines to help you decide when to use a list box and when to use a combo box.

- Use a drop-down or simple combo box when you want to show the user a list of items to select from but do not want to limit the user's input to the items on the list.

- Use a list box or a drop-down list combo box when you want to limit the user's selection to a list of items. The drop-down list combo box generally takes less space than a list box (because the list doesn't appear until the user clicks the down arrow), so use it when you want to conserve space on the form.

Tutorial 12-9: Creating combo boxes

In this tutorial you will create each of the three styles of combo box.

Step 1: Start Visual C# .NET and begin a new Windows application project. Name the project Combo Box Demo.

Step 2: Set the form up like the one shown in Figure 12-49. Note that you are to draw three combo boxes: `countriesComboBox` (drop-down combo box), `playsComboBox` (a simple combo box), and `artistsComboBox` (a drop-down list combo box).

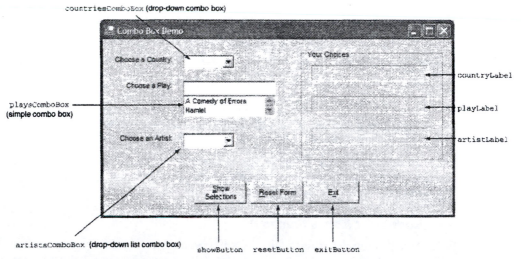

Figure 12-49 Combo Box Demo form

Step 3: Enter the following items into the Items property of the `countriesComboBox` combo box: **England**, **Ireland**, **Scotland**, and **Wales**.

Step 4: Enter the following items into the Items property of the `playsComboBox` combo box: **Hamlet, Much Ado About Nothing, Romeo and Juliet, A Comedy of Errors**, and **The Merchant of Venice.**

Step 5: Enter the following items into the Items property of the `artistsComboBox` combo box: **Michelangelo, Raphael**, and **da Vinci.**

Step 6: The `showButton_Click` event procedure should perform the following tasks:

■ Copy the selected item or typed text from the `countriesComboBox` combo box to the `countryLabel` Text property.

■ Copy the selected item or typed text from the `playsComboBox` combo box to the `playLabel` Text property.

■ Copy the selected item from the `artistsComboBox` combo box to the `artistLabel` Text property.

Enter the following code for the `showButton_Click` event procedure.

```
private Sub showButton_Click(object sender, System.EventArgs e)
{
    // This procedure displays the combo box selections.
    coutryLabel.Text = countriesComboBox.Text;
    playLabel.Text = playsComboBox.Text;
    artistLabel.Text = artistsComboBox.Text;
}
```

Step 7: The `resetButton_Click` event procedure should deselect any items that are selected in the combo boxes. As with list boxes, this is accomplished by setting the SelectedIndex property to 1. The procedure should also set the Text property of `countryLabel`, `playLabel`, and `artistLabel` to `""`. Enter the following code for the `resetButton_Click` event procedure.

```
private void resetButton_Click(object sender, System.EventArgs e)
{
    // This procedure clears selections in the
    // Combo Boxes and resets the labels to .
    // Reset the combo boxes.
    countriesComboBox.SelectedIndex = -1;
    countriesComboBox.Text = ;
    playsComboBox.SelectedIndex = -1;
    playsComboBox.Text = ;
    artistsComboBox.SelectedIndex = -1;
    // Note: artistsComboBox.Text is read-only.

    // Reset the labels.
    countryLabel.Text = ;
    playLabel.Text = ;
    artistLabel.Text = ;
}
```

NOTE: If the user types characters into a combo box's text input area, those characters are not cleared by setting the SelectedIndex to 1. You must set the Text property to " " to accomplish that.

Step 8: The `exitButton_Click` event procedure should end the application. Write the code for that event procedure.

Step 9: Run the application. Experiment with the combo boxes by trying a combination of text input and item selection. For example, select an item from the `countriesComboBox` list and type text into the `playsComboBox`' text input area. Click the `showButton` button to see what you have entered.

Step 10: End the application when you are finished experimenting with it.

 # CHECKPOINT

12.14 What is the index of the first item stored in a list box or combo box's Items property?

12.15 Which list box or combo box property holds the number of items stored in the Items property?

12.16 Which list box or combo box property holds the index of the item that has been selected from the list?

Review Questions and Exercises

Multiple Choice and True or False

1. When the user types input into a TextBox control, it is stored in what property?

   a) Input   c) Value

   b) Text   d) Keyboard

2. In code, you move the focus to a control with what method?

   a) `MoveFocus`   c) `ResetFocus`

   b) `SetFocus`   d) `Focus`

3. What form property allows you to select a button that is to be clicked anytime the user presses the Enter key while the form is active?

   a) DefaultButton   c) CancelButton

   b) AcceptButton   d) EnterButtom

4. What form property allows you to select a button that is to be clicked anytime the user presses the Escape key while the form is active?

   a) DefaultButton   c) CancelButton

   b) AcceptButton   d) EnterButton

5. You can modify a control's position in the tab order by changing what property?

    a) TabIndex   c) TabPosition

    b) TabOrder   d) TabStop

6. A group box's title is stored in what property?

    a) Title   c) Text

    b) Caption   d) Heading

7. In code you should test this property of a radio button or a check box to determine whether it is selected.

    a) Selected   c) On

    b) Checked   d) Toggle

8. Use this method to display a message box and determine which button the user clicked to dismiss the message box.

    a) `MessageBox.Show`

    b) `MessageBox.Button`

    c) `Message.Box`

    d) `MessageBox.UserClicked`

9. You display input boxes with the intrinsic _____ function.

    a) `InBox`   c) `InputBox`

    b) `Input`   d) `GetInput`

10. An input box returns the value entered by the user as a _____.

    a) string   c) single

    b) integer   d) `boolean`

11. Visual C# .NET automatically adds a _____ to a list box when it contains more items than can be displayed.

    a) Larger list box   c) Second form

    b) Scroll bar   d) Message box

12. A list box or combo box's index numbering starts at

    a) 0   c) 1

    b) 1   d) any value you specify.

13. This property holds the index of the selected item in a list box.

   a) Index

   b) SelectedItem

   c) SelectedIndex

   d) Items.SelectedIndex

14. The _____ method erases one item from a list box.

   a) `Erase`   c) `Items.RemoveItem`

   b) `Items.Remove`   d) `Clear`

15. When the ListBox control's _____ property is set to true, it causes the ListBox control to display its list in multiple columns.

   a) Columns   c) ColumnList

   b) Multicolumn   d) TableDisplay

16. A _____ has a rectangular area that functions like a text box.

   a) List box   c) Combo box

   b) Drop-down list box   d) Input label

17. With this style of combo box, the list of items does not drop down, but is always displayed.

   a) Drop-down combo box

   b) Simple combo box

   c) Drop-down list combo box

   d) Simple drop-down combo list box

18. The combo box's _____ property will contain the user's text input or the item selected from the list.

   a) Input   c) List

   b) Caption   d) Text

19. True or False: The TextBox control's Text property holds the text entered by the user into the TextBox control at runtime.

20. True or False: You can access a TextBox control's Text property in code.

21. True or False: GroupBox and Label controls have a TabIndex property, but they are skipped in the tab order.

22. True or False: When you assign an access key to a button, the user can trigger a Click event by typing Alt+ the access key character.

23. True or False: The statement messageLabel.BackColor = Green will set messageLabel control's background color to green.

24. True or False: To group controls in a group box, draw the controls first, then draw the group box around them.

25. True or False: Clicking on a radio button selects it, and leaves any other selected radio button in the same group selected as well.

26. True or False: Radio buttons that are placed inside a group box are treated as one group, separate and distinct from any other groups of radio buttons.

27. True or False: When a group of radio buttons appears on a form (outside of a group box), any number of them can be selected at any time.

28. True or False: You may have one or more check boxes on a form, and any number of them can be selected at any given time.

29. True or False: If you do not provide a value for an input box's title, an error will occur.

30. True or False: If the user clicks an input box's Cancel button, the function returns the number –1.

31. True or False: To create a checked list box, you draw a regular list box and set its Checked property to true.

32. True or False: A drop-down list combo box allows the user to either select an item from a list or type text into a text input area.

Programming Challenges

1. Miles-per-Gallon Calculator

Create an application that calculates a car's gas mileage. The application's form should have Text-Box controls that let the user enter the number of gallons of gas the tank holds, and the number of miles it can be driven on a full tank. When a calculateButton MPG button is clicked, the application should display the number of miles that the car may be driven per gallon of gas. The form should also have a Clear button that clears the input and results, as well as an Exit button that ends the application. The application's form should appear as in Figure 12-50.

Figure 12-50 Miles-Per-Gallon calculator

Use the following set of test data to determine whether the application is calculating properly:

Gallons	Miles	Miles-Per-Gallon
10	375	37.50
12	289	24.08
15	190	12.67

2. Stadium Seating

There are three seating categories at an athletic stadium. For a baseball game, Class A seats cost $15 each, Class B seats cost $12 each, and Class C seats cost $9 each. Create an application that allows the user to enter the number of tickets sold for each class. The application should be able to display the amount of income generated from each class of ticket sales and the total revenue generated. The application's form should resemble the one shown in Figure 12-51.

Figure 12-51 Stadium Seating form

Use the following set of test data to determine whether the application is calculating properly:

Ticket sales	Revenue
Class A: 320	Class A: $4,800.00
Class B: 570	Class B: $6,840.00
Class C: 890	Class C: $8, 010.00
	totalLabel Revenue: $19,650.00
Class A: 500	Class A: $7,500.00
Class B: 750	Class B: $9,000.00
Class C: 1,200	Class C: $10,800.00
	totalLabel Revenue: $27,300.00
Class A: 100	Class A: $1,500.00
Class B: 300	Class B: $3,600.00
Class C: 500	Class C: $4,500.00
	totalLabel Revenue: $9,600.00

3. Fat Gram Calculator

Create an application that allows the user to enter the number of calories and fat grams in a food. The application should display the percentage of the calories that come from fat. If the calories from fat are less than 30% of the total calories of the food, it should also display a message indicating the food is low in fat. (Display the message in a label or a message box.) The application's form should appear similar to Figure 12-52.

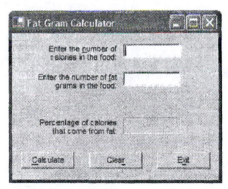

Figure 12-52   Fat Gram Calculator form

One gram of fat has 9 calories, so:

Calories from fat = fat grams * 9

The percentage of calories from fat can be calculated as:

Percentage of calories from fat = Calories from fat / total calories

Input validation: Make sure the number of calories and fat grams are not less than 0. Also, the number of calories from fat cannot be greater than the total number of calories. If that happens, display an error message indicating that either the calories or fat grams were incorrectly entered.

Use the following set of test data to determine if your application is calculating properly:

Calories and Fat	Percentage Fat
200 calories, 8 fat grams	Percentage of calories from fat: 36%
150 calories 2 fat grams	Percentage of calories from fat: 12% (a low-fat food)
500 calories, 30 fat grams	Percentage of calories from fat: 54%

4. Sum of Numbers

Create an application that displays a form similar to Figure 12-53.

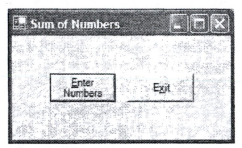

Figure 12-53   Sum of Numbers form

When the Enter Numbers button is clicked, the application should display the input box shown in Figure 12-54.

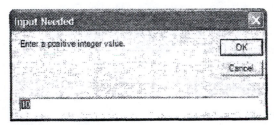

Figure 12-54   Sum of Numbers input box

The input box asks the user to enter a positive integer value. Notice that the default input value is 10. When the OK button is clicked, the application should display a message box with the sum of all the integers from 1 through the value entered by the user, as shown in Figure 12-55.

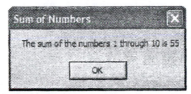

Figure 12-55 Sum of Numbers message box

If the user enters a negative value, the application should display an error message. Use the following set of test data to determine whether your application is calculating correctly.

Value	Sum
5	15
10	55
20	210
100	5050

5. Distance Calculator

If you know a vehicle's speed and the amount of time it has traveled, you can calculate the distance it has traveled as follows:

Distance = Speed * Time

For example, if a train travels 40 miles per hour for three hours, the distance traveled is 120 miles. Create an application with a form similar to Figure 12-56.

Figure 12-56   Distance Calculator

When the user clicks the Calculate button, the application should display an input box asking the user for the speed of the vehicle in miles per hour, followed by another input box asking for the amount of time, in hours, that the vehicle has traveled. It should then use a loop to display in a list box the distance the vehicle has traveled for each hour of that time period. Figure 12-57 shows an example of what the application's form should look like.

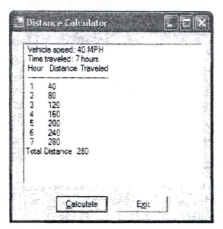

Figure 12-57   Distance Calculator completed

Input validation: Do not accept a value less than one for the vehicle's speed or the number of hours traveled.

Use the following set of test data to determine if your application is calculating correctly.

Vehicle Speed: **60**

Hours Traveled: 7

Hour	Distance Traveled
1	60
2	120
3	180
4	240
5	300
6	360
7	420

Appendix A:
ASCII/Unicode Characters

The following table lists the first 127 Unicode character codes, which are the same as the ASCII (American Standard Code for Information Interchange) character set. This group of character codes is known as the *Latin Subset of Unicode*. The code columns show character codes and the character columns show the corresponding characters. For example, the code 65 represents the letter A. Note that the first 31 codes, and code 127, represent control characters that are not printable.

Code	Character	Code	Character	Code	Character	Code	Character	Code	Character
0	NUL	26	SUB	52	4	78	N	104	h
1	SOH	27	Escape	53	5	79	O	105	i
2	STX	28	FS	54	6	80	P	106	j
3	ETX	29	GS	55	7	81	Q	107	k
4	EOT	30	RS	56	8	82	R	108	l
5	ENQ	31	US	57	9	83	S	109	m
6	ACK	32	(Space)	58	:	84	T	110	n
7	BEL	33	!	59	;	85	U	111	o
8	Backspace	34	"	60	<	86	V	112	p
9	HTab	35	#	61	=	87	W	113	q
10	Line Feed	36	$	62	>	88	X	114	r
11	VTab	37	%	63	?	89	Y	115	s
12	Form Feed	38	&	64	@	90	Z	116	t
13	CR	39	'	65	A	91	[	117	u
14	SO	40	(	66	B	92	\	118	v
15	SI	41	)	67	C	93	]	119	w
16	DLE	42	*	68	D	94	^	120	x
17	DC1	43	+	69	E	95	_	121	y
18	DC2	44	,	70	F	96	`	122	z
19	DC3	45	-	71	G	97	a	123	{
20	DC4	46	.	72	H	98	b	124		
21	NAK	47	/	73	I	99	c	125	}
22	SYN	48	0	74	J	100	d	126	~
23	ETB	49	1	75	K	101	e	127	DEL
24	CAN	50	2	76	L	102	f		
25	EM	51	3	77	M	103	g		

Appendix B:
Operator Precedence and Associativity

This table shows the precedence and associativity of all the C# operators. The table is divided into groups, and each operator in a group has the same precedence. The groups of operators are arranged from the highest precedence at the top of the table to the lowest precedence at the bottom of the table. For example, the first group of operators shown is

```
. () [] ++ -- new typeof checked unchecked
```

This group of operators has the highest precedence of all the operators. Each of the operators in this group has the same precedence.

Operator	Description	Associativity
.	membership	left-to-right
()	parenthesized expression	left-to-right
[]	array subscript	left-to-right
++	postfix increment	left-to-right
--	postfix decrement	left-to-right
new	object creation	left-to-right
typeof	type_of	left-to-right
checked	checked	left-to-right
unchecked	unchecked	left-to-right
+	unary plus	left-to-right
-	unary minus	left-to-right
!	logical NOT	left-to-right
~	bitwise complement	left-to-right
++	prefix increment	left-to-right
--	prefix decrement	left-to-right
(type)	cast	left-to-right

Operator	Description	Associativity
*	multiplication	left-to-right
/	division	left-to-right
%	remainder	left-to-right
+	addition	left-to-right
+	string concatenation	left-to-right
-	subtraction	left-to-right
<<	left shift	left-to-right
>>	signed right shift	left-to-right
<	less than	left-to-right
>	greater than	left-to-right
<=	less than or equal to	left-to-right
>=	greater than or equal to	left-to-right
is	type comparison	left-to-right
as	type comparison	left-to-right
==	equal to	left-to-right
!=	not equal to	left-to-right
&	bitwise AND	left-to-right
&	logical AND	left-to-right
^	bitwise XOR	left-to-right
^	logical XOR	left-to-right
|	bitwise OR	left-to-right
|	logical OR	left-to-right
&&	conditional AND	left-to-right
||	conditional OR	left-to-right
? :	conditional	right-to-left
=	assignment	right-to-left
+=	combined assignment	right-to-left
-=	combined assignment	right-to-left
*=	combined assignment	right-to-left
/=	combined assignment	right-to-left
<<=	combined assignment	right-to-left
>>=	combined assignment	right-to-left
&=	combined assignment	right-to-left
^=	combined assignment	right-to-left
|=	combined assignment	right-to-left

Appendix C:
C# Key Words

abstract	as	base
bool	break	byte
case	catch	char
checked	class	const
continue	decimal	default
delegate	do	double
else	enum	event
explicit	extern	false
finally	fixed	float
for	foreach	goto
if	implicit	in
int	interface	internal
is	lock	long
namespace	new	null
object	operator	out
override	params	private
protected	public	readonly
ref	return	sbyte
sealed	short	sizeof
stackalloc	static	string
struct	switch	this
throw	true	try
typeof	uint	ulong
unchecked	unsafe	ushort
using	virtual	volatile
void	while	

Appendix D
Introduction to .NET
Framework SDK

This appendix serves as a quick reference for performing the following operations using the .NET Framework SDK to create C# console applications using the DOS command line:

- Creating & Saving a new program
- Compiling & Executing a program
- Compiling & Executing a multi-file program

Creating & Saving a New Program

To create a new program using .NET Framework SDK you need to download the latest version from:

> http://www.microsoft.com/downloads

The latest version at this writing was version 1.1.4322.

You will also need to type your source code into a simple text editor like Notepad.

1. Type your C# program into the editor as like Figure D-1:

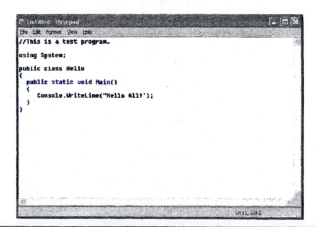

Figure D-1

2. Go to file to Save As. Select the location where you want to save your program. Also make sure you save the program the same name as your class name. Include your program name in double quotes to prevent the default .txt extension. Under the Save as type box select All Files. Figure D-2 shows an example.

Figure D-2

3. Click Save when finished. Your saved program should be named as Hello.cs as seen in Figure D-3.

```
//This is a test program.

using System;

public class Hello
{
  public static void Main()
  {
    Console.WriteLine("Hello All!");
  }
}
```

Figure D-3

4. Now, you need to compile the program from the DOS prompt. Open the Command Prompt window. Change the directory to where your program is located. Figure D-4 demonstrates this.

Figure D-4

5. Next you need to locate the csc.exe program is on your system. Once found you need to set the path to the program. You can do this by changing the System Properties under Windows to set the path. If you do not wish to permanently set the path, you can set the path for the current session only. To do this you would type:

```
path =c:\Windows\Microsoft.NET\Framework\v1.1.4322
```

Figure D-5 shows the path command.

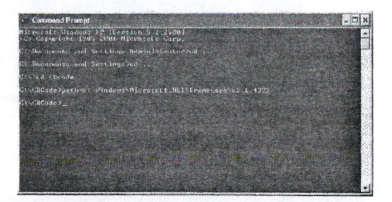

Figure D-5

6. Now you are ready to compile your program. At the prompt invoke the compiler by typing:

```
csc Hello.cs
```

If your program was successful your program will return a new command prompt. If it was not successful, go back to your source code and make changes and try compiling again. Figure D-6 shows a successful compilation.

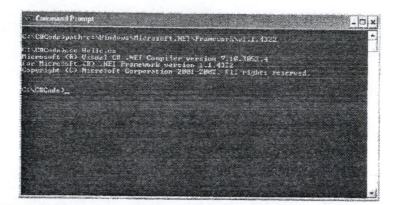

Figure D-6

7. To execute your program, after it has been compiled successfully. Type the file name without the extension. In this case it is just

```
Hello
```

Figure D-7 shows a successful run.

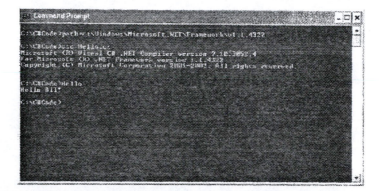

Figure D-7

Compiling & Executing Multi-file Programs

The compiler has many different output options. Using these options we can compile multi-file programs.

Each multi-file program should be saved with the .cs extension. Each class that does that does not hold a Main() method will be compiled into a library (.dll) file. We have two classes Rectangle.cs and RectangleDemo.cs under the C#Code directory. The file RectangleDemo.cs holds the Main() method. We compile Rectangle.cs file first. To do this we type at the command line:

```
C:\C#Code\csc /t:library Rectangle.cs
```

The /t is shorthand for target and with the :library will create a .dll file named Rectangle.dll. We use this .dll file then to compile the RectangleDemo class with the following command:

```
C:\C#Code\csc /r:Rectangle.dll RectangleDemo.cs
```

The /r is shorthand for reference. We reference the Rectangle.dll file in order to compile the RectangleDemo.cs file. To execute the RectangleDemo program type

```
RectangleDemo
```

at the command line.

You follow the same general format for more than two files.

Appendix E
Introduction to
Microsoft Visual C# .NET

This appendix serves as a quick reference for performing the following operations using the Microsoft Visual C# .NET integrated development environment (IDE) to create C# console applications:

- Starting a new project and entering code
- Saving a project to disk
- Compiling & Executing a project
- Opening an existing project

Starting a New Project

The first step in creating a program with Visual C# .NET is to start a *project*. A project is a group of one or more files that make up a software application. (Even if your program consists of no more than a single source code file, it still must belong to a project.)

To start a project:

1. Launch Microsoft .NET. The IDE window opens and allows for a number of options, which are shown in Figure E-1. Click the **New Project** button in the main window as shown in Figure E-1. (If you do not see the New Project button, click **File** on the menu bar, then click **New**, then click **Project**.)

2. The New Projects dialog box appears, as shown in Figure E-2. Under Project Types (the left pane) select **Visual C# Projects**. Under Templates (the right pane), scroll down to and select **WIN 32 Project**.

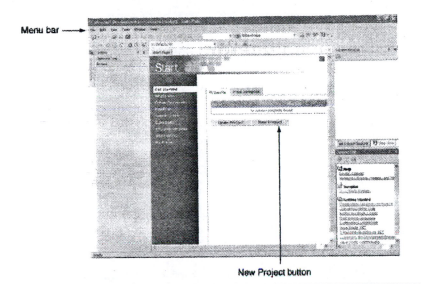

Figure E-1

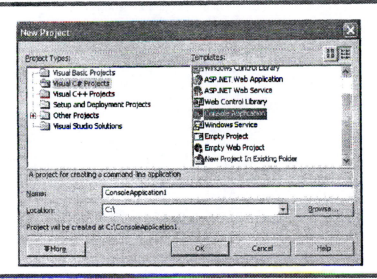

Figure E-2

3. When you create a project, Visual C# .NET creates a folder where all the project files are normally stored. The folder is called the *project folder* and it has the same name as the project. The Location text box lets you type in or browse to a location on your system where the project folder will be created. If you do not want to keep the default location, click the **Browse...** button to select a different one. Once you have selected a folder the dialog box should appear similar to Figure E-3.

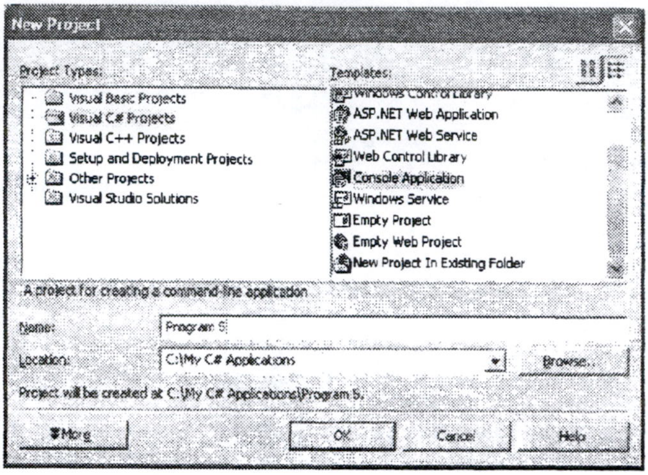

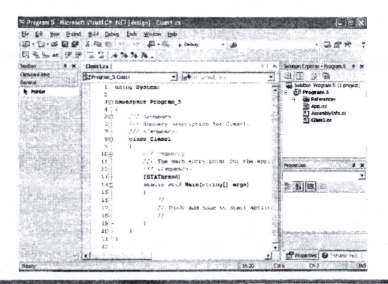

Figure E-3

Enter the name of the project (such as Lab6, or Program5) in the Name text box. (Do not enter an extension for the filename.) Figure E-3 shows an example. Click the **OK** button if you are satisfied with the name and directory for the project.

4. This will take you to the main screen with an empty project as shown in Figure E-4.

Figure E-4

5. Now you should delete the existing code present. Highlight the code and press Delete. Figure E-5 shows an example of the dialog box with this step completed.

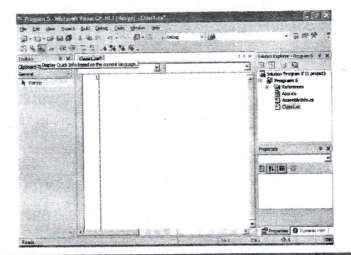

Figure E-5

6. Now type in your C# program. Highlight the code and press Delete. Figure E-6 shows an example of a completed C# program.

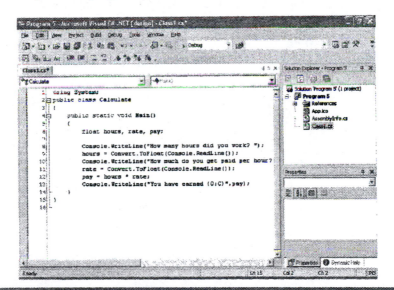

Figure E-6

Saving Your Project to Disk

It is important to periodically save your work. To do so, click File on the menu bar, then click Save All on the File menu. This saves your program as the default name Class1.cs. Rename the file Calculate.cs. To do this double click on Class1.cs in the Solution Explorer Window and rename the file. Figure E-7 shows an example of the renamed file.

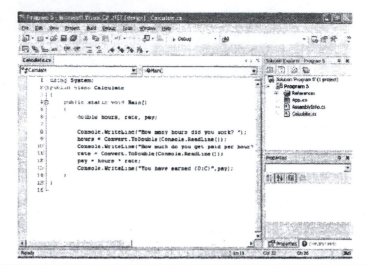

Figure E-7

Compiling and Executing

Once you have entered a program's source code, you may compile and execute it by any of the following methods:

- Click the **Debug** menu item and choosing **Start Without Debugging** as shown in Figure E-8.

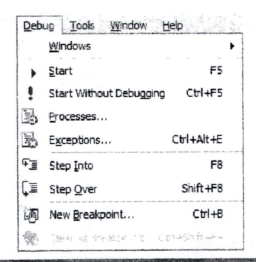

Figure E-8

- by pressing **Ctrl+F5**

The Output window shown in Figure E-9 appears at the bottom of the screen. This window shows status messages as the program is compiled. Error messages are also displayed in this same area.

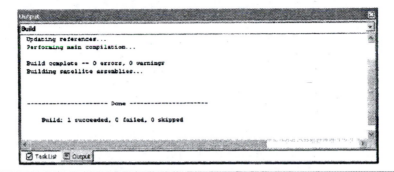

Figure E-9

If the program compiles successfully, an MS DOS window appears and the program runs. This is illustrated in Figure E-10.

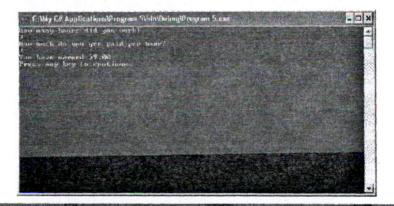

Figure E-10

Opening an Existing Project

To open an existing project, click **File** on the menu bar, then click **Open Solution**. Use the resulting dialog box to browse to the folder containing your project. In that folder you should see a solution file. This file has the same name that you gave the project, and the .sln extension. Double-click this file to open the project.

NOTE: If the source file does not open in the editor, double-click the name of the file in the Solutions Explorer window.

Appendix F:
Answers to Checkpoints

Chapter 1

1.1 Because the computer can be programmed to do so many different tasks.

1.2 The Central Processing Unit (CPU), main memory, secondary storage devices, input devices, output devices.

1.3 Arithmetic and Logic Unit (ALU), and Control Unit

1.4 Fetch: The CPU's control unit fetches the program's next instruction from main memory.

Decode: The control unit decodes the instruction, which is encoded in the form of a number. An electrical signal is generated.

Execute: The signal is routed to the appropriate component of the computer, which causes a device to perform an operation.

1.5 A unique number assigned to each section of memory. The address is used to identify a location in memory.

1.6 Program instructions and data are stored in main memory while the program is operating. Main memory is volatile, and loses its contents when power is removed from the computer. Secondary storage holds data for long periods of time—even when there is no power to the computer.

1.7 It means that an operating system is capable of running multiple programs at once.

1.8 A key word has a special purpose, and is defined as part of a programming language. A programmer-defined symbol is a word or name defined by the programmer.

1.9 Operators perform operations on one or more operands. Punctuation symbols mark the beginning or ending of a statement, or separates items in a list.

1.10 A line is a single line as it appears in the body of a program. A statement is a complete instruction that causes the computer to perform an action.

1.11 Because their contents may be changed.

1.12 The original value is overwritten.

1.13 A compiler is a program that translates source code into an executable form.

1.14 Syntax errors are mistakes that the programmer has made that violate the rules of the programming language. These errors must be corrected before the compiler can translate the source code.

1.15 The C# compiler translates C# source code into an intermediate language called Microsoft Intermediate Language (MSIL).

1.16 The Just In Time (JIT) is a compiler that reads C# MSIL instructions and executes them as they are read. In other words, it interprets the MSIL instructions.

1.17 The program's purpose, input, process, and output.

1.18 Before you create a program on the computer, you should first create it in your mind. Try to imagine what the computer screen will look like while the program is running. If it helps, draw pictures of the screen, with sample input and output, at various points in the program.

1.19 A cross between human language and a programming language. Pseudocode is especially helpful when designing an algorithm. Although the computer can't understand pseudocode, programmers often find it helpful to write an algorithm in a language that's "almost" a programming language, but still very similar to natural language.

1.20 A compiler translates source code into an executable form.

1.21 A runtime error is an error that occurs while the program is running. These are usually logical errors, such as mathematical mistakes.

1.22 Syntax errors are found by the compiler.

1.23 You can provide sample data, and predict what the output should be. If the program does not produce the correct output, a logical error is present in the program.

1.24 Data and the code that operates on the data.

1.25 The data contained in an object.

1.26 The procedures, or behaviors, that an object performs.

1.27 Encapsulation refers to the combining of data and code into a single object.

1.28 Data hiding refers to an object's ability to hide its data from code that is outside the object. Only the object's methods may then directly access and make changes to the object's data. An object typically hides its data, but allows outside code to access the methods that operate on the data.

Chapter 2

2.1
```
// A crazy mixed up program
using System;
public class Columbus
{
    public static void Main()
    {
        Console.WriteLine("In 1492 Columbus sailed the ocean blue.");
    }
}
```

2.2 Columbus.cs

2.3
```
using System;
public class Hello
{
    public static void Main()
    {
        Console.WriteLine("Hello World");
    }
}
```

2.4
```
//  Example
//  August 22, 2005
using System;
public class MyName
{
    public static void Main()
    {

        Console.WriteLine("Herbert Dorfmann");

    }
}
```

2.5 C

2.6 A

2.7
```
// Its a mad, mad program
using System;
public class Success
{
    public static void Main()
    {
        Console.Write("Success\n");
        Console.Write("Success ");
        Console.Write("Success\n");
        Console.WriteLine("\nSuccess");
    }
}
```

2.8
```
The works of Wolfgang
        include the following
        The Turkish March and Symphony No. 40 in G minor.
```

2.9
```
// August 22, 2005
public class PersonalInfo
{
    public static void Main()
    {
        Console.WriteLine("Herbert Dorfmann");
        Console.WriteLine("123 Elm Street");
        Console.WriteLine("My Town, NC  21111");
        Console.WriteLine("919-555-1234");
    }
}
```

2.10 Variables: `little` and `big`.

Literals: `2`, `2000`, `"The little number is "` and `"The big number is "`

2.11 `The value is number`

2.12 `99bottles` is illegal because it starts with a number.

`r&d` is illegal because the `&` character is illegal.

2.13 They are not the same because one begins with an uppercase S while the other begins with a lowercase s. Variable names are case-sensitive.

2.14 ▪ `short`

   ▪ `int`

   ▪ 22.1 because it is stored as a `double`.

2.15 `6.31E17`

2.16 Append the `F` suffix to the numeric literal, such as:

`number = 7.4F;`

2.17 `true` and `false`

2.18 a) `char letter;`

   b) `letter = 'A';`

   c) `Console.WriteLine(letter);`

2.19 The code for 'C' is 67.

The code for 'F' is 70.

The code for 'W' is 87.

2.20 `'B'` is a character literal.

2.21 You cannot assign a string literal to a `char` variable. The statement should be:

`char letter = 'Z';`

2.22 | **Expression** | **Value** |
|---|---|
| `6 + 3 * 5` | 21 |
| `12 / 2 - 4` | 2 |
| `9 + 14 * 2 - 6` | 31 |
| `5 + 19 % 3 - 1` | 5 |
| `(6 + 2) * 3` | 24 |
| `14 / (11 - 4)` | 2 |
| `9 + 12 * (8 - 3)` | 69 |

2.23 Integer division. The value 23.0 will be stored in `portion`.

2.24 a) `x += 6;`

   b) `amount -= 4;`

   c) `y *= 4;`

   d) `total /= 27;`

   e) `x %= 7;`

2.25 a) No

b) Because the result of basePay + bonus results in an int value, which cannot be stored in the short variable totalPay. You can fix the problem by declaring totalPay as an int, or casting the result of the expression to a short.

2.26 a = (float)b;

2.27 string city = "San Francisco";

2.28 stringLength = city.Length;

2.31 lowerCity = city.ToLowerCase();

2.32 To write a single line comment you begin the comment with //. To write a multi-line comment you begin the comment with /* and end it with */.

2.33 string name;

```
// Ask the user to enter the name of a favorite pet.
Console.Write("Enter the name of your favorite pet: ");
name = Console.ReadLine();
```

2.34 Because the ReadLine method returns a string.

2.35 number = Convert.ToInt32(str);

Chapter 3

3.1 A value-returning method returns a value back to the code that called it, and a void method does not.

3.2 Method call

3.3 Method header

3.4 If the user enters 5 the program will display "Able was I." If the user enters 10 the program will display "I saw Elba." If the user enters 100 the program will display "I saw Elba."

3.5
```
public static void MyName()
{
    Console.WriteLine("Mary Catherine Jones");
}
```

3.6 An argument is a value that is passed into a method. A parameter is a special variable that holds the value being passed into the method.

3.7 b and c will cause a compiler error because the values being sent as arguments (a double and a long) cannot be automatically converted to an int.

3.8 Only d is written correctly.

3.9 Only a copy of an argument's value is passed into a parameter variable. A method's parameter variables are separate and distinct from the arguments that are listed inside the parentheses of a method call. If a parameter variable is changed inside a method, it has no affect on the original argument.

3.10 99 1.5
99 1.5
0 0.0
99 1.5

3.11 `double`

3.12 `public static int Days(int years, int months, int weeks)`

3.13 `public static double Distance(double rate, double time)`

3.14 `public static long LightYears(long miles)`

3.15 A recursive algorithm requires multiple method calls. Each method call requires several actions to be performed by the C# compiler. These actions include allocating memory for parameters and local variables, and storing the address of the program location where control returns after the method terminates. All of these actions are known as overhead. In an iterative algorithm, which uses a loop, such overhead is unnecessary.

3.16 A case in which the problem can be solved without recursion.

3.17 Cases in which the problem is solved using recursion.

3.18 When it reaches the base case.

3.19 C2

3.20 F2

3.21 N2

Chapter 4

4.1 Classes are the blueprints.

4.2 Objects are the cookies.

4.3 The memory address of the object.

4.4 A `string` object.

4.5 a) `Car`

b) `make` and `yearModel`

c) `SetMake`, `SetYearModel`, `GetMake`, and `GetYearModel`

d) `make` and `yearModel`

e) `SetMake`, `SetYearModel`, `GetMake`, and `GetYearModel`

4.6 `limo.SetMake("Cadillac");`

4.7 Creates an instance of an object in memory.

4.8 An accessor is a method that gets a value from a class's field but does not change it. A mutator is a method that stores a value in a field or in some other way changes the value of a field

4.9 When the value of an item is dependent on other data and that item is not updated when the other data is changed, it is said that the item has become stale.

4.10

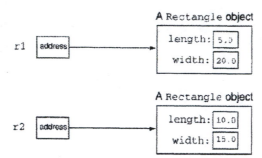

4.11 It has the same name as the class.

4.12 It has no return type, not even void.

4.13 Assume that the following is a constructor, which appears in a class.

a) `ClassAct`

b) `act = new ClassAct(25);`

4.14 Overloaded methods must have different parameter lists. Their return types do not matter.

4.15 A method's signature consists of the method's name and the data types of the method's parameters, in the order that they appear.

4.16 This is the second version of the method.
This is the first version of the method.

4.17 Only one.

Chapter 5

```
5.1   if (y == 20)
          x = 0;
5.2   if (hours > 40)
          payRate *= 1.5;
5.3   if (sales >= 10000)
          commission = 0.2;
5.4   if (max)
          fees = 50;
5.5   if (x > 100)
      {
          y = 20;
          z = 40;
      }
5.6   if (a < 10)
      {
          b = 0;
          c = 1;
      }
```

```
5.7   if (myCharacter == 'D')
          Console.WriteLine("Goodbye");
5.8   if (x > 100)
          y = 20;
      else
          y = 0;
5.9   if (y == 100)
          x = 1;
      else
          x = 0;
5.10  if (sales >= 50000.0)
          commission = 0.2;
      else
          commission = 0.1;
5.11  if (a < 10)
      {
          b = 0;
          c = 1;
      }
      else
      {
          b = -99;
          c = 0;
      }
```

5.12 1 1

5.13

If the customer purchases this many books...	this many coupons are given.
1	1
2	1
3	2
4	2
5	3
10	3

```
5.14  if (amount1 > 10)
      {
          if (amount2 < 100)
          {
              if (amount1 > amount2)
                  Console.WriteLine(amount1);
              else
                  Console.WriteLine(amount2);
          }
      }
```

5.15
```
if (x > 0)
{
    if (y < 20)
    {
        z = 1;
    }
    else
    {
        z = 0;
    }
}
```

5.16

Logical Expression	Result (*true* or *false*)
true && false	false
true && true	true
false && true	false
false && false	false
true || false	true
true || true	true
false || true	true
false || false	false
!true	false
!false	true

5.17 T, F, T, T, T

5.18
```
if (speed >= 0 && speed <= 200)
    Console.WriteLine("The number is valid");
```

5.19
```
if (speed < 0 || speed > 200)
    Console.WriteLine("The number is not valid");
```

5.20
```
if (name.Equals("Timothy"))
    Console.WriteLine("Do I know you?");
```

5.21
```
if (name1.CompareTo(name2) < 0)
    Console.WriteLine("{0} {1}", name1, name2);
else
    Console.WriteLine("{0} {1}", name2, name1);
```

5.22 a)
```
z = x > y ? 1 : 20;
```

b)
```
population = temp > 45 ? base * 10 : base * 2;
```

c)
```
wages = hours > 40 ? wages * 1.5 : wages * 1;
```

d)
```
Console.WriteLine(result >=0 ? "The result is positive" :
                              "The result is negative");
```

5.23
```
// Here is the switch statement.
switch(userNum)
{
    case 1 : Console.WriteLine("One");
             break;
    case 2 : Console.WriteLine("Two");
             break;
    case 3 : Console.WriteLine("Three");
             break;
    default: Console.WriteLine("Error: invalid number.");
             break;
}
```

5.24
```
switch(selection)
{
    case 'A' : Console.WriteLine("You selected A.");
               break;
    case 'B' : Console.WriteLine("You selected B.");
               break;
    case 'C' : Console.WriteLine("You selected C.");
               break;
    case 'D' : Console.WriteLine("You selected D.");
               break;
    default  : Console.WriteLine("Not good with letters, eh?");
               break;
}
```

5.25 Because it uses greater-than and less-than operators in the comparisons.

5.26 The case expressions must be a literal or a const variable which must be one of the integral data types. In this code, relational expressions are used.

5.27 That is serious.

Chapter 6

6.1 a) 2   b) 2   c) 1   d) 8

6.2 0 times

6.3 This must be a trick question. The statement that prints "I love C# programming!" is not in the body of the loop. The only statement that is in the body of the loop is the one that prints "Hello World". Because there is no code in the loop to change the contents of the count variable, the loop will execute infinitely, printing "Hello World". So, "I love C# programming!" is never printed.

6.4
```
// Assume that input is a string reference variable,
// number is an int,
Console.Write("Enter a number in the range " +
              "of 10  25: ");
number = Convert.ToInt32(Console.ReadLine());
```

```csharp
while (number < 10 || number > 25)
{
    Console.WriteLine("That number is not in the range.");
    Console.Write("Enter a number in the range " +
                "of 10  25: ");

    number = Convert.ToInt32(Console.ReadLine());
}
```

6.5 `// Assume that input is a string reference variable,`
`// ch is a char`

```csharp
Console.Write("Enter Y, y, N, or n: ");

ch = Convert.ToChar(Console.ReadLine());
while (ch != 'Y' && ch != 'y' && ch != 'N' && ch != 'n')
{
    Console.WriteLine("Try again.");
    Console.Write("Enter Y, y, N, or n: ");

    ch = Convert.ToChar(Console.ReadLine());
}
```

6.6 `// Assume that input is a string reference variable,`

```csharp
Console.Write("Enter Yes or No: ");
input = Console.ReadLine();
while ((!input.Equals("Yes")) && (!input.Equals("No")))
{
    Console.Write("Please enter Yes or No: ");
    input = Console.ReadLine();
}
```

6.7 Initialization, test, and update.

6.8 a) count = 1

b) count <= 50

c) count++

d) `for (int count = 1; count <= 50; count++)`
`    Console.WriteLine("I love to program");`

6.9 a) 0

2
4
6
8
10

b) -5
   -4
   -3
   -2
   -1
   0
   1
   2
   3
   4

c) 5
   8
   11
   14
   17

6.10
```
for (int i = 1; i <= 10; i++)
    Console.WriteLine("Chloe Ashlyn");
```

6.11
```
for (int i = 0; i <= 100; i += 5)
    Console.WriteLine(i);
```

6.12
```
// Assume that input is a string reference variable

int number = 0, total = 0;
for (int i = 1; i <= 7; i++)
{
    Console.Write("Enter a number: ");

    number = Convert.ToInt32(Console.ReadLine());
    total += number;
}
Console.WriteLine("The total is {0}", total);
```

6.13 The variable x is the loop control variable and y is the accumulator.

6.14 You should be careful to choose a value that cannot be mistaken as a valid input value.

6.15 Data is read from an input file, and data is written to an output file.

6.16
```
using System.IO;
```

6.17 StreamWriter

6.18
```
StreamWriter outputFile = new StreamWriter("MyName.txt");
outputFile.WriteLine("Jim");
outputFile.Close();
```

6.19 StreamReader

6.20
```
StreamReader inputFile = new StreamReader("MyName.txt");
string str;
str = inputFile.ReadLine();
if (str != null)
    Console.WriteLine(str);
inputFile.Close();
```

Chapter 7

7.1 a) `int[] employeeNumbers = new int[100];`

b) `double[] payRates = new double[25];`

c) `float[] miles = new float[14];`

d) `char[] letters = new char[1000];`

7.2 An array's size declarator must be a non-negative integer expression. The first statement is incorrect because the size declarator is negative. The second statement is incorrect because the size declarator is a floating-point number.

7.3 0 through 3

7.4 The size declarator specifies the number of elements in the array. A subscript identifies a specific element in the array.

7.5 The subscript is outside the range of valid subscripts for the array.

7.6 When the statement executes, it crashes the program and displays a runtime error message.

7.7 1
2
3
4
5

7.8 `double[] array = { 1.7, 6.4, 7.9, 3.1, 8.2 };`

There are five elements in the array.

7.9 `result = numbers1[0] * numbers2[3];`

7.10 `for (int i = 0; i < array.Length; i++)`
`    array[i] = -1;`

7.11 `int size;`
`string input;`
`Console.Write("Enter the size of the array: ");`
`size = Convert.ToInt32(Console.ReadLine());`
`values = new double[size];`

7.12 `for (int i = 0; i < a.Length; i++)`
`        b[i] = a[i];`

7.13 `MyMethod(numbers);`

7.14 `public static void Zero(int[] array)`
`{`
`    for (int i = 0; i < array.Length; i++)`
`        array[i] = 0;`
`}`

7.15 `Rectangle[] rectArray = new Rectangle[5];`
`for (int i = 0; i <= rectArray.Length; i++)`
`{`
`    // Initialize each rectangle with the values`
`    // i and i+1 for length and width.`
`    rectArray[i] = new Rectangle(i, i+1);`
`}`

7.16 The selection sort first looks for the smallest value in the array. When it finds it, it moves it to element 0.

7.17 Only once.

7.18 The sequential search steps through each element of the array, starting at element 0, looking for the search value. The binary search requires that the array be sorted in ascending order. It starts by looking at the middle element. If it is not the search value, and is greater than the search value, then the lower half of the array is searched next. If the middle element is not the search value, and is less than the search value, the upper half of the array is searched next. This same technique is repeated on the half of the array being searched until the element is either found or there are no more elements to search.

7.19 10,000 comparisons

7.20 Move the items that are frequently searched for to the beginning of the array.

7.21
```
const int RACKS = 50;
const int SHELVES = 10;
const int VIDEOS = 25;
// Create an array to hold video numbers.
int[,,] videoNumbers = new int[RACKS,SHELVES,VIDEOS];
```

Chapter 8

8.1 Each instance of a class has its own copy of the class's instance fields. A static field does not belong to any instance of the class, and there is only one copy of a static field in memory, regardless of the number of instances of the class.

8.2 It isn't necessary for an instance of the class to be created in order to execute the method.

8.3 They cannot refer to non-static members of the class. This means that any method called from a static method must also be static. It also means that if the method uses any of the class's fields, they must be static as well.

8.4 The object's memory address.

8.5 Although the object's address is passed by value, the method has access to the object referenced by that address.

8.6
```
public static void ShowBalance(BankAccount a)
{
    Console.WriteLine("Balance: {0}",a.GetBalance());
}
```

8.7
```
public static Rectangle GetRectangle()
{
    return new Rectangle(0.0, 0.0);
}
```

8.8 The Car class is the aggregate class because it contains an instance of another class: Engine.

8.9 Because code outside the class can get the return value and gain direct access to the field. This is not true for fields that are string objects because string objects are immutable.

8.10 No, it is not advisable. This is because the variable will contain the value null prior to being assigned an address. Any operation with the variable that would require the existence of an object, such as calling an instance method, will cause an error.

8.11 The this variable will reference the distance2 object.

8.12 When you store classes in a namespace, you can make them available to all applications without copying them and storing them in each application's folder or directory.

8.13 Each class must have a using statement that identifies the namespace that the class belongs to.

Chapter 9

9.1 `little = Char.ToLowerCase(big);`

9.2
```
if (Char.IsDigit(ch))
    Console.WriteLine("digit");
else
    Console.WriteLine("Not a digit");
```

9.3 A

9.4
```
string input;
char choice;
Console.Write("Do you want to repeat the " +
              "program or quit? (R/Q)");

choice = Convert.ToChar(Console.ReadLine());
choice = Char.ToUpperCase(choice);
while (choice != 'R' && choice != 'Q')
{
    Console.Write("Do you want to repeat the " +
                  "program or quit? (R/Q) ");

    choice = Convert.ToChar(Console.ReadLine());
    choice = Char.ToUpperCase(choice);
}
```

9.5 $

9.6
```
int total = 0;
for (int i = 0; i < str.Length; i++)
{
    if (Char.IsUpperCase(str[i])))
        total++;
}
```

9.7
```
public static bool EndsWithGer(string str)
{
    bool status;

    if (str.EndsWith("ger"))
        status = true;
    else
        status = false;
    return status;
}
```

9.8
```
public static bool EndsWithGer(string str)
{
    bool status;
    string strUpper = str.ToUpperCase();

    if (strUpper.EndsWith("GER"))
        status = true;
    else
        status = false;
    return status;
}
```

9.9   You would use the Substring method.

9.10 The IndexOf method searches for a character or substring, starting at the beginning of a string. The LastIndexOf method searches for a character or substring, starting at the end of a string. This means that the IndexOf method returns the index of the first occurrence of a character or substring, and the LastIndexOf method returns the index of the last occurrence of a character or substring.

9.11 The Substring method returns a reference to a substring. The GetChars method stores a substring in a char array.

9.12 The Concat method.

9.13 The ToCharArray method returns all of the characters in the calling object as a char array.

9.14 The fellow student is wrong. The replace method will return a reference to a string which is a copy of str1, in which all of the o characters have been replaced with u characters. The original string in str1 will not be changed however. The code will produce the following output:

```
To be, or not to be
Tu be, ur nut tu be
```

9.15 WilliamtheConqueror

9.16 Once you create a string object, you cannot change the object's value.

9.17 It would be more efficient to use StringBuilder objects because they are not immutable. Making a change to a StringBuilder object does not cause a new object to be created.

9.18 StringBuilder city = new StringBuilder("Asheville");

9.19 The Append method.

9.20 The Insert method.

9.21 While the string class's Replace method replaces the occurrences of one character with another character, the StringBuilder class's Replace method replaces a specified substring with a string.

9.21 The tokens are "apples", "pears", and "bananas". The delimiter is the space character.

9.23
```
string str = "/home/rjones/mydata.txt"
char[] tokens = {'/'};
string[] strtok = str.Split(tokens);
```

9.24 An exception is an object that is generated as the result of an error or an unexpected event.

9.25 To throw an exception means to generate an exception object.

9.26 Unless an exception is detected by the application and dealt with, it causes the application to halt.

9.27 The Exception class.

9.28 Classes that extend the ApplicationException class are for exceptions that are thrown when a critical error occurs. An application should not try to handle these exceptions. Exception classes that extend the SystemException class are general exceptions that an application can handle.

9.29 A try block is one or more statements that are executed and can potentially throw an exception. A catch block is code that appears immediately after a catch clause, and is executed in response to a particular exception.

9.30 The program will resume with the code that appears after the entire try/catch construct.

9.31 Each exception object has a method named Message that can be used to retrieve the error message for the exception.

9.32 Statements in the finally block are always executed after the try block has executed and after any catch blocks have executed if an exception was thrown. The finally block executes whether an exception is thrown or not.

9.33 Because method B does not handle the exception, control is passed back to method A. Method A doesn't handle the exception either, so control is passed back method Main. Because Main doesn't handle the exception, the program is halted and the default exception handler handles the exception.

9.34 All of the data stored in a text file is formatted as text. In a binary file, data is stored in its raw binary format.

9.35 To write data to a binary file you use the BinaryWriter class. To read data from a file you use the BinaryReader class.

9.36 With sequential access, when a file is opened for input, its read position is at the very beginning of the file. This means that the first time data is read from the file, the data will be read from its beginning. As the reading continues, the file's read position advances sequentially through the file's contents. In random file access, a program may immediately jump to any location in the file without first reading the preceding bytes.

9.37 FileStream

Chapter 10

10.1   Vehicle is the base class and Truck is the derived class.

10.2   a) Shape is the base class, Circle is the derived class.

      b) SetArea, GetArea, SetRadius, GetRadius

      c) area

      d)
c.SetRadius(9.0);	legal
s.SetRadius(9.0);	illegal
Console.WriteLine(c.GetArea());	legal
Console.WriteLine(s.GetArea());	legal

10.3   The base class constructor (class A) will execute first, then the derived class constructor (class B) will execute.

10.4   You are on the ground.
      You are in the sky.

10.5   The ground is green
      The sky is blue

10.6   When the base class method is inadequate for the derived class's purpose.

10.7   A derived class may call an overridden base class method by prefixing its name with the base key word and a dot (.).

10.8   It overrides the base class method.

10.9   It overloads the base class method.

10.10 Protected members of class may be accessed by methods in a derived class, and by methods in the same namespace as the class.

10.11 Private members may be accessed only by methods in the same class. A protected member of a class may be directly accessed by methods of the same class or methods of a derived class.

10.12 Because any class that inherits from the class, or is in the same package, has unrestricted access to the protected member.

10.13 When you accidentally leave out the access specifier, the member will have package access.

10.14 ClassD still inherits from Object, because all classes ultimately inherit from Object.

10.15 Because those methods are members of the Object class.

10.16 a) Legal, because a Cube is a Rectangle.

        b)
Console.WriteLine(r.GetLength());	Legal
Console.WriteLine(r.GetWidth());	Legal
Console.WriteLine(r.GetHeight());	Illegal
Console.WriteLine(r.GetSurfaceArea());	Illegal

        c) Illegal, because a Rectangle is not a Cube. The Cube class has capabilities beyond those of the Rectangle class, so a Cube variable cannot reference a Rectangle object.

10.17 Abstract methods are used to ensure that a derived class implements the method.

10.18 Override the abstract method.

10.19 An abstract class serves as a base class for other classes. It represents the generic or abstract form of all the classes that inherit from it.

10.20 An abstract class cannot be instantiated. It must serve as a base class.

10.21 To specify behavior for other classes.

10.22 It cannot be instantiated.

10.23 An interface only specifies methods, it does not define them. In addition, all members of an interface are public.

10.24 `public class Customer : Relatable`

10.25 `public class Employee : Payable, Listable`

Chapter 11

11.1 The Solution Explorer window shows a file-oriented view of a project. It allows you to quickly navigate among the files in your project.

11.2 The Properties window shows, and allows you to change, most of the currently selected object's properties, and those properties' values.

11.3 The Dynamic Help window displays a list of help topics that changes as you perform operations. The topics that are displayed are relevant to the operation you are currently performing.

11.4 It means that an application responds to events that occur, or actions that take place, such as the clicking of a mouse.

11.5 A property is data stored in an object. A method is an action that an object performs.

11.6 Because the default name is not descriptive. It does not indicate the purpose of the control.

11.7 A Text Box.

11.8 Text1

11.9 Text

11.10 With the form selected, double-click the Label control tool in the toolbox.

11.11 The title bar shows [run], which indicates that Visual C# .NET is in run time.

11.12 1) On the Visual Studio .NET Start Page click the name of the project.

2) On the Visual Studio .NET Start Page click the Open Project button, then use the Open Project dialog box to locate the project's solution or project file. Select the file and click Open.

3) Click File on the menu bar, then click New, then click Project. Use the Open Project dialog box to locate the project's solution or project file. Select the file and click Open.

11.13 If a control will be accessed in code, or will have code associated with it (such as an event procedure), you will assign it a name. Otherwise, keep the control's default name.

11.14 `SecretAnswerLabel.Visible = False;`

11.15 The background color of the Label's text changes.

11.16 The color of the Label's text changes.

Chapter 12

12.1 Text

12.2 `MessageLabel.Caption = InputText.Text;`

12.3 Hello Jonathon, how are you?

12.4 You can make a form appear more organized by grouping related controls inside group boxes.

12.5 f, g, a, b, I, h, e, c, d

12.6 c, a, d, b

12.7 By examining its Checked property. If the property is set to true, the radio button is selected. If the property is set to false, the radio button is not selected.

12.8 By examining its Checked property. If the property is set to true, the Check Box is selected. If the property is set to false, the Check Box is not selected.

12.9 `input = InputBox("Enter a number", "Please Respond", 500);`

12.10 `input = InputBox("Enter a number", "Please Respond", 500, 100, 300);`

12.11 0

12.12 Items.Count

12.13 SelectedItem

12.14 0

12.15 Items.Count

12.16 SelectedIndex

Appendix G: Answers to Odd-Numbered Review Questions

Chapter 1

Multiple Choice

1. b
3. a
5. b
7. c
9. a
11. a
13. d

Find the Error

1. The algorithm performs the math operation at the wrong time. It multiplies width by length before getting values for those variables.

Algorithm Workbench

1. Display "What is the customer's maximum amount of credit?"
   Input maxCredit.
   Display "What is the amount of credit used by the customer?"
   Input creditUsed.
   availableCredit = maxCredit − creditUsed.
   Display availableCredit.

3. Display "What is the account's starting balance?"
   Input startingBalance.
   Display "What is the total amount of the deposits made?"
   Input deposits.
   Display "What is the total amount of the withdrawals made?"
   Input withdrawals.
   Display "What is the monthly interest rate?"

Input interestRate.
balance = startingBalance + deposits – withdrawals.
interest = balance * interestRate.
balance = balance + interest.
Display balance.

Predict the Result

1.   7

Short Answer

1.   Main memory, or RAM, holds the sequences of instructions in the programs that are running and the data those programs are using. Main memory, or RAM, is usually volatile. Secondary storage is a type of memory that can hold data for long periods of time—even when there is no power to the computer.

3.   An operating system is a set of programs that manages the computer's hardware devices and controls their processes. Windows and UNIX are examples of operating systems. Application software refers to programs that make the computer useful to the user. These programs solve specific problems or perform general operations that satisfy the needs of the user. Word processing, spreadsheet, and database packages are all examples of application software.

5.   Because machine language programs are streams of binary numbers, and high-level language programs are made up of words.

7.   *Syntax errors* are mistakes that the programmer has made that violate the rules of the programming language. *Logical errors* are mistakes that cause the program to produce erroneous results.

9.   A program that translates source code into executable code.

11.   Machine language code is executed directly by the CPU. Intermediate code (MSIL) is executed by the JIT.

13.   Object-oriented programming

15.   The object's methods.

17.   No

21.   `csc LabAssignment.cs`

Chapter 2

Multiple Choice and True/False

1.   c

3.   a

5.   b and c

7. c

9. a

11. a

13. True

15. True

Predict the Output

1. 0
    100

3. I am the incredible computing
    machine
    and I will
    amaze you.

5. 23
    1

Find the Error

- The comment symbols in the first line are reversed. They should be /* and */.

- The word class is missing in the second line. It should read public class MyProgram.

- main should be Main

- The Main header should not be terminated with a semicolon.

- The fifth line should have a left brace, not a right brace.

- The first four lines inside the Main method are missing their semicolons.

- The comment in the first line inside the Main method should begin with forward slashes (//), not backward slashes.

- The last line inside the main method, a call to WriteLine, uses a string literal, but the literal is enclosed in single quotes. It should be enclosed in double quotes, like this: "The value of c is".

- (0) should be {0}

- The last line inside the Main method passes C to WriteLine, but it should pass c (lowercase).

- The class is missing its closing brace.

Algorithm Workbench

1. `double temp, weight, age;`

3. a) `b = a + 2;`

   b) `a = b * 4;`

   c) `b = a / 3.14;`

   d) `a = b - 8;`

   e) `C = 'K';`

   f) `c = 66;`

5. a) `3.287E6`

   b) `-9.7865E12`

   c) `7.65491E-3`

7. ```
   int speed, time, distance;
   speed = 20;
   time = 10;
   distance = speed * time;
   Console.WriteLine(distance);
   ```

9. ```
   string str;
   double income;

   // Ask the user to enter his or her desired income
   Console.Write("Enter your desired annual income: ");
   str = Console.ReadLine();
   income = Convert.ToDouble(str);
   ```

11. `total = (float)number;`

Short Answer

1. Multi-line style.

3. It does not regard uppercase letters as being the same character as their lowercase equivalents. So programmers will not declare variables like this.

5. The values of the variables can be changed during program execution.

7. The purpose of the variable and size of the value.

9. One is a single line comment the other is a multi-line comment

11. You only have to declare the constant once.

Chapter 3

Multiple Choice and True/False

1. b

3. a

5. b

7. d
9. True
11. False
13. True
15. False
17. False

Find the Error

1. The header should not be terminated with a semicolon.
3. The method should have a `return` statement that returns a `double` value.

Algorithm Workbench

1. `DoSomething(25);`
3. The value 3 will be stored in a, 2 will be stored in b, and 1 will be stored in c.
5. `result = Cube(4);`
7.
```
public static double TimesTen(double num)
{
    return num * 10.0;
}
```

Short Answer

1. A large complex problem is broken down into smaller manageable pieces. Each smaller piece of the problem is then solved.
3. An argument is a value that is passed into a method when the method is called. A parameter variable is a variable that is declared in the method header, and receives the value of an argument when the method is called.
5. When an argument is passed to a method, the address of the argument is passed. The method can access the actual argument.
7. Fixed.
9. Number.

Chapter 4

Multiple Choice and True/False

1. a
3. d
5. b
7. d

9.   b

11.   c

13.   b

15.   True

17.   False

Find the Error

1.   The constructor cannot have a return type, not even void.

3.   The parentheses are missing. The statement should read:

```
Rectangle box = new Rectangle();
```

5.   The square methods must have different parameter lists. Both accept an int.

Algorithm Workbench

1.   a) UML diagram:

```
┌─────────────────────────────────┐
│              Pet                │
├─────────────────────────────────┤
│ - name : string                 │
│ - animal : string               │
│ - age : int                     │
├─────────────────────────────────┤
│ + SetName(n : string) : void    │
│ + SetAnimal(a : string) : void  │
│ + SetAge(a : int) : void        │
│ + GetName() : string            │
│ + GetAnimal() : string          │
│ + GetAge() : int                │
└─────────────────────────────────┘
```

b)   Class code:

```
public class Pet
{
    private string name;    // The pet's name
    private string animal;  // The type of animal
    private int age;        // The pet's age

    /*
       SetName method
       --parameter n The pet's name.
    */
```

```
public void SetName(string n)
{
    name = n;
}

/*
    SetAnimal method
    --parameter a The type of animal.
*/

public void SetAnimal(string a)
{
    animal = a;
}

/*
    SetAge method
    --parameter a The pet's age.
*/

public void SetAge(int a)
{
    age = a;
}

/*
    GetName method
    --return The pet's name.
*/

public string GetName()
{
    return name;
}

/*
    GetAnimal method
    --return The type of animal.
*/

public string GetAnimal()
{
    return animal;
}

/*
    GetAge method
    --return The pet's age.
*/
```

```
      public int GetAge()
      {
          return age;
      }
  }
```

3. a) `public Square()`
```
        {
            sideLength = 0.0;
        }
```

   b) `public Square(double s)`
```
        {
            sideLength = s;
        }
```

Short Answer

1. A class is a collection of programming statements that specify the attributes and methods that a particular type of object may have. You should think of a class as a blueprint that describes an object. An instance of a class is an actual object that exists in memory.

3. An accessor method is a method that gets a value from a class's field but does not change it. A mutator method is a method that stores a value in a field or in some other way changes the value of a field.

5. Methods that are members of the same class.

7. It looks in the current folder or directory for the file Customer.exe. If that file does not exist, the compiler searches for the file Customer.cs and compiles it. This creates the file Customer.exe, which makes the Customer class available. The same procedure is followed when the compiler searches for the class.

9. If you do not write a constructor for a class, Java automatically provides one.

11. By their signatures, which includes the method name and the data types of the method parameters, in the order that they appear.

13. They are specific to C#. They are properties that allow us to not have to use the traditional and methods with classes.

Chapter 5

Multiple Choice and True/False

1. b
3. a
5. c
7. a
9. a

11.　a

13.　c

15.　False

17.　True

19.　True

Find the Error

1.　Each if clause is prematurely terminated by a semicolon.

3.　The conditionally-executed blocks of code should be enclosed in braces.

5.　The ! operator is only applied to the variable x, not the expression. The code should read

```
if (!(x > 20))
```

7.　The statement should use the || operator instead of the && operator.

Algorithm Workbench

1.
```
if (y == 0)
x = 100;
```

3.
```
if (sales < 10000)
commission = .10;
else if (sales <= 15000)
commission = .15;
else
commission = .20;
```

5.
```
if (amount1 > 10)
{
    if (amount2 < 100)
    {
        if (amount1 > amount2)
        {
            Console.WriteLine(amount1);
        }
        else
        {
            Console.WriteLine(amount2);
        }
    }
}
```

7.
```
if (temperature >= -50 && temperature <= 150)
    Console.WriteLine("The number is valid.");
```

9.
```
if (title1.compareTo(title2) < 0)
    Console.WriteLine(title1 + " " + title2);
else
    Console.WriteLine(title2 + " " + title1);
```

11.　C, A, B

Short Answer

1. Conditionally executed code is executed only under a condition, such as an expression being true.

3. By indenting the conditionally executed statements, you are causing them to stand out visually. This is so you can tell at a glance what part of the program the `if` statement executes.

5. A flag is a `boolean` variable that signals when some condition exists in the program. When the flag variable is set to false, it indicates the condition does not yet exist. When the flag variable is set to true, it means the condition does exist.

7. It takes two `boolean` expressions as operands and creates a boolean expression that is true only when both subexpressions are true.

9. They determine whether a specific relationship exists between two values. The relationships are greater-than, less-than, equal-to, not-equal-to, greater-than-or equal-to, and less-than-or-equal-to.

Chapter 6

Multiple Choice and True/False

1. a
3. c
5. a
7. b
9. c
11. a
13. a
15. d
17. a
19. True
21. False
23. False
25. True

Find the Error

1. The conditionally executed statements should be enclosed in a set of braces. Also, the variable `again` is tested in the while loop before it is ever given a value.

3. The expression being tested by the `do-while` loop should be `choice == 1`. Also, the do-while loop must be terminated by a semicolon.

Algorithm Workbench

1.
```
int product = 0, num;
while (product < 100)
{
    input = Console.ReadLine();
    num = Convert.ToInt32(input);
    product = num * 10;
}
```

3. The following code simply prints the numbers, separated by spaces.
```
for (int x = 0; x <= 1000; x += 10)
    Console.Write("{0} ",x);
```

The following code prints the numbers separated by commas.
```
for (int x = 0; x <= 1000; x += 10)
{
    if (x < 1000)
        Console.Write("{0}, ",x);
    else
        Console.Write(x);
}
```

5.
```
double total = 0;
for (int num = 1, denom = 30; num <= 30; num++, denom--)
    total += num / denom;
```

7.
```
int x;
do
{
    Console.Write("Enter a number: ");
    input = Console.ReadLine();
    x = Convert.ToInt32(input);
} while (x > 0);
```

9.
```
for (int count = 0; count > 50; count++)
    Console.WriteLine("count is {0}", count);
```

11.
```
int number;
Console.Write("Enter a number in the range " +
              "of 1 through 4: ");
input = Console.ReadLine();
number = Convert.ToInt32(input);
while (number < 1 || number > 4)
{
    Console.Write("Invalid number. Enter a " +
                  "number in the range " +
                  "of 1 through 4: ");
    input = Console.ReadLine();
    number = Convert.ToInt32(input);
}
```

13.
```
StreamWriter outFile = new
            StreamWriter("NumberList.txt");
for (int i = 1; i <= 100; i++)
    outFile.WriteLine(i);
outFile.Close();
```

15.
```
StreamReader inFile = new
            StreamReader("NumberList.txt");
string input;
int number, total = 0;
input = inFile.ReadLine();
while (input != null)
{
    number = Convert.ToInt32(input);
    total += number;
    input = inFile.ReadLine();
}
Console.WriteLine("The total is {0}", total);
inFile.Close();
```

Short Answer

1. In postfix mode the operator is placed after the operand. In prefix mode the operator is placed before the variable operand. Postfix mode causes the increment or decrement operation to happen after the value of the variable is used in the expression. Prefix mode causes the increment or decrement to happen first.

3. A pretest loop tests its test expression before each iteration. A posttest loop tests its test expression after each iteration.

5. The while loop is a pretest loop and the do-while loop is a posttest loop.

7. The do-while loop.

9. An accumulator is used to keep a running total of numbers. In a loop, a value is usually added to the current value of the accumulator. If it is not properly initialized, it will not contain the correct total.

11. There are many possible examples. A program that asks the user to enter a business's daily sales for a number of days, and then displays the total sales is one example.

13. Sometimes the user has a list of input values that is very long, and doesn't know the number of items there are. When the sentinel value is entered, it signals the end of the list, and the user doesn't have to count the number of items in the list.

15. There are many possible examples. One example is a program that asks for the average temperature for each month, for a period of five years. The outer loop would iterate once for each year and the inner loop would iterate once for each month.

17. After the WriteLine method writes its data, it writes a newline character. The Write method does not write the newline character.

19. Append means to add on to an existing file.

Chapter 7

Multiple Choice and True/False

1. b
3. b
5. c
7. a
9. d
11. d
13. True
15. False
17. True
19. True
21. True

Find the Error

1. The size declarator cannot be negative.
3. The loop uses the values 1 through 10 as subscripts. It should use 0 through 9.

Algorithm Workbench

1.
```
for (int i = 0; i < 20; i++)
    Console.WriteLine(names[i]);
```
3. `int[,] grades = new int[30,10];`
5.
```
double total = 0.0;          // Accumulator
// Sum the values in the array.
for (int row = 0; row < 10; row++)
{
    for (int col = 0; col < 20; col++)
        total += values[row, col];
}
```

Short Answer

1. The size declarator is used in a definition of an array to indicate the number of elements the array will have. A subscript is used to access a specific element in an array.
3. a) 2

    b) 14

    c) 8

5. Because this statement merely makes array1 reference the same array that array2 references. Both variables will reference the same array. To copy the contents of array2 to array1, the contents of array2's individual elements will have to be assigned to the elements of array1.

7. Yes, the statements are okay.

9. N/2 times

Chapter 8

Multiple Choice and True/False

1. c

3. a

5. b

7. c

9. False

11. False

Find the Error

1. The static method SetValues cannot refer to the nonstatic fields x and y.

Algorithm Workbench

1. a)
```
public string ToString()
{
    string str;
    str = "Radius: " + Radius +
        " Area: " + GetArea;
    return str;
}
```

   b)
```
public bool Equals(Circle c)
{
    bool status;

    if (c.Radius == radius)
        status = true;
    else
        status = false;

    return status;
}
```

```
c)  public bool GreaterThan(Circle c)
    {
        bool status;

        if (c.GetArea > GetArea
            status = true;
        else
            status = false;

        return status;
    }
```

Short Answer

1. Access a nonstatic member.

3. When a variable is passed as an argument, a copy of the variable's contents is passed. The receiving method does not have access to the variable itself. When an object is passed as an argument, a reference to the object (which is the object's address) is passed. This allows the receiving method to have access to the object.

5. Nothing

7. An object that refers to itself.

Chapter 9

Multiple Choice and True/False

1. b

3. a

5. a

7. c

9. c

11. c

13. d

15. c

17. a

19. True

21. True

23. True

25. True

27. False

29. False

Algorithm Workbench

1. ```
   if (Char.ToUpper(choice) == 'Y')
   ```
   Or
   ```
   if (Char.ToLower(choice) == 'y')
   ```

3. ```
   int total = 0;
   for (int i = 0; i < str.Length(); i++)
   {
       if (Char.IsDigit(str[i]))
           total++;
   }
   ```

5. ```
   public static bool DotCom(string str)
   {
       bool status;
       if (str.EndsWith(".com"))
           status = true;
       else
           status = false;
       return status;
   }
   ```

7. ```
   public static void UpperT(StringBuilder strBuff)
   {
       for (int i = 0; i < strBuff.Length; i++)
       {
           if (strBuff[i] == 't')
               strBuff.SetCharAt(i, 'T');
       }
   }
   ```

9. AD

Short Answer

1. This will improve the program's efficiency by reducing the number of string objects that must be created and then removed by the garbage collector.

3. Converts a number to a string.

5. One reason is that they are not as easy to use as variables for simple operations. For example, to get the value stored in an object you must call a method, whereas variables can be used directly.

7. Yes

9. StreamWriter

Chapter 10

Multiple Choice and True/False

1. b
3. d
5. a
7. b
9. a
11. a
13. True
15. False
17. False
19. True
21. False

Find the Error

1. The Car class header should use the word extends instead of expands.
3. Because the Vehicle class does not have a default constructor or a no-arg constructor, the Car class constructor must call the Vehicle class constructor.

Algorithm Workbench

1. `public class Poodle : Dog`
3.
```
public abstract class B
{
    private int m;
    protected int n;

    public void SetM(int value)
    {
        m = value;
    }

    public void SetN(int value)
    {
        n = value;
    }

    public int GetM()
    {
        return m;
    }
```

```
    public int GetN()
    {
        return n;
    }

    public abstract double Calc();
}

public class D : B
{
    private double q;
    protected double r;

    public void SetQ(double value)
    {
        q = value;
    }

    public void SetR(double value)
    {
        r = value;
    }

    public double GetQ()
    {
        return q;
    }

    public double GetR()
    {
        return r;
    }

    public double Calc()
    {
        return q * r;
    }
}
```

5.  ```
    SetValue(10);
    ```

    Or

    ```
    base.SetValue(10);
    ```

7.  ```
    public class Stereo : SoundSystem, CDPlayable,
                                       TunerPlayable,
                                       CassettePlayable
    ```

Short Answer

1. When an is-a relationship exists between objects, the specialized object has all of the characteristics of the general object, plus additional characteristics that make it special.

3. Dog is the base class and Pet is the derived class.

5. No.

7. Overloading is when a method has the same name as one or more other methods, but a different parameter list. Although overloaded methods have the same name, they have different signatures. When a method overrides another method, however, they both have the same signature.

9. At runtime.

11. An abstract class is not instantiated itself, but serves as a base class for other classes. The abstract class represents the generic or abstract form of all the classes that inherit from it.

Chapter 11

Multiple Choice and True/False

1. True

3. False

5. True

7. True

9. True

Short Answer

1. The Text property simply displays text on a control. The Name property, however, is the control's internal name. You access and manipulate a control in code by using its name.

3. ▪ Click the view code button on the Solution Explorer window.

   ▪ Click View on the menu bar, then click the Code command.

   ▪ Press the F7 key while the Form window is visible.

5. One method is to double-click the control's button on the toolbar. This causes a default-sized control to appear in the center of the form. You then move and resize the control as desired. Another method is to single-click the control's button on the toolbar, and then draw it on the form with the mouse cursor.

Chapter 12

Multiple Choice and True/False

1. b
3. b
5. a
7. b
9. c
11. b
13. c
15. b
17. b
19. False
21. False
23. False
25. False
27. False
29. False
31. False

Index

Symbols

==. *See* Equality
! operator. *See* Logical NOT operator
&& operator. *See* Logical AND operator
++ operator. *See* Increment operators
-- operator. *See* Decrement operators
|| operator. *See* Logical OR operator

A

Abstract classes, 559–565
Abstract methods, 559–565
    body, writing (mistake), 576
    header, format, 559
    overloading mistake, 577
    overriding, 561
Accept buttons, 674
    setting, 674
Access key, 671
    assignment. *See* GroupBox control; Labels;
        Multiple buttons; Radio buttons
    setting, 674
    usage, labels (usage), 672–673
Access modifier, 545
Access specification, showing. *See* Unified Modeling
    Language
Access specifier, 160–161
Accessor method, 171
Accumulator
    initialization mistake, 315
    variable, 483
Add method, 410–412
Addition operator, 60
Aggregate objects, creation, 420
Aggregation, 417–428. *See also* Objects; Unified
    Modeling Language diagrams

Algorithm
    definition, 7
    dissection, 133
    variables, usage, 364
Align submenu, 679–680
Alphabetic button, 633
American Standard Code for Information
    Interchange (ASCII) characters, 717
Ampersand (&)
    character, display. *See* Buttons
    usage, 671
AND operator. *See* Logical AND operator
Append method, 468
    overloaded StringBuilder class versions, 468
Application
    building, example, 614–634
    ending, 630
    event procedures, 613
    examination, 652–654
    check boxes, usage, 689–690
    planning phase, 620
    purpose, defining, 614
    running. *See* Controls
    tutorial, 629–630
    visualization, 615
args (parameter), 377
Arguments, 110
    data type compatibility, 112–113
    object, 411, 413
    passing, 524. *See also* Constructors; Methods;
        Multiple arguments
    mistakes, 143
    value/reference, usage, 115–122
    polymorphic acceptance, 557
    providing, mistakes, 198

Arithmetic operators, 59–65, 238
ArithmeticException (class), 477, 487
array
    numbers, elements, 348
    parameter, 349
Arrays. *See* Multidimensional arrays; Objects; One-
    dimensional array; Ragged arrays;
    Searching arrays; Sorting arrays; Two-
    dimensional array
    answers, 744–745
    array, 365
    bounds, 476
    contents
    inputting/outputting, 331–335
    processing, 337–345
    copying, 343–345
    creation, 370
    declaration, 354, 369. *See also* Three-dimensional
        array declaration
    elements, 334
    accessing, 330–331
    display, 372
    processing, 337
    usage, 340
    initialization, 335–336
    introduction, 328–337
    length, 340
    modification, 347
    multiple dimensions, 376–377
    passing. *See* Methods
    ascending order sort, 360
    processing algorithm, usage, 462
    programming challenges, 383–387
    reference variable, 328
    reassignation, 342–343
    returning. *See* Methods
    review questions/exercises, 379–383
    answers, 764–765
    scanning, 358
    searching, 357–365
    size
    change, 329
    declarator, 329, 331
    user specification, 341–342
    sorting, 357–365
    traversing, for loop (usage), 346
    value, 357

ASCII. *See* American Standard Code for
    Information Interchange
Assignment
    operation, 343
    operators, 238
    statement, 41, 56, 101, 415
Associativity, 63, 718–719. *See also* Logical
    operators
Attributes, 154. *See also* Objects
Auto hide
    feature, 600
    initiation, tutorial, 601–602
Auto list box, 642
    disabling, 644

B

Backslash characters, 307
Base class, 511
    access, 541
    constructor, 516, 519–521
    calling, 522–531
    default constructor, absence, 529
    derived class, is-a relationship, 555
    inheritance, 518
    methods, 531–539
    overriding, 538
    overriding, mistake, 576
    virtual declaration, 534
    no-arg constructor, absence, 529
    private members, 518
base (key word), 522–523
base (statement), 524
Binary files, 301, 488–492
    data
    reading, 491–492
    writing, 489–491
Binary format. *See* Raw binary format
Binary numbers, 7
Binary operators, 59
Binary search, 363
    algorithm, 363–365
    performing, 364
BinaryReader class, instance, 491
BinaryWriter class, instance, 490
Binding, 184
boolean
    data type, 54–55
    value, returning, 127–128, 446, 454
    variable, 234

Boolean expression, 212, 232, 238, 300
mistakes, 258
boolean (expression), 219, 225, 231, 250
control, 286
enclosure, mistakes, 315
evaluation, 239
false return, 277
parentheses, enclosure (mistakes), 258
result, 412
testing, 283
usage, 239, 274–276
Boolean (property), 635
Boolean variable, 217
BooleanExpression, 274
Bounding box, 622
Braces
mismatch, 89–90
set, 162
usage, 230. *See also* Curly braces; Statements
break (statement), 254
omission, mistake, 259
usage, 300
Buttons
& character, display, 672
access key, assignment. *See* Multiple keys
determination. *See* Users
keyboard access keys, assignment, 671–672

C

C#
answers, 732–733
console application, 31
exception, 475
introduction, 1
operators, 237
programming challenges, 25
review questions/exercises, 21–24
answers, 752
standard namespaces, 435
statement, 274
virtual machine, compiler (interaction), 12
C# fundamentals, 27
answers, 733–736
programming challenges, 96–98
review questions/exercises, 91–95
answers, 753–755

C# program, 163
compiling/running, 12–13
components, 28–34
Main method, 377
writing, 301
Calling object, 461
substring copy, 460
Calling string
object, 464
usage, 455
Cancel buttons, 674
setting, 674
Capitalization, purpose, 46
case (section)
mistake, 258
case (statement), 253
fall through, 254
CaseExpression, 251
mistakes, 258
Case-sensitive comparison, 455
Cast operators, 68–70
catch block (clause), 478
catch (clause), 478–482
control, 484
inclusion. *See* try
ordering mistake, 498
writing, mistake, 498
Categorized button, 633
C/C++ syntax, usage, 374
Center in Form submenu, 680
Central processing unit (CPU)
usage, 3–4
waste, 233
Chain of inheritance. *See* Inheritance
char (argument), 446
char (array), reference (returning), 461
char (class), usage. *See* Characters
char (data type), 55–56, 446
char (value), returning, 452
Characters
case conversion, 452–454
comparison, 218–219
conversion, char class (usage), 446–454
deletion. *See* StringBuilder object
ending position, 461
position

reverse order, 459
searching
    IndexOf method, usage, 458–459
    LastIndexOf method, usage, 458–459
    testing, 446–454
    methods, application, 449
Char.IsDigit method, 452
Char.IsLetter method, 451
Check boxes, 686, 688–690
    usage. *See* Application
CheckBox control, 688
CheckChanged event. *See* **Radio buttons**
Checked list boxes, 701–703
CheckOnClick property, 702
Classes, 154
    abstraction, 560
    answers, 737–738, 745–746
    body, 30
    code, writing, 160
    construction, 159–171
    definition, 30
    Equals method, benefit, 403
    error, 434
    fields, code (writing), 160–161
    has-a relationship, 420
    header, 30, 32
    colon, usage, 514
    inheritance, 541, 549, 553
    insecure status, 424
    instance, 157, 394, 477
    interfaces
    comparison, 565
    usage, 566
    members. *See* Static class members
    layout, 173
    names, 46, 164
    operation, 415
    programming challenges, 202–208, 439–443
    review questions, 198–202, 436–439
    answers, 756–759, 765–766
    storage, 431
    usage, 157–158. *See also* Objects
    usefulness, increase, 192
clearButton_Click event procedure, 665–666
Click (event), 637
    occurrence, 588

CLR
    determination, 556
    usage, 478, 484, 488
Code, 648. *See also* **Unicode**
    block, 247
    data, separation, 156
    entering/compiling, 17
    errors, checking, 593
    printing, 651
    template, 642
    usage. *See* Pseudocode; Text property
    window, 642, 648
    writing. *See* Classes
    mistakes, 315
Colon
    purpose, 140. *See also* Semicolon
    usage, 248. *See also* Classes
Combined assignment operators, 65–67
    space, insertion, 90
Combo boxes, 701, 703–708. *See also* **Drop-down combo box; Simple combo box**
    contrast. *See* List boxes
    creation, 706–708
    styles, 704
    usage. *See* User input
Comma delimited number, 142
Command-line arguments, 377–378
Comments, 80–82. *See also* **Multi-line comments**
    process, 81–82
    usage, 32, 33
    writing, 162
Common Language Specification (CLS), 49
Compare method, overloading, 246
CompareTo method, usage, 244–246
Compiler, 67. *See also* **Just-in-time compiler**
    error, 126
    informing, 431, 433
    interaction. *See* C#
    usage, 29, 434
Compound operators, 66
Computer systems, 3–6
Concat method, usage, 464
Concatenation, 184
Conditional expression, 248
    value, usage, 249
Conditional loop, 285

Conditional operator, 248–249
Conditionally executed action, 211, 216
Conditionally executed statements. *See* Multiple
    conditionally executed statements
Conditions (formation), relational operators
    (usage), 212–213
Console, 34
    application. *See* C#
    class, 35
const (key word), 72–73
Constructors, 179–183. *See also* Default
    constructor; StreamReader; StreamWriter
    constructor; string
    ++ operator, usage, 392
    addition, 182
    arguments
    acceptance, 180
    passing, 185
    issues. *See* Inheritance
    overloading, 184–192, 522
    calling, this (usage), 430
    providing, 189
    showing. *See* Unified Modeling Language
    diagrams
    writing. *See* No-arg constructor
Contents button, 656
Context-sensitive help, 658
continue (statement), usage, 300
Controls, 609–614
    addition/movement. *See* Group boxes
    characters, 37
    creation, 616
    deletion, tutorial, 625–626
    demonstration, application (running), 610–611
    display, 640
    input, receiving, 667
    list, 591, 615–616, 635
    locking, 650–651
    method, list, 592–593
    naming rules/conventions, 613
    properties, value (defining), 591
    selection/movement. *See* Multiple controls
    variable, 335
    modification, avoidance. *See* for
    usage, 287. *See also* for
Convert class methods, usage, 313

Copy method, 415–417
count (variable), 338
Countable class, 391
    instances, creation, 393
Count-controlled loop, 285
    elements, 286
Cube class, 525
    Rectangle class, inheritance relationship, 525
Cube constructor, 527
Curly braces, usage, 433
custNumber (argument), 451

D
Data
    appending. *See* Files
    binary format storage, 489
    hiding, 155
    items, 472
    processing. *See* Two-dimensional array
    reading. *See* Files
    staleness, avoidance, 172
    writing, 301. *See also* Files
Data types, 47–48–59. *See also* boolean; char;
    Floating-point data types; Integer
    compatibility. *See* Arguments; Parameters
    conversion, 67–71
    ranking, 113
    usage. *See* Unified Modeling Language diagrams
Date string application, construction, 664–667
DateString label, 665
DateTester (class), 473
Debug menu, usage, 629
Decimal data type, 51
Decision structures, 210
    answers, 738–741
    coding, 211
    programming challenges, 264–268
    review questions, 259–264
    answers, 759–761
Decision-making power, 249
Decrement, meaning, 270
Decrement operators (-- operators), 270–273
    mistakes, 315
    usage, 338
Deep copy, performing, 416

Default constructor, 182
  absence, 52. *See also* Base class
  writing, mistakes, 198
Default error message, retrieval, 481–482
Default exception handler, 476
Default name, 611
Default radio button, setting, 688
default (section), 253
Default (string value), 691
DefaultButton (argument), 683
Definition, knowledge, 102
Delimiter, 303
  semicolon, usage, 472
  usage, 474. *See also* Multiple delimiters
Derived class, 511
  constructor, 519–521
  header, 524
  usage, 524
  creation, 514
  inheritance, 518
  is-a relationship. *See* Base class
  method
  inheritance, 531
  version, invoking, 534
Design window, 602
  opening (tutorial), 600
Diamond symbol, 210
Digits, number determination, 462
directionsButton control, placement (tutorial),
      638–642
directionsButton_Click event method, 636–638
directionsLabel control, 635, 651
  placement, tutorial, 638–642
directionsLabel.Visible (property), 638
Divide and conquer, 100, 130
Division operator, 60
Docked windows, 603
Dot notation, usage, 197
Dot operator, 394
double (argument), acceptance, 547
double (data type), 400, 483
Double (literal), 52
Double method, 487
Double (parameter variable), 186
Double precision data type, 51
Double quotation marks, usage, 42, 73

doubles (array), 365
  creation, 352
do-while (loop), 282–285
  usage, 301
Drop-down combo box, 704

Drop-down list combo box, 705
  text property, 706
Dynamic binding
  performing, 556
  relationship. *See* Polymorphism
Dynamic help, 654–655
  usage, tutorial, 655–658
  window, 603

E

E notation, 53–54
Elements
  access. *See* Two-dimensional array
  number, 329
  value, 358–359
  display, for loop (usage), 353
else (clause), 222
Empty parentheses, usage, 143
Encapsulation, 19, 155
EndsWith method, 455–458
Equality (==), usage. *See* string
  mistakes, 258
Equality operator (== operator), 241, 412
  usage, mistake, 379
Equals method, 403, 412–415, 429, 553
  benefit. *See* Classes
Equals method, usage, 241–244
Errors, 89–91. *See also* Compiler; Off-by-one errors
  correction, 17. *See also* Runtime errors; Syntax
        errors
  message
  customization, 486
  retrieval. *See* Default error message
  occurrence, 483
  recovery, exception handlers (usage), 485
Escape sequence, 37, 38. *See also* Newline escape
        sequence
Event
  handlers, 637
  method, 588, 637

procedures. *See* Application
   writing, tutorial, 642–647
   response, 634–638
Event-driven programming, 588–593
   tutorial, 588
Exception (class), 477
Exceptions, 446, 475
   answers, 746–748
   catching, inability, 488
   detection, 476
   error, 476
   handler, 476. *See also* Default exception handler
   compatibility, 488
   usage. *See* Errors
   handling, 475–488. *See also* Multiple exceptions
   process, 486
   programming challenges, 503–507
   review questions/exercises, 498–503
   answers, 766–767
   throwing, 475–488
ExceptionType (class name), 486
ExceptionType parameter Name (code), 478
exitButton controls, placement (tutorial), 638–642
exitButton_Click method, code template, 645

F

f (parameter), usage, 430
Factorials, 136, 137
FCL. *See* Framework Class Library
FeetInches class, 403
FeetInches method, 410
Fields, 563. *See also* Objects
   declarations, 173
   variables, 173
Filename, passing, 490, 491
filename (reference), 310
FileNotFoundException
   class, 478
   object, 483
Files, 270, 446
   access. *See* Random file access; Sequential file access
   answers, 741–743, 746–748
   closing, 310
   data

   appending, 306–307
   reading, 308–313
   writing, 302–307
   end, detection, 310–312
   input, introduction, 301–314
   location, specifying, 307–308
   mode, passing, 490, 491
   opening, 490
   operations, 488–497
   output, introduction, 301–314
   pointer, 495–497
   programming challenges, 322–325, 503–507
   review questions/exercises, 316–321, 498–503
   answers, 761–763, 766–767
FileStream class, 495
   reading/writing, 494–495
   usage, 493
finally (clause), 485–486
   ordering mistake, 498
Flags, 217–218
float (data type), 400
Float variable, 51, 52
Floating windows, 603
Floating-point data types, 51–54, 140
Floating-point literals, 52–53
Floating-point numbers, 51
Flowchart
   creation. *See* Methods
   usage, 211
Focus method, 667
   usage, 667–668
Font size
   change. *See* Label
   reduction, 665
Font style, change. *See* Label
for (loop), 285–294
   body, control variable modification (avoidance), 290
   control variable, usage, 288
   creation. *See* User-controlled for loop
   format, 286
   initialization, 346
   expression, variable declaration, 290
   pretest loop, 289
   usage, 301. *See also* Arrays; Elements
foreach (loop), 346–347

Form grid, 677–681
Format
  menu, 678–679
  specifier, 42, 140
FormBorderStyle property, setting, 649–650
  tutorial, 650–651
Forms
  creation, 616
  formatting, 675, 677–681
  tab order, control, 668
Forward slashes, usage, 81
Framework Class Library (FCL), 34–40, 100, 552
fullName (variable), 461
Functional decomposition, 130

G

Garbage collector, 467
General class, 511
Generalization, 510
get (key word), usage, 194–197
get property, writing, 425
GetAccount method, 402
GetArea method, writing, 169–170
GetArray method, 352
GetLength method
  calling, 390
  usage, 371, 372
  writing, 166–169
Getters, 171
GetValues method, 350
GetWidth method, writing, 166–169
goodSoFar (variable), 451
Graphical user interface (GUI), 587
  design, 672–673
  focus, 681, 686
  environment, 588
  user convenience, 672–673
GridSize setting, change, 598
Group boxes, 675–681
  controls
  addition, 675–676
  movement, 676
  creation, 675–676
  tab order, 676
GroupBox control, 675
  access key, assignment, 676

Grouping, parentheses (usage), 64

H

Hardware, usage, 3–6
Has-a relationship. *See* Classes
Help menu, 658
Hidden windows, 600–601
Hierarchical method calls, 108–109
Horizontal spacing submenu, 680

I

Icon (value), 683
Identifiers, 45–46
IDEs. *See* Integrated development environments
if (expression), 216
if (statement), 210–219. *See also* Nested if
    statements
  examples, 215–216
  execution, 226, 230
  explanation, 212
  logic, 230
  mistakes, 258
  programming style, 216
  usage, 225
  while loop, comparison, 275
if-else (statement), 219–221, 248
  chain, 222
  logic, 221
if-else-if (statement), 222–226, 250
  comparisons, performing, 413
  construction, 223
if-else-if (structure), 228
Increment, meaning, 270
Increment operators (++ operators), 270–273
  mistakes, 315
  usage, 338. *See also* Constructors
Index, 695
  button, 656
IndexOf method, 457
  usage. *See* Characters; Substring
Infinite loop, 277–278
Inheritance, 485
  answers, 749–750
  chains, 546–552
  constructor issues, summary, 529
  definition, 510–522

is-a relationship, 510–519
  process, 516
  programming challenges, 582–586
  relationship, 551, 574. *See also* Cube class
  reverse order, inability, 521
  review questions/exercises, 577–582
  answers, 768–770
  usage, 511
Initialization. *See* **Arrays**
  expression, 286
  multiple statements, usage, 292–293
  list, 335
  values, 370
Inner loops, 299
Input boxes, 691–701
Input devices, 3, 6
Input validation, 279
  performing, logic, 280
  while loop, usage, 279–282
Insert method, 468–470
  usage, 469
Insertion, starting point, 469
Instance. *See* **Classes**
  fields, 175–179
  mistakes, 435
  review, 390
  scope, 192–194
  methods, 162, 175–179
  headers, 178
  mistakes, 435
  review, 390
  variables, 177
instanceCount field, 392
InstanceCount property, calling, 393
int (argument), 537
  acceptance, 461
  passing, 539
int (data type), 400
int (field), 403
int (parameter variable), 349
int (value), 490
Integer
  array
  allocation, 343

creation, 342
  element (confusing), mistake, 379
  selection sort, performing, 360
  data types, 49–51
  division, 62
  expression, 250
  literals, 51
  value, 495
  variable, 275
  declaration, 110
Integrated development environments (IDEs), 14, 594
  window, 726
Intellisense, 642
Interfaces, 565–576
  comparison. *See* Classes
  definition, format, 565
  implementation. *See* Multiple interfaces
  inheritance, 574
  reference variable
  limitation, 575–576
  usage, 574
  relationship. *See* Polymorphism
  usage. *See* Unified Modeling Language
I/O error, 485
IOException (class), 477
  catching, 485
Is-a relationship. *See* **Base class; Inheritance**
  reverse order, inability, 558
IsValid method, 451
Item indexing, 695
item (string representation), 468
Items.Add method, 696
Items.Clear method, 697
Items.Count property, 694
Items.Insert method, 696–697
Items.Remove method, 697
Items.RemoveAt method, 697
Iteration, 276, 283, 300, 334
  number, 285, 299
  control, 342

J

Just-in-time (JIT) compiler, 12

K

Key words (reserved words), 10, 45, 720
   mistakes, 90
Keyboard
   access keys, assignment. *See* Buttons
   input, reading, 85–89

L

Labels
   access keys, assignment, 673
   control
     addition, tutorial, 618–620
   focus, receiving (inability), 670
   font size/style, change, 624–625
   moving/sizing, 620–622
   TextAlign property, setting, 622–624
   usage. *See* Access key
LastIndexOf method, 457
   usage. *See* Characters; Substring
lastName (variable), 461
Late binding, 556
Layout toolbar, 605–607
Leading spaces, usage, 465
Leading whitespace character, 464
   entering, 474
Left brace (opening brace), 30
Left-to-right associativity. *See* **Operators**
Length field, 390. *See also* **One-dimensional array;**
     Ragged arrays; Rectangular two-
     dimensional arrays
   usefulness, 340
Letters, number determination, 462
Lexicographical comparison, 245–246
Library, 431
Lines (reading), ReadLine method (usage), 308–310
Lines/statements, usage, 11
List boxes, 691, 693–701. *See also* **Checked list boxes**
   combo boxes, contrast, 706
   creation, tutorial, 697–701
ListBox control, 693
   creation, 693
Literals, 40, 44–47. *See also* **Double literal; Floating-**
     point literals; Integer; string; Strings
Load (event procedure), 681
Local reference variables. *See* **Uninitialized local**
     reference variables

Local variables, 79, 122–124, 451
   declaration, mistakes, 198
   initialization, parameter values (usage), 124
   lifetime, 123–124
Locking controls, setting, 649–650
   tutorial, 650–651
Logical AND operator (&& operator), 232–234
Logical errors, 17
Logical NOT operator (! operator), 237
Logical operators, 231–240
   associativity, 237–238
   left-to-right associativity, 238
   precedence, 237–238
   usage, 234. *See also* Numeric ranges
Logical OR operator (|| operator), 235–236
Loops, 270. *See also* **Nested loops**
   answers, 741–743
   body, 276
   control variable, 451
   creation, 278
   definition, 273–274
   execution, 284, 354
   header, 286
   iteration, 294
   location, 299
   notation, 346
   programming challenges, 322–325
   repetition, 276
   review questions/exercises, 316–321
   answers, 761–763
   usage, 345, 458
   decision, 300–301

M

Machine language, 7
Main memory, 3–5
Main method, 397. *See also* **C# program**
   usage, 377–378
Make Same Size submenu, 680
malicious (variable), 425
maxValue variable, value (storage), 292
Menu bar, 604
Message box, 681–685
   display, 700
Message (property), 481, 486
MessageBox.Show method, 681

Messages, runtime display, 652–654
MessageString (argument), 486
Methods, 99. *See also* Recursive method
   answers, 736–737
   arguments
   arrays, passing, 348–351
   objects, passing, 396–400
   passing, 110–122
   arrays, returning, 352–353
   body, 32, 102
   calling, 103–107
   declaration, 398
   flowchart, creation, 592–593
   header, 31, 32, 162, 398
   usage, mistakes, 143
   introduction, 100–109
   list. *See* Control
   local variables, hiding, 122
   modifiers, 103
   name, 103
   objects, returning, 400–403
   overloading, 184–192
   mistakes, 198
   summary, 190
   overriding, 531
   parameter variable, change (mistake), 143
   programming challenges, 148–152
   pseudocode, creation, 592–593
   return value, obtaining, 424
   review questions/exercises, 144–147
   answers, 755–756
   signature, 184, 534
   string (object references), passing, 118–121
   two-dimensional arrays, passing, 373–374
   usage. *See* Problem solving
   value, returning, 124–129
Microsoft Intermediate Language (MSIL), 12
Mixed integer operation, 70
Mixed mathematical expressions, 71
Mnemonic, 671
Modifiers, writing (mistake), 143
Modulus operator, 60
Multi-class programs, compiling, 163
Multidimensional arrays, 365–377
Multi-file programs, compiling/execution, 724–725

Multi-line comments, 82
Multiple arguments, passing, 113–114
Multiple buttons, access key (assignment), 672
Multiple conditionally executed statements, 217
Multiple controls, selection/movement, 678
Multiple delimiters, usage, 474
Multiple exceptions
   catching, mistakes, 498
   handling, 482–486
Multiple interfaces, implementation, 570
Multiplication operator, 60
Mutator method, 171

N
Name property, 611–612
name (variable), creation, 466
Named constants (creation), const (usage), 72–73
namespace (key word), 433
Namespaces, 29, 431–435. *See also* C#
   location, 431
   statement, 90
Narrowing conversion, 68
Negotiation operator, 59
Nested if statements, 228–231
Nested loops, 298–300
.NET Framework SDK, introduction, 721–725
new (key word), usage, 402
Newline characters, 303, 304
Newline escape sequence, 38
No-arg constructor, 186, 354, 519
   absence, 522. *See also* Base class
   usage, 523
   writing, 182–183, 428
Nonletter argument, 452
Non-negative integer expression, 329
Nonnegative number, defining, 136
Nonstatic methods, reference variable (availability), 429
No-parameter constructor, writing (mistakes), 198
NOT operator. *See* Logical NOT operator
null (references)
   usage
   avoidance, 426–428
   mistake, 436
   variable, 426

Numbers
formatting, 140–142
string
input, conversion, 86–89
values, conversion, 313–314
variable, 276, 277
numbers (array), 475
numbers (variable), 343
Numeric code, 218
Numeric ranges (checking), logical operators (usage), 239
Numeric score
determination, 511–514
level, 547
nonadjustment, 545

O
Object class, 552–554
Object-oriented programming (OOP), 18–20, 154, 663
procedure, 161
usage, 155
Objects, 154
address, returning, 402
aggregation, 417
answers, 737–738, 745–746
arrays, 353–357
attributes, 19
box, 633
calling, 411
construction, 179
creation, 157–158. *See also* Aggregate objects
classes, usage, 73–74
example, 156–157
fields, 154
methods, 19, 155
modification, mistake, 435
passing. *See* Methods
programming challenges, 202–208, 439–443
referencing, 354, 415, 425. *See also* Variables
returning. *See* Methods
reusability, 156
review questions, 198–202
answers, 756–759, 765–766
review questions/exercises, 436–439

software entity, 154
specialized version, 510
string, determination, 455
type, 328
variable referencing, 426
Off-by-one errors, 335, 340
causing, mistake, 379
Offending method, 488
One-dimensional array, 365
Length field, 371
reference, 375
On-screen elements, creation, 587
Operands
requirements, 59
usage, 56
Operating system pathname, 473
Operators, 10. *See also* **Arithmetic operators; Binary operators; Negotiation operator; Unary operators**
precedence, 62–64, 238, 718–719
usage, 213
OR expression, 235
OR operator. *See* **Logical OR operator**
Order submenu, 680–681
Outer loop, 299
Output
devices, 3, 6
file, 301
layout, 37
parameters, 116, 117
performance, 35
Overloading, overriding (contrast/distinction), 536–539
override (key word), 410, 534

P
Parameters
data type compatibility, 112–113
list, 103, 113, 185
notation, usage. *See* Unified Modeling Language
setting, 135
value, 138
usage. *See* Local variables
variable, 110, 114, 165. *See also* Double parameter variable; string

contents, 397
name, 166
scope, 113
Parentheses
mismatch, 89–90
mistakes, 198
set, 164
usage, 249
Pass by value, meaning, 397
Passed by reference, meaning, 116
Passed by value, meaning, 115
PictureBox control, insertion, 626–628
Polymorphic reference variable, 555
Polymorphism, 555–559
dynamic binding, relationship, 556–558
interfaces, relationship, 571–576
Postfix mode, 271
prefix mode, contrast, 272–273
Posttest loop, 283
Precedence, 62. *See also* **Logical operators;**
Operators
Prefix mode, 271
contrast. *See* Postfix mode
Pretest loop. *See* **for loop; while loop**
Priming read, 280
Primitive variables, 415
Private base class member, access mistake, 576
Private fields
references, returning (avoidance), 421–425
Private methods, 157, 405
Problem solving
focus, 614–638
methods, usage, 130–133
Procedural programming, 154
Procedures, 154
Processing algorithm, usage. *See* **Arrays**
Program
compiling/execution. *See* Multi-file programs
components, 9–14. *See also* C# program
crashing, 428
creation/saving, 721–724
definition, 7–8
design, 2
model
design tools, usage, 16
logical errors, checking, 17

output, 164
purpose, defining, 15, 590
results, validation, 17
running
test input data, usage, 17
visualization, 16
Programmer-defined constructor, 511
Programmer-defined names, 10, 613
Programming, 609–614. *See also* **Procedural**
programming
decision making, 222
languages, 7–8
customized profile, creation, 595
elements, 9–11
problems, 472
process, 15–18
reasons, 2–3
statements, 251
style, 83–85. *See also* if statement; while loop
Projects
compiling/execution, 730–731
disk organization, 630–631
disk saving, 729–730
initiation, 726–729
opening, 631–633, 731
saving, 628–629
Prompt (argument), 691
Properties
defining, 194
usage, 196
window, 603, 633
opening (tutorial), 600
Protected members, 540–545
Pseudocode
creation. *See* Methods
usage, 16. *See also* Selection sort
Public field, 340
Public methods, 157
Punctuation, 11
Pushpin icon, usage, 602

Q
Question mark, usage, 248
Quotation marks, 43–44
mismatch, 89–90
usage. *See* Double quotation marks

R

Radio buttons, 686–690
    access key, assignment, 687
    CheckChanged event, 688
    properties, 687
    selection, code (usage), 688
    setting. *See* Default radio button
    TabIndex value, assignment, 687
    usage, code usage, 698
RadioButton control, 686
Ragged arrays, 374–376
    creation, 374
    Length field, 375–376
Ragged two-dimensional arrays, 375
Random access files, 488, 493–497
    creation/interaction, 493
Random file access, 493
Raw binary format, 489
Read operation, 280
Read position, 309
ReadLine method, 310. *See also* StreamReader
    usage. *See* Lines
Rectangle class, 390, 525
    inheritance relationship. *See* Cube class
Rectangle constructor, 527
Rectangular two-dimensional arrays, 365–370
    Length field, 371–372
Recursion, 133–140
    application, 136–139
Recursive method, 133–134
ref (key word), 398, 399
Reference
    parameters, 116
    returning. *See* string
    avoidance. *See* Private fields
    variable, 116, 118, 397, 574. *See also* Arrays;
        Polymorphic reference variable;
        Uninitialized reference variable
    availability. *See* Nonstatic methods
    declaration, 329
    name, 429
Relational operators, 238
    usage. *See* Conditions
Remove method, 471
Replace method, 464, 471

Return
    data type, 401
    statement, 125, 138
    type, 103, 402
    mistakes, 143
    value, 244
return (statement), writing (mistake), 143
Row/column subscripts, reversal mistake, 379
Running totals, 294–298
Runtime errors, 695
    correction, 17

S

Same class operations, 403–417
Scientific notation, 53–54, 142
Scope, 79–80. *See also* Instance; Variables
scores (array), 366
Scroll bars, movement, 611
Search algorithm, usage, 357
Search button, 656
Search value, 362
SearchArray program, 361
Searching arrays, 361–362
Secondary storage, 3, 5
Security hole
    creation, 421
    prevention, 425
SelectedIndex property, 695
SelectedItem property, 695
Selection sort, 357
    algorithm, 357–360
    pseudocode, usage, 360
    performing. *See* Integer
Self-documenting programs, 45
Semicolon
    absence, 90
    mistakes, 143, 197, 258, 315
    purpose, 32
    usage, 41. *See also* Delimiter
    care, 216–217
Sentinel values, 294–298
    mistake, 315
    usage, 296–298
Sequence structure, 210
Sequential file access, problem, 493

Sequential search algorithm, 361–362
set (key word), usage, 194–197
SetLength method, 194
    calling, 178
    writing, 161–165
Setters, 171
SetWidth method, 194
    writing, 165–166

Shadowing, 192–193
    overcoming, this (usage), 430
Shallow copy, 343, 416
Short-circuit evaluation, 233
ShowArray method, 350
ShowValue
    calling, 349
    method, 538
Signatures. *See* Methods
    specification, 566
Simple combo box, 704–705
Simulated clock, example, 299
Single precision data type, 51
Size declarator, 366
SizeMode property, 626–627
Sizing handles, usage, 619
Software
    classes, 560
    engineering, 18
    usage, 3–6
Solutions
    closing, 630
    disk organization, 630–631
    file, 631
Solutions Explorer
    opening (tutorial), 600
    window, 602
    usage, 645
Sorted property, 696
Sorting algorithm, usage, 357
Sorting arrays, 357–360
Source code, 37
Source file, 12
Space, insertion (mistakes), 198
Specialization, 510
Specialized class, 511
Split method, usage, 471, 473. *See also* string
Standard output (device), 34

Standard toolbar, 604–605
Starting value, 296
StartsWith method, 455–458
Statements
    block
    braces, usage, 278
    creation, 217
    contrast, 142
    execution, 167
    writing, error, 164–165
Static class members, 390–396
Static fields, 390–393
static (key word), placement, 392
Static members, 390–391
Static methods, 390, 393–396
    convenience, 396
    creation, 394
str (parameter), 471
StreamReader
    class, 483
    ReadLine method, 485
    constructor, 308, 480
    object, 308
StreamWriter class, usage, 306
StreamWriter class Write method, 304–306
StreamWriter class WriteLine method, 303
StreamWriter constructor, 306–307
String
    tokens, extraction, 472
string
    argument, acceptance, 537
    assignation, 465
    class, 74
    constructor, 183
    indexer, 451
    methods, 463
    searching ability, 457
    comparison
    ==, usage, 241
    case, ignoring, 246
    methods, mistakes, 497
    length, determination, 451
    literal, 307
    methods, 454–466
    parameter variable, 189
    parsing, Split method (usage), 472–475
    position (perception), mistakes, 497

reference variables, 247, 427
representation. *See* item
trimming, 474
type, 73–79
values, conversion. *See* Numbers
variable, 75
storage, 120
string (object), 118, 309
comparison, 241–246
contents, 241
change, inability, 466
creation, 74–78
immutability, 119, 467
modified copy (returning), methods (usage),
   463–465
reference, 244, 460–461
passing. *See* Methods
returning, 128–129
StringBuilder class, 466–472
limitation, 468
overloaded versions. *See* Append method
StringBuilder methods, 468–471
StringBuilder objects
character, deletion, 471
methods, 478
passing. *See* Write method; WriteLine method
size, 467
substring, deletion, 471
Strings
appearance, 36
length, 246
literals, 55
returning, 410
strl (object), copy, 464
Strongly typed language, 52, 67
Subclasses, 511
Subexpressions, 233, 235, 248
Subscripts, 369
invalid usage, mistake, 379
loop control, 372
notation, 346
usage, 347
numbering, 330
numbers, storage. *See* Variables

usage, 354
validity, 362
Substring
copy. *See* Calling object
deletion. *See* StringBuilder object
extraction, 460–463
methods, 460–461
searching, 454–460
IndexOf method, usage, 459–460
LastIndexOf method, usage, 459–460
starting position, 460
Subtraction operator, 60
Superclasses, 511
switch (statement), 250–258
SwitchExpression, 251
mistakes, 258
Syntax errors, correction, 593
System (namespace), 446, 552
System.Array class, 371
SystemException, 477
System.IO namespace, 491
System.Text namespace, 466

T

Tab order. *See* **Group boxes**
change, tutorial, 668–671
control. *See* Forms
selection, 668
TabIndex property, usage, 668
TabIndex values
assignment. *See* Radio buttons
contrast, 669
Telephone (class), 469
Test expression, 286
Text Box, clearing, 663–664
Text colors, change, 648–649
Text Editor, usage, 12, 489, 644
Text file, 301, 488
Text input, gathering, 661–675
Text processing, 446
answers, 746–748
programming challenges, 503–507
review questions/exercises, 498–503
answers, 766–767

Text property, 640, 703. *See also* Drop-down list combo box
  code usage, 663
  modification, code (usage), 651–654
TextAlign property, setting. *See* Label
TextBox control, usage (tutorial), 661–664
this (keyword), 430
this (reference variable), 429–431
  usage. *See* Constructors; Shadowing
Three-dimensional (3D) array declaration, 376
Three-dimensional (3D) rendering, 156
throw (statement), 486
Time sharing, 6
Title bar, 603–604
Title (string), 691
ToCharArray method, 461–462
Tokenizing, 473
Tokens
  extraction, 473–474. *See also* string
  usage, 473
ToLower method, 452
Toolbar. *See* Layout toolbar; Standard toolbar
Toolbox, 607
Tooltips, usage, 607–608
ToString method, 403–410, 553
totalSales variable, 296
ToUpper method, 452, 453
Trailing else, 222
  omission, 258
Trailing spaces, usage, 465
Trailing whitespace character, 464
  entering, 474
Trim method, usage, 464–465
try (block), 478, 480–482
  code, inclusion, 483
  ordering mistake, 498
  statement execution, mistake, 498
try (key word), 478
try (statement)
  catch (clause), inclusion, 485
  searching, 484
  usage, 477
try/catch (construct), 478, 480
Tutorial application, initiation, 616–618

Two-dimensional array, 365. *See also* Ragged two-dimensional arrays; Rectangular two-dimensional arrays
  data, processing, 366
  declaration, 366
  elements, access, 367
  initialization, 370
  passing. *See* Methods
  usage, 368
Two-dimensional arrays
  elements, display, 372
Two-dimensional int array, reference, 373

U

UML. *See* Unified Modeling Language
Unary operators, 59, 231
  set, 270
Unconditional operators, 239
Unicode, 55–56
  characters, 717
  usage, 218
Unified Modeling Language (UML), 159
  interfaces, usage, 570
Unified Modeling Language (UML) diagrams, 186
  access specification, showing, 172
  aggregation, 421
  constructors, showing, 181
  data type, usage, 172–173
  depiction, 551
  example, 403
  parameter notation, usage, 172–173
  usage, 511, 514
Uninitialized local reference variables, 181–182
Uninitialized reference variable, 181
Update expression, 286
  forms, 290
  multiple statements, usage, 292–293
User input (obtaining), combo box (usage), 705–706
User interface, design, 590, 615
User-controlled for loop, creation, 291–292
User-controlled loop, 285
Users, button determination, 684–685
using (key word), 434
using (statement), 435

V

Value

assignation, 166

insertion, 468

returning, 166. *See also* Methods

truncation, 69

usage. *See* Conditional expression

Value-returning methods, 100–102, 124, 127

defining, 125–126

mistakes, 143

Variables, 40–47. *See also* **Local variables**

address, assignment, 518

assignment/initialization, 56–58

change, 117

contents, 489

count, 289

declaration, 41, 49, 247–248. *See also* for

mistakes, 197

statement, 57

incrementation, 273

names, misspelling, 90

object referencing, 412

references, 398

scope, 247–248

subscript numbers, storage, 332

usage, 11–12. *See also* Algorithm

value, holding, 58

Vertical spacing submenu, 680

Visible (property), 635

Visual C# development environment, 587

Visual C# .NET

controls, 588, 609–610

customization, 597

environment, 594, 599–608

familiarity, tutorial, 608

exiting, 630

help, usage, 654–658

initiation, 616

introduction, 726–731

windows application, development (steps), 589–593

Visual Studio, 594–608

files, storage, 596

initiation, tutorial, 594–599

void (method), 100–102

defining, 102–103

W

while (loop), 273–279

comparison. *See* if statement

incompleteness, 274

iteration, 340

pretest loop, 277

programming style, 278

usage, 300. *See also* Input validation

usefulness, 279

Whitespace characters. *See* **Leading whitespace character; Trailing whitespace character**

number determination, 462

Widening conversion, 68

Width field, 390

Windows applications, 661

answers, 750–751

design/creation, 589

introduction, 587

programming, 613–614

challenges, 659–660, 711–716

review questions/exercises, 658–659, 708–711

answers, 770–771

visualization, 590

Write method, 34–40, 331. *See also* **StreamWriter class Write method**

StringBuilder object, passing, 467

usage, 488

WriteByte method, 495

WriteLine method, 34–40, 272, 331. *See also* **StreamWriter class WriteLine method**

display, 273

StringBuilder object, passing, 467

usage, 303, 304, 488

WriteLine statement, 283

X

Xpos (integer), 691

Y

Ypos (integer), 691